Urban
Political
Analysis

Urban Political Analysis

A Systems Approach

Edited by

DAVID R. MORGAN
University of Oklahoma

and

SAMUEL A. KIRKPATRICK
University of Oklahoma

FP THE FREE PRESS, NEW YORK
COLLIER-MACMILLAN LIMITED, LONDON

The Free Press
A Division of The Macmillan Company
866 Third Avenue, New York, New York 10022

COLLIER-MACMILLAN CANADA LTD., TORONTO, ONTARIO

Library of Congress Catalog Card Number: 74–156838

Printing number
1 2 3 4 5 6 7 8 9 10

Preface

THIS VOLUME on urban politics contains several features which we think should be noted. First, a specific conceptual framework—systems analysis—has been employed as an organizing and unifying device throughout the book. Second, the readings were deliberately selected to reflect the best empirical research now taking place in the field of local politics. Third, extensive supplementary textual material is provided through an introductory essay and at the beginning of the remaining sections to provide continuity and integrate the articles into a more complete whole. We have tried to incorporate these features into the volume without doing violence to the ideas contained in the individual articles chosen for inclusion.

Several other assumptions have guided us in this undertaking. We believe that today's college student is capable, with some assistance, of understanding and appreciating the scholarly research in most academic disciplines. For some years the undergraduate student has been successfully grappling with sophisticated analytic concepts and techniques used in mathematics and the natural sciences. Yet we have continued to "talk down" to the student in the social sciences (perhaps not so much in economics) by providing largely descriptive material or perhaps expecting him to memorize the conventional wisdom of the past as "the answers" to complex social questions. While it may be fashionable in some quarters to think that students will respond only to entertaining or "fun" topics in the classroom, we also know they are deeply concerned with social issues of the day. If social science has a contribution to make in helping us understand today's problems, an early exposure to its various analytic approaches, techniques, and research findings is a must. Until recently, the concerned student was not likely to find much exciting or theoretically meaningful research activity in the field of "municipal government." Scholars in this subarea of political science had long been preoccupied with the proper administration of urban affairs or with suggesting various reform measures designed to improve city government. In recent years, however, the "lost world" of local government has been rediscovered and some of the best work in political science is now taking place in this field. This volume amply demonstrates that the study of local politics not only has rejoined the mainstream of political science but that it can be creative and stimulating as well. Because of this development, the insights found in these selections, as well as the methodology and techniques employed, will be useful in the study of political phenomena generally.

We will save until later our remarks concerning systems as an important conceptual framework. At this point we might note that the systems approach in political science has found increasing acceptance in a wide number of areas, attesting to its flexibility and usefulness. An important aspect of this widespread acceptance is the usefulness of the systems framework as a pedagogical device in the classroom. Moreover, many of the more important advances in applying this approach to concrete problems have come from the fields of state and local politics, the very places where a few years ago only barren soil was being tilled.

In addition to the contributors to our volume, several people should be recognized here for their assistance in preparing the manuscript. In particular, Philip Coulter, University of Massachusetts; James Clarke, University of Arizona; Robert Lineberry, University of Texas at Austin; and F. Ted Hebert, University of Oklahoma, deserve our thanks for their valuable comments on our undertaking. Several of our graduate students have provided valuable commentary on the essays: Mary Ann Armour, C. Kenneth Meyer, and James Visser. Larry Edwards and Cherrie Flury assisted in the more routine, yet cumbersome tasks involved in the compilation of readings. David Harrop of The Free Press also merits our appreciation for his excellent editorial assistance. Finally, our wives, Carolyn and Pam, deserve our greatest gratitude for their encouragement, support, and very real help.

DRM

NORMAN, OKLAHOMA   SAK

Contents

A Systems Framework
for the Analysis of Urban Politics

Urban Politics and the Role of Theory

SINCE WORLD WAR II political science has achieved considerable progress in the development and application of empirically oriented methods and techniques for the analysis of political behavior. This approach with its strong emphasis on scientific rigor, quantification, and comparative studies has now begun to make significant inroads into one of the last major strongholds of traditional, prescriptive political science: the study of state and local politics.[1] For example, a recent evaluation of the state of political science concluded that "rather than being the laggard of the discipline ... the study of the state and local politics has reentered the mainstream of political research."[2] Much credit for the increasingly sophisticated nature of this research is due Charles Adrian, Oliver Williams, Edward Banfield, Robert Wood, James Q. Wilson, Scott Greer, and others who have contributed so heavily to the revival and subsequent growth of stimulating, fruitful, and exacting studies of local politics.[3] Yet, while much of this research is comparative and increasingly dependent upon adroit use of statistical techniques, there remains a decided void in empirical theory construction for local political systems. The study of urban politics, perhaps more than other areas of political science, stands in particular need of empirically based theories because of its normative, reform-oriented, case-study heritage. While this is not the place to consider the problems of empirical theory building, a review of recent literature reveals that efforts have been made to develop conceptual frameworks, models, and approaches for the study of urban politics. Since this book uses a particular analytic approach, it might be profitable to briefly examine some of these attempts at theory construction. Following this, a systems approach will be outlined, and its utility as an analytic

(All footnotes will be found at the end of respective introductions and selections)

and organizing framework for studying urban political processes will be considered.

For our purposes we might group the various theoretical approaches to urban politics into three broad categories: limited propositions, middle-range theory or models, and broad conceptual frameworks.[4] The first group of studies includes statements of relationship between limited observations or events which have a low level of generality. The second category, middle-range theory or model construction, represents an effort to devise propositions which help explain certain aspects of the total urban political process, such as the decision-making process or power relationships within a community. The third class of studies attempts to formulate overall conceptual schemes or frameworks for analyzing and explaining events in the realm of urban politics.

LIMITED PROPOSITIONS

Much of the urban-related research involving statements of singular or limited relationship consists of efforts to link community socioeconomic characteristics to certain dependent variables, such as (1) voting behavior on specific urban issues; (2) attitudes toward urban problems or governmental change; and (3) expenditure patterns of local governments. This type of research ordinarily depends upon gathering quantifiable data from voting records, survey research, or reports of public expenditures by city. Community factors which are assumed to influence these dependent variables are often taken from census sources or from collections of information about city characteristics such as is found in the *Municipal Year Book*. Even though we might place studies of this kind in the limited theoretical category, their importance should not be minimized. To the contrary, some of the best recent empirical research in urban politics is of this genre.

Studies of the influence of election systems and electoral behavior on the course of local politics have yielded useful insights. For example, a considerable body of evidence has been accumulated to show that non-partisan elections operate to the benefit of a community's middle class and business interests as opposed to that of the working class or ethnic groups.[5] Other studies of local voting behavior rather uniformly suggest that high education and social status are associated with support for local referenda issues[6] and with favorable attitudes toward greater metropolitan political centralization.[7] One study has also indicated that political alienation was related to an unfavorable attitude and a negative vote on metropolitan governmental consolidation.[8]

Studies of the socioeconomic correlates of local government expenditures might also be grouped under the heading of lower-level theory. These studies of the spending patterns of selected cities are based on the premise that the urban environment as represented by certain socioeconomic characteristics influences a city's policy commitments, reflected by its spending behavior.[9] Thus municipal expenditures are used as a way of operationalizing or measuring local policy outputs. Despite the inclusion of these public policy studies in the limited proposition category, they owe a considerable debt to a broader conceptual approach, the Easton input-output analytic framework, which will be considered subsequently.

MIDDLE-RANGE THEORY

In the field of local politics there are relatively few good illustrations of the level of analysis which can properly be labeled as middle-range theories, partial theories, or conceptual models. Perhaps much of the literature devoted to the study of community power belongs here although some would undoubtedly maintain that the decision-making approach should be considered as a broad-gauge theoretical framework.[10] In some respects community power studies form a separate collection of literature in political science and sociology which has not been fully incorporated into the larger body of studies in urban politics. Nevertheless, the "who governs?" investigations have not been without certain theoretical contributions which might be noted. For instance, Robert Agger and his associates in *The Rulers and the Ruled* set forth a multiphase model of the process of political decision making with particular application to the local level.[11] And Robert Dahl's now classic study of decision making and community power relationships in New Haven, *Who Governs?*, still stands as one of the best theoretical and methodological studies on local politics yet produced.[12]

Also to be included in the category of middle-range theory is an approach most accurately described as urban political ecology. Studies of this sort, normally confined to a single metropolitan area, are concerned with the processes by which individual units of local government seek to cope with their metropolitan environment. In a study of the Philadelphia area, Oliver Williams (with others) made extensive comparisons of census and fiscal data in measuring the effect of metropolitan cultural and structural differentiation on the policy choices of certain suburban Philadelphia cities.[13] Robert Wood's *1400 Governments* dealt with the structural factors (particularly size, level of industrialization, and population characteristics) influencing the revenue and expenditure policies of the suburban communities in the New York metropolitan region.[14] Above all, studies of this type focus on the processes by which local political institutions adjust and adapt to their social as well as physical environment.

BROAD CONCEPTUAL FRAMEWORKS

Several attempts to explain the functioning of the metropolitan political system using broadly conceived theoretical approaches have appeared in recent years. As a case in point, it has been suggested that concepts and terminology derived from the study of international relations might be conducive to a better understanding of how and why the various cities within a metropolis interact in the way that they do. Matthew Holden has contended that important similarities exist between the metropolitan system and the international political system since both are examples of interaction between rather than within diplomatic systems.[15] Another inclusive conceptual approach to the analysis of metropolitan politics has been adapted from economic theory. Individual units of government within a metropolitan complex are considered as being in competition with each other for residents as well as business and perhaps industry. The decentralized structure of metropolitan government, according to this theme, is the result of market-like competitive forces which sustain the existence of separate communities in order to serve specialized purposes (e.g., industrial suburbs, high-status residential suburbs) arising from a heterogeneous metropolitan setting.[16]

At least two other broad approaches which have had limited application to urban politics might be mentioned at this point—game theory and communication or cybernetics theory. Norton Long is usually credited with being the first to characterize the metropolis as a territorial system of games involving a number of local "players": government, business, the press, and so on. The players use each other in pursuit of their own strategies and goals with the result that much of what takes place in the metropolis consists of "undirected cooperation of particular social structures, each seeking particular goals, and, in doing so, meshing with others."[17]

As a branch or outgrowth of cybernetics, a communications approach to the analysis of political behavior emphasizes the paramount place of message transmission in the political system.[18] Although its primary application has been at the international level, limited use has been made of information flows and transactions among community-level institutions as a way of studying local political integration and community growth.[19]

Finally, the study of urban and metropolitan politics from a systems perspective has been urged.[20] A conceptual framework in which the entire urban area is viewed as comprising a set of interrelated components interacting over time and thus becoming a "system" is not unique to urban research. A few years ago, Bebout and Bredemeier suggested the use of a Parsonian structural-functional frame of reference as an inclusive approach to understanding the way in which the central city relates to its surroundings.[21] Using this form of analysis, the focus is on the processes by which the city maintains its integrity as an ongoing system through a series of devices such as coercion, bargaining, legal-bureaucratic relations (especially with the state and federal government) and by inducing citizen support through identification with the needs and goals of the city. Robert Wood has also offered an exploratory scheme for analyzing urban politics which goes beyond a mere concern for decision making to include the inputs (generators of activity) to the local political system and its outputs (the consequences of public action).[22]

None of the above systemic approaches, however, owes its primary conceptual origin to David Easton, generally regarded as the intellectual father of the systems approach as developed in political science.[23] Since Easton's approach has been widely adapted to a variety of types and levels of political research, a number of advantages should accrue to the application of a framework for urban politics based substantially upon his work.

Systems Analysis

The search for new strategies, methods, and concepts for describing and understanding the political process has increasingly drawn political scientists toward broader approaches to analysis. Less attention is being devoted to the details of single political processes, such as "judicial review," "legislative apportionment," or "the role of city bosses," while there is more concern for the characteristics and performance of entire political systems. Political analysts are recognizing that such things as voting behavior or the legislative process cannot be fully understood without more exact information on how these processes function in various settings. Comparison lies at the core of scientific investigation, and political scientists are more concerned than ever with developing appropriate analytical frameworks which will permit sophisticated comparative studies in a variety of geographical areas. Systems analysis has found wide acceptance in political science by providing the conceptual scheme so essential for placing political phenomena in this perspective. The pervasiveness of a systems orientation to political analysis was suggested in Gabriel Almond's presidential address before the American Political Science Association in 1966:

> The emerging analytical framework in contemporary political theory is the concept of system whether it is employed at the level of subnational, regional, or structural units such as communities, legislative bodies or committees, at the level of national political units, or at the level of the international political system.[24]

Beginning with his book, *The Political System*, published in 1953, Easton has continued to describe, amplify, and refine his particular approach to systems analysis, sometimes referred to as input-output analysis. Following his lead, a number of political scientists have resorted to the concept of system as a research strategy and a variety of studies have embraced this analytical scheme in recent years. For example, in the field of American politics alone, applications of the systems approach in one form or another have been made to American national government, American state politics, the legislative process, congressional committee activity, and judicial decision making.[25]

THE DEVELOPMENT OF A SYSTEMS APPROACH
AND RELATED CONCEPTS

Although systems analysis in political science has been developed by a relatively small group of scholars, the roots of such an approach are widely dispersed and its evolution is attributable to many factors. One of these factors is primarily theoretical. For many years political science built upon a basic set of prescriptive or normative "theories" about the ideal polity. Since World War II, however, the discipline has undergone a rather substantial shift from a normative approach to a concern for empirical analysis. The subsequent emphasis on empirical measurement and data collection was also devoid of theory for a period of time. In the 1950s, however, serious questions were raised about collecting facts and applying them to situations prematurely without theory.[26] From our increased concern with theory we developed renewed emphasis on approaches or frameworks, the category which most adequately describes systems analysis.

Whereas a theory is a systematic statement of relationships between political phenomena, providing criteria of relevance, guiding the search for data and giving meaning to the real world, an approach is a less rigorous means for classifying, ordering, and structuring political information.[27] When these classifications and conceptualizations are developed into models of the real world, theories begin to emerge.[28] The ultimate goal is the explanation and prediction of political phenomena by relating them in ordered patterns. Modern political science is concerned with finding empirical (observable) regularities which cannot be adequately depicted or known without a mental framework, As such a framework, systems analysis developed as a consequence of our need to establish criteria for recognizing problems, define facts, and screen out irrelevant factors, and bring order to our perceptions of what is political.

Another influential factor in the development of systems analysis is related to an increased recognition of the continuity of nature and the interactive aspects of physical, biological, psychological, social, economic, cultural, and political phenomena.[29] The approach, as an outgrowth of cybernetics, the science of communication and control, developed as a reaction to compartmentalized knowledge and disciplinary boundaries. Emphasis was placed on interdisciplinary research, building a common language of science, a broad focus, and unifying themes.

A systems view of politics can also be seen as a logically developed alternative to previous definitions of "political." For centuries, political philosophers explicated the meaning of politics and even more recent attempts in this process created mixed degrees of satisfaction and confusion. In many respects, Easton's definition of politics and the accompanying system components represents another progression in our search for what is political. This search has recently included emphasis on power, influence, and the influential;[30] the legal environment of government;[31] decision making and nondecision making;[32] the conflict of groups and interest;[33] and politics as symbolism.[34] The systems viewpoint utilized here contends that politics is the "authoritative allocation of values."[35] The political system, according to this definition, distributes and allocates a wide variety of values which the members of that system consider important (e.g., freedom, safety, resources, skill) and it does so authoritatively. That is, the decisions of the political system are accepted as binding or legitimate, and despite the fact that government is only one of several agents of social control (e.g., family, church, school), it is the only legitimate societal institution with the ultimate sanction—the use of force.

The integral concept stemming from the development of general systems theory and its application to political science is that of a system. A *system* is any set of interrelated and interacting objects, elements, or variables. Furthermore, their *interactions* are usually characterized by predictable patterns or sequences—that is, interactions are nonrandom. General systems concepts can be categorized as either descriptive, or as those dealing with dynamics, regulation, and breakdown.[36] The descriptive components make distinctions about kinds of systems (e.g., open, closed), the hierarchical levels of systems (e.g., one system can be a subsystem of another), internal organization (e.g., interdependence, centralization), and the interaction of systems with their environments. Basically, the components of any system can be reduced to its *environment, inputs* emanating from that environment, the conversion of inputs into *outputs*, and the *feedback* of information through the environment back to the system. Although the character of system components varies, this analogy holds for social as well as biological or physical systems. When the concepts are made politically specific, a *political system* is viewed as a bounded set of interdependent roles and structures whose interactions authoritatively allocate values for society. When we speak of an *urban political system*, we refer primarily to the local legitimate distribution of values. Nevertheless, that system is a subsystem of a larger system and it has an environment composed of systems with different content (e.g., social, biological). Allocations of values are rules and *rules* are the result of decision making. The political system must not only make rules, but apply them and adjudicate them. *Rule making, rule application,* and *rule adjudication* are examples of functions which the political system must perform to assure its maintenance. Other functions frequently associated with any political system include the necessity of expressing interests and desires (*interest articulation*), bringing wants and demands together for action (*interest aggregation*), inculcating the values of the system (*political socialization*), training new leadership (*political recruitment*), and communicating in a system composed of information flows (*political communication*).[37] Therefore, interaction in this system is any communication of information between actors, and political interactions are oriented toward the authoritative allocation of values. Complexes of interactions create communication networks and information can flow from higher to lower status roles, such as elite to mass (*downward communication*), from lower to higher (*upward communication*), or between roles of generally equal status (*horizontal communication*). This information flow is the "stuff" of which decisions are made and the most influential members of the political system are usually, by definition, ones that control the information flow process.

We have also come to view component sets of interactions and expectations held by actors in this system as roles. These *roles* are defined by the actor and the expectations of others. Furthermore, every role has a *status* in this system and a *structure* is a set of interdependent roles. Many complex structures with legal bases are called *institutions*. For example, a bureaucracy is a structure with actors performing rather formalized roles.

Finally, there are those concepts which deal with the way the system responds to stress. *Stress* is a disturbance which endangers the system's ability to persist or prevents the system from operating in its characteristic way. A characteristic of any system is its ability to cope with stress, and in this respect all political systems are *adaptive systems*. A basic process of cybernetics is *homeostasis*—that is, the ability of the system to achieve a steady state or maintain equilibrium. Like a thermostat in a heating system, the political system has homeostatic mechanisms which reduce stress. If they fail to operate effectively, the subsequent modification of roles creates a system transformation known as a *step-level function*, altering its characteristic behavior. There is output failure when this system unsuccessfully generates outputs to cope with stress. One cause of such failure might be *demand input overload*, a situation in which demands are too numerous (*volume stress*) or too difficult (*content stress*) to process.

In summary, the following diagram is a typical representation of the political system. The core of this system is the "black box" of *authoritative decision makers* and decision-making agencies which are influenced by the inputs to the system emanating from a diverse environment of other systems. These systems may be within the same society (*intrasocietal*) or outside that society (*extrasocietal*). The inputs are *demands* placed on decision makers, and *apathy* which assures the decision makers freedom to interpret the meaning of inputs. *Supports* for this system are either material (e.g., taxes), behavioral (obedience to laws), participatory (e.g., voting), or deferential (e.g., respect for authority). Various structures such as political parties and interest groups transmit inputs by performing various functions (e.g., interest aggregation and interest articulation). The results of decision making is *outputs* or policy, which in turn influences

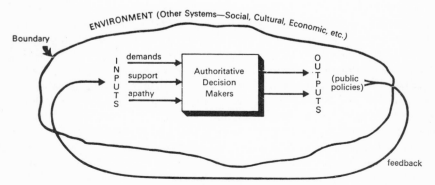

Figure 1.   Partial Model of a Local Political System

new inputs from the environment through the process of feedback. Some-times these outputs are *substantive* (e.g., a new tax) or *symbolic* (e.g., medal of honor). Since information and energy interchange is the basic component of any system, its *boundary* is defined by the fact that it requires more energy to transverse it than to travel an equivalent distance inside or outside that boundary. In a political system, the boundary is dependent upon the extent to which certain interactions lead to the authoritative allocation of values. In time of war, for example, much of the economic system is infused into the political system. Furthermore, all political systems are *open systems* in that they cannot function without environmental interaction.

We have alluded to general systems theory and its applications to political systems in order to expose the reader to a growing body of concepts and language which assists us in the analysis of politics. The remaining examples will utilize these concepts yet focus on authoritative allocation which rests in the hands of the people (democratic system) and is specifically urban.

USES AND LIMITATIONS OF A SYSTEMS APPROACH

A systems approach appears to offer several explicit advantages in the search for understanding political life generally and urban political behavior specifically. First, as Easton emphasizes, the idea of a political system compels the researcher to separate political activity from other forms of social behavior—at least for purposes of analysis. In this sense the political system is regarded as a self-contained set of political interactions imbedded in, but analytically distinct from, the larger environment in which it is found. At the level of urban politics, therefore, the systems analyst would concentrate only on those processes and interactions through which binding or authoritative decisions are made for the community as a whole. In the United States, those formal activities and agencies involved in making authoritative decisions at the local level are well known and highly visible—for example, city councils, mayors, city managers, and so forth.

In addition to analytically separating interactions which involve authoritative allocation of values from a larger environment, systems analysis focuses attention on the specific set of components or units making up a particular political system. Identifying the distinct funda-mental elements of a political system is actually an integral part of distinguishing that system from its larger environment. This process is not, however, a simple matter. It involves the crucial notion of a boundary which encompasses the political system indicating, at least for purposes of analysis, what we have included or excluded from the system.[38]

A systems approach requires that the political researcher take a com-prehensive look at all the dimensions and components of the authoritative allocation process. In more traditional local government research, policy outcomes and feedback were slighted in an overemphasis on formal government structure and more recently by a preoccupation with "who governs?" Not only is a broad perspective necessitated by systems analysis, but the approach draws attention to the relationship between system components and between the political system and its environment. Each unit of the system must be studied from the standpoint of its relationship to the other elements since, by definition, each part affects other parts. In addition, it is essential to know how the political system is related to other systems outside its boundary since this outside environment furnishes the inputs for political activity. Thus a systems approach has the advantage of constantly calling the researcher's attention to the larger whole, the functioning of the entire system and its relation with its environment.

A systems framework is also highly compatible with rigorous empirical research, providing a rich vein of concepts and working models to be used in a variety of substantive areas. Thus it may prove of significant value as a heuristic device or as an aid to understanding in the search for empirically verifiable propositions. In this connection, systems analysis has become increasingly associated with recent advances in mathematics and in the use of computer techniques. In general, the systems approach, stemming from interdisciplinary attempts to establish common forms of language and analysis across a variety of substantive applications, has infused new concepts into the language of political analysis; encouraged new ways of looking at political phenomena in the context of all relevant variables; enabled comparative analysis through common knowledge of different systems; facilitated the gathering of data and the empirical examination of politics; developed microanalysis in conjunction with macroanalysis; and, most important, stimulated us to raise new queries, otherwise unasked, about basic political phenomena.

The above utility of systems analysis notwithstanding, a persuasive argument can be made that a systems approach is not a real theory. A theory, strictly speaking, has explanatory power. And, as the critics of systems theory are fond of pointing out, systems analyses are not really explanatory—they are essentially heuristic aids, guides in the search for testable generalizations.[39] Nevertheless, systemic analysis should not be greatly faulted on this account, since deductive theory, in the sense used by the natural sciences, is almost unknown in the social sciences. A true deductive theory requires one or more basic axioms or postulates from which other postulates necessarily follow. But, as Eugene Meehan has pointed out, "If political science were limited to deductive theory there would be no political theory."[40]

Other shortcomings of systems analysis are mentioned from time to time. The approach is of limited value in goal determination since it is basically concerned with systems persistence and not with the direction the system may be headed. Another criticism which has been leveled at systems analysis concerns its lack of usefulness in dealing with matters of control, power, and influence. Oran Young admits, for instance, that the concentration on persistence and survival detracts from an interest in "who gets what" and results in the charge that the approach harbors a status quo bias.[41] Finally, it may be argued that certain systems concepts are not easily operationalized, making it difficult to apply the approach to certain concrete problems of analysis.[42] For example, the notion of a boundary separating the political system from its environment is particularly troublesome for many to visualize and would seem almost impossible to operationalize. Despite these constraints, a growing body of system-oriented research testifies to the usefulness of a systems framework for political analysis.[43]

The Components of a Political System

A political system, as indicated previously, consists of several major attributes which may be distinguished analytically: inputs, outputs, decision-making agencies and processes, and feedback. Inputs consist of those activities emanating from the environment which get channeled into the decision-making structures as the "raw material" to keep the system functioning. From another perspective inputs present themselves as stimuli to which decision makers react. The decision-making or conversion portion of the systems paradigm can be viewed in two ways. In one sense it represents those officials and official agencies within a society charged with the legal responsibility for making public decisions and policies. Some systems analysts, however, prefer to focus less on the official structures (such as city councils or mayors) and more on the process of conversion itself; that is, the interactions which take place as the inputs are transformed into outputs. Easton, for example, comes within this latter category. Outputs, in the simplest sense, are decisions and acts of public officials which may take the form of laws, administrative decrees, and court decisions. The feedback loop or process is what gives the political system its dynamic quality. The operation of the system does not stop with the production of outputs. Instead, governmental decisions and policies affect other systems surrounding the political system (the environment) which may in turn generate new forms of inputs for the political system to process. In addition, certain forms of outputs or policies might return as feedback directly to the decision makers as a new input without necessarily going through the outside environment. The environment was described as being made up of a network of other systems (e.g., economic, social, cultural) which surround and influence the political system. Since the political system is an open one, it constantly engages in a series of transactions and exchanges across the boundary which separates the system from its environment. These specific elements of the political system will now be examined in greater detail.

ENVIRONMENT AND BOUNDARY

The environment is important in systems analysis primarily because it serves as a major source of inputs to the system. Easton has suggested a broad twofold division: intrasocietal and extrasocietal.[44] In the case of urban political systems, extrasocietal forces would represent those occurrences taking place outside the community itself, such as in the national or regional economy, which eventually influence the local polity. Federal and state government programs which affect cities would be another example of an extrasocietal environmental influence. The intrasocietal environment at the local level would include those characteristics found entirely within the community—such as the prevailing social structure, size of the community, density, age levels, or peculiar cultural norm—all of which help determine the volume and content of the inputs for the urban political system. Even though the local political system is an open system involved in a continuing interaction with its environment, for purposes of analysis these outside forces must be considered as constants or parameters which at any given time are unchanging. For instance, if we are interested in determining the effects of a community's ethnic composition on certain programs of local government, we must accept the level of ethnicity in that city at a particular time as fixed.

The notion of a system boundary, as indicated, presents certain difficulties and ambiguities. The concept is essentially an analytical construct determined largely by what the researcher desires to include or exclude as part of the system under investigation. In Easton's words, the boundary of a political system is "a symbol or spatial embodiment of the criteria of inclusion-exclusion ... a summary way of referring phenomenally to what we have included in or left out of a system."[45] It is not the same as a physical boundary, such as a city limit or the outer limits of a Standard Metropolitan Statistical Area. Unlike the boundaries of a physical system such as a solar system, a system of social interactions is troublesome to isolate because it is ordinarily so diffused throughout the larger society. At the local level it is not unrealistic to assume that the boundary of the political system is constantly shifting and reforming. For example, in its stated purposes the local Chamber of Commerce is not a part of the local political system; it may even explicitly disavow political activity. Yet in several large cities this organization has a history of rather extensive involvement in certain enterprises which have important consequences for local politics, such as taking the lead in support of municipal bond elections and even buying real estate for highway right of way for later resale to the city.[46] Specific groups, therefore, may be only intermittently concerned with the political process, moving in and out of the political system depending upon the particular circumstances at the time. Despite these conceptual complications the notion of a boundary isolating these sets of interactions which are political from those which are not is essential to systems analysis.

For purposes of urban political analysis, the environmental influences have been grouped into the following categories: political structure, socio-economic characteristics, and political culture. These parameters generate and condition the inputs (except those which arise within the system itself) for the local political system.

Political structure. As a part of the American federal system, no urban area in the United States constitutes a self-contained political system. State and federal policies along with the complex web of interrelated governmental units existing in metropolitan areas impose important outside constraints on the local polity. State environmental influences may include prohibition of certain forms of local government or imposition of tax and debt limitations. State government also establishes ground rules for annexation, new municipal incorporations, the creation of special districts, as well as providing the authorization for interlocal agreements and contracts. The availability of state financial assistance may also serve to stimulate certain forms of demands at the local level and provide an important source of support for the city government.[47]

National government activities increasingly have a far-reaching impact on local politics. The bewildering maze of recent federal programs for urban areas has often resulted in consequences which have not always been anticipated at the local level. For example, the local OEO (anti-poverty) programs which have included provisions for "maximum feasible participation" by the poor have sometimes resulted in certain demands on local decision makers which they had not necessarily expected.[48]

Another major environmental influence in metropolitan areas is the existence of a variety of local political jurisdictions with often competing, overlapping, and duplicating service responsibilities. Over the years metropolitan reformers have vigorously opposed this "crazy-quilt" pattern of local government within the metropolis, arguing that it was inefficient, illogical, and debilitating.[49] Recent less-normative research has begun to question this long-assumed causal relationship between fragmented metropolitan government and the "urban crisis."[50] Moreover, new insights have been offered concerning the forces which help perpetuate the polycentric metropolis and the values it may protect. For example, Oliver Williams and associates have argued that the spatially separate economic and life-style differentiation characteristic of metropolitan areas leads to differing and conflicting suburban policies which serve as a barrier to greater metropolitan political integration.[51]

Socioeconomic characteristics. Just as variations in the political structure help determine the level and kinds of demands made on the urban political system, so differences in community demographic and economic features exert a differential effect on local politics. Some urban areas are characterized by large, diverse populations arranged spatially in an often confused and seemingly incompatible pattern. The effects of size and heterogeneity on local government may take several forms. Campbell and Sacks, for example, report that local governments in a metropolitan setting spend more money per capita, raise more taxes per capita, have greater per capita debt, and receive less state aid than localities in nonmetropolitan areas.[52] Empirical research by Scott Greer and others demonstrates that people with differing social status and life styles also differ with respect to community participation and political behavior.[53] Metropolitan subareas of high social rank undoubtedly do not make the same sort of demands on their local governments as do neighborhoods of low income or ethnic composition. Patterns of socioeconomic variation such as homogeneity or heterogeneity are sometimes taken to indicate the presence of social cleavages in the community from which pressures may emerge for particular policy decisions by local government. To the extent that managing conflict in matters of public importance is a basic function of urban government,[54] the nature and dimension of social and economic divisions within the city's border will be of utmost importance to those with official decision-making responsibilities.

A number of impressive public policy studies have used various socio-economic characteristics (income, urbanization, education, etc.) as input variables within a research format analogous to Easton's input-output framework. In the approach being outlined here, however, it seems more appropriate to follow the suggestion of Jacob and Lipsky, who argue that socioeconomic measures should be considered as environmental factors which may lead to the articulation of demands and support, rather than as input variables *per se*.[55]

Political culture. Another dimension of the local political environment is its political culture. The research on the impact of cultural forces on local politics has been quite limited, in part because of the elusive and nebulous nature of the concept of political culture. One of the better statements on this subject has been offered by James Q. Wilson:

> Very broadly, a political culture might be thought of as a widely shared, patterned view of the proper scope and behavior of public institutions and specifically of what ways of behaving on public matters (getting votes, casting votes, promising programs, administering services, managing conflict) would be thought legitimate.[56]

Several studies on urban politics have at least tangentially included the effects of underlying values and norms as they influence public policy formation and execution.[57] A particularly interesting example of the impact which certain belief systems may have on local government has been offered by Robert Wood in his now classic examination of life and politics in suburbia. Wood contends that a firm commitment by most suburbanites to the belief that small government close to home is best (a "grassroots" political ideology) has been effectively used to defend the existence of the multitude of small political units surrounding so many metropolitan areas. He insists that this grassroots political orientation "has been powerful enough, at least to date, to blunt the edge of all reform efforts to bring suburban governments into the twentieth century."[58] Although the usefulness of certain attempts to use political culture at the local level have been questioned,[59] an approach which takes into account the value commitments of groups within the community should aid in the analysis of the local political system.

INPUTS

The inputs of a political system can best be summarized under two broad categories: demands and supports.[60] As mentioned previously, the inputs furnish the raw material which the political system processes. If people did not want or expect government to do certain things there would be little need for a government at all. Thus demands can be considered the requests made by citizens individually and collectively for decisions or policies which require action on the part of some government agency or official. Various groups often find they are unable to resolve problems privately and therefore request, sometimes reluctantly, the involvement of those charged with making binding decisions for the whole society. The need for authoritative decisions does not always arise outside the system; some demands may be internally inspired (withinputs).[61] For example, employees of the local government, perhaps through collective bargaining, may insist upon higher wages and better working conditions. This action would most assuredly be a demand, but one originating within the political system itself. Demands must be expressed, either explicitly or implicitly, and should be distinguished from expectations concerning the "rules of the game" (e.g., government officials are expected to be honest; this is not ordinarily a demand), public opinion (which may not yet be articulated in demand form), ideology, or mere preferences.[62]

Demands, although an essential form of input, can under certain conditions also become a source of stress for the political system. Demand input overload might occur when the number of demands exceeds the capacity of a particular system to process them. An example at the urban level might be a situation in which a large quantity of demands were put forth by one segment of the community, perhaps by the blacks, creating considerable stress (volume stress) because of the difficulty a city government might encounter in immediately meeting all of them. Stress on the system may also develop when the content of the demands is especially complex, controversial, or difficult to produce. Again, the insistence of minority groups that cities provide certain economic benefits—better jobs, housing, and so on—as Nathan Glazer has observed, may in all likelihood be beyond the capacity of the local government to furnish.[63] This situation might be seen as a form of content stress arising out of input overload.

The political system is not without certain mechanisms which serve to reduce, regulate, and channel demands made upon it. The prevailing local political ideology—beliefs, values, and myths—may serve as a potentially important barrier preventing certain demands from being seriously considered by local decision makers. Although it is difficult to empirically verify, defenders of the status quo frequently employ existing local political beliefs to discredit controversial proposals, according to Bachrach and Baratz. This thwarting of latent or even manifest challenges to the current allocation of values has been termed "nondecision-making" by the two authors.[64] Other methods for managing demands may involve the use of channeling structures—such as the mass media, interest groups, or political parties—which serve to focus demands and aggregate diffuse requests for action by local decision makers. Other structural characistics of local government such as the electoral system (partisan or non-partisan), the form of government (mayor or council-manager), and the constituency type (election at-large or by ward) should also be included among those arrangements which shape and limit the nature of local demands. These mechanisms and processes keep political officials from being inundated with a disorderly flood of demands.

If the political system is to successfully convert the demands made upon it into outputs, a certain degree of "support" for the system is essential. This support may be expressed by supportive actions (overt support) or supportive attitudes (covert support). Active commitment to the political system at the local level might include voting in city elections, willingly paying taxes, or even defending the actions of the local police. Less observable support might assume the form of a set of favorable attitudes or predispositions with respect to the local political system. A great deal of research documents that many citizens possess very little in the way of strong feelings for the local community as such. Sentiments of loyalty, patriotism, and so on in this country are ordinarily directed at the higher levels of the system. Findings at the urban level on the correlates of support are interesting. For instance, we know that high income, education, and occupational status are positively associated with knowledge of local civic affairs, voting turnout, and greater civic involvement generally.[65] At the same time, however, when we examine the urban populace with respect to where they fall on a local-cosmopolitan continuum, we also note that the better educated, high-status groups are more likely to be oriented toward the larger world outside the local community.[66] Bollens and Schmandt have also argued that even the suburbanite's commitment to a separate suburban government comes not from a sense of community, but from fear of "higher taxes, invasion by Negroes and other core city 'undesirables,' downgrading of the local public school system, or loss of certain privileges peculiar to the suburban enclave."[67]

Support for the political system, according to Easton, may be low or even negative, as certain recent events in American cities amply indicate. Particularly in recent years, extensive manifestations of system disaffection ranging from sit-ins to widespread looting and rioting have erupted in many large urban areas. The causes have been many but might be subsumed under the term *output failure* which takes place when political authorities cannot or will not effectively cope with the demands of various aggrieved groups either in terms of quantity or quality.[68]

Gabriel Almond has offered an alternative scheme for grouping inputs into four functional categories: (1) political socialization and recruitment; (2) interest articulation; (3) interest aggregation; (4) political communication.[69]

Political socialization is "the process of induction into the political culture. Its end product is a set of attitudes—cognitions, value standards, and feelings—toward the political system, its various roles, and role incumbents."[70] Although political socialization is considered an input function in Almond's scheme, Irish and Prothro reason that, in actuality, political socialization should be regarded as *both* an input and an output of the political system. They suggest that the political system itself through its decisions and policies generates so much reinforcement of prevailing political norms and values that the socialization process must be considered as a system output as well as an input.[71]

Political recruitment may be considered as a further extension of the political socialization process. Every modern government must devise ways of drawing persons from the larger society into positions of civic leadership. At the local level, knowledge of the recruitment process comes primarily from studies of the background characteristics of local decision makers. City managers have been shown to be very much like other administrative elites in this country with respect to social attributes—that is, highly educated, white, male, native-born, predominantly Anglo-Saxon and Protestant.[72] Surveys of city council members, especially those from small and medium-sized communities with nonpartisan elections, reveal that in most instances these officials are true amateurs with respect to previous political experience. Often they are merchants or real estate and insurance salesmen instead of professional politicians, attracted to part-time public office by a sense of civic duty rather than an interest in the power and perquisites of elective office.[73]

Every government to remain viable must in some way recognize those matters which are of concern to its citizens. For diffuse claims and demands of various individuals and groups to be effective, they must not only be expressed but drawn together in such a manner as to present relatively few alternative policy proposals for government action. These interest articulation and interest aggregation functions are the crucial tasks performed by interest groups and political parties in modern societies. Interest groups assume the primary responsibility of articulating political demands while parties seek to form the largest possible interest-group coalitions.[74] Much of what is known about interest-group activity in urban politics comes from community power studies in which a major concern has often been to determine which private groups or associations "really" control the city. In this respect, Claire Gilbert, relying on a secondary analysis of power structure data from 166 communities, concludes that American cities have increasingly become pluralistic. She found that power over community decisions lies less and less in the hands of a few with a resulting increase in importance of the "broker" who can bring together various community elements.[75] Aside from the sometimes tangential consideration of the role of interest groups as articulators of public demands found in local power studies, systematic research on interest groups has been limited.[76] Not so in the case of political parties, in which considerable attention has been devoted to the effects of partisan or nonpartisan elections on local politics. An examination of nonpartisan elections in Newark, for instance, revealed that the absence of a party label for local candidates increased voter awareness of ethnic and religious considerations.[77] Nonpartisan elections also appear to be associated with lower levels of voting turnout,[78] an increase in the relative strength of

Republicans,[79] and an enhanced political role for the press, civic associations, and city bureaucrats.[80]

URBAN POLITICAL DECISION MAKERS AND STRUCTURES

Inputs cannot automatically transform themselves into outputs or public policies without the direct intervention of official agencies and structures. At the level of urban policies, decision-making bodies play distinctive and readily recognizable roles. Every city government has some form of legislative body (a city council, commission, or board of aldermen), an executive or administrative head (either elected or appointed), a judicial system, and a public bureaucracy if the city is of any size. Moreover, in many urban areas a vast plethora of local governmental agencies exist which may have complete autonomy from the city government, including a separate school system, county government, and a variety of special districts. These official agencies of local government have one thing in common: they are all engaged in converting certain demands into public policies.

Some recent empirical studies of urban political phenomena have minimized the direct influence of local government structure on public policy outcomes,[81] partially as a reaction to the overemphasis of formal government agencies found in so many early local government studies. The early community power research also tended to slight the importance of elected local officials, stressing instead the dominance of informal private sources of power, particularly the economic notables.[82] Recently, however, many urban scholars have begun to reconsider the impact of city government on local politics. James Q. Wilson has suggested that we still need to "understand the political linkages between demography (or attitudes) and policy."[83] In systems terms we cannot overlook the "black box" which converts demands and supports into binding policy decisions.

A considerable amount of research exists on the role of the city manager in the policy-making process, with the general conclusion being that the manager and his staff are inevitably involved in policy initiation as well as policy execution.[84] Less research exists on the way in which city councils make policy decisions.[85] One study reveals the council to be a largely passive partner or even a negative one, either going along with the city manager's proposals or, in the case of some members, taking an active opposition role to the manager's ideas.[86] Mayors have been studied less systematically than councils despite the insistence of some urban scholars that in the large city, at least, the mayor's role is crucial in providing needed policy leadership.[87] Research on strictly urban-level courts is almost nonexistent although there are studies which deal with the impact of higher court decisions at the local level.[88]

The reintroduction of variables which attempt to measure the influence of political structures in the policy process has been characteristic of the best current empirical research on urban politics. Research of this type considers governmental and political characteristics to be intervening variables which modify the effects of socioeconomic and cultural factors on local public policy.[89] Outputs in this scheme, as suggested previously, often take the form of municipal expenditures, while inputs are represented by such things as community educational levels, income, percent nonwhite, percent foreign born, and so on. The intervening political structure variables are likely to include type of local election (partisan or nonpartisan), form of government (mayor-council, manager, or commission), and constituency type (ward or at-large). One of the hypotheses tested is that government structure exerts an independent effect on the level and scope of public politics and that socioeconomic characteristics alone cannot account for as much variation in local policy as political structure and socioeconomic characteristics taken together can explain. A basic criticism of research of this type is that the attempts to operationalize political or government features have been overly simple or crude.[90] Nevertheless, municipal policy research which seeks to take account of the influence of political decision-making structures and processes has done much to pull the study of local politics back into the political science mainstream.

URBAN POLICY OUTPUTS

Outputs of the political system are the decisions and actions taken by the official decision makers in response to the changing demands and supports generated by the environment and by the political system itself. At the community level these outputs are the laws (city ordinances), administrative actions, or court decisions which determine local public policy. Perhaps a distinction should technically be made between decisions, outputs, outcomes, and policies, although the terms are often used interchangeably. To Easton, binding decisions and implementing actions constitute outputs which he differentiates from their *consequences* or outcomes.[91]

Two broad categories of outputs have been identified: rewards and deprivations.[92] *Rewards* consist of the goods and services which a person might receive or be able to receive from his government. At the local level these might include such tangible facilities as fire stations, streets, school buildings, or garbage trucks. Or rewards might take intangible forms such as local health services or welfare payments. *Deprivations*, on the other hand, would not only include taxes to pay for government services but also such things as regulations and restrictions imposed by local authority to maintain public order and protect the peace. A moment's thought would indicate that many local policies may simultaneously reward and deprive, the most common example of which might be the traffic ordinance limiting an individual's driving behavior to make it possible to get from place to place with some degree of convenience and safety.

Additional categories for analysis of public policies have also been suggested. Theodore Lowi has presented a threefold policy typology which includes the following: distributive policies, redistributive, and regulatory.[93] Lewis Froman, on the other hand, would divide community policies into two broad groups, areal and segmental, with the first having communitywide application and the latter affecting only limited geographical sections or certain groups in the locality.[94] Very little research using either Lowi's or Froman's concepts has been undertaken in the field of local politics. Another approach to developing analytical categories for urban policies would be to employ the technique of factor analysis which seeks to group variables on the basis of underlying similarities. Some interesting research using factor analysis has been undertaken on state politics,[95] but its use in urban politics has been virtually nonexistent.[96]

The general approach to the analysis of public policies at both the state and local level has increasingly followed the lead of Dawson and Robinson who declared several years ago that "public policy is the major dependent variable that political science seeks to explain."[97] Primarily because of data availability, most of the policy outcomes used as dependent variables have consisted of government revenue and expenditures, both in the aggregate and for particular policy areas. For example, the entire book, *Metropolitan America*, is devoted to an explanation of the differences in fiscal behavior from city to city and between cities and suburbs.[98] The particular dependent variables employed in the study were per capita education expenditures, per capita noneducation expenditures, per capita education tax proxy (education expenditures less state aid), and per capita noneducation tax proxy (noneducation expenditure less state aid). Other municipal-level studies have dealt with such policy areas as planning, health, police and fire, parks and recreation, as well as education.[99] The model typically followed in this research, as indicated previously, uses community socioeconomic characteristics as the independent variables (or inputs) along with the intervening political variables in a regression and correlation analysis to show how much policy variation among cities can be "explained" by the presence of these sets of independent variables. Basically, the assumption is that differing levels of local service are "caused" by variations in the community's socioeconomic environment together with its governmental characteristics. One of the classic studies of this type is Thomas Dye's analysis of educational policies in a large number of American cities (contained in this volume).

Jacob and Lipsky have suggested that recent policy-oriented studies of state and local politics have at least one shortcoming: the failure to be concerned with differences in distribution of benefits among a population. They argue that even programs which apparently benefit most of the community—such as education and highway construction—have a variable incidence of benefits. Consequently, political scientists are urged to collect and analyze data concerning distribution of program benefits as well as the overall levels of public services.[100] There is no suggestion that urban scholars abandon the policy focus in their research. To the contrary, policy-oriented research has opened virtually a whole new dimension for important scholarly work in urban politics which should continue to bring significant advances in our knowledge of local political systems.

FEEDBACK

Feedback is a crucial concept in all of systems analysis. In political research the terms is ordinarily used to indicate the capacity of the system to respond to stress by modifying or redirecting its own behavior. The feedback process—or feedback loop, as it is sometimes called—begins with the outputs of the system which have an effect on other systems or on the political system itself. Information about the impact of governmental decisions and policies must then return to the authorities (as inputs) so that the political system may adapt its behavior to changing demands (through producing new outputs). In effect, the feedback process is what gives the political system its dynamic quality and it may be viewed as a series of succeeding steps: (1) production of outputs by the political system; (2) response by members of the larger society (the environment); (3) communication of information about responses to the decision makers; (4) possible action (new outputs) by the political authorities in response to the information received.

Easton insists that the very persistence of the political system depends upon keeping this dynamic process functioning. Anything that delays, distorts, or severs the flow of information to the authorities seriously interferes with their capacity to act and may result in a serious reduction of support for the system. Feedback, therefore, provides a key link in what Easton terms a "goal-setting, self-transforming and creatively adaptive system."[101]

Policy research at both the state and local level has been especially negligent in studying the effects of feedback. At the community level, for example, almost no efforts have been made to systematically measure the effects of public policies on the environment which might subsequently produce a response by the local government. Planning and zoning along with industrial promotion are among the more obvious policies by which a city copes with its environment. By the careful use of zoning and land use controls a city may be able to significantly influence its future socio-economic composition. Robert Wood, in his study of the New York City region, concluded that planning and zoning were particularly important devices by which local jurisdictions kept "undesirables" out and encouraged "desirables" to come in.[102] A municipality's search for industry may also generate pressures on the local polity. An example of this recently occurred in an overwhelmingly white residential community in a border state which had apparently been successful in attracting a large branch plant of a highly prestigious national corporation. One crucial factor, however, in the minds of many who had sought the industry was the adoption of a local open housing policy. Thus the community's commitment to acquiring new industry resulted in the demand—by some at least—for a controversial local policy in hopes of assuring the location of the desired plant.

The structure of a democratic system suggests that political figures constantly engage in the process of measuring the public's reaction to various government proposals and programs. Their very political lives may depend on their sensitivity to this feedback process. Yet, as common as this phenomena is in everyday political life, very little academic research has been devoted to a rigorous analysis of the feedback process, largely because of the difficulty in measuring its effect.[103] The challenge of devising imaginative and fruitful ways of empirically measuring the feedback concept lies waiting for the enterprising urban scholar.[104]

Conclusion

The purpose of this introductory essay has been to outline a systems approach to the study of urban politics. It has been necessary for us to avoid certain details and perhaps to unduly simplify important systems concepts. Therefore, we urge those who are interested in a more detailed discussion of systems analysis to go directly to other works which can generally be understood by the nonspecialist.

At this point, perhaps, we should be reminded that the systems paradigm is not a political theory in the strictest sense but rather an approach or framework for analysis. This is not to detract from its usefulness, however, but only to recognize its purposes and limitations. It is also important to note that serious research gaps exist, and certain problems need to be overcome to make maximum use of the systems approach to local politics. In particular, political scientists must continue to search for more theoretically sophisticated models of the relationships between various components of the political system. There is considerable agreement that our knowledge of the conversion process is inadequate—not only with respect to *how* certain inputs get transformed into outputs, but *why* some and not others. Feedback was also singled out as a concept which has thus far been greatly underresearched. The final essay in the volume deals with the research problems and gaps which currently plague state and local studies based on a systems approach. Despite certain problems which will undoubtedly accompany any attempt to use a theoretical framework for empirical research, the increasing popularity of systems analysis testifies to its usefulness in studying a variety of political institutions and processes.

Notes

1. One of the first criticisms of the failure of students of local government to keep pace with advances in the general field of political science was Allan R. Richards, "Local Government Research: A Partial Evaluation," *Public Administration Review*, 14 (1954), 271–77. Other early critics include Lawrence J. R. Herson, "The Lost World of Municipal Government," *American Political Science Review*, 51 (1957), 330–45; Robert J. Daland, "Political Science and the Study of Urbanization," *ibid.*, pp. 491–509; and Coleman Woodbury, "Great Cities, Great Problems, Great Possibilities?", *Public Administration Review*, 18 (1958), 332–40. Also see Gladys Kammerer, "The Politics of Metropolis: Still a Frontier," *ibid.*, 23 (1963), 240–46; Wallace Sayer and Nelson Polsby, "American Political Science and the Study of Urbanization," in Philip Hauser and Leo Schnore (eds.), *The Study of Urbanization* (New York: John Wiley, 1965), pp. 115–56; James Q. Wilson, "Problems in the Study of Urban Politics," in Edward Buehrig (ed.), *Essays in Political Science* (Bloomington: Indiana University, 1966), pp. 131–50; H. Paul Friesema, "The Metropolis and the Maze of Local Government," *Urban Affairs Quarterly*, 2 (1966), 68–90; and Norton Long, "Political Science and the City," in Leo Schnore and Henry Fagin (eds.), *Urban Research and Policy Planning* (Beverly Hills, Calif.: Sage, 1967), pp. 243–62.

2. Herbert Jacob and Michael Lipsky, "Outputs, Structure, and Power: An Assessment of Changes in the Study of State and Local Politics," *Journal of Politics*, 30 (1968), 510–39.

3. See Charles R. Adrian, "Some General Characteristics of Nonpartisan Elections," *American Political Science Review* 46 (1952), 766–76; Adrian, "A Typology of Nonpartisan Elections," *Western Political Quarterly*, 12 (1959), 449–58; Oliver P. Williams and Charles R. Adrian, *Four Cities: A Study in Comparative Policy Making* (Philadelphia: University of Pennsylvania Press, 1963); Williams, Harold Herman, Charles Liebman, and Thomas Dye, *Suburban Differences and Metropolitan Policies: A Philadelphia Story* (Philadelphia: University of Pennsylvania Press, 1965); Edward C. Banfield, "The Politics of Metropolitan Area Organizations," *Midwest Journal of Political Science*, 1 (1957), 77–91; Banfield, *Political Influence* (New York: The Free Press, 1961); Banfield and James Q. Wilson, *City Politics* (Cambridge: Harvard–M.I.T. Press, 1963); Wilson, "Planning and Politics: Citizen Participation in Urban Renewal," *Journal of the American Institute of Planners*, 29 (1963), 210–36; Wilson and Banfield, "Public-Regardingness as Value Premise"; *American Political Science Review*, 58 (1964), 876–87; Robert C. Wood, *Suburbia: Its People and Their Politics* (Boston:

Houghton-Mifflin, 1958); Wood, *1400 Governments* (Cambridge: Harvard University Press, 1961); Scott Greer, "The Social Structure and Political Process of Suburbia," *American Sociological Review*, 25 (1960), 514–26; Greer, *Governing the Metropolis* (New York: John Wiley, 1962); and Greer, *Metropolitics: A Study of Political Culture* (New York: John Wiley, 1963).

4. The discussion of the three analytic categories of urban studies included here has been influenced by a similar discussion found in Henry J. Schmandt, "Toward Comparability in Metropolitan Research," in Thomas R. Dye (ed.), *Comparative Research in Community Politics* (Proceedings of the Conference on Comparative Research in Community Politics, University of Georgia, 1966), pp. 6–41.

There appears to be little doubt about the lack of a related group of general statements concerning the urban political process which would provide a formalized deductive theory in the sense used by philosophers of science. Eugene J. Meehan, for example, argues that there are no deductive theories in either political science or sociology. Therefore, our use of the term *theory* is somewhat loose and inexact, more nearly conforming to what Meehan considers as "quasi-theory" or probabilistic explanation. See his *The Theory and Method of Political Analysis* (Homewood, Ill.: Dorsey, 1965), particularly chaps. 4 and 5.

5. Robert Salisbury and Gordon Black, "Class and Party in Partisan and Nonpartisan Elections: The Case of Des Moines," *American Political Science Review*, 57 (1963), 584–92; and Williams and Adrian, *Four Cities*, pp. 53–56.

6. Walter C. Kaufman and Scott Greer, "Voting in a Metropolitan Community: An Application of Social Area Analysis," *Social Forces*, 38 (1960), 196–204; Alvin Boskoff and Harmon Zeigler, *Voting Patterns in a Local Election* (Philadelphia: J. B. Lippincott, 1964); Richard A. Watson and John H. Romani, "Metropolitan Government for Metropolitan Cleveland: An Analysis of the Voting Record," *Midwest Journal of Political Science*, 5 (1961), 365–90; and James A. Norton, "Referenda Voting in a Metropolitan Area," *Western Political Quarterly*, 16 (1963), 195–212.

7. David A. Booth, *Metropolitics: The Nashville Consolidation* (East Lansing: Institute for Community Development, Michigan State University, 1963); and Brett W. Hawkins, "Public Opinion and Metropolitan Reorganization in Nashville," *Journal of Politics*, 28 (1966), 408–18.

8. Edward L. McDill and Jeanne C. Ridley, "Status, Anomia, Political Alienation, and Political Participation," *American Journal of Sociology*, 58 (1962), 205–17.

9. Werner Z. Hirsch, "Expenditure Implications of Metropolitan Growth and Consolidation," *Review of Economics and Statistics*, 41

(1959), 232–41; Seymour Sacks and William F. Hellmuth, Jr., *Financing Government in a Metropolitan Area* (New York: The Free Press, 1961); and Louis H. Masotti and Don R. Bowen, "Communities and Budgets: The Sociology of Municipal Expenditures," *Urban Affairs Quarterly*, 1 (1965), 39–58.

10. Terry N. Clark, for example, employs a broad analytical scheme for the analysis of community power which is derived from the structural-functional approach of the sociologists Talcott Parsons, Robert Merton, and Robert Bales. See his "Who Governs, Where, When, and With What Effects?" in Clark (ed.), *Community Structure and Decision-Making: Comparative Analyses* (San Francisco: Chandler, 1968), pp. 15–24. Herbert Simon has used a decision-making framework for political analysis. See his *Administrative Behavior*, 2nd ed. (New York: The Macmillan Company, 1957); *Models of Man* (New York: John Wiley, 1957); and "Political Research: The Decision-Making Framework," in David Easton (ed.), *Varieties of Political Theory* (Englewood Cliffs, N.J.: Prentice-Hall, 1966), pp. 15–24.

11. Robert Agger, Daniel Goldrich, and Bert Swanson, *The Rulers and the Ruled* (New York: John Wiley, 1964), pp. 40–51.

12. Robert A. Dahl, *Who Governs? Democracy and Power in an American City* (New Haven: Yale University Press, 1961).

13. Williams *et al.*, *Suburban Differences and Metropolitan Policies.*

14. Wood, *1400 Governments.*

15. Matthew Holden, Jr., "The Governance of the Metropolis as a Problem in Diplomacy," *Journal of Politics*, 26 (1964), 627–48.

16. Vincent Ostrom, Charles M. Tiebout, and Robert O. Warren, "The Organization of Government in Metropolitan Areas: A Theoretical Inquiry," *American Political Science Review*, 55 (1961), 831–42; and Robert O. Warren, "A Municipal Services Market Model of Metropolitan Organization," *Journal of the American Institute of Planners*, 30 (1964), 193–204.

17. Norton E. Long, "The Local Community as an Ecology of Games," *American Journal of Sociology*, 54 (1958), 251–61. See also Paul A. Smith, "The Games of Community Politics," *Midwest Journal of Political Science*, 9 (1965), 37–60.

18. Karl W. Deutsch, *The Nerves of Government* (New York: The Free Press, 1963).

19. Richard L. Meier, *A Communications Theory of Urban Growth* (Cambridge: M.I.T. Press, 1962), and James V. Toscano, "Transaction Flow Analysis in Metropolitan Areas: Some Preliminary Explorations," in Philip E. Jacob and Toscano (eds.), *The Integration of Political Communities* (Philadelphia: J. B. Lippincott, 1964), pp. 98–119.

20. Robert Gutman, "Urban Studies as a Field of Research," *American Behavioral Scientist*, 6 (1963), 9–14.

21. John E. Bebout and Harry C. Bredemeier, "American Cities as Social Systems," *Journal of the American Institute of Planners*, 29 (1963), 64–76.

22. Robert C. Wood, "The Contributions of Political Science to Urban Form," in Werner Z. Hirsch (ed.), *Urban Life and Form* (New York: Holt, Rinehart & Winston, 1963), pp. 99–128.

23. See David Easton, *The Political System* (New York: Alfred A. Knopf, 1953); Easton, "An Approach to the Analysis of Political Systems," *World Politics*, 9 (1957), 383–400; Easton, *A Framework for Political Analysis* (Englewood Cliffs, N.J.: Prentice-Hall, 1965); and Easton, *A Systems Analysis of Political Life* (New York: John Wiley, 1965).

24. Gabriel A. Almond, "Political Theory and Political Science," *American Political Science Review*, 60 (1966), 876.

25. For example, see William C. Mitchell, *The American Polity* (New York: The Free Press, 1962); Marian D. Irish and James W. Prothro, *The Politics of American Democracy*, 4th ed. (Englewood Cliffs, N.J.: Prentice-Hall, 1968); Herbert Jacob and Kenneth Vines, *Politics of the American States* (Boston: Little, Brown, 1965); Roland Young, *The American Congress* (New York: Harper & Brothers, 1958); Richard Fenno, "The House Appropriations Committee as a Political System: The Problems of Integration," *American Political Science Review*, 56 (1962), 310–24; and Glendon Schubert, *Judicial Policy-Making: The Political Role of the Courts* (Glenview, Ill.: Scott, Foresman, 1965).

26. Easton, *Political System.*

27. For elaboration of these concepts see Abraham Kaplan, *The Conduct of Inquiry* (San Francisco: Chandler, 1964); Robert Dubin, *Theory Building* (New York: The Free Press, 1969); Meehan, *Political Analysis*; Fred M. Frohock, *The Nature of Political Inquiry* (Homewood, Ill.: Dorsey Press, 1962); Anatol Rapoport, "Various Meanings of Theory," *American Political Science Review*, 52 (1958), 972–88; and Arthur S. Goldberg, "Political Science as Science," in Nelson W. Polsby, Robert A. Dentler, and Paul A. Smith (eds.), *Politics and Social Life* (Boston: Houghton Mifflin, 1963), pp. 26–36.

28. Conceptual applications to urban politics are summarized in Samuel A. Kirkpatrick, "Multidimensional Aspects of Local Political Systems," *Western Political Quarterly*, 23 (1970), 808–28.

29. Norbert Wiener, *The Human Use of Human Beings: Cybernetics and Society* (New York: Doubleday, 1950); Stafford Beer, *Cybernetics and Management* (New York: John Wiley, 1959); and Walter Buckley (ed.), *Modern Systems Research for the Behavioral Scientist* (Chicago: Aldine, 1968).

30. Charles E. Merriam, *Political Power* (New York: Collier Books, 1934); and Harold D. Lasswell, *Politics: Who Gets What, When, How* (New York: McGraw-Hill, 1936).

31. Charles S. Hyneman, *The Study of Politics* (Urbana: University of Illinois Press, 1959).

32. Dahl, *Who Governs?*; and Peter Bachrach and Martin S. Baratz, "Decisions and Nondecisions," *American Political Science Review*, 57 (1963), 632–43.

33. David B. Truman, *The Governmental Process* (New York: Alfred A. Knopf, 1951).

34. Murray Edelman, *The Symbolic Uses of Politics* (Urbana: University of Illinois Press, 1964).

35. Easton, *Political System*.

36. Oran R. Young, *Systems of Political Science* (Englewood Cliffs, N.J.: Prentice-Hall, 1968), chap. 2.

37. Gabriel A. Almond and James S. Coleman (eds.), *The Politics of the Developing Areas* (Princeton, N.J.: Princeton University Press, 1960), pp. 3–64.

38. Easton, *Framework for Political Analysis*, pp. 63–69.

39. Meehan, *Political Analysis*, p. 153; and Jerone Stephens, "The Logic of Functional and Systems Analysis in Political Science," *Midwest Journal of Political Science*, 13 (1969), 367–94.

40. Meehan, *Political Analysis*, p. 134.

41. Oran Young, *Systems of Political Science*, p. 48.

42. Anatol Rapoport, "Some System Approaches to Political Theory," in David Easton (ed.), *Varieties of Political Theory* (Englewood Cliffs, N.J.: Prentice-Hall, 1966), pp. 131–33.

43. An approach closely related to Easton's systems approach — structural-functionalism — has also received considerable attention in recent years among political scientists. Originating with anthropology and coming to political science through the writings of such eminent sociologists as Talcott Parsons and Robert Merton, functionalism, as it is often called, is basically concerned with designating and analyzing those functions performed by various structures of a particular system which contribute to system stability or equilibrium. Harold Kaplan, in his book on Metro Toronto, has been one of the few to use an explicitly structural functional framework for the analysis of urban politics. See his *Urban Political Systems: A Functional Analysis of Metro Toronto* (New York: Columbia University Press, 1967).

44. Easton, *Framework for Political Analysis*, pp. 69–75.

45. *Ibid.*, p. 66.

46. Ronald L. Stewart, "The Influence of the Business Community in Oklahoma City Politics" (unpublished Masters thesis, Oklahoma State University, 1967), pp. 70–112, documents the extensive involvement of the local Chamber of Commerce in the politics of one such city.

47. For a consideration of state-urban relations see Council of State Governments, *State Responsibility in Urban Regional Development* (Chicago, 1962); Harold Herman, *New York State and the Metropolitan Problem* (Philadelphia: University of Pennsylvania Press, 1963); Norman Beckman and Page L. Ingraham, "The States and Urban Areas," *Law and Contemporary Problems*, 30 (1965), 76–102; and Alan K. Campbell (ed.), *The States and the Urban Crisis* (Englewood Cliffs, N.J.: Prentice-Hall, 1970).

48. For recent examples see J. David Greenstone and Paul Peterson, "Reformers, Machines, and the War on Poverty," in James Q. Wilson (ed.), *City Politics and Public Policy* (New York: John Wiley, 1968), pp. 267–92; James J. Vanecko, "Community Mobilization and Institutional Change: The Influence of the Community Action Program in Large Cities," *Social Science Quarterly*, 50 (1969), 609–30; Fremont J. Lyden and Jerry V. Thomas, "Citizen Participation in Policy-Making: A Study of a Community Action Program," *ibid.*, pp. 631–42; Murray Seidler, "Some Participant Observer Reflections on Detroit's Community Action Program," *Urban Affairs Quarterly*, 5 (1970), 183–205; and Peter Bachrach, "A Power Analysis: The Shaping of Antipoverty Policy in Baltimore," *Public Policy*, 18 (1970), 155–86.

49. Recent examples of the metropolitan reform literature include Committee for Economic Development, *Modernizing Local Government* (New York, 1966); Advisory Commission on Intergovernmental Relations, *Metropolitan America: Challenge to Federalism* (Washington, D.C.: Government Printing Office, 1966); and Committee for Economic Development, *Reshaping Government in Metropolitan Areas* (New York, 1970).

50. See Vincent Ostrom, Charles M. Tiebout, and Robert Warren, "The Organization of Government in Metropolitan Areas: A Theoretical Inquiry," *American Political Science Review*, 55 (1969), 831–42; Thomas R. Dye, "Metropolitan Integration by Bargaining Among Sub-Areas," *American Behavioral Scientist*, 5 (1962), 11–13; and H. Paul Friesema, "The Metropolis and the Maze of Local Government," *Urban Affairs Quarterly*, 2 (1966), 68–90.

51. Williams *et al.*, *Suburban Differences and Metropolitan Policies*.

52. Alan K. Campbell and Seymour Sacks, *Metropolitan America: Fiscal Patterns and Governmental Systems* (New York: The Free Press, 1967), p. 95.

53. Morris Axelrod, "Urban Structure and Social Participation," *American Sociological Review*, 21 (1956), 13–18; John M. Foskett, "The Influence of Social Participation on Community Programs and Activities," in Marvin Sussman (ed.), *Community Structure and Analysis* (New York: Thomas Y. Crowell, 1959), pp. 311–30; Greer, "Surburbia"; Greer and Peter

Orleans, "The Mass Society and the Parapolitical Structure," *American Sociological Review*, 27 (1962), 634–46; Robert R. Alford and Harry M. Scoble, "Sources of Local Political Involvement," *American Political Science Review*, 62 (1968), 1192–1206.

54. Banfield and Wilson, *City Politics*, pp. 18–32, stresses the role of conflict management by city government.

55. Jacob and Lipsky, "Outputs, Structure, and Power," p. 514.

56. Wilson, "Introduction," *City Politics and and Public Policy*, p. 12.

57. Williams and Adrian, *Four Cities*, pp. 23–36, and Wilson and Banfield, "Public-Regardingness as Value Premise."

58. Wood, *Suburbia*, p. 13.

59. See Wolfinger and Field, "Political Ethos," for a criticism of Wilson and Banfield's "public-regarding" thesis.

60. Easton, *Systems Analysis of Political Life*, Part 2 and 3.

61. Easton, *Framework for Political Analysis*, pp. 114–15.

62. Easton, *Systems Analysis of Political Life*, pp. 41–47.

63. Nathan Glazer, "Race in the City," in Brian J. L. Berry and Jack Meltzer (eds.), *Goals for Urban America* (Englewood Cliffs, N.J.: Prentice-Hall, 1967), pp. 85–98.

64. Peter Bachrach and Morton Baratz, "Two Faces of Power," *American Political Science Review*, 56 (1962); Bachrach and Baratz, "Decisions and Non-decisions: An Analytical Framework," *ibid.*, 57 (1963), 641–51.

65. John C. Bollens (ed.), *Exploring the Metropolitan Community* (Berkeley and Los Angeles: University of California Press, 1961), pp. 284–312; William Erbe, "Social Involvement and Political Activity: A Replication and Elaboration," *American Sociological Review*, 29 (1964), 198–215; and Robert R. Alford and Eugene C. Lee, "Voting Turnout in American Cities," *American Political Science Review*, 62 (1968), 796–814.

66. William M. Dobriner, "Local and Cosmopolitan as Contemporary Suburban Character Types," in Dobriner (ed.), *Suburban Community*, pp. 132–43; and Thomas R. Dye, "The Local-Cosmopolitan Dimension and the Study of Urban Politics," *Social Forces*, 41 (1963), 239–46.

67. John C. Bollens and Henry J. Schmandt, *The Metropolis: Its People, Politics, and Economic Life* (New York: Harper & Row, 1965), p. 221.

68. Easton, *Systems Analysis of Political Life*, pp. 230–31.

69. Almond, "Functional Approach to Comparative Politics," pp. 26–52.

70. *Ibid.*, pp. 27–28.

71. Irish and Prothro, *Politics of American Democracy*, pp. 15–17.

72. Lloyd M. Wells, "Social Values and Political Orientations of City Managers: A Survey Report," *Southwestern Social Science Quarterly*, 48 (1967), 443–50.

73. Robert T. Daland, *Dixie City: A Portrait of Political Leadership* (University: Bureau of Public Administration, University of Alabama, 1956); and Eugene E. Lee, *The Politics of Nonpartisanship: A Study of California City Elections* (Berkeley and Los Angeles: University of California Press, 1960), pp. 50–69.

74. Almond, "Functional Approach to Comparative Politics," pp. 33–45.

75. Claire W. Gilbert, "Some Trends in Community Politics: A Secondary Analysis of Power Structure Data from 166 Communities," *Southwestern Social Science Quarterly*, 48 (1967), 373–82.

76. Nicholas A. Masters, "The Politics of Union Endorsement of Candidates in the Detroit Area," *Midwest Journal of Political Science*, 1 (1957), 136–50. See William H. Form, "Organized Labor's Place in the Community Power Structure," *Industrial and Labor Relations Review*, 12 (1959), 526–39; Salisbury, "St. Louis Politics"; Charles S. Liebman, "Electorates, Interest Groups and Local Government Policy," *American Behavioral Scientist*, 5 (1961), 8–11; Betty H. Zisk, Heinz Eulau, and Kenneth Prewitt, "City Councilmen and the Group Struggle: A Typology of Role Orientations," *Journal of Politics*, 27 (1965), 618–46; and Schley R. Lyons, "Labor in City Politics: The Case of the Toledo United Auto Workers," *Social Science Quarterly*, 49 (1969), 816–28.

77. Gerald M. Pomper, "Ethnic and Group Voting in Nonpartisan Municipal Elections," *Public Opinion Quarterly*, 30 (1966), 79–87.

78. Eugene C. Lee, "City Elections: A Statistical Profile," *Municipal Year Book, 1963* (Chicago: International City Managers' Association, 1963), pp. 74–84.

79. Oliver P. Williams and Charles R. Adrian, "The Insulation of Local Politics Under the Nonpartisan Ballot," *American Political Science Review*, 53 (1959), 1052–63. However, Peter Orleans, "Urban Politics and the Nonpartisan Ballot; A Metropolitan Case," in Scott Greer *et al.* (ed.), *The New Urbanization* (New York: St. Martin's Press, 1968), pp. 287–98, found that the nonpartisan ballot favored incumbent council members who, in this city, were predominantly Democrats.

80. Lee, *The Politics of Nonpartisanship*, pp. 76–96; and Banfield and Wilson, *City Politics*, p. 334.

81. See Amos Hawley, "Community Power and Urban Renewal Success," *American Journal of Sociology*, 68 (1963), 422–31; Masotti and Bowen, "Communities and Budgets"; and Dennis J. Palumbo and Oliver P. Williams, "Predictors of Public Policy: The Case of Local Public Health," *Urban Affairs Quarterly*, 2 (1967), 75–93.

82. The classic study of this type remains

Floyd Hunter, *Community Power Structure* (Chapel Hill: University of North Carolina Press, 1953).

83. Wilson, "Introduction," *City Politics and Public Policy*, p. 5.

84. See C. A. Harrell and D. G. Weiford, "The City Manager and the Policy Process," *Public Administration Review*, 19 (1959), 101–107; Duane Lockard, "The City Manager, Administrative Theory and Political Power," *Political Science Quarterly*, 72 (1962), 224–36; and David A. Booth, *Council-Manager Government in Small Cities* (Chicago: International City Managers' Association, 1968), pp. 91–114.

85. See J. Lieper Freeman, "A Case Study of the Legislative Process in Municipal Government," in John Wahlke and Heinz Eulau (eds.), *Legislative Behavior: A Reader in Theory and Research* (New York: The Free Press, 1959), pp. 228–37; Bryan T. Downes, "Issue Conflict, Factionalism and Consensus in Suburban City Councils," *Urban Affairs Quarterly*, 4 (1969), 477–97; and Heinz Eulau, "The Informal Organization of Decisional Structures in Small Legislative Bodies," *Midwest Journal of Political Science*, 13 (1969), 341–66.

86. Charles R. Adrian, "Leadership and Decision-Making in Manager Cities: A Study of Three Communities," *Public Administrative Review*, 18 (1958), 208–13.

87. Edward C. Banfield and Morton Grodzins, *Government and Housing in Metropolitan Areas* (New York: McGraw-Hill, 1958), pp. 160–66, and Henry W. Maier, *Challenge to the Cities* (New York: Random House, 1966).

88. See Frank J. Sorauf, "Zorach v. Clauson: The Impact of a Supreme Court Decision," *American Political Science Review*, 53 (1959), 777–91; and Clement E. Vose, "Interest Groups, Judicial Review, and Local Government," *Western Political Quarterly*, 19 (1966), 85–100.

89. Especially good examples of this kind of research are Thomas R. Dye, "Governmental Structure, Urban Environment, and Educational Policy," *Midwest Journal of Political Science*, 11 (1967), 353–80; and Dye, "Urban School Integration: A Comparative Analysis," *Urban Affairs Quarterly*, 4 (1968), 141–67.

90. Jacob and Lipsky, "Outputs, Structure, and Power," pp. 516–18.

91. Easton, *Systems Analysis of Political Life*, pp. 351–52.

92. Irish and Prothro, *Politics of American Democracy*, p. 12.

93. Theodore J. Lowi, "American Business, Public Policy, Case Studies, and Political Theory," *World Politics*, 16 (1964), 677–715.

94. Lewis A. Froman, Jr., "An Analysis of Public Policies in Cities," *Journal of Politics*, 29 (1967), 94–108.

95. See Ira Sharkansky and Richard I. Hofferbert, "Dimensions of State Politics, Economics, and Public Policy," *American Political Science Review*, 63 (1969), 867–79.

96. An exception is Palumbo and Williams, "Predictors of Public Policy."

97. Richard E. Dawson and James A. Robinson, "Inter-Party Competition; Economic Variables, and Welfare Policies in the American States," *Journal of Politics*, 25 (1963), 266.

98. Campbell and Sacks, *Metropolitan America*. Also see Roy W. Bahl, *Metropolitan City Expenditures: A Comparative Analysis* (Lexington: University of Kentucky Press, 1969).

99. See Donald A. Krueckeberg, "A Multivariate Analysis of Metropolitan Planning," *Journal of the American Institute of Planners*, 35 (1969), 319–25; Robert L. Lineberry, "Community Structure and Planning Commitment: A Note on the Correlates of Agency Expenditures," *Social Science Quarterly*, 50 (1969), 723–30; Palumbo and Williams, "Predictors of Public Policy"; Chester B. Rogers, "Environment, System and Output: The Consideration of a Model," *Social Forces*, 48 (1969), 72–87; Heinz Eulau and Robert Eyestone, "Policy Maps of City Councils and Policy Outcomes: A Developmental Analysis," *American Political Science Review*, 62 (1968), 124–44; Werner Z. Hirsch, "Determinants of Public Education Expenditures," *National Tax Journal*, 13 (1960), 29–40; and Seymour Sacks and David Ranney, "Suburban Education: A Fiscal Analysis," *Urban Affairs Quarterly*, 2 (1966), 103–19.

100. Jacob and Lipsky, "Outputs, Structure, and Power," pp. 516–17.

101. Easton, *Framework for Political Analysis*, pp. 128–32.

102. Wood, *1400 Governments*, pp. 93–95.

103. Some excellent studies have been done in the area of congressional-constituency relationships. See, for example, Warren E. Miller and Donald E. Stokes, "Constituency Influence in Congress," *American Political Science Review*, 57 (1963), 45–56; Lewis A. Froman, Jr., *Congressmen and Their Constituencies* (Chicago: Rand McNally, 1963); and Charles F. Cnudde and Donald J. McCrone, "The Linkage between Constituency Attitudes and Congressional Voting Behavior: A Causal Model," *American Political Science Review*, 60 (1966), 66–72. See also John W. Kingdon, "Politicians' Beliefs About Voters," *ibid.*, 61 (1967), 137–45.

104. A most promising start in this direction is Edmund P. Fowler and Robert Lineberry, "Canadian City Politics: Public Policy Analysis and the Problem of Reciprocal Causation" (paper delivered at the 65th Annual Meeting of the American Political Science Association, New York, 1969).

The Urban Environment

URBAN POLITICAL ACTIVITY is continuously conditioned and regulated by the nature of the environment within which it functions. The environment consists of the manifold societal subsystems which lie outside the political system but may interact with it at various times in such a way as to affect the process of authoritative allocation of values. Such societal subsystems as the economic system, the social structure, the religious climate, cultural influences, and state and federal government policies and regulations all help form the environment in which the local political system must operate.

A basic tenet of systems analysis dictates that a system must be distinguishable from its environment and yet remain open to influences from it. In the case of a political system, we are concerned with identifying and abstracting from the larger society those behavioral patterns and activities through which values are authoritatively allocated. Yet this statement alone does not solve the problem of what interactions should be included or excluded as part of the political system. The notion that some processes are "in" the system and some are not inevitably brings us to a consideration of a "boundary" which demarks the limits of the political system. As an open system, the polity is subjected to environmental influences which cross the boundary as exchanges, interactions, or flows from one system to the other. But the empirical referents, or tangible indicators, of the political system boundary are not always readily identifiable. In dealing with local political systems in this country, where a rather high degree of structural differentiation exists, a useful way of conceptualizing the boundary between the local polity and its immediate environs is through the use of role distinctions. For example, the local city council may consist of part-time, largely amateur decision makers who devote most of their energy to their business or occupation rather than to their official civic responsibilities. However, we consider these two roles—one primarily in the economic subsystem and the other in the political—to be largely separate and distinct. The local merchant, when he sits in deliberation on the city council, is expected to consider the problems of the municipality from a different perspective than he could if he were concerned only with his role of buying and selling merchandise. In fact, there are laws and unwritten norms dealing with conflict of interest, hopefully to insure that roles which are supposed to be separate are kept that way. This example is not to imply, however, that the boundary of the local political system is fixed and unchanging. To the contrary, boundary shifts characterize every political system, particularly the smaller urban system. Specifically, in many smaller, homogeneous communities the local government may be virtually an extension of the downtown business and commercial interests who view the city government as just another device to enhance local trade interests and/or keep taxes down.[1]

Another form of boundary permeability, which might be termed vertical as opposed to horizontal, takes place when the policies and regulations of upper levels of government intrude upon local decision processes. There was a time when most of the vertical exchanges took place between the state government and its legal creation, the municipality. But recently a growing amount of activity has developed between the federal government and urban areas as the problems of the big cities are increasingly viewed as national in scope. In addition, decisions of the U.S. Supreme Court have had a far-reaching impact upon the actions of local government, from restrictions on police behavior to school district boundary changes to achieve racial integration.

At a broader level of analysis, a set of four categories for classifying the boundary transactions by which urban areas get the things they need and want from the outside has been offered by Bebout and Bredemeier in their discussion of American cities as social systems.[2] The term they use for this is system "adaptation," which is part of the vocabulary of functional analysis. The four devices are coercive mechanisms, bargaining mechanisms, legal-bureaucratic mechanisms, and identification or solidarity mechanisms. In their discussion of these processes, the authors indicate that the central city has largely attempted to cope with its environment by bargaining, for example, with its noncitizens who may work there (commuters), other parallel social systems (e.g., adjoining cities, the business community, the state university), and the more inclusive systems of which it is a part—the county, region, state, and nation. They argue that this technique is increasingly less useful for the central city because its bargaining position has become so weak that it cannot effectively compete with so many potent outside forces without help, particularly from the state and federal government. Even though these concepts of boundary interchange are applied to the city as a social system rather than as a strictly political unit, the categories might also be used in discussing the ways in which the urban polity reacts with its environment.

At this point we might again consider those basic elements which make up the environment surrounding the urban political system. Applying Easton's suggested dichotomy of extrasocietal and intrasocietal forces at the urban level, we might group environmental influences in the following manner:

Intrasocietal Subsystems
(1) local economic base
(2) community social structure
(3) local cultural influences
(4) local physical character-
    istics

Extrasocietal Subsystems
(1) federal government
(2) state government
(3) state and regional economic,
    cultural, and social systems
(4) other contiguous or nearby
    local political systems.

The above listing is not intended to be exhaustive, but at least suggests the general kinds of outside subsystems which may impinge upon the operation of local government. For purposes of analysis, in this volume we have grouped environmental influences into three broad categories which we feel represent the most pervasive and significant outside pressures affecting urban politics. These are political structure, local political culture, and socioeconomic characteristics.

Political Structure

Political structure, in the analytic scheme being developed here, refers primarily to the effects of other political units, both horizontal and vertical, on the authoritative allocation of values at the local level. Some research and a considerable amount of speculation has been generated concerning the impact of metropolitanization and suburbanization on urban politics. Perhaps the most obvious result of the decentralized pattern of local government in metropolitan areas has been that no single political jurisdiction has control over or is responsible for the entire area or even a very large part of it. Many observers have long believed that this kind of polycentric governmental arrangement is dysfunctional for the metropolis, contributing to such problems as lack of coordination of public services, local tax inequities, imbalance in land-use patterns, and the failure to develop areawide political leadership. On the other hand, certain political scientists have recently begun to question whether the "fragmented" metropolitan political structure is intrinsically pathological and have suggested that, in fact, numerous arrangements exist which encourage and facilitate negotiation and bargaining among various local political units.[3] The decentralized political structure of the metropolis has also been defended as providing spheres of choice for individuals and groups who may find particular subareas better suited for their interests or needs[4] although, as Oliver Williams and associates have indicated, this has largely been a choice for whites only.[5] Despite these provocative arguments, considerable evidence shows that the existence of a multiplicity of governmental units in a metropolitan area results in differences in local fiscal and taxing patterns which, almost without exception, appear to be detrimental to the central city. The Advisory Commission on Intergovernmental Relations' analysis of this situation, which included in-depth case studies of twelve metropolitan areas, established that not only did central city–suburban fiscal disparities exist but that in several categories the disparities were growing.[6] Thus the debate continues between those who insist that a polycentric political structure is basically an unhealthy and undesirable political environment for local government and those who aver that the appearance of new coordinating mechanisms such as councils of governments (COG) will add to the already flourishing system of intergovernmental cooperation which now characterizes most metropolitan areas.

Other studies which have focused on relationships among local governments in metropolitan areas have found that interjurisdictional cooperation occurs more often where there are no major socioeconomic inequalities between the municipalities involved.[7] Further research suggests that cooperation may take place between communities with widely differing socioeconomic characteristics so long as the service area involved does not significantly affect social or life-style values, such as police radio agreements or other arrangements for providing neutral system maintenance functions (e.g., communications lines, transportation networks).[8] Interlocal relations, therefore, appear to be a function of both community socioeconomic distance and the type of service involved.

In any analysis, state government must be considered as a significant part of the large environment which helps determine the scope and direction of the local political system. At the most basic level, the local government is legally the creature of the state which establishes the ground rules for its operation through provisions of the state constitution, statutory law, judicial decisions, and administrative regulations. Beyond this, the state is deeply involved in furnishing various kinds of financial aid for local government, particularly in the areas of education, welfare, and highways. In 1967, for example, of the $60 billion spent by local government, $15 billion came from strictly state revenues, the major portion of which (60 per cent) went to elementary and secondary schools.[9] It would be a mistake to assume that local governments are merely passive receptacles for state largess which is channeled to them equally. To the contrary, in the case of state aid to education, existing formulas for assistance in many states permit substantial variations in per-pupil expenditures and generally ignore the need for additional help to those districts where the poor tend to congregate.[10] Apparent discrepancies of this sort between central cities and noncentral cities have often been cited among the reasons why big cities have so frequently turned to Washington for help rather than to the state governments. Nevertheless, most of the outside money which cities get continues to come from the states and not from the federal government and, in addition, about twice as much federal money reaches the cities through the states than is received directly from the federal government.[11]

Despite the extensive commitment of state funds to urban areas, there is little systematic research on how this form of assistance affects local programs and activities. It has been discovered that enormous variation occurs from state to state with respect to the allocation of expenditure responsibility to local governments. For example, in 1966 state expenditures were 70.4 percent of total state and local expenditures in Hawaii while representing only 22.9 percent of combined state and local spending in New York.[12] It has also been shown that those cities which rely more heavily on local sources of revenue are more likely to reflect higher per capita expenditures for all local functions, especially noneducation activities.[13] Recent research concerned with local fiscal behavior has found it useful to include the percentage of local spending emanating from state funds (state aid) as one of the independent variables in a multiple regression equation to explain variations in local spending. Campbell and Sacks indicate that the per capita municipal expenditures for New York as reported in the 1963 census were $332.34 compared to Chicago's $122.92. The discrepancy is, in large part, accounted for by differences in fiscal assignment responsibilities between the two states. Welfare and education are largely city functions in New York while in Illinois the two are generously assisted by the state. Yet only limited information is available on just how these differences in financing urban services effect the scope and quality of those services, So, despite the admonition of those troubled by the "urban crisis" that states must do more for the cities, little empirical data exists which would help us assess the impact of greater state involvement in local affairs.[14]

Since the 1930s, the federal government has assumed an ever larger role in dealing with the problems found in the nation's cities. This development has progressed so far that Roscoe Martin has insisted that the cities be considered as "partners in the federal system."[15] Much of the investigation of federal-local relations has dealt with the impact of federal programs on the structure of local government. Some observers have felt that federal influence in metropolitan areas has been a major contributing cause of the decentralized nature of metropolitan political structure. Urban sprawl has been made easier, the argument goes, as a result of two crucial federal programs—the mortgage financing policies of federal lending agencies (FHA and VA) and the federal highway program.[16] York Wilbern, however, has suggested that federal mortgage underwriting programs have been more a product of social and economic forces (including the automobile) rather than the cause of changing urban residential patterns.[17] Nevertheless, there is considerable agreement that prior to 1966 most federal aid to local areas did not encourage regional or areawide approaches to the planning and administration of urban development programs. Nearly two-thirds of the physical development programs surveyed in 1964 by the Advisory Commission on Intergovernmental Relations either accepted whatever areas of jurisdiction were made

available by the states and cities (usually strictly local), or in some instances required limited local jurisdictions.[18] The failure of federal programs to do much more than merely augment local funds for ongoing
local projects came as no surprise to some. Robert Wood, in 1961, had
observed that federal programs tended to follow rather than guide local
decisions for urban development; that in the absence of an overall national
strategy for metropolitan development, federal efforts facilitated accommodation to existing political structures and helped maintain the decentralized metropolitan political system.[19] Michael Danielson's research
on federal-metropolitan relations in the area of mass transportation
suggests that it would not be an easy matter for the federal government
to impose areawide policy making and planning on metropolitan areas
because of the absence of consensus among the many metropolitan
interests represented in Washington. The conflicting interests and objectives among groups representing the suburbs, the central city, and other
metropolitan agencies which make the creation of a metro-wide political
jurisdiction difficult to achieve locally also affect those in Washington
who deal with urban problems. Danielson concludes that the higher
political levels are constrained by the same values and commitments to
local autonomy which are so powerful at the politically fragmented and
differentiated grass roots.[20]

Beginning with the Housing and Urban Development Act of 1966, the
federal government began to take steps to induce greater metropolitan-
wide planning by providing for the review of most municipal federal
grant applications by either an areawide planning agency or a metropolitan
council of governments (COG). This legislation brought about a tre-
mendous increase in the number of COGs around the country which
began to undertake comprehensive planning in such areas as water and
air pollution, transportation, sewage disposal, and crime, among others.
Since COGs are regarded as essentially voluntary in nature, they have
no legislative or taxing authority over individual communities in the
area or over the metropolitan area itself. Their basic functions include
providing a basis for interlocal communication, developing regional
planning, serving as the reviewing agency for local grant applications,
and promoting cooperation among member governments.[21] So far, few
COGs have paid little more than passing attention to social problems
and issues, although there is apparently some indication that at least in
some locales these items will increasingly be considered.[22]

The recent concern for poverty and civil unrest in many of the nation's
cities has resulted in a vast proliferation of federal programs and aid
for various social purposes with apparently mixed consequences. Even
the earlier urban renewal program, which many thought would result in
more and better housing for the poor in urban areas, has actually de-
stroyed more housing units than it has replaced.[23] Theodore Lowi has
argued, along with others, that federal public housing and urban renewal
policies have enabled cities to remove Negroes and other "undesirable"
lower classes from locations sought by businesses, apartment builders,

and various public agencies.[24] Newer programs designed to benefit the poor directly, such as the "war on poverty," have also had diverse effects on the intended recipients and on the city governments as well. The most controversial component of the Economic Opportunity Act of 1964, and the one which affected existing local political structures most, was the section authorizing Community Action Programs which were to involve the poor directly in formulating and executing programs for their benefit. This provision for maximum feasible participation of the poor led in some places to the development of autonomous neighborhood organizations which demanded a voice in those urban activities affecting their well-being or, more likely, not reaching the more disadvantaged areas of the city. The creation of indigenous neighborhood power blocs which were not under the control of the usual political organizations was vigorously resisted by local political leaders and often by city hall itself. Most city officials apparently considered poverty as a strictly economic condition and were unwilling to accept the idea that a dispersal of political power to certain lower-class groups was desirable. Greenstone and Peterson have argued, however, that the antipoverty program contains two divergent and not entirely compatible goals: (1) to end poverty by distributing material goods; and (2) to reduce the virtual exclusion of low-income groups from political life by distributing political power. They found, in their study of the antipoverty effort in the nation's four largest cities, that those cities which had the most centralized political structure were less willing to share political power with the poor but at the same time were the most successful in distributing material perquisites.[25] Despite the apprehension of the local political leadership—or perhaps because of it—a recent evaluation of the actual results of community action programs in twelve large cities concluded that

> the actual programs operated under the heading of community action programs were for the most part traditional social service, opportunity, or educational programs, and did not directly provide the poor with the opportunity or the skill to obtain and exercise the power required to bring about observable changes in their living conditions.[26]

James Venecko has used the rigorous tools of social science in an effort to gain some further insights into the ingredients of successful community action programs. He surveyed urban CAP programs in fifty U.S. cities of 50,000 or over and found the most successful were in areas where previous political activity had been relatively high, where neighborhood centers were actively involved in community organizing, and where militant activities had been minimal. Even under these conditions he concluded that the critical addition the CAP program provides may be only

> protection from active resistance to the efforts of neighborhood residents, integration of the activities which may be somewhat diffuse, legitimacy for suspect activities, moral support, and perhaps simplest of all, financial backing.[27]

At this point it might be appropriate, in concluding our discussion of federal-urban programs, to note the overall absence of cumulative, comparative, and rigorous empirical studies dealing with the impact of the federal government upon urban areas. The kind and quality of data are just not available to undertake the task of arriving at even tentative general statements about the interactions which actually take place between various levels of government in this country.

The two articles included under political structure discuss various factors affecting interlocal relationships and the effects of certain federal government programs on the organization of local government. The first, by Dye and others, directs our attention to some of the consequences of urban social and economic differentiation which often coincide with political boundaries in many large metropolitan areas. The hypothesis is that intermunicipal cooperation in a metropolitan area (Philadelphia, in this case) is a function of the socioeconomic differences reflected among the various political subdivisions within the area. The study concludes that even though demands for greater governmental integration in metro areas continue, the existence of highly differentiated and spatially segregated political subunits, each espousing separate public policies, may operate to maintain the present "fragmented" structure of local government and inhibit the growth of intergovernmental cooperation. Daniel Elazar, in the next selection, is also concerned with local government fragmentation and the possible role of the federal government in contributing to the proliferation of separate political units at the local level. It has been commonly assumed, he suggests, that federal action has played a major role in fragmenting local government, although this assumption has been largely untested. To study this phenomenon, he examines the participation of the state of Illinois and its local governments in three traditional federal programs: airport construction, public housing, and urban renewal. The author finds that federal law permits considerable local organizational flexibility in the recognition that there may be no one best form of local government to implement these programs. However, the actual form which Illinois cities adopt to implement these federally funded activities seems to depend primarily on the local political situation. Thus, while fragmentation at the local level tends to be high, it is the result of local decisions and not undue federal influence.

Local Political Culture

Political culture has become an important concept in political science since Gabriel Almond wrote in 1956 that "every political system is embedded in a particular pattern of orientations to political action."[28] The basic idea was borrowed from anthropology and, while fairly easy to define, political scientists have had difficulty in operationalizing and applying the notion. The concept is not a new theory of politics but instead is an attempt to focus attention on the symbolic, evaluative, and cognitive responses people have to the political system, and on the relationship of these orientations to other aspects of politics.[29] Most of the work dealing with political culture has been done in the field of comparative politics[30] so that much of what exists in the local politics literature is only tentative and suggestive. For our purposes we might start with Robert Alford's definition of local political culture as the "value commitments of groups within the community as a whole, expressed through laws and policies."[31] These widely shared local norms concerning politics may include such things as governmental functions considered appropriate, the legitimacy of political demands by certain groups, an interest in political innovation, and expectations about political participation and the proper role for bureaucracy. All of these factors contribute to a local "climate" or "style" of politics which may significantly condition and regulate the kinds of demands and supports which reach local decision makers.

Two of the most widely known studies in urban politics which explore certain dimensions of local political culture, although not necessarily referred to as such, are by Williams and Adrian, and Wilson and Banfield. In *Four Cities*, Williams and Adrian attempt to distinguish a typology of basic roles for local government by examining policy differences among four middle-sized Michigan communities.[32] The four roles were designated as (1) promoting economic growth; (2) providing or securing life's amenities; (3) maintaining (only) traditional services; and (4) arbitrating among conflicting interests; and the four cities were ranked along these dimensions from high to low. These fundamental orientations as to what was expected of local government were apparently the product of past events and circumstances bringing certain groups to power who gradually conditioned the locality to accept certain political habits, styles, and perspectives which became the dominant local culture. For example, city Alpha (one of the four) was largely controlled by professional and business types who were principally interested in civic amenities and growth. On the other hand, city Delta was a poorer community with a large ethnic population concerned primarily with having local government provide only minimal traditional services. None of the four cities, however, represented the perfect prototype of a particular role orientation. Even though the community's economic base was an important factor in determining its basic role orientation, the authors concluded that economic differences alone could not account for the variations in public policies manifested by the four cities. Local political values played an indispensable part.

The Wilson and Banfield study in this volume examines certain aspects of local political culture by concentrating on the value premises underlying the choices made by certain classes of voters.[33] Their basic proposition is that certain subgroups in American cities constituted largely along ethnic and income lines tend to take a more "public-regarding" attitude toward local government than other groups. This middle-class ethos developed primarily as a result of the reaction of white, Anglo-Saxon Protestants to the machine-dominated politics of the big city and supported such things as the council-manager plan, nonpartisanship, at-large elections, and the civil service in an effort to reorient city government to broader community or "public" concerns and away from the narrower, privatistic interests associated with the ethnic politics of bosses and machines. Wilson and Banfield examined a series of referenda votes (on such things as county building, parks, hospitals, etc.) in several large cities as a way of testing their thesis that these two basic orientations, private- and public-regarding, are still viable influences in big city politics. They found that upper-income voters did react in a public-regarding way and vote against their self-interest narrowly conceived, while other groups, largely lower-income and ethnic, took a narrower, less community-wide perspective and voted against the bond measures. Analysis of the voting data convinced the authors that income was not the sole determinant of the public- or private-regarding ethos, that ethnic attributes, or culture, was also a major contributing factor.

Wilson and Banfield employ the statistical technique of correlation analysis to show relationships between percentage voting "yes" in selected referenda elections and certain other variables (e.g., ethnic characteristics, percentage of dwelling units owner-occupied). The Pearson product-moment correlation (r) is a standard measure of linear correlation (where a constant change in one unit is associated with a constant change in another unit) which indicates the strength of relationship between variables. The correlation coefficient varies between zero (no relationship) to a $+1$ or -1 (perfect relationship) so that the closer the coefficient is to one (either $+$ or $-$) the stronger the association between variables. The closeness or the degree of relationship is essentially the proportion of the variation in the dependent variable which can be attributed to variation in the independent variable. A finding that two variables are closely related does not necessarily mean that one is *causing* the other.

Robert Alford has also considered political culture as an explanatory variable in local politics and reached a conclusion somewhat at odds with the above writers.[34] First, he suggests that variations in political culture, as well as community social structure, are largely a function of the local economy. In the four medium-sized Wisconsin cities which he studied, differences existed concerning the extensiveness of the local bureaucracy and the degree of civic participation. The highly bureaucratized, participatory communities he terms "modern," the nonbureaucratic, low participatory communities he calls "traditional." Both types manifested a set of distinctive public policies. However, Alford found no characteristic set of attitudes or orientations on the part of community leaders and the general citizenry associated with residence *per se* which was not due to the socioeconomic differences among groups. Social class, education, religion, party identification, and the like apparently account for variations in the way these groups perceive political events regardless of the community in which they live.

In summary, the values and attitudes of political elites and the larger public toward the local polity obviously affect the conduct of political affairs in a given community. Whether these attitudes form a patterned, recurring normative structure unique to a particular locale, and thus a local political culture, has not been fully determined. The major obstacle at this point is that the concept of local political culture has not been satisfactorily operationalized so as to permit its use in comparative, empirical research.[35] Undoubtedly, further research in this potentially fruitful area will be necessary to establish the extent to which this concept can add a useful dimension to a systematic body of knowledge about local politics.

Socioeconomic Characteristics

More extensive research has been done on the effects of socioeconomic factors on local politics than on the other major environmental components discussed earlier. In fact, much of the recent input-output-oriented urban research has used various community socioeconomic characteristics directly as system inputs even though the term "environment" is often used. Undoubtedly, this practice has resulted in some conceptual fuzziness since, according to Easton, demands and supports must serve as the link between the environment and the political system. In other words, "median family income" or "percent nonwhite" are abstractions which cannot in themselves press demands on political leaders; some person or group must articulate the wants and desires which are fed into the political system. Such demands, obviously, are difficult to systematically measure, especially on a comparative basis, so that researchers in both state and local politics have resorted to the use of environmental characteristics in place of more elusive input variables. These researchers are saying that, irrespective of the precise way in which demands get expressed, local government reacts to variations in its socioeconomic setting. This approach has not been without its critics;[36] yet, at this stage in the development of an empirically based urban political science, it seems a necessary if not essential step.

Social scientists have long recognized the fundamental importance of economic factors in shaping political decisions. Alford has recently attested to this in the following words:

> The economic base of a city influences the population composition of a city—its occupational structure, educational level, amount of home ownership and geographic mobility, the amount of wealth—and thus the potential for certain kinds of issues and responses to them by government and by local groups.[37]

Most recent studies attempting to assess the impact of community socioeconomic composition on local politics have focused on revenue and expenditure policies. Robert Wood's *1400 Governments* is a good example of this kind of analysis.[38] In his study of sixty-four municipalities in five New Jersey counties (in the New York region), he found seven major socioeconomic factors (using a factor analysis of twenty-two separate characteristics) associated with variations in urban spending. About 83 percent of community expenditure differences was attributable to the community size factor. When that dominant trait was held out or controlled, the rest of the variance was associated principally with differences in industrialization, housing density, and age (of the population) in that order. Campbell and Sacks, Dye, Bahl, and Rodgers have all demonstrated that a relatively few community socioeconomic variables can explain a fairly sizable proportion of the variation in spending among a large number of American cities.[39] Robert Lineberry has shown, however, that not all expenditure areas are closely related to municipal socioeconomic factors, as in the case of city planning expenditures where twenty-four variables could explain only 14 percent of the variation in planning costs among 190 cities of over 50,000 population.[40]

Other studies have explored the relationships between socioeconomic environment and other dimensions of urban politics. For example, a wealth of research documents the socioeconomic correlates of reform government. Wealthier, better-educated, white-collar communities tend to employ the council-manager plan with a nonpartisan ballot and at-large elections. Cities with large ethnic populations, higher levels of manufacturing, and low mobility are more likely to have traditional or nonreform local government structures.[41] Terry Clark has shown that there are certain interesting correlations between community composition and decision-making structures.[42] Two basic findings emerged from his study of fifty-one large U.S. cities: (1) the larger the city, the more decentralized the decision-making structure; and (2) the more diverse the economy of the city, the more decentralized the decision-making structure. A study of riot behavior in American cities reveals that the socioeconomic environmental context in which hostile outbursts took place tended to be quite different from that found in communities with no incidents.[43] Finally, Thomas Dye's work on the correlates of racial segregation in public schools in both northern and southern cities identified a series of environmental features associated with segregated schools.[44] In all, a large body of research supports the proposition that socioeconomic characteristics are among the most significant forces influencing the policies, structure, and decision-making processes of local political systems. The article found in this section by Alford and Scoble, "Political and Socioeconomic Characteristics of American Cities," is an excellent summary of the major community features associated with the three basic forms of municipal government found in this country. White, Anglo-Saxon, Protestant, growing, mobile cities are more likely to be council-manager cities; and ethnically and religiously diverse but nonmobile industrial cities are more likely to be mayor-council cities. The commission form (where the legislative body is composed of members elected as heads of particular functional departments) is associated with declining population, low mobility, low white-collar composition, low educational level, and low ethnic and religious diversity.

Obviously, environmental forces other than the ones considered above help determine the scope and conduct of urban politics. Historical and geographical factors, for example, will inevitably affect the demands and supports funneled into the local system. All of these environmental factors are so interrelated and connected that at times the outcome of particular struggles over local issues will result from the interplay of a variety of forces and conditions.

Notes

1. See Arthur J. Vidich and Joseph Bensman, *Small Town in Mass Society* (Princeton, N.J.: Princeton University Press, 1958) for numerous examples of the difficulty small-town officials have in keeping their roles separate.

2. John E. Bebout and Harry C. Bredemeier, "American Cities as Social Systems," *Journal of the American Institute of Planners*, 29 (1963), 64–76.

3. See, for example, Vincent Ostrom, Charles Tiebout, and Robert Warren, "The Organization in Metropolitan Areas: A Theoretical Inquiry," *American Political Science Review*, 60 (1961), 831–42; and Thomas R. Dye, "Metropolitan Integration by Bargaining among Sub-Areas," *American Behavioral Scientist*, 5 (1962), 11–13.

4. Edward C. Banfield and Morton Grodzins, *Government and Housing in Metropolitan Areas* (New York: McGraw-Hill, 1958).

5. Oliver P. Williams et al., *Suburban Differences and Metropolitan Policies* (Philadelphia: University of Pennsylvania Press, 1965).

6. Advisory Commission on Intergovernmental Relations, *Fiscal Balance in the American Federal System*, Vol. 2, *Metropolitan Fiscal Disparities* (Washington, D.C., 1967).

7. Thomas R. Dye et al., "Differentiation and Cooperation in a Metropolitan Area," *Midwest Journal of Political Science*, 7 (1963), 145–55; and Vincent L. Marando, "Inter-Local Cooperation in a Metropolitan Area: Detroit," *Urban Affairs Quarterly*, 4 (1968), 185–200.

8. James V. Toscano, "Transaction Flow Analysis in Metropolitan Areas; Some Preliminary Explorations," in Philip E. Jacob and James Toscano (ed.), *The Integration of Political Communities* (Philadelphia: J. B. Lippincott, 1964), pp. 98–119; and Oliver P. Williams, "Life Style Values and Political Decentralization in Metropolitan Areas," *Southwestern Social Science Quarterly*, 47 (1967), 299–310.

9. Advisory Commission on Intergovernmental Relations, *State Aid to Local Government* (Washington, D.C., 1969), p. 3.

10. *Ibid.*, p. 13.

11. *Ibid.*, p. 3.

12. Advisory Commission on Intergovernmental Relations, *Fiscal Balance in the American Federal System*, Vol. 1 (Washington, D.C., 1967), p. 265.

13. Yong H. Cho, "The Effect of Local Government Systems on Local Policy Outcomes in the United States," *Public Administration Review*, 27 (1967), 31–38.

14. For example, Ira Sharkansky, "Environment, Policy, Output and Impact: Problems of Theory and Method in the Analysis of Public Policy" in Sharkansky (ed.), *Policy Analysis in Political Science* (Chicago: Markham, 1970), pp. 61–79, in his study of educational policies in Georgia found that output levels (attendance, graduation and dropout rates) were not identical with levels of expenditures (spending per pupil) or for that matter with other environmental variables used to measure the availability of economic resources within each school district.

15. Roscoe C. Martin, *The Cities and the Federal System* (New York: Atherton, 1965), p. v.

16. See the discussion in Leonard E. Goodall, *The American Metropolis* (Columbus, Ohio: Charles E. Merrill, 1968), pp. 23–24.

17. York Willbern, *The Withering Away of the City* (Bloomington: Indiana University Press, 1964), p. 13.

18. Advisory Commission on Intergovernmental Relations, *Impact of Federal Urban Development Programs on Local Government Organization and Planning* (Washington, D.C., 1964), chap. 3.

19. Robert C. Wood, *The Federal Government and the Cities* (Washington, D.C.: George Washington University, 1961), pp. 51–59.

20. Michael N. Danielson, *Federal-Metropolitan Politics and the Commuter Crisis* (New York: Columbia University Press, 1965), pp. 183–89.

21. International City Managers' Association, *Councils of Governments*, Report 296, September 1968, p. 7.

22. John C. Bollens and Henry J. Schmandt, *The Metropolis: Its People, Politics, and Economic Life*, 2nd ed. (New York: Harper & Row, 1970), p. 367.

23. See Charles Abrams, *The City is the Frontier* (New York: Harper & Row, 1965), chap. 8.

24. Theodore J. Lowi, *The End of Liberalism* (New York: W. W. Norton, 1969), chap. 9.

25. J. David Greenstone and Paul E. Peterson, "Reformers, Machines, and the War on Poverty," in James Q. Wilson (ed.), *City Politics and Public Policy* (New York: John Wiley, 1968), pp. 267–92.

26. Kenneth B. Clark and Jeannette Hopkins, *A Relevant War Against Poverty: A Study of Community Action Programs and Observable Social Change* (New York: Harper & Row, 1969), p. 235.

27. James J. Vanecko, "Community Mobilization and Institutional Change: The Influence of the Community Action Program in Large Cities," *Social Science Quarterly*, 50 (1969), 609–30 (quotation is from p. 630). See also the entire issue (No. 3) which is devoted to the theme of Planned Social Intervention.

28. Gabriel A. Almond, "Comparative Political Systems," *Journal of Politics*, 18 (1956), 396.

29. Samuel C. Patterson, "The Political Cultures of the American States," *Journal of Politics*, 30 (1968), 187–209.

30. The classic work is still Gabriel Almond and Sidney Verba, *The Civic Culture: Political Attitudes and Democracy in Five Nations* (Princeton, N.J.: Princeton University Press, 1963).

31. Robert R. Alford, "The Comparative Study of Urban Politics," in Leo F. Schnore (ed.), *Social Science and the City* (New York: Praeger, 1968), pp. 263–302.

32. Oliver P. Williams and Charles R. Adrian, *Four Cities: A Study in Comparative Policy Making* (Philadelphia: University of Pennsylvania Press, 1963).

33. James Q. Wilson and Edward C. Banfield, "Public-Regardingness as a Value Premise in Voting Behavior," *American Political Science Review*, 58 (1964), 876–87.

34. Robert R. Alford, *Bureaucracy and Participation: Political Cultures in Four Wisconsin Cities* (Chicago: Rand McNally, 1969).

35. Ira Sharkansky, "The Utility of Elazar's Political Culture," *Polity*, 2 (1969), 66–83, has recently attempted to give operational referents to Daniel Elazar's impressionistic discussion of state political culture found in *American Federalism: A View from the States* (New York: Thomas Y. Crowell, 1966). See also Samuel A. Kirkpatrick, "Multidimensional Aspects of Local Political Systems: A Conceptual Approach to Public Policy," *Western Political Quarterly*, 23 (1970), 808–28, for a discussion of local dimensions of political culture.

36. Herbert Jacob and Michael Lipsky, "Outputs, Structure, and Power: An Assessment of Changes in the Study of State and Local Politics," in Marian Irish (ed.), *Political Science: Advance of the Discipline* (Englewood Cliffs, N.J.: Prentice-Hall, 1968), pp. 324–25. For an elaboration of this problem in terms of group dynamics see James W. Clarke, "Urban Policy Output Models" (unpublished paper delivered at the annual meeting of the American Society for Public Administration, Philadelphia, April 1970).

37. Alford, *Bureaucracy and Participation*, p. 155.

38. Robert C. Wood, *1400 Governments: The Political Economy of the New York Metropolitan Region* (Cambridge: Harvard University Press, 1961).

39. Alan K. Campbell and Seymour Sacks, *Metropolitan America: Fiscal Patterns and Governmental Systems* (New York: The Free Press, 1967); Thomas R. Dye, "Governmental Structure, Urban Environment and Education Policy," *Midwest Journal of Political Science*, 12 (1967), 353–80; Roy W. Bahl, *Metropolitan City Expenditures: A Comparative Analysis* (Lexington: University of Kentucky Press, 1969); and Chester B. Rodgers, "Environment, System and Output: The Consideration of a Model," *Social Forces*, 48 (1969), 72–87.

40. Robert L. Lineberry, "Community Structure and Planning Commitment: A Note on the Correlates of Agency Expenditures," *Social Science Quarterly*, 50 (1969), 723–30.

41. See the summary of these finding₋ in Lewis A. Froman, Jr., "An Analysis of Public Policies in Cities," *Journal of Politics*, 29 (196.), 94–108.

42. Terry N. Clark, "Community Structure, Decision-Making, Budget Expenditures, and Urban Renewal in 51 American Communities," *American Sociological Review*, 33 (1968), 576–93.

43. Bryan T. Downes, "The Social Characteristics of Riot Cities: A Comparative Study," *Social Science Quarterly*, 49 (1968), 504–20.

44. Thomas R. Dye, "Urban School Segregation: A Comparative Analysis," *Urban Affairs Quarterly*, 4 (1968), 141–66.

I. Political Structure

GOVERNMENTAL "FRAGMENTATION" at the local level is a matter of considerable concern among those interested in local government today. Indeed, it has become a major bugbear of reformers—from the Advisory Commission on Intergovernmental Relations to the Council on Economic Development—and is reputed to be one of the major sources of local failure to meet local problems adequately. It has been observed that until the advent of the "Great Society" most of the major federal-aided programs in American cities have been handled by local government agencies established for the specific purpose of implementing each program. The truth of this need not be documented. Indeed, students of intergovernmental relations have frequently commented on the proliferation of special districts established at the local level for the specific purpose of implementing specific federal-city programs. It is also generally assumed that this proliferation of governments has been a product of federal pressure; if not directly at least by subtle encouragement, because of the demands made by the federal grant programs involved. Thus it is assumed that federal action has played a major role in fragmenting local government, affecting municipal organization in new and deleterious ways. Even federal officials have come to endorse this view and deplore it.

The argument of federal responsibility—culpability is the thought usually expressed—has generally remained an unexamined one, yet even cursory examination of the historical record and contemporary activities at the local level leads to a challenge of orthodox notions.

Three formal federal-local relationships will be considered here: airport construction, public housing, and urban renewal.[1] In all three fields, the Congress of the United States has made it legally possible for the federal government and the localities to deal directly with each other to implement specific programs, provided that the localities in every case have the authorization of their respective states to engage in such action.[2] This does not mean that the states are excluded from participation in those fields. In the field of

"Fragmentation" and Local Organizational Response to Federal-City Programs*

Daniel J. Elazar

airport construction, the states have the option of entering into an active three-way partnership by directing the channeling of all federal funds through state agencies for reallocation to the localities.[3] In the other two programs, the states' minimum task is to provide the requisite enabling legislation and to establish means for the creation of local

"'Fragmentation' and Local Organizational Response to Federal-City Programs," by Daniel J. Elazar, is reprinted from Urban Affairs Quarterly, 2 (June 1967), 30–46, by permission of the publisher, Sage Publications, Inc.

*This article is based largely on data collected for the author's study of comparative metropolitan political systems in Illinois, conducted under the auspices of the Institute of Government and Public Affairs, University of Illinois, which will be published as the "Cities of the Prairie" series. The general background material utilized in this article is based on the following sources: (1) the author's personal files; (2) the reports of the (Kestnbaum) Commission on Intergovernmental Relations (June 1955), particularly An Advisory Committee Report on Local Government, A Description of Twenty-five Federal Grant-in-Aid Programs, Summaries of Survey Reports on the Administrative and Fiscal Impact of Federal Grants-in-Aid, and the specific reports cited in the following pages; (3) Morton Grodzins, The American System: A New View of Government in the United States, ed. by Daniel J. Elazar (Chicago: Rand McNally, 1966); (4) Edward C. Banfield and Morton Grodzins, Government and Housing in Metropolitan Areas (New York: McGraw-Hill, 1958); (5) Metropolitan Problems and Urban Development (Hearings before a subcommittee of the Committee on Government Operations, House of Representatives, 86th Cong., 1st sess., June 3, 9, 19, and July 21, 1959); (6) Charles R. Adrian, Governing Urban America (New York: McGraw-Hill, 1961).

administrative units to handle each program. Since Congress has specifically charged the states with responsibility for both programs, it is within the power of the latter to opt to participate further by prescribing the form of local administrative agency to handle them by contributing funds to supplement the federal grants, or by actively involving their agencies in the operations of the programs in other ways.

While the acts of Congress establishing these programs require the designation of local agencies to handle program implementation in the local community, with the exception of the public housing legislation they do not explicitly require the establishment of new governments or even new agencies to do so. While this has frequently been the end result of the federal legislation, the reasons for it, as we will see, are not reflective of federal "coercion" or even of strictly federal influences.

Three Programs in Illinois

The state of Illinois and its local governments have participated in all three programs virtually since their inception. Their experiences with those programs, while not necessarily typical of the experiences of other states and localities (in the sense of being the same in all essential respects as the others), conform reasonably to the nationwide pattern. Furthermore, the Illinois experience may represent the "hard case" in direct federal-local relations, in which state intervention has been more pronounced despite the existence of strong local governments.

AIRPORT GOVERNMENT
IN ILLINOIS METROPOLITAN AREAS

When the Federal Airport Act of 1946 was drafted to allow the states to opt for channeling all funds to local airport projects, the state of Illinois, which has been involved in airport construction since the initiation of governmental activity in the field after World War I, chose to exercise that option. Since then, with one exception, all federal funds

for airport development in Illinois have not only been formally channeled through the state but have been channeled through the governor's office, where they have been allocated according to decisions made at the state level. Governors have responded to local pressures or refused to do so, utilizing federal funds (which have to be matched by a relatively small state contribution, usually 25 percent of the total cost of the project) to implement state (or personal political) policies. State policy is not only important in the distribution of funds, it is also a major factor in determining or limiting the manner in which localities are able to organize for the government of their airports. In this respect, Illinois is very permissive, as the following examples should indicate.[4] Furthermore, the localities have taken advantage of that permissiveness to develop unique kinds of airport governments suited to local needs.

Among the metropolitan areas of over 100,000 population wholly or partly within Illinois, eight have undertaken airport development programs since the end of World War II, with the aid of federal funds. They are Champaign-Urbana, Chicago, Decatur, Joliet, Peoria, Rock Island–Moline, Rockford, and Springfield. Their experiences in the administrative organization of their respective airport programs are illustrative of the flexibility of federal law, the variability of state roles, and the local penchant for "fragmentation."[5] In every case, the localities involved determined the form of local organization for air service.

Three types of airport government can be found in these eight metropolitan areas. There are four special airport districts (Peoria, Rock Island–Moline, Rockford, and Springfield) all located in Illinois' leading downstate medium-size metropolitan areas, the ones with the largest volume of air traffic for their size. Except for the Rock Island County Airport District, which embraces the entire county, the city-county districts were drawn to include central cities and suburban areas without including the entire county.[6] In two cases (Decatur and Joliet) the airports are nominally governed by the local park districts which were used because they possessed readily adaptable tax bases that were available at the time the airports were developed. Both of these airports are relatively small operations though the Decatur Airport does have scheduled airline service. Champaign-Urbana is served by an airport owned and operated by the University of Illinois. This unique arrangement virtually excludes the regular local governments of that metropolitan area from any role in this federal program.

Though they were stimulated by earlier federal airport aid programs, the majority of these airport governments were developed before passage of the Federal Airport Act of 1946. Though all have received federal assistance in varying degrees, the forms of their organization and the options they have taken have been designed to meet specific local needs within the framework prescribed or allowed by state law, not as a consequence of federal grants as such. Furthermore, since Illinois has opted to channel federal funds through the state and the governor's office, the federal grant program is made to conform to state policy rather than allowing it to freely make itself felt in the various urban areas of the state. By and large, this appears to be a successful arrangement from both the state and local point of view. The state exercises some control over the distribution of airport facilities, governors gain an additional political lever, "states rights" are maintained, localities get more outside funds because the state helps them vis-à-vis the federal bureaucracy and also supplements the federal grants, and smaller cities are assured of their share in the federal grants.

Chicago, the one super-metropolis in Illinois, unlike its medium size counterparts, has an airport program virtually (but not entirely) independent of the general state-local program described above.[7] The city owns and operates three airports directly— O'Hare, Midway, and Meigs Field. They are operated under the city's Department of Public Works. All three airports have been substantial beneficiaries of federal aid and have received state assistance as well. However, Illinois law provides that federal aid to Chicago airports may be provided directly to the city of Chicago without going through the state's mediating agency. This law, which reflects Chicago's political influence in the state legislature, provides the city with the flexibility it desires and also recognizes Chicago's special financial and administrative capabilities which enable the city to properly handle direct relations with the federal government, something that the other cities with more limited aviation agencies cannot do so well.

PUBLIC HOUSING PROGRAMS
IN ILLINOIS METROPOLITAN AREAS

Whereas the federal airport construction program was not institutionalized in its present form until after World War II, the current low-rent public housing program was formalized during the New Deal, dating as it does from the Federal Housing Acts of 1933 and 1937. Federal requirements for the local government and administration of public housing projects are somewhat more detailed than in the case of the airports but are still quite flexible, leaving much discretion to the states, which must make provision for the creation of local housing authorities under state law.

The state of Illinois did not become actively involved in the public housing program after the end of World War II though the State Housing Board was actually established in 1933 to facilitate cooperation with the federal housing programs of the depression years. In 1934, the state provided for the organization of local housing authorities, granting the state board power to oversee local housing boards. Until 1945, when $10 million was appropriated for the board's activities to stimulate public housing projects, the agency's role was clearly secondary to that of the federal government. In the 1934 act, the Illinois legislature granted counties as well as cities the right to establish housing authorities, thus broadening the potential base of public housing in the state beyond that in many other states.[8]

The Chicago Housing Authority has clearly been the most active public housing agency in the state since its creation in 1937 as an independent municipal corporation with special powers from the state legislature for action in the field of slum clearance and low-rent public housing. Its creation was in direct response to the Federal Housing Act of that year. It was established as an independent municipal corporation in order to (1) acquire power to issue bonds since the city government proper had reached the limit of its bonding powers and (2) protect the public housing program from the most deleterious pressures of organized politics in Chicago.[9] The authority is governed by a five-man board of commissioners, appointed by the mayor and subject to the approval of the Illinois State Housing Board. It has, over the years, developed and implemented one of the nation's major public housing programs, but because of its *structural* insulation from the city power system, it has done so in a manner not always best calculated to conform to the desires and interests of the political and business leadership of Chicago.

Public housing activity in the downstate medium-size metropolitan areas follows much the same pattern. Control over public housing is vested in a city, county, or joint city-county housing authority, which is organized under state law and is governed by a board appointed by the governing body(s) that was responsible for its creation. Except for East St. Louis, which has continued to be involved in the construction of relatively large-scale public housing projects, after initial flurries of activity at the time of their respective inceptions the local housing authorities have been very conservative bodies, interested in managing existing projects within the framework of established patterns (including the maintenance of racial segregation) and definitely not interested in new starts unless forced to become active in that direction. By and large, the housing authority boards have abdicated operational responsibilities to hired managers and do little more than review the managers' activities perfunctorily. Many of the managers have developed a "landlord" outlook which leads them to adopt policies that will maximize profits rather than provide public service.

A few examples of this should suffice. The Champaign County Housing Authority, whose board is directly responsible to the Champaign County Board of Supervisors (which means, in practice, that it is virtually independent) did the bulk of its work before 1946 and has since become extremely conservative. On a televised panel discussion of race and housing in Champaign-Urbana early in 1963, the representative of the authority presented an even more conservative posture toward racial integration of housing than did the representative of the local real estate board.[10] In 1961, the Champaign County Housing Authority was finally forced into a new start by the city of Champaign in conjunction with an urban renewal project. For all intents and purposes, the authority is an entirely local operation, making policy locally and reflecting local values. Its only serious problems are those generated locally or local manifestations of the nationwide Negro drive for integration.

The Springfield Housing Authority is exclusively a city agency, like that of Chicago. In addition to operating one large (599-unit) housing project, it has also been designated as Springfield's urban renewal agency, which has channeled its current activities into the fields of land clearance and redevelopment and away from an aggressive public housing policy. Nevertheless, the local decision to utilize the authority for these expanded purposes has made it an important force on the newest frontiers of urban redevelopment.

The public housing authority in Decatur had been forced into purely custodial activities by local rejection of an expanded public housing program in the 1950s. Then, in the early 1960s, Decatur's very energetic city manager began to develop an urban renewal program which was planned to include a public housing project for the aging. The public housing authority was revived to undertake it, apparently to the satisfaction of the board members. By involving the housing authority, the city manager was actually saving it from oblivion, since the Decatur voters had earlier voted the repeal of a city ordinance providing for the erection of a new public housing project on the grounds that it was "socialistic" and an unwarranted expenditure of public funds. While the authority's director wished to proceed with his work, his public prevented him from doing so until the city manager could mobilize support for additional public housing from a different angle.

Public housing in Rockford is handled by two separate agencies, a city housing board and a county housing authority. The Illinois State Housing Board was instrumental in securing the creation of the Rockford Housing Board shortly after World War II when the state was still actively involved in the public housing field. It is appointed by the mayor with State Housing Board approval. Its major efforts have been to encourage self-help conservation projects in the blighted areas of the city. Since Rockford has never entered into any formal urban renewal program, the city housing board has become the *de facto* urban renewal agency locally. However, though it is empowered to do so, it manages no public housing projects so has virtually no formal relations with the federal government. The local public housing projects are owned and operated by the Winnebago County Housing Authority, which is responsible to the county board of supervisors. Though originally built in an area outside of Rockford's city limits, the public housing units have all since been annexed to the city but have remained under the county housing authority, which is one of the most "landlord" oriented in the state.

In the field of public housing, as in the field of airport construction the influence of the federal government in determining the organizational forms of local housing authorities appears to be confined to the issuance of general regulations, legitimizing a number of possible alternatives. On the other hand, the state's role is of great importance, since it is put in the position of dictating the means by which its local subdivisions can conform to federal provisions

and the extent to which it will be involved in the program. In Illinois, as in most states, this has led to the creation of a uniform system of housing authorities with quasi-independent powers but not completely separated from the general local governments, city or county. Actually it is within the option of each locality to choose which of the two governments is to control the housing program, and by utilizing the less formal mechanisms of local politics, to determine the extent of that control and the character of the program itself.

URBAN RENEWAL
IN ILLINOIS METROPOLITAN AREAS

Since 1954, the public housing and urban renewal programs have become closely connected. In most cities, such new public housing projects as have been started have been erected on sites cleared through the urban renewal program and in conjunction with it. Federal law itself makes provision for the development of public housing in conjunction with the urban renewal program. In the metropolitan areas of Illinois no new governments have been established to handle urban renewal programs. Urban renewal, where it has been initiated, has either been handled by existing governments and their agencies (including public housing authorities) or through newly created agencies within existing governments. City governments have been involved in urban renewal projects most frequently, with the city councils, planning departments, or public housing authorities being designated the local urban renewal agency under the federal requirements.

Without exception, federal aid for urban renewal has not led to increased fragmentation of local government in the lesser metropolitan centers of Illinois. Thus, in Alton, Champaign, Decatur, and Rock Island, the city council is the designated urban renewal agency. In Springfield, the housing authority has that power. Chicago is the only city in which fragmentation has occurred on a large scale, for strictly local considerations.

The Sources of
Local Governmental Fragmentation

In all three programs in Illinois, the degree of fragmentation at the local level tends to be high. At the same time, the fragmentation that does exist has been determined locally. In this respect, Illinois communities are simply following classic patterns of local government in the United States. Since the beginning of local government in this country, there has been a tendency to formally fragmentize the institutions of local government. These fragmentizing tendencies are actually rooted in the British experience and were transplanted to these shores, along with the general paraphernalia of local government, by the early American colonists.[11] Two reasons for this are apparent, one historical and distinctive to the Anglo-American experiences in general, the other immediate and particularly American.

Classical city government in the West originated in the ancient Greek, Hellenistic, and Roman city-state or its medieval equivalent on the European continent. In its original form it represented both local and central governmental authority, being politically sovereign to a measurable degree. As such, its governmental institutions were of necessity centralized.[12] The origins of local—including municipal—government in the Anglo-American world more closely approximate the "city" governments of the Israelite tribal confederacy as described in the Bible in which supralocal government (either tribal, or monarchial) existed prior to the institution of local government over fixed local territory as we know it.[13] Accordingly, local government in the countries of this tradition was instituted to serve specific and immediate purposes alone, while central government, or sovereign, authority remained vested in higher echelons of the civil society. Furthermore, local government was instituted in piecemeal fashion as new tasks developed for local authorities to undertake. Since there was no demand for the development of a general government at the local level, there was no particular reason for consolidating such functions under a single authority. So the number of local government authorities multiplied as new ones were created under different conditions to handle most new tasks. This condition prevailed undiminished in Great Britain until the first reform of local government in 1832.

For obvious reasons, the British system was transplanted to the American colonies where local government also developed after the establishment of central governments in the individual colonies. A similar process of development then ensued on these shores. Counties and towns were the first local governments to be instituted by the early settlers. Municipal government was added later in a manner purposely designed so as not to supersede either the counties or, in many cases, even the towns (or townships).

Special-purpose governments were also instituted virtually from the beginning. As the number of tasks requiring local governmental action expanded rapidly in the nineteenth century, many, if not most, of them were allocated to special purpose governments, from school districts to fire protection districts, or to quasi-independent agencies of the municipalities.[14]

In fact, the first example of federal influence on localities that led to the creation of special local governments came early in the nineteenth century with the common school land grant program inaugurated in 1802.[15] As in present-day programs, the federal government did not dictate the exact form of local organization, allowing the formation of either special school districts in the townships or school boards attached to municipal governments but, by demanding the creation of permanent school funds to be administered by local authorities for school purposes only, it virtually forced the creation of separate local agencies. Generally speaking, the smaller communities adopted the former approach and the larger cities, the latter. For neither did this mean a departure from local norms, even then.

Not only was there no apparent need for governmental consolidation at the local level, but it was often politically expedient to create such special-purpose governments rather than add functions to existing municipal governments. This was particularly true when the demand for new local government services came to the state legislature directly from specialized interest groups rather than via the existing local governments. In such cases, the leaders of the existing governments frequently were not interested in acquiring new programs (unless they were programs that promised them some form of reward) while the proponents of the new programs were interested in gaining direct control over their administration, often in the hope of avoiding the assimilation of *their* programs into local political patterns. Furthermore, a program administered through an independent local government was assured of continued financial support through possession of an authorized tax levy of its own. It was also assured continued representation in the political system through its formal leadership, if in no other way.[16]

Except in much of the South, where local government has always been more limited and less fragmentized, this approach to local government has remained the dominant one in American society, despite periodic efforts at local governmental consolidation generated by nationwide "reform" movements or by special local considerations.[17] By and large, the same reasons that encouraged the early development of formally fragmentized local government remain valid in the minds of those local citizens who are politically articulate and concerned. Their attitude is reinforced even in the larger cities by a basic conception of local or municipal government as a vehicle for providing services or, among the more sophisticated, as a means for organizing a local community politically. Even the municipal government is rarely conceived by the public to be "the government of the city" in the classic sense.

Federal demands for separate local agencies or governments to handle federal-aided programs, where they exist, cannot be said to represent a new departure on the local scene but a reinforcement of a traditional approach. Indeed, when the question is raised as to why the federal government makes this demand for any given program in the first place, the answer is likely to be that the interests which have promoted federal aid have also promoted its local administration in this way so that their local representatives may achieve some measure of control over the program locally.[18] Certainly this is true of the federal-aid airport program (whose supporters even fought hard to prevent its channelization through the states, and lost). It is somewhat less true in the case of the urban renewal and public housing programs, though, even in those cases, the desire for programmatic autonomy on the local level was an important consideration.

The Impact on Municipal Organization

One major criticism of the organization of the federal-aided programs like the ones discussed here has been the charge that they have an adverse effect on the coordination of local government activities. The extent to which this approach to local government organization has affected municipal organization generally depends on the local political situation in each individual city. In theory, the formal fragmentation introduced by these programs should prevent the concentration of municipal authority and the introduction of the type of "energy" in government" advocated by Hamiltonians and contemporary students of public administrations. However, where a strong political organization exists, as in Chicago, or a well-organized oligarchy "controls" civic life as reported by Floyd Hunter in Atlanta, the handicaps of fragmentation are frequently overcome by the political or civic leadership. This is no less true in the case of the federal-aided programs.[19] In cities with less centralized political systems, there is very likely a high degree of actual fragmentation of government in the local community in any case and this carries over into the federal-aided programs as well.

Moreover, the variations in the organization of these programs have differential effects on the character of local control, some having been organized as separate departments within the regular structure of municipal government. This form is almost invariably associated with the largest cities where internal consolidation of governments is generally the norm. These cities, which most closely approximate the classical city in their consciousness of being civic entities as well as in the scope of their concerns, tend to be governed more centrally in general. There have been organized semiautonomous agencies which are formally responsible to the municipality but actually possess substantial autonomy in their budgeting and operations. These are found primarily in the medium-large cities (perhaps 250,000–750,000 in population range) though in some of the immediately larger and immediately smaller cities as well. They represent a compromise, of sorts, between the first and third forms. Created by the municipality, it ultimately remains its creature while at the same time enjoying some degree of the autonomy its supporters generally desire. Still others have been organized as independently established local governments.

They are found most frequently in medium size and smaller cities, as well as in nonurban communities. As special districts, autonomous local governments created by the state legislature or by local referendum pursuant to state statute, they are more than nominally independent of the other local governments. Occasionally responsible directly to the voters, they are more frequently responsible, in fact, to their board alone. When the power of appointment is spread among several other governments, this usually enables the interests most concerned with controlling the special district board to gain position and power, often by simply filling a power vacuum. Such boards are more frequently kept responsible by community norms than through political organization.

In any case, regardless of the extent of overall political control, organizational separation by program leads to a substantial degree of governmental specialization by interest. In most cases those people with special concern for the implementation of each program are given some priority in appointments to the governing body of the department, agency, or district responsible for the program's administration. In the case of the airport districts in Illinois, no matter how they are formally organized, they are almost inevitably dominated by the businessmen who make the most extensive use of the airport facilities.

In those cities (usually the larger ones) where public housing programs are still active, they are generally administered and governed by those reasonably sympathetic with public housing and its goals. In those cities (usually the smaller ones) where public housing programs were "single-shot" affairs and where the completed projects must simply be administered, control has frequently passed into the hands of those uninterested in, or even opposed to, public housing and its goals. (Indeed, the relegation of the program to maintenance status may well be a consequence of the capture of the housing board by those opposed to public housing.)

Urban renewal programs are still too new to have passed through their expansion stage into quiescence. If they pass the planning stage, it almost invariably is an indication that they are administered and governed by people sympathetic to the urban renewal idea (whether for reasons of idealism or personal profit). Generally speaking, urban renewal programs are still controlled in a reasonably close manner by the municipal chief executive or council regardless of their formal organizational structure because they are still new programs which have not yet settled into a firm place in the local government constellation. Even so, real estate and building interests usually figure prominently in their administration, often through an "advisory board." In this connection, it should be noted that the more routinized a program has become, the more likely it is that its governors and administrators will be left alone by both federal and local authorities.

In so far as the exercise of local control is concerned, "local control" itself means different things to different people. The opportunity for some local group to exercise substantial control over federal-aided programs is almost always present. The degree to which the presently utilized forms of organization affect the extent and locus of local control depends on the political system of each city much more than on the attitudes of the federal government.

Federalism and "Proper" Forms of Local Organization

In light of all this, it would be hard to conclude that there is one "proper" form of municipal or local government organization to deal with these programs. It is entirely possible that there has been, in effect, a sorting out of organizational forms by city size that for most cities is quite reasonable.[20] Whether this is so or not, a consideration of the local political system in each city would, strictly speaking, be necessary to determine the proper organizational form (or, more accurately, the consequences likely to flow from use of different forms) in each case.

This is not an effort to beg the question. In this respect, the problem of properly organizing the federal-aided programs is no different than that of organizing any other municipal programs. It is conceivable that, under circumstances that are quite legitimate, each of the forms might be most appropriate. In the largest cities, for example, the administration of urban renewal and public housing programs is probably best handled through an executive department in the city government that is directly responsible to the mayor. The central importance of both urban renewal and public housing in cities of the size and condition of our largest ones, and the natural interrelationship of the two programs makes their central coordination a reasonable idea. Furthermore, the problem of public responsibility in the largest cities is best handled by concentrating authority in the hands of a powerful and responsible chief executive through an administrative organization of executive departments. In medium size and cities whose fiscal responsibility is considerably more restricted, it is

quite possible that the virtues of providing an independent tax or bonding power base for the maintenance of the local share of the support for federal-aided programs outweigh the administrative disadvantages of separate organization. If this were the case, the special district device would be most appropriate.

All in all, the possibilities for proper organization of federal-aided programs are varied but they should not be considered separately from the problems of administrative organization in each locality. In this respect, the organizational flexibility allowed by federal law is good and should be maintained or even increased.

One more point of federal impact must be noted. The federal government does exert a potentially negative influence on municipal governmental organization through the impact of its own administrative structure. While the federal administration is organized in reasonably hierarchical and bureaucratic fashion from the federal perspective, at the local level the federal government is represented by the outermost projections of its bureaucratic pyramid—a profusion of specialized agencies and bureaus, each with its own programmatic concerns and professional biases. Quite frequently—one is tempted to say, invariably—the federal bureaucratic fragmentation, which is a legitimate organizational concomitant of the administration of the several different programs, becomes a source of extreme fragmentation and disharmony at the community level as the different federal line agencies make differing demands upon local governments. The problem is especially acute when the Urban Renewal Administration, the Public Housing Administration, and the Federal Housing Administration each deal with separate local "counterpart" agencies, pulling them apart from one another. It is even worse when all three federal agencies make their differing demands upon the same local agency.[21]

Cities, which are lucky enough or smart enough to hire astute administrators to handle their share of the federal-city programs, can frequently turn this fragmentation of federal demands to local advantage by playing one federal agency off against another. This is, in essence, a political solution to a problem generated by the administrative structure. While some would deplore this, it is suggested that this is precisely why we have noncentralized democratic political institutions—to provide another, more locally responsible means of handling the problems of government, particularly those generated by the necessities of bureaucractic organization.

There is no "single best way" for a city to exercise its rights of political access and control as a means of influencing the federal programs which affect it. Perhaps the most universally used means—and the most effective—is the cities' use of their congressional representatives, either individually or collectively, to go to bat for them in Washington. Some cities, particularly some of the larger ones, have found it helpful to maintain their own paid respresentatives in Washington to lobby directly for them or to provide expert assistance for the city's congressional delegation.[22] This method can be quite helpful. It can also be quite hazardous since a poorly qualified city representative may alienate already touchy members of Congress who view such lobbying activities as an infringement upon their own "casework" bailiwicks. In any case, only a few of the largest cities are in a position to consider the appointment and maintenance of such representatives for their use only.

What is absolutely necessary, regardless of the organizational devices used to influence Washington, is good local political leadership, leadership that can make intelligent decisions as to the most desirable local programmatic goals, can assess various possible strategies that will help them achieve those goals, and can make reasonable good decisions as to what strategy to pursue. As yet, there is no administrative or organizational substitute for such leadership.

Notes

1. Background material on the public housing and urban programs includes Banfield and Grodzins, *op. cit.;* Housing and Home Finance Agency, *Program for Community Improvement* (*Workable Program*), 1960; Urban Renewal Administration, *Approaches to Urban Renewal in Several Cities,* 1954; Jack Levin, *Your Congress and American Housing* (Library of Congress, 1952); George Dugger and P. Ford, *Urban Renewal Administration* (Berkeley: University of California Press, 1957); Martin Millspaugh and Gurney Breckenfield, *The Human Side of Urban Renewal* (Baltimore: Fight-Blight, 1958); William Gerberding, "The States and Housing" (Master's thesis, Department of Political Science, University of Chicago, 1956). Also useful are the chapters on housing and urban renewal in each annual issue of *The Municipal Year Book,* particularly for bibliographic purposes. For background material on the national airport program, *A Staff Report on Federal Aid to Airports,* submitted to the Commission on Intergovernmental Relations (June 1955) and "Airport Construction" chap. 6, in *A Description of Twenty-five Federal Grant-in-Aid Programs* submitted to the Commission on Intergovernmental Relations (June 1955). The discussion of these selected programs should in no way obscure the myriad direct federal-local relationships that have developed in other fields, including some that are formally federal-state programs (e.g., highways) and some that are not formally shared programs at all (e.g., flood control).

2. As late as 1963, Iowa cities were unable to participate in federal-aided low-rent public housing programs for lack of legislative authorization (see *Journal of Housing,* January 1960).

3. The history of the struggle to obtain this channeling provision provides an excellent example of the relative power of the states vis-à-vis the large cities in American national politics. For an analysis of the inclusion of this provision in the Federal Airport Act of 1946, see Morton Grodzins, "American Political Parties and the American System," *Western Political Quarterly,* 13 (December 1960), 974–98.

4. *Illinois Revised Statutes,* chap. 15, "Aviation."

5. The data for the seven downstate metropolitan areas is available in the author's files, by city.

6. Rockford's airport is located on the site of a former U.S. Army camp which was deactivated after service in the two world wars and transferred to the airport authority under the federal surplus property program.

7. Chicago's major airport construction project, the development of O'Hare International Airport, is described in Malcolm Wise, "Jet Age Chaos," *Chicago Sunday Sun-Times,* November 13, 1960 (history of intergovernmental collaboration in the construction of O'Hare Field, emphasizing the delays), and Allen Alderman, "O'Hare International Airport and the Impact of Federalism" (term paper prepared for course

n the American Federal System, University of Illinois, 1962).

8. Illinois could do this by virtue of the flexibility of the federal laws. This flexibility has permitted a wide range of state-local responses, varying from a high level of state involvement to almost total neglect of the program. In Michigan, for example, the municipal housing commissions are integrated into the general city governments. In Mississippi, on the other hand, the program is regarded as a "federal" one and the legally autonomous local housing authorities are in much closer relationship with the federal government than with the state or the local governments. As of 1962, Kansas had not entered the program and, while South Carolina permits municipalities to participate in it, local antagonism has prevented them from doing so except in a few cases. Washington has an active state public housing administration dedicated to stimulating the program and city and county activity falls under its general jurisdiction. For information on the variations in state-local responses and in the forms of local government organization for federal-aided programs as established in state law see *Local Government Structure in the United States* (U.S. Bureau of the Census, 1954) and John E. Stoner, "Local Government Relations" (paper delivered at the APSA meeting, September 1962). Federal policy, in essence, has been to allow the states to determine the forms of local government to be developed for the public housing program, providing that the agency created can enter into legal agreements, directly or indirectly. In this respect, state involvement is considerably more important than the passage of enabling legislation might indicate when taken alone. More information on public housing programs illustrating this and other points may be found in *Summaries of Survey Reports on the Administrative and Fiscal Impact of Federal Grants in Aid* submitted to the Commission on Intergovernmental Relations (June 1955). Information on the Illinois public housing program as of 1950 can be found in *Staff Memorandum No. 33* on the State Housing Board for the (Schaefer) Commission to Study State Government.

9. For a detailed study of the public housing program in Chicago, covering both its political and administrative aspects, see Martin Meyerson and Edward C. Banfield, *Politics, Planning, and the Public Interest* (New York: The Free Press, 1955).

10. Personal observation by the author.

11. For a discussion of early fragmentation in local government see Adrian, *Governing Urban America;* and Clyde F. Snider, *Local Government in Rural America* (New York: Appleton Century-Crofts, 1957).

12. For a discussion of classical city government see Leo Strauss, *Natural Right and History* (Chicago: University of Chicago Press, 1954);

and Lewis Mumford, *The City In History* (New York: Harcourt, Brace, & World, 1961).

13. Unfortunately, the Bible and the Israelite civilization it describes have not been studied by political scientists to the same extent that the Greco-Roman civilizations have been, hence there is little in the way of authoritative material for citation in support of this statement. The view implied in this statement is the author's, developed through his analysis of the books of *Joshua* and *Judges* (of his unpublished manuscript, "A Political Commentary on the Book of Joshua"). For a discussion of the historical and archeological evidence for this view see William F. Albright, *From Abraham to Ezra* (New York: Harper Torchbooks, 1962) and Harry M. Orlinsky, *Ancient Israel* (Ithaca: Cornell University Press, 1957). It is this author's view that the Israelite system provides an alternate "classic" pattern of government which may be examined with equally useful results as the examination of the "classic" Greek pattern, and was so examined, in part, by the originators of governmental patterns in what is now the United States.

14. See Snider, *Local Government in Rural America*, and Daniel J. Elazar, *Cities of the Prairie: The Cities in Their Setting* (forthcoming).

15. Daniel J. Elazar, *The American Partnership* (Chicago: University of Chicago Press, 1962).

16. *Ibid.*

17. See *Local Government Structure in the United States* (U.S. Bureau of the Census, 1957).

18. See Grodzins, *American System.*

19. See Meyerson and Banfield, *Public Interest*, and Floyd W. Hunter, *Community Power Structure* (Chapel Hill: University of North Carolina Press, 1953). For a selected discussion of this phenomenon see Oliver Williams and Charles Press, *Democracy in Urban America* (Chicago: Rand McNally, 1961).

20. For a discussion of this point in relation to the organization of general-purpose city governments, see John Kessel, "Governmental Structure and Political Environment: A statistical Note About American Cities," *American Political Science Review*, 56 (September 1962), 615–20.

21. The effects of this federal bureaucratic fragmentation and the other negative influences of the present structure of federal-city relations in the urban renewal and housing fields are ably discussed with particular reference to the Puerto Rican experience by Joseph M. Heikoff of the University of Illinois Bureau of Community Planning in his unpublished manuscript "Urban Renewal in Puerto Rico: The First Ten Years."

22. Philadelphia and San Francisco have maintained paid representatives in Washington in the past, as indicated in the hearings of the (Fountain) Subcommittee on Intergovernmental Relations of the House Committee on Government Operations, 1956–58.

Differentiation and Cooperation in a Metropolitan Area*

Thomas R. Dye, Charles S. Liebman, Oliver P. Williams, and Harold Herman

A DISTINGUISHING CHARACTERISTIC of metropolitan areas is areal specialization, or differentiation among spatially defined subpopulations with respect to class or status, life style, and economic function. To sociologists the relationship between specialization and urbanization is a commonplace. Their analysis has commonly centered on isolating the types of specialization and their discrete effects. Ecologists have described functionally differentiated zones and sectors and have even identified specific behavioral patterns associated with the residents of particular areas. To the political scientist,

Thomas R. Dye, Charles S. Liebman, Oliver P. Williams, and Harold Herman, "Differentiation and Cooperation in a Metropolitan Area." Reprinted from the Midwest Journal of Political Science, 7 (May 1963), 145-55, by permission of the Wayne State University Press.

*Revised version of a paper presented at the 1962 annual meeting of the American Political Science Association. This paper is from a larger study by the authors on urban differentiation and political choice in a metropolitan area. The technique of comparing agreeing and nonagreeing pairs of municipalities was developed in the Seminar on Interdisciplinary Research in Political Integration, University of Pennsylvania, under the leadership of Professor Karl Deutsch. We wish to express our appreciation to James Toscano for his helpful cooperation in sharing his data and findings for his study approaching cooperative arrangements from a different perspective. See his "Transaction Flow Analysis in Metropolitan Areas," Memorandum No. 4, University of Pennsylvania Studies of Social Values and Public Policy.

one of the most interesting attributes of metropolitan areas is the fact that urban specialization very often coincides with political boundaries. Not only has the familiar bedroom community become incorporated as a political entity, but within metropolitan regions one can also find industrial enclaves, recreational resorts, commercial centers, intellectual retreats, racial and ethnic ghettoes, company towns, and religious colonies which correspond roughly with local political units.

A central hypothesis of this paper and of the larger study upon which it is based is that social and economic differentiation among communities in a metropolitan area is associated with differing local governmental policies. Local governmental decisions in a metropolitan area are made at hundreds of decision centers, each set in a separate social and economic environment, each responding to different types of interests, and each struggling to maintain a separate existence. As a result of these differing conditions, local governments can be expected to select differing policy alternatives designed to cope with specific interests within their constituencies.

Yet because of the interdependency of urban communities, some interests express themselves through demands for integrative or cooperative actions among local governments. Frequently, it is suggested that certain services can be administered more economically and planned more intelligently when handled on an areawide basis, or at least on a multijurisdictional basis. These arguments are often encountered with regard to schools, water supply, police protection, waste disposal, libraries, and street maintenance. Cooperative responses of local communities to jointly felt pressures of urbanization are not uncommon. The popular forms of cooperative responses among urban communities include the interjurisdictional agreement and joint authorities.

Students of political integration at the international level have suggested that policy concensus is the basis of viable political integration. If this same proposition is operative at the intermunicipal level and if the pattern of local policy choices is associated with social and economic differences among municipalities, then one should be able to observe the effect of urban differentiation on integrative arrangements in a metropolitan area. In short, it is our hypothesis that intermunicipal cooperation in a metropolitan area is a function of social and economic distance. Intermunicipal cooperation will tend to occur more frequently among communities which are similar in character and less frequently among highly differentiated communities. In this paper, we shall attempt to set forth this hypothesis about the effect of urban differentiation on patterns of intermunicipal cooperation in an operational manner and to test it with reference to characteristics of local governments within the Philadelphia metropolitan area.

There are 238 municipalities covering the Pennsylvania sector of the Philadelphia metropolitan area. Although they range in size and density from the core city of Philadelphia with nearly two million persons to sparsely populated rural townships with less than three hundred inhabitants, each of these local governments has substantially the same legal powers with which to structure its internal life and to cope with social and economic diversity. Recognizing that specialization and differentiation increases with urbanization, a distinction was made between the urban and semirural portions of the metropolitan area. The definition of urban as opposed to semirural was established at five hundred persons per square mile, a figure chosen to approximate the state of urbanization of an area when urban services are generally initiated by the local government. According to this classification there were 90 urban and 135 semirural municipalities composing the study's sample; 12 communities were dropped from analysis because of large institutional populations which interfered with social and economic measurement.

In addition to the development of satisfactory measures of social, life style, and economic diversities, several other conditions were required for the hypothesis to be tested:

(1) To have a cooperative arrangement, the potential cooperators must have or want to have the same service (if one community has a police force and another neither has nor wants one, there is no basis for a cooperative operation of a police radio transmitter). (2) For a particular service, some municipalities must have selected a cooperative approach and others rejected it (there must be a basis for comparing cooperating and noncooperating communities). (3) While not absolutely essential, local governments must generally be contiguous for cooperation to be feasible. Thus in the analysis which follows, only the relationships between contiguous municipalities are subject to examination.

For the purposes of this paper, urban differentiation was operationally defined by three indices; these indices were selected for their relevance to decisions involving one or more of the most common types of interjurisdictional agreements. They are "social rank," market value per capita, and party voting.

1. "*Social rank.*" This is an adaptation of an objective measure of community social status developed by sociologists Eshref Shevky and Wendell Bell which gives equivalent weight to occupational and educational attributes of a community's population. The occupational factor is the percent of employed males in professional, managerial and sales occupations. The educational factor is the percent of persons over 25 years old with one or more years of college education. The percentages for each factor are first standardized in a range from 0 to 100 which assigns a zero score to the community with the lowest percent in the college age or status occupational class and 100 to the highest community. Once the two standard scores are computed, they can be averaged. Thus every local unit is assigned a social rank score.

2. *Market value per capita.* A measure of community wealth which indicates the kind of financial resources which a municipality would bring to a cooperative enterprise.

3. *Party vote.* Partisan officials are the negotiators of cooperative arrangements.

The percent Republican of the total vote for governor in 1950 was used to identify the general partisan orientation of each community.

Cooperation is defined here as the joint financing of a service facility which is operated administratively as a single system. A cooperative arrangement may take the form of a contract, a joint authority, or a joint board. *Noncooperative* is defined as the lack of any cooperative arrangement between contiguous municipalities which provide similar services. In the study area there are numerous cooperative arrangements for particular services. These arrangements represent local choices and are not imposed by higher legal authorities. The principal functional areas of cooperation are schools, sewers, police radio, libraries, water and solid waste disposal. Only in the first three areas is there a large enough number of cases to accommodate statistical analysis. Fortunately, these three functional areas represent three distinctly different kinds of local policies. Schools are an expression of the life style of a community but sewers and police radio systems are not. Both schools and sewers represent large financial commitments but police radio systems do not.

With 238 municipalities in the study area, there are 28,203 possible pairs of municipalities and therefore that same number of possible intermunicipal relationships. But if our analysis of intermunicipal relationships is limited to geographically contiguous municipalities, this figure is reduced to 534, the total number of pairs of contiguous municipalities.[1] This reduction was accomplished by inspecting a map of the area. Using the density classification, there were 198 pairs in the urban area, 294 in the rural and 42 pairs comprised of one urban and one rural municipality.

Since each of the 534 pairs consists of two municipalities and each municipality is described by three measures of urban differentiation, it was possible to identify quantitatively the social and economic distance involved in each pair of municipalities along three separate indices. The

absolute difference in index scores between paired municipalities constituted the measures of social and economic distance; three measures of social and economic distance were available for each pair—namely, social rank, per capita market value, and party voting. The smaller the difference in any index for a pair of communities, the more similar the communities in that pair are to each other, and the less social and economic distance exists between them. The larger the differences in index scores between two municipalities in a pair, the more dissimilar these municipalities are said to be. The central hypothesis of this paper can now be stated in operational terms. *If intermunicipal cooperation in a metropolitan area is a function of social and economic distance between communities, the mean of the differences in index values will be smaller for cooperating than for noncooperating pairs of municipalities.*

Table 1 presents the data on school arrangements. For the hypothesis to be borne out, the mean of the differences for cooperating pairs must always be less than for noncooperating ones. Table 1 indicates that this is the case to the greatest extent in the urban area, is barely corroborated in the semirural one, and is only partially so in the rural-urban —the area comprised of those mixed pairs of rural and urban municipalities.

The major incentive for cooperative school arrangements is the pooling of resources in constructing high schools. Both from a capital financing and a curricular standpoint, small municipalities have greater difficulty building high schools independently. As the number of pairs in the various categories of Table 1 indicate, the total incidence of agreement is greater in the semirural than the urban areas (urban 26 and semirural 162). This difference however, cannot be explained merely by the differences in size of urban and semirural municipalities. According to current Pennsylvania state policy, school districts should have at least 5,000 pupils. This means that ideally most municipalities with under 25,000 persons should be parties to joint arrangements. According to this standard only 12 urban and one semirural municipality are large enough to have independent systems. In fact there are many more than twelve urban municipalities with independent systems, but none in the semi-rural area. Indeed, many urban municipalities which are quite small maintain their independence through *ad hoc* tuition arrangements with various neighboring governmental units.

Our hypothesis suggests that the more extensive use of cooperative school arrangements in the semirural area is a function, in part, of the lesser social distance among pairs there than is found in the urban area. Note that in the "TOTAL" column the mean of the differences is larger for each index value for the urban area. Urban specialization tends to create sharp social breaks which follow municipal boundaries. Thus the intermunicipal social distances influence not only the pattern of cooperation, but also its extent. Only 26 out of 198 urban pairs had agreements, while 162 out of 294 rural ones did. The urban-rural pairs lie in between with 13 out of 29 cooperating. The 26 urban pairs which did cooperate were atypical for the sample area. The mean differences in social rank for the entire urban area is 16.0, but only 10.4 for the cooperating communities. A similar pattern holds for the other three variables, although not always at a high level of significance.

In the urban-rural area, the mean differences in market value per capita between cooperating and noncooperating pairs is in the opposite direction of that expected. Since none of the differences in market value per capita in any of the three sample areas are at a .10 level of significance, the difference in the urban-rural area might have arisen solely due to chance. It may also be a function of the market value index which does not always coincide with the year in which an agreement took place; variances of as much as ten years between index and agreement year are included.[2] Most communities do not experience rapid demographic changes. However, along the fringes of the urban area the most rapid shifts take place. Fringe area industrialization and large housing developments are the most

common form which these changes take. It is likely that some disparities in market value per capita have taken place subsequent to the development of joint school systems. The hypothesis is supported even in this changing area with regard to social rank and the related variable, party voting. Either populations channeling into fringe areas are not upsetting the social balance of agreeing pairs, or changes in social composition occur at a slower rate than any of our other indexes. Our observation is that both these propositions are true.

In the semirural area, the differences in means are all in the expected direction but at less than a .10 level of significance. Additional applications of the social rank concept to the Philadelphia metropolitan area suggest an explanation for this apparent difference between urban and semirural behavior. We suspect that social rank is not as determinative an influence in the public policies of semirural areas as in urban areas, where the closeness, size, and more frequent interactions of populations evoke greater consciousness of differences in community social status.

Education is one of the more vital policy areas through which local communities may express particular cultural and social styles of living. Another service, which is essential for urban living, but which has very little to do with life style, is the disposal of sewage. The analysis was repeated for sewage disposal agreements. One of the conditions for analysis was that both potential parties to an agreement must provide the service in question; thus only sewered communities are included in the sample. The condition confined the sample to the contiguously urbanized area around the core city. A review of the first portion of Table 2 under the heading "TOTAL" indicates that there is little difference between agreeing and non-agreeing pairs with respect to social rank and party vote. There are significant differences with respect to community wealth. The conclusion might be drawn that municipalities do not mind negotiating with neighbors of differing social rank and party over matters of as little social significance as

TABLE 1. Schools—Mean Differences among Pairs of Cooperating and Noncooperating Municipalities

	URBAN			RURAL-URBAN			SEMIRURAL		
	Cooperating	Non-cooperating	Total	Cooperating	Non-cooperating	Total	Cooperating	Non-cooperating	Total
1. Social rank	10.4	16.9	16.0‡	8.6	14.1	12.8†	7.3	7.8	7.5
2. Market value per capita	$1,131	$1,467	$1,424	$1,685	$1,437	$1,515	$957	$994	$974
3. Percent Republican	9.0	11.5	11.2*	7.1	10.2	9.2*	8.0	8.8	8.4
Number of pairs	26	172	198	13	29	42	162	132	294

*Differences between cooperating and noncooperating pairs of municipalities are significant at the .10 level of significance.
‡Differences between cooperating and noncooperating pairs of municipalities are significant at the .05 level of significance.
†Differences between cooperating and noncooperating pairs of municipalities are significant at the .01 level of significance.

TABLE 2. Sewer Agreements—Mean Differences among Pairs of Cooperating and Noncooperating Municipalities

	TOTAL			DELAWARE RIVER OUTLET			OTHER OUTLETS		
	Cooperating	Non-cooperating	Total	Cooperating	Non-cooperating	Total	Cooperating	Non-cooperating	Total
1. Social rank	15.9	15.3	15.6	17.4	11.9	16.1	11.2	18.0	15.0†
2. Market value per capita	$1,223	$1,829	$1,440†	$1,278	$2,194	$1,506†	$1,057	$1,537	$1,324
3. Percent Republican	10.5	11.4	10.8	11.2	10.3	10.8	8.5	12.3	10.6*
Number of pairs	113	63	176	85	28	113	28	35	63

*Differences between cooperating and noncooperating pairs of municipalities are significant at the .01 level of significance.
†Differences between cooperating and noncooperating pairs of municipalities are significant at the .05 level of significance.

sewage, but are concerned about their neighbors wealth because the maintenance and future expansion of the joint system will be influenced by the tax situation of the members. However, as the remaining portions of the table show, this is only partially true.

The municipalities along the Delaware River are old industrial locations. They frequently have substantial tax bases, but low social ranking populations. As one goes up the tributary streams from the river, the social rank rises. Since sewage "runs down hill," the low status communities have had a monopoly of the access points for sewer trunks to the river. For the higher status upstream communities to solve their problems, they must deal with the lower status downstream communities. Table 2 lists all sewered communities with systems emptying directly into the Delaware River from the Delaware-Pennsylvania state boundary to Bensalem Township, which represents the strip of prewar river front development. These are labeled "DELAWARE RIVER OUTLET."

These pairs of municipalities with sewer agreements have higher mean social rank difference (though not significantly higher) than the pairs of municipalities without sewer agreements. However, with regard to taxable wealth (market value per capita) the agreeing municipalities in the Delaware River Outlet sample have a significantly smaller mean difference than the pairs of municipalities without sewer agreements. Joint sewer systems are rarely financed by uniform tax rates applying to all participating municipalities. Rather, the shares to be paid by each municipality are worked out at the time of the agreement. Nevertheless, as was indicated above, the economic well-being of cooperating municipalities is a matter of vital concern to the partners. High-status municipalities in the Delaware River Outlet sample had no choice but to negotiate agreements with low-status communities, but it would appear that they sought to cooperate with those low-status communities that were high in taxable resources.

The differences in party voting between agreeing and nonagreeing pairs in the Delaware River Outlet sample is similar to the social rank pattern. This is not surprising since there is a .703 coefficient of correlation between social rank of each municipality and the percent Republican in the election used for the party affiliation index.

The remainder of the sewered communities not in the Delaware River Outlet sample are shown in Table 2 under the heading "OTHER OUTLETS." These municipalities are located further up the streams from the Delaware River and along the Schuylkill and its tributaries. In these areas, municipalities frequently have a range of choice in deciding which other communities, if any, they will join in building sewerage systems. Here there is no solidly built-up riparian industrial strip monopolizing river access.

Agreements among these communities occur between those of similar status (social rank). It is interesting that although the agreeing communities also resemble each other more closely than do the nonagreeing communities with respect to taxable wealth, the difference between agreeing and nonagreeing communities is not statistically significant, even at the .10 level. It would appear that where a range of choice does exist, status is a more important determinant of agreement than is taxable resources.

Party voting again shows the same pattern as social rank. The question may be raised whether it is social rank or the party affiliation of the negotiators which influences the pattern of cooperative arrangements. The data indicates that social rank is the more important variable. In both school and sewer agreements, whenever there are significant differences between agreeing and nonagreeing municipalities with respect to social rank, there are also significant differences (up to the .10 level) with respect to party voting. But, in each instance, differences in social rank are greater (they are at a higher level of statistical significance) than are differences in party voting.

School and sewage systems have entirely differing social and cultural connotations, but both involve expensive capital facilities. Thus in each case the formation of co-

TABLE 3. Police Radio Agreements—Mean Differences among Cooperating and
Noncooperating Municipalities*

	Cooperating	Non-cooperating	Total
1. Social rank	14.2	17.1	15.9
2. Market value per capita	$1,645	$1,304	$1,445
3. Percent Republican	11.3	11.5	11.4
Number of pairs	80	114	194

*None of the differences were significant at the .10 level.

operative systems means as least protracted negotiations among the leadership representing the communities, though perhaps little general public involvement in the case of sewer systems. The formation of a cooperative police radio network involves very modest financial contributions from participating municipalities, is of concern primarily to police technicians, and is a subject which generally should involve the general public very little. Here the pattern of cooperation indicates no preference for similar municipalities among cooperating pairs. Table 3 gives the results for all pairs which have police radios. Only pairs from the urban area are thereby included. For this rather minor service, social and economic distances apparently do not control the pattern of cooperation.

The interjurisdictional agreement and the joint authority are the most popular forms of metropolitan political integration at the present time. Operations performed with data on these forms of integration in the Philadelphia Metropolitan Area tend to support the hypothesis that intermunicipal cooperation is a function of social and economic distance. Areal specialization appears to be an important obstacle to cooperative relations among urban communities. It was observed that cooperative arrangements are more frequent in the relatively undifferentiated semirural sectors of the metropolitan area and less frequent in the highly differentiated urban sectors. It was also observed that what cooperation did occur among the urbanized communities of the metropolitan area tended to occur among communities which were socially and economically similar rather than dissimilar. In

addition, our findings indicate that social distance is a more important determinant of cooperation than is economic distance.[3]

These findings suggest that social and economic differentiation among urban communities may be fundamental to the whole question of metropolitan government. The highly differentiated character of metropolitan communities may operate to maintain our present "fragmented" structure of local government and to inhibit the growth of intergovernmental cooperation. Of course, social science, at least since Durkheim, has been acutely aware that interdependence is a concomitant of specialization and that our interdependent system must be organized in some manner. The demand for effective organization of metropolitan areas is likely to continue. But, because of the highly differentiated character of urban communities, integrative demands are likely to be accommodated through patterns of cooperation which least conflict with the divisive effects of differentiation.

Notes

1. There were 66 pairs of contiguous municipalities which were eliminated because each involved at least one of the 12 municipalities with high institutional populations.

2. Methodologically, data for indices of agreeing pairs should be gathered at the time agreements occur. Aside from nonavailability of data in all years, there is a problem of selecting the proper year for an index of noncooperating pairs.

3. For a discussion of changes in social and economic variables affecting interjurisdictional cooperation, see the authors' "Social Status, Tax Resources and Metropolitan Cooperation," *National Tax Journal*, 16 (March 1963), 56–62.

2. Local Political Culture

Public-Regardingness as a Value Premise in Voting Behavior*

James Q. Wilson and Edward C. Banfield

OUR CONCERN HERE is with the nature of the individual's attachment to the body politic and, more particularly, with the value premises underlying the choices made by certain classes of voters. Our hypothesis is that some classes of voters (provisionally defined as "subcultures" constituted on ethnic and income lines) are more disposed than others to rest their choices on some conception of "the public interest" or the "welfare of the community." To say the same thing in another way, the voting behavior of some classes tends to be more public-regarding and less private- (self- or family-) regarding than that of others. To test this hypothesis, it is necessary to examine voting behavior in situations where one can say that a certain vote could not have been private-regarding. Local bond and other expenditure referenda present such situations: it is sometimes possible to say that a vote in favor of a particular expenditure proposal is incompatible with a certain voter's self-interest narrowly conceived. If the voter, nevertheless, casts such a vote and if there is evidence that his vote was not in some sense irrational or accidental, then it

Reprinted with permission from the *American Political Science Review*, 58 (December 1964), 876–87.

This is a preliminary report of a study supported by the Joint Center for Urban Studies of M.I.T. and Harvard University and the Rockefeller Foundation. The writers wish to acknowledge assistance from Martha Derthick and Mark K. Adams and comments from James Beshers, Anthony Downs, Werner Hirsch, Hendrik Houthakker, H. Douglas Price, and Arthur Stinchcombe. This paper was originally presented at the Second Conference on Urban Public Expenditures, New York University, February 21–22, 1964.

must be presumed that his action was based on some conception of "the public interest."

Our first step, accordingly, is to show how much of the behavior in question can, and cannot, be explained on grounds of self-interest alone, narrowly conceived. If all of the data were consistent with the hypothesis that the voter acts as if he were trying to maximize his family income, the inquiry would end right there. In fact, it turns out that many of the data cannot be explained in this way. The question arises, therefore, whether the unexplained residue is purposive or "accidental." We suggest that for the most part it is purposive, and that the voters' purposes arise from their conceptions of "the public interest."

I

We start, then, from the simple—and admittedly implausible—hypothesis that the voter tries to maximize his family income or (the same thing) self-interest narrowly conceived. We assume that the voter estimates in dollars both the benefits that will accrue to him and his family if the proposed public expenditure is made and the amount of the tax that will fall on him in consequence of the expenditure; if the estimated benefit is more than the estimated cost, he votes for the expenditure; if it is less, he votes against it. We assume that all proposed expenditures will confer some benefits on all voters. The benefits conferred on a particular voter are "trivial," however, if the expenditure is for something that the particular voter (and his family) is not likely to use or enjoy. For example, improvement of sidewalks confers trivial benefits on those voters who are not likely to walk on them.

Insofar as behavior is consistant with these assumptions—that is, insofar as the voter seems to act rationally in pursuit of self-interest narrowly conceived—we consider that no further "explanation" is required. It may be that other, entirely different hypotheses would account for the behavior just as well or better. That possibility is not of concern to us here, however.

No doubt, our assumptions lack realism. No doubt, relatively few voters make a conscious calculation of costs and benefits. Very often the voter has no way of knowing whether a public expenditure proposal will benefit him or not. In only one state which we have examined (Florida) do ballots in municipal referenda specify precisely *which* streets are to be paved or *where* a bridge is to be built. Even if a facility is to serve the whole city (e.g., a zoo, civic center, or county hospital), in most cities the ballot proposition is usually so indefinite that the voter cannot accurately judge either the nature or the amount of the benefits that he would derive from the expenditure. Similarly, it is often difficult or impossible for the voter to estimate even the approximate amount of the tax that will fall upon him in consequence of the expenditure. Some states (e.g., Illinois and California) require that the anticipated cost of each undertaking be listed on the ballot (e.g., "$12,800,000 for sewer improvements"). Of course, even when the total cost is given, the voter must depend on the newspapers to tell, or figure out for himself—if he can—how much it would increase the tax rate and how much the increased tax rate would add to his tax bill. Ohio is the only state we have studied where the voter is told on the ballot how the proposed expenditure will affect the tax rate ("17 cents per $100 valuation for each of two years"). Almost everywhere, most of the expenditure proposals are to be financed from the local property tax. Occasionally, however, a different tax (e.g., the sales tax) or a different tax base (e.g., the county or state rather than the city) is used. In these cases, the voter is likely to find it even harder to estimate how much he will have to pay.

We may be unrealistic also both in assuming that the voter takes only *money* costs into account (actually he may think that a proposed civic center would be an eyesore) and in assuming that the only money costs he takes into account are *taxes* levied upon him (actually, if he is a renter he may suppose —whether correctly or incorrectly is beside the point—that his landlord will pass a tax increase on to him in a higher rent).

The realism of the assumption does not really matter. What does matter is their usefulness in predicting the voters' behavior. It is possible that voters may act *as if* they are well informed and disposed to calculate even when in fact they are neither. If we can predict their behavior without going into the question of how much or how well they calculate, so much the better.

II

On the assumptions we have made, one would expect voters who will have no tax levied upon them in consequence of the passage of an expenditure proposal to vote for it even if it will confer only trivial benefits on them. Having nothing to lose by the expenditure and something (however small) to gain, they will favor it. In the *very* low-income[1] wards and precincts of the larger cities, a high proportion of the voters are in this position since most local public expenditures are financed from the property tax and the lowest-income people do not own property. We find that in these heavily non-homeowning districts the voters almost invariably support all expenditure proposals. We have examined returns on thirty-five expenditure proposals passed upon in twenty separate elections in seven cities and have not found a single instance in which this group failed to give a majority in favor of a proposal. Frequently the vote is 75 to 80 percent in favor; sometimes it is over 90 percent. The strength of voter support is about the same no matter what the character of the proposed expenditure.[2]

In all of the elections we have examined, non-homeowners show more taste for public expenditures that are to be financed from property taxes than do homeowners. Table 1 shows by means of product-moment (Pearsonian *r*) coefficients of correlation the strength and consistency of this relationship over a wide variety of issues in several elections in Cleveland and Chicago.[3] As one would expect, when an expenditure is to be financed from a source other than the property tax the difference between homeowner and

TABLE 1.   Relationship between Percentage of Ward Voting "Yes" and Percentage of Dwelling Units Owner-occupied; Various Issues in Cleveland and Chicago

Issue and Date	Simple Correlation Coefficient (r)
Cleveland (33 wards):	
Administration Building (11/59)	—0.86
County Hospital (11/59)	—0.77
Tuberculosis Hospital (11/59)	—0.79
Court House (11/59)	—0.85
Juvenile Court (11/59)	—0.83
Parks (11/59)	—0.67
Welfare Levy (5/60)	—0.72
Roads and Bridges (11/60)	—0.77
Zoo (11/60)	—0.81
Parks (11/60)	—0.57
Chicago (50 wards):	
County Hospital (1957)	—0.79
Veterans' Bonus (1957)	—0.49
Welfare Building (1958)	—0.67
Street Lights (1959)	—0.83
Municipal Building (1962)	—0.78
Urban Renewal Bonds (1962)	—0.79
Sewers (1962)	—0.79
Street Lights (1962)	—0.81

non-homeowner behavior is reduced. This is borne out in Table 2 in which we have compared wards typical of four major economic groups in Cook County (Illinois) in their voting on two issues: first, a proposal to increase county hospital facilities and, second, a proposal to construct a state welfare building. The measures were alike in that they would benefit only indigents; they were different in that their costs would be assessed against different publics: the hospital was to be paid for from the local property tax, the welfare building from state sources, largely a sales tax. Middle-income homeowners showed themselves very sensitive to this difference; the percentage favoring the state-financed measure was twice that favoring the property-tax-financed one. Low-income renters, on the other hand, preferred the property-tax-financed measure to the state-financed one.

Let us turn now to the behavior of voters who do own property and whose taxes will therefore be increased in consequence of a public expenditure. One might suppose that the more property such a voter has, the less likely it is that he will favor public expenditures. To be sure, certain expenditures confer benefits roughly in proportion to the value of property and some may even confer disproportionate benefits on the more valuable properties; in such cases one would expect large property owners to be as much in favor of expenditures as the small, or more so. Most expenditures, however, confer about the same benefits on large properties as on small, whereas of course the taxes to pay for the expenditure are levied (in theory at least) strictly in proportion to the value of property. The owner of a $30,000 home, for

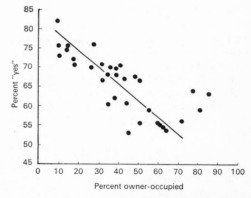

Source of housing data: U.S. Census of Housing, 1960. Figure reprinted from Edward C. Banfield and James Q. Wilson, City Politics (Cambridge: Harvard University Press. 1963), p. 238.

Figure 1. Relation between percentage voting "yes" on proposition to provide increased county hospital facilities (November 1959) and percentage of dwelling units owner-occupied in the 33 wards of Cleveland.

example, probably gets no more benefit from the construction of a new city hall or the expansion of a zoo than does the owner of a $10,000 one; his share of the tax increase is three times as much, however. Very often, indeed, there is an inverse relation between the value of a property and the benefits that accrue to its owner from a public expenditure. The probability is certainly greater that the owner of the $10,000 house will some day use the free county hospital (patronized chiefly by low-income Negroes) than that the owner of the $30,000 house will use it.

TABLE 2. Voting Behavior of Four Major Economic Groups
Compared in Cook County

Group	PERCENT "YES" VOTE	
	County Hospital (1957)	State Welfare Building (1958)
	(%)	(%)
High-Income Homeowners*		
Winnetka	64	76
Wilmette	55	70
Lincolnwood	47	64
Middle-Income Homeowners†		
Lansing	30	54
Bellwood	21	55
Brookfield	22	51
Middle-Income Renters‡		
Chicago Ward 44	65	71
Chicago Ward 48	61	72
Chicago Ward 49	64	74
Low-Income Renters§		
Chicago Ward 2	88	73
Chicago Ward 3	87	76
Chicago Ward 27	87	78

*Three suburbs with the highest median family income ($13,200 to $23,200) among all suburbs with 85 percent or more home ownership.
†Three suburbs with lowest median family income ($8,000 to $8,300) among all suburbs with 85 percent or more home ownership.
‡Three wards with highest median family income ($6,200 to $6,800) among all wards with less than 15 percent home ownership (none of the three wards is more than 4 percent Negro).
§Three wards with lowest median family income ($3,100 to $4,100) among all wards with less than 15 percent home ownership (Negro population of wards ranges from 59 to 99 percent).

Since normally the *ratio* of benefits to costs is less favorable the higher the value of the property, one might expect to find a positive correlation between the percentage of "no" votes in a neighborhood and the median value of homes there.

This expectation is not borne out by the facts, however. Table 3 gives partial correlation coefficients relating the percent voting "yes" in the wards of Cleveland and the suburban wards and towns of Cuyahoga County to the median family income in those wards and towns.[4] It shows that the higher the income of a ward or town, the more taste it has for public expenditures of various kinds. That the ratio of benefits to costs declines as income goes up seems to make no difference.[5]

The same pattern appears in a 1960 Flint, Michigan, vote on additional flood control facilities. This is shown graphically in Figure 3. Although there is a considerable dispersion around the line of regression, in general the

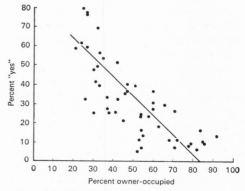

Figure 2. Relation between percentage voting "yes" on proposition to provide additional sewer facilities (1962) and percentage of dwelling units owner-occupied in wards of Chicago.

TABLE 3. Partial Correlations between Median Family Income of Ward and Percentage "Yes" Vote on Various Measures, Cleveland and Suburbs

Area and Issue	Partial Correlation*
Cleveland (33 wards):	
Administration Building	+0.49
County Hospital	+0.64
Tuberculosis Hospital	+0.57
Court House	+0.49
Juvenile Court	+0.66
Parks	+0.48
Welfare Levy	+0.70
Roads and Bridges	+0.61
Zoo	+0.59
Cuyahoga County Suburbs (90 wards and towns):	
Administration Building	+0.47
County Hospital	+0.54
Tuberculosis Hospital	+0.43
Court House	+0.60
Juvenile Court	+0.59
Parks	+0.52
Welfare Levy	+0.35
Roads and Bridges	+0.60
Zoo	+0.62

*Controlling for proportion of dwelling units owner-occupied.

higher the home value—and accordingly the more the expected tax—the greater the support for the expenditure.[6]

It may be argued that because of the phenomenon of the diminishing marginal utility of money these findings are not really anomalous. The richer a man is, perhaps, the smaller the sacrifice that an additional dollar of taxation represents to him. Thus, even though the well-to-do voter may get no more benefit than the poor one gets and may have to pay a great deal more in taxes, an expenditure proposal may nevertheless be more attractive to him. He may be more willing to pay a dollar for certain benefits than his neighbor is to pay fifty cents because, having much more money than his neighbor, a dollar is worth only a quarter as much to him.

Differences in the value of the dollar to voters at different income levels account in part for the well-to-do voter's relatively strong taste for public expenditures. They can hardly account for it entirely, however.

For one thing, they do not rationalize the behavior of those voters who support measures that would give them only trivial benefits while imposing substantial costs upon them. The suburbanite who favors a county hospital for the indigent which he and his family will certainly never use and for which he will be heavily taxed is not acting according to self-interest narrowly conceived no matter how little a dollar is worth to him.

Moreover, if the well-to-do voter places a low value on the dollar when evaluating some expenditure proposals, one would expect him

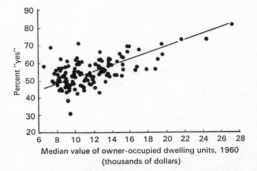

Note: Only property owners and their spouses could vote. Source of housing data: U.S. Census of Housing, 1960. Figure reprinted from Banfield and Wilson, City Politics, p. 239.

Figure 3. Relation between percentage voting "yes" on proposition to provide additional flood control facilities (November 1960) and median value of owner-occupied dwelling units in the precincts of Flint, Michigan.

to place the same low value on it when evaluating all others. In fact, he does not seem to do so; indeed, he sometimes appears to place a *higher* value on it than does his less-well-off neighbor. Compare, for example, the behavior of the Cook County (Illinois) suburbanites who voted on a proposal to build a county hospital (an expenditure which would confer only trivial benefits on them and for which they would be taxed in proportion to the value of their property) with the behavior of the same suburbanites who voted on a proposal to give a bonus of $300 to Korean War veterans (an expenditure from which the well-to-do would benefit about as much as the less-well-to-do and for which they would not be taxed disproportionately, since the bonus was to be financed from state, not local, revenues, and the state had neither an income tax nor a corporate profits tax). As Figures 4 and 5 show, the higher the median family income of a voting district, the larger the percentage voting "yes" on the welfare building (the rank-order correlation was +0.57) but the *smaller* the percentage voting "yes" on the veterans' bonus (the rank-order correlation was +0.71).

In Cuyahoga County, Ohio, the same thing happened. There the higher the median family income, the larger the percentage voting for all the expenditure proposals except one—a bonus for Korean War veterans. On this one measure there was a correlation of −0.65 between median family income and percentage voting "yes."

Thus, although it is undoubtedly true that the more dollars a voter has, the more he will pay for a given benefit, the principle does not explain all that needs explaining. When it comes to a veterans' bonus, for example, the opposite principle seems to work: the more dollars the voter has, the fewer he will spend for a given benefit of that sort.

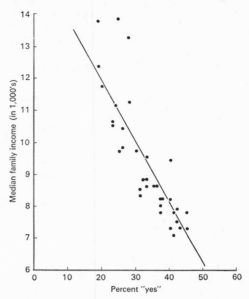

Figure 5. Relation between percentage voting "yes" on proposition to approve a $300 bonus for veterans of Korean War (1958) and median family income in the suburban cities and towns of Cook County, Illinois, in which two-thirds or more of the dwelling units are owner-occupied.

That there is a positive correlation between amount of property owned (or income) and tendency to vote "yes" does not, of course, imply that a majority of property owners at *any* income level favors expenditures: the correlation would exist even if the highest income voters opposed them, provided that at each lower level of income voters opposed them by ever larger majorities. In fact, middle-income homeowners often vote against proposals that are approved by both the very poor (renters) and the very well-to-do (owners). Table 4 gives a rather typical picture of the response of the various income groups to proposals that are to be financed from the property tax in Cuyahoga County (Ohio).

Not infrequently the highest-income districts support expenditure proposals by very large majorities—indeed, sometimes by majorities approaching those given in the propertyless slums. Table 5 compares the percentage voting "yes" in the high-income, high-home-ownership precincts of three city-county areas with the percentage of all

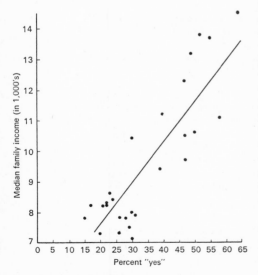

Figure 4. Relation between percentage voting "yes" on proposition to provide increased county hospital facilities (1957) and median family income in the suburban cities and towns of Cook County, Illinois, in which two-thirds or more of the dwelling units are owner-occupied.

TABLE 4.   Voting Behavior of Four Major Economic Groups Compared in Cuyahoga County

Group	PERCENT "YES" VOTE	
	County Hospital (1959)	County Court House (1959)
	(%)	(%)
*High-Income Homeowners**		
Pepper Pike	69	47
Beachwood	72	47
Middle-Income Homeowners†		
Olmstead Township	51	28
Garfield Heights (Ward 4)	48	29
Lower-Middle-Income Renters‡		
Cleveland Ward 31	76	66
Low–Income Renters§		
Cleveland Ward 11	73	63
Cleveland Ward 17	74	62

*Two suburbs with highest median family income ($15,700 and $19,000) of all suburbs with 85 percent or more home ownership.

†Two suburbs with lowest median family income ($6,800 and $7,000) of all suburbs with 85 percent or more home ownership.

‡The one ward with less than 15 percent home ownership and which is less than 10 percent Negro (median income: $4,700).

§Two wards with lowest median family incomes ($3,400 and $3,600) of all wards with less than 15 percent home ownership (Negro population of wards was 90 and 97 percent).

TABLE 5. Percentage Voting "Yes" on Expenditures in Home-owning, Upper-income "Old-stock" Precincts in Various Counties

County, Issue, and Date	Percent "Yes" Vote in Upper-Income Precincts	Percent "Yes" Vote in County as a Whole
	(%)	(%)
Detroit-Wayne County		
Sewers (8/60)	83.6	64.3
Increase school tax limit	52.0	39.0
Build schools (4/63)	52.0	33.4
Increase sales tax (11/60)	78.6	47.8
Kansas City—Jefferson County		
Increase school taxes (11/60)	68.6	54.9
Build jails (3/62)	86.3	78.0
Sewage treatment plant (11/60)	93.2	81.6
Miami-Dade County		
Highways (5/60)	71.2	53.0
Schools (1955)	90.8	92.1

voters in these areas who voted "yes."[7]
Except for Detroit and Dade County, where
only property owners and their spouses may
vote on expenditures, the city-county totals
include large numbers of renters. Even so,
the high-income precincts are comparatively
strong in their support of all expenditures.

III

When we hold constant the percentage of
home ownership, percentage of nonwhites,
and median family income, a negative
correlation appears between the percentage
of voters in the wards of Cleveland who are
of foreign stock and the percentage of the
total vote in those wards that is "yes." This
is shown in column 1 of Table 6.[8] Of the
many foreign stocks in Cleveland, the Poles
and Czechs have the strongest distaste for
expenditures. Column 2 of Table 6 shows
how markedly the presence of Poles and
Czechs in a voting district affects the "yes"
vote.[9] In the suburbs, the correlation is only
slightly weaker, but significant at the .001
level in all but two cases and in these at the
.01 level. The complete correlation table
shows that in all but three cases the percentage of Poles and Czechs is a more
important influence on voting than median
family income, and is second in influence

only to home ownership. In two of the three
exceptional cases, indeed, it was *more* important than home ownership.

The findings in columns 3 of Table 6 are
surprising. We expected a positive correlation
between percentage of Negroes and the
strength of the "yes" vote. Deficiencies in
the data may possibly account for the
absence of any correlation: there are not
enough home-owning Negroes or enough
very low-income whites in Cleveland to make
a really satisfactory matching of wards
possible.

In order to get a closer view of ethnic
voting, it is necessary to forego general
correlations and instead to examine individual precincts known to be predominantly
of a single ethnic group. In Tables 7 and 8 we
show how selected "ethnic" precincts belong-
ing to two income and home-ownership
classes voted in several elections in the
Chicago and Cleveland areas.[10] There is a
remarkable degree of consistency in the
influence of both ethnicity and income or
home ownership, whether viewed on an
intra- or intercity basis. In Chicago, for
example, the low-income renters in *every*
case voted more favorably for expenditures
than did the middle-income homeowners of
the same ethnic group. Within the same economic class, however, ethnicity makes a striking difference. Low-income Negro renters

TABLE 6. *Partial Correlations between Selected "Ethnic" Variables and Percentage Voting "Yes" on Expenditures in Cleveland and Cuyahoga County Wards and Towns**

ISSUE	FOREIGN STOCK		POLISH-CZECH		NEGRO	
	City	Suburbs	City	Suburbs	City	Suburbs
Admin. Building	−0.40	ns†	−0.54	−0.17	ns	ns
County Hospital	ns	ns	−0.79	−0.40	ns	ns
TB Hospital	ns	−0.22	−0.74	−0.46	ns	ns
Court House	−0.47	ns	−0.58	−0.28	ns	ns
Juvenile Court	−0.46	ns	−0.74	−0.40	ns	ns
Parks (1959)	−0.41	ns	−0.62	−0.31	−0.49	ns
Welfare Levy	−0.58	ns	−0.71	−0.49	ns	ns
Roads and Bridges	−0.48	ns	−0.66	−0.40	ns	ns
Zoo	−0.62	ns	−0.71	−0.40	ns	ns
Parks (1960)	ns	ns	ns	−0.50	ns	ns

*These are partial correlation coefficients derived from a regression analysis in which home ownership, median family income, and two "ethnic" variables have been held constant.

†If the correlations were not significant at the .05 level (student's *t*), "ns" is entered in the table. The critical values were based on 27 degrees of freedom for the city data and 84 degrees of freedom for the suburban data.

TABLE 7. Percentage of Various "Ethnic" Precincts Voting "Yes" on Selected Expenditures in Chicago

ETHNIC GROUP AND NUMBER OF PRECINCTS	PERCENT VOTING "YES" ON:				
	Co. Hosp. (6/57)	Vets' Bonus (11/58)	Urban Renewal (4/62)	City Hall (5/62)	School (4/59)
	(%)	(%)	(%)	(%)	(%)
Low-Income Renters*					
Negro (22)	84.9	80.2	88.6	82.3	97.8
Irish (6)	61.3	55.3	45.7	46.3	79.4
Polish (26)	60.1	54.6	57.1	53.8	81.8
Middle-Income Homeowners†					
Negro (13)	66.8	54.9	69.6	49.8	88.9
Irish (6)	54.6	44.1	22.0	27.2	64.2
Polish (38)	47.4	40.0	14.6	15.2	58.3

*Average median family income under $6,000 per year; at least two-thirds of all dwelling units renter-occupied.
†Average median family income between $7,500 and $10,000 a year for whites; over $6,000 a year for Negroes. At least 80 percent of all dwelling units owner-occupied.

TABLE 8. Percentage of Various "Ethnic" Precincts Voting "Yes" on Selected Expenditures in Cleveland and Cuyahoga County

ETHNIC GROUP AND NUMBER OF PRECINCTS	PERCENT VOTING "YES" ON:				
	Co. Hosp. (11/59)	Court House (11/59)	Parks (11/59)	Welfare Levy (5/60)	Vets' Bonus (11/56)
	(%)	(%)	(%)	(%)	(%)
Low-Income Renters*					
Negro (16)	78.6	67.3	52.6	85.9	89.9
Italian (10)	68.8	53.3	43.5	49.9	74.8
Polish (6)	54.9	39.9	28.1	33.7	71.6
Middle-Income Homeowners†					
Negro (8)	68.1	54.0	39.6	73.2	79.2
Italian (7)	59.3	49.7	41.1	56.8	66.8
Polish (12)	52.9	35.8	34.3	46.4	61.7
Upper-Income Homeowners‡					
Anglo-Saxon (11)	70.6	51.4	57.2	64.8	53.7
Jewish (7)	71.7	47.1	48.4	64.5	56.8

*Average median family income less than $6,000 per year; at least two-thirds of all dwelling units renter-occupied.
†Average median family income between $7,000 and $9,000 a year for whites; over $6,000 a year for Negroes. At least 75 percent of all dwelling units owner-occupied.
‡Average median family income over $10,000 per year; over 85 percent of all dwelling units owner-occupied.

are in *every* case more enthusiastic by a wide margin about public expenditures than low-income Irish or Polish renters. Middle-income Negro homeowners are in *every* case more enthusiastic about the same proposals than middle-income Irish or Polish homeowners. (In passing, it is worth noting that Negroes are two or three times more favorable toward urban renewal—despite the fact that they are commonly the chief victims of land clearance programs—than Irish or Polish voters.)

Essentially the same relationships appear in Table 8 for Cleveland–Cuyahoga County. With one exception (Italians voting on the welfare levy), low-income renters in an ethnic group are more favorable to expenditures than middle-income homeowners in the same ethnic group. Low-income Negro renters are the most favorable to all proposals and middle-income Negro homeowners are more favorable to them than are the other middle-income ethnic groups. Aside from the veterans' bonus (a special case), both the "Anglo-Saxon" and the Jewish upper-income homeowners are more favorable to expenditures than any middle-income group except the Negro.

IV

We have shown both that a considerable proportion of voters, especially in the upper income groups, vote against their self-interest narrowly conceived and that a marked ethnic influence appears in the vote. Now we would like to bring these two findings together under a single explanatory principle.

One such principle—but one we reject—is that the voters in question have acted irrationally (either in not calculating benefits and costs at all or else by making mistakes in their calculations) and that their irrationality is a function of their ethnic status. According to this theory, the low-income Polish renter who votes against expenditures proposals that would cost him nothing and would confer benefits upon him and the high-income Anglo-Saxon or Jewish homeowner who favors expenditures proposals that will cost him heavily without benefiting him would both behave differently if they thought about the matter more or if their information were better.

A more tenable hypothesis, we think, is that voters in some income and ethnic groups are more likely than voters in others to take a public-regarding rather than a narrowly self-interested view of things—i.e., to take the welfare of others, especially that of "the community," into account as an aspect of their own welfare.[11] We offer the additional hypothesis that both the tendency of a voter to take a public-regarding view and the content of that view (e.g., whether or not he thinks a Korean war veterans' bonus is

in the public interest) are largely functions of his participation in a subculture that is definable in ethnic and income terms. Each subcultural group, we think, has a more or less distinctive notion of how much a citizen ought to sacrifice for the sake of the community as well as of what the welfare of the community is constituted; in a word, each has its own idea of what justice requires and of the importance of acting justly. According to this hypothesis, the voter is presumed to act rationally; the ends he seeks are not always narrowly self-interested ones, however. On the contrary, depending upon his income and ethnic status they are more or less public-regarding.[12]

That his income status does not by itself determine how public-regarding he is, or what content he gives to the public interest, can be shown from the voting data. As we explained above, generally the higher a homeowner's income the more likely he is to favor expenditures. This is partly—but only partly—because the value of the dollar is usually less to people who have many of them than to people who have few of them. We suggest that it is also because upper-income people tend to be more public-regarding than lower-income people. We do not think that income per se has this effect; rather it is the ethnic attributers, or culture, empirically associated with it. It happens that most upper-income voters belong, if not by inheritance then by adoption, to an ethnic group (especially the Anglo-Saxon and the Jewish) that is relatively public-regarding in its outlook; hence ethnic influence on voting is hard to distinguish from income influence.

In the three scatter diagrams which comprise Figure 6 we have tried to distinguish the two kinds of influence. For this figure, we divided all wards and towns of Cleveland and Cuyahoga County in which 85 or more percent of the dwelling units were owner-occupied into three classes according to median home value. Diagram 6a shows the voting where that value was more than $27,000; diagram 6b shows it where it was $19,000–27,000, and diagram 6c shows it where it was less than $19,000. The hori-

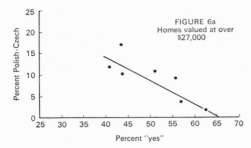

FIGURE 6a
Homes valued at over
$27,000

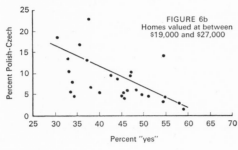

FIGURE 6b
Homes valued at between
$19,000 and $27,000

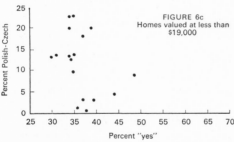

FIGURE 6c
Homes valued at less than
$19,000

Figure 6. Relation between percentage voting "yes" on proposition to provide additional zoo facilities (1960) and proportion of ward or town population which is of Polish or Czech foreign stock in Cuyahoga County, Ohio; at three median home-value levels (only wards and towns with 85 percent or more owner-occupied dwellings used).

zontal and vertical axes are the same for all diagrams; each diagram shows the relationship between the percentage of voters in the ward or town who are Polish-Czech (vertical axis) and the percentage of "yes" vote on a proposal to expand the zoo (horizontal axis). In the group of wards and towns having the lowest medium home value (diagram 6c) the presence of Polish-Czech voters made little difference; these wards and towns were about 65 percent against the proposal no matter how many Poles and Czechs lived in them. In both groups of higher home-value wards and towns, however, Poles and Czechs were

conspicuously less favorable to the proposal than were the rest of the voters. Among the non-Polish-Czech voters in these higher home-value wards and towns, Angle-Saxons and Jews were heavily represented; therefore, it seems plausible to conclude that, as compared to Poles and Czechs in these two income groups, the Anglo-Saxons and Jews were decidedly public-regarding.

Another interpretation of the behavior of the Poles and Czechs is possible, however. It may be that they had the welfare of the community in view also but defined it differently than did the Anglo-Saxons and the Jews. They may have thought that the particular expenditure proposed—or, for that matter, all public expenditures—would do the community more harm than good. (This would rationalize the behavior of those low-income renters—see Table 8—who voted against proposals giving them benefits without any costs.)[13] Whatever may be true of the Poles and Czechs, it seems clear that upper-income Anglo-Saxons, and to a somewhat lesser degree Jews, tend to vote on public-regarding grounds *against* some proposals (notably those, like veterans' bonuses and city employees' pension benefits and pay increases) that they regard as serving "special interests" rather than "the community as a whole."

When we know more about each of the various subcultures—especially about the nature of the individual's attachment to the society, his conception of what is just, and the extent of the obligation he feels to subordinate his interest to that of various others (e.g., the community)—we should doubtless be able to make and test more refined hypotheses about voting behavior.

Appendix

We chose the "ethnic" precincts for Tables 7 and 8 by inspecting census tract data and then visiting the precincts that appeared to be predominantly of one ethnic group to get confirmatory evidence from well-informed persons and from a view of the neighborhoods. We could have used a less impressionistic method (e.g., counting the proportion of ethnic names on voter registration lists), but since we wanted only to identify precincts that are predominantly of one ethnic group, not to place them on a scale of ethnicity, this did not appear necessary.

Having identified the "ethnic" precincts, we divided them into two (sometimes three) income groups on the basis of census data. As we indicate on the tables, with one exception we used the same cutting points to separate the income levels of all ethnic groups. The exception was the Negro. The income distribution among Negroes is so skewed to the low end of the scale that "middle income" has to be defined differently for Negroes than for whites. We identified "middle-income Negro" precincts by selecting from among all precincts that were at least 85 percent Negro and had an owner-occupancy rate of at least 80 percent those few with the highest median family incomes. Some of these precincts turned out to have median incomes as low as $6,000 a year, which is about $1,000 less than any of the "middle-income white" precincts had. If we had made the cutting point higher, however, we would not have had enough middle-income Negro precincts to work with. In our opinion, Negroes with incomes of $6,000 are about as likely to "feel" middle income as are whites with incomes of $7,000.

Notes

1. Median family income under $3,000 per year. Needless to say, most voters in this category are Negroes.

2. The cities and elections examined are:
Cleveland—Cuyahoga County: Nov. 1956; Nov. 1959; May 1960; Nov. 1960.
Chicago—Cook County: June 1957; Nov. 1958; Nov. 1959; April 1962.
Detroit—Wayne County: August 1960; Feb. 1961; April 1961; April 1963.
Kansas City: Nov. 1960; March 1962.
Los Angeles: Nov. 1962.
Miami: Nov. 1956; May 1960.
St Louis: March 1962; Nov. 1962; March 1963.

3. The degree of association was also calculated using a nonparametric statistic (Kendall's

tau). The relationship persists but at lower values. Since we are satisfied that the relationship found by *r* is not spurious, we have relied on it for the balance of the analysis because of its capacity to produce partial correlation coefficients.

4. Only two measures of tax liability can be got from the census: median home value and median family income. We have used the latter for the most part. The census classifies all homes valued at over $25,000 together, thereby collapsing distinctions that are important for us. We think, too, that people are more likely to know their incomes than to know the current market value of their homes, and that therefore the census information on incomes is more reliable. Finally, in neighborhoods populated mostly by renters, median home values are likely to be unrepresentative of the class character of the neighborhood: this is so, for example, where a few owner-occupied slums exist in a district of luxury apartments.

5. Other studies which suggest that upper-income groups may have a greater preference for public expenditures than middle-income groups include Oliver P. Williams and Charles R. Adrian, *Four Cities: A Study in Comparative Policy Making* (Philadelphia: University of Pennsylvania Press, 1963), chap. 5; Alvin Boskoff and Harmon Zeigler, *Voting Patterns in a Local Election* (Philadelphia: J. B. Lippincott, 1964), chap. 3; Richard A. Watson, *The Politics of Urban Change* (Kansas City, Mo.: Community Studies, 1963), chap. 4; and Robert H. Salisbury and Gordon Black, "Class and Party in Non-Partisan Elections: The Case of Des Moines," *American Political Science Review*, 57 (September 1963), 591. The Williams-Adrian and Salisbury-Black studies use electoral data; the Boskoff-Zeigler and Watson studies use survey data. See also Otto A. Davis, "Empirical Evidence of 'Political' Influences Upon the Expenditure and Taxation Policies of Public Schools," Graduate School of Industrial Administration of the Carnegie Institute of Technology, January 1964 (mimeo); and William C. Birdsall, "Public Finance Allocation Decisions and the Preferences of Citizens: Some Theoretical and Empirical Considerations" (unpublished Ph.D. thesis, Department of Economics, Johns Hopkins University, 1963). A difficulty with the Davis and Birdsall studies is the size (and thus the heterogeneity) of the units of analysis—entire school districts in one case, entire cities in the other.

6. Michigan is one of the few states which restricts the right to vote on expenditures to property owners and their spouses. Because the Flint returns were tabulated on a precinct basis, demographic data had to be obtained from block rather than tract statistics; since median family income is given only for tracts, median value of owner-occupied homes had to be used. Possibly the flood control benefits would be

distributed roughly in proportion to the value of properties; about this we cannot say. However, it is worth noting that the vote in Flint on other expenditures which presumably would *not* distribute benefits in proportion to the value of properties (e.g., parks) followed the same pattern.

7. We isolated all precincts in census tracts having median family incomes of at least $10,000 a year, with at least 70 percent home ownership (the central city of Chicago was excepted here), and at least 70 percent of the population third- (or more) generation native born.

8. A person is of "foreign stock" if he was born abroad or if one or both of his parents was born abroad. We believe that the reason why a significant relationship does not appear for the suburbs is that there is a considerable number of Jews among the foreign stock of the suburbs. In the central city, there are practically no Jews. Like other Jews, Jews of Eastern European origin tend to favor expenditures proposals of all kinds. Their presence in the suburbs, therefore, offsets the "no" vote of the non-Jews of foreign stock.

9. Since no home-owning ward or town in Cuyahoga County is more than 25 percent Polish-Czech according to the 1960 census, it may be that no inferences can be drawn from the voting data about Polish-Czech behavior. Three considerations increase our confidence in the possibility of drawing inferences, however. (1) Only first- and second-generation Poles and Czechs are counted as such by the Census; but third- and fourth-generation Poles and Czechs tend to live in the same wards and towns; thus the proportion of the electorate sharing Polish-Czech cultural values (the relevant thing from our standpoint) is considerably larger than the census figures suggest. (2) When other factors are held constant, even small increases in the number of Poles and Czechs are accompanied by increases in the "no" vote; nothing "explains" this except the hypothesis that the Poles and Czechs make the difference. (3) When we take as the unit for analysis not wards, but precincts of a few hundred persons that are known to contain very high proportions of Poles and

Czechs, we get the same results. Because we are using ecological, not individual, data, we are perforce analyzing the behavior of ethnic "ghettos" where ethnic identification and attitudes are probably reinforced. Poles in non-Polish wards, for example, may behave quite differently.

10. The method by which these precincts were selected is given in the Appendix. Unfortunately, it proved impossible to identify relatively homogeneous precincts typical of other ethnic groups at various income levels and degrees of home-ownership. For example, middle-income Jews tend to be renters, not homeowners, and there are practically no low-income Jewish precincts in either city. A complete list of these precincts is available from the authors.

11. Cf. Anthony Downs, "The Public Interest: Its Meaning in a Democracy," *Social Research*, 29 (Spring 1962), 28–29.

12. The proposition that "subculture" can be defined in ethnic and income terms is highly provisional. We are looking for other and better criteria and we think we may find some. But so far as the present data are concerned, ethnic and income status are all we have.

13. Two other explanations are possible and, in our opinion, plausible. One is that the low-income renters may have taken into account costs to them other than taxes—e.g., the cost (perhaps monetary) of changes in the neighborhood that would ensue from expenditures. (Irish objections to urban renewal in Chicago may have been due, not to a fear of higher taxes, but to fear of neighborhood "invasion" by Negroes displaced from land clearance projects.) The other is that in these precincts a much higher proportion of renters than of homeowners may have stayed away from the polls. In Cleveland (though not, interestingly, in Chicago) voter turnout is highly correlated with home ownership and almost all white renter precincts have at least a few homeowners in them. Conceivably —we think it unlikely—all those who voted in some "renter" precincts were actually owners.

3. Socioeconomic Characteristics

Political and Socioeconomic Characteristics of American Cities

Robert R. Alford
and Harry M. Scoble*

Robert R. Alford and Harry M. Scoble, *"Political and Socioeconomic Characteristics of American Cities,"* Municipal Year Book, 1965. Copyright, 1965, by the International City Managers' Association. Reproduced by permission.

*We are indebted to Leo Schnore, Herbert Jacob, and Jane Hood for critical comments, and to the National Science Foundation, through the Computing Center at the University of Wisconsin, for assistance with the data.

WHY SHOULD POLITICAL and socioeconomic characteristics of a city be related to its form of government? For several reasons, we cannot assume that any set of factors will correlate with the form of government: (1) Changing the constitutional framework of local government is difficult, especially if it has been changed quite recently. Although there is little evidence on this score, it seems a fair assumption that neither activists nor voters will be prepared to make frequent changes. (2) State laws prescribe one or another form or make change difficult. (3) Such change is difficult to translate into successful political action, even if the city contains a majority of social groups likely to favor a certain form. (4) As a consequence of the above, a city is likely to possess a given form for many years, through periods of considerable social and economic change.

Nevertheless, as will be shown, such relationships exist, and this paper attempts a partial explanation. This article extends to all U.S. cities over 25,000 population (in 1960) the findings and implications of several previous studies concerning the relationship between forms of government and socioeconomic characteristics of American cities. Liebman analyzed the economic functions of twenty-one Cook County (Illinois) suburbs, Kessel examined growth rates, economic base, and foreign-born population of cities between 25,000 and 250,000 population, and Schnore and Alford studied the relation between a number of population and economic characteristics of suburbs and their form of government. For reasons of space no direct citations will be made, but a number of ideas come from these previous publications.[1]

Forms of City Government

We must make certain initial assumptions about the character of these forms of government, assumptions which cannot here be defended in detail. The council-manager form is assumed to be more "business-like" and less "politicized" than either the commission or the mayor-council form, in the sense that the manager form implies agreement upon the major goals of city government by dominant social groups. By *politicized* we mean that the form encourages or allows interest group representation, by *professionalized* that it encourages efficient implementation of specified goals. We have no evidence concerning the actual differences in performance of city services, or whether certain groups actually have less potential influence over city decisions under the council-manager form than in the other forms. The fact that manager cities are less likely to have partisan elections, and more likely to have at-large rather than ward elections, means that other features of the governmental framework are consistent with an assumption of consensus on an "anti-political" governmental structure by dominant groups.

The commission form is essentially non-political, but of a different character than the council-manager form, stressing "nonprofessional" implementation of agreed-upon goals. This type of government is probably less likely to be able to handle new goals or new problems than the manager form, since its commissioners head administrative departments. The commission form is usually regarded as obsolete, and its declining incidence is consistent with this view. Only 15 percent of American cities have the commission form, and it will be treated here, for the most part, as a residual category.

The mayor-council form may be regarded as an intermediate type, less centralized than the council-manager form, more centralized than the commission form, and allowing for a variety of forms of political representation and levels of administrative efficiency. When combined with the other aspects of the most professionalized, nonpolitical form—nonpartisanship and at-large elections—it may be quite similar to a manager form.

Three major variables may be related to one or another form of government: (1) the *social heterogeneity* of the population (along such lines as religion, race, or ethnicity); (2) its *class composition* (the proportion of persons in white-collar occupations, or with college education); and (3) its population *growth and mobility*. Social heterogeneity—the existence of sizeable groups with diverse political cultures and demands—favors a more politicized, less centralized, less professionalized form because there is not as great a consensus among politically active groups upon the proper goals of city government and a greater need for access and representation from diverse groups. A relatively high proportion of middle-class persons favor a less politicized form because such groups are less likely to have political demands inconsistent with the centralized, efficient form. Population growth and mobility favor a less politicized form because cities are facing new problems requiring administrative and managerial skills, at the same time that a low proportion of the population is settled into stable social and political groups.

These hypotheses do not imply that the council-manager form is only possible where all major social groups agree upon the proper goals for city government. Certainly most city managers must deal with many social

and political cleavages. Also, the very existence of the manager form may represent a victory for one social group over another. The fact (to be shown) that the manager form is *less* likely rather than more likely in heavy working-class cities indicates that the simple presence of a majority of one social class does not create a consensus favoring the manager form (assuming, of course, that our hypotheses about the nature of the forms are correct). The social class composition of a city may be regarded as an element of social heterogeneity, if there is a large enough working class to provide a political base of opposition for the "natural" leaders of a community: the educated professional and business groups.[2]

Our basic assumption is that the more cleavage in a city—regardless of the source— the more highly politicized a government it is likely to have, if the sources of social and political diversity have channels of political expression. Unfortunately, we have no independent measure of whether the mayor-council form allows more interest-group representation and influence than the council-manager form.

This paper sorts out the relative importance of some of these factors for the form of government of American cities. Some factors, such as statutory control by the states, serve to confound the relations here discussed, but we have not been able to take them into account. All of the characteristics dealt with can be plausibly interpreted as fitting some theory about the relation of political forms to their economic and social "environment." The problem, of course, is that in some instances the characteristics of cities are so highly correlated that it is impossible to separate them after the fact (so to speak) by comparing the effects of certain characteristics while simultaneously holding other characteristics "constant." If almost all eastern cities are heavily industrialized, with a high proportion of foreign-born persons, a low proportion of migrant persons, and a fairly low average level of education, and almost all western cities are just the opposite, then clearly the effect of one factor cannot be distinguished from another.

But it would be significant if we should discover that it is the occupational composition of the population, rather than its mobility, which is related to the adoption of the council-manager plan. Only a few such interrelations can be discussed in this paper.

Empirical Indicators

The indicators used can be summarized as follows:

Occupation and education. The existence of a high proportion of white-collar persons or of persons with at least a high school education suggests that a politically important segment of the electorate will favor a professional manager, since the ideals and goals of the manager are not inconsistent with their view of city government. The manager form is consistent with an antipolitical and efficient running of the business of government typical of a white-collar, business political point of view.

Growth. Growing cities have a smaller proportion of the population with stable roots in the community and connections with groups with political demands. Therefore, the population is likely to have a more instrumental approach to city government and is more likely to accept or want professional administration of city services.

Size. The larger the city, the more socially heterogeneous it is likely to be, and therefore the more likely to have competing interest groups demanding political access, and the more likely to have a "politicized" form.

Mobility. Cities with highly mobile populations, like cities which are growing, are less likely to have stable political groupings, and more likely to have populations which demand efficient, business-like government rather than a government responsive to traditional groups' desires for representation and access. Growth is associated with mobility, but there can be high mobility without high growth. We have no data on the type of mobility, nor on which groups are mobile, and these may be more important than the sheer quantity of movement.

Ethnic diversity. Cities with higher proportions of persons of recent foreign origin are more likely to be politically and culturally heterogeneous, and they require "political" rather than "administrative" forms.

Religious diversity. Cities with higher proportions of children going to private schools—a crude measure of religious diversity—are, again, more likely to be politically and culturally heterogeneous.

Racial diversity. Cities with higher proportions of nonwhites are certainly, at this stage of American history, likely to be politically and culturally heterogeneous.

The last three are measures of social heterogeneity. The first is a good indication of the degree of ethnic diversity in the city, and the second represents as a good a measure of religious diversity as we have from census data. Probably most of the children in private schools are Catholic, except in the Midwest where many are Lutheran. Regardless of which religious group (or any other private group) has its own schools, this is an indication of local cleavage along lines which might well be politically relevant and require a more politicized form of government. Nonwhites as recorded by the census are not all Negroes, but this generally is a good index of the Negro composition of a city.

It must be emphasized that we are not arguing that any of these characteristics of cities "cause," in any direct sense, the adoption of a particular form of government. The social and political *processes* involved must be inferred from the crude cross-sectional indicators that are available.

Different forms of government are not evenly distributed in the major regions of the United States. As expected, the Far West, the newest and most rapidly growing region of the nation, has a far higher proportion of manager cities than any other region; the East has the lowest (see Table 6*). Whether the associations of certain other factors with governmental forms are merely due to their regional character will be seen later.

_____
* All tables are at the end of this selection.

Initial Findings

All of the suggested relations between social and economic characteristics of cities and their forms of government are borne out by the tables that follow, which were selected from a range of possible measures of the major factors: social heterogeneity, class composition, and population growth and mobility. Because of space limitations, certain two-variable tables have been omitted if they are repeated in later three-variable tables. Thus form of government by region is given in the totals column of Table 6, by mobility in Table 8, by occupational composition in Table 7, by foreign parentage in Table 11, and by nonwhite composition in Table 12.[3]

Table 1 shows the relation of forms of government to the metropolitan status and employing character of cities. No clear relationship is shown, and, although other tables will not be given, there seems to be no independent influence of these two factors upon the adoption of a form of government when other characteristics are examined simultaneously.

Consistent with the hypothesis that social heterogeneity increases with the size of cities, and therefore the incidence of professionalized government should drop, Table 2 shows that fewer large cities have the council-manager plan. There are no striking differences of form among the middle-sized cities.

Growth is clearly related to form of government, as seen in Table 3. Growing cities are more likely to have the council-manager form, less likely to have commission and mayor-council forms. Similarly, cities with highly mobile populations are considerably more likely to have managers than cities with stable populations. (See Table 8. The association of mobility and form remains exactly the same when size of city is controlled).

Turning to the economic and social class character of cities, we see in Tables 7 and 4 that both indicators used—white-collar proportion and educational attainment—are consistent with the generalizations advanced.[4] Cities with a high proportion of white-collar persons, or high-school educated persons, are considerably more likely to have manager forms than cities with low proportions.

Tables 11 and 5 show that only two measures of social heterogeneity are clearly related to form of government: the proportion of the native-born population which has one or both foreign-born parents, and the proportion of elementary school children which is attending private school.

Cities with a high proportion of nonwhite population (more than 15 percent) are somewhat more likely to have the commission form, and cities with a low proportion of nonwhites are slightly more likely to have a mayor-council form, but the differences are neither great nor consistent (see Table 12).

Up to this point, we have shown that nearly all of the characteristics of cities considered are related to their forms of government. High mobility, low private school population, high white-collar population, low proportion of native-born persons of foreign parentage, high level of population growth, high level of education, and smaller size are all associated with the council-manager rather than the mayor-council form, and in roughly that order of association, judging from the percentage-point differences shown in the tables. The three major factors —social heterogeneity, class composition, and growth or mobility—are all important, regardless of which indicator is used. The only exception is nonwhite composition.

Interrelationships of the Factors

It is the task of this section to consider which of these factors are independently related to form of government, and which are related only because they are correlated with others.

Is the apparent association of mobility with forms of government due simply to the fact that Far West cities have more mobile populations and are also more likely to have the council-manager form? Regions differ greatly in the mobility of their cities' populations, as Table 6 shows, but the effect of mobility does not disappear. The manager form is generally more likely in more mobile cities, and both commission and mayor-council forms are less likely, regardless of the region.

In eastern cities higher mobility reduces the incidence of commission and increases the likelihood of manager forms, but it is not associated with the mayor-council form. In the Midwest, the commission form is not related to mobility. In the Far West, where most cities have managers, the manager form is only slightly more likely in high mobility cities. It may be noted that no cities at all in the Far West have the lowest level of mobility in the tripartite division used here.

Thus, mobility remains important, even within regions, although there is a strong association of both mobility and form of government with the region in which a city is located.

Table 7, showing the interrelations of occupational composition, population mobility, and form of government, may clarify the connections of these variables further. The table shows that mobility is closely related to occupational composition: heavily white-collar cities have far more mobile populations than heavily blue-collar cities. As we have already shown, both mobility and occupational composition are closely related to the form of government. The question is: What is the nature of the relation of these two factors to form of government? Are white-collar populations more likely to have manager forms simply because they are more mobile, and therefore have less stake in local government policies and will relinquish control to a professional manager? This 'table may help specify the conditions under which a white-collar population is related to a particular form of government, or explain why there is such a connection.

The table shows that among mobility cities, the proportion of white-collar persons in the city makes little or no difference in the form of government, but that a small difference does remain in the less mobile cities. The association of mobility with form, however, is hardly reduced at all. The average percentage-point difference for the manager form attributable to mobility, controlling for occupational composition, is $+45$, for mayor-council $+36$, while the average percentage-point difference attributable to occupational composition, controlling for mobility, is $+11$ for the manager form, $+6$ for the mayor-council form. Thus mobility is more significantly related to forms of government than is occupational composition.

The interrelations of population change (both growth and decline) and mobility as they relate to forms of government must now be examined. Mobility is certainly related to growth, as Table 8 shows, but the two characteristics of a city may be somewhat independent (particularly in these data, because the growth data do not take account of annexations, and the measure of mobility is migration from different counties in the United States between 1955 and 1960). No cities have both high mobility and a decline in population, as Table 8 shows, although such a combination is possible if many more persons leave than enter. Considering both of these indicators of growth and mobility simultaneously allows some control for the lack of information on annexations.

Table 8 shows that mobility is far more important than population change as a factor in forms of government. When mobility is controlled, the effect of population change is reduced. On the other hand, the association with mobility remains high, even when population change is controlled. We infer that the association of population change with form of government depends upon mobility. Growth or decline without much mobility, by annexations or by out-migration without in-migration, is not strongly related to the form of government.

Now let us bring together the two major factors—mobility and religious diversity—which have been found to be most closely related to forms of government. Again, they are related, because the more mobile cities have fewer children in private school. There is probably more reliance in such cities upon government to provide essential services than on traditional institutions based upon religious and ethnic subcommunities. Many of these cities are in the Far West, of course. While it may seem to fly in the face of common sense, such an association may be a sign of less cultural and political heterogeneity in mobile cities. Stable populations may be more likely to develop institutions based upon whatever religious and ethnic subcultures exist.

Table 9 shows the relations of mobility and religious diversity, as measured by the proportion of elementary school children in private school, to form of government. Both factors are independently and strongly related to forms of government. The average percentage-point difference for mobility, controlling for private school population, is +35 and +18 percent for manager and mayor-council forms, respectively, and +27 and +35 percent for private school population, controlling for mobility. What is perhaps more important is the fact that they are additive in their effects. Taking both factors into account provides a high level of predictability of the form of government of a city. Of cities with the lowest mobility and the highest proportion of children in private school, 18 percent have a manager form, 16 a commission form, 66 percent a mayor-council form, as contrasted with 78, 9, and 13 percent, respectively, in cities with the highest mobility and the lowest proportion of children in private schools. Fully 55 percent of the few cities with low mobility and few children in private schools have the commission form.

Although the proportion of children in private school in a city is closely related to its form of government, this association is reduced when the same relationship is examined within regions (see Table 10). Such a finding is difficult to interpret. Does this mean that the original association of religious diversity with form of government is spurious? Or merely that the region in which a city is located is correlated highly with both the religious composition of the community, its mobility, and its form of government? We do not really know what it means for a city to be located in a given region, aside from historical patterns of growth and development, and possibly the diffusion of political forms from adjacent and older cities.

Table 11 shows the relations of the ethnic diversity of cities (as measured by the proportion of persons who are native-born of either foreign or mixed parentage) to mobility and form of government. Here, as in Table 9, we see a difference in the social characteristics of commission and mayor-council forms. Unlike the mayor-council form, commission forms are considerably less likely to be found in cities with high ethnic diversity, and taking the mobility of the population into account increases this difference considerably. Fully 46 percent of the twenty-six least mobile, least ethnically diverse cities have the commission form. This is consistent with the findings of Table 9.

Although cities with a lower proportion of persons of foreign ancestry have more mobile populations, both factors independently correlate with forms of government. Mobility however, is far more closely related to governmental form than is foreign parentage.

Table 12 shows that foreign parentage is related to form of government, even when the proportion of nonwhites in the cities is controlled, for both mayor-council and council-manager forms. The average percentage-point difference for foreign parentage is +28 for the manager form, +22 for the mayor-council form. When, in contrast, foreign parentage is controlled, and the association of nonwhite composition with forms is examined, differences are small or even reversed from the expected direction. (Also, when region is controlled, there is no relation between governmental form and nonwhite composition.) A high proportion of nonwhites does not, therefore, lead to a greater likelihood of a mayor-council form of government. It is possible that this is because nonwhites have not hitherto had an effective political voice. Ethnic groups of European origin and Catholics seem to be the sources of social heterogeneity related to form of government.

Conclusion

To summarize: white, Anglo-Saxon, Protestant, growing, and mobile cities are highly likely to be manager cities; ethnically and religiously diverse but nonmobile industrial cities are highly likely to be mayor-council cities. The commission form is associated with declining population, low mobility, a low white-collar composition and a low educational level, and low ethnic and religious diversity. Native, probably Protestant, declining industrial cities are thus highly likely to be commission cities.

Some possible causal connections of these factors with governmental form may be suggested, subject to the qualifications already given. Mobility appears to explain the association of economic and class composition with form. It is apparently through mobility that a political base is changed, because mobile blue-collar cities are as likely to have managers as mobile white-collar cities. Similarly, mobility seems to explain how population growth and decline affect form of government. It is not just growth, but primarily the fact of a sizable mobility on the part of a city's population which destroys the potential political opposition to a professional city manager. Mobility does not explain, however, why the religious composition of a city is related to forms of government.

We may conceive of both population growth and mobility as intervening variables, serving to loosen the social and political ties of persons to their community and rendering ineffective those characteristics of the population which would otherwise bring forth political demands. Class composition and social heterogeneity or homogeneity are stable long-term characteristics of a city's population. Growth and mobility are more likely to be temporary characteristics, although it is obvious that they may ultimately change the class composition and heterogeneity of a city. For purposes of our present investigation, all of these variables can be regarded as snapshots of processes of social and political change.

Unfortunately, we have no data on changes in form of government, but we may venture a concluding speculation. We would expect more change in forms of government in certain types of cities, where the political influence of different social groups varies over time and the city "vacillates" between a concern for efficiency and a concern for representation of group interests. Thus we would expect that highly mobile and heterogeneous cities would experience considerable pressure for change in form of government. Growing but heavily blue-collar cities should exhibit similar conflicts since they face the "cross-pressures" of (1) need for an efficient, professionalized administration to solve their problems of growth, and (2) need for a political form well adapted to providing representation for diverse subcultures and subcommunities. Such cities have no stable set of "predispositions" toward a given form of government but are pushed in several different directions, much like the "cross-pressured" voters in the classic voting studies.

TABLE 1. *Form of Government by Metropolitan Status* *

FORM OF GOVERNMENT	CENTRAL CITY			SUBURB			INDEPENDENT CITY	
	Employing	Balanced	Dormitory	Employing	Balanced	Dormitory	Employing	Balanced
	(%)	(%)	(%)	(%)	(%)	(%)	(%)	(%)
Manager	45	31	58	42	38	53	53	55
Commission	16	21	15	21	10	12	15	13
Mayor-council	39	48	27	37	52	35	32	32
100%† =	(103)	(86)	(26)	(57)	(50)	(107)	(96)	(100)

*Information on metropolitan status was not available for 49 cities. The categories are those presented in the *1959 Municipal Year Book*. An INDEPENDENT city (I) is not located in a Standard Metropolital Statistical Area, as designated by the Bureau of the Budget; a CENTRAL city (C) and a SUBURB (S) are likewise designated by the Bureau of the Budget according to certain criteria. DORMITORY (D), BALANCED (B), and EMPLOYING (E) cities are classified according to the number of persons who work in a city as compared with the number of working people who live there. An independent city, by definition, cannot be a dormitory city.

†In this and subsequent tables, "100%" indicates that percentages add up to 100 and that the total number of cities, by categories, is shown in parentheses.

TABLE 2. *Form of Government by Size of City*

FORM OF GOVERNMENT	SIZE (thousands)			
	25–50	50–100	100–200	200+
	(%)	(%)	(%)	(%)
Manager	51	48	45	37
Commission	14	16	17	12
Mayor-council	35	36	38	51
100%=	(338)	(174)	(69)	(59)

TABLE 3. *Form of Government and Population Change*

FORM OF GOVERNMENT	POPULATION DECLINE			POPULATION GROWTH		
	High (7–29%)	Medium (4–6%)	Low (0–3%)	Low (0–15%)	Medium (16–44%)	High (45%+)
	(%)	(%)	(%)	(%)	(%)	(%)
Manager	26	30	30	39	48	70
Commission	36	27	14	17	12	8
Mayor-council	38	43	56	44	40	22
100%=	(50)	(40)	(37)	(152)	(181)	(178)

Note: Percentages refer to population loss or gain in the city from 1950 to 1960. These changes may reflect alterations in city boundaries, which were not taken into account in this study.

TABLE 4. *Form of Government and Education*

FORM OF GOVERNMENT	PERCENT COMPLETING HIGH SCHOOL		
	Low (18–40%)	Medium (41–49%)	High (50–89%)
	(%)	(%)	(%)
Manager	33	49	67
Commission	21	12	10
Mayor-council	46	39	23
100%=	(247)	(203)	(190)

Note: Percentages refer to the proportion of the population aged 25 and over with four years of high school or more.

TABLE 5. Form of Government and Private School Population

FORM OF GOVERNMENT	PRIVATE SCHOOL POPULATION		
	Low (0–9%)	Medium (10–24%)	High (25–69%)
	(%)	(%)	(%)
Manager	67	50	24
Commission	15	15	16
Mayor-council	18	35	60
100%=	(185)	(282)	(173)

Note: Percentages refer to the proportion of the elementary school population which is in a private school.

TABLE 6. Form of Government* by Region† and Mobility

REGION	MOBILITY‡			TOTAL
	Low (2–11%)	Medium (12–20%)	High (21–58%)	
East	(%)	(%)	(%)	(%)
Manager	16	29	42	21
Commission	30	13	0	24
Mayor-council	54	58	58	55
100%=	(111)	(38)	(12)	(161)
Total	69	24	7	100
Midwest	(%)	(%)	(%)	(%)
Manager	33	32	64	37
Commission	7	11	11	10
Mayor-council	60	57	25	53
100%=	(63)	(88)	(28)	(179)
Total	35	49	16	100
Far West	(%)	(%)	(%)	(%)
Manager	(1)	76	84	81
Commission	(0)	10	3	5
Mayor-council	(1)	14	13	14
100%=	(2)	(42)	(71)	(115)
Total	2	36	62	100
South	(%)	(%)	(%)	(%)
Manager	31	57	71	61
Commission	31	20	15	19
Mayor-council	38	23	14	20
100%=	(16)	(83)	(86)	(185)
Total	9	45	46	100

Note: The average (for all regions) percentage-point difference for mobility is +26 for the manager form, +14 for the mayor-council form. The figure 26 was reached by subtracting 16 percent from 42 percent in the first row of the table, then 33 from 64, 76 from 84, 31 from 71. The resulting numbers, 26, 31, 8, and 40, were added together, and divided by four to produce +26. This is a crude quantitative measure of the association of mobility with the manager form, controlling for region. The figure +14 was produced by a similar procedure for the mayor-council rows. This procedure was used in tables to follow, and the "average percentage-point difference" is given at the foot of each table. The same procedure for columns instead of rows produces the association of the other variable with form of government. A plus indicates that the association is in the direction of the hypothesis.

*Information on form of government was not available for 3 eastern cities, 11 midwest cities, 16 far west cities, and 6 southern cities.

†All 676 cities over 25,000 population are included in the regions: "East" (Maine, New Hampshire, Vermont, Massachusetts, Connecticut, Rhode Island, New York, New Jersey, Pennsylvania, Maryland, Delaware, District of Columbia) ; "Midwest" (Ohio, Indiana, Illinois, Michigan, Wisconsin, Minnesota, Iowa, North Dakota, South Dakota, Nebraska) ; "Far West" (Montana, Idaho, Colorado, Utah, Wyoming, Arizona, New Mexico, California, Oregon, Washington, Nevada, Alaska, Hawaii) ; "South" (Texas, Oklahoma, Kansas, Missouri, Arkansas, Alabama, Louisiana, Mississippi, Florida, Georgia, North Carolina, South Carolina, Virginia, West Virginia, Kentucky, Tennessee).

‡Mobility refers to the residents five years old and older who were living in a different county on April 1, 1955.

TABLE 7. Form of Government by Proportion in White-Collar Occupations and Mobility

PROPORTION IN WHITE-COLLAR OCCUPATIONS*	MOBILITY			TOTAL
	Low (2–11%)	Medium (12–20%)	High (21–58%)	
Low (15-35%)	(%)	(%)	(%)	(%)
Manager	17	37	79	32
Commission	25	16	14	20
Mayor-council	58	47	7	48
100%=	(127)	(77)	(28)	(232)
Total	55	33	12	100
Medium (36-42%)	(%)	(%)	(%)	(%)
Manager	32	46	69	51
Commission	18	12	9	12
Mayor-council	50	42	22	37
100%=	(38)	(96)	(67)	(201)
Total	19	48	33	100
High (43-85%)	(%)	(%)	(%)	(%)
Manager	36	57	73	62
Commission	16	16	9	13
Mayor-council	48	27	18	25
100%=	(25)	(74)	(94)	(193)
Total	13	38	49	100

Note: Average percentage-point difference for mobility: council-manager form, +45; mayor-council, +36. Average percentage-point difference for occupational composition: manager, +11; mayor-council, +6.
*White collar refers to persons employed in professional, technical, managerial, clerical, and sales occupations.

TABLE 8. Form of Government by Mobility and Population Change

MOBILITY	POPULATION DECLINE			POPULATION GROWTH			TOTAL
	High (7–29%)	Medium (4–6%)	Low (0–3%)	Low (0–15%)	Medium (16–44%)	High (45%+)	
Low (2–11%)	(%)	(%)	(%)	(%)	(%)	(%)	(%)
Manager	19	25	26	25	19	28	23
Commission	40	31	16	16	11	5	22
Mayor-council	41	44	58	59	71	67	55
100%=	(42)	(32)	(19)	(51)	(27)	(21)	(192)
Total	22	17	11	27	14	11	100
Medium (12–20%)	(%)	(%)	(%)	(%)	(%)	(%)	(%)
Manager	—	—	27	40	47	63	47
Commission	—	—	13	20	12	9	14
Mayor-council	—	—	60	40	41	28	39
100%=	(8)	(8)	(15)	(83)	(93)	(43)	(250)
Total	3	4	6	33	37	17	100
High (21–58%)	(%)	(%)	(%)	(%)	(%)	(%)	(%)
Manager	—	—	—	72	61	81	73
Commission	—	—	—	6	15	7	9
Mayor-council	—	—	—	22	24	12	18
100%=	(0)	(0)	(3)	(18)	(61)	(114)	(196)
Total	—	—	2	9	31	58	100

Note: Average percentage-point difference for population change: manager, +18; mayor-council, +23. Average percentage-point difference for mobility: manager, +47; mayor-council, +46.

TABLE 9. Form of Government by Mobility and Proportion of Children in Private School

MOBILITY	PRIVATE SCHOOL POPULATION			TOTAL
	Low (0–9%)	Medium (10–24%)	High (25–69%)	
Low (2–11%)	(%)	(%)	(%)	(%)
Manager	27	30	18	23
Commission	55	25	16	22
Mayor-council	18	45	66	55
100%=	(11)	(77)	(104)	(192)
Total	6	40	54	100
Medium (12–20%)	(%)	(%)	(%)	(%)
Manager	56	47	35	47
Commission	18	14	11	14
Mayor-council	26	39	54	39
100%=	(73)	(123)	(55)	(251)
Total	29	49	22	100
High (21–58%)	(%)	(%)	(%)	(%)
Manager	78	74	28	73
Commission	9	6	29	9
Mayor-council	13	20	43	18
100%=	(101)	(82)	(14)	(197)
Total	51	42	7	100

Note: Average percentage-point difference for private school population: manager, +27; mayor-council, +35. Average percentage-point difference for mobility: manager, +35; mayor-council, +18.

TABLE 10. Form of Government by Region and Proportion of Children in Private School

REGION	PRIVATE SCHOOL POPULATION			TOTAL
	Low (0–9%)	Medium (10–24%)	High (25–69%)	
East*	(%)	(%)	(%)	(%)
Manager	—	26	17	21
Commission	—	26	22	24
Mayor-council	—	48	61	55
100%=	(1)	(77)	(83)	(161)
Total	—	48	52	100
Midwest*	(%)	(%)	(%)	(%)
Manager	42	43	30	37
Commission	17	9	9	10
Mayor-council	41	48	61	53
100%=	(12)	(90)	(77)	(179)
Total	7	50	43	100
Far West*	(%)	(%)	(%)	(%)
Manager	89	78	—	81
Commission	4	6	—	5
Mayor-council	7	16	—	14
100%=	(44)	(68)	(3)	(115)
Total	38	59	3	100
South*	(%)	(%)	(%)	(%)
Manager	62	64	40	61
Commission	19	19	20	19
Mayor-council	19	17	40	20
100%=	(128)	(47)	(10)	(185)
Total	69	25	6	100

Note: Average percentage-point difference for private school population: manager, +10; mayor-council, +14.
*See Table 5 for listing of states in each region.

TABLE 11. Form of Government by Mobility and Foreign Parentage

| FOREIGN PARENTAGE* | MOBILITY | | | TOTAL |
	Low (2–11%)	Medium (12–20%)	High (21–58%)	
Low (0–9%)	(%)	(%)	(%)	(%)
Manager	27	47	72	54
Commission	46	17	15	20
Mayor-council	27	36	13	26
100%=	(26)	(108)	(79)	(213)
Total	12	51	37	100
Medium (10–19%)	(%)	(%)	(%)	(%)
Manager	31	54	75	59
Commission	26	14	3	11
Mayor-council	43	32	22	30
100%=	(35)	(81)	(88)	(204)
Total	17	40	43	100
High (20–40%)	(%)	(%)	(%)	(%)
Manager	21	37	70	32
Commission	16	11	10	14
Mayor-council	63	52	20	54
100%=	(131)	(62)	(30)	(223)
Total	59	28	13	100

Note: Average percentage-point difference for mobility: manager, +46; mayor-council, +26. Average percentage-point difference for foreign parentage: manager, +6; mayor-council, +20.
*Persons native-born of foreign or mixed parentage.

TABLE 12. Form of Government by Foreign Parentage and Nonwhite Composition

| NONWHITE | FOREIGN PARENTAGE | | | |
	Low (0–9%)	Medium (10–19%)	High (28–40%)	
Low (less than 1.0%)	(%)	(%)	(%)	(%)
Manager	—	56	32	39
Commission	—	6	10	10
Mayor-council	—	38	58	51
100%=	(7)	(50)	(89)	(146)
Total	5	34	61	100
Medium Low (1.0–4.9%)	(%)	(%)	(%)	(%)
Manager	61	59	42	53
Commission	14	15	16	15
Mayor-council	25	26	42	32
100%=	(36)	(72)	(64)	(172)
Total	21	42	37	100
Medium High (5.0–14.9%)	(%)	(%)	(%)	(%)
Manager	57	63	27	50
Commission	12	6	17	11
Mayor-council	31	31	56	39
100%=	(58)	(52)	(48)	(158)
Total	37	33	30	100
High (15.0–79.0%)	(%)	(%)	(%)	(%)
Manager	53	60	14	49
Commission	25	20	18	23
Mayor-council	22	20	68	28
100%=	(112)	(30)	(22)	(164)
Total	68	18	14	100

Note: Average percentage-point difference for foreign parentage: manager, +28; mayor-council, +22. Average percentage-point difference for nonwhite composition: manager, +7; mayor-council, −4.

Notes

1. See Charles Liebman, "Functional Differentiation and Political Characteristics of Suburbs," *American Journal of Sociology,* 66 (March 1961), 485–91; John H. Kessel, "Governmental Structure and Political Environment," *American Political Science Review,* 56 (September 1962), 615–20; Leo F. Schnore and Robert R. Alford, "Forms of Government and Socioeconomic Characteristics of Suburbs," *Administrative Science Quarterly,* 8 (June 1963), 1–17.

2. See Edward Banfield and James Q. Wilson, *City Politics* (Cambridge: Harvard University Press, 1963), chap. 13, for a summary of the relevant literature, and a discussion of how the white, Anglo-Saxon, Protestant middle-class ethos favors the "good government," council-manager form. See also Eugene Lee, *The Politics of Nonpartisanship* (Berkeley: Univeristy of California Press, 1960); Gladys Kammerer *et al.,* *City Managers in Politics: An Analysis of Manager Tenure and Termination* (University of Florida Monographs: Social Sciences, No. 13, Winter 1962); and Charles R. Adrian, *Governing Urban America* (New York: McGraw-Hill, 1961).

3. One methodological qualification must be kept in mind. The cities have been divided into three approximately equal groups on most variables. A comparison of the association of a variable with form of government can be made by simply adding up percentage differences, but a different set of cutting points would result in different percentages and possibly different relative weights of the variables. There is little reason to assume that any relationships found here would reverse or disappear with a rearrangement of the data, but it is possible that some of the internal comparisons would shift slightly. Before these divisions into three groups and the three-variable tables were made, the two-variable associations of each factor with form of government were examined with a more detailed breakdown into eight or nine classifications, and no serious internal reversals were noted. There is reason to believe, therefore, that the arbitrary cutting points do not affect the relationships presented and discussed.

4. From data not given on relation of form of government to the economic base of cities, as defined in the 1959 *Municipal Year Book,* industrial and manufacturing cities are much less likely to have the council-manager form than are retail and diversified cities.

III

Inputs of the Urban
Political System

URBAN POLITICAL DECISION MAKERS and the values which they allocate as public policy are linked to the environment of the political system through a network of inputs. The inputs emanating from environmental systems provide information for the political system to process; it is environmental influences which narrow into inputs. These are considered political when they relate to political roles or the authoritative allocation of values. Therefore, political inputs are a reflection of everything in the environment which is politically relevant. For example, urban political inputs include linkages to environmental economic systems (such as demands for lower taxes) as well as linkages to political systems at other levels (such as higher court orders to integrate urban schools). At the most general level of analysis, these inputs are individual and collective responses to the environment of the urban system, to the activity of other political systems, to urban public policy outcomes fed back through the environment, and to certain activities within the urban system itself (withinputs such as internal demands for metropolitan governmental reorganization).

Inputs to the urban political system—specifically, demands and supports—can be categorized as either manifest or latent. *Manifest demands* are expressed opinions or requests in support of, or in opposition to, a particular allocation of values. In urban political systems, as in others, demands appear as vocal and visible forms of activity which are often mistaken for the only form of political activity. However, demands may take a variety of forms, some of which are more visible than others. This range includes individual letters, contacts, and communications with decision makers (perhaps less visible); appearances, hearings, and confrontations with authorities or the regime; as well as mass demonstrations, strikes, and riots (highly visible). Even though *latent demands* are not expressed, they are still important determinants of manifest demands. Expectations about government, political ideologies, preferences, and public opinion are all forms of latent demands.[1] Although many opinions, preferences, or interests are never converted into more visible, manifest demands, a variety of factors may effectuate such conversion. For example, individuals with intense opinions will be more likely to express them, certain political events may stimulate such conversion (e.g., riots, announcements of political candidacy), and certain urban political cultures may be characterized by patterns of political socialization which develop norms encouraging demand expression (e.g., town meetings in smaller New England cities or mass demonstrations in highly differentiated urban communities). Whether public opinions and preferences are expressed or unexpressed, they are nevertheless important inputs for the urban system.

Supports may also be viewed as either manifest or latent. This suggests that there are overt means for supporting demands, candidates, policies, or local regimes, such as voting and paying taxes, as well as more covert modes of allegiance, such as loyalty or patriotism. A passive urban system (where things are politically stagnant) would contain few manifest demands and a high level of latent support. A less passive system would at least show supportive actions (manifest support) accompanying supportive attitudes (latent support). Although the concept of latent support is difficult to operationalize, its content varies from one political system to another. For example, on the local level concepts of patriotism or loyalty created by common bonds such as war or space ventures are less important forms of latent support. On the urban level, we may find such support in the form of loyalty to local autonomy and the preservation of private property and interests.

Inputs may take either an individual or collective form. For example, individual demands include personal contacts with decision makers and letters to the mayor or council, whereas collective demands are expressed in group form through political parties, pressure groups, or even organized strikes or demonstrations. We call the presence of such inputs—political involvement, and their absence—apathy. The latter, however, may sometimes be interpreted as latent support rather than as a mere absence of involvement.

With these fine distinctions in mind, we have categorized the readings for this chapter into four sections: (1) Public opinion—a latent demand or support which is often developed into more manifest forms expressed by individuals or collectivities. In the absence of such conversion, public opinion is nevertheless an input. (2) Political involvement and apathy— the presence or absence of various forms of demand and support expression in the urban community. (3) Interest aggregation and articulation—the primary functions performed by collective mechanisms for the expression of demands and supports. These mechanisms are nongovernmental input agencies which channel and mediate inputs—that is, political parties and pressure groups. (4) The urban electoral system—the formal input structure or agency of government which has been institutionalized as a regular means for the channeling of political inputs. The electoral system is also important for the performance of political recruitment and communications functions.

Public Opinion

Public opinion is a set of latent or unarticulated demands and supports for the urban political system. It is a complex of beliefs held by a large number of persons on issues of public importance.[2] Attitudinal support is a necessary prerequisite for the survival of urban systems, and attitudinal demands are essential for the ongoing process of public policy making. The core of the demand process is the expression of these complexes of individual and group views about political allocations.

The most important aspect of public opinion (as latent demands and supports) is its content,[3] that is, how an individual or collectivity feels on an issue which relates to the local allocation of values. This may be an opinion about a political candidate, a particular public policy, or a whole set of political activities. Underlying these more specific attitudes are individual feelings of political efficacy (the extent to which one believes he can influence the system), political salience (the extent to which politics is important), political alienation (the degree to which one feels powerless and estranged from politics), and awareness of public needs and problems. These are important components of local political cultures as we have previously defined them.[4]

Intensity, the degree of feeling one maintains on an issue or other political object, is also an important dimension of public opinion. The more intense one feels about urban politics, the greater the likelihood opinion will emerge as explicit demands. More concerned individuals are likely to hold the most intense opinions, as are those who hold more extreme views.[5] Political action associated with more intense and extreme opinions is generally the most visible form of action in urban politics. When such intensity is accompanied by nonaction it may represent a maladjustment in the system (e.g., political alienation).

Stability as a property of opinion is vital for the urban system across time. In many urban areas the content and intensity of opinion varies according to environmental conditions and political events. In recent years we have witnessed changes in the form of demand expression (e.g., riots) which are symptomatic of underlying opinion instability.

Finally, the local distribution of opinions is vital for the urban political process. Sets of opinions which coincide have the potential for developing into stressful demands. Although the climate of American opinion has been characterized by noncongruent cleavages[6] (i.e., the failure of opinions to divide neatly along the same racial, social, religious, or economic group), particular urban areas with low levels of heterogeneity may display enduring splits between religions or races characterized by sets of opinions that fall on opposite sides of these groups, further stimulating polarization and stress.

For the most part, the above concepts of public opinion have not been subjected to serious empirical testing at the urban level.[7] This is a reflection of the paucity of survey research studies on urban America,[8] the lack of comparative analyses which are so crucial to empirical research, and the apparent heterogeneity of opinions that exist among urban areas.[9] Nevertheless, political scientists continue to recognize the importance of public opinion on the local level. For example, James Q. Wilson comments that "the city is the best place to explore the kinds of attachments citizens have to the polity—their sense of obligation or duty, their conception of the public interest, and the extent to which (or the circumstances in which) their preferences in community programs are the product of rational self-interest or of learned cultural norms."[10] The most developed attitudinal literature tends to focus on forms of local alienation indicating the extent to which locals feel normless, powerless, or estranged from politics,[11] and on attitudes toward governmental reorganization.[12] One of the most crucial yet underdeveloped research areas in urban politics relates to attitudinal impact upon public policy. In democratic political systems we assume some degree of translation of public opinion into public policy, yet the extent to which public policy reflects the actual opinions of the public varies. The lack of direct translation hypothesized by theories of direct democracy and grass roots ideology is usually a result of important mediating factors. Studies of national politics suggest that classical requirements for such translations are lacking[13] (e.g., an issue-oriented, active, informed, and rational public), and that political processes are sufficiently complex so as to thwart high congruence between opinion and policy. Such a classical scheme of opinion-policy linkages has been called a "rational-activist" model.[14] It assumes an informed public sensitive to leadership errors, exercising coercion through the electoral process. The relationships are simple and direct: the public expresses opinion and votes, and leaders provide policy. More complex models, however, take into account the group and pluralistic aspects of contemporary politics, emphasizing aggregating and articulating mechanisms. For example, the public votes for a party which provides preference satisfaction for the public, and the party in turn provides electoral support for leaders who make policy with party interests in mind. Pressure groups also serve as linkages in the opinion-policy process, pressuring leaders to enact certain demands.

With these concepts in mind we have selected two essays on public opinion in urban politics. They treat the content of public attitudes toward specific and timely urban issues: governmental reorganization and attitudinal supports for the urban system among urban blacks and whites.

The Hawkins' study on public opinion about metropolitan reorganization focuses on the reasons why urban area voters are hesitant to approve reorganization plans, the nature of voter attitudes underlying opposition and support for such plans, and the conditions which favor consolidation.

The findings suggest that support for reorganization is associated with public dissatisfaction with services, higher voter education levels, the failure to anticipate higher taxes as a consequence of reorganization, and greater voter understanding of urban area problems.

The research of Cataldo, Johnson, and Kellstedt attempts to measure support for the political system among black Americans with a view toward developing more suitable public policies to soothe racial tension and meet black policy demands. More specifically, the authors seek to discover the extent to which blacks have confidence in the system's capacity to meet their needs, black policy preferences, and the disparity between their policy demands and those of urban whites. They conclude that blacks do not lack confidence in the system or in themselves; they respond to politics more in terms of accomplishment and hope than despair. Nevertheless, there are basic policy demand differences between blacks and whites: the former favor integration and more governmental responsibility in certain functional areas, their views of justice and civil liberties are distinct from whites, and they show less satisfaction with governmental performance. As a consequence, the authors suggest that system support among blacks especially depends upon the performance of government.

Political Involvement and Apathy

Active citizen involvement in urban politics is an important aspect of manifest supports and demands flowing into the political system. It is characterized by a wide range of activities, both individual and collective, which impinge upon the policy-making process. In many respects, involvement is a social role which varies between groups and cities, depending upon one's role definition (including others' expectations) and political socialization. Manifest demands and supports, therefore, may be a consequence of a variety of factors: economic (self-interest), cultural (the norm of businessman participation), social (organization activity), physical (an attractive place to live), or psychological (motivation).

The other side of political involvement, apathy, is also an input of the political system. Its presence is used as an indication of support by some decision makers or as an indication of true lack of interest or even alienation. That is, a silent public is often used as a functional device by formal decision makers to justify their own perceptions of citizen wants and demands. When apathy is treated as noninvolvement, we can isolate a set of influential factors similar to those for involvement. For example, low voter turnout and low political participation are directly linked to lower individual levels of socioeconomic status.[15] Yet there may be other factors which are more unique to political apathy: it may be a function of local control patterns, boss rule, closed elite decision making, or, in general, impermeable groups and policy subsystems;[16] apathy may also be a reflection of consensual local political cultures where there are low levels of issue and societal cleavage; it may be influenced by conflicting group memberships and conflicting social pressures which lead one to withdraw from politics;[17] or apathy may be due to psychologically related predispositions, such as low political efficacy, low trust in public officials, high political cynicism, or feelings of powerlessness or alienation.[18]

The above factors testify to the complexity of political involvement and apathy. Furthermore, some citizens may engage in the voting act yet refrain from other forms of participation, while other individuals may fail to vote, yet participate in local groups. The absolute level of this involvement varies from city to city; nevertheless, some important generalizations have been made about local participation. Despite the prevalent grass roots myth of high involvement on local political affairs, it has been found that only 11 percent of the citizens are highly involved in such affairs,[19] and that about 60 percent of the public does little more than vote or talk politics.[20] Early studies by the Lynds[21] found that political issues are blurred, that elections are not lively centers of public interest, and that there is general apathy and repugnance to politics. Hunter's classic research[22] characterized the local citizen as apathetic and silent, partially because leaders were unwilling to open the doors of political participation. Coleman[23] contends that citizens react negatively—that is, they become participants when they have an objection to voice—and Polsby[24] notes that political issues are entirely uninteresting to most people. Even writers of the pluralist school, such as Robert Dahl,[25] cite the general indifference of the mass public and the relatively low salience of city politics. In these respects, urban America appears as a mere microcosm of the larger society.

Although there is a wide range of urban involvement inputs, most research has dealt with the extremes along this continuum: voting and riots. Research on the act of urban voting has attempted to explain vote direction—that is, why people vote as they do—and voter turnout. Furthermore, analysts have used a variety of data sources for their generalizations. Yet, for the most part, local voting studies have lagged behind more sophisticated studies of national voting behavior.[26] That is, developments in national voting behavior research have not been fully applied to the study of local elections or statewide referenda issues.[27] In the first place, many local voting studies still focus on an areal unit and rely on aggregate data for purposes of analysis. There are several reasons for this continued reliance on aggregate techniques for local elections.[28] First, and most apparent, aggregate information, in contrast with survey data, can be obtained for a variety of elections with relative ease and without great expense. Second, this accessibility and inexpensiveness of aggregate data invites replicative and comparative studies. And, third, aggregate data are the "hardest" form of electoral information we have. That is, the aggregate researcher avoids "interview bias" by not interacting directly with his basic sources of information, and the data have not been "constructed" strictly for research purposes since recorded votes are at the very heart of the official election process.

Local and state electoral studies have not followed trends in national voting studies in one other way. While recent national election analysis has deemphasized the importance of social class as an explanatory variable,[29] local election studies continue to find social variables useful in explaining voting behavior differentials.[30] Although the findings are far from unanimous, Boskoff and Zeigler have suggested that status has persisted as a primary predictive device in local voting behavior because referenda voting may be more closely tied to social variables than other kinds of elections. This appears particularly likely if the referenda election has generated a considerable amount of controversy.[31] Pomper has also shown that in a local nonpartisan election involving personalities, the absence of party labels appeared to enhance ethnic and religious influences.[32] However, Jennings and Zeigler found in their study of a series of elections in Atlanta that social class was generally a better predictor in partisan (national elections) than in referenda elections.[33]

Issue-related elections which take place only at the state and local level in our society have not been extensively studied by political scientists despite their importance for basic activities of government, such as funds for capital improvements and other public works. Moreover, referenda elections may provide the average citizen his only opportunity to express his views toward some special community controversy, such as fluoridation of water or open housing. Referenda election studies are ordinarily of the aggregate variety, with the exception of a few studies of political alienation which have used survey techniques to tap attitudes toward certain kinds of local political issues.[34] The aggregate studies have used several community characteristics to explain local voting patterns. For example, in a study of the metropolitan district sewer issue in St. Louis, Kaufman and Greer used the three components of social area analysis (social rank, ethnicity, and familism) developed by Shevky and Bell[35] to analyze voting responses in St. Louis city and county. Using census tract information and election figures in a multiple regression analysis, they found high social rank (based on education and occupation) to be related to a "yes" vote on the sewer district issue.[36] Later studies confirm that areas with high socioeconomic status tend to support community referenda issues whether they be of the "good government" type (metropolitan reform or city manager plan) or for physical improvements.[37]

Rather conclusively, research on local voting behavior supports the proposition that social diversity among urban populations is translated into differences in voting behavior. Some studies suggest that the widest voting cleavage based upon social distinctions exists in partisan elections, while findings from other studies indicate that the voting spread related to social differences is greatest where a controversial local referenda issue is being contended.

Although political scientists have been concerned with linking certain personal and environmental factors with the way in which one votes in urban areas, they have also been concerned with whether one votes at all. In general, there is more nonvoting (e.g., three-fourths of qualified voters) in local elections than in state or national elections[38] and rates of turnout are particularly low in referenda elections. The latter usually involve complex issues, frequently beyond the grasp of local voters; as a consequence, the reaction is often one of alienation and powerlessness. As we have suggested previously, there are many factors which contribute to low voter turnout. Women, the young and very old, lower socioeconomic status individuals, and those who are highly mobile or do not own their homes are least likely to vote.[39] The increased nationalization of politics, the importance of foreign affairs, the growth of presidential powers, and mass media developments have all served to divert attention away from city politics. Organizational activity is also important. Although Americans are frequently described as joiners, as many as one third of our city dwellers belong to no voluntary associations;[40] those who do belong are most likely to vote.[41] Evidence also suggests that turnout is a function of the amount of opposition generated in the voter's mind, with individuals becoming involved primarily to protest decision makers' actions.[42] Finally, turnout has been treated as a function of political structure and electoral system arrangements. For example, nonpartisanship has been positively related to low voter turnout,[43] as has council manager and non-popularly-elected mayoral political structures.[44]

Aside from explanations of voter choice and turnout, urban riots have been the subject of recent attention in the social sciences. Whereas we have previously treated riot ideology as opinion input, the overt acts associated with riots represent a manifest form of involvement in the political system. Violent behavior generates a set of demands which are particularly stressful for the system. When previous demands are unanswered, low system support is created and active opposition arises. Stress may be caused by demand input overload which involves demands which are too complex and difficult for the system to process (content stress) or too numerous for the system to process (volume stress). When these demands are ineffectively converted into policy output—that is, when authorities are unresponsive or when the response is symbolic or when the lag in the conversion process is significant—the subsequent output failure leads to continued decrease in support for the system. When this low support is intensified by active demand expression, riotous conditions often occur.

Riots, as one form of civil violence at the extreme end of the involvement continuum, differ from coups or revolutions in that they are not attempts to seize power or overthrow governments. Urban riots are attacks on the "symbols and agencies of political domination and social control."[45] Neither are they merely another form of criminal activity, pathology, or crowd psychology. They are manifest and directed demands which may be an important source of inputs for those whose demands are infrequently heard (e.g., the black and poor). Several influential factors may lead to these riotous forms of demand expression. One is general dissatisfaction and alienation from the political order and the host of social and psychological conditions which create it. These usually include deprivation or the perceived unjust allocation of values (e.g., money, power); yet riotous behavior may be motivated by hope as well as despair. That is, one's expectations or the gap between the real and the ideal are potentially important so that the system must either achieve the ideal or quell the expectations. Riots as demand expression may also develop apart from attempts to seize power where positive attachment to the system exists and where legitimacy is sufficiently high to prevent violence from becoming a revolution. In this situation, the system is still capable of responding in a riot situation. These conditions, however, must be accompanied by factors which facilitate tumultuous action, such as leadership, cultural norms, group conflict, or the breakdown of consensual forms, plus particular precipitating events or immediate causes, such as an arrest or shooting. Furthermore, riotous action has been traced to environmental influences which are basically (1) economic, including unemployment or underemployment; (2) social, such as weak family structures (particularly among blacks), a low sense of community, and the lack of a politically oriented middle class (where, for example, the Negro middle class does not identify with the Negro lower class and therefore fails to provide leadership); or (3) political structure factors which reduce the influence in at-large, nonpartisan elections. These environmental factors are frequently accompanied by ineffectiveness in other input structures or channels, such as lack of black organizations, which may further contribute to riots as a means of demand expression.[46]

The article by Alford and Lee contained in this volume is more narrowly concerned with turnout as a form of urban involvement, related to variations in political structure and population characteristics. Turnout is tested for its dependence upon such political structure characteristics as form of government and type of election, as well as social structure (e.g., education, ethnicity), community continuity (a city's age and patterns of mobility), and regional variations. Higher voter turnout is found in cities with unreformed political structures and where class and ethnic cleavages are salient. This reinforces earlier findings that participation is lower when the effectiveness of political parties as aggregating mechanisms has been impaired. Greater turnout is also associated with greater community continuity and less educated populations. Although the latter finding is at the aggregate rather than individual level and contrary to many research findings, the authors contend that it is a reflection of more basic economic cleavages.

Interest Aggregation and Articulation

The remaining two sections of this introductory essay focus on the input mechanisms for demands and supports. This section treats a set of formal and informal nongovernmental aggregating and articulating mechanisms for political inputs: political parties, pressure groups, and reference groups. The final section deals with the structured, legal, and governmental set of mechanisms for channeling inputs: the electoral system.

Local political parties can be viewed from a variety of perspectives, all of which relate to concepts of systems analysis. In many respects, the party is a social organism: a group of individuals with specific roles within a boundaried social unit, a set of actors performing tasks through communication channels. The political party is also a political subsystem with its own authority structure and power distribution, performing its own functions for recruitment, goal definition, and conflict resolution. Finally, the party has been treated as a decision-making system by which values are allocated with varying degrees of legitimacy or authoritativeness.[47]

Both the functional and structural properties of political parties on the urban level provide important information about their role as input mechanisms. At the broadest level of analysis, parties perform the function of aggregating or bringing together individual interests, demands, or supports so that they may be effectively heard and converted into public policy. In association with this function, they provide a means for electing members to public office, a means for recruiting new decision makers into the political system, and a means for communication of political information. Along with other societal agencies such as the family, church, and school, they perform the system function of political socialization by inculcating system values, teaching political attitudes, and providing symbols and points of reference for political activities. In urban areas, they have also played a social role with political side-benefits, such as sponsoring local clubs or Boy Scout troops. Parties perform the less obvious functions of simplifying choices for the individual voter by narrowing the range of candidates and compromising the clashes of political interests by aggregating diversity.[48]

Although the above party functions tend to be performed in all urban areas, structural properties tend to vary along a structural dimension, depending upon environmental constraints and local political cultures. Therefore, four basic images may be identified along a structural dimension for local aspects of political parties.[49] (1) One image of the party is as a "clientele-oriented structure," an open and personalized structure based upon clientele support which is permeable and adaptive, characterized by low internal control, a multiplicity of factions, and mixed ideologies. (2) The party can also be seen as a "structural system" which converts socioeconomic interests into political power through an alliance of substructures seeking political recognition and control. Substructures compete; each subgroup has its own demands which are channeled into larger coalitions for winning elections. (3) Another image views the party as a "reciprocal deference structure" rather than a monolithic or clearly ordered authority system. Heterogeneity is reflected in a diffusion of power throughout various strata. No clear hierarchy exists, and there is a significant amount of deference to local structural organization. (4) Finally, in some respects the party consists of sets of plural elites which are not monolithic but differentiated and for which there is not merely a circulation of elites but rather an unstable tenure for leaders.

These images of the urban political party have largely replaced the classical view of machine politics, party bosses, clear hierarchies, cohesive groups, and political patronage. Although much empirical research remains to be conducted, the emerging view of the local party is one which emphasizes leaders (vs. bosses), low party discipline, open organizations, and the important role of the mass media. A variety of influences have encouraged this open and multifaceted view. One factor which tempers effective party involvement and control is the existence of cleavages within the political parties over candidates, issues, race, and religion.[50] The most important factor, however, appears to be structural: the decentralized nature of the American party system and the fragmentation of urban political structures. The higher levels of partisan structure in the United States derive their strength from the local units. The urban and national segments of the party are linked by middlemen—that is, local party leaders and activists who often share attitudes with national leaders[51]—yet partisan candidates must be tailored to their constituencies in order to win. Therefore, compliance with the weak national party policy which does exist is not enforced, and we find instances of considerable polity differences between Democrats and between Republicans who wish to be elected from different urban areas. This picture is most congruent with the "reciprocal deference" view of party structure characterized by Eldersveld: "More than any other social organization, the critical action locus of the party structure is at its base. And since there is a high potential for inefficiency, indifference, and displacement of group (leadership) goals with personal goals among activists at the base, leaders defer."[52] Party control has also been constrained by the decline of patronage power which causes party leadership to be less involved in urban politics.[53] Furthermore, some local party leaders feel that local concerns are beyond the range of party politics and that intense involvement on the local level may be dysfunctional, costly and dangerously involving local issues which could ruin national bases of support. Despite this changing image of urban politics, special local political parties have arisen only sporadically. These usually emerge as reform parties (e.g., La Guardia's Fusion party in New York City) which tend to articulate issues rather than aggregate interests, and therefore few have survived.[54]

In general, a wide diversity of partisan organizational structures exist on the urban level, ranging from uninformed groups of activists to remnants of the old urban machine. These structures or input channeling mechanisms are a further reflection of urban heterogeneity and structural differentiation such as varying population characteristics (e.g., immigrant flow and machine politics), degree of urban development, and different electroal systems (partisan, nonpartisan).

To this point, we have discussed the political party as an input mechanism for the political system. There is another channel, however, for demand expression which is explicitly concerned with the specifics of public policy: the interest or pressure group. These groups are characterized by shared interests which are the bases for membership and their primary function of interest articulation makes them distinct from political parties. For the most part, they are concerned with the policy-making process rather than the power-contesting process; that is, their primary function is to articulate member demands through collective actions rather than to elect members to public office. In many respects, they perform a policy function in an undisciplined, uncohesive, and decentralized party system. Although we tend to emphasize the primacy of formal secondary groups, the importance of more removed reference groups such as common ethnic or religious bonds must also be recognized.

The group approach to politics has been the subject of much attention in contemporary political science;[55] nevertheless, empirical research beyond a community power approach has been neglected on the local level. In discussing past findings, Scott Greer[56] contends that we cannot make uniform statements about the greater or lesser role of social and political groups. He argues that formal and community organizational involvement is weak while involvement in kin and friendship groups is high. From this he concludes that democratic processes are rare in urban democracy and that shared decision making occurs in families and friendship groups whereas participation in the urban community, formal and work organizations involve only a minority of citizens. The presence of informal, personalized networks does not preclude the existence of local organizations with professional and oligarchical leadership which try to influence political parties and decision makers. In this sense, the organization becomes a "holding company" for the interests of members who exercise an occasional veto in plebiscites. Greer contends that these patterns of "bureaucratic leadership," "plebiscitary membership," and the "privatized citizen" are incongruent with prevailing normative views of democratic society. Yet his thesis is less pessimistic than an atomistic view of urban society in which man is anomic and adrift in mass society.

These findings argue for a modified view of grass roots democracy in the context of highly complex and differentiated urban areas. Yet these fine distinctions fail to negate the influence of groups as articulating mechanisms; rather, they suggest that involvement is less widespread than previously thought. Empirical evidence suggests that community influence is mediated through primary and secondary groups, more so than organized party activities. Such group members are more exposed to dominant opinions and the groups serve to reinforce opinions, whether they are democratic or antidemocratic.[57] Political inputs emanating from group activity of this sort are more likely to be issue-oriented, reflecting common ideological, economic, professional, or other interests. Therefore, the nature of pressure groups varies on the urban level. In addition, certain kinds of groups are more commonly found in an urban situation.[58] For example, there are reform groups such as local civic associations and the League of Women Voters which are concerned with efficiency and economy in government, nonpartisanship, and home rule; and a host of neighborhood associations, such as homeowners, businessmen, or taxpayer groups which are usually stimulated by economic interests involving such issues as taxes, zoning, and minorities.

Other groups are less urban-specific, yet they are decentralized and organized locally. The business community spawns particularly powerful groups—service agencies, bankers, contractors, realtors, and others frequently brought together by the Chamber of Commerce. Previous urban experiences indicated that the businessman and politician were synonymous. However, it has been suggested that the role of business groups has changed as the urban political system has changed.[59] With rapid urban growth, industrialization, and heterogeneity, more demands have been made on the urban political system; and, as a consequence, the professional politician has risen to power. These trends also led to the creation of other groups for channeling new demands so that business interests were no longer alone. The points of urban politicization have become more dispersed, widespread, and less monolithic, with a subsequent diffusion of political involvement and conflict between groups. Other groups such as professional associations (especially medical and legal), newspapers, and labor have come to play an increasingly important role. This is particularly true for labor as it appears to be moving through a transition stage with regard to local involvement. Empirical studies have rather consistently emphasized the labor union's low concern for local politics, their ineffectiveness due to low status, their disunity and overlapping memberships, and their narrow concern for economic interests.[60] Others have argued that the political power of labor is considerably less than its economic power and numerical size.[61] Nevertheless, the impact and participation of labor now tends to vary, depending upon local strength and the structure of the urban system.[62] In Detroit one finds intensive and widespread union involvement in the political system. In such instances, the local AFL-CIO Council and its Committee on Political Education (COPE) functions as a political party—it drafts and endorses local candidates and has a precinct organization. This intensive involvement has often been stimulated by dominant business influence in the leadership structure of certain cities. In cities with a more differentiated labor supply, one union may dominate (e.g., the St. Louis Teamsters) while in other cities the withdrawal of unions from political activities may occur (e.g., Houston).

Finally, minority group participation has become increasingly salient in urban politics, whether the group is merely a referent (such as race or ethnicity) or actively organized (e.g., NAACP). They have brought forth a new set of demands for acceptance and services resulting from long-term deprivation of the rewards of public policy outputs. In place of the need satisfaction once provided by the urban machine, the urban system today is providing varying degrees of substantive (e.g., jobs) and symbolic (e.g., a minority candidate) rewards in response to new demands for employment, open housing, school integration, and so on, and new demand tactics (e.g., sit-ins, boycotts). Unorganized ethnic identifications continue to be a more important influence on voting behavior in nonpartisan elections than party identification.[63]

In general, a variety of forces shape the structure and function of pressure groups in urban politics. Four basic factors have appeared in empirical research. First, the urban political structure affects group activity—for example, the bifurcated governmental structure in St. Louis has enabled two different interest groups to align with the same dominant political party because each group seeks control of different segments of the government structure, thereby minimizing conflict.[64] Second, group characteristics, tactics, organization, cohesion, leadership skill, resources, and stability all impinge upon the group's degree of effectiveness. Third, predispositions of policy makers influence group success; formal decision makers must be predisposed to filter interest group demands and convert them into public policy. Since about three fourths of such urban decision makers are either neutral or negative toward interest groups, they must be highly salient and valued in order for councilmen to react. Many listen if the group is respected—that is, based upon the group's strength as they perceive it.[65] Fourth, group control apparently varies with particular policy areas. For example, there may be less elite control in distributive policy areas (e.g., contracts) or in regulatory policies (e.g., land use regulation) than in redistributive policies (e.g., local income tax, welfare programs).[66] Although many such questions remain to be empirically verified, a systems framework suggests the utility of examining input patterns from an output perspective.[67]

In the reading section to follow, we have included two essays on aggregating and articulating mechanisms in urban politics. One is a broad overview of urban party politics, the other is an urban labor union case study.

The Greenstein article traces the rise and character of disciplined urban party organizations and the factors which have influenced it: cultural patterns, urban growth, free suffrage, and the services performed by the urban machine. A variety of reasons are suggested for the decline of such cohesive parties, including the decline of patronage and lower voter turnout, and the emerging patterns of contemporary urban party politics (e.g., nonpartisanship, reform movements).

Although a variety of tactics are available to labor unions, the Lyons article deals with one means for articulation: support for candidates and policies. The focus is the union's strength in the urban nonpartisan electoral process, its range of political activities, its means of political communication with members, and the general impact of union endorsements on members. The author finds that union power is supported mostly by older members, that union endorsement is not a significantly influential factor in voting, that party identification is more important than union identification, and that union political involvement is generally unimportant to members, thereby reinforcing a pattern of limited electoral involvement by union members.

The Urban Electoral System

The urban electoral system is the formal and legal input agency of local government, providing for a regularized means of political recruitment and the communication of electoral demands to the political system. Although parties and pressure groups are important input channels, they are not the agents of urban governments. Yet political parties, in particular, must work within the context of this electoral system which, through its laws and election machinery, attempts to set the boundaries of direct political activity. This does not mean, of course, that the political system converts only those inputs which are channeled through the formal electoral mechanism. More than ever, urban political systems are finding it necessary to respond to demands and supports which are articulated in forms other than electoral power.

The components of urban electoral systems are particularly complex and governed by a variety of factors. To begin with, urban elections are strongly influenced by the decentralized electoral system in this country which is characterized by a variety of state laws that prescribe qualifications for voting (e.g., residence, age, citizenship). Methods of nomination vary in response to state and local party rules: a simple declaration of candidacy (with some use of voter petitions) is permitted in over half of the American cities. The direct primary (mostly nonpartisan) is slightly less frequent, and party caucus and convention procedures are found in less than 3 percent of our cities.[68] These methods for nominating candidates assume particular importance in one-party areas where primaries perform electoral functions. In addition, a wide variety of local arrangements affect the urban electoral system in several ways: the type of election or ballot (partisan or nonpartisan), the nature of election districts (e.g., single-member, multimember, at-large), and requirements for electoral success (e.g., majority or plurality). These latter two factors appear to be less important than the first and remain less well investigated. Since they are treated in one of the readings to follow (Gilbert and Clague), we will focus our attention on the partisan-nonpartisan dimension.

Partisan elections are used in only 40 percent of our cities.[69] This widespread nonpartisanship is a result of governmental reform movements stressing efficiency, independent voting, and local decisions made without the constraints of partisan differences or the confusion of national affairs and local affairs. The possibility that national affairs and trends may influence local politics suggests that the timing as well as the type of urban elections is of crucial importance.[70] Urban electoral independence and the goals of nonpartisanship appear to be difficult to achieve if city elections coincide with national and state elections. The concurrence of partisan elections leads to urban voting patterns similar to state and national partisan patterns. Although there is evidence that local partisan politics reflects national politics, the lack of urban independence may be influenced by local historical circumstances and electoral realignments as well.[71] In situations where urban elections are isolated yet partisan, higher offices are perceived to be more important to urban voters, local voting patterns are different, and urban turnout is sharply reduced.[72] The most common (over one half of U.S. cities over 5,000 in population) pattern of timing involves the use of nonpartisan elections which do not occur at the same point in time as other elections. The basic consequence of this pattern is lower voter participation for local elections. Although nonpartisan elections often reflect partisan tendencies in higher elections, the use of local isolated or nonconcurring nonpartisan elections does insulate urban politics to some degree.[73]

In many respects, nonpartisanship is a consequence of one-party dominance at the urban level which encouraged reformers to contend that one-party systems were less effective and that independent and nonpartisan systems should be a goal. However, where nonpartisan electoral systems are adopted, it may only indicate that the electoral system has imposed a formal constraint which does not necessarily insure a lack of partisanship in the voters' mind or in the real world of political interrelationships. Indeed, latent partisanship has been found to be an important factor in many local nonpartisan elections. In some urban systems, it is evident that one cannot win without party support.[74] but in others this support may be mustered through interest groups with little formal organizational party activity or through individual effort. Furthermore, party affiliation remains an important factor in nonpartisan election systems and latent partisanship is most important in cities with a nonpartisan ballot where the parties have the potential to be competitive.[75]

In general, the consequences of nonpartisanship are complex and varied. Reform goals of efficiency and less party activity have been only partially met, yet where they appear, other reform structures (e.g., council-manager system) tend to accompany them. The role of party identification is somewhat reduced, creating a candidate or issue focus, yet latent partisanship remains quite real. Nonpartisan systems also provide few cues for the voters, often leading to voter confusion. There are few differences in recruitment practices and no greater job security.[76] Finally, nonpartisanship has produced few changes in the nature of urban public policy outputs or the ideological milieu of city politics.[77]

Our final reading on urban political inputs attempts to deal with some of the above electoral system factors. In a study of twenty-four of the nation's largest cities, Gilbert and Clague investigate the impact of urban electoral systems on electoral competition from a comparative perspective among cities, and between cities and broader electoral systems on the state and national level.[78] After presenting a typology representing the diversity of electoral systems, they examine a variety of potentially influential community arrangements (partisanship and nonpartisanship, type of district, and majority and plurality requirements) and their impact on the closeness of electoral margins and patterns of incumbency. Some of their findings suggest that large multimember districts increase the likelihood of enduring factionalism and that partisan elections and closed primaries reduce competition, as do strong national party preferences. In general, they find that urban electoral systems have some effect on electoral competition, but that it varies according to national party preferences, the locale, and local interests and traditions.

Notes

1. It should be noted that this conceptualization differs slightly from David Easton's contention that demands must be expressed in order to be called demands. See *A Systems Analysis of Political Life* (New York: John Wiley, 1965), chap. 3.

2. Bernard C. Hennessey, *Public Opinion*, 2nd ed. (Belmont, Calif.: Wadsworth, 1970), p. 25.

3. A similar discussion of opinion characteristics appears in Robert E. Lane and David O. Sears, *Public Opinion* (Englewood Cliffs, N.J.: Prentice-Hall, 1964), pp. 6–10.

4. For an expanded treatment see Samuel A. Kirkpatrick, "Multidimensional Aspects of Local Political Systems: A Conceptual Approach to Public Policy," *Western Political Quarterly*, 23 (1970), 808–28.

5. See V. O. Key, Jr., *Public Opinion and American Democracy* (New York: Alfred A. Knopf, 1964), chap. 9.

6. *Ibid*, chap. 7.

7. A body of local attitude studies is now developing. For example, Henry J. Schmandt and William Standing, *Citizen Images of the Fox River Valley* (Madison: Survey Research Laboratory, University of Wisconsin, 1962); Henry Teune, "The Learning of Integrative Habits." in Philip E. Jacob and James V. Toscano (eds.), *The Integration of Political Communities* (New York: J. B. Lippincott, 1964), pp. 247–83; Robert Putnam, "Political Attitudes and the Local Community," *American Political Science Review*, 60 (1966), 640–54; and Joseph Zikmund, "A Comparison of Political Attitude and Activity Patterns in Central Cities and Suburbs," *Public Opinion Quarterly*, 31 (1967), 69–75.

8. For a review of current developments in local survey research see Robert E. Agger, "Proposal for an International Study," in Thomas R. Dye (ed.), *Comparative Research in Community Politics* (Proceedings of the Conference on Comparative Research in Community Politics, University of Georgia, 1966), pp. 71–90; and Peter H. Rossi, "The NORC Permanent Community Sample," *ibid.*, pp. 109–34.

9. Although there has been a recent de-emphasis on interstate heterogeneity of opinion, such as Robert E. Crew, Jr. (ed.), *State Politics* (Belmont, Calif.: Wadsworth, 1968), pp. 11–12, the question becomes more complex with more narrowly prescribed environments such as those existing on the urban level.

10. "Problems in the Study of Urban Politics," in Edward H. Buehrig (ed.), *Essays in Political Science* (Bloomington: Indiana University Press, 1966), p. 142.

11. For example, Murray B. Levin, *The Alienated Voter: Politics in Boston* (New York:

Holt, Rinehart, & Winston, 1960); and Edward L. McDill and Jeanne C. Ridley, "Status, Anomia, Political Alienation and Political Participation," *American Journal of Sociology*, 68 (1962), 205–13.

12. For example, John C. Bollens (ed.), *Exploring the Metropolitan Community* (Berkeley: University of California Press, 1961); Daniel R. Grant, "A Comparison of Prediction and Experience with Nashville Metro," *Urban Affairs Quarterly*, 1 (1965), 34–54; Brett W. Hawkins, "Public Opinion and Metropolitan Reorganization in Nashville," *Journal of Politics*, 28 (1966), 408–18; and Amos H. Hawley and Basil G. Zimmer, *The Metropolitan Community: Its People and Government* (Beverly Hills, Calif.: Sage, 1970), chap. 6. See also Marian Roth and G. R. Boynton, "Communal Ideology and Political Support," *Journal of Politics*, 31 (1969), 167–85.

13. For a summary see Samuel A. Kirkpatrick, "Issue Orientation and Voter Choice in 1964," *Social Science Quarterly*, 49 (1968), 87–102.

14. Norman R. Luttbeg (ed.), *Public Opinion and Public Policy* (Homewood, Ill.: Dorsey Press, 1968), pp. 1–9.

15. Oliver Williams and Charles Adrian, "The Insulation of Local Politics Under the Non-partisan Ballot," *American Political Science Review*, 53 (1959), 1052–63.

16. These concepts are developed more completely in Kirkpatrick, "Multidimensional Aspects of Local Political Systems."

17. Richard M. Merelman, "Intimate Environments and Political Behavior," *Midwest Journal of Political Science*, 12 (1968), 382–401; and Samuel A. Kirkpatrick, "Political Attitudes and Behavior: Some Consequences of Attitudinal Ordering," *Midwest Journal of Political Science*, 14 (1970), 1–24.

18. James Reichley, *The Art of Government: Reform and Organization Politics in Philadelphia* (New York: Fund for the Republic, 1958); Levin, *Alienated Voter;* and Joel D. Aberbach, "Alienation and Political Behavior," *American Political Science Review*, 62 (1969), 86–100.

19. Morris Janowitz, *The Community Press* (New York: The Free Press, 1952).

20. Lester Milbrath, *Political Participation* (Chicago: Rand McNally, 1965), pp. 18ff.

21. Robert S. Lynd and Helen M. Lynd, *Middletown* (New York: Harcourt, Brace, 1929) and *Middletown in Transition* (New York: Harcourt, Brace, 1937).

22. Floyd Hunter, *Community Power Structure* (Chapel Hill: University of North Carolina Press, 1953).

23. James S. Coleman, *Community Conflict* (New York: The Free Press, 1957).

24. Nelson W. Polsby, *Community Power and Political Theory* (New Haven: Yale University Press, 1963).

25. *Who Governs?* (New Haven: Yale University Press, 1961).

26. For example, Angus Campbell *et al.*, *The American Voter* (New York: John Wiley, 1960).

27. For more extensive developments of this theme see David R. Morgan, *Demographic Correlates of Suburban Voting: The Oklahoma City Metro Area* (Norman, Okla.: Bureau of Government Research, University of Oklahoma, 1970).

28. Austin Ranney, "The Utility and Limitations of Aggregate Data in the Study of Electoral Behavior," in Ranney (ed.), *Essays on the Behavioral Study of Politics* (Urbana: University of Illinois Press, 1962), pp. 91–102, discusses the advantages and limitations of aggregate voting analysis.

29. See Robert R. Alford, "The Role of Social Class in American Voting Behavior," *Western Political Quarterly*, 16 (1963), 180–94, for an argument that social class influence on American voting behavior has not declined.

30. See Robert H. Salisbury and Gordon Black, "Class and Party in Partisan and Non-Partisan Elections," *American Political Science Review*, 57 (1963), 584–92.

31. Alvin Boskoff and Harmon Zeigler, *Voting Patterns in a Local Election* (Philadelphia: J. B. Lippincott, 1964), pp. 15–29.

32. Gerald Pomper, "Ethnic and Group Voting in Nonpartisan Municipal Elections," *Public Opinion Quarterly*, 30 (1966), 79–87.

33. M. Kent Jennings and Harmon Zeigler, "Class, Party, and Race in Four Types of Elections," *Journal of Politics*, 28 (1966), 391–407.

34. McDill and Ridley, "Status, Anomia," pp. 205–17; and John E. Horton and Wayne Thompson, "Powerlessness and Political Negativism: A Study of Defeated Referendums," *American Journal of Sociology*, 68 (1966), 485–93.

35. Eshref Shevky and Wendell Bell, *Social Area Analysis* (Stanford, Calif.: Stanford University Press, 1955).

36. Walter C. Kaufman and Scott Greer, "Voting in a Metropolitan Community: An Application of Social Area Analysis," *Social Forces*, 38 (1960), 196–204.

37. Richard A. Watson and John H. Romani, "Metropolitan Government for Metropolitan Cleveland: An Analysis of the Voting Record," *Midwest Journal of Political Science*, 5 (1961), 365–90; James A. Norton, "Referenda Voting in a Metropolitan Area," *Western Political Quarterly*, 16 (1963), 195–212; Hawkins, "Public Opinion in Nashville," pp. 408–18; and Eugene S. Uyeki, "Patterns of Voting in a Metropolitan Area, 1938–1962," *Urban Affairs Quarterly*, 1 (1966), 65–77.

38. Robert E. Lane, *Political Life* (New York: The Free Press, 1959), pp. 318ff.

39. For a discussion of these findings in an urban context see John C. Bollens and Henry J. Schmandt, *The Metropolis* (New York: Harper & Row, 1965), pp. 223–24.

40. Morris Axelrod, "Urban Structure and Social Participation," *American Sociological Review*, 21 (1956), 13–18. See also Robert R. Alford and Harry M. Scoble, "Sources of Local Political Involvement," *American Political Science Review*, 62 (1968), 1192–1206.

41. Herbert Maccoby, "The Differential Political Activity of Participants in a Voluntary Association," *American Sociological Review*, 23 (1958), 524–32.

42. L. W. O'Rourke, *Voting Behavior in the Forty-five Cities of Los Angeles County* (Los Angeles: Bureau of Government Research, University of California, 1953).

43. Eugene C. Lee, *The Politics of Nonpartisanship* (Berkeley: University of California Press, 1960).

44. Eugene C. Lee, "City Elections: A Statistical Profile," in *Municipal Year Book, 1963* (Chicago: International City Managers' Association, 1963), pp. 74–84.

45. Don R. Bowen and Louis H. Masotti, "Civil Violence: A Theoretical Overview," in Masotti and Bowen (eds.), *Riots and Rebellion: Civil Violence in the Urban Community* (Beverly Hills, Calif.: Sage, 1968), p. 15. Many of our ideas parallel the theoretical treatment in this essay.

46. E. S. Evans, "Ghetto Revolts and City Politics," in Masotti and Bowen (ed.), *Riots and Rebellion*, pp. 389–407.

47. These distinctions appear in Samuel J. Eldersveld, *Political Parties: A Behavioral Analysis* (Chicago: Rand McNally, 1964), chap. 1.

48. Frank J. Sorauf, *Political Parties in the American System* (Boston: Little, Brown, 1964), chap. 1.

49. Eldersveld, *Political Parties*, chap. 1.

50. Bollens and Schmandt, *The Metropolis*, pp. 205–206.

51. Thomas A. Flinn and Frederick M. Wirt, "Local Party Leaders: Groups of Like Minded Men," *Midwest Journal of Political Science*, 9 (1965), 77–98.

52. Eldersveld, *Political Parties*, p. 10.

53. Frank J. Sorauf, "The Silent Revolution in Patronage," *Public Administration Review*, 20 (1960), 28–34.

54. J. Leiper Freeman, "Local Party Systems: Theoretical Considerations and a Case Analysis," *American Journal of Sociology*, 64 (1958), 282–89.

55. For a brief description of this trend see Alan C. Isaak, *Scope and Methods of Political Science* (Homewood, Ill.: Dorsey Press, 1969), chap. 13.

56. "Individual Participation in a Mass Society," in Roland Young (ed.), *Approaches to*

the Study of Politics (Evanston: Northwestern University Press, 1958), pp. 329–42.

57. Putnam, "Political Attitudes and the Local Community," pp. 640–54.

58. These distinctions are elaborated by Charles R. Adrian and Charles Press, *Governing Urban America*, 3rd ed. (New York: McGraw-Hill, 1968), pp. 121ff.

59. Bollens and Schmandt, *The Metropolis*, pp. 198ff.

60. Joel Seidman, Jack London, and Bernard Karsk, "Political Consciousness of a Labor Union," *Public Opinion Quarterly*, 15 (1952), 692–702.

61. William H. Form, "Organized Labor's Place in the Community Power Structure," *Industrial and Labor Relations Review*, 12 (1959), 537ff.

62. Kenneth E. Gray and David Greenstone, "Organized Labor in City Politics," in Edward C. Banfield (ed.), *Urban Government* (New York: The Free Press, 1961), pp. 368–79. See also Nicholas A. Masters, "The Politics of Union Endorsement of Candidates in the Detroit Area," *Midwest Journal of Political Science*, 1 (1957), 136–50.

63. Pomper, "Ethnic and Group Voting," pp. 79–87. See also Raymond Wolfinger, "Some Consequences of Ethnic Politics," in M. Kent Jennings and L. Harmon Zeigler (eds.), *The Electoral Process* (Englewood Cliffs, N.J.: Prentice-Hall, 1966), pp. 42–55; and Wolfinger, "The Development and Persistence of Ethnic Voting," *American Political Science Review*, 59 (1965), 896–909.

64. Robert H. Salisbury, "St. Louis Politics: Relationships Among Interests, Parties and Governmental Structure," *Western Political Quarterly*, 13 (1960), 498–507.

65. Betty H. Zisk, Heinz Eulau, and Kenneth Prewitt, "City Councilman and the Group Struggle: A Typology of Role Orientations," *Journal of Politics*, 27 (1965), 618–46.

66. Theodore J. Lowi, "American Business, Public Policy, Case Studies and Political Theory," *World Politics*, 16 (1964), 677–715.

67. See Kirkpatrick, "Multidimensional Aspects of Local Political Systems."

68. William O. Winter, *The Urban Polity* (New York: Dodd, Mead, 1969), p. 255.

69. Adrian and Press, *Governing Urban America*, p. 96.

70. A discussion of this timing factor appears in Thomas A. Flinn, *Local Government and Politics* (Glenview, Ill.: Scott, Foresman, 1970), pp. 40ff.

71. Thomas A. Flinn, "Continuity and Change in Ohio Politics," *Journal of Politics*, 24 (1962), 521–44.

72. O'Rourke, *Voting Behavior*.

73. Salisbury and Black, "Partisan and Non-partisan Elections," pp. 584–92; and Williams and Adrian, "Insulation of Local Politics," pp. 1052–63.

74. Charles Adrian, "A Typology of Non-partisan Elections," *Western Political Quarterly*, 12 (1959), 449–58.

75. Salisbury and Black, "Class and Party," pp. 584–92; and Heinz Eulau, Betty H. Zisk, and Kenneth Prewitt, "Latent Partisanship in Nonpartisan Elections: Effects of Political Milieu and Mobilization," in Jennings and Zeigler (eds.), *Electoral Process*, pp. 208–38.

76. A. Clarke Hagensick, "Influences of Partisanship and Incumbency on a Nonpartisan Elections System," *Western Political Quarterly*, 17 (1964), 117–24.

77. John Kessel, "Government Structure and Political Environment," *American Political Science Review*, 56 (1962), 615–20; and Charles E. Gilbert, "Some Aspects of Nonpartisan Elections in Large Cities," *Midwest Journal of Political Science*, 6 (1962), 345–62.

78. For a study of the impact of environmental factors on electoral structure, see Phillips Cutright, "Nonpartisan Electoral Systems in American Cities," *Comparative Studies in Society and History*, 5 (1963), 212–26.

1. Public Opinion

RECENT YEARS have witnessed an enormous outpouring of literature on the nation's metropolitan areas, much of it designed to offer solutions to the problems of governing such areas. In spite of extensive interest in reform, however, few major structural changes have occurred when a vote was required. From 1950 to 1961, for example, there were six failures in seven attempts that contemplated the consolidation of two previously independent governments.[1]

Why have metropolitan area voters been so reluctant to approve reorganization proposals? What kinds of voter attitudes underlie opposition and support? These are the fundamental questions of this study. Its focus is on voter attitudes toward metropolitan reorganization; and the author's purpose is to contribute to an understanding of the conditions under which major reorganizations are probable and the conditions under which they are improbable. It is also hoped that the following analysis will help to meet the objections of those students of metropolitics who are critical of reform-oriented research, and who complain that there has been little systematic research into voter attitudes for and against reorganization.[2]

On June 28, 1962, the voters of Nashville and Davidson County, Tennessee, attracted nationwide attention by approving a consolidation charter. In 1958 they had rejected a similar charter despite the heavy support of the area's civic and business leaders.[3] Following the 1958 defeat the city of Nashville annexed some 85,000 county residents. The city's morning newspaper, the *Tennessean*—a long-time foe of Nashville Mayor West—portrayed the annexation as an assault on county residents and began a crusade for another vote on consolidation. Supported by the *Tennessean* and a well-organized (though heterogeneous and unstable) citizens' committee, the proponents of "Metro" soon succeeded in placing a second consolidation charter before the voters.

The campaign that followed was marked by the efforts of Metro's proponents to stigmatize the governmental status quo and

Public Opinion and Metropolitan Reorganization in Nashville

Brett W. Hawkins

to personalize the issue by attacking Mayor West. The proponents also conducted a block-by-block canvas for votes. Metro's opponents, on the other hand, hoped to use the reputedly well-oiled West organization to obtain a "no" vote in the city. (West himself believed that the adoption of Metro would spell the end of his tenure as mayor, as indeed it did.) The opponents also expected a heavy "no" vote from city Negroes who feared the dilution of their influence in a consolidated city-county.

Subsequently the city voters approved the charter by 56 percent and the county voters by 58 percent.

Voter Attitude Hypotheses

In this section, four voter attitude hypotheses gleaned from the relevant literature are compared with data from 181 interviews in the Nashville area. Only the data from 181 interviews are considered. "Don't know" and "no answer" responses are discarded in all cases, and for purposes of this paper null hypotheses are rejected when the probability value for chi square is less than .05.[4] It is also important to understand that the present research was conducted *after* the 1962 consolidation vote. Consequently, in addition to any sampling error that might be present, the *ex post facto* nature of the research was

Reprinted with permission from The Journal of Politics, *28 (May 1966), 408–18.*

likely to introduce a bias in favor of the actual outcome of the referendum (in this case on the pro-Metro side). Such discrepancies are common in *ex post facto* research.[5]

1. DISSATISFACTION WITH PUBLIC SERVICES UNDER FRAGMENTED STRUCTURE

It is frequently assumed that the impetus for governmental change in metropolitan areas is generated by widespread dissatisfaction with services.[6]

In St. Louis a large proportion indicated some dissatisfaction (approximately 80 percent had some suggestion for change) but there was very little consensus as to changes desired and there was no significant criticism of most major services.[7]

One hypothesis implied by findings of dissatisfaction is that *voters who are dissatisfied with services are more likely to support reorganization than voters who are satisfied.* This is perhaps the most common hypothesis and is the one tested here.

Each Nashville area respondent was first asked what he thought of his services at the present time. The question was intentionally left open-ended in order to provide a measure of the saliency of this issue among respondents. Fifty-four percent answered "inadequate."[8] These results were then compared with answers to the question on how the respondents voted. Table 1 shows this relationship.

These data show much greater support for reorganization among voters not satisfied with their services than among satisfied voters, and thus the data confirm the

hypothesis as stated. It is worth emphasizing, however, that even among those expressing satisfaction more than half voted for consolidation.

2. ANTICIPATION OF HIGHER TAXES WITH REORGANIZATION

It seems likely that voters will oppose reorganization when they feel that higher taxes will follow. Other attitudes are possible, however, including the belief that reorganization will save money by ending duplication and waste. It is nonetheless generally assumed in the literature that voter anticipation of higher taxes is associated with opposition to reorganization. Thus the hypothesis tested here is that *voters who anticipate higher taxes with reorganization are more likely to oppose it than those who do not anticipate higher taxes.*

To discover something of the saliency of this issue compared with others, all Nashville area respondents were asked to state the most important reason causing them to vote either for or against Metro. Among those voting against it, 23.7 percent said that their decision was based on the belief that consolidation would cost them more in taxes. Although this percentage is not large (76.3 percent expressed other reasons), it was the modal reason.

Each respondent was also asked to say what he thought would happen to taxes "as a result of Metro." In Table 2 these responses are compared with those from the question on how the respondents voted.

It is clear from Table 2 that a majority of those who indicated that they anticipated

TABLE 1. Relationship between Dissatisfaction with Services and Support for Reorganization in Nashville, 1962

	PERCENT	
	Satisfied with Services	Not Satisfied with Services
Vote		
For reorganization	52.6	81.1
Against reorganization	47.4	18.9
N(=100%)	76	90

$X^2 = 14.09$, $df = 1$, $p < .001$

TABLE 2. *Relationship between Anticipation of Higher Taxes with Reorganization and Opposition to Reorganization in Nashville, 1962*

| | PERCENT | |
	Anticipating Higher Taxes	Not Anticipating Higher Taxes
Vote		
For reorganization	41.4	85.7
Against reorganization	58.6	14.3
$N (=100\%)$	70	98
$X^2 = 34.38, df = 1, p < .001$		

higher taxes with reorganization voted "no," whereas those who did not anticipate higher taxes voted "yes." The sample data therefore support the hypothesis.

The author also considered the possibility that this correlation represents as much the satisfaction or dissatisfaction with services variable as the anticipation or nonanticipation of higher taxes. If this were true it would suggest that opposition to metropolitan reorganization can be explained equally well with either variable.

The data in Table 3 lend some support to this hunch. Thus 92.7 percent of those both dissatisfied with their services and *not* anticipating higher taxes were "yes" voters, whereas only 26.3 percent of those both satisfied with their services and anticipating higher taxes were "yes" voters. In the latter group more than 7 out of 10 were "no" voters.

On the other hand, it appears that the anticipation of higher taxes variable is still relevant when the satisfaction with services variable is held constant, because among all voters dissatisfied with their services a much higher percentage of those not anticipating higher taxes (NAT) were for reorganization than those anticipating higher taxes (AT). Furthermore, among all satisfied voters a much higher percentage of NATs were "yes" voters than of ATs. Thus given the wording of the hypothesis, it is not required that the hypothesis be rejected from these data.

In any case, the Nashville data do suggest that more research is needed into these relationships.

3. RURAL AND SUBURBAN SUSPICION OF THE CITY

It is frequently assumed that fringe distaste for the central city is fairly widespread, thus providing a base for antireorganization sentiment where reorganization can be viewed as a device for enabling the city to reach out and swallow up the fringe. Survey research in this area suggests that such

TABLE 3. *Relationship of Satisfaction with Services to Anticipation of Higher Taxes in Nashville, 1962*

| | PERCENT | | | | | |
| | SATISFIED WITH SERVICES | | | DISSATISFIED WITH SERVICES | | |
	Anticipating Higher Taxes	Not Anticipating Higher Taxes	Total	Anticipating Higher Taxes	Not Anticipating Higher Taxes	Total
Vote						
For reorganization	26.3	87.5	52.6	63.3	92.7	81.1
Against reorganization	73.7	12.5	47.4	36.7	7.3	18.9
$N (=100\%)$	38	32	76	30	55	90
	$X^2 = 24.79, df = 1, p < .001$			$X^2 = 9.61, df = 1, p < .01$		

distaste is in fact widespread. It turned up in Flint, Michigan, for example.[9]

The hypothesis implied from such findings is that where there is suspicion there will be resistance to reorganization. The hypothesis tested here, therefore, is that *fringe voters who are suspicious of the central city are more likely to oppose reorganization than those who are not.* (This hypothesis uses the word "suspicious" only to convey the anti-city attitudes widely attributed in the literature to fringe residents.)

All respondents outside the city of Nashville were asked to indicate whether they agree or disagreed with the following statements printed on a card:

1. This community (or area) is really a separate community from Nashville and should have a separate government.
2. On the whole, big city politics are more corrupt than smaller city politics.
3. As a rule, it is better to live in small communities with small governments than large communities with large governments.

Responses of agreement were regarded as indicating some degree of suspicion. These data were then compared with those from the question on how respondents voted. Space prohibits a complete presentation of results, but they were very similar from all three measures of suspicion. Table 4 presents the results using measure number 3.

If our measures of suspicion are valid, there is clearly a higher incidence of opposition among those who expressed suspicion than among those who did not. These data, therefore, support the hypothesis.

4. VOTER IGNORANCE AND UNFAMILIARITY WITH LOCAL GOVERNMENT

In the literature, there is strong documentation for the conclusion that many voters are ignorant about government. In Flint, Hawley and Zimmer were brought to the tentative conclusion that resistance to unification rested largely in ignorance of government and what to expect from it.[10] The proposition implied from such findings is that voter ignorance is associated with resistance to reorganization. The hypothesis tested here is that *less knowledgeable voters are more likely to oppose reorganization than more knowledgeable voters.*

Among the measures of knowledgeability used in Nashville were two fixed-alternative questions designed to test the respondents' familiarity with the proposed consolidation charter.

The data from these two questions, compared with those on how the respondents voted, were in conflict as to their support for the hypothesis. In the first case the less knowledgeable voters (LKVs), 26 in all, split evenly in their support for the charter, whereas the more knowledgeable voters (MKV), 104 in all, supported it. Thus, although the LKVs did not oppose reorganization, they did vote against it proportionately more than the knowledgeable voters. In the second case, however, the LKVs heavily supported the proposal and the MKVs split evenly. The data from the second measure, therefore, offer nothing in the way of confirmation of the hypothesis.

A third measure of voter ignorance was an open-ended question asking the respon-

TABLE 4. *Relationship between Suspicion of the Central City among Fringe Voters and Opposition to Reorganization in Nashville, 1962*

	PERCENT	
	Suspicious	Not Suspicious
Vote		
For reorganization	37.5	75.0
Against reorganization	62.5	25.0
(N=100%)	32	40
$X^2=8.80$, $df=1$, $p<.01$		

TABLE 5. Relationship between Voter Education Level and Opposition to Reorganization in Nashville, 1962

			PERCENT		
	Grades 1–8	Grades 9–11	High-School Graduate	Some College	College Graduate
Vote					
For reorganization	33.3	57.7	71.4	80.8	95.7
Against reorganization	66.7	42.3	28.6	19.2	4.3
	30	26	63	26	23
$X^2 = 25.36$, $df = 4$, $p < .001$					

dents what other courses of action, beside Metro, might metropolitan areas take to deal with some of their problems.[11] Of those whose answers were knowledgeable (only 29 in all), an overwhelming 86.2 percent supported reorganization. The "unknowledgeable" also supported it, however, although in less striking fashion.

A final test of the hypothesis was to compare education (measured by last grade in school) to voting. The results are presented in Table 5.

Except for those in the grade school category, all groups supported Metro in a clear pattern of increasing support with increasing education and decreasing support with decreasing education. Clearly, this is some support for the hypothesis, although the measure used (years in school) is not a measure of knowledge about government.

The author also considered the possibility that this correlation is as much "income"

as "education." If this were true, the poorly educated voters (anti-Metro) would be predominantly the same persons as those in the very low income brackets. Table 6 shows the support for Metro at each intersection of the two stratified populations.

Since the pro-Metro percentages generally increase across the rows and not down the columns—that is, the percentages increase with increasing education—these data suggest that education was a more relevant variable than income. Even so, the income categories used in this study were probably too broad to permit any very meaningful conclusions as to whether it is "really" low income or low education that is primarily associated with opposition to metropolitan reorganization.

No consistent pattern emerges from all these data on voter knowledgeability and attitude toward reorganization. It therefore seems possible to conclude that voter ignorance (at least of government) and

TABLE 6. Relationship of Income to Education Level and Support for Metro in Nashville, 1962

REPORTED ANNUAL INCOME	PRESENT SUPPORT FOR METRO				
	Grades 1–8	Grades 9–11	High-School Graduate	Some College	College Graduate
Under $3,000	($n=13$) 38.5	($n=3$) 66.7	($n=1$) 100	($n=2$) 100	($n=1$) 100
$3,000–5,999	($n=9$) 33.3	($n=10$) 60.3	($n=20$) 70.0	($n=3$) 66.7	($n=5$) 100
$6,000–9,999	($n=3$) 66.7	($n=10$) 50.0	($n=23$) 60.9	($n=12$) 75.0	($n=7$ 100
$10,000–14,999	($n=4$) 0.0	($n=3$) 66.7	($n=7$) 57.1	($n=6$) 83.3	($n=6$) 83.3
$15,000 and over	($n=1$) 0.0	($n=0$) —	($n=4$) 100	($n=3$) 100	($n=4$) 100

opposition are not significantly associated, perhaps because ignorance is subject to manipulation and can go either way. On the other hand, the sample data do suggest that voter support is associated with greater knowledge about local government and with higher education.

Aggregate Voting Behavior

A breakdown of the aggregate voting figure reveals some important geographic variations. Thus when the central city is broken down into old city (7 wards) and annexed area (3 wards) the results are striking. And when the country outside (15 civil districts) is then broken down into unincorporated suburban areas, rural areas, and incorporated cities further important variations appear. See Table 7.

There are a number of plausible explanations for these figures. In the old city, it appears that West's political organization carried the day, with assistance from most Negro voters (the 13 city precincts with a nonwhite majority voted "no" by 56.8 percent in aggregate). Of course, the whites in the city also voted "no," and by a very similar margin (55.6 percent in 29 precincts). Thus, while the data provide little evidence that the racial factor was of great importance, it is quite possible that whites and Negroes voted similarly for different reasons; the whites in support of West and the Negroes in fear of losing their voting power.

In the recently annexed areas it is possible that anti-city and anti-West sentiments,

whether clearly separated by the voters or not, resulted in the 72 percent "yes" vote. In the county, it appears that the unincorporated suburban areas, which may have felt threatened by further annexations, played a part comparable to that of the annexed areas in the city; that is, they pushed the entire area into the "yes" column. Annexation, one can argue, made it possible for the proponents of change to stigmatize successfully the status quo and to champion Metro as a device for eliminating not only future annexations but also the formentor of such evils—namely, Mayor West. In a word, most county residents perhaps voted for consolidation to fend off being annexed involuntarily.

The reader will recall, however, that the sample data presented above showed not support but opposition from fringe area residents who were suspicious of the central city. Possible explanations for this are that the sample may have been off and that the questionnaire measures of suspicion may have uncovered only the extraordinarily "suspicious" who would not vote for governmental integration under any circumstances.

Turning to incorporated cities, it is interesting to note that the three high-income cities voted "yes" whereas the three lower-income cities voted "no." Two of the latter, however, were several miles from the central city. It is, therefore, possible that the higher education or income levels in the former, plus their perhaps less locally oriented populations, were the deciding factors.

TABLE 7. Relationship between Geographic Area, by Groups of Precincts, and 1962 Metro Vote

	PERCENT WITHIN CITY			PERCENT OUTSIDE CITY			
	Old City	Annexed Area	Total	Unincorporated Suburban Area	Rural Area	Incorporated Suburban Cities	Total
Number of precincts	(42)	(27)	(69)	(53)	(20)	(6)	(79)
Vote							
For reorganization	45.2	72.2	57.4	62.6	34.0	47.3	56.0
Against reorganization	54.8	27.8	42.6	37.4	66.0	52.7	44.0
Number of voters (=100%)	19,960	16,726	36,686	19,706	4,040	4,662	28,408

Conclusions

The outcome in Nashville of a proposed reorganization was not the usual one. Therefore, voter attitudes underlying support for metropolitan reorganization are perhaps the most important findings of this study. The interview data suggest that such support is associated with (1) voter dissatisfaction with services, (2) the non-acticipation by voters of higher taxes stemming from reorganization, (3) voter education levels higher than grade school, and (4) voter understanding of "metropolitan problems."

A common sense conclusion from the aggregate voting data, in addition, is that annexation transformed the usual "no" vote of fringe residents (an anti-city vote) into a "yes" vote. The relevant interview data contradict this conclusion, however. Doubtless more research is required into the character and correlates of fringe "suspicion."

Scott Greer has suggested that the available alternatives for bringing about metropolitan reform are (1) to manipulate the electorate through redefining (or misdefining) the issues and (2) to bring about change through *fiat*. The former course, he finds, was taken in Dade County, the latter in Toronto.[12]

The Nashville experience perhaps falls into the Dade County category. Certainly the annexation of 85,000 county residents helped Metro's proponents to put the issue on a personal, barely relevant, nonrational basis—namely, for or against Mayor West. The insertion of a "devil," moreover, simplified the task of selling a highly complicated governmental reorganization. It is certainly true, in any case, that the circumstances that pertained to Nashville from 1958 to 1962 have not been common to proposals for governmental reorganization in metropolitan areas. This, in turn, lends some support to Robert C. Woods' proposition that "program expansion of urban governments" not initiated from without the system, or by highly mobilized elite groups, is random—"the result of accident, not design."[13]

Notes

1. Advisory Commission on Intergovernmental Relations, *Factors Affecting Voter Reactions to Governmental Reorganization in Metropolitan Areas* (Washington, 1962), pp. 7, 26.

2. See, for example, Scott Greer, "Dilemmas of Action. Research on the 'Metropolitan Program,' " Morris Janowitz (ed.), *Community Political Systems* (New York: The Free Press, 1961), p. 188.

3. See David A. Booth (ed.), *Metropolitics: The Nashville Consolidation* (East Lansing, Mich.: Institute for Community Development and Services, 1963).

4. The interview schedule used in this study was precoded for punch card tabulation and included both open and fixed alternative questions. The sample was drawn randomly from the official list of registered voters in Davidson County. Inasmuch as the hypotheses tested relate to the attitudes of voters, only those registrants whose cards indicated that they had actually voted in the referendum were chosen. (If the choice happened to fall on a nonvoter, the next card was chosen, and so on.)

5. Herbert Hyman, *Survey Design and Analysis* (New York: The Free Press, 1955), p. 151. See also F. Mosteller *et al.*, *The Pre-Election Polls of 1948* (New York: Social Science Research Bulletin No. 6, 1949), p. 213.

6. Henry J. Schmandt *et al.*, *Metropolitan Reform in St. Louis: A Case Study* (New York: Holt, Rinehart, Winston, 1961), p. 63.

7. Greer, "Dilemmas of Action Research," pp. 197, 198.

8. Sewage disposal and street and road maintenance were most often mentioned as needing improvement.

9. Amos H. Hawley and Basil G. Zimmer, "Resistance to Unification in a Metropolitan Community," in Morris Janowitz (ed.), *Community Political Systems* (New York: The Free Press, 1961), pp. 170, 182.

10. *Ibid.*, p. 182.

11. Answers coded by the author as "knowledgeable" included annexation by the central city, partial consolidation, and intergovernmental cooperation. "Unknowledgeable" answers included "make studies," more civic spirit by the citizenry, better leadership, and the levying of higher city taxes.

12. Scott Greer, *Metropolitics: A Study of Political Culture* (New York: John Wiley, 1963), p. 199.

13. Robert C. Wood, "The Contributions of Political Science to Urban Form," *Urban Life and Form*, ed. Werner Z. Hirsch (New York: Holt, Rinehart, Winston, 1963), p. 113.

Political Attitudes of Urban Blacks and Whites: Some Implications for Policy Makers[*]

*Everett C. Cataldo,
Richard M. Johnson,
and Lyman A. Kellstedt*

A PRIMARY OBJECTIVE of policy makers is to develop programs that are workable and useful for the target populations at which they are aimed. At the present time, those responsible for developing programs to deal with the urban crisis have an especially heavy burden. As the report of the Kerner Commission has warned: "Our nation is moving toward two societies, one black, one white—separate and unequal."[1] A continuation of present policies, the Kerner Commission report warns, will lead to "the continuing polarization of the American community and, ultimately, the destruction of basic democratic values."[2]

Given the present structure of urban problems, black Americans have been and will continue to be the target population of

This article draws on experience and data derived from an ongoing study of agencies of social change and political behavior in Buffalo. The study has been supported by the State University of New York and the Office of Economic Opportunity in Washington, Contract No. 50–6056–A. Computing time and facilities were contributed by the Computing Center of the State University of New York at Buffalo, which is partially supported by NIH Grant FR–00126 and NSF Grant GP–7318. Special appreciation is due to James Hottois and Ronald Johnson for their assistance in the preparation of this article. This selection is a revised version of a paper delivered at the 1968 annual meeting of the American Political Science Association. Reprinted with permission of the authors and the American Political Science Association.

many of the programs aimed at dealing with our urban ills. Blacks have been told to be patient, to "cool it" in the language of the streets, while programs are developing. Moreover, blacks are being urged to participate in the processes of developing and even administering the programs of which they will be direct beneficiaries. To remain patient and to participate fully, blacks will need a full measure of faith in America's capacity to deal with their problems; they will need to feel that progress has been made or to feel reasonably optimistic that it can be made. Without this kind of confidence in the political system and willingness to work within it among blacks, little hope can be held out that programs developed at any level of government will reverse the trend stated so starkly in the Kerner Commission report.

To secure this confidence in the long run, policy makers will have to develop programs that bear a close relationship to the problems of urban life as seen by black Americans themselves. This is no easy task. For one thing, policy makers may have no detailed knowledge of what the policy preferences of blacks actually are. But even if their preferences are known all obstacles to effective policy making are not necessarily removed. The reactions of the white majority must also be taken into account. Orienting policies along racial lines runs the risk of offending other segments of society, and setting a "backlash" into motion. To try to move boldly in directions preferred by blacks, therefore, may bring massive resistance by the white majority. On the other hand, to deal with blacks in a way preferred by most whites might make the polarization between the races only more dramatic and make the gloomy warning of the Kerner Commission a reality.

For programs aimed at the problems of urban America to succeed, then, three conditions must exist. The first condition is that black citizens have faith in the resolve and ability of America to deal with their problems in more than just a token way. The second condition is that the programs themselves must bear a close relationship to the problems and policy preferences of blacks. The third condition is that the policies and their outcomes not meet massive resistance by the white majority.

Here we shall explore the implications for policy makers of these conditions. In particular, the following questions will be investigated: To what extent do blacks demonstrate the requisite confidence in America's capacity to meet their needs? Do they view developments in the nation and in their own communities with hope or with despair? What are the policy preferences of blacks with respect to the problems they share as a group? To what extent do their preferences correspond to or differ from those of whites? The data brought to bear on these questions are taken from a survey of attitudes conducted in the Buffalo area in the winter of 1966–67, with a sample of over a thousand blacks and whites. Since this is a single-city study, we are aware of the dangers of generalizing our findings to other settings and will make no effort to do so. On the other hand, Buffalo is a significant research site for these kinds of question. In size, it ranks in the top twenty urban areas in the United States, and it is the second largest urban area in New York State. Moreover, it was one of eight U.S. cities which experienced major disorders in 1967, as classified by the Kerner Commission.[3]

I

First, we examine the degree to which blacks may be developing confidence in the ability of the system to meet some of their needs, and in their own ability to develop

within their milieu. If individuals lack such confidence, it should be reflected in a lack of accomplishment and hope as they view their own life situations and developments within their political communities. Do blacks view their life situation with alarm; do they look upon their present circumstances with despair and a lack of hope for the future? Are they pessimistic about developments in the nation and their own community? How do they compare with whites in these matters?

For a summary measure of perceived life situation, Cantril's "Self-Anchoring Striving Scale" was used.[4] Respondents were given the following statement:

Think for a moment of the best possible life you could imagine. The very best and worst life could be seen as the top and bottom of a ladder. Imagine that the top of the ladder represents the best possible life for you and the bottom the worst possible life for you.

Respondents were then asked to place themselves on a ladder of eleven rungs ranging from 0–10 in terms of where they felt themselves to be at the present time, where they thought they were five years in the past, and where they thought they would be five years in the future. Table 1 shows how whites and blacks placed themselves on the "ladder of life" in terms of low, medium, and high categories.

Both racial groups see themselves better off presently than in the past and even better off in the future than at present. A larger percentage of blacks than whites, however, place themselves low on the ladder in the past and at the present. But the gap between white and black placements is far narrower for the present than for the past. In terms of

TABLE 1. Comparison of Black-White Personal Ladder Placements*

LADDER STEPS	PAST		PRESENT		FUTURE	
	Whites	Blacks	Whites	Blacks	Whites	Blacks
	(%)	(%)	(%)	(%)	(%)	(%)
0–4	30	50	13	23	9	9
5–7	44	33	56	49	34	32
8–10	26	15	31	27	57	60

*Totals on this and subsequent tables may not add up to 100 percent due to roundings.

TABLE 2. U.S. Ladder Placements, by Race

LADDER STEPS	PAST		PRESENT		FUTURE	
	Whites	Blacks	Whites	Blacks	Whites	Blacks
	(%)	(%)	(%)	(%)	(%)	(%)
0–4	8	21	16	14	14	15
5–7	41	37	42	42	28	25
8–10	51	42	42	45	59	60

TABLE 3. Buffalo Ladder Placements, by Race

LADDER STEPS	PAST		PRESENT		FUTURE	
	Whites	Blacks	Whites	Blacks	Whites	Blacks
	(%)	(%)	(%)	(%)	(%)	(%)
0–4	32	54	29	28	19	11
5–7	48	34	57	57	38	37
8–10	20	12	14	16	44	53

future placements, differences between whites and blacks practically disappear.

A similar technique was used to gauge respondents' sense of development of the United States and the Buffalo community. In terms of their greatest hopes and worst fears for the United States and Buffalo, respondents were asked again to make ladder placements with respect to the past, present, and future. Tables 2 and 3 show United States and Buffalo ladder placements by race.

The trend for blacks that was noted on the personal ladder is evident here as well. With respect both to Buffalo and the United States, blacks perceive the present situation better than the past, and see things improving even more in the future. The jump between present and future is particularly dramatic with respect to Buffalo. The pattern differs for whites. Fewer give high placements to either the United States or Buffalo in the present than they did in the past. The U-shaped distributions, however, suggest a restoration of confidence in the future for whites. While the future ratings for the United States are practically identical for both racial groups, blacks give Buffalo a higher rating for the future. Neither group rates Buffalo as highly as the United States at any juncture.

Data presented thus far would appear to indicate a relatively strong sense of progress and optimism for the future for blacks. To measure these things somewhat differently, however, past ratings were subtracted from present ratings and present ratings were subtracted from future ratings. Present-past differences comprise our "sense of progress" index; future-present differences comprise the "sense of optimism" index. Table 4 compares whites and blacks along these dimensions with respect to their personal life situation.

TABLE 4. Sense of Personal Progress and Optimism for the Future, by Race

Sense of Progress: Present-past Ladder Ratings	Whites	Blacks
	(%)	(%)
Worse	19	16
Same	36	26
Better	45	57
Sense of Optimism for the Future: Future-present Ladder Ratings	Whites	Blacks
	(%)	(%)
Worse	10	8
Same	37	26
Better	53	65

As can be seen, the sense of personal progress and sense of optimism for the future is strong for both blacks and whites. Fifty-seven percent of the blacks as compared with 45 percent of the whites see themselves better off in the present than they were in the past. Comparable figures on the sense of optimism index are 65 percent for blacks and 53 percent for whites. Thus, while both groups are reasonably high on these indexes, the tendency is for blacks to view things even more positively than whites.

Sense of progress and sense of optimism indexes were also constructed for the United States and Buffalo. Table 5 compares whites and blacks for the United States.

TABLE 5. Sense of Progress and Optimism for the Future: U.S.

Sense of Progress	Whites	Blacks
	(%)	(%)
Worse	44	28
Same	33	26
Better	23	46

Sense of Optimism	Whites	Blacks
	(%)	(%)
Worse	18	19
Same	38	38
Better	44	43

As the table shows, blacks have a far greater sense of progress with respect to developments in the United States. Only 23 percent of the whites see things as better, while 46 percent of the blacks responded in those terms. Nearly one half of the whites see the present as worse than the past, whereas only about one quarter of the blacks view recent developments as pessimistically. Both racial groups are nearly identical in their sense of optimism: 44 percent of the whites view the future optimistically, and 43 percent of the blacks do so.

As Table 6 shows, both whites and blacks display a sense of progress for Buffalo, and a sense of optimism for the future of the Buffalo community, with blacks scoring even higher than whites on these indexes.

TABLE 6. Sense of Progress and Optimism for the Future: Buffalo

Sense of Progress	Whites	Blacks
	(%)	(%)
Worse	37	20
Same	26	18
Better	38	62

Sense of Optimism	Whites	Blacks
	(%)	(%)
Worse	15	9
Same	17	10
Better	68	81

Controls for social status do not alter the observed relationships between whites and blacks. With only two exceptions, at each income and education level blacks sense greater progress and express more optimism than whites with respect to the self, the United States, and Buffalo. Moreover, there is little overall relationship between social status and feelings of progress and optimism for either racial group, as Table 7 shows. The correlation of .20 between education and personal optimism for blacks suggests a somewhat more favorable evaluation of the future among better educated blacks. Perhaps this reflects awareness of the special opportunities available to them though the efforts of business and industry to hire "qualified"—that is, educated—blacks either to avoid charges of job discrimination or to identify with the rising expectations of blacks.

Any hopes among policy makers that blacks will participate actively in developing and administering programs designed to benefit them can be bolstered if a tendency exists for blacks to participate highly in community politics. Furthermore, high rates of political participation can be interpreted as additional evidence of system support on the part of blacks, and as evidence of a willingness among them to work for advancement within the established political framework. Our respondents were asked to indicate the extent to which they engaged in a number of conventional political activities. Responses were scored on the basis of a four-

TABLE 7. Sense of Progress and Optimism for the Future for the Self, U.S., and Buffalo Community Correlated with Income and Education, by Race

| | INCOME | | EDUCATION | |
	Whites	*Blacks*	*Whites*	*Blacks*
Person progress	0.09	0.15	0.03	0.01
U.S. progress	− 0.11	− 0.07	− 0.05	− 0.07
Buffalo progress	0.00	0.10	0.02	0.01
Personal optimism	0.05	0.07	0.10	0.20
U.S. optimism	0.00	0.06	0.01	0.05
Buffalo optimism	0.01	0.08	0.01	0.13

point scale. Table 8 shows mean scores on these items for both blacks and whites. As can be seen, whites score higher than blacks on some of these activities, but the reverse is also true. In general, blacks participate in politics equally as highly as whites in the Buffalo community. Of similar importance, blacks in our sample who were found to be "riot prone"[5] participated in conventional political activities to the same extent, generally, as those blacks who were not. As Table 9 shows, riot-prone and non-riot-prone blacks are quite similar in their rates of political participation. Small percentage differences exist between the groups on certain items, the riot-prone being higher on some, the non-riot-prone higher on others. These differences, however, tend to cancel each other out.

If blacks lacked confidence in themselves and in the system in large measure, it would have been reflected in the measures of progress, optimism, and political participa-tion. We simply do not see in these data a black community despairing of how far it has come and where it is going: nor do we see a black community that has lost faith in the United States or its own city. What we see, rather, are blacks with a definite sense of accomplishment and hope for the future as they view their own life situations and developments within their political com-munities. We should conclude, however, with a cautionary note. We are not dealing with a static situation. It may be that advantages over the past several years in civil rights legislation and increased attention by govern-ment to the problems of urban blacks are mainly responsible for the progress and optimism that blacks feel. A failure to develop and implement more programs along these lines, in both the public and private sectors, could lead to a diminished sense of con-fidence, to frustration, and to an abandon-ment of conventional means of political action for more exclusive reliance on unconven-

TABLE 8. Political Participation Scores for Blacks and Whites

Item	Whites	Blacks
1. Keep informed about politics	3.00	2.73
2. Engage in political discussion	2.39	2.34
3. Discuss politics between elections as well as at election time	2.23	2.13
4. Inform others about politics	1.91	2.10
5. Registered to vote	3.37	3.45
6. Vote in elections	3.48	3.66
7. Tried to influence political decisions other than by voting	1.56	1.44
8. Were asked for advice and information about politics	1.46	1.53
9. Join and support a political party	2.16	2.32
10. Take an active part in a political campaign	1.57	1.68
11. Participate in a political party between elections as well as at election time	1.68	1.72

TABLE 9. *Riot-Prone and Non-Riot-Prone Blacks Percentage Indicating Fairly Regular Involvement in Conventional Political Activities**

Item	Non-Riot-Prone	Riot-Prone
	(%)	(%)
1. Keep informed about politics	64	56
2. Engage in political discussion	40	47
3. Discuss politics between elections	28	27
4. Inform others about politics	34	33
5. Vote in elections	90	90
6. Join and support a political party	44	42
7. Take an active part in a political campaign	17	25
8. Participate in a political party between elections	19	18
9. Registered to vote †	80	88
10. Tried to influence political decisions other than by voting	17	9
11. Asked for advice about politics	28	27

*Sample size for the non-riot-prone is 199; for the riot-prone it is 67.
†The registration item asked specifically if respondents were registered to vote in the election of November 1966; some respondents who reported that they voted fairly often or regularly in a general sense, may not have been registered to vote in that particular election, thus explaining the discrepancy between items 5 and 9.

tional and disruptive behavior.[6] The consequences of raising hopes and then dashing them by inaction may be worse than if hope had never been held out in the first place.

II

We move now to a consideration of postures toward issues of public policy and governmental action. To what extent do blacks and whites differ in their perceptions of programs undertaken to deal with the problems of urban life? Are there two societies in terms of attitudes about what needs to be done? The recently published *Supplemental Studies for The National Advisory Commission on Civil Disorders*[7] presents data that bear on these questions. Blacks were more likely than whites to express dissatisfaction with the adequacy of city services and to question the sincerity of the efforts of governmental officials to solve urban problems.[8] What do we find in Buffalo, using a more complete set of measures?

A number of policy concerns were presented to our respondents for evaluation. They were asked to evaluate their utility on a five-point scale. These data are summarized in Table 10.

Both whites and blacks see utility in social security, equal employment opportunities, the War on Poverty, and, to a lesser extent, welfare. One can understand why the gaps between the racial groups might not be great on these issues. After all, whites as well as blacks benefit from social security and welfare. Moreover, we would expect whites in Buffalo to endorse highly equal employment opportunities. Buffalo has a high white ethnic concentration, and many of these people have felt the effects of job discrimination themselves. It is somewhat surprising and encouraging that the War on Poverty is viewed as helpful by 80 percent of the whites in our sample. Perhaps what this means is that the poverty program has gained legitimacy in the eyes of most urbanites, white and black.

When we look at issues that are highly racial in their content, however, considerable gaps are seen to exist between the races. Blacks overwhelmingly approve the notion of integration generally and plans aimed specifically at bringing it about in housing and in the schools. (The 4-4-4 Plan in a state mandated integration plan for the Buffalo schools.) Whites express far less approval of these policies, particularly the ones aimed at integrating the schools. For whites, approval of integration increases as status increases.

TABLE 10. Policy Concerns by Race

Items	Race	Harmful	Neutral	Helpful	N
		(%)	(%)	(%)	(%)
1. Social security	Whites	1	4	95	709
	Blacks	0	1	99	260
2. Equal employment	Whites	1	9	90	707
opportunities	Blacks	1	1	98	261
3. War on poverty	Whites	6	13	80	654
	Blacks	5	4	91	323
4. Welfare payments	Whites	18	18	64	658
	Blacks	7	6	87	243
5. Open housing	Whites	21	26	53	620
	Blacks	2	4	94	242
6. Integration	Whites	25	32	43	612
	Blacks	6	8	86	243
7. School bussing to facilitate	Whites	56	19	26	631
integration	Blacks	17	16	67	228
8. 4-4-4 plan	Whites	60	17	22	425
	Blacks	13	16	71	153

There is little relationship for whites between status and endorsement of open housing. On the other hand, there is an inverse relationship for whites between status and bussing to integrate the schools.

To explore further attitudes toward governmental performance, respondents were asked to evaluate government in terms of how effectively it performed a series of basic functions and to indicate how important a responsibility government had to perform such functions. Table 11 shows that

TABLE 11. Conceptions of Governmental Responsibility*

Item	Race	Essential or Important Responsibility	Some Responsibility	Should't Do at All
		(%)	(%)	(%)
1. Providing justice	Whites	97	3	0
for all	Blacks	98	2	0
2. Securing civil rights	Whites	91	7	2
and liberties	Blacks	97	3	0
3. Providing a change to	Whites	79	17	4
make a good living	Blacks	94	5	1
4. Make it possible for a	Whites	72	18	10
person with the means	Blacks	93	6	1
to live where he wishes				
5. Seeing to it that every-	Whites	84	12	4
one who wants a job	Blacks	91	8	1
can have one				
6. Insuring equal oppor-	Whites	78	17	5
tunity to participate in	Blacks	88	10	2
making political deci-				
sions				
7. Providing welfare	Whites	72	24	4
services	Blacks	85	13	2
8. Facilitating social	Whites	56	29	15
mobility	Blacks	64	28	8
9. Trying to even out	Whites	39	30	31
differences in wealth	Blacks	51	29	20
and prestige				

*Sample sizes for these percentages range from 697 to 718 for whites, and 255 to 266 for blacks.

blacks and whites agree on the things government has the greatest and least responsibility to do. Both groups are nearly unanimous in holding government highly responsible for providing justice and securing civil rights and liberties. Both groups see government least responsible in the areas of social mobility and redistribution of wealth and status. It is important to note, however, that blacks see government as having more responsibility to act in each instance. In other words, the appropriate scope of governmental activity is greater for blacks than it is for whites on each of these dimensions. The largest difference between the racial groups is found on government's role in making it possible for a person with the means to live where he wishes.

With respect to evaluation of actual governmental performance, Table 12 shows that blacks are far less satisfied than whites in each of these areas except for welfare. The gaps between the races on evaluations are considerably greater than the gaps on conceptions of governmental responsibility. While evaluations of governmental performance are higher for whites than for blacks, their expectations of governmental action are lower. We might infer from this that whites see government as more nearly fulfilling its responsibilities than do blacks. In short, whites are far more satisfied with governmental activity than are blacks.

As was seen, both racial groups were nearly unanimous in holding government highly responsible in the areas of civil rights and justice. This is not surprising given the prevailing ideology of Americans. These are abstract notions, however, and may mean different things to different people. With what things are these abstract notions associated? Table 13, which displays correlations for each racial group between government's responsibility to provide civil rights and justice and its responsibility to perform the other activities, provides a clue.

As can be seen, for blacks there is a cluster of activities associated with rights and justice. For many blacks, providing justice and securing civil rights involves governmental responsibility to assist in providing opportunities in the areas of jobs, income, and housing. For whites no such clustering is observable. Civil rights and justice are correlated highly with each other, but not with anything else. Except for correlations with each other, for whites civil rights correlates most highly with providing welfare,

TABLE 12. Evaluations of Governmental Performance*

Item	Race	Effective	Ineffective
		(%)	(%)
1. Providing justice for all	Whites	79	21
	Blacks	60	40
2. Securing civil rights and liberties	Whites	78	22
	Blacks	55	45
3. Providing a chance to make a good living	Whites	85	15
	Blacks	71	29
4. Make it possible for a person with the means to live where he wishes	Whites	75	25
	Blacks	40	60
5. Seeing to it that everyone who wants a job can have one	Whites	63	37
	Blacks	43	57
6. Insuring equal opportunity to participate in making political decisions	Whites	74	26
	Blacks	68	32
7. Providing welfare services	Whites	79	21
	Blacks	90	10
8. Facilitating social mobility	Whites	66	34
	Blacks	36	64
9. Trying to even out differences in wealth and prestige	Whites	43	57
	Blacks	33	67

*Sample sizes on which these percentages are based range from 650 to 716 for whites, and 225 to 267 for blacks.

TABLE 13. Conceptions of Civil Rights and Justice: Comparison of Correlation Coefficients by Race

Item	Race	Civil Rights	Justice
1. Providing justice for all	Whites	0.457	1.000
	Blacks	0.617	1.000
2. Securing civil rights and liberties	Whites	1.000	0.457
	Blacks	1.000	0.617
3. Providing a chance to make a good living	Whites	0.153	0.150
	Blacks	0.397	0.356
4. Make it possible for a person with the means to live where he wishes	Whites	0.234	0.141
	Blacks	0.345	0.387
5. Seeing to it that everyone who wants a job can have one	Whites	0.169	0.160
	Blacks	0.325	0.353
6. Insuring equal opportunity to participate in making political decisions	Whites	0.236	0.231
	Blacks	0.315	0.271
7. Providing welfare services	Whites	0.269	0.099
	Blacks	0.131	0.125
8. Facilitating social mobility	Whites	0.203	0.118
	Blacks	0.177	0.173
9. Trying to even out differences in wealth and prestige	Whites	0.023	−0.028
	Blacks	0.094	0.019

and justice correlates most highly with the opportunity to participate in political decisions. In other words, whites give a much more limited and conventional content to these basic notions while to blacks they encompass the very basics of life.

Although blacks construe these notions of justice and civil rights much more broadly than whites, they do not seem to extend them to the area of social mobility or to the redistribution of wealth and status. For many blacks, then, it is apparently "opportunity" which is the important element in their conception of rights and justice.

How do these data relate to the "two-societies" notion? In certain important attitudinal respects we do see two societies, one black and one white. First of all, blacks overwhelmingly approve the notion of integration generally and plans aimed specifically at bringing it about, and whites do not; second, blacks see government as more responsible for performing certain functions; third, blacks are less satisfied than whites with governmental performance; and finally, and most importantly, blacks and whites seem to differ significantly on the very nature of government's central responsibilities in providing justice and securing civil rights and liberties.

III

The data presented in this paper do not show a sense of despair and hopelessness on the part of most blacks. Rather, blacks appear to have observed considerable progress in the past few years both personally and in terms of the nation and the local community. While blacks occupied lower ladder positions than whites in the past, they share with most whites the predilection to view the future optimistically. Moreover, blacks show as much willingness as whites to participate in politics. From these data it can be inferred that most blacks see their lives and their futures in the context of developments within their community and nation, and that, by and large, they have positive affect for the political system that persists in spite of their comparatively negative evaluations of governmental performance.

Most important, blacks see their everyday life situations inextricably tied to governmental performances. The very basics of life —jobs, housing, education—and the "good life" in general, are seen as being related to positive governmental action. For blacks, the very definition of basic concepts such as justice, civil rights, and civil liberties involves the providing of opportunities for a better life, and are seen as part of government's basic responsibilities to help provide. This view differs markedly from the conceptions of many whites who look askance at governmental activity to improve the lot of blacks, especially, as we have seen, those measures aimed at the integration of blacks into American life. A common response among whites is to ask why government should do those things. Correct or not, the myth is still prevalent among white Americans that people get ahead through individual initiative, hard work, and perseverance alone, and that advancement is to be sought through private and not public means. Even many ethnic Americans do not know or have forgotten that their people made minimal gains economically and/or socially until they took over City Hall. Blacks, on the other hand, cannot look to a history in which their people have achieved progress through implementing the Protestant ethic. They do have, however, a recent history where personal improvement to some degree has come in the wake of governmental action. Consequently, concerted efforts will be continued on the part of blacks to improve their life situations through involvement in the political process. Hence, we see basic differences in white-black value structures in this regard.

The positive affect noted on the part of blacks should provide some degree of solace for policy makers. In these times of emphasis on urban violence and the need for law and order, many individuals appear to find it easy to forget that the vast majority of blacks are loyal Americans who see their personal future and the future of their nation and community as inseparable. As Kenneth Clark said in *Dark Ghetto:*

> An inescapable reality is the fact that the American Negro is inextricably American. In spite of the psychological appeals of identification with Africa, and the temporary props to a sagging ego which can be found in occasional discussions and seminars about "our African heritage," the American Negro is no more African than he is Danish, or Irish, or Indian. He is American. His destiny is one with the destiny of America. His culture is the culture

of Americans. His dilemmas are essentially the dilemmas of Americans.[9]

In short, few blacks see their salvation in the destruction of American society.

It is possible to suggest, however, that the maintenance of system support is to some extent tied to specific governmental performance. What has been done to deal with problems of poverty and race relations may be increasingly viewed among blacks as too little, and too late. For policy makers to deal with these problems effectively by attempting to make policy which is meaningful for blacks will undoubtedly meet the opposition of many whites whose orientation to the political process is much different. Thus the problem becomes one not only of creating policy which is beneficial to one segment of society, but also one of creating a climate of acceptance of policy among those who are not the immediate beneficiaries. This climate involves not only approval of the policy itself, but acceptance of policy outcomes which involve the admission of blacks into full participation in the ongoing life of the community. For whites, therefore, acceptance of policy outcomes involves accepting blacks in places of employment, in the schools, and in their neighborhoods. The creation of this climate of acceptance among whites remains a principal unsolved problem for policy makers.

Notes

1. *Report of the National Advisory Commission on Civil Disorders* (New York: Bantam Books, 1968), p. 1.

2. *Ibid.*

3. *Ibid.*, pp. 113, 158.

4. For a full discussion of this technique see Hadley Cantril, *The Pattern of Human Concerns* (New Brunswick, N.J.: Rutgers University Press, 1965), pp. 22ff.

5. Respondents were asked the extent to which they felt responsibility to "riot if necessary to get public officials to correct political wrongs." Responses were scored on a four-point scale

according to the intensity with which such responsibility was felt. Those who scored two, three, or four on the scale were classified as riot-prone.

6. See the authors' "Social Strain and Urban Violence" in Louis Masotti and Don R. Bowen (eds.), *Riots and Rebellion: Civil Violence in the* *Urban Community* (Los Angeles: Sage, 1968), pp. 295, 297.

7. Washington, D.C.: Government Printing Office, 1968.

8. *Supplemental Studies*, p. 8.

9. Kenneth Clark, *Dark Ghetto* (New York: Harper & Row, 1965), p. 219.

2. Political Involvement and Apathy

Voting Turnout in American Cities*

Robert R. Alford and Eugene C. Lee

WRITING about local elections in 1968, Charles R. Adrian and Charles Press report that "it is not known whether . . . state and national voting-population characteristics fit municipal voting, too."[1] Although a number of important studies of politics and elections in individual communities have emerged in recent years, the data are far from sufficient to permit more than the most speculative generalizations about the nature of the local electorate.[2] This study draws back the curtain, albeit only a bit, on one aspect of local political participation—voting turnout. The data presented constitute, so far as we know, the first attempt at a comprehensive comparison among American cities with respect to turnout. As will be suggested and become obvious, the breadth of the data is not matched by their depth; data were received from only 80 percent of the 729 cities above 25,000 population in 1962, and we were able to utilize comparative turnout figures from only 282 of these. While relationships are suggested between turnout, political and governmental structure, and characteristics of the population, these relationships must be regarded more as

leads to future research, than as clear and unambiguous findings.

Previous work by the present authors has pointed to the importance of the political and social variables included in this analysis of American cities. Lee suggested in a study of nonpartisan elections and politics in California cities that nonpartisanship might tend to reduce voter participation.[3] In a study of American cities, this hypothesis was confirmed in a preliminary analysis of the same data used in this article.[4] The median turnout in partisan elections was 50 percent, compared to 30 percent in nonpartisan cities; in addition, the related characteristics of council-manager government and the appointed mayor were also seen to have a negative relationship to voter participation. It was not possible, however, to determine whether these relationships were independently associated or, rather, merely reflected underlying characteristics of the cities themselves.

Parallel work on form of government by Alford and others posited the existence of a relationship between form of government and socioeconomic characteristics. For example, "white, Anglo-Saxon, Protestant, growing, and mobile cities are highly likely to be manager cities; ethnically and religiously diverse but nonmobile industrial cities are highly likely to be mayor-council cities." Other features of so-called "reform" type local government—nonpartisan elections, at-large elections, small city councils, local elections which are not concurrent with state or national elections—have a similar social base.[5] In this paper, the data and theoretical notions derived from these previous works are combined. The paper also draws upon two as yet unpublished studies, one of which included a factor analysis and multiple regression of these data.[6]

Reprinted with permission from The American Political Science Review, *62 (September 1968), 796–814.*

**The authors are indebted to Michael T. Aiken, Ruth B. Dixon, Daniel N. Gordon, Willis D. Hawley, Robert L. Lineberry, Donald B. Rosenthal, Peter W. Sperlich, Frederick M. Wirt, and Raymond E. Wolfinger for comments and suggestions above and beyond the normal call of collegial duty. Their willingness to be of assistance in no way renders them responsible for the results. The senior author wishes to thank the Institute for Research on Poverty, University of Wisconsin, for research assistance.*

Concepts and Data

THE MEANING OF VOTING TURNOUT

Voting turnout in local elections is the most direct measure of participation in the electoral process, and possibly an indicator of other forms of political participation. We assume that a high level of voting turnout implies several things about the characteristics of the local electorate, although we do not have the data directly to test these assumptions.

For example, where there is a high level of voting turnout, one might assume there has been communication of political information to voters both about the particular election and about the political system of which elections form a part. This political information might be conveyed through a variety of reference groups—neighborhood groups, ethnic groups, political parties, voluntary associations—or through mass media such as television, radio, and the press. Whether such political communication exists or not, either the community as a whole or particular groups within it possess norms which define voting as appropriate and proper behavior. Voting turnout is defined thus as the dependent variable, although it would be just as legitimate to turn the question around and attempt to determine the consequences of higher versus lower levels of voting turnout. A few studies have dealt with this question, particularly with reference to referenda, finding that higher turnout is associated with negative voting.[7] There is no necessary connection between the causes and the consequences of different levels of voting turnout, however.

Varying levels of voting turnout in American cities may also be a consequence of political organization at the local level. For example, the more activity there is of groups interested in electoral outcomes, the more activity of party or other organizations seeking to get out the vote or to mobilize support behind slates of candidates, the higher voting turnout may be. On the other hand, high turnout may occur because of norms encouraging vote turnout held by members of other groups in the community with very little activity of political organizations *per se*.

As the above assumptions indicate, we see voting turnout as linked to the political and social structure of the local community. It seems possible, however, that relationships of characteristics of a community with voting turnout may be cancelled out by idiosyncrasies of a particular election: the personality of the mayor, the issues which happen to be salient at the moment, the accident of having a controversial referendum or bond issue on the ballot, whether or not the local election happens to be held at the same time as a particularly important state or national election. Unfortunately, comparative data are not available to test such "situational" factors influencing voting turnout, and we shall assume that the correlations that we discuss are only reduced by the operations of these situational factors, and not reversed.[8] It seems plausible to infer that if unique electoral issues and personalities account for most of the variation between cities in voting turnout, there should not be consistent associations between turnout and structural features of the local government and community. As indicated below, however, this is not the case, and relationships do exist. Given the nature of the data in the study, particularly the fact that they relate to only one election for each city, the fact that even modest relationships can be discovered on a national basis is significant.

Our perspective here is one which looks at a "population of elections," not a "population of individual voters," as V. O. Key put it. Correlatively, electorates are not merely "arithmetic sums of individuals," but rather "units playing special and significant roles in the political process and therefore worthy of analysis in their own right," in Austin Ranney's words.[9] We are thus not inferring from our data on voting turnout anything about the characteristics of individual voters, nor do we invoke any social-psychological properties of individuals to explain our ecological correlations between characteristics of cities and the level of voting turnout. It would certainly be possible to develop propositions about the intervening processes of communication, definition of the political situation, and the formation of political identities in individuals and groups which connect structural features of American cities to the probability of high or low voting turnout, but these tasks are beyond our scope. We attempt, therefore, to avoid the pitfalls of "the ecological fallacy" (the generalization from group data to individuals) and "the contextual fallacy" (the prediction of group action from the characteristics of individuals).[10]

THE DATA

It is essential to an understanding of the data reported below that the nature of the original turnout figures and the ambiguity of certain of the variables be clearly understood.

1. No national source either collects or reports local voting statistics; few states do so. The data utilized here were collected by the International City Managers' Association in late 1962 from approximately 80 percent of the nation's 729 cities above 25,000 population.[11] The missing cities tended disproportionately to be partisan, mayor-council and eastern, all characteristics noted below as being associated with high voting turnout.

2. For the bulk of the report, data are utilized only for those cities whose local election was *not* held concurrently with a state or national election, for we do not know for concurrent elections whether the turnout figures represent only the local increment—for example, the vote for mayor—or the vote in the larger race—for example, a vote for governor in 1962. Thus a valid comparison of concurrent and nonconcurrent elections is impossible, and it is essential to use the narrower base, even though it reduces the number of cities to be analyzed by one-third.

3. An understatement of the mayor-council vote may result from the fact that in an undetermined (but quite small) number of such cities, only ward elections were held in 1961–62, which—in an unspecified (but even smaller) number of cities—involved only a portion of the city.

4. The data do not distinguish, either in mayor-council or manager cities, those elections in which a mayor appeared separately on the ballot from those in which he did not. The presence of the mayor on the ballot

CHARACTERISTICS	CITIES IN 1960		CITIES REPORTING TURNOUT		CITIES WITH NON-CONCURRENT ELECTIONS USED IN THIS STUDY	
	No.	Percent	No.	Percent	No.	Percent
Form of Government:		(%)		(%)		(%)
Mayor-council	259	38	30	30	73	26
Commission	77	11	37	9	30	11
Council-manager	330	50	261	61	179	63
		100		100		100
Form of Election:						
Partisan	193	29	99	23	50	18
Nonpartisan	479	71	329	77	232	82
		100		100		100
Region:						
East	164	24	84	20	43	15
Midwest	190	28	122	29	67	24
South	191	28	118	28	95	34
Far West	131	19	104	24	77	27
		100		100		100
Total	(676)	100	(428)	100	(282)	100

Note: See Table 1 for the states comprising each region. By 1962, when the voting data were obtained, there were 729 cities over 25,000 population.

tends to increase voter turnout,[12] and the separately elected mayor is more likely to be found in mayor-council cities than in council-manager cities. Thus the fact that in a small number of the mayor-council cities the mayor was not on the ballot in the election here reported tends to understate voter turnout in mayor-council cities, insofar as the impact of the mayor is concerned.

5. The data do not indicate whether the election reported was a runoff or a primary. (Approximately 20 percent of the nation's cities employ a runoff if no candidate receives a majority in the initial general election.) The consequences of this fact for turnout are not known. The local elections reported were held in 1961 and 1962, while the demographic data derive from the 1960 census. Thus, as much as two years may have elapsed from the census to the election, so that changes in population characteristics in the intervening period are not reflected. Inasmuch as the voter-registration ratio is used as a measure of turnout, rather than the voter-adult population ratio the impact of such changes is minimized insofar as the turnout percentages themselves are concerned. However, similar flaws exist with reference to the registration figures. States employ different laws, and cities and counties often administer the laws quite independently. Thus the registration base in one city may be full of deadwood, another up-to-date, and the resulting percentage turnout figures be incomparable.

6. Finally, the use of *partisan* and *nonpartisan* as terms to describe the form of elections is a measure, not of the reality of political party activity, but merely of the form of ballot. While we assume that the existence of the party label on the ballot— the definition of a partisan election generally employed—is associated with a higher degree of party activity than is the case in which the nonpartisan ballot is employed, we have no evidence to support the assumption. "As some formally partisan cities are nonpartisan in fact, so some formally nonpartisan cities are *de facto* partisan in varying degrees."[13] Party activity may have a closer relationship to voter participation than the ballot form,

but we have no way of assessing this on a comparative basis. Thus we are forced to utilize a legal definition of partisan and nonpartisan elections, rather than an actual measure of partisan involvement. Similarly, the mayor-council form of government, associated with a separately elected mayor, includes mayors with widely varying powers and, theoretically, a wide range of impact upon the electorate and, indirectly, upon voter turnout. Again, however, we must employ a legal definition rather than a test of actual mayoral influence which might, in fact, be more significant.

While none of these shortcomings appears crucial to us, they do suggest the tentative nature of both the data and the findings themselves, as well as the need for additional controls in subsequent studies.

CORRELATES OF VOTING TURNOUT

We shall consider three general categories of factors which may be related to the level of voting turnout in American cities: *political structure, social structure*, and *community continuity*. In addition, we shall include region as a separate category, although one of a totally different theoretical nature. The first two categories encompass a variety of possible specific factors related either to the institutions of government, party, and elections or to the demographic and group composition of the community. The third category is of a different order, referring to the development over time of interrelationships, contacts, or communications between different elements of political or social structure.

First, *political structure*. Institutions which allow greater access to political leaders and, theoretically, greater responsiveness to political demands should encourage higher levels of voting turnout. So, too, should the existence of institutions explicitly designed to mobilize the electorate. We shall follow the assumptions of the recent literature in taking the existence of *mayor-council form* of government[14] and *partisan elections* as indicating a greater probability of responsiveness "to class, racial, and religious cleavages . . .

the enduring conflicts of political life."[15] We have already noted that earlier analysis of some of the data presented in this paper showed that the presence of the "reformist" institutions—council-manager government and nonpartisan elections—was associated with lower voting turnout.[16] The causal direction of the relationship is difficult to infer, however, since the activity of groups which favor certain political forms may influence both political structures themselves and also the level of turnout, or, on the other hand, once in existence, a political structure may be sufficiently inaccessible and unresponsive to discourage electoral participation.

Second, *social structure*. The existence in a community of groups which provide a social base for political organization would seem to be an important element of social structure which might be associated with voting turnout. Which elements or characteristics of population heterogeneity have an impact on turnout is an important theoretical question; we can only suggest a few possibilities, not all of which are testable with the data available. Religion, ethnicity, education, occupation, neighborhood, and race are obvious and standard bases of social differentiation in American communities. Yet it is not self-evident that variations in any or all of them should be systematically related to levels of voting turnout, at least as measured by aggregate and crude indicators such as those available for comparative studies. It may be, too, that variations in religious or ethnic composition expressed as a percentage of the total population are inadequate measures to relate to voting turnout. Very low or very high ethnicity, for example, may suggest little social cleavage and low turnout; figures between these two extremes, however, might reveal a divided community, high cleavage, and high turnout. Only limited data exist on the numbers and social organization of religious or ethnic groups, or on the voluntary associations based on persons with similar occupation or education vis-à-vis aggregate data on their proportion in the electorate. We must, therefore, infer something about social structure from census data

on the socioeconomic and ethnic composition of the communities.

We shall use the *ethnic* composition of a city, as measured by the proportion of foreign-born persons and persons of foreign or mixed parentage, and the educational composition of the city as our two indicators of social structure.

Arguments and some data on the persistence of ethnic voting are provided in several recent articles; the point is made that the political system is not merely a dependent variable, but that parties and candidates may continue to serve as a "mediator and mobilizer of minority symbols and interests."[17] Although admittedly a very inadequate measure, the proportion of persons of foreign stock is closely related ($r = .62$) to the only indicator of religious composition of a city which is available from the census (the proportion of children in private schools), and we shall use the former as a more direct measure of the religious-ethnic characteristics of a city.

Education would seem to be associated with voting turnout, if the logic of the oft-reported individual correlation of education with political participation can be extended to the ecological or aggregate level.[18] We might expect higher voting turnout in cities with a higher proportion of better-educated persons. Yet such persons are often in a minority in a city and, therefore, their behavior alone may not be able markedly to determine the absolute level of voting turnout. The opposite hypothesis also seems plausible: the higher the proportion of *less* well-educated persons and workers in a community, the higher the voting turnout, for these groups could form the social base for political movements likely to have a stake in influencing local leaders through elections. Here is a case which provides a direct test of alternative hypotheses suggested by an analytical framework which includes both individual level data and ecological level data.

Third, *community continuity*. The longer a community has existed, the more likely it is that there are groups, institutions, and individuals with a stake in the city's political and governmental structures. Similarly, regardless of the age of the community, the more stable the population within the city, the greater the likelihood that such political attachments will exist. Thus both the age of a city and the stability of its population would seem to have a probable relationship to voting turnout. We shall use two indicators to measure the continuity of the local social and political systems of American communities: *the age of the city* and *the geographic mobility* of its population. The age of the city, as measured by the decade in which the city reached 25,000 population, is a direct measure of the length of time that a social and political organization has existed on a given territorial site. City age does not measure, however, the age of either form of government or form of elections, both of which may have been altered one or more times during the life of the city. Thus only indirect statements may be made about the continuity of *particular* political institutions. Geographic mobility—as measured by the proportion of the population who moved to their present home from a different county between 1955 and 1960—is an indirect indication of the continuity of a given set of families and households in a community. Where such mobility is low, a high level of out-migration may or may not have taken place, and thus geographic mobility may not be a good measure of population change. However, for that very reason it is appropriate for our purposes. The "residue" of families left behind is the appropriate population which is attached or unattached to the electoral system. Conversely, a city which has experienced a high level of movement of its population from one county to another probably contains many residents who have lost their ties to social groups and political networks which have been their channels of communication of political stimuli.

Finally, *region*. It is difficult both conceptually and analytically to suggest or to test the notion that "region" has an independent relationship to voting turnout. As Lineberry and Fowler suggest, "Region as a variable is an undifferentiated potpourri of socio-

economic, attitudinal, historical and cultural variations."[19] Nevertheless, while not capable of adequate analysis in this study, the possibility remains that such factors as political tradition or culture—the previous existence of particular institutions, the impact of previous events, or the existence of particular value systems—may have a relationship to the character of the community and, thus, to voter participation.[20] For example, our data do not permit us to measure the existence—past or present—of leaders or bosses, of citizen organizations and community controversies that may have an enduring impact upon patterns of community politics, including voting turnout. Such characteristics may not be randomly distributed throughout the country and may not be adequately "explained" by normal demographic data. Thus the oft-asserted likelihood that working-class eastern and midwestern cities are more likely to have political machines with a stake in controlling local elections and getting out the vote is not revealed by the data available in this broad national survey.[21] Similarly, we cannot assess the possible impact, suggested by David Rogers, that many southern communities have an authoritarian and conservative value system, reflected in a rigid class structure and one-party politics, all of which would be likely to have an effect on voter participation.[22] Nor are our data adequate for us to have confidence that the "independent effect" of region can be isolated. Nevertheless, the regional differences suggested below may well hide more important variables than those which are available from census data.

Findings

Table 1 displays the correlations of the various indicators of social and political structure and community continuity with four different measures of voting turnout in American cities. In order to avoid the problem of variations in registration from city to city, both the proportion of registrants voting and of adults voting are shown. Also, because cities with elections which are concurrent with state or nation elections have higher turnout than those with nonconcurrent elections, cities are divided into those two categories. Thus we have two independent replications based on two populations of cities.

All four general factors are associated with the level of voting turnout regardless of whether the proportion of adults or registrants voting is considered, and regardless of whether the local election was concurrent or nonconcurrent. With regard to political structure, cities without the council-manager form and with partisan elections have higher voting turnout than cities with other forms. With respect to social structure, cities with highly ethnic populations and *less* well

TABLE 1.　Correlates of Local Voting Turnout in American cities, 1961–62* (Cities over 25,000 population in 1960)

Characteristic	Cities With:	REGISTRANTS VOTING		ADULTS VOTING	
		Nonconcurrent Elections	Concurrent Elections	Nonconcurrent Elections	Concurrent Elections
Political Structure					
Non-council-manager vs. council-manager		0.43	0.34	0.50	0.35
Partisan vs. nonpartisan elections		0.28	0.43	0.29	0.38
Social Structure					
Ethnicity: Percent of the population native of foreign or mixed parentage, 1960		0.32	0.36	0.51	0.49
Education: Percent of persons 25 years old and over who completed four years of high school or more, 1960		−0.28	−0.16	−0.15	−0.22
Community					
Mobility: Percent migrant to a different county, 1955–60		−0.32	−0.32	−0.40	−0.49
Age of city: Decade in which the city reached 25,000 population		0.27	0.27	0.28	0 23
Regional Location					
East		0.39	0.58	0.45	0.51
Midwest		0.04	−0.13	0.21	0.02
South		−0.15	−0.29	−0.44	−0.45
Far West		−0.19	−0.25	−0.10	−0.20
Mean registrants voting		46.9%	59.0%		
Mean adults voting				31.2%	43.5%
N=		(282)	(142)	(294)	(146)

*Entries are product-moment correlations of the actual percentages of registrants voting or adults voting in the last local election held in the given city. Cities in which the local election was held concurrently with a state or national election are separated from those in which it was not concurrent. The Ns shown are approximate for a few correlations, since not all data were available on political structure. The direction of the correlation is indicated by the italicized word. The two political structure variables and regional location were treated as dummy variables (presence or absence of the attribute named) for the correlations. All other correlations were computed from the actual percentages. Data on political structure were obtained from the *Municipal Year Book*, 1963, and all other data are from the 1960 U.S. Census of Population. The correlations are not significantly altered if commission cities are grouped with manager cities for the purpose of constructing a mayor-council/nonmayor-council dummy variable.

States comprising the indicated regions are as follows:

East: Maine, New Hampshire, Vermont, Massachusetts, Connecticut, Rhode Island, New York, New Jersey, Pennsylvania, Maryland, Delaware, District of Columbia.

Midwest: Ohio, Indiana, Illinois, Michigan, Wisconsin, Minnesota, Iowa, North Dakota, South Dakota, Nebraska.

Far West: California, Oregon, Washington, Nevada, Alaska, Hawaii, Montana, Idaho, Colorado, Utah, Wyoming, Arizona, New Mexico.

South (and border): Texas, Oklahoma, Kansas, Missouri, Arkansas, Louisiana, Alabama, Mississippi, Florida, Georgia, North Carolina, South Carolina, Virginia, West Virginia, Kentucky, Tennessee.

educated populations have higher voting turnout. With respect to community continuity and region, cities with stable populations, which are older, and which are located in the East have higher voting turnout than cities with a high level of inmigration, which are younger, and which are located in the Far West or South.

The same general patterns are found if other related indicators are used, such as the percent of foreign born, the percent of persons with five years of education or less, the percent of college graduates, the percent of children in private school, or the decade in which the city reached 10,000 population. Nor do other dividing lines for regions alter the general relationships.

We shall present only the proportion of *registrants voting* in subsequent tables, because we are concerned with the factors which bring eligible voters to the polls, not with the factors which influence the possibility of registration. Analytically, the two bases are distinct in terms of their relevance for political processes, since it is possible for a city to have an extremely high proportion of registrants voting but a very low proportion of adults voting (particularly in the South), although not vice versa. The act of registration is of course, an important aspect of political participation.[23] In any event, the correlation between adults and registrants voting in this study is high (.81), and separate analysis of the data shows that the relationships described here would not be altered by the use of the "adult" base.

As noted above, we shall report further data only for those cities whose local election was not held concurrently with a state or national election. The correlation of concurrence with the proportions of registrants voting was .30, with adults voting .35. The mean voting turnout of adults in cities with concurrent elections was 43.5 percent, for nonconcurrent elections 31.2 percent, and the "advantage" of concurrent elections is maintained in every subgroup we examined. Concurrent elections are slightly more likely in the East, in cities with partisan elections and a mayor-council form of government, and in older cities, all characteristics themselves linked to higher voter turnout. But, as Table 1 shows, the association does not account for the correlations of these other characteristics with voter turnout. While not included here, all subsequent tables shown were also separately computed for cities with concurrent elections, and the same patterns of relationships hold.

POLITICAL STRUCTURES
AND VOTING TURNOUT

Table 2 attempts to assess the *independent* influence of political structural characteristics upon the level of voting turnout. The table shows that the overall correlations of political structure and voting turnout remain while controlling for each demographic characteristic and the four regions, although the magnitudes change. (The single disappearance of the association occurs for form of election in the Far West; in that region, only 6 of the 77 cities with nonconcurrent elections also had partisan elections.) We may summarize Table 2 simply by noting that both aspects of political structure—the form of government and the form of elections—are related to the proportions of registrants voting, even when important characteristics of social structure and region are held constant.

The correlations suggest that form of government has a stronger relationship to turnout than form of elections. In an attempt to assess this more adequately, Table 3 examines each structural variable, holding the other constant. Form of government does have a more significant relationship to turnout than form of election. The election of a mayor (which occurred in 77 percent of the mayor-council cities in the nonconcurrent elections covered by this study) may be a stronger motivating force in relation to turnout than the existence of the partisan ballot. The latter is much more ambiguous in terms of its practical meaning; a partisan ballot, as we have noted, may mask a wide range of party activity, ranging from the total absence of political party organization to total mobilization. Thus, it is not surprising

TABLE 2. *Correlates of Registrants Voting with Political Structures Controlling for Social Structure, Community Continuity, and Region.* *(Cities with Nonconcurrent Local Elections)*

CHARACTERISTIC	CONTROLLING FOR SOCIAL STRUCTURE AND COMMUNITY CONTINUITY				CORRELATION WITHIN REGION				ALL CITIES
	Ethnicity	Education	Mobility	Age of City	East	Midwest	South	Far West	
Nonmanager vs. council-manager form of government	0.38	0.37	0.34	0.38	0.40	0.38	0.28	0.30	0.43
Partisan vs. nonpartisan elections	0.27	0.25	0.23	0.25	0.14	0.40	0.27	−0.01	0.28
N=	(279)	(279)	(279)	(279)	(43)	(67)	(95)	(77)	(282)

*See Table 1 for the states comprising each region and the measures of each variable. Entries are product-moment correlates of the percentage of registrants voting with the two characteristics of political structure indicated. Entries under "Social Structure and Community Continuity" are partial correlations, controlling for each of the variables indicated. The direction of the correlation is indicated by the italicized word.

TABLE 3. The Correlation of Registrants Voting with Each Element of Political Structure.* (Cities with Nonconcurrent Elections)

CHARACTERISTIC	CORRELATION WITHIN FORM OF ELECTION		CORRELATION WITHIN FORM OF GOVERNMENT	
	Partisan	Nonpartisan	Nonmanager	Manager
Nonmanager vs. manager form of government	0.45	0.36	—	—
Partisan vs. nonpartisan elections	—	—	0.24	0.11
N=	(50)	(232)	(103)	(179)

*Entries are product-moment correlates of the percentage of registrants voting with each aspect of political structure, controlling for the other. The direction of the correlation is indicated by the italicized word.

that the more clear-cut variable demonstrates a clearer relationship.

These findings are consistent with those reported by Ruth Dixon, utilizing the same base data as in this study. Analyzing all cities, regardless of the concurrency of the election, she reported a correlation of −.48 between council-manager form of government and percent of adults voting and −.38 between adult turnout and the nonpartisan ballot. Furthermore, in a multiple-correlation regression including eight political variables, form of government accounted for 22 percent of the variance in turnout, concurrency of election for an additional 11 percent, type of election for 3 percent, and form of registration for 2 percent. The author notes Lord Bryce's suggestion that "the most important single factor in affecting turnout is the color and appeal of the candidates," and goes on to state that "the predictive power of these governmental variables is considerable in view of the multitude of factors that are brought into play in influencing citizens to vote."[24]

SOCIAL STRUCTURES AND VOTING TURNOUT

Table 4 shows the correlates of measures of ethnicity and of educational level with the voting turnout of registered persons in cities with nonconcurrent elections. Although several of the correlations are very weak, cities with more highly ethnic or less well-educated populations generally have higher levels of voting turnout, regardless of form of government and elections and in each of the four regions. (Again, the Far West does not have many cities with a highly "ethnic" population.)

In noting the relationship between ethnic populations and the existence of mayor-council form of government, Kessel had

TABLE 4. Correlates of Registrants Voting and Social Structure, Controlling for Political Structure and Region* (Cities with Nonconcurrent Local Elections)

Characteristic	Correlation within								All Cities
	FORM OF GOVERNMENT		FORM OF ELECTION		REGION				
	Nonmanager	Manager	Partisan	Nonpartisan	East	Midwest	South	Far West	
Ethnicity	0.38	0.15	0.26	0.33	0.29	0.09	0.21	−0.06	0.32
Education	−0.23	−0.15	−0.43	−0.20	−0.32	−0.33	−0.19	−0.03	−0.28
N=	(103)	(179)	(50)	(232)	(43)	(67)	(95)	(77)	(282)

*Entries are product-moment correlates of the actual percentages for each city. States comprising the regions are given in Table 1 with the measures of ethnicity and education.

suggested that the foreign-born "would be especially dependent on political activity because of its exclusion from alternative agencies of community integration."[25] Although our data are not strictly comparable, the parallel existence of a relationship between ethnicity and turnout would seem to support Kessel's assumptions.

However, the findings relating education to turnout appear to fly in the face of accepted conventional wisdom. If voting turnout reflects an "adding up" of the predispositions of individuals in cities to participate in politics, then we would expect that education would be closely correlated with voting turnout. This is not the case. Although not high, the ecological or aggregate correlation of registrants voting with education is the opposite of the well-known individual correlation.[26] (Use of other measures of education does not alter this generalization.)

Voting turnout (registrants voting) is thus *inversely* correlated with the educational level of a city. We conclude that high educational level of the city as a whole either has no effect or reduces the level of voting turnout. Although better-educated individuals may indeed vote more frequently than less-educated individuals, less well-educated communities vote more (or at least not less) than well-educated communities. We leave for further study the question of whether the relationship between education and voter turnover is curvilinear, a question unanswered by the existence of the single correlation. It may well be that turnout is lowest at either end of the aggregate educational scale but proportionally higher in communities falling between these two extremes.

COMMUNITY CONTINUITY
AND VOTING TURNOUT

Table 5 shows the correlates of the age of the city and the geographic mobility of its population with voting turnout, holding form of political structure and region constant. The older the city and the less mobile its population, the lower the voting turnout, regardless of either form of government or form of election.

Mobility remains highly correlated with voting turnout in the East and Midwest, but drops to nothing in the South and Far West. The age of the city, however, is not correlated with voting turnout in any region except the Far West.

Such findings do not necessarily mean that these factors have no influence in those regions, but rather that we must reconceptualize their relationships to each other and to voting turnout. Community continuity does not appear to be a "factor" influencing voting turnout in the same way as contemporary features of the social and political structure of the city, but rather— we suggest—indicates a greater probability that stable communication networks linking social and political groups to political leaders in a community may have developed.

TABLE 5.   *Correlates of Registrants Voting and Indicators of Community Continuity, Controlling for Political Structure and Regions.* (*Cities with Nonconcurrent Elections*)

| Characteristic | Correlation within Political Structure | | | | Correlation within Region | | | | All Cities |
| | FORM OF GOVERNMENT | | FORM OF ELECTIONS | | East | Midwest | South | Far West | |
	Non-manager	Manager	Partisan	Non-partisan					
Mobility	−0.23	−0.16	−0.41	−0.26	−0.49	−0.47	−0.03	−0.06	−0.32
Age of city	0.11	0.24	0.22	0.24	0.15	0.18	0.03	0.34	0.27
N=	(103)	(179)	(50)	(232)	(43)	(67)	(95)	(77)	(282)

*Entries are product-moment correlations of the actual percentages for each city. States comprising the regions are given in Table 1 with the measures of mobility and city age. The direction of the correlation is in terms of the *age* of the city; thus, the earlier the city reached 25,000 population, the higher the turnout.

TABLE 6.   Correlations of Regional Location of a City and Selected Characteristics Related to Voting Turnout.* (Cities with Nonconcurrent Elections)

CHARACTERISTIC	REGION			
	East	Midwest	South	Far West
Political Structure				
Council-*manager* form vs. non-council-manager form	−0.29	−0.33	0.23	0.32
Nonpartisan vs. partisan	−0.13	−0.20	0.13	0.18
Social Structure				
Ethnicity	0.56	0.14	−0.60	0.06
Education	−0.23	0.03	−0.21	0.41
Community Continuity				
Mobility	−0.34	−0.22	0.17	0.32
Age of city	0.29	0.12	−0.10	−0.26
Mean registrants voting	64%	48%	43%	41%
Mean adults voting	49%	37%	23%	30%
N=	(43)	(67)	(95)	(77)

*Note that the table does *not* present correlates relating the characteristics to turnout, but shows the relationship of the characteristics to region. Entries are product-moment correlations of each variable listed with the regional location of a city, treated for computation purposes as four different dummy variables. Thus, "East"-"Not East" is a "variable" for purposes of computation of the correlations. See Table 1 for the states comprising the regions and the measures. The total number of cases is 282.

Also, sets of norms encouraging political participation may have developed as a consequence of the existence of networks of access to and influence upon political leaders. These, in turn, may bear some relationship to voting turnout, but a relationship too complex to be revealed by the gross data here employed.

The above findings concerning the positive relationship of mobility and ethnicity and the negative relationship of education to voter turnout are corroborated in a separate study by Dixon. Using multiple-correlation regression involving clusters of related demographic factors, she concluded that "the single most important factor to be considered in predicting the voter turnout of a city is the residential mobility pattern of its inhabitants, which alone can account for 31 percent of the variability in turnout. Knowing the ethnic composition of the city increases the power of prediction an additional 19 percent . . . [while] the factors 'age composition', 'social status' [which included education as a variable], 'employment stability' and 'city size' contribute little or no information about whether a city has high or low turnout in local election."[27]

REGION

The regional location of a city is associated with a wide variety of political and social characteristics, as Table 6 shows, and many of these characteristics are also associated with voting turnout. Eastern cities are older, have more out-migration and little in-migration, and have more persons native of foreign-born parentage. In addition, they are more likely to have partisan elections and less likely to have the council-manager form of government. Western cities are at the other extreme in all of these characteristics. Thus it is no surprise to find that important differences exist among regions with respect to voter turnout, as has been suggested in tables presented above. The distinction is most apparent in a comparison of eastern and far western cities. Eastern location is positively correlated with all the variables associated with high turnout. Eastern cities have a mean turnout figure of 64.0 percent, compared to but 41.2 percent in the Far West. Nevertheless, the table also reveals once again the difficulty of dealing theoretically and analytically with region as an independent variable. Since we are unable to control for other than a very limited number of these variations, we only note the regional characteristics but offer little by way of explanation other than our previous reference to the possible existence of such factors as political tradition and culture.

SOCIOPOLITICAL STRUCTURES, HISTORICAL CONTINUITY, REGION, AND VOTING TURNOUT

In the pages above, relationships of varying strength have been noted between form of government, form of elections, ethnicity, education, and mobility and voting turnout. Age of city was seen to have little relationship independent of other characteristics, while region did seem associated with turnout but presented both theoretical and analytical problems which could not be resolved by the data here available. In the tables to follow, we review some of the above findings by the use of other data, in this case the mean turnout in various categories and subcategories of cities. (The substitution of median for mean does not alter the results; the two have a correlation of .97). The demographic variables previously utilized are dichotomized above and below the median value for all cities in the United States, in order to develop a primitive typology of cities along the dimensions we have distinguished.

In Table 7, the average voting turnout is shown for cities classified simultaneously by form of government, form of elections, and the four demographic variables. In every comparison, the relationships appear as predicted. Holding all other variables constant, both partisan elections and non-manager (typically mayor-council) government show a higher turnout than nonpartisan elections and manager government. Similarly, again paralleling the results indicated above, the average turnout among cities with high ethnicity, low education and low mobility is higher (with one minor exception) than among cities with reverse characteristics. Older cities, regardless of their form of government or election, are more likely to have higher voting turnout

than younger cities, although the mean differences are not as great as for the political structural characteristics.

Table 8 presents average turnout data by form of government and form of elections, classified according to region. As indicated above, region is itself related to various demographic characteristics themselves associated with turnout; multivariate analysis is thus handicapped by the small size of the frequencies in many of the subcategories. Again, partisan nonmanager cities tend to command a larger turnout than nonpartisan and manager cities. However, the impact of other variables hidden under the "region" label is similarly indicated. In the East, for example, the average turnout in nonpartisan nonmanager cities is higher than in partisan mayor-council cities. Whether this reflects the impact of form of government—for example, the possibility that the office of mayor "means" more in the East than in other parts of the country—or the association of these cities with demographic variables associated with turnout, or a number of other possibilities, cannot be determined with any degree of confidence from these data. Similarly, in the Far West, average turnout in nonpartisan-manager cities is the same as that in the very small number of partisan-manager cities, in contrast to the general pattern. Here, the ambiguous nature of "partisan" as well as "region" is evidenced as well as the difficulty of generalizing from the very small number of deviant cases. It may well be that partisanship is lacking in those few western cities, ballot form notwithstanding, that there is a "spill-over" effect from the prevailing nonpartisan policy of the area. Again, the data utilized here do not permit an evaluation of these important distinctions.

In Table 9, demographic and regional variables are examined simultaneously. Again, the mean turnout figures reported for the nation as a whole are consistent with the findings already noted: older cities with high ethnicity, low education, and low mobility show higher turnout than cities with the opposite characteristics. However, the relationships are reduced sharply and some-

TABLE 7. *Mean Percent of Registrants Voting, by Social Structure and Political Structure.* * *(Cities with Nonconcurrent Local Elections)* % and (N)

CHARACTERISTIC		PARTISAN			NONPARTISAN			ALL CITIES		
		Nonmanager	Manager	All	Nonmanager	Manager	All	Nonmanager	Manager	All
Ethnicity	High	65 (19)	45 (9)	58 (28)	58 (44)	42 (57)	49 (101)	60 (63)	42 (66)	51 (129)
	Low	62 (15)	49 (7)	58 (22)	48 (25)	40 (106)	41 (131)	53 (40)	40 (113)	44 (153)
Education	High	59 (10)	45 (10)	52 (20)	53 (42)	39 (110)	43 (152)	54 (52)	39 (120)	44 (172)
	Low	66 (24)	50 (6)	62 (30)	57 (27)	44 (53)	48 (80)	61 (51)	44 (59)	52 (110)
Mobility	High	60 (10)	40 (10)	50 (20)	52 (26)	39 (122)	41 (148)	54 (36)	39 (132)	42 (168)
	Low	65 (24)	58 (6)	64 (30)	56 (43)	44 (41)	50 (84)	59 (67)	46 (47)	54 (114)
Age of city	Old	66 (21)	47 (10)	60 (31)	57 (41)	43 (63)	49 (104)	60 (62)	44 (73)	51 (135)
	Young	60 (13)	45 (6)	55 (19)	51 (28)	38 (100)	41 (128)	54 (41)	39 (106)	43 (147)
All cities		64 (34)	47 (16)	58 (50)	55 (69)	40 (163)	44 (232)	57 (103)	41 (179)	282

*1. "Low ethnicity" means that there were less than 15 percent of persons in the city native of foreign-born or mixed parentage in 1960. "High ethnicity" more than 15 percent. This figure is the median for all 676 cities in the United States over 25,000 population in 1960.
2. Educational level was dichotomized, with "low education" comprising cities which had 43 percent or more who had completed high school in 1960.
3. Mobility was dichotomized with "low mobility" comprising cities which had 15 percent or less persons 5 years and over who were migrant from a different county between 1955 and 1960, "high mobility" those cities with more than 15 percent migration.
4. Cities which reached 25,000 population by the census of 1930 are classified as "older," those in the censuses of 1940 to 1960 as "younger."

TABLE 8. Mean Percent of Registrants Voting, by Region and Political Structure. (Cities with Nonconcurrent Elections) % and (N)*

REGION	PARTISAN			NONPARTISAN			ALL CITIES		
	Nonmanager	Manager	All	Nonmanager	Manager	All	Nonmanager	Manager	All
East	66 (11)	— (1)	67 (12)	69 (19)	54 (12)	63 (31)	68 (30)	56 (13)	64 (43)
Midwest	61 (16)	53 (5)	59 (21)	49 (28)	35 (18)	43 (46)	53 (44)	39 (23)	48 (67)
Far West	— (1)	39 (5)	40 (6)	56 (7)	40 (64)	41 (71)	55 (8)	40 (69)	41 (77)
South	69 (6)	43 (5)	57 (11)	47 (15)	40 (69)	41 (84)	53 (21)	40 (74)	43 (95)
Total	64 (34)	47 (16)	58 (50)	55 (69)	40 (163)	44 (232)	57 (103)	41 (179)	47 (282)

* See Table 1 for states comprising the regions.

TABLE 9. Mean Percent of Registrants Voting, by Region and Social Structure. (Cities with Nonconcurrent Elections)% and (N)*

REGION	ETHNICITY		EDUCATION		MOBILITY		AGE OF CITY		ALL CITIES
	High	Low	High	Low	High	Low	Old	Young	
East	64 (41)	— (2)	56 (17)	69 (26)	52 (9)	67 (34)	66 (31)	60 (12)	64 (43)
Midwest	48 (40)	49 (27)	45 (41)	53 (26)	41 (25)	53 (42)	52 (39)	43 (28)	48 (67)
South	53 (10)	42 (85)	41 (45)	45 (50)	43 (70)	43 (25)	42 (45)	43 (50)	43 (95)
West	40 (38)	43 (39)	41 (69)	39 (8)	41 (64)	41 (13)	48 (20)	39 (57)	41 (77)
Total	51 (129)	44 (153)	44 (172)	52 (110)	42 (168)	54 (114)	51 (135)	43 (147)	47 (282)

*See Table 7 for explanation of demographic categories, Table 1 for stages comprising the regions and the other measures.

times reversed when region is controlled. The tendency of eastern cities to have a higher turnout, even when demographic characteristics are held constant, suggests again that the history and traditions of a region, its political culture, in short, may be as important variables as those which we have been able to utilize in this exercise. Our gross data do not allow a more extensive exploration of the links between the political and social structure of cities and their origins and development within a particular region.

In sum, the tables utilizing mean turnout data are generally consistent with the findings based on correlations. The fact that these two approaches yield much the same results gives confidence in our conclusion that, regardless of the vulnerability of the data and the generally modest nature of the relationships, there is an association between voter turnout and the variables utilized. Cities with partisan elections, mayor-council (or nonmanager) government, high ethnicity, low education, low mobility, and eastern location tend to have a higher voting turnout than cities with nonpartisan elections, council-manager government, low ethnicity, high education, high mobility, and far western location.

Conclusions

Voting turnout is generally higher in cities with either or both "unreformed" political structures and more explicit class or ethnic cleavages. Voting turnout is higher, not lower, in cities with less well educated populations, perhaps because in those cities political cleavages based on economic interests are more explicit and visible than in middle-class suburbs or other communities likely to have high proportions of college-educated persons. Cities with more stable populations also have higher levels of voting turnout, possibly because of the greater likelihood of integration of the different elements of social and political structure. Whether or not there are direct links of community continuity—as represented by popu-

lation stability—and stages of development to accessible and responsive political structures and to the existence and organization of social cleavages is a question we cannot answer from our own data. However, some evidence on the matter of integration can be inferred from a recent study.

Lineberry and Fowler found that cities with "reformed" political structures were less likely to be responsive to cleavages in their population than unreformed cities. Specifically, they found that there were higher correlations of ethnicity and religion (as measured indirectly by private school attendance) with taxation and expenditures in cities with the mayor-council form of government and partisan or ward elections. They suggest that reformed cities have "removed" the influence of party as a mechanism for aggregating interests and, therefore, they expected that the "effects" of social composition would be seen more clearly in unreformed cities. In brief, they suggest that the *political* structures of un-reformed cities are likely to be more integrated with their *social* structures than those of reformed cities and that "the electoral institutions of reformed governments make public policy less responsive to the demands arising out of social conflicts in the population."[28] The fact that voting turnout tends to relate independently and positively both to "unreformed" political institutions and to characteristics of community cleavage is consistent with Lineberry and Fowler's conclusions.

With respect to partisanship, it comes as no surprise to find that in the absence of the political party label on the ballot and the assumed reduced likelihood of party organization and activity, voter turnout is generally less. Although there are many advocates of nonpartisanship who would espouse the thesis that local citizen participation should be just as great without the "artificial" injection of partisan politics, the fact remains that the party remains an agent of political mobilization, both symbolically and practically. To some, this is unfortunate. Richard Childs, perhaps the leading exponent of non-partisanship and one of its "founding fathers," takes the view that "in partisan local elections, two prominent national party organizations consider it their noble duty to combat the other organization, disparage its achievements, advance rival candidates, and the 'outs' consider it necessary to oust the 'ins,' no matter how good a record the 'ins' may have been making. No matter how meaningless the contest for office may be in a given year, both forces must be marshalled for a fight. But what good is that, even if it does bring out a high percentage of the adult population to the polls?"[29]

Regardless of the various merits of non-partisan elections, and there are many,[30] Child's view overlooks the fact that elections and participation in the electoral process are not just a means to an end—the election of qualified citizens to public office—but an end in themselves. In fact, one may well ask in 1968 whether a high rate of participation in local elections and the possible reduction of a sense of alienation of many citizens from their community would not more than offset the possible loss of an outstanding candidate.

Insofar as relatively greater turnout in non-manager cities is concerned, both the theoretical and analytical questions are more elusive. The separate election of the mayor would seem to be the prime factor distinguishing manager and mayor-council cities (although there are some manager cities with a separately elected mayor and some mayor-council cities with an appointed mayor). Yet mayors have a wide range of roles in American cities, ranging from figurehead to strong executive; it would seem that these varying roles and the public's response to them would bear a direct relation to voter interest and turnout, but our data provide no assistance to assess such relationships. Nor do we have data, other than these gross turnout figures, to assess the importance of a separately elected chief executive to the community. Does the existence of an election for mayor serve to increase a citizen's attachment to and interest in the political life of the community? Does the personalization of politics around a contest between two individuals, so familiar at the state and national levels, serve in some sense as a bridge between the

citizen and his government? We can only hint at the host of the social-psychological questions which the existence or non-existence of a contest for mayor may suggest.

An alternative, but not mutually exclusive explanation is that electoral politics is simply regarded as less important in council-manager cities than in nonmanager communities. Council-manager theory notwithstanding, it may well be that the citizen feels that the manager has, in fact, reduced the scope of authority and responsibility of the city's elected officials. The manager hires and fires the department heads; the manager submits the budget and, in so doing, resolves many of the basic resource allocation policies before the council ever sees the document. Such matters may well fall on the administration side of the ancient administration-policy dichotomy, but they represent in many citizens' minds the stuff of city government and politics. Their removal, rightly or wrongly, from the overt political scene may be one explanation of the apparent relationship of the council-manager form to lower voter turnout. In a similar fashion, it could well be that the result of the manager plan and an effective manager is to so "manage" conflict and issues that they do not become political and, eventually, electoral issues. A resulting depressant effect on voter attention and participation would be a likely by-product.

In general, relatively high levels of voting turnout are probably the result of the combined influences of sustained and continuous political organization of parties, wards, neighborhoods, voluntary associations with local political concerns, and simply traditional behavior by social groups which does not require the mobilizing influence of political organization. Where there is high turnout without high activity of parties and interest groups, votes may be "available" for manipulation by political elites, because in such cities individuals vote because of their party identification and not their involvement in political organizations. Where there is a high level of activity of political organizations *without* high turnout, on the other hand, we might expect that the lack of electoral sanctions would result in a high level of competition and conflict between the relatively better-educated leaders of the active organizations.

Paradoxically, voting turnout may *not* necessarily be a good index of the politicization of the electorate. Voting may be a form of traditional behavior produced by membership in ethnic and other groups which have a certain party identification as part of their group identity. In such cases, a high vote turnout need not mean high issue consciousness or a high level of political conflict. Conversely, voting turnout may be low without denying the possibility of a high level of conflict and concern with issues among the minority of voters who have a high level of political interest.

Thus, it is possible that a high level of action on such policies as urban renewal and poverty programs may be found in cities with low conflict and issue concern but high voting turnout, precisely because votes can be delivered by political leaders, and bargains and negotiations between local leaders and state and national leaders are possible. A highly active community may have so much conflict that activity leads to stalemate, because leaders are not able to mobilize clear majorities or count on the passive acquiescence of majorities. This argument is consistent with that of Crain and Rosenthal concerning the impact of high levels of education upon participation, conflict, and stalemate in fluoridation and other decisions. Although they noted exceptions at the highest educational level, they argued that high-status cities, precisely because they have citizens ready and able to participate in politics, will be less likely to be able to innovate new community programs and less able to make decisions because of higher levels of conflict which lead to stalemate.[31] The authors examined data on various types of community decisions—urban renewal, fluoridation, school desegregation, and others—which are related to the educational level of the population in the cities, and found that by and large the cities with better-educated populations have been *less* likely to undertake such programs.

Unfortunately, they did not have data on the key intervening variable in their theoretical proposition: political participation. Our data indicates that, in fact, cities with higher levels of education among the population are *less* likely to have high voting turnout than cities with low levels of education. This finding casts doubt upon the plausible assumption that political participation at the level of the city as a whole has the same relationship to education that it does at the individual level. But if, in fact, there is *less* political participation in cities with high levels of education, this explanation of differences in decision-making processes cannot rest upon a presumed correlation between education and participation.

As suggested, the answer may partly rest on the possibility that voting turnout may be a poor indicator of other forms of the political activity of groups in cities. Groups composed of better-educated persons may have other channels through which to influence policy than mere voting turnout. Effective political participation by such groups might tend to resolve issues before they become relevant to a campaign and election. In any event, our findings about relatively low turnout in better-educated cities do at least raise questions about the assumption that correlations at the individual level can be casually extended to the level of community social organization. Crain and Rosenthal make the same methodological point in a different substantive context, suggesting that the greater likelihood of better-educated persons to accept innovation may not be true when the same factors are measured at the community "ecological" level.[32]

An investigation of the individual correlations of education and political participation in cities with different demographic and economic characteristics is clearly called for. It may well be true—and we suspect—that in *all* cities, the better educated are more likely to vote than the less well educated, despite the higher overall levels of voting turnout in less well-educated cities. In high turnout cities, for example, the better-educated stratum in those cities may respond to the political mobilization of the ethnic less-educated majorities by even higher political participation than the majority social groups themselves exhibit. Nor would one expect that in middle-class, better-educated, Far West Cities with low vote turnout, there would necessarily be any counterresponse by the less well-educated elements in those cities to participate at higher levels. The very fact of the recent migration of less well-educated persons to western cities should serve to break their ties to the local ethnic neighborhood organizations or other community groups which sustained high voting participation in the eastern cities from which they came. Thus a plausible case can be made for expecting the "normal" pattern of individual correlation between education and political participation in both types of cities. It would be possible to compute possible ranges of variations of the individual-level correlations, given certain marginal distributions of educational composition and voting turnout levels in cities, but that problem is beyond our present scope.

A final word on the implications of our data for the controversy over local political subcultures. The operations and functions of a political "ethos" or political culture at the local level may be best understood through a historical perspective of the continuity of social and political structures and the norms of behavior which they enforce, rather than through the current attitudes of social groups in a community. We have noted the difference in direction of the correlation between education and voting turnout at the city and individual levels. This may indicate that the consequences of structural features of a political system, derived in turn from its history, may be visible in collective patterns of political behavior, such as partisan strength, levels of voting turnout, or referenda outcomes, but not at all visible in correlations of political attitudes with individual characteristics.

Banfield and Wilson's original article[33] used ecological data on ethnic and class composition of tracts, in relation to referenda voting, which we would regard as appropriate

kinds of data for inferences to collective processes, but their theoretical framework was based upon assumptions about *individual* behavior, not necessary to and even possibly misleading about the actual causal processes involved. Wolfinger and Field questioned that certain ethnic groups hold "private-regarding" or "public-regarding" values, and therefore favor certain political structures in their community. They noted that when a region was controlled, the correlations between ethnicity and various aspects of political structure and governmental functions presumed to be predicted by the "ethos" hypothesis vanished. And they suggested that regional variations in the age of cities may explain more than the "ethos" of groups residing in cities. As they put it, "regional variations may reflect to some extent interaction between cities' natural histories and prevailing political enthusiasms at crucial periods in those histories."[34] Our data indicating significant regional differences, particularly the tendency of eastern cities to have relatively high voting turnout regardless of form of government, method of balloting and social characteristics is consistent with this view. Whereas region may not be a useful analytical tool, *as such*, the variations among regions suggest the need to introduce into the conceptual framework and research design a recognition of such phenomena as Wolfinger and Field describe.

The regional or even the state location of a city may not be sufficient to identify its political culture accurately. Samuel C. Patterson has recently suggested that while there may be interstate variations in basic political orientations, there are also important variations within states. A few studies have analyzed this topic.[35]

We have suggested that there is likely to be variation in community political systems linked to the regional location of the city, its age, and the extent of out-migration or in-migration. Sheer length of existence, as well as the proportion of the population which has lived in the city for a long or a short time, would seem to be plausibly related to the degree to which there is historical continuity of leadership patterns and policy-making patterns in a city. Again, these are indirect indicators, because, for example, some cities may have experienced what amounts to a revolution in leadership continuity in certain periods of their history. But we hypothesize that our indicators would correlate with more direct measures of continuity of leadership and policy making.

Over a period of years, we suggest, communication networks between social groups and political leaders develop which have some continuity, although incumbents may change. Political roles and institutionalized locations for those roles develop which are linked to the historical success of certain groups in winning electoral victories or exerting informal influence over policy-making processes. High voting turnout may be one consequence of the development over time of these links of social groups to political organization.

Notes

1. Charles R. Adrian and Charles Press, *Governing Urban America*, 3rd ed. (New York: McGraw-Hill, 1968), p. 95.

2. Alvin Boskoff and Harmon Zeigler's study, *Voting Patterns in a Local Election*, provides a brief review of the state of the literature: (Philadelphia: J. B. Lippincott, (1964), chap. 1. See also Lester W. Milbrath, *Political Participation* (Chicago: Rand McNally, 1965); but note that references to city elections are infrequent.

3. Eugene C. Lee, *The Politics of Nonpartisanship* (Berkeley: University of California Press, 1960), chap. 9 and 11.

4. Eugene C. Lee, "City Elections: A Statistical Profile," in *Municipal Year Book* (Chicago: International City Managers' Association, 1963), 74–84.

5. Robert R. Alford and Harry M. Scoble, "Political and Socioeconomic Characteristics of American Cities," in *Municipal Year Book* (Chicago: International City Managers' Association, 1965), p. 95. See also Leo F. Schnore and Robert R. Alford, "Forms of Government and Socioeconomic Characteristics of Suburbs," *Administrative Science Quarterly*, 8 (June 1963), 1–17; and John Kessel, "Governmental Structure and Political Environment: A Statistical Note about American Cities," *American Political Science Review*, 66 (September 1962), 615–620. Robert L. Lineberry and Edmund P. Fowler present data at some variance with the above and

suggest that there are not significant class differences between reformed and unreformed cities, although there is "some support for the argument that reformed cities are more homogeneous." However, as they suggest, varying samples may produce varying conclusions. In any event, the differences between these studies are not central to this analysis of voting participation. See their "Reformism and Public Policies in American Cities," *American Political Science Review*, 61 (September 1967), 706.

6. Ruth B. Dixon, "Predicting Voter Turnout in City Elections" (unpublished M.A. thesis in sociology, University of California, Berkeley, 1966); Ruth B. Dixon, "The Reform Movement in American City Government: Has Democracy Been Sacrificed to Efficiency?" (unpublished paper, Department of Sociology, University of California, Berkeley, 1965).

7. Maurice Pinard, "Structural Attachments and Political Support in Urban Politics: The Case of Fluoridation Referendums," *American Journal of Sociology*, 68 (March 1963), 518. A similar study reported that in cities with high levels of citizen participation, associated with a well-educated population, the local government was frequently immobilized from making decisions on such issues as bond referenda and fluoridation controversies. Robert L. Crain and Donald B. Rosenthal, "Community Status as a Dimension of Local Decision-Making," *American Sociological Review*, 32 (December 1967), 970–84.

8. See Robert R. Alford, "The Comparative Study of Urban Politics," in Leo F. Schnore and Henry Fagin (eds.), *Urban Research and Policy Planning* (Beverly Hills, Calif.: Sage, 1967), 263–302, for an analytic scheme which distinguishes "situational" from "cultural" and "structural" factors in explaining decisions, policies and roles of government in urban politics. Situational factors themselves have causes and may be patterned, of course, but, by definition, are not predictable from structural or cultural factors. Voting turnout figures for four Wisconsin cities in April and November elections from 1950 to 1964 ranged from 14 percent to 91 percent, which is partly explainable by situational factors. See Robert R. Alford, with the collaboration of Harry M. Scoble, *Bureaucracy and Participation: Political Cultures in Four Wisconsin Cities* (Chicago: Rand McNally, forthcoming), chap. 7.

9. V. O. Key, Jr., "The Politically Relevant in Surveys," *Public Opinion Quarterly*, 24 (1960), 54–61; and Austin Ranney, "The Utility and Limitations of Aggregate Data in the Study of Electoral Behavior," in Ranney (ed.), *Essays in the Behavioral Study of Politics* (Urbana: University of Illinois Press, 1932), p. 99.

10. Crain and Rosenthal, "Community Status," p. 984.

11. The following table compares characteristics of American cities above 25,000 population in 1960 and the cities used in this study.

12. Lee, "City Elections," p. 81.

13. Charles E. Gilbert and Christopher Clague, "Electoral Competition and Electoral Systems in Large Cities," *Journal of Politics*, 24 (May 1962), 330.

14. We use "mayor-council" and "non-manager" interchangeably, although the category includes some thirty commission cities, 10.6 percent of the total of nonmanager communities with nonconcurrent elections.

15. Lineberry and Fowler, "Reformism and Public Policies," p. 715. This article provides a succinct summary of these hypotheses.

16. Lee, "City Elections," pp. 74–84. Ecological data from Des Moines, Iowa, show a similar pattern; see Robert H. Salisbury and Gordon Black, "Class and Party in Partisan and Non-Partisan Elections: The Case of Des Moines," *American Political Science Review*, 57 (September 1963), 589–90.

17. Michael Parenti, "Ethnic Politics and the Persistence of Ethnic Identification," *American Political Science Review*, 61 (September 1967), 717. An earlier statement of this thesis is found in Raymond E. Wolfinger, "Some Consequences of Ethnic Politics," in M. Kent Jennings and Harmon Ziegler (eds.), *The Electoral Process* (Englewood Cliffs, N.J.: Prentice-Hall, 1966). See also Raymond E. Wolfinger, "The Development and Persistence of Ethnic Voting," *American Political Science Review*, 59 (December 1965), 896–908. Robert Lane has suggested that "the seat of ethnic politics is the local community, not the national capitol." See his *Political Life* (New York: The Free Press, 1959), p. 239.

18. See, for example, *ibid.*, p. 222; Boskoff and Zeigler, *Voting Patterns*, p. 16: Milbrath, p. 122.

19. Lineberry and Fowler, "Reformism and Public Policies," p. 707.

20. For an example of the use of "political culture" as a variable in categorizing American states, see Daniel J. Elazar, *American Federalism: A View from the States* (New York: Thomas Y. Crowell, 1966).

21. We are indebted to Raymond Wolfinger for bringing this point to our attention.

22. David Rogers, "Community Political Systems: A Framework and Hypothesis for Comparative Studies," in Bert E. Swanson (ed.), *Current Trends in Comparative Studies* (Kansas City, Mo.: Community Studies, 1962), p. 39.

23. Stanley Kelley, Jr., Richard E. Ayres, and William G. Bowen, "Registration and Voting: Putting First Things First," *American Political Science Review*, 61 (June 1967), 359–79.

24. Dixon, "The Reform Movement."

25. Kessel, *op. cit.*, p. 617.

26. It should be noted that while these correlations are based upon measures of education as a continuous variable, the measure itself is not continuous for a given city, but rather a single proportion of persons who have achieved a given level of education. See Robert R. Alford and Harry M. Scoble, "Sources of Local Political Involvement," *American Political Science Review* (forthcoming) for an analysis of the relative importance of a variety of factors, including education, for political involvement.

27. Dixon, "Predicting Voter Turnout," pp. 50–52.

28. Lineberry and Fowler, *op. cit.*, p. 716.

29. Letter to one of the authors dated January 29, 1964.

30. Lee, *Politics of Nonpartisanship*, chap. 11.

31. Crain and Rosenthal, "Community Status," 970–84.

32. *Ibid.*

33. James Q. Wilson and Edward C. Banfield, "Public-Regardingness as a Value Premise in Voting Behavior," *American Political Science Review*, 58 (December 1964), 876–87.

34. Raymond E. Wolfinger and John Osgood Field, "Political Ethos and the Structure of City Government," *American Political Science Review*, 60 (June 1966), 326. While we take full note of the Wolfinger-Field vs. Banfield-Wilson controversy as to the use and abuse of "ethos," we make no attempt here to enter into their discussion as to what the latter pair said or implied in *City Politics*. The issue is discussed in letters to the editor of each pair in the December 1966, issue of *American Political Science Review*. See "Communications," 998–1000.

35. Samuel C. Patterson, "The Political Cultures of the American States," *Journal of Politics*, 30 (February 1968), 204–07; Alford with the collaboration of Harry M. Scoble, "Characteristics of American Cities." and Oliver P. Williams and Charles R. Adrian, *Four Cities* (Philadelphia: University of Pennsylvania Press, 1963).

3. Interest Aggregation and Articulation

The Changing Pattern of Urban Party Politics

Fred I. Greenstein

ABSTRACT: Disciplined urban party organizations, capable of controlling politics and government in their communities, have been one of our more interesting indigenous political growths. This political form probably could not have arisen in the United States had it not been for certain broad cultural patterns, such as the absence of strong traditional authorities. These cultural patterns were necessary but not sufficient for the growth of party machines. The immediate determinants were the organizational requirements of urban growth, the inability of existing city governments to meet these requirements, the presence of a market—among both businessmen and voters—for the services of the old-style politician, and the existence of free suffrage. Old-style urban parties have declined only partly as a consequence of direct attacks upon them. A variety of social and political changes have sapped the resources of old-style parties and, in many communities, have reduced voter interest in those resources still available to the parties. Further insight into the functions of old-style parties may be had by looking at certain of their present-day alternatives—the politics of nonpartisanship and new-style reform politics within the Democratic party.

Highly organized urban political parties are generally conceded to be one of America's distinctive contributions to mankind's repertory of political forms. Just as the two major national parties in the United States are almost universally described in terms of their *dis*organization—their lack of an authorita-

Reprinted with permission from the Annals of the American Academy of Political and Social Science, *353 (May 1964), 1–13.*

tive command structure—the municipal parties have, until recently, been characterized by most observers in terms of their hierarchical strength. E. E. Schattschneider once summarized this state of affairs in the memorable image of a truncated pyramid: a party system which is weak and ghostlike at the top and solid at the bottom.[1]

This essay deals with the disciplined, largely autonomous local political parties which sprang up in many American cities in the nineteenth century. Much of the literature on these political configurations is heavily pejorative, concerned more with excoriation than explanation. Even the basic nomenclature, "boss" and "machine," is laden with negative connotations, although recently there has been a turn toward nostalgic romanticization of the "vanishing breed" of city bosses.[2]

Here, for reasons which I shall indicate, the attempt shall be to delineate rather than to pass moral judgment: What was the nature of old-style urban party organization? Why did this political pattern develop and how did it operate? What contributed to its short-run persistence in the face of reform campaigns? Under what circumstances have such organizations disappeared and under what circumstances have they continued into the present day—or even undergone renaissances? What are the present-day descendents of old-style urban party organizations?

Analytic delineation invariably involves oversimplification. This is doubly necessary in the present case, because our knowledge of the distribution of types of local party organization is scant. We have no census of local political parties, either for today or for the putative heyday of bosses and machines. And there is reason to believe that observers have exaggerated the ubiquity of tightly organized urban political parties in past generations, as well as underestimated somewhat their contemporary prevalence.

Old-Style Party Organization: Definitional Characteristics

Ranney and Kendall have persuasively argued that the imprecision and negative connotations of terms like *boss* destroy their usefulness. What, beyond semantic confusion, they ask, can come from classifying politicians into "bosses" versus "leaders"? Such a distinction leads to fruitless preoccupation with the purity of politicians' motives rather than the actuality of their behavior; it overestimates the degree to which figures of the past such as Richard Croker, William Tweed, and Frank Hague were free of public constraints; and it obscures the fact that *all* effective political leaders, whether or not they are popularly labeled as bosses, use quite similar techniques and resources.[3]

Granting these points, it still seems that a recognizable and noteworthy historical phenomenon is hinted at by the venerable terms *boss* and *machine*. If the overtones of these terms make us reluctant to use them, we might simply speak of an "old style" of party organization with the following characteristics:

1. There is a disciplined party hierarchy led by a single executive or a unified board of directors.

2. The party exercises effective control over nomination to public office, and, through this, it controls the public officials of the municipality.

3. The party leadership—which quite often is of lower-class social origins—usually does not hold public office and sometimes does not even hold formal party office. At any rate, official position is not the primary source of the leadership's strength.

4. Rather, a cadre of loyal party officials and workers, as well as a core of voters, is maintained by a mixture of material rewards and *nonideological* psychic rewards—such as personal and ethnic recognition, camaraderie, and the like.[4]

The Rise of Old-Style Party Organization

This pattern of politics, Schattschneider comments, "is as American as the jazz band . . . China, Mexico, South America, and southern Italy at various times have produced figures who played roles remotely like that of the American boss, but England, France, Germany, and the lesser democracies of Europe have exhibited no tendency to develop this form of political organization in modern times."[5] What then accounted for the development of old-style party organization in the United States?

The Crokers, Tweeds, and Hagues and their organizations probably could not have arisen if certain broad preconditions had not existed in American society and culture. These include the tradition of freewheeling individualism and pragmatic opportunism, which developed in a prosperous, sprawling new society unrestrained by feudalism, aristocracy, monarchy, an established church, and other traditional authorities. This is the state of affairs which has been commented on by countless observers, even before de Tocqueville, and which has been used to explain such disparate phenomena as the failure of socialism to take hold in the United States, the recurrence of popularly based assaults on civil liberties, and even the peculiarly corrosive form which was taken by American slavery.[6]

It also is possible to identify five more direct determinants of the form that urban party organization took in the nineteenth century, three of them consequences of the Industrial Revolution and two of them results of political institutions and traditions which preceded industrialization.

MASSIVE URBAN EXPANSION

Over a relatively brief span of years, beginning in the mid-nineteenth century, industrial and commercial growth led to a spectacular rise in the number and proportion of Americans concentrated in cities. A thumbnail sketch of urban expansion may be had by simply noting the population of urban and rural areas for each of the twenty-year periods from 1840 to 1920:

	URBAN POPULATION	RURAL POPULATION
	(*in millions*)	
1840	1.8	15.2
1860	6.2	25.2
1880	14.1	36.0
1900	30.1	45.8
1920	54.2	51.6

These statics follow the old Census Bureau classification of areas exceeding 2,500 in population as urban. Growth of larger metropolitan units was even more striking. In 1840 slightly over 300,000 Americans lived in cities—or, rather, a single city, New York —with more than a quarter of a million residents; by 1920 there were twenty-four cities of this size, containing approximately twenty-one million Americans.

The sheer mechanics of supporting urban populations of this magnitude are, of course, radically different from the requirements of rural life. There must be extensive transportation arrangements; urban dwellers are as dependent upon a constant inflow of food and other commodities as an infant is on the ministrations of adults. A host of new administrative functions must be performed as the population become urbanized: street construction and maintenance, bridges, lighting, interurban transportation, sanitary arrangements, firefighting, police protection, and so forth. Overwhelming demands suddenly are placed on governments which, hitherto, were able to operate with a minimum of effort and activity.

DISORGANIZED FORMS OF URBAN GOVERNMENT

The forms of government which had evolved in nineteenth-century America were scarcely suitable for meeting the demands of mushrooming cities. Governmental structures reflected a mixture of Jacksonian direct democracy and Madisonian checks and balances. Cities had a multitude of elected officials (sometimes they were elected annually), weak executives, large and unwieldy councils and boards. The formal organization of the cities placed officials in a position permitting and, in fact, encouraging them to checkmate each other's efforts to make and execute policies. Since each official was elected by appealing to his own peculiar constituency and had little incentive to cooperate with his associates, the difficulties caused by the formal limitations of government were exacerbated. In a period when the requirements for governmental action were increasing geometrically, this was a prescription for chaos.

NEEDS OF BUSINESSMEN

A third aspect of mid-nineteenth-century American society which contributed to the formation of old-style party organizations was the needs of businessmen. There was an increasing number of merchants, industrialists, and other businessmen, licit and illicit, who needed—and were willing to pay for— the appropriate responses from city governments. Some businessmen wanted to operate unrestrained by municipal authority. Others desired street-railway franchises, paving contracts, construction work, and other transaction connected with the very growth of the cities themselves.

NEEDS OF DEPENDENT POPULATIONS

The needs of the bulk of the nineteenth-century urban population were not for profits but for the simple wherewithal to survive and maintain a modicum of dignity. It is difficult in the relatively affluent society of our day to appreciate the vicissitudes of urban life several generations ago: the low wages, long hours, tedious and hazardous working conditions, and lack of security which were the lot of most citizens. Even for native-born Americans, life often was nasty and brutish But many urbanites were first- and second-generation immigrants who, in addition to their other difficulties, had to face an alien culture and language. Between the Civil War and World War I, the United States managed to absorb twenty-five million foreigners.

UNRESTRICTED SUFFRAGE

Urban dwellers were not totally without resources for their own advancement. The American tradition of unrestricted male franchise was, in the long run, to work to their advantage. Although it doubtless is true that few city dwellers of the day were aware of the importance of their right to vote, politicians *were* aware of this. Because even the lowliest of citizens was, or could become a voter, a class of politicians developed building upon the four conditions referred to above: the requirements of organizing urban life, the inability of existing governments to meet these requirements, and the presence of businessmen willing to pay for governmental services and of dependent voting populations in need of security from the uncertainties of their existence.

The old-style urban party leader was as much a product of his time and social setting as was the rising capitalist of the Gilded Age. Building on the conditions and needs of the day, the politician had mainly so supply his own ingenuity and coordinating ability in order to tie together the machinery of urban government. If a cohesive party organization could control nominations and elect its own agents to office, the formal fragmentation of government no longer would stand in the way of municipal activity. The votes of large blocs of dependent citizens were sufficient to control nomination and win elections. And the financial support of those who sought to transact business with the city, as well as the revenues and resources of the city government, made it possible to win votes. The enterprising politican who could succeed in governing a city on this basis was a broker *par excellence*; generous brokers' commissions were the rule of the day.

The importance of out-and-out vote-buying on election day as a source of voter support can easily be overestimated. Party organizations curried the favor of voters on a year-long basis. In a day when "better" citizens espoused philosophical variants of Social Darwinism, urban politicians thought in terms of an old-fashioned conception of the welfare state. In the familiar words of Tammany sachem George Washington Plunkitt:

What holds your grip on your district is to go right down among the poor families and help then in the different ways they need help. I've got a regular system for this. If there's a fire in Ninth, Tenth or Eleventh Avenue, for example, any hour of the day or night, I'm usually there with some of my election district captains as soon as the fire engines. If a family is burned out I don't ask whether they are Republicans or Democrats, and I don't refer

them to the Charity Organization Society, which would investigate their case in a month or two and decide they were worthy of help about the time they are dead from starvation. I just get quarters for them, buy clothes for them if their clothes were burned up, and fix them up till they get things runnin' again. Its philanthropy, but it's politics, too—mighty good politics. Who can tell how many votes one of these fires bring me? The poor are the most grateful people in the world, and, let me tell you, they have more friends in their neighborhoods than the rich have in theirs.[7]

With numerous patronage appointees (holders not only of city jobs but also of jobs with concerns doing business with the city), party organizations could readily administer this sort of an informal relief program. And, unlike many latter-day charitable and governmental relief programs, the party's activities did not stop with the provision of mere physical assistance.

I know every man, woman and child in the Fifteenth District, except them that's been born this summer—and I know some of them, too. I know what they like and what they don't like, what they are strong at and what they are weak in, and I reach them by approachin' at the right side.
For instance, here's how I gather in the young men. I hear of a young feller that's proud of his voice, thinks that he can sing fine. I ask him to come around to Washington Hall and join our Glee Club. He comes and sings, and he's a follower of Plunkitt for life. Another young feller gains a reputation as a baseball player in a vacant lot. I bring him into our baseball club. That fixes him. You'll find him workin' for my ticket at the polls next election day. Then there's the feller that likes rowin' on the river, the young feller that makes a name as a waltzer on his block, the young feller that's handy with his dukes—I rope them all in by givin' them opportunities to show themselves off. I don't trouble them with political arguments. I just study human nature and act accordin'.[8]

This passage reflects some of the ways in which party activities might be geared to the *individual* interests of voters. *Group* interests were at least as important. As each new nationality arrived in the city, politicians rather rapidly accommodated to it and brought it into the mainstream of political participation. Parties were concerned with the votes of immigrants virtually from the time of their arrival. Dockside naturalization and voter enrollment was not unknown.

But if the purposes of the politicans was to use the immigrants, it soon became clear that the tables could be turned. In Providence, Rhode Island, for example, a careful study of the assimilation of immigrant groups into local politics shows that, within thirty years after the arrival of the first representative of a group in the city, it began to be represented in the councils of one or both parties. Eventually, both of the local parties came to be dominated by representatives of the newer stocks. Thus, in 1864 no Irish names appear on the lists of Democratic committeemen in Providence; by 1876 about a third of the names were Irish; by the turn of the century, three-quarters were Irish. In time, the Republican party became the domain of politicians of Italian ancestry.[9] Perhaps the most dramatic example to date of urban party politics as an avenue of upward social mobility was in the antecedents of President Kennedy, whose great-grandfather was an impoverished refugee of the Irish potato famine, his grandfather a saloon keeper and a classical old-time urban political leader, his father a multimillionaire businessmen, presidential advisor, and ambassador to the Court of St. James's.

When the range of consequences of old-time party organizations is seen, it becomes apparent why moral judgments of "the boss and the machine" are likely to be inadequate. These organizations often were responsible for incredible corruption, but they also— sometimes through the very same activities— helped incorporate new groups into American society and aided them up the social ladder. The parties frequently mismanaged urban growth on a grand scale, but they *did* manage urban growth at a time when other instrumentalities for governing the cities were inadequate. They plied voters, who might otherwise have organized more aggressively to advance their interests, with Thanksgiving Day turkeys and buckets of coal. But, by siphoning off discontent and softening the law, they probably contributed to the generally pacific tenor of American

politics. It seems fruitless to attempt to capture this complexity in a single moral judgment. One can scarcely weigh the incorporation of immigrant groups against the proliferation of corruption and strike an overall balance.

Why Reformers Were "Mornin' Glories"

Stimulated by high taxes and reports of corruption and mismanagement on a grand scale, antiboss reform movements, lead by the more prosperous elements of the cities, became increasingly common late in the nineteenth century. Compared with the regular party politicians of their day, reformers were mere fly-by-night dilettantes —"mornin' glories."[10] They lacked the discipline and the staying power to mount a year-long program of activities. Perhaps more important, the values of the reformers were remote from—in fact, inconsistent with —the values of the citizens whose support would be needed to keep reform administrations in office. Reformers ordinarily saw low taxes and business-like management of the cities as the exclusive aim of government. To the sweatshop worker, grinding out a marginal existence, these aims were at best meaningless, at worst direct attacks on the one agency of society which seemed to have his interests at heart.

The Decline of Old-Style Party Organization

Although in the short run old-style party organizations were marvelously immune to the attacks of reformers, in recent decades the demise of this political form has been widely acclaimed. Because of the absence of reliable trend data, we cannot document "the decline of the machine" with precision. The decline does seem to have taken place, although only partly as a direct consequence of attempts to reform urban politics. Events have conspired to sap the traditional resources used to build voter support and to make voters less interested in these resources which the parties still command.

DECLINE IN THE RESOURCES
OF OLD-STYLE URBAN POLITICIANS

Most obviously, job patronage is no longer available in as great a quantity as it once was. At the federal level and in a good many of the states (as well as numerous cities), the bulk of jobs are filled by civil service procedures. Under these circumstances, the most a party politician may be able to do is seek some minor form of preferment for an otherwise qualified job applicant. Furthermore, the technical requirements of many appointive positions are sufficiently complex to make it inexpedient to fill them with unqualified personnel.[11] And private concerns doing business with the cities are not as likely to be sources of patronage in a day when the franchises have been given out and the concessions granted.

Beyond this, many modern governmental techniques—accounting and auditing requirements, procedures for letting bids, purchasing procedures, even the existence of a federal income tax—restrict the opportunities for dishonest and "honest" graft. Some of these procedures were not instituted with the explicit purpose of hampering the parties. Legislation designed deliberately to weaken parties *has*, however, been enacted— for example, nomination by direct primary and nonpartisan local elections, in which party labels are not indicated on the ballot. Where other conditions are consistent with tight party organization, techniques of this sort seem not to have been especially effective; old-style parties are perfectly capable of controlling nominations in primaries, or of persisting in formally nonpartisan jurisdictions. But, together with the other party-weakening factors, explicit antiparty legislation seems to have taken its toll.

DECLINE OF VOTER INTEREST
IN REWARDS AVAILABLE TO THE PARTIES

Even today it is estimated that the mayor of Chicago has at his disposal six thousand to ten thousand city patronage jobs. And there are many ways of circumventing good government, antiparty legislation. An additional element in the decline of old-style organization is the increasing disinterest of many citizens in the rewards at the disposal of party politicians. Once upon a time, for example, the decennial federal census was a boon to those local politicians whose party happened to be in control of the White House at census time. The temporary job of door-to-door federal census enumerator was quite a satisfactory reward for the party faithful. In 1960 in many localities, party politicians found census patronage more bother than boon; the wages for this task compared poorly with private wages, and few voters were willing to put in the time and leg work. Other traditional patronage jobs— custodial work in city buildings, employment with departments of sanitation, street repair jobs—were becoming equally undesirable, due to rising levels of income, education, and job security.

An important watershed seems to have been the New Deal, which provided the impetus, at state and local levels as well as the federal level, for increased governmental preoccupation with citizen welfare. The welfare programs of party organizations were undercut by direct and indirect effects of social security, minimum wage legislation, relief programs, and collective bargaining. And, as often has been noted, the parties themselves, by contributing to the social rise of underprivileged groups, helped to develop the values and aspirations which were to make these citizens skeptical of the more blatant manifestations of machine politics.

Varieties of
Contemporary Urban Politics

Nationally, in 1956, the Survey Research Center found that only 10 percent of a cross section of citizens reported being contacted personally by political party workers during that year's presidential campaign. Even if we consider only nonsouthern cities of over 100,000 population, the percentage is still a good bit less than 20.[12] This is a far cry from the situation which would obtain if party organizations were well developed and assiduous. But national statistics conceal a good bit of local variation. A survey of Detroit voters found that only 6 percent of the public remembered having been approached by political party workers; in fact, less than a fifth of those interviewed even knew that there *were* party precinct officials in their district.[13] Reports from a number of other cities—for example, Seattle and Minneapolis—show a similar vacuum in party activity.[14]

In New Haven, Connecticut, in contrast, 60 percent of the voters interviews in a 1959 survey reported having been contacted by party workers.[15] The continuing importance of parties in the politics of this municipality has been documented at length by Robert A. Dahl and his associates.[16] New Haven's Mayor Richard C. Lee was able to obtain support for a massive urban redevelopment program, in spite of the many obstacles in the way of favorable action on such programs elsewhere in large part because of the capacity of an old-style party organization to weld together the government of a city with an extremely "weak" formal charter. Lee commanded a substantial majority on the board of aldermen and, during the crucial period for ratification of the program, was as confident of the votes of Democratic aldermen as a British prime minister is of his parliamentary majority. Lee was far from being a mere creative creature of the party organization which was so helpful to him, but he also was effectively vetoed by the party when he attempted to bring about governmental reforms which would have made the mayor less dependent upon the organization to obtain positive action.[17]

Further evidence of the persistence of old-style party activities came from a number of other studies conducted in the late 1950s. For example, in 1957 party leaders from eight New Jersey counties reported performing a wide range of traditional party services, in response to an ingeniously worded questionnaire administered by Professor Richard T. Forst.[18]

Services Performed by New Jersey Politicians

The Service	Percentage Performing It "Often"
Helping deserving people get public jobs	72
Showing people how to get their social security benefits, welfare, unemployment compensation, etc.	54
Helping citizens who are in difficulty with the law. Do you help get them straightened out?	62

There was even some evidence in the 1950's of a rebirth of old-style urban party activities —for example, in the once Republican-dominated city of Philadelphia, where an effective Democratic old-style organization was put together. Often old-style organizations seem to exist in portions of contemporary cities, especially the low-income sections. These, like the reform groups to be described below, serve as factions in citywide politics.[19]

Why old-style politics persists in some settings but not others is not fully clear. An impressionistic survey of the scattered evidence suggests, as might be expected, that the older pattern continues in those localities which most resemble the situations which originally spawned strong local parties in the nineteenth century. Eastern industrial cities, such as New Haven, Philadelphia, and many of the New Jersey cities, have sizable low-income groups in need of traditional party services. In many of these areas, the legal impediments to party activity also are minimal: Connecticut, for example, was the last state in the union to adopt direct primary legislation, and nonpartisan local election systems are, in general, less common in industrial cities than in cities without much manufacturing activity.[20] Cities in which weak, disorganized parties are reported—like Seattle, Minneapolis, and even Detroit (which, of course, *is* a manufacturing center of some importance)—are quite often cities in which nonpartisan institutions have been adopted.

Some New-Style
Urban Political Patterns

In conclusion, we may note two of the styles of politics which have been reported in contemporary localities where old-style organizations have become weak or non-existent: the politics of nonpartisanship and the new "reform" factions within some urban Democratic parties. Both patterns are of considerable intrinsic interest to students of local government. And, as contrasting political forms, they provide us with further perspective on the strength and weaknesses of old-style urban politics.

THE POLITICS OF NONPARTISANSHIP

The nonpartisan ballot now is in force in 66 percent of American cities over 25,000 in population. Numerous styles of politics seem to take place beneath the facade of nonpartisanship. In some communities, when party labels are eliminated from the ballot, the old parties continue to operate much as they have in the past; in other communities, new local parties spring up to contest the nonpartisan elections. Finally, nonpartisanship often takes the form intended by its founders: no organized groups contest elections; voters choose from a more or less self-selected array of candidates.

In the last of these cases, although nonpartisandship has its intended effect, it also seems to have had—a recent body of literature suggests[21]—a number of unintended side effects. One of these is voter confusion. Without the familiar device of party labels to aid in selecting candidates, voters may find it difficult to select from among the sometimes substantial list of names on the ballot. Under these circumstances, a bonus in votes often goes to candidates with a familiar-sounding name—incumbents are likely to be reelected, for example—or even candidates with a favorable position on the ballot. In addition, campaigning and other personal contacts with voters become less common, because candidates no longer have the financial resources and personnel of a party organization at their disposal and therefore are dependent upon personal financing or backing from interest groups in the community.

Nonpartisan electoral practices, where effective, also seem to increase the influence of the mass media on voters; in the absence of campaigning, party canvassing, and party labels, voters, become highly dependent for information as well as advice on the press, radio, and television. Normally, mass communications have rather limited effects on people's behavior compared with face-to-face communication such as canvassing by party workers.[22] Under nonpartisan circumstances, however, he who controls the press is likely to have much more direct and substantial effect on the public.

Ironically, the "theory" of nonpartisanship argues that by eliminating parties a barrier between citizens and their officials will be removed. In fact, nonpartisanship often attentutates the citizen's connections with the political system.

THE REFORM DEMOCRATS

The doctrine of nonpartisanship is mostly a product of the Progressive era. While nonpartisan local political systems continue to be adopted and, in fact, have become more common in recent decades, most of the impetus for this development results from the desire of communities to adopt city-manager systems. Nonpartisanship simply is part of the package which normally goes along with the popular city-manager system.

A newer phenomenon on the urban political scene is the development, especially since the 1952 presidential campaign, of ideologically motivated grass-roots party organizations within the Democratic party.[23] The ideology in question is liberalism: most of the reform organizations are led and staffed by college-educated intellectuals, many of whom were activated politically by the candidacy of Adlai Stevenson. In a few localities, there also have been grass-roots Republican organizations motivated by ideological considerations: in the Republican case, Goldwater conservatism.

New-style reformers differ in two major

ways from old-style reformers: their ideological concerns extend beyond a preoccupation with governmental efficiency alone (they favor racial integration and improved housing and sometimes devote much of their energy to advocating "liberal" causes at the national level); second, their strategy is to work within and take control of the parties, rather than to reject the legitimacy of parties. They do resemble old-style reformers in their preoccupation with the evils of "bossism" and machine politics.

There also is an important resemblance between the new reform politician and the old-style organization man the reformer seeks to replace. In both cases, very much unlike the situation which seems to be stimulated by nonpartisanship, the politician emphasizes extensive face-to-face contact with voters. Where reformers have been successful, it often has been by beating the boss at his own game of canvassing the election district, registering and keeping track of voters, and getting them to the polls.[24]

But much of the day-to-day style of the traditional urban politician is clearly distasteful to the new reformers: they have generally eschewed the use of patronage and, with the exceptions of campaigns for housing code enforcement, they have avoided the extensive service operations to voters and interest groups which were central to old-style party organizations. For example, when election district captains and other officials of the Greenwich Village Independent Democrats, the reform group which deposed

Services Performed by New York Reform Democrats[25]

The Service	Percentage Performing It "Often"
Helping deserving people get public jobs	0
Showing people how to get their social security benefits, welfare, unemployment compensation, etc.	5
Helping citizens who are in difficulty with the law. Do you help get them straightened out?	6

New York Democrat County Leader Carmine DeSapio in his own election district, were asked the same set of questions about their activities used in the New Jersey study, strikingly different responses were made.

The successes of this class of new-style urban party politician have vindicated a portion of the classical strategy of urban party politics, the extensive reliance upon canvassing and other personal relations, and also have shown that under some circumstances it is possible to organize such activities with virtually no reliance on patronage and other material rewards. The reformers have tapped a pool of political activists used by parties elsewhere in the world—for example, in Great Britain—but not a normal part of the American scene. One might say that the reformers have "discovered" the British Labor constituency parties.

It is where material resources available to the parties are limited—for example, California—and where voter interest in these resources is low, that the new reformers are successful. In practice, however, the latter condition has confined the effectiveness of the reform Democrats largely to the more prosperous sections of cities; neither their style nor their programs seem to be successful in lower-class districts.[26] The areas of reform Democratic strength are generally *not* the areas which contribute greatly to Democratic pluralities in the cities. And, in many cities, the reformers' clientele is progressively diminishing as higher-income citizens move outward to the suburbs. Therefore, though fascinating and illuminating, the new reform movement must at least for the moment be considered as little more than a single manifestation in a panorama of urban political practices.[27]

Conclusion

The degree to which *old-style* urban party organizations will continue to be a part of this panorama is uncertain. Changes in the social composition of the cities promise to be a major factor in the future of urban politics. If, as seems possible, many cities become lower-class, nonwhite enclaves, we can be confident that there will be a continuing market for the services of the service-oriented old-style politician. Whether or not this is the case, many lessons can be culled from the history of party politics during the years of growth of the American cities—lessons which are relevant, for example, to studying the politics of urbanization elsewhere in the world.[28] In the nineteenth century, after all, the United States was an "emerging," "modernizing" nation, facing the problems of stability and democracy which are now being faced by countless newer nations.

Notes

1. E. E. Schattschneider, *Party Government* (New York, 1942), pp. 162–69.
2. Among the better known accounts are Frank R. Kent, *The Great Game of Politics* (Garden City, N.Y., 1923, rev. ed., 1930); Sonya Forthall, *Cogwheels of Democracy* (New York, 1946); Harold F. Gosnell, *Machine Politics* (Chicago, 1937); and the many case studies of individual bosses. For a recent romanticization, see Edwin O'Connor's novel, *The Last Hurrah* (Boston, 1956).
3. Austin Ranney and Willmoore Kendall, *Democracy and the American Party System* (New York, 1956), pp. 249–52.
4. This last definitional criterion explicitly departs from the characterization of a "machine" in James Q. Wilson's interesting discussion of "The Economy of Patronage," *Journal of Political Economy*, 59 (August 1961), 370*n.*, "as that kind of political party which sustains its members through the distribution of material incentives (patronage) rather than nonmaterial incentives (appeals to principle, the fun of the game, sociability, etc.)." There is ample evidence that for many old-style party workers incentives such as "the fun of the game," "sociability," and even "service" are of central importance. See, for example, Edward J. Flynn, *You're the Boss* (New York, 1947), p. 22; James A. Farley, *Behind the Ballots* (New York, 1938), p. 237; and the passage cited in note 8 below. The distinction between "material" and "nonmaterial" incentives would probably have to be discarded in a more refined discussion of the motivations underlying political participation. So-called material rewards, at base, are nonmaterial in the sense that they are valued for the status they confer and for other culturally defined reasons.

5. Farley, *Behind the Ballot*, p. 106.
6. See, for example, Edward A. Shils, *The Torment of Secrecy* (Glencoe, Ill., 1956) and Stanley M. Elkins, *Slavery* (Chicago, 1959, reprinted with an introduction by Nathan Glazer, New York, 1963).
7. William L. Riordon, *Plunkitt of Tammany Hall* (originally published in 1905; republished New York, 1948, and New York, 1963; quotations are from the 1963 edition), pp. 27–8.
8. *Ibid.*, pp. 25–26.
9. Elmer E. Cornwell, Jr., "Party Absorption of Ethnic Groups: The Case of Providence, Rhode Island," *Social Forces*, 38 (March 1960), 205–10.
10. Riordon, *Plunkitt of Tammany Hall*, pp. 17–20.
11. Frank J. Sorauf, "State Patronage in a Rural County," *American Political Science Review*, 50 (December 1956), 1046–56.
12. Angus Campbell, Philip E. Converse, Warren E. Miller, and Donald E. Stokes, *The American Voter* (New York, 1960), pp. 426–27. The statistic for nonsouthern cities was supplied to me by the authors.
13. Daniel Katz and Samuel J. Eldersveld, "The Impact of Local Party Activity on the Electorate," *Public Opinion Quarterly*, 25 (Spring 1961), 16–17.
14. Hugh A. Bone, *Grass Roots Party Leadership* (Seattle, 1952); Robert L. Morlan, "City Politics: Free Style," *National Municipal Review*, 38 (November 1949), 485–91.
15. Robert A. Dahl, *Who Governs?* (New Haven, 1961), p. 278.
16. *Ibid.;* Nelson W. Polsby, *Community Power and Political Theory* (New Haven, 1963); Raymond E. Wolfinger, *The Pylitics of Progress* (forthcoming).
17. Raymond E. Wolfinger, "The Influence of Precinct Work on Voting Behavior," *Public Opinion Quarterly*, 27 (Fall 1963), 387–98.
18. Frost deliberately worded his questionnaire descriptions of these services favorably in order to avoid implying that respondents were to be censured for indulging in "machine tactics." Richard T. Frost, "Stability and Change in Local Politics," *Public Opinion Quarterly*, 25 (Summer 1961), 231–32.
19. James Q. Wilson, "Politics and Reform in American Cities," *American Government Annual, 1962–63* (New York, 1962), pp. 37–52.
20. Phillips Cutright, "Nonpartisan Electoral Systems in American Cities," *Comparative Studies in Society and History*, 5 (January 1963), 219–21.
21. For a brief review of the relevant literature, see Fred I. Greenstein, *The American Party System and the American People* (Englewood Cliffs, N.J., 1963), pp. 57–60.
22. Joseph T. Klapper, *The Effects of Mass Communication* (New York, 1960).

23. James Q. Wilson, *The Amateur Democrat* (Chicago, 1962).

24. There is another interesting point of resemblance between old- and new-style urban party politics. In both, an important aspect of the motivation for participation seems to be the rewards of sociability. Tammany picnics and New York Committee for Democratic Voters (CDV) coffee hours probably differ more in decor than in the functions they serve. An amusing indication of this is provided by the committee structure of the Greenwich Village club of the CDV; in addition to the committees dealing with the club newsletter, with housing, and with community action, there is a social committee and a Flight Committee, the latter being concerned with arranging charter flights to Europe for club members. See Vernon M. Goetcheus, *The Village Independent Democrats: A Study in the Politics of the New Reformers* (unpublished senior distinction thesis, Honors College, Wesleyan University, 1963), pp. 65–66. On similar activities by the California Democratic Clubs, see Robert E. Lane, James D. Barber, and Fred I. Greenstein, *Introduction to Political Analysis* (Englewood Cliffs, N.J., 1962), pp. 55–57.

25. Goetcheus, *op. cit.*, p. 138.

26. DeSapio, for example, was generally able to hold on to his lower-class Italian voting support in Greenwich Village; his opponents succeeded largely by activating the many middle- and upper-class voters who had moved into new high-rent housing in the district.

27. Probably because of their emphasis on ideology, the new reform groups also seem to be quite prone to internal conflicts which impede their effectiveness. One is reminded of Robert Michels' remarks about the intransigence of intellectuals in Europe socialist parties. *Political Parties* (New York, 1962, originally published in 1915), Part 4, chap. 6.

28. On the significance of the American experience with old-style urban politics for the emerging nations, see Wallace S. Sayre and Nelson W. Polsby, "American Political Science and the Study of Urbanization," Committee on Urbanization, Social Science Research Council, mimeo, 1963, pp. 45–48.

Do UNIONS HAVE any influence over the political behavior of their rank-and-file members? Systematic analysis of this question has produced conflicting findings. Unions with limited political power and memberships that feel political action is not an appropriate union function have been reported in some studies.[1] On the other hand, overwhelming support of union political activities by rank-and-file workers in St. Louis and by the auto workers in Detroit has also been reported.[2] Most of these studies have been made within the context of presidential elections; consequently, it is difficult to separate the appeals of the Democratic party from those of the union, since they are generally reinforcing. It is proposed that a more appropriate test of union strength in the electoral process would be within local, nonpartisan elections where it can reasonably be expected that the appeal of partisanship is lessened. Therefore, in this study an effort was made to determine whether a union, the United Auto Workers (UAW), exercised any influence over the political attitudes and electoral behavior of its membership in two local, nonpartisan elections: a primary and a general election.

The setting for the study was the industrial city of Toledo, Ohio. In the primary the UAW endorsed the passage of a fair housing ordinance which was placed on the ballot for voter approval. In the general election the UAW endorsed the incumbent mayor, a Republican, for reelection, as well as five Democrats and two Republicans for seats on the city council. In light of the fact that 60 percent of the UAW members were Democrats and that, at the time of the endorsement, no community in the nation had successfully passed a fair housing ordinance by referendum, the endorsements represented stringent tests of the union's ability to influence the political behavior of its membership.

Methodology

Interviews were held with 314 members of the UAW living in the Toledo Metropolitan

Labor in City Politics: The Case of the Toledo United Auto Workers*

Schley R. Lyons

area during September and October 1967. The interviewers employed a fixed schedule including open-ended, multiple choice, and one-word response items. The procedure utilized in drawing a representative sample of the UAW membership consisted of assigning to everyone on the mailing list of the *Toledo Union Journal* (the UAW's weekly newspaper and its primary communication tool) a number ranging from 1 to 29,389. From this list 525 random numbers were selected.

Following a minimal effort of three callbacks at home and an attempt to secure interviews with the respondents on the job, 76 percent of the potential interviews were completed, 12 percent of the sample refused to participate, and 12 percent were not locatable.[3] Immediately following the general election of November 1967, questionnaires were sent to 264 persons who had been previously interviewed; of these, 129 (49 percent) were returned.[4]

The primary analytical tool utilized in the study was a pro-union political orientation rating. Responses to three sets of questions were combined to yield a score or rating for each individual in the sample. The questions and their scoring were as follows.

Reprinted with permission from the Social Science Quarterly, 49 (March 1969), 816–28.

*The author wishes to express his appreciation to Region 2B of the United Auto Workers and the Urban Studies Research Committee, the University of Toledo, for providing the funds which made this study possible.

			Score
I.	A.	Do you vote for candidates and issues endorsed by the union?	
		Yes (see next question)	
		No	−1
		Don't know	0
	B.	How often do you vote for the candidates and issues endorsed by the union?	
		Always	+3
		Most of the time	+2
		Occasionally	+1
		Hardly ever	0
		Don't know	0
II.	A.	Which one of these would you say was the most important in giving you information and ideas about local politics and local candidates?	
		Selected *Toledo Union Journal*	+1
		Did not select *Journal*	−1
	B.	Which of these on the list would you say you trust the most?	
		Selected *Toledo Union Journal*	+2
		Did not select *Journal*	0
	C.	Which of these do you trust the least?	
		Selected *Toledo Union Journal*	−2
		Did not select *Journal*	0
III.		People have different opinions in regard to the things that unions should be concerned with at the local level. On the whole, what do you think about the following things?	
	A.	Try to get union members elected to city council	
		Should do	+1
		Should not do	−1
	B.	Endorse local councilmen in councilmanic races	
		Should do	+1
		Should not do	−1

The rating of attitudes toward the union in local politics was based upon numerical scores ranging from +8 to −6. These scores were aggregated into categories: high or positive union political orientation (+3 to +8, $N = 106$); intermediate or neutral union political orientation (0 to +2, $N = 117$); and low or anti-union political orientation (−1 to −6, $N = 91$). No special significance should be attached to the number in each category since this was determined by the arbitrary cutting points selected. Those scoring high on the pro-union political rating were the union members most likely to support the union politically. If no relationship exists between a high score on the rating and membership support of union endorsements, the political influence of the union over the rank-and-file workers would be judged to be minimal or nonexistent.

Analysis revealed that high orientation scores were by no means randomly distributed among the rank and file. Negroes scored higher on the rating than Caucasians. Older members of the union, especially those 50 years and over, and those with the longest tenure in the union scored higher than younger members. There was evidence that a members' political loyalty to the union did not erode after retirement, since the retirees as a group scored higher on the rating than active members. Union members with less than a high school education scored higher than those with more education, and rank-and-file workers identifying themselves as Democrats scored higher than those identifying themselves as Republicans or as independents (see Table 1).

In order to evaluate the discriminating ability of the rating, respondents were asked whether they would be willing to follow the advice and recommendations of the union within the following legislative areas: medicare, water pollution control, workman's compensation, minimum wages, control of

TABLE 1. *Association between Pro-Union Political Orientation Rating of UAW Members and Selected Characteristics*

SELECTED CHARACTERISTICS	PRO-UNION POLITICAL ORIENTATION RATING			N
	High	Intermediate	Low	
Race	(%)	(%)	(%)	
Caucasian	31	39	30	283
Negro	58	22	19	31
				314
	$X^2 = 9.10$; $p < .02$			
Age	(%)	(%)	(%)	
50 years or over	47	30	22	134
40–49 years	35	45	20	80
30–39 years	12	55	32	49
29 years or under	18	25	57	51
				314
	$X^2 = 44.76$; $p < .001$			
Length of Time in Union	(%)	(%)	(%)	(%)
25 years or more	49	32	19	84
16–25 years	38	36	26	94
6–15 years	25	37	37	59
5 years or less	12	44	44	52
				289
	$X^2 = 24.96$; $p < .001$			
Union Status	(%)	(%)	(%)	
Active	30	40	30	266
Retired	52	23	25	48
				314
	$X^2 = 9.07$; $p < .02$			
Education	(%)	(%)	(%)	
13 years or more	21	45	34	29
12 years	30	30	39	102
8 to 11 years	33	42	26	141
7 years or less	54	34	12	41
				313
	$X^2 = 17.86$; $p < .01$			
Partisanship	(%)	(%)	(%)	
Democrat	46	35	20	189
Republican	18	43	39	28
Independent	14	42	44	77
				294
	$X^2 = 32.07$; $p < .001$			

crime in the streets, aid to education, open housing regulation, and repeal of Section 14B of the Taft-Hartley Act. The association between a high score on the rating and a stated willingness of the UAW members to follow the recommendations of the union was statistically significant in each case. Uniformly, a majority of those scoring low on the rating indicated an unwillingness to follow union recommendations. With the single exception of open housing, the associations remained statistically significant after controls were introduced for race and partisanship. The significant association between a high score on the rating and willingness to follow the union's preference in the open housing issue was due primarily to respondents who identified with the Democratic party; among Republicans and independents in this particular issue, the rating was not a discriminating device, Age was the variable which most clearly distinguished union members who claimed to follow the political recommendations of the union from those who did not.

Union Political Activities and Membership Support

It is obvious that rewards accruing to the membership on the political front have a lower visibility than do products of collective bargaining—increased wages, improved working conditions, and enhanced fringe benefits. Correspondingly, UAW workers in Toledo overwhelmingly supported union activities which were directly job-oriented, with the exception of working for a guaranteed annual income, one of the major new goals of the UAW leadership. In the broader social and political fields union goals were supported by a smaller segment of the workers. Nevertheless, the most significant finding was not that the proportion of the membership supporting noneconomic activities declined, but that approximately two of every three workers supported such activities (see Table 2).

Workers who scored high on the pro-union political orientation rating supported union involvement in non-job centered activities more frequently than did those with intermediate or low scores. There was also an association between a high score on the rating and support of a guaranteed annual wage (see Table 3).

After controls were introduced for race and partisanship, two of the relationships were altered. Although the age variable seemed to account for most of the differing attitudes toward union involvement in non-job-centered activities, in the area of social and recreational activities partisanship was also an important consideration, since among Republicans and independents the rating was not a discriminating device. Likewise in the guaranteed-annual-wage issue, identification with the Democratic party, as well as age, was an important factor in distinguishing those who supported the proposal from those who did not.

TABLE 2. Percentage of Rank-and-File Support for Selected Union Activities

Selected Activities	Membership Support
	(%)
Work for better health, pension, and insurance benefits	95
Work for better conditions in the shop	94
Try to get higher wages for workers	91
Work for a guaranteed annual wage	57
Try to get more money made available to schools	77
Try to improve housing opportunities for all people	76
Endorse candidates in local councilmanic elections	70
Endorse candidates for any kind of political office	68
Try to get union members elected to city council	56
N=	(314)

TABLE 3. *Association between Pro-Union Political Orientation Rating and Support of Selected Union Activities*

| SELECTED ACTIVITIES | PRO-UNION POLITICAL ORIENTATION RATING | | | N |
	High	Intermediate	Low	
Improve Social and Recreational Activities	(%)	(%)	(%)	
Should do	38	38	24	212
Should not do	24	38	38	95
				307
	$X^2 = 8.22$; $p < .02$			
Endorse Candidates for Any Kind of Political Office	(%)	(%)	(%)	(%)
Should do	44	46	10	214
Should not do	12	13	74	88
				302
	$X^2 = 122.92$; $p < .001$			
Improve Housing Opportunities for All People	(%)	(%)	(%)	
Should do	39	37	24	239
Should not do	16	32	52	64
	$X^2 = 22.91$; $p < .001$			303
Work for Increased Financial Aid to Schools	(%)	(%)	(%)	
Should do	39	37	24	243
Should not do	14	39	47	67
				310
	$X^2 = 19.63$; $p < .001$			
Work for a Guaranteed Annual Wage	(%)	(%)	(%)	
Should do	39	41	20	180
Should not do	26	23	42	120
				300
	$X^2 = 17.88$; $p < .001$			

The Union and the Transmission of Political Information

Among the UAW members the daily newspaper and local television were considered more important sources of local political information than the *Toledo Union Journal* (a weekly newspaper). However, the union newspaper was rated more important as a political informational source than radio, magazines, speeches, personal talks, leaflets, and things sent in the mail. Of all the communication media, the workers trusted the union newspaper the most; 32 percent of the sample trusted the union newspaper, 25 percent trusted local television, and 21 percent trusted the daily newspaper.

Age was the only characteristic which was significantly associated with the union newspaper being considered the most important source of political information. Workers 50 years of age and over relied on the union newspaper for political information more than those who were younger (see Table 4). Several characteristics were significantly associated with trust of the union news-

TABLE 4. *Association between Age of UAW Members and Dependence on* Toledo Union Journal *for Information about Local Politics*

	Considered Union Journal *Important*	Did Not Consider Union Journal Important	N
Age	(%)	(%)	
50 years or over	40	60	132
40–49 years	28	72	80
30–39 years	16	84	49
29 years or under	14	86	50
			311

$$X^2 = 17.36; p < .001$$

paper. Men trusted the union newspaper more than women, union members over 40 years of age trusted the newspaper more than younger members, and those who identified themselves as Democrats trusted the newspaper more than those who identified themselves as Republicans or as independents (see Table 5).

Although the weekly union newspaper competed surprisingly well against the daily newspapers and television in terms of its importance to, and trust by, the rank and file, did it transmit political messages effectively to the workers? Since the union newspaper was the primary communication link between the leadership and the rank and file, one indicator of effectiveness would be the level of comprehension demonstrated by the rank and file in regard to the union's political activity and endorsement policies.

Sixty-nine percent of the respondents knew that the UAW endorsed candidates

TABLE 5. *Association between Selected Characteristics of UAW Members and Trust of the* Toledo Union Journal

Selected Characteristics	Those Who Trusted Union Newspaper Most	Those Who Did Not Trust Union Newspaper Most	N
Sex	(%)	(%)	(%)
Male	28	62	229
Female	23	77	56
			285

$$X^2 = 4.08; p < .05$$

Age	(%)	(%)	
50 years or over	44	56	113
40–49 years	35	65	75
30–39 years	23	77	48
29 years or under	24	76	49
			285

$$X^2 = 9.73; p < .05$$

Partisanship	(%)	(%)	
Democrat	44	56	177
Republican	16	84	25
Independent	21	79	67
			269

$$X^2 = 15.37; p < .001$$

for local political office. The lack of knowledge about this aspect of the union's activities was associated with age and the length of time the respondents had been members of the union. Forty-seven percent of the union members under 30 years of age did not know the union endorsed candidates for local political office, and 48 percent of those who had been members of the UAW for less than five years were unaware of this political activity. There was a significant association between a high score on the pro-union political orientation rating and knowledge-ability of the union's practice of endorsing candidates for local political office. However, this association disappeared among the Republicans and independents when partisanship was controlled. The significant association between a high score on the rating and knowledgeability of union endorsement practices was due primarily to Democratic respondents (see Table 6).

In response to the question, "Do you know the candidates whom your union has endorsed for city council?" 17 percent of the sample answered in the affirmative. The only pattern that emerged from the variables investigated was that men (20 percent) claimed to be more knowledgeable about the primary endorsement than did the female members of the union (8 percent). When the subsample that answered affirmatively to the first question was handed a card listing the

names of twelve primary candidates and was asked to point out those candidates endorsed by the union, only fifteen male respondents were able to select correctly as many as four out of seven candidates.

In a subsequent question about the fair housing ordinance—which was placed on the primary ballot for voter approval or rejection and which had received extensive coverage in the union and daily newspapers and over TV and radio (fifteen separate articles on fair housing appeared in the *Toledo Union Journal*)—96 percent of the sample had either heard or read about it. However, only 44 percent of the sample knew that the union was on record as favoring approval of the ordinance. Sex again was the only characteristic that demonstrated some variance when compared to knowledgeability of union activity. Forty-nine percent of the men knew that the union had taken a position on the issue while only 27 percent of the women did so.

Impact of UAW Political Endorsements on the Rank and File

Forty-five percent of them stated they voted for candidates and issues endorsed by the union; 22 percent claimed to vote for union endorsements either always or most of the time. Of all the variables investigated, age

TABLE 6. *Association between Pro-Union Political Orientation Rating of UAW Members and Knowledgeability of Union's Endorsement Practices and Support for the Fair Housing Ordinance*

| | PRO-UNION POLITICAL ORIENTATION RATING | | | |
	High	Intermediate	Low	N
Knowledgeable	(%) 40	(%) 36	(%) 24	218
Not knowledgeable	20	39	41	95
				313
		$X^2 = 14.66$; $p < .001$		
For fair housing	(%) 50	(%) 27	(%) 23	60
Against fair housing	25	36	39	88
				148
		$X^2 = 9.95$; $p < .01$		

and length of time in the union were clearly the best indicators of a willingness to follow union endorsements. Among those workers 40 years of age and over, 52 percent stated that they voted for issues and candidates endorsed by the union, while only 30 percent of those under 40 years of age did so. Among those with 25 or more years of membership in the union, 60 percent claimed they voted union endorsements, while only 25 percent of the workers with less than five years of membership in the union did so.[5]

Among the workers who were knowledgeable about the union's endorsement practice but who stated they did not vote its endorsements, one out of two felt voting was a private affair and beyond the scope of the union's proper concern and one out of three expressed opposition to the political policies supported by the union. However, this latter group represented only 7 percent of the sample.

Latent support among the rank-and-file membership for the political goals of the union is one step removed from the acid test of actually delivering the votes in elections. Did those union members who indicated a willingness to vote union endorsements, who trusted the political messages transmitted by the union newspaper, and who supported union involvement in local political affairs actually support the positions endorsed by the UAW in the primary and general elections in significantly greater numbers than those in the membership with lesser union identification? In the primary 29 percent of the sample favored the passage of the fair housing ordinance while 43 opposed it and 27 percent were undecided. There was a significant association between a pro-fair-housing position and a high pro-union political orientation rating. One of every two workers who supported the passage of fair housing scored high on the orientation rating even though only one of every three in the sample were included in that category (see Table 6). However, once race was controlled the significant association between a pro-fair-housing position and a high orientation rating disappeared for Caucasian members. No Negro in the sample opposed

the passage of the fair housing ordinance.

In the general election 22 percent of the sample voted for the union-endorsed incumbent Republican mayor, 42 percent voted for the Democratic challenger, and 36 percent did not vote.[6] Since a high score on the political orientation rating reflected a stated willingness to vote union endorsements, it is notable that those union members scoring high on the rating did not vote for the union-endorsed candidate in greater numbers than did those scoring low. In addition, the rating was not an aid in distinguishing voters from nonvoters. Partisanship was the most discriminating variable since 76 percent of the Democrats voted for the Democratic candidate for mayor and 77 percent of the Republicans voted for their party's nominee. In the race for city council, 61 percent of the sample voted for at least four of the seven candidates endorsed by the union; workers with high, intermediate, and low scores on the rating voted for approximately the same percentages of endorsed candidates: 64, 60, and 59 percent respectively. None of the respondents voted for all seven endorsed candidates.

Summary and Conclusions

This study of the attitudes and political behavior of rank-and-file members of one union within the context of two local nonpartisan elections suggest the following:

1. The political power of the union rested primarily on the support provided by its older members, 50 years of age and over, both active and retired. Partisanship appeared to be a second important variable in several of the relationships studied, but for the most part those workers who lived through the Depression and who could remember firsthand the union's struggle for recognition were those most likely to support the union politically. The influx of younger people into the union seriously threatens its future political viability.[7]

2. Although roughly one of every two union members claimed to vote at least occasionally for union-endorsed candidates,

in the two elections studied, 29 percent supported the passage of the fair housing ordinance and 22 percent voted for the union-endorsed mayoralty candidate. The significant association between a high score on the political orientation rating and support of fair housing was due to Negroes almost unanimous support of fair housing, an issue in which they obviously had a direct stake. After race was controlled, the statistically significant association disappeared among Caucasian respondents. There was no association between a high score on the rating and membership support of union-endorsed candidates in the mayoralty and councilmanic races. The union endorsements had no more impact on those who scored high on the rating than on those who scored low. The union was unable to "deliver," through the mechanism of an endorsement, the votes of those who were most likely to support it politically. Among the workers in the two local nonpartisan elections, the most salient factor in the voting decisions appeared to be party identification, not union identification.

3. Approximately one in three workers stated the union newspaper was the most important source of information about local politics and the medium they trusted most. Awareness of UAW political activity, however, was limited. One in three did not know that the union endorsed candidates for local political office; fewer than one out of two knew the union took a public position on fair housing; and only one in twenty could name as many as four of seven candidates endorsed by the union for city council in the primary. Union involvement in local politics was remote and unimportant to most of the rank-and-file workers.

4. The union membership approved of the union speaking out on local political issues and candidates. Even though fewer than one of every three supported the passage of the fair housing ordinance, 56 percent approved of the union taking a position on the ordinance and only 25 percent disapproved. Fewer than one in four supported the candidate endorsed for mayor but two of three approved of the practice of endorsing candidates. Political activity on the part of the union was unlikely to create disunity in the membership and threaten union solidarity on "bread and butter" issues.

The findings in this study support the proposition that unions in local nonpartisan elections have limited political power at the polls. The value of the union endorsement was minimal unless it reinforced the workers existing predispositions. A high rate of rank-and-file followership in an election is more likely to be an attribute of the leadership "reading" its membership correctly, rather than leading it. Nevertheless, among the membership widespread approval was expressed for the union being involved in politics. A majority of workers recognized the "right" of the union leadership to make political endorsements but they felt no particular obligation to support these endorsements at the polls.

Notes

1. For example, see Ruth Alice Hudson and Hjalmar Rosen, "Union Political Action: The Union Member Speaks," *Industrial and Labor Relations Review*, 7 (April 1954), 418; Joel Seidman, Jack London, Bernard Karsh, and Daisy Tagliacozzo, *The Worker Views His Union* (Chicago: University of Chicago Press, 1958), p. 264; Richard Norman Baisden, "Labor Unions in Los Angeles Politics" (unpublished Ph.D. dissertation, University of Chicago, 1958), p. 464. Samuel J. Eldersveld, in a study of Wayne County, Michigan, suggested that efforts by the union leadership to mobilize the labor vote could alienate rank-and-file members in some circumstances and might be dysfunctional. (See his *Political Parties: A Behavioral Analysis* [Chicago: Rand McNally, 1964], pp. 503–512.) For a study of a probably unique stituation in which a peculiar racial cleavage in the local union limited the ruling minority to Negroes, see J. David Greenstone, "Political Norms and Group Process in Private Government: The Case of a Local Union," *Midwest Journal of Political Science*, 9 (November 1965), 339–60.

2. Arnold M. Rose, *Union Solidarity* (Minneapolis: University of Minnesota Press, 1952), p. 100; Arthur Kornhauser, Harnold Sheppard, and Albert Mayer, *When Labor Votes* (New York: University Books, 1956), p. 262; and Harold Sheppard and Nicholas Masters, "The Political Attitudes and Preferences of Union Members: The Case of the Detroit Auto

Workers," *American Political Science Review*, 53 (June 1959), 443.

3. Of the initial 525 names in the sample, 110 were not potential interviewees due to the following factors: 32 persons were on the mailing list but were not union members; 34 persons had moved from the Toledo area; 5 were ill or in the hospital; 23 were laid off or fired; 7 were deceased; 3 were in the military service; and 6 had language or hearing difficulties. Of the 415 potential interviews, 314 were completed. Fifty persons were not located and 51 persons refused to be interviewed. It was possible to collect some data on 48 of the 51 persons who refused to participate in the survey from their employment personnel folders. On the bases of the data available, it was felt the nonresponse was not likely to bias the sample:

Selected Characteristics of Respondents and Nonrespondents by Percentages

	Respondents N = 314	Nonrespondents N = 48
Males	79	75
Caucasians	90	98
Resident of city	84	90
Married	80	80
Age		
50 or over	43	48
40–49	25	24
30–39	16	13
29 or under	16	15
Education		
13 years or more	9	0
12 years	32	41
8 to 11 years	45	49
7 years or less	13	10
Skill of occupation		
Skilled	21	13
Semiskilled	57	47
Unskilled	6	21
Retired	15	19

4. The original sample included 50 UAW members who lived in the suburban areas surrounding the city of Toledo. Since they could not participate in the city's general election, they were dropped from the sample.

5. Age and length of time in the union were so highly intercorrelated that it was not possible to determine independent effect. On the 214 respondents over 40 years of age, only 7 had been members of the union less than 5 years while only 10 of 100 respondents under 40 years of age had been in the union as long as 15 years.

6. The analysis of the general election is based upon a sample of 129 respondents who returned mail-back questionnaires. There is evidence that the study of relationships rather than the estimation of population parameters is less affected by nonresponse bias in survey research. Mail-back bias appears to be a broad, fairly uniform factor that cuts across socioeconomic and other research variables and may not disturb relationships among the variables being investigated. See Edward A. Suchman, "An Analysis of 'Bias' in Survey Research," *Public Opinion Quarterly*, 16 (Spring 1962), 108; and Schley R. Lyons, "Mailed Questionnaires as an Adjunct to the Interview: A Methodological Note," *Social Science*, 43 (October 1968), 234–35.

7. The lack of identification with the union on the part of the younger members does not appear to the unique with the UAW in Toledo. The professional pollster John Kraft, in a study of twelve international unions in which 1,700 union members were interviewed, found unions in general were experiencing difficulty in communicating with their younger members. For a discussion of the Kraft Report see Alexander E. Barkan, "The Union Member: Profile and Attitudes," *The American Federationist*, 74 (August, 1967), 1–6.

4. The Urban Electoral System

Electoral Competition and Electoral Systems in Large Cities

Charles E. Gilbert
and Christopher Clague

IT IS OFTEN ALLEGED that neither electoral competition nor voter choice is effective in an urban environment, and that "while the machines' influence has waned, they are still the major political force in most urban communities."[1] So far as *local* elections in large cities are concerned, however, we have almost no systematic or comparative information—nothing to compare with our data on national and state elections and political structures. This paper results from an attempt to assemble and analyze election returns and related data from several large cities. A general description of the political systems of these cities is contained in Section 1, and the analysis that follows is limited to the influence of electoral systems on electoral competition.

The basic data for the study are election returns over the post-war period for mayor and seats in city councils in twenty-four of our largest cities. The election series were compiled from both newspapers and official sources, but primarily from newspapers. For most cities the series begin with the year 1945 or the closest election thereto. The cities include all those over 500,000 in population by the 1950 census (with the exception of Washington), plus seven other cities of 300,000 or more.[2] These cities are located in all sections of the country and comprehend a wide variety of electoral systems, governmental institutions, demographic character-

Reprinted with permission from Journal of Politics, 24 (*May 1962*), 323–49.

istics, and patterns of political organization. The selection of cities studied here should not be taken as a sample. Our information and, in most cases, our inferences are confined to these cities alone.

I

There is great variation in the political structures of our major cities; but there are also some recurring broad patterns. Political "competition" thus occurs in differing forms as well as in different degree in our several cities; and *electoral* competition is influenced by the variant political structures. Here we essay an introductory outline of these broad types of political structure. Our purpose is twofold: to place the election data and electoral systems in context, and to try to identify the major factors determining context. Thus the outline that follows is not derived from the electoral data themselves; it stems from a systematic perusal of newspapers and from the limited monographic and periodical literature.[3]

1. One type is that of the dominant (usually Democratic) organization which is relatively cohesive, strongly controlled, and secure. Examples are Chicago and Pittsburgh. Cohesion, control, and security are always relative, but these two cities certainly score high today. So does Philadelphia despite the distinguishing characteristic discussed just below.[4]

2. A second type differs from the first but marginally, so some say; others find the difference crucial. This type also "enjoys" Democratic party dominance, but with the difference that a "good government," anti-organization, and programmatic element holds some offices of at least substantial influence. The pattern is thus partly one of uneasy alliance between two new traditional sets of urban political forces: those underlying the "organization," and those based in the interests and ideologies of reform. Probably the position of the anti-organization element depends in large part on the "enlightenment" and support of downtown businessmen. There is something of a

political division of labor in which certain citywide aspects of policy are left to the executive (for the division is typically a governmental division also), while local benefits and political patronage are primarily left to the political professionals and the council. The two groups sometimes contest primaries, but there are incentives to co-operation in general elections and in most phases of the conduct of government. In these several respects Philadelphia and St. Louis are similar, though St. Louis's Democratic organization is much weaker and less centralized.[5] Perhaps New York City (which is, on the whole, *sui generis*) can be said to be moving in this direction, and a number of cities conform to the pattern in a more fragmentary fashion.

3. A third type is the partisan (effectively one-party) city with two or more enduring factions (plus, perhaps, some more ephemeral and peripheral factions). Baltimore is the best example, and New Orleans could be placed in this class.[6] A more-or-less one-party state politics, state political factions, the habit and statewide incidence of primary competition, or such electoral requirements as runoff primaries or multimember districts may help explain this structure; but this study can offer no evidence on these points.

4. A fourth type differs significantly from the third. Here, the dominant (Democratic) party is weakened or divided, not by enduring factions, but by shifting coalitions based on ward organizations which are often weak themselves, or by relatively weak control of city-wide primaries because ethnic blocs or other interest groups rival the influence of party organization. Democratic parties in Buffalo and Cleveland share the latter infirmity, which is probably augmented in Cleveland by nonpartisan primary elections.[7] Cities in this category may be more subject to occasional two-party competition than any of the preceding types.

5. Some cities are characterized by organized and enduring competition between a *local* party (or "association") and one of the two national parties. Cincinnati and Kansas City (both formally nonpartisan) are the two chief examples—though the 1957 defeat of

"PR" in Cincinnati may have altered this pattern, and the 1959 "organization" victory in Kansas City has certainly changed the competitive balance. In Kansas City, Republicans have been active in the Citizens' Association and in Cincinnati the Democrats were locally merged in the Charter "party" until the defeat of PR. In each city the local party has been called a cover for opposing partisans by "regulars" of the dominant national party; but the charge is not wholly accurate in either city and seems least well founded in Cincinnati. Up to 1957 this political structure gave rise to sharp and regular competition in Cincinnati, while in Kansas City party alternation in power has been secular rather than regular. One reason for this may be the chronic factionalism in Kansas City's Democratic organization.[8]

6. A sixth type is that of the more-or-less party-competitive city. Interestingly enough, no city in our selection clearly falls into this category over the entire period, although two cities belonged to it for several years. One—Buffalo—was closely contested over most of the period, but now seems dominantly Democratic due in part to demographic movements and the redrawing of council district lines by the Democratic majority. The other—Indianapolis—has been moving more slowly toward Democratic predominance; but its electoral system, together with the state political environment, probably help to keep it in the competitive category.[9] Neither city is subject to strong organization "control," as distinguished from electoral dominance; and party factionalism and nationality politics in Buffalo especially tend to undermine Democratic control.

7. A final partisan category comprises two cities in one-party regions which are formally partisan but informally nonpartisan. Houston and Memphis are the two cities.[10] These cities have in common their location in one-party areas and the repressive effects of race on political competition. There are no permanent factions today—at least not formally organized or publicly advertised; though personal factions form on occasion, and one or more "slates" appear in about half of Houston's elections.[11] Presumably

TABLE 1. *Party Division of City Governments*

City	Election Year	Council	Mayor
Baltimore	1943	20–0 D	R
	1947	20–0 D	D
	1951	20–0 D	D
	1955	20–0 D	D
	1959	20–0 D	D
Buffalo	1945	11–4 R	R
	1947	8–7 R	
	1949	8–7 R	R
	1951	9–6 D	
	1953	9–6 D	D
	1955	11–4 D	
	1959	13–2 D	D
Chicago	1943	39–9 D	D
	1947	32–17 D	D
	1951	33–16 D	D
	1955	38–11 D	D
	1959	46–3 D	D
Kansas City†	1944	8–1 Reform	R
	1946	7–2 R	R
	1948	7–2 R	R
	1951	7–1 R†	R
	1955	8–1 R	R
	1959	5–3 R†	R
New Orleans‡	1942	4–0 RDO	RDO
	1946	3–1 CCDA	CCDA
	1950	6–1 CCDA	CCDA
	1954	5–2 CCDA	CCDA
	1958	6–1 CCDA	CCDA
Philadelphia	1943	20–2 R	R
	1947	22–0 R	R
	1951	14–3 D	D
	1955	14–3 D	D
	1959	15–2 D	D
Pittsburgh	1945	9–0 D	D
	1947	9–0 D	D

City	Year	Council	Party
Cincinnati*	1945	5–4	R
	1947	5–4	R
	1949	5–4	R
	1951	5–4	R
	1953	5–4	C
	1955	5–4	C
	1957	5–4	R
	1959	5–2–2	R–C–D
Cleveland	1945	19–14	D
	1947	10–12	D
	1949	22–10	D
	1951	21–11	D
	1953	20–13	D
	1955	22–11	D
	1957	22–11	D
	1959	25–8	D
Indianapolis	1947	6–3	D
	1951	6–3	R
	1955	6–3	D
	1959	6–3	D

City	Year	Council	Party	
Kansas City†	1949	9–0	D	D
	1951	9–0	D	D
	1953	9–0	D	D
	1955	9–0	D	D
	1957	9–0	D	D
	1959	9–0	D	D
St. Louis	1945	23–6	R	R
	1947	20–8	R	R
	1949	15–15	D	D
	1951	17–12	D	D
	1953	20–9	D	D
	1955	25–4	D	D
	1957	25–4	D	D
	1959	25–4	D	D

*In Cincinnati, R is Republican party; C is Charter party; D is Democratic party.

†In Kansas City, R is Reform (later called Citizens' Association) and D is the Democratic organization itself, an alliance of factions. In 1951 one councilman was both R and D; and in 1959 three councilmen were both R and D (thus these two years could be listed as 8–1 and 0–8).

‡In New Orleans, RDO is "Regular Democratic Organization," and CCDA is "Crescent City Democratic Association" (the Morrison faction).

the bifactionalism of Louisiana politics has helped to exempt New Orleans from this category.

These, then, are the principal partisan types. Interparty competition appears to have declined in several cities during the postwar period and has not increased in any. Several cities that were closely contested in the 1930s—either regularly or occasionally—have become dominantly Democratic.[12] As Table 1 shows, all of the cities that have undergone changes in party control of government during the period have gone Democratic. In addition, two less regularly partisan cities underwent a basic shift in the balance of political power: New Orleans in 1946, and Kansas City in 1959. Finally the demise of PR in Cincinnati had at least the temporary effect of reactivating the Democratic party locally, diminishing the Charter vote, and thus enhancing the Republican control of council.

As the outline indicates, however, electoral "dominance" is not the same thing as organization "control," and control in the wards or districts does not always mean citywide control. These differences show up in primary elections, which are in general more closely contested in cities of types 3 and 4 than of types 1 and 2. Moreover, many city councils exhibit frequent factionalism and/or personal independence, except for cities of types 1 and 2. Mayors and councils (or important factions in councils) are often at odds, except in cities of type 1 and the (formally nonpartisan) cities of type 5.[13] City parties and factions often fail as solvents of the separation of powers or crystallizers of legislative purpose in both partisan and nonpartisan cities.

8. Thirteen of our cities employ nonpartisan elections. As some formally partisan cities are nonpartisan in fact, so some formally nonpartisan cities are *de facto* partisan in varying degrees. The starting points in an analysis of nonpartisanship must be the writings of Charles Adrian. His typology of nonpartisan elections covers most of our cities, and readers are referred to it for a more detailed treatment.[14] A number of our cities, as distinguished from those already

mentioned, are quite effectively nonpartisan.

Readers may feel that a total of eight types for twenty-four cities is neither heroic nor heuristic; but we hope that the outline will meet the twofold purpose set out above. It should indicate that the organization of electoral competition differs among our major cities, and that it varies in importance *vis-à-vis* primary elections and other intraorganization contests, intragovernmental rivalry, and nonpartisan competition among interests that is not always reflected in elections.

The outline should also suggest some factors influencing the role and degree of electoral competition in large cities. Four principal types of influence can be provisionally identified. One is that of electoral behavior relating to larger jurisdictions, principally state and national and especially national. A second conglomerate influence is that of the interests involved in city politics —demographic groupings, economic interests, and ideologies. Organizational traditions and allegiances affecting party cohesion make a third factor. A fourth is that of local government institutions and, in particular, electoral systems. While this characterization of influences (especially the second) is a broad one, it probably contains the more universal of the factors which, in the outline above, effects electoral competition and thus, with less tangible local traditions, interact within the cities and determine their "type."[15] In what follows we attempt to relate electoral systems to electoral competition.

II

The influence of electoral systems on electoral competition is difficult to analyze because of both the prevailing variety of city electoral systems and the lack of agreement about how to define "competition." There is a wide variety of electoral arrangements in use in American cities: partisan and nonpartisan; single-member districts, multimember districts, and at-large elections; majority or mere plurality requirements; and the occasional waiving of general elections if a candidate obtains a majority in the primary. These methods are used in various combinations.[16] Two differences are most basic, however, and make possible some comparative analysis. These are the (often overlapping) differences between partisan and nonpartisan elections and, respecting city councils, between district and at-large election. Most of the following analysis has to do with these differences.

The other obstacle to analysis is the practical meaning to be given to *competition*. In partisan politics, competition has been understood in any or all of several senses: closeness of elections, frequency of turnover, and/or division of governmental offices. Under comparable conditions these may all be dealt with in one graphic index.[17] In this study, any effort to identify comparable conditions and arrive at a common index is defeated by the very variety of electoral arrangements being studied. However, Section 1 and Table 1 have indicated that few partisan cities score high on frequency of party turnover, and that divided party control of city governments almost never occurs. At the same time we have to contend with the nonpartisan cities—no index of party competition will serve for those that are effectively nonpartisan. Thus two aspects of competition alone seem susceptible of broadly comparative study here. One is the closeness of electoral margins, which is reduced in comparability by the variety of electoral systems; but which is dealt with just below. The other is the influence of incumbency in elections, considered in the following section.

Table 2 contains the basic data for general elections, with the cities grouped by electoral systems. We have tried to present the data in as comparable a form as possible. Computing election margins (percentages) for single-member district cities is a relatively straightforward affair, though it should be noted that not all such cities narrow the field to straight fights in general elections. The percentages for nonpartisan at-large elections, however, are the margins between the lowest of the several winning candidates on the one hand and all other winning candi-

dates plus an equal number of losing candidates on the other hand; that is, each at-large election is treated as a number of (hypothetical) straight fights. The percentages for partisan at-large elections represent the margin between the lowest winner and the highest loser. (In the partisan at-large cities the dispersion of the vote over "slates" is characteristically small; in the nonpartisan at-large cities the differences among winning —and losing—margins are characteristically large.) Some other electoral variations present further obstacles to comparability, and these are noted in Table 2. The number of cities (and, for several cities, the number of elections) is small in each category; but, subject to that limitation some comparisons can be made between partisan and nonpartisan, district and at-large systems.[18]

1. First, overall comparison of categories 1 and 2 indicates that partisan *versus* nonpartisan elections are not in themselves associated with substantially different electoral margins in single member districts; the variation within each category far exceeds the small overall differences between the partisan and nonpartisan groups. Two more tentative observations may be in order, the first of which concerns the variations *within* categories 1 and 2. In the partisan case this cannot be accounted for by minor electoral arrangements—large or small councils, or the ratio of councilmen to constituents—and it thus appears to be associated with other factors in the outline of Section 1.[19] Among the few SMD nonpartisan cities there is a bare suggestion that size of district may be a factor in election margins. Los Angeles, with very large districts, shows the widest margins generally, and Milwaukee is smallest on both counts. Dallas, Denver, and Minneapolis are intermediate but closer to Milwaukee in both respects. In the absence of parties the advantages of incumbents in organization and communication may increase with size of district and difficulty of identifying common dissatisfactions and concerting opposition.[20]

A second suggestion concerns the nonpartisan cities alone. An overall look at Table 2 indicates that the two cities that are

TABLE 2. Electoral Margins for City Council Seats

	50–55%		55.1–60%		>60%		No contest		<>N
	N	%	N	%	N	%	N	%	
I. "Partisan" Els.									
by Districts:									
Baltimore*	3	13.0	5	21.0	16	67.0			24
Buffalo†‡	24	29.6	18	22.2	39	48.0			81
Chicago	47	18.8	26	10.4	135	54.0	42	16.8	250
Cleveland	62	29.2	36	17.0	94	44.5	20	9.4	212
Kansas City†	5	25.0	2	10.0	13	65.0			20
New Orleans	7	41.2	3	17.6	7	41.2			17
Philadelphia	11	23.9	11	24.9	24	52.2			46
St. Louis	27	24.1	22	19.6	63	56.3			112
Totals and grand means	186	24.4	123	16.1	391	51.3	62	8.1	762
II. Nonpartisan Els.									
by Districts:									
Dallas‡	12	20.7	6	10.3	31	53.4	9	15.5	58
Denver‡	11	25.6	9	21.0	23	53.5			43
Los Angeles‡	12	12.2	10	10.2	66	67.3	10	10.2	98
Milwaukee	37	30.8	35	29.2	47	39.2	1	0.8	120
Minneapolis	25	24.0	25	24.0	54	51.9			104
Totals and grand means	97	22.9	85	20.1	221	52.2	20	4.9	423
III. At-large Els.									
Straight Fights:									
Kansas City†	11	55.0	7	35.0	2	10.0			20
Portland§	3	50.0	1	16.7	2	33.3			6

	50–45%		44.9–40%		<40%				
IV. Nonpartisan									
At-Large Els.									
Mixed Fights:									
Boston	16	40.0	13	32.5	11	27.5			40
Detroit	16	33.3	17	35.4	15	31.5			48
Houston†	4	40.0	4	40.0	2	20.0			10
San Francisco	3	8.3	5	13.9	28	77.8			36
Seattle	10	37.0	7	25.9	10	37.0			20
Total and grand means	49	30.4	46	28.6	66	40.1			161
V. Partisan At-large									
Els. Mixed Fights:									
Indianapolis	2	50.0	2	50.0					4
Pittsburgh	2	25.0			6	75.0			8

*Multimember districts or partisan mixed fights. Lowest winner *v.* highest loser.
†City elects or has elected both at-large and by districts.
‡Vote for top two candidates where there is no clear majority; otherwise runoff vote.
§ Most elections won in primary and not shown here. Commission government.

formally nonpartisan but *de facto* more-or-less partisan use district elections.[21] Moreover, the newspaper coverage of campaigns and elections indicates that, of the more-or-less effectively nonpartisan cities, the most patent (if occasional) party involvement in councilmanic campaigns occurred in some—though not all—of the district cities.[22] This *may* indicate that if one wants to enforce nonpartisanship the at-large council increases the likelihood of doing so. It is almost certain that other variables are involved, and it is quite possible for formal or informal factions to enter slates in at-large elections; but, where the "factions" are basically the regular political parties, one might expect their organization to be less offensive and at least equally effective in district rather than at-large election. In any event—the foregoing suggestions apart—our first point is that, given district elections, partisan or non-partisan ballots, *per se* do not appear to affect their closeness.

2. Second, we compare district and at-large elections. It seems sensible to hold constant the partisan-nonpartisan factor. Cities with partisan, at-large ballots are too few and too disparate (types 6 and 1, respectively) to be useful, so the comparison is confined to nonpartisan cities in category 2 *versus* categories 3 and 4. This still leaves two types of at-large elections, which we shall term "straight fights" and "mixed fights" (categories 3 and 4 respectively of Table 2). It appears that in general (with the unexplained exception of San Francisco) margins are closer in at-large than in district cities, assuming that the computational device underlying category 4 is not misleading.[23] However, since the electoral system of category 4 (basically a multimember, citywide district system) is fundamentally different from the systems of categories 2 and 3 (which usually involve straight fights) no method of calculation can make the two systems entirely comparable.

There is another way of contrasting the results of district and at-large elections. That is to see whether electoral margins for district offices and at-large (citywide) offices in the same city tend consistently to differ in one direction or the other. Table 3 presents the findings for cities with district councilmen (and includes cities with at-large councilmen with the relevant margins computed between the lowest winner and the highest loser). It indicates that, in both partisan and nonpartisan cities, the mean electoral margins of district councilmen tend to exceed those of mayors. Cleveland is the single clear exception, and its importance is probably qualified by an electoral idiosyncrasy of that city.[24] For whatever the finding is worth, the differ-

ence in means can probably be regarded as statistically significant; and the difference is especially marked in the partisan cities.[25] By itself the difference in the means is not surprising, since, as will later be seen, the mayor's political position appears less secure than the councilman's for reasons that are broader than electoral systems alone. Similar results are obtained, however, wherever mean district outcomes can be matched against citywide offices other than mayor (e.g., at-large councilmen, or council presidents in some cities). Thus the mean margins for district councilmen exceed those for at-large councilmen in all the cities with mixed councilmanic systems—the partisan cities of Buffalo and Philadelphia, and the well-defined cities of Houston and Kansas City.[26]

Mean electoral margins should be larger for districts than for cities because there is ordinarily less demographic diversity in districts than in cities. In this respect the (partisan) city situation is similar to that of congressional elections contrasted with presidential elections. The relative homogeneity of many districts may permit firmer organization "control" at the local level—that is, more monopolization by a party or candidate of communications and organizational resources.[27] On the other hand, relative homogeneity may entail more organizational or candidate responsiveness to an alert population at the local level. In either case, effective competition is inhibited.

The district system does allow the minority party to hold out in some districts, and it may have slowed the rate of change to Democratic dominance in such cities as Buffalo and St. Louis. But the number of minority party districts has steadily dwindled in all our partisan cities due to prevailing patterns of urban ecology and, on occasion, to gerrymandering.[28] It seems doubtful that the district system in partisan cities substantially assists citywide organization control, despite the possibilities for control at the local level. Factional alignments may occur among ward or district leaders,[29] and the position of Pittsburgh among the type (1) cities shows the possibility of effective citywide organization control in the at-large system.[30] Further

TABLE 3. *Mean Electoral Margins for District Councilmen and Mayors*

City	Council	N	Mayor	N	Difference		Cities With At-Large Councils Lowest Winner v. Highest Loser		
							Council	Mayor	Difference
Baltimore*	65.0	24	61.4	4	3.6	Boston	50.8	58.5	−7.7
Buffalo†	59.8	81	55.9	4	3.9	Detroit	50.2	62.4	−12.2
Chicago§	67.8	209	59.2	5	8.6	Houston	55.0	58.2	−3.1
Cleveland§	62.6	190	64.3	6	−1.7	San Francisco	57.2	58.3	−1.1
Dallas†§	65.5	49	63.0	4	2.5	Seattle	57.2	53.7	−3.5
Denver†	64.0	43	62.2	5	1.8				
Houston†§	60.1	30	58.9	7	1.2	Indianapolis	54.2	55.6	−1.4
Kansas City	65.0	20	58.5	4	6.5	Pittsburgh	60.4	61.1	−0.7
Los Angeles†§	69.5	88	62.4	4	7.1				
Milwaukee§	59.8	119	59.1	5	0.7	Kansas City	57.2	58.5	−1.3
Minneapolis	61.6	104	61.6	8	—	Portland	55.7	56.5	−0.1
New Orleans‡	62.2	14	58.5	4	3.7				
Philadelphia	61.7	30	58.8	5	2.9				
St. Louis	64.6	112	63.2	9	1.4				
Grand Totals and Means	63.4	14	60.4	14	3.0				

*Multimember districts. Lower winner v. highest loser.
†Top two candidates where winner has majority; otherwise runoff election is used.
‡All candidates included where winner has majority; otherwise runoff election is used.
§Uncontested seats are not included. Cf. Table 3.

discussion of our fragmentary findings on closeness of elections may be delayed until they can be contrasted with the data on incumbency.

III

One readily observable aspect of competition that is common to nearly all electoral systems is the role of incumbency—the frequency with which incumbents run for reelection. (I_1), and the frequency with which those running are reelected (I_2).[31] These two ratios, together with the overall survival ratio (I_0), are displayed in Table 4. The ratios refer to primary and general elections combined. It appears that incumbent councilmen run again, and run successfully with great

frequency; though this was probably to be expected.[32]

For mayors the two incumbency ratios are lower. That for mayors seeking reelection (I_1) is 72/98 or .735; that for success when reelection is sought (I_2) is 53/72 or .736. Thus, overall (I_0), incumbent mayors succeed themselves only slightly more than half the time (54%). No city in our selection had the same mayor over the entire fifteen-year period, and most cities had several mayors.[33] One reason for this is voluntary retirement. We do not know why mayors tend voluntarily to retire more frequently than councilmen. Some retirements have evidently been strategic—incumbents saw (or thought they saw) the handwriting on the wall,—in some cases the electoral margins of that incumbent mayor having dwindled over time. The other

TABLE 4. *Incumbency Ratios for City Councilmen (in Descending Order of I_2 Ratio)*

City	I_2	I_1	I_0	No. of Seats	No. of Elections
San Francisco	96.8	94.0	90.9	33	6
Pittsburgh	96.7	90.9	87.9	33	7
Dallas	96.0	44.7	43.0	58	7
Kansas City	93.5	77.5	72.5	40	5
Portland	93.3	88.0	82.4	17	8
Seattle	92.1	95.0	87.5	40	8
Cincinnati	92.0	85.0	75.5	45	5
Detroit	89.2	82.2	73.5	45	5
Boston	87.6	87.3	76.5	102	7
Los Angeles	87.2	88.7	77.3	97	8
Cleveland	85.8	91.0	77.7	264	8
Chicago	84.6	80.0	68.0	250	5
Denver	84.5	71.1	60.0	45	5
Memphis	83.3	75.0	62.5	16	4
Minneapolis	82.0	89.0	73.0	100	8
Philadelphia	81.5	68.4	55.3	95	5
Houston	79.1	67.2	53.1	64	8
Buffalo	77.3	47.8	41.3	46	4
Baltimore	73.4	80.0	58.8	80	4
Milwaukee	72.9	93.0	67.8	115	5
St. Louis	69.8	83.0	58.0	112	8
New Orleans	68.3	86.4	59.1	22	4
Indianapolis	60.3	85.2	44.4	36	4
MEAN	84.0	80.5	67.2	(Mean and median are for cities, not candidates.)	
MEDIAN	84.6	85.0	68.0		

Note:
I_2 = Incumbents reelected/incumbents running.
I_1 = Incumbents running for reelection/all incumbents.
I_0 = Incumbents reelected/all incumbents.

principal reasons for voluntary retirement are probably age (which may affect mayors more than councilmen and proportionately more mayors than councilmen), and attractive political alternatives.[34] There have been a few cases of pressure from the local political organization.

In most of our cities incumbents have been beaten in primaries or generals, and this has happened more than once in the period in several cities. In only a few has it been the case that incumbents won repeatedly *and* that there was no pattern of fairly frequent retirement. Nearly all of our cities have had close and hard-fought mayoralty campaigns from time to time. It seems a safe if not surprising conclusion that mayors are at once more "visible" and more vulnerable than are councilmen. Citizen dissatisfactions accumulate, and certain issues—characteristically crime and corruption—are effectively used against incumbents. Sometimes an incumbent who has enjoyed solid newspaper support loses this backing as issues arise and interests are alienated, and—particularly in nonpartisan cities—this withdrawal of press support (or even opposition) is likely to spell electoral disaster. The administrative difficulties and political dilemmas that confront most mayors are impressive—this is evident in the newspaper reports we have read. Thus the contemporary emphasis on the need to organize city executives for political leadership is understandable.[35] And the contrasts in security of tenure between mayors and a number of councilmen may help to sharpen executive-legislative rivalry in some cities—perhaps especially in the nonpartisan cities.[36]

1. Electoral systems appear to influence incumbency. We find that nonpartisan, and especially at-large, elections tend to increase the security of incumbent councilmen. Looking first at nonpartisanship. it is sometimes suggested that nonpartisan elections add to the advantages of incumbency because familiarity with the candidate's name is about the only cue available to the voter, and because the organizational disadvantages of non-incumbents are increased. It is also argued that nonpartisanship augments the advantages of incumbency by removing organiza-

tional labels, thus facilitating buck-passing and frustrating electoral accountability.[37]

Are nonpartisan elections, then, associated with higher incumbency ratios for councilmen in our cities? Inspection of Table 4 indicates that, among the partisan cities, only in the two strongly "organized" type (1) cities of Chicago and Pittsburgh are the two ratios, I_1 and I_2, as high as those in the effectively nonpartisan cities. In the other partisan cities one or both ratios are lower and especially the I_2 ratio. Also, when the incumbency ratios in the effectively nonpartisan cities combined are compared, for the period as a whole, with the combined ratios of the clearly partisan cities, the differences in proportions are statistically significant at the 5 percent level.[38]

A survey of the data reveals two factors that help account for the more frequent defeat of partisan incumbents. One factor is that of occasional party overturns in such cities as St. Louis (1949) and Philadelphia (1951); the other factor is the occasional defeat of incumbents in primary fights, especially in factional partisan cities. One interesting aspect of the primary defeats is that they sometimes result from either tacit or explicit withdrawal of organization support in situations of demographic change within districts or (in strongly "organized" cities) as a disciplinary measure. It seems doubtful that these factors can account for the more frequent voluntary retirement of partisan incumbents, and we do not know how to account for it.[39]

It appears, then, that partisan incumbents may be more frequently defeated than nonpartisan incumbents for reasons, among others, of inter- or intraparty competition. In general, the more competitive and the factional, type-3 partisan cities stand lowest in Table 4 and the type-1 cities stand high.[40] The defeats of nonpartisan incumbents seem largely to be accounted for by three factors: (1) withdrawal of support or development of opposition by newspapers and/or civic organizations; (2) instances of general dissatisfaction in which one or more at-large councilmen share in a mayor's or an administration's defeat; and (3) instances of sectional dissatisfaction in which district councilmen fail to survive the aftermath of annexations, assessments, or crises in city services. For district councilmen particularly, the issues resulting in defeat are often quite specific.[41]

There are two further evidences that nonpartisanship favors incumbents. One is the fact that—in nonpartisan cities, including such de facto nonpartisan cities as Houston and Memphis—ex-incumbents occasionally run for mayor or council and nearly always run strongly. This phenomenon almost never occurs in partisan cities. A second finding is that, in partisan council elections at-large (as in Indianapolis, Pittsburgh, or Baltimore's multi-member districts) the vote spread between incumbents and nonincumbents of the same party is always very small; while in nonpartisan cities the spread in at-large elections between winning candidates who are incumbents and those who are not is characteristically large.

There is, however, an important qualification or complement to our findings on nonpartisanship. This is that, within the nonpartisan cities, the survival rate of incumbents in cities with at-large councils is much higher than in those with district councilmen, and the difference is clearly significant at the 1 percent level.[42] This would suggest that a sizable portion of the partisan-nonpartisan difference can be accounted for by another electoral variation—district versus at-large elections. The difficulty is that our level of statistical significance diminishes with the number of elections as we complicate the analysis and that the number of cities involved is perhaps uncomfortably small.[43]

Of our two partisan at-large cities, one (Indianapolis) has low incumbency ratios, while the other (Pittsburgh) has high ratios. This suggests that partisanship can work either way in at-large electoral systems, depending on how competitive is the city in question. It seems possible that those nonpartisan cities that employ at-large elections are more effectively nonpartisan in council races than those using the district system—in part, at least, because of at-large elections.[44] This has been claimed for the at-large system for nonpartisan cities;[45] and it would protect incumbents against occasional party inter-

ventions. Finally, and for what it is worth, the case of Boston may be instructive. Boston (nonpartisan) is the only one of our cities to have exchanged one electoral system for another during the period—from twenty-two districts to nine seats at-large in 1951. In three district elections, 1945–59, its I_2 ratio was 82.7, and in the four at-large elections, 1953–59, the ratio was 96.8; and the contrast is heightened by the fact that many of the post-1951 incumbents were new, the old district councilmen having retired with the district system.[46]

There is also some suggestion in the data that small districts make reelection more difficult for incumbents—at least for nonpartisan incumbents. This could be because the area involved is small enough for voters to identify dissatisfactions held in common, to organize for electoral action, and to know or recognize the candidate challenging the incumbent. All three factors, and especially the last, are likely to be absent, relatively speaking, in at-large systems—particularly in at-large elections which (like those in question here) are of the "mixed fight" variety. But the difference would seem, a priori, to be less a matter of candidate "visibility" than of the ability of voters to identify grievances and to mobilize.[47]

To summarize: nonpartisanship, and, especially, at-large elections in nonpartisan cities appear to favor incumbent councilmen. The two influences often work together. Partisan incumbents in our cities were generally less likely to run for reelection than were nonpartisan incumbents. These generalizations are supported, though not strongly, by our tests of statistical significance. Needless to say, such tests do not eliminate other influences on incumbency—either idiosyncratic ones, or a more general political culture related to nonpartisanship and at-large elections and favoring incumbency. They do not "prove" the propositions discussed here; they only indicate that they are tenable, assuming that the theory underlying them is sound.

2. Among mayors, however, incumbents are apparently no more advantaged by nonpartisan than by partisan elections. Statis-

tical tests cannot help us here for the numbers are small and other important variables cannot be removed. Of these, the most important is probably the fact that most of the partisan cities are dominantly Democratic in state and national elections today, while a majority of the nonpartisan cities exhibit a close balance in presidential and other elections.[48]

Nonetheless, the cities in which incumbent mayors were most frequently defeated were invariably nonpartisan cities either formally or *de facto*, and incumbents lost at least once in the postwar period in all the nonpartisan cities but one. Of the nonpartisan cities that were hardest on incumbents not all were cities of close party balance in presidential elections. Party intervention figured in a number of these defeats (e.g., in Los Angeles, Minneapolis, Portland, and Seattle) and such intervention, on an occasional and at least *sub rosa* basis, seems a normal part of nonpartisan elections in most large cities.[49] It probably adds to the insecurity of incumbents in most cases because its public reception and practical effects are uncertain and it is thus used more openly in behalf of challengers. Thus, in nonpartisan cities where the parties are closely balanced in state and national elections, incumbent mayors may be disadvantaged simply because local elections are not as nonpartisan as they are supposed to be. But in several cases of defeat of nonpartisan incumbents no evidence of overt partisanship was reported.

Three nonpartisan cities—Boston, Detroit, and Milwaukee—are dominantly Democratic in state and national elections. In Detroit and Milwaukee incumbent mayors rarely met serious challenge in the postwar period and party intervention was minimal, while in Boston Democratic factionalism was a factor in closely contested elections and the defeat of two incumbents. In Houston, a *de facto* nonpartisan city, incumbents were beaten twice and there were other tight contests.

The only clear cases of defeat of incumbents in partisan cities occurred in primaries rather than in general elections; and in each case the candidate of the dominant Democratic party won the general election. Incumbents in type-1 and type-2 cities always won their elections. On the other hand, voluntary retirement—sometimes in face of mounting public criticism and/or organization pressure—occurred more often in partisan cities, perhaps indicating that party organization provides superior political intelligence.[50]

Looking further back, the history of incumbent mayors in the nineteen-twenties and thirties is mixed. Several of the partisan cities were more closely competitive than they are today and a few partisan incumbents were beaten in party overturns. The nonpartisan cities stood at two extremes. Five of them—Denver, Houston, Milwaukee, Portland, and San Francisco—had mayors of long tenure; but the five cities that were hardest on incumbents (Boston, Detroit, Los Angeles, Minneapolis, and Seattle) were all nonpartisan cities. Prominent among the factors leading to defeats and close calls for nonpartisan incumbents were depression dissatisfactions, charges of corruption, party intervention and factionalism, together with business-labor and inter-labor rivalries and more broadly liberal-conservative conflicts. It appears that, once serious political controversy broke loose, nonpartisan mayors were highly vulnerable; though in some cities nonpartisanship probably helped to depress controversy and forestall the consolidation of opposition.

This experience will not bear a simple interpretation; but we think it strongly suggests without strictly supporting the following propositions: (1) In nonpartisan cities incumbents' prospects improve as elections are more effectively nonpartisan (more generally, as contests are less organized). This applies to both mayors and councilmen. (2) Party intervention in nonpartisan elections is most probable in cities where the party balance is close in state and national elections—perhaps because it is most effective against incumbents under those conditions. (3) In cities where one party is dominant in state and national contests, effectively nonpartisan elections make possible (though not inevitable) closer contests and more frequent defeats of incumbents. Finally, (4) the relation between partisan or nonpartisan elections and incumbency is too complex for generalization. Where party competition is close and regular, incumbents should be insecure under partisan elections; but such competition rarely occurs—largely for reasons of national party alignments, but probably in part because incumbency conveys organizational advantages on the "ins." In nonpartisan elections, too, incumbents are probably favored in the relative absence of serious local controversy and conflict of interests. In some circumstances nonpartisanship appears to help in forestalling controversy, conciliating interests, forging local coalitions across national party lines, and engrossing the major channels of organization and communication. Just as often, however, city management provokes public dissatisfactions and alienates interests; while the absence of national party lines and allegiances can make for unstable coalitions, easy slippage of interests and individuals from support of the incumbent (there is usually a realistic alternative), and relative isolation of the incumbent in controversy without benefit of party organization efforts and popular party loyalties. Thus nonpartisan elections can cut either way for incumbents, and the principal conditioning factor appears to be the pattern of interests in nonpartisan cities.[51]

IV

The comparative study of city politics is highly complex. City electoral systems are not strictly comparable in all respects, and they can rarely be isolated as influences in the broader context of city politics. The overall structure of competition varies widely, and degree of competition cannot be defined or measured by more than a few common attributes.

Presumably, electoral "competition" is valued not primarily for its own sake, but as facilitating governmental accountability and voter choice (or, in combination, "voter sovereignty"). Yet electoral systems commonly affect attributes of governmental performance other than strict "accountability"

and they structure voter choice in different ways. Thus most systems of electoral competition may be said to differ in kind as well as in degree. Of electoral competition *in general* it can probably be said that we seek situations in which voters and challengers think that more than one candidate has a "good" (i.e., supportable) chance of winning, and in which incumbents think their chances of losing are "good" if they fail to conform to voters' tastes.[52] Of the usual scholarly indicators of this state of affairs, only closeness of elections will do in the nonpartisan situation, and we have, therefore, supplemented it by the prevalence of continued incumbency in both partisan and nonpartisan systems. Of the two, incumbency is the more useful, since how close is "close" can vary with local political conditions.[53] Both indicators have a large element of self-fulfilling prophecy in them so far as voter sovereignty is concerned. And an observer might take a series of elections high on incumbency and low on closeness as indicating an impairment of voter sovereignty when it merely reflects voter satisfaction. There seems to be no single or compound indicator of electoral competition equally meaningful for all observers and all electoral systems; but, with their serious limitations, closeness and incumbency seem best for our purposes.

It seems clear that, *ceteris paribus*, electoral systems have some effect on several aspects of competition. It cannot be clearly demonstrated, but there is good reason to believe that PR in Cincinnati favored a highly competitive system under "type 5" conditions and Kansas City's partial use of at-large council seats under similar conditions has been said to foster hard-fought elections but with less frequent factional alternation in control.[54] Baltimore's "type 3" factionalism seems to be favored by large, multimember districts, some of them subject to factional control and some to interfactional competition or coalition. It seems probable that the guarantee of one-third Indianapolis' at-large council seats to the minority party has abetted party competition in that city, and that Buffalo's limitations on incumbency and partial use of at-large elections have had a similar effect. (Yet each of these last-named devices are found in lesser degree in Philadelphia, which is not at all a competitive city.) The problem is that other things are almost never equal. There is thus a host of combined effects to deal with, and some "other things" may overbear the "normal" tendencies of electoral systems.

In general, such factors as prevailing (national) party preferences, the pattern of local interests, and local traditions of political organization appear to outweigh the influence of electoral systems on electoral competition; this even applies on occasion to the important partisan-nonpartisan distinction.[55] But some electoral arrangements are of great importance under certain circumstances, and we have sought to identify the most influential arrangements and circumstances.

Two suggestions from this study may be worth mentioning in conclusion. One is that our findings on nonpartisan elections and incumbency (especially in at-large councils) are consistent with the notion that nonpartisan systems often foster a pluralistic politics of *immobilisme*, that partisanship provides more effective citywide leadership in large cities, and that some response to public pressures in partisan systems occurs within the party organization rather than in government, leaving a little more scope for governmental initiative. But it should be noted, too, that most of the partisan cities have more-or-less secure majorities based in national political alignments; they are less competitive than the nonpartisan cities.

These majorities hold up despite significant differences among partisan cities in degree of organization control as distinguished from electoral dominance. In the cities where they now obtain, formally or de facto, partisan elections and closed primaries probably curtail competition by dividing it between primary and general elections: the turnout in primaries is normally low and the "opposition" is divided in two parties and elections; and normal party preference (largely relevant to national politics) damps competition in general elections.[56] This suggests that, so far as they can be distinguished, party prefer-

ence is at least as important an influence on electoral competition as is party organization; though variations in party organization appear to be of great importance for other characteristics of city government.

Notes

1. Irvin Ross, "Big City Machines and Liberal Voters," *Commentary*, 10 (October 1950), 301–308.
2. See Table 4 below for the full list of cities. The exclusion of Washington needs no explanation. New York City is not included in most series because of its division into boroughs and its peculiar legislative arrangement. New York politics and elections have been much studied— see especially Sayre and Kaufman, *Governing New York City* (New York, Russell Sage Foundation, 1960), on which we have relied for most of our New York data. The availability of newspapers on microfilm and the extent of their electoral coverage largely determined which cities below 500,000 population were included. In the case of almost all elections, we read what election coverage there was over at least a two-week pre-election period. As a rule, with some exceptions, we examined only one newspaper for each city.
3. Besides the regularly published literature, the series of *City Politics Reports* now being compiled and mimeographed by the Joint Institute for Urban Studies of Harvard and M.I.T. under the editorship of Edward C. Banfield provide an excellent introduction to the diversity and possibilities for comparative study in the field of city politics. These reports have been extremely useful to us in this study. They are hereafter cited as *City Politics Reports*, followed by the name of the city covered in the particular report.
4. Chicago elections are formally nonpartisan for council but not for mayor. Of the large literature on Chicago politics, cf. M. Meyerson and E. Banfield, *Politics, Planning, and the Public Interest* (Glencoe, Ill., 1955); and W. R. Gable, *The Chicago City Council: A Study of Urban Politics and Legislation* (1953), and R. G. Geisler, *Chicago Democratic Voting, 1947–57* (1958), both unpublished Ph.D. dissertations, University of Chicago. For Pittsburgh, see F. Hawkins, "Lawrence of Pittsburgh: Boss of the Melon Patch," *Harpers*, July 1956; and for Philadelphia, J. Reichley, *The Art of Government* (New York: Fund for the Republic, 1959).
5. On this pattern in St. Louis, see the St. Louis *Post Dispatch*, editorial of March 8, 1959; R. H. Salisbury, "St. Louis Politics," *Western Political Quarterly*, 13 (1960), 498–507; and *City*

Politics Reports: St. Louis. For Philadelphia, see Reichley, *Art of Government.*

6. On Baltimore, see Edwin Rothman, *Factional Machine Politics: William Curran and the Baltimore City Democratic Organization, 1929–46* (unpublished Ph.D. dissertation, Johns Hopkins University, 1948). On New Orleans, see L. Reissman, K. H. Silvert, and C. W. Wing, Jr., *The New Orleans Voter* (New Orleans: Tulane Studies in Political Science, Vol. 25, 1955), chap. 1.

7. St. Louis's relatively weak and decentralized political organization should perhaps place the city in this category rather than in (2); it has elements of both types. Cleveland elections are effectively partisan though formally nonpartisan; but the nonpartisan primary appears to afford more opportunity for opposition to either party organization, or even to both of them.

8. See Ralph Straetz, *PR Politics in Cincinnati* (New York, 1958); A. Theodore Brown, *The Politics of Reform—Kansas City's Municipal Government, 1925-1950* (Kansas City, Community Studies, 1958); and the *City Politics Reports* on Cincinnati and Kansas City.

9. Three of the city's nine councilmen must be from the minority party.

10. On Houston, see *City Politics Reports: Houston.* Memphis is more difficult to locate since its emergence from the Crump period. It has commission government with four-year terms, which would seem to make electoral competition difficult to organize.

11. A 1955 change in Houston's election law made it possible to vote for city "slates" by simply pulling one lever on the voting machine.

12. Baltimore, Chicago, and Pittsburgh have been dominantly Democratic and well organized —either centrally or factionally—since the early thirty's or earlier; and Philadelphia was strongly Republican (though threatened in the mid-thirty's). Buffalo, Cleveland, Indianapolis, New York, and St. Louis have more complicated histories in which competition—at least for citywide offices—in the 1930s was, for reasons peculiar to each city, either close or contingent; but each (with the exception of Buffalo and Indianapolis) has settled down to Democratic dominance in our period.

13. In neither of the type-5 cities is the separation of powers a real problem. Both are manager cities, and Cincinnati's mayor is elected by council from among its membership.

14. "A Typology of Non-partisan Elections," *Western Political Quarterly,* 12 (1959), 449. See also "Some General Characteristics of Non partisan Elections," *American Political Science Review,* 46 (1952), 766; and (with O.P. Williams) "The Insulation of Local Politics under the Non-partisan Ballot," *ibid.* 53 (1959), 1052.

15. Cf. J. L. Freeman, "Local Party Systems: Theoretical Considerations and a Case Analysis,"

American Journal of Sociology, 64 (1958), 282, for a similar characterization, except that the third factor is omitted.

16. To illustrate: Chicago uses nonpartisan elections for council and partisan contests for mayor, and winners of primary majorities need not run in the general. Several cities—both partisan and nonpartisan—have both at-large and district councilmen. In some cities—e.g., Kansas City and Portland—at-large councilmen run straight fights for separate seats in general elections; but in most at-large systems the city as a whole may be considered a multimember district. Other electoral wrinkles will be noted below where they are more pertinent.

17. Ranney and Kendall, *Democracy and the American Party System* (New York, 1956), chap. 7; J. A. Schlesinger, "A Two-dimensional Scheme for Classifying the State According to Degree of Inter-party Competition," *American Political Science Review,* 49 (1955), 1120, and "The Structure of Competition," *Behavioral Science,* 5 (1960), 197.

18. The number of cases is too small, on the whole, for useful comparisons across combinations of partisan-nonpartisan on the one hand and district-at-large on the other.

19. In general, the cities of types 1 and 2 (Chicago, Philadelphia, and St. Louis) show wider margins than those of types 4 (Buffalo and Cleveland). Baltimore's type-3 factionalism tends to show up in primaries rather than generals, while the New Orleans elections recorded here are, in fact, primaries.

20. While the wider margins shown for Los Angeles in Table 2 result in some part from our using only top two candidates in districts where several were running, the Los Angeles margins remain wider if the alternative procedure is used. On the advantages of incumbents, see Section III below and, for Los Angeles, the relevant *City Politics Report.* Los Angeles districts are extremely large, averaging more than 125,000 and frequently redistricted (a rarity among large cities). "Communities widely separated both in geography and interests are often thrown together into a single district." W. Crouch and D. McHenry, "Los Angeles," in W. Robson (ed.), *Great Cities of the World* (London, 1955), p. 304.

21. The cities are Chicago and Cleveland (of which the former holds officially partisan elections for mayor). Kansas City (type 5 above) could be added as a city that combines district and at-large elections. The other type (5) city— Cincinnati—is the only "partisan" nonpartisan city in our selection which is not a district city. It is not included in Table 2 because it employed PR through most of the period and was the only city in our selection to do so.

22. The cities were Denver, Milwaukee, and Minneapolis.

23. The device was described above. "Factions" or "slates" regularly appear in Minneapolis elections and occasionally in Houston elections; but this factor does not seem to affect the electoral margins. The practice of manifold organizational endorsements of candidates in San Francisco elections helps account for the wide dispersion of the vote there that shows up in the computation of category 4.

24. In recent years, candidates receiving a majority of the total vote in the primary have not had to run in the general election; but this is only so where there are more than two contestants in the primary.

25. The statement is a guarded one because of the possibility that the two series are not entirely independent. Student's "t" was used to test, and the means of the individual cities were not weighted by the number of elections involved. The difference is significant at .05 for all cities using district elections, and clearly significant at .01 for the partisan cities. Only *contested* seats are included in the means—cf. Table 2.

26. New Orleans shifted between at-large and district councils during the period, and the mean district margins exceeded the mean at-large margins. In Buffalo and Philadelphia the majority faction normally sweeps the at-large seats (or as many as it is allowed by statute). During the period of close party competition in Buffalo there was some ticket-splitting in this respect (apparently related to nationality appeals), but this no longer seems to occur. Pittsburgh's at-large council has been unanimously Democratic since the 1930s; and in the more part-competive city of Indianapolis the at-large council is regularly divided between the parties in the most lopsided manner allowed by the electoral system (i.e., 6–3, rather than 5–4).

27. But cf. the somewhat contrasting suggestions above about size of district and electoral margins in the nonpartisan case.

28. Cf. Table 1 above. Philadelphia, despite district elections, underwent a rapid and wholesale change in 1951. Its district lines were thoroughly redrawn before the 1951 election, and the old Republican organization had been badly weakened and discredited. The 1959 overturn in Kansas City was accomplished when several at-large Citizens' Association incumbents accepted endorsement from the Democratic organization as well and later voted in council with the latter group.

29. This has been the case in St. Louis, which has twenty-eight rather small districts. It seems quite possible that Baltimore's system of *multi-member* districts has abetted factionalism within, as well as among, the six districts of that city.

30. In the two partisan at-large cities of Indianapolis and Pittsburgh, the governing party has occasionally conducted primary election purges of incumbent councilmen who

had opposed the city administration, and one or two Philadelphia at-large councilmen have been threatened with this treatment. We find no record of this in the case of district councilmen, and it could be that election of councilmen at-large in Indianapolis and Pittsburgh either invests the administration with some sense of responsibility for the integrity of the entire ticket or affords the central party organization stronger sanctions against recalcitrants.

31. A few cities limit incumbency. In Buffalo incumbents cannot run again for mayor or at-large council seats, and Philadelphia has a two-term limit for mayors.

32. But cf. C. S. Hyneman, "Tenure and Turnover of Legislative Personnel," *Annals of the American Academy of Political and Social Science*, 195 (1938), 21, for evidence (at p. 23) that state legislators in ten states had much lower overall incumbency ratios than those in our cities over the period 1925–35. The principal difference was in I_1. Over the three most recent elections to the lower house of Congress, on the other hand, the two mean incumbency ratios were, respectively, 92.5 and 91.9, which are *higher* than those for city councilmen.

33. Two of our cities—Buffalo and (since 1951) Philadelphia—have charter limits on the number of terms a mayor may serve.

34. On the matter of alternatives and political advancement, cf. Adrian, Characteristics of Nonpartisan Elections."

35. See, for example, Editors of Fortune, *The Exploding Metropolis* (New York, 1958), chap. 3.

36. Actually, despite electoral insecurity and close elections in some cities, three-fourths of the mayors elected during the period served two or more terms; and in most of our cities the term is four years. We do not have long-run (pre-1945) data on councilmen. More than half of our councilmen served *at least* three terms; and it is clear that in most city councils there is a nucleus of long-time, more-or-less career members.

37. Cf. Adrian, "Characteristics of Nonpartisan Elections."

38. Not at the 1 percent level. The test was made for seven "partisan" cities (Baltimore, Buffalo, Chicago, Indianapolis, Philadelphia, Pittsburgh, and St. Louis), and ten "nonpartisan" cities (Boston, Dallas, Denver, Detroit, Los Angeles, Milwaukee, Minneapolis, Portland, San Francisco, and Seattle). For the two groups, $I_{1p} = .773$ and $I_{1np} = .845$; $I_{2p} = .80$ and $I_{2np} = .843$. $N_{1np} = .635$; $N_{1p} = .657$. A test of the differences between the means of the individual city means in the two groups, using student's "t" also yielded a significant deviate. It is not completely clear that the assumptions underlying both tests are fully satisfied here.

39. We offer two tentative suggestions: occasional organization pressure; and promotion

up the political ladder. On the latter, see Adrian, "Characteristics of Nonpartisan Elections," note 37.

40. Partisanship in Cleveland, which stands relatively high, appears to be less salient in councilmanic than in mayoral elections—particularly in the primaries, where occasionally most or all of the entries are of one party.

41. Another occasional threat to nonpartisan incumbents can be the intervention of party organizations in the elections. For example, such intervention seems to be on the increase in Denver where, in 1959, four incumbent councilmen lost (a rare occurrence in Denver).. All were Republicans or Independents in districts where the Democratic organization was strong. See Denver *Post* for June 17, 1959.

42. "At-large" elections here mean the type in which the entire city is treated as a multi-member district; i.e., "mixed fights." The result holds only for the ratio, I_2; and the test was made only for cities using the at-large or district system entirely. For at-large cities, $I_2 = 93.5$, and for district cities, $I_2 = 80.2$. There were four cities in each group. A test of the four nonpartisan district cities against four partisan district cities reveals a not statistically significant difference between the ratios, I_2; though the ratios for partisan cities tend to be lower.

43. Thus the difference between the two groups is heavily influenced by Milwaukee's I_2 ratio, which is quite low. But the difference remains significant at the 5 percent level when Milwaukee is excluded.

44. Cf. the discussion above at notes 23 and 24.

45. Cf. R. S. Childs, *Civic Victories* (New York, 1952), *passim*. The at-large system as a *sole* system seems to be more often used in non-partisan than in partisan cities. Cf. Straetz, *PR Politics in Cincinnati*, pp. 54–58, for the view that, in Cincinnati, the PR (and at-large) election system has also aided incumbents and several-time candidates. "The name is important, especially on the office-type ballot or the non-partisan ballot, and the candidates whose names have appeared on previous ballots hold a great advantage." Cincinnati's incumbency ratios are very high.

46. The I_1 ratios were high in both cases. Cf. the *City Politics Report* on Boston for a discussion of the effects of at-large elections.

47. On this point and the general point about at-large councils, cf. C. S. Hyneman, "Tenure and Turnover of Legislative Personnel." Hyneman found some tendency for state legislators to serve and survive for longer periods in large districts and in multimember districts.

48. In our selection, all the northern non-partisan cities west of the Mississippi were closely contested in postwar presidential elections.

49. Cf. Adrian, "Typology of Non-partisan Elections." As this paper was written in the summer of 1961 incumbent mayors were defeated in Los Angeles and Minneapolis, and in each case (especially the latter) some party intervention was reported.

50. One case of retirement under organization pressure in a strongly organized type-1 city was that of Kelly in Chicago (1947). All of the party overturns in the postwar period occurred when incumbents were not running.

51. Whether the mayoralty is by charter "strong" or "weak" seems to have little relation to length of incumbency, although such electoral arrangements as two-year terms and at-large councils probably add to the insecurity of incumbent mayors.

52. What probability a voter thinks is "support-able" probably reflects the intensity of his preferences, even assuming that his assessment of the probability itself is uninfluenced by this factor. And voter "tastes" may be specific or general, and *could* include a liking for candidates who appear to be independent of voter tastes.

53. It would seem that, where party organization is tight, party preferences are traditional, and the independent vote is small, an election would have to be closer to further voter sovereignty than under contrasting conditions. In some cities, elections are not characteristically close when incumbents are turned out.

54. Cf. Straetz, *PR Politics in Cincinnati*; and the *City Politics Report* on Kansas City (chap. 2, pp. 3–4, and Document 11).

55. Cf. the contrasting degrees in which non-partisan elections are effective in, e.g., Chicago and Cleveland; Cincinnati and Kansas City; and Boston and Detroit. Yet such factors as partisan or nonpartisan mayoral primaries, "PR," and at-large council seats seem to be relevant to the varying degree of electoral competition in these cities, as suggested above.

56. Our data on primary election turnout indicate that it is often highest in the most effectively organized cities, such as Pittsburgh or factional Baltimore; and that it rarely amounts to more than 50 percent of the dominant party registration even in those cities. As a percentage of the population 21 years of age and older it averages less than half the general election turnout in all partisan cities but Pittsburgh and Baltimore.

Urban Political Decision Makers and Structures

THE URBAN POLITICAL PROCESS is characterized by two basic activities, power contesting and policy making, which interrelate to ensure the functional maintenance of the local political system. To this point, we have focused on the first of these two activities, in particular, partisan and group efforts to influence those in positions of authority through input processes which form the core of power-contesting. While the articulation of interest and the programmatic aspects of partisan efforts can also be considered as elements of policy making,[1] the most salient aspects of this second basic activity involve the authoritative allocation of values and their implementation by urban decision makers and agencies. This allocation is crystallized in the conversion process where demands are transformed into public policy. To many, this process is the heart of urban political activity, yet it remains the most nebulous and underresearched area in political analysis.

Formal decisions in urban politics are made by sets of political actors occupying authority roles. These actors regularly engage in system activities: they are objects of demands and supports, they are perceived as having responsibility for certain matters, and their actions are binding within the limits of their roles.[2] In highly developed political systems, such as those in urban areas, roles are likely to be highly differentiated. Decision makers, therefore, occupy a variety of roles and perform a variety of functions. Because the mayor and city council are the most visible and accessible points of linkage in the system, their political functions and roles are most complex. On the other hand, the roles performed by court justices and bureaucratic administrators are more circumscribed and formalized. Similarly, various urban authorities differ in the inclusiveness of their decision-making responsibilities. For example, in "strong mayor" cities, the mayor could be located at the most inclusive end of this continuum, and minor bureaucratic decision makers would locate at the other extreme. This set of formal decision makers has the responsibility for selecting urban system objectives and committing their efforts and resources to realizing these objectives. The objectives and roles of formal policy makers are defined by demands and support emanating from various sources within the community which are converted into legitimate and binding decisions. The thrust of the urban system is maintenance of this conversion process. The flexibility of policy making is defined not only by direct environmental inputs, but by a whole set of external and internal resources.[3] Some environmental-related resources which shape the conversion process include available goods and services, technological developments, and the entire urban economy. Policy making is also shaped by internal resources such as ability, competence, and organizational skills of the authorities, plus a set of culturally prescribed and experimental decision rules which develop across time. Therefore, the actual decision-making process is a complex phenomenon constrained and influenced by sets of resources and demands and characterized by a multiplicity of decision-making models ranging from the most rational and comprehensive models in which alternatives are known and weighed and outcomes are anticipated to the more nebulous and incremental processes where decision making is a "muddling through" process.[4]

Thus decision making at the urban level is a complex process in which policy outcomes are a mixture of the "public interest"; community characteristics; the social, economic, and psychological characteristics of decision makers and their perceived role; structural decision-making arrangements; constituency relationships; and the underlying political culture. Yet the visibility of structural and legal components led most early studies to focus almost exclusively on the formal institutions of municipal government, largely ignoring informal political processes and the broader socioeconomic influences affecting the local polity. The early reform heritage in political science contributed to a penchant for finding the "best" form of city government, one which would insure freedom from inefficiency, corruption, and boss domination while providing for economical, business-like administration. In the 1950s, however, a few perceptive critics began to raise questions concerning the narrow scope of local government studies with their limited methodology and preoccupation with formal institutional arrangements.[5] Students and practitioners of municipal government were being bypassed as newer trends and developments were taking place in political science and research findings emanating from other social science disciplines, especially sociology and psychology, were generating valuable new insights into man's behavior. Increasingly, it became apparent that the limited case study with its heavy emphasis on formal government arrangements and the administration of local services had to give way to a broader approach using modern research techniques which would take into account informal power arrangements, the socioeconomic environment of the local government, and the variations in public policy found among a large number of cities.

The studies of community power which began to reappear in the 1950s (especially those by sociologists) were considerably less certain than political scientists had been of the importance of local public officials in making basic community decisions. Devoted primarily to discovering who actually controls local affairs, these early community power studies almost invariably found that local business elites were really running things while those who held formal political authority had little independent power, especially on important issues.[6] These findings did not go unchallenged, however, as a number of political scientists such as Robert Dahl, Edward Banfield, Nelson Polsby, and others began to provide evidence that decision making in many large American cities was not elite-dominated but, in fact, was largely fragmented, issue-related, and coalition-centered with elected local officials often playing an important role.[7] Thus the emergence of community decision making as a focal point for local research had the result—at least among political scientists—of providing a renewed interest in those officially charged with making local decisions. Other empirically based urban research continues to suggest that the perceptions, orientations, and values of decision makers,[8] as well as certain institutional arrangements which centralize or decentralize the decision process, have an important influence on urban policy. Studies dealing with fluoridation of water and urban renewal, for example, indicate that centralized decision arrangements may contribute to swifter action while decentralized systems which permit extensive public involvement may act more slowly or not at all.[9] Thus knowledge about the officials and agencies which participate in the demand conversion process is essential to our understanding of the urban political system.

City Councils

In a narrow and technical sense, the task of the municipal legislative body is to formulate local public policy. Yet city councils, more than other legislative bodies in this country, are not really equipped to play a prominent role in policy innovation. With the possible exception of those in the largest cities, most city councils are but "faint and modified copies" of legislative bodies found at the state and national level. Manned by amateurs conducting city business in their spare time, attention to routine business tends to absorb the spare time and energy most individuals bring to their council positions. Thus Williams and Adrian conclude in their study of four medium-sized Michigan communities that "most councilmen were quite willing for the drama of city policy formation to be played off-stage where they and their colleagues were scarcely identified as participants." When council members do become involved in rule making, their actions are often negative and symbolic and sometimes accompanied by a focus on patronage and narrow policy matters.[10]

Municipal governing bodies are concerned with other system activities beyond their involvement in matters of policy leadership. In many respects, council functions are more differentiated and less clearly defined than their analogous institutions on the state or national level. Although we made an initial distinction between rule making, rule application, and rule adjudication, these distinctions are often more conceptual than real at the urban level. As suggested above, municipal policy initiation and leadership is frequently supplied by groups and agencies other than the city council which merely ratifies, modifies, or rejects proposals generated from other sources. The grass roots political ethos which encourages continuous citizen participation in matters of local policy is another factor which contributes to the complex pattern of policy making at the urban level. In addition to this involvement of outside forces in the policy process, the council may also share in other aspects of rule application and adjudication. Certain structural characteristics of the city government are particularly important in shaping the nature of council functions—that is, the role of the council varies according to the form of government and the size of city as well. In many small "weak mayor" cities,[11] councilmen may play an active role in supervising a variety of administrative activities, while in larger, reform cities (especially with a city manager), the council may confine its interests almost exclusively to broader public issues. In council-manager cities, the council is particularly dependent upon leadership by the manager and the administration so that it tends to concentrate on reviewing departmental activities.[12] The most extreme form of functional overlap, however, is found in cities with a commission form of government where the council acts as both a legislative and executive body.

City councils do play a variety of important roles in the urban political process even though policy leadership largely resides in other hands. At the very least, no matter where policy alternatives originate, the final authority to adopt or reject lies with the city council. Moreover, there is a growing awareness that local officials, including councilmen, possess a wide latitude for discretion in policy matters permitting them to follow a variety of courses of action. Kenneth Prewitt, drawing on the comprehensive study of city councils in the San Francisco Bay area, recently offered the provocative thesis that a number of councilmen are prone to consider their public service as a form of civic duty or obligation not unlike a leadership position in a local civic organization.[13] Prewitt suggests that this perspective on the nature of council responsibilities leads to several behavioral traits which have far-reaching implications for democratic political theory. Councilmen who adhere to this norm of "volunteerism" are (1) more likely to vote against perceived majority public opinion; (2) less sensitive to public pressures; (3) less likely to reflect concern with forthcoming elections in making policy decisions; (4) less likely to want constituents and other groups involved in policy making; and (5) less interested in performing services for constituents. Prewitt attributes these characteristics primarily to the absence of political ambition on the part of these elected officials which tends to produce a feeling of freedom from obligation except to one's own concept of the good of the community. Obviously, volunteerism in this sense is incompatible with the notion of electoral accountability which is such a basic part of democratic ideology. Prewitt and Eulau, in an earlier report on the same data from the San Francisco area, had observed that city size and diversity apparently influenced the responsiveness of city councils to outside influences.[14] Governing bodies in larger, more diverse communities were more likely to act in response to interest groups or attentive publics than were those councils from smaller, homogeneous cities where there was a tendency to rely on the council's own image of community requirements. The authors also observed that those cities with a higher percent of forced turnover of council members through electoral defeat tended to be more responsive to public pressures and petitions. The medium-sized and larger cities in their Bay area study ($N = 82$) were more likely to have higher rates of forced turnover than the smaller communities.

The article by Eulau and Eyestone contained in this volume also deals with the city councils from the San Francisco area. Consistent with the above findings, this study indicates that a city's policy development is strongly affected by the preferences, orientations, and expectations of its city council—what the authors term the "policy maps" of the council members. Five levels of urban policy development are identified—retarded stage, emergent phase, transitional stage, maturing phase, and advanced stage—which were found related to city size and growth rate. Larger and faster growing cities were in the more developed policy stages except that the most developed cities showed a falling off in growth rate. The authors suggest, however, that policy development is not solely the result of size, growth, or resource capability, that councilmen's policy preferences act as intervening variables to help shape the final policy commitments of the community.[15]

Municipal Executives and Administrators

Municipal executives, administrators, and bureaucrats are continually involved in converting demands, putting decisions into effect, and supervising their implementation. These administrative officials and structures not only produce authoritative outputs in the form of rules, regulations, and binding decisions, they also participate in the process of reducing and combining demands so as to sharpen and limit the issues with which the local system must contend. The mayor has primary responsibility for rule application in mayor-council cities, but he also performs important legislative functions by recommending policy to the council. His control over administration varies, with "strong mayors" having the greatest degree of formal authority over substantive and budgetary policy. Robert Dahl's now classic study of New Haven, *Who Governs?*, spells out the dominant role of the mayor in policy initiation and leadership in that city.[16] Dahl depicts how Mayor Richard Lee gradually assumed increasing control over urban renewal and development (New Haven became a nationwide leader in this area) and exercised growing influence in the domain of public education. In the article found in this portion of the book, Rosenthal and Crain examine the role of the mayor in an especially controversial policy area, fluoridation of the municipal water supply. They conclude that the position taken by this elected official was frequently crucial in determining the community's decision on fluoridation. One reason for the mayor's preeminence in this policy area was his symbolic representation of the "public interest" which often provided a welcome cue for the voter in making a decision on a fluoridation referendum.

The above studies are concerned primarily with mayors who function within a mayor-council government and are not intended to assess the role of the mayor under council-manager government where a somewhat different picture emerges. Under the original theory of council-manager government, the appointed city manager was to be the chief administrative official responsible for routine municipal operations, free from interference by the elected mayor and council who were only to establish broad policy guidelines. Under this arrangement, the mayor was to be little more than a figurehead who, in addition to his ceremonial duties, would preside over council meetings and be permitted to appoint citizens (with council approval) to a limited number of boards and commissions. The extent to which the mayor was to be a community leader and policy innovator was not completely resolved by those who supported the manager plan. In many ways, he was only first among equals since he was frequently elected to his post for a limited period (often for a year) by his fellow council members. In many instances, mayors were apparently willing to follow the largely passive role which seemed to be called for under council-manager government. Charles Adrian's study of three Michigan cities found policy leadership rather firmly in the hands of the manager and his administration, with the mayor playing no special leadership role.[17]

Additional research reveals, however, that different activity patterns may prevail with respect to policy leadership in various cities so that managers and mayors may both play important policy roles depending on a variety of factors. In large council-manager cities, the likelihood seems greater that the mayor might become more extensively involved in innovation and leadership.

Early proponents of council-manager government did not want the mayor to become too powerful for fear that he would be tempted to meddle in administrative affairs which were to be the exclusive domain of the professional manager. Only recently have researchers begun to explore whether mayors (particularly those who are popularly elected) pose a threat to the basic tenets of the council-manager plan. Gladys Kammerer, in a study of ten council-manager cities in Florida, has argued that a significant "role collision" is likely to develop in council-manager cities where the mayor is popularly elected. The author stresses the variety of roles a city manager must play which, she suggests, are not solely the product of the community's political style or the manager's own qualifications or personality but are also dependent upon certain institutional-structural arrangements found within the local government. She concludes that conflict with the manager is more likely where popularly elected mayors exist than where mayors are selected from within the council.[18] However, David Booth's study of 140 council-manager cities of 10,000 or less found no basic differences in the policy leadership role played by the mayor whether he was elected by the people or chosen by his council peers.[19] Thus he concluded that mayors chosen by the electorate were not a threat to the manager. One reason for the differences in these two studies, both empirically based, might be that Booth's cities were all small while those in the Florida study included several larger cities. Size of city could be an important variable, as popularly elected mayors in large cities might be likely to assume a more active leadership role than their smaller town counterparts. A case study in point is one focusing on the resignation of the city manager of Dallas, Texas, after fourteen years of service, shortly following the election of a well-known, highly regarded business executive to the mayor's post.[20] The new mayor was a strong-willed leader who had definite ideas about certain basic approaches to running the city which were in conflict with those of the city manager. The mayor had been swept into office with a 73 percent vote: the council apparently agreed with him so the manager resigned. Ronald Loveridge's study, contained in this section, suggests that managers and council members may inevitably clash because they have differing conceptions of what the manager's functions should be. The basic disagreement is over how active the manager should be in policy innovation: managers rather uniformly adhere to a policy innovator and advocate role, while council members tend to see the manager's role essentially as that of a staff administrator whose prime task is (or should be) the execution of council policy.

The manager's role as policy initiator and community leader has been the subject of continuing debate and study. Early devotees to the manager concept apparently saw a substantially limited role for the manager in these areas for two basic reasons. First, those who strongly supported council-manager government were also likely to have considered city government as primarily a service-rendering agency, not a vehicle for resolving basic community conflicts.[21] Thus the manager must be almost exclusively concerned with administering an organization dedicated to providing good, yet efficient, public services. Second, the manager was to be strictly subordinate to the council in the area of policy determination so as to assure the separation of politics from administration, a foremost goal of the early reformers who backed the plan.[22] In recent years, however, the politics-administration dichotomy has been viewed as increasingly unrealistic and the manager's involvement in matters of policy increasingly apparent. A recent overview of the city manager profession acknowledged the situation in these words:

> Today there is little debate about whether the manager should play the role of community leader; widespread agreement exists about the necessity and inevitability of such a role.[23]

Empirical research supports this view. Booth asked a large number of small community managers about their participation in policy formation and found that in 60 percent of the cities the managers emerged as activists in general policy initiation.[24] Data accumulated by Deil Wright on forty-five city managers in large cities (over 100,000 population) clearly established the manager as the dominant policy initiator in most of the cities studied.[25] Wright also asked managers to rank three basic roles—management, policy involvement, and community leadership—according to (1) amount of time spent on each; (2) personal preference; and (3) the extent to which each role actively contributed to the successful performance of the manager's overall job. His findings show the management category ahead of the other two roles in each of the three comparisons. Thus it would seem inappropriate to characterize even the city manager of large cities as primarily a policy leader and innovator. To the contrary, it appears that in his own view at least the manager still sees his fundamental job as that of administering the various services and enterprises of the municipality.

LOCAL BUREAUCRACY

Several recent studies reveal how much influence the local bureaucracy may have on public policy. John Gardiner reports that the primary factor leading to a high or low rate of traffic law enforcement among a large group of cities of over 25,000 population is the departmental norm or policy fostered by the chief of police and his commanding officers.[26] This observation parallels some of James Q. Wilson's on police behavior where he establishes that levels of "professionalism" within two American police departments affected the use of police discretion in dealing with juvenile offenders.[27] Inculcation of professional norms apparently makes police less discriminatory but more severe in their treatment of juveniles. The level or degree of bureaucratization apparently has an impact on the functioning of a variety of municipal operations (e.g., planning and zoning, rates of traffic arrest, gambling, and juvenile arrests) in four Wisconsin cities studied by Robert Alford.[28] The most developed of the four communities in terms of levels of bureaucracy and political participation also had the largest antipoverty program, had done the most with urban renewal, had the only public low-rent housing project, and was a nationwide leader in fluoridation of water. Alford concludes that cities with more highly developed bureaucratic structures and high levels of political participation are more likely to be innovators in various substantive policy areas. Martha Derthick's study of the administration of public assistance programs in a group of Massachusetts cities led to the conclusion that, although federal and state regulations reduced the margin for local discretion, the values and attitudes of local agency heads did produce some differences in program operation among certain cities.[29] In two contrasting cases, with one city consistently near the top and the other at the bottom on assistance expenditures, Derthick found differences attributable to the kinds of goals defined by agency executives and the methods used to achieve them. One agency was rule-oriented and internally authoritarian while the other was client-oriented and permissive. The lenient agency had a comparatively generous program financially while the more legalistic agency had a frugal one. In a study of the legislative process in Los Angeles in this volume, Harry Reynolds concluded that the career city administrators were active in all phases of local lawmaking. They tended to dominate the initiation, synthesizing, and legislative manipulation phases of bill enactment. Moreover, the author's evidence suggests rather complete acquiescence by the city council in this arrangement, partly because of the bureaucracy's monopoly of technical competence and also because of their skill in cultivating council good will. Thus studies of this kind rather vividly point up how bureaucratic norms and values may seriously impinge upon substantive municipal policy areas.

Studies of bureaucratic behavior in large cities emphasize the ways in which employee groups bring pressure on elected policy makers in order to become as nearly independent and self-directing as possible. Drawing on their study of New York City, Sayre and Kaufman suggest several ways a large urban bureaucracy might seek this basic goal: (1) by preventing "political interference" or meddling by special interests or outside groups; (2) by playing a prominent role in policy enactment as a way of protecting group values and procedures against "amateurs" and "innovators"; and (3) by exercising as much control as possible over work conditions to prevent disturbance of settled work patterns.[30] The authors conclude that large city bureaucracies have become an important conservative force to reckon with in city politics in any effort to bring about substantial change.

There is no doubt that as cities increase in size and the operation of municipal functions becomes increasingly complex, urban bureaucracies will loom ever more important as a force in the determination of local public policy. Yet it would surely be inaccurate to characterize the bureaucratic structures of local government, even in large cities, as monolithic giants unmovable by the course of normal political events and pressures. Bollens and Schmandt argue instead that, like so much of the local political structure, bureaucracies in metropolitan areas are highly pluralistic. County and city agencies contend over policy areas; administrative heads of agencies supplying urban services vie with each other over territory and scope of programs; and school units, sewer districts, and county agencies all have special and competing interests to defend. In this interplay of forces, each segment or subunit of bureaucratic structure cultivates its own clientele relationships and thus affords points of access for influencing the political process to the various contending private groups and forces operating within the larger community.[31]

Urban Courts

In the American political system, with its strong attachment to separation of powers, the courts are sharply differentiated from other political institutions. In part because of the belief that courts must preserve their objectivity and neutrality, the concept of a separate and independent judiciary has been extended to every level of our political system. Undoubtedly, this arrangement has contributed to the rather common notion that judges do not (or, at least, should not) "make law" or policy but merely interpret it. In recent years, however, political scientists have begun to recognize that the ideal of a neutral, value-free judiciary which only "discovers" the law is a myth, that judges in this country, along with legislators and executives, actually do make policy decisions affecting important social, economic, and political values. The involvement of courts in policy making (or demand conversion in systems terminology) has been more extensively studied at the national level, where particular interest has been focused on the U.S. Supreme Court, than at other levels of government in our system. Yet, even at the local level, judicial action may protect certain basic social values (e.g., the right of peaceful assembly, or "law and order") or reward certain individuals or groups (through a favorable decree in a civil law suit) or impose sanctions on members of the local polity (perhaps for violation of the local criminal code).

Despite the absence of comprehensive studies of the local judicial process, certain general observations can be made from some of the more limited studies which have been done. First, most people who come into contact with the court system in this country do so at the local level. While public attention focuses on sensational felony cases and on the conduct of trials in the prestigious felony courts, 90 percent of the nation's criminal cases are heard in the lower trial courts.[32] Second, Glendon Schubert has argued that our judicial systems are poorly designed to cope with the "politico-legal" problems arising in metropolitan areas. Overburdened, complicated structural arrangements in many large urban areas have contributed to excessive delays in the judicial process. Further, he observed that the municipal legal system is notorious for its "failure to grow rapidly enough to accommodate the increasing demands made upon it."[33] Third, there is general agreement that disparities exist within the local legal process which operate to the disadvantage of indigents, Negroes, and less educated groups. Stuart Nagel, analyzing a mass of data from all fifty states, concluded that although indigency and race overlap, "generally, the poor suffer even more discrimination than Negroes in criminal justice; and Negroes may suffer more from lack of money than from race."[34] Fourth, it now seems apparent that the local judicial process is not equipped to deal with large-scale civil disorders. In the large cities shaken by civil disorders during the summer of 1967, recurring breakdowns occurred in the judicial mechanisms for processing, prosecuting, and protecting arrested persons. For example, arraignments in the major riot cities were often delayed several days, thus denying defendants the right to prompt bail. Sentences meted out during the riots tended to be harsher than in those cases disposed of later—a policy which adversely affected the poorest defendants who agreed to immediate trials because they were unable to raise bail.[35] Finally, in the area of civil activity, Kenneth Dolbeare has examined the purposes of the groups who resort to civil litigation at the local level.[36] His study of court trials in a suburban New York county from 1948 to 1963 revealed that parties initiating litigation were mostly individuals and small businesses bringing suit against local governments for purposes of private economic advantage. Over half the suits involved zoning and land use controversies.

The study of local judicial behavior by Martin Levin included in this part of the volume compares the behavior of—and especially the sentences imposed by—criminal court judges from two urban areas where judges are selected by different political processes. In one city, selection was dominated by the local bar association; in the other, the local party system exercised strong influence over judicial selection. Significant differences were found as those judges chosen through the party-dominated arrangement tended to impose more lenient sentences than those judges selected by the other method. Thus this study indicates that different kinds of local political structures and methods of judicial selection may affect rule adjudication, a process often thought to be somewhat removed from "politics."

Notes

1. These conceptual distinctions are explored in Henry S. Albinski and Laurence K. Pettit, *European Political Processes* (Boston: Allyn & Bacon, 1968), p. 89ff.

2. David Easton, *A System Analysis of Political Life* (New York: John Wiley, 1965), p. 212.

3. *Ibid.*, p. 448, for an extension of external and internal distinctions.

4. For a discussion of these two models of decision making, see Charles E. Lindblom, *The Policy-Making Process* (Englewood Cliffs, N.J.: Prentice-Hall, 1968), chaps. 3 and 4.

5. See, in particular, Lawrence J. R. Herson, "The Lost World of Municipal Government," *American Political Science Review*, 51 (1957), 330–45.

6. In addition to Floyd Hunter, *Community Power Structure* (Chapel Hill: University of North Carolina Press, 1953), representative examples include E. Digby Baltzell, *Philadelphia Gentlemen* (New York: The Free Press, 1958); Robert O. Schulze and Leonard Blumberg, "The Determination of Local Power Elites," *American Journal of Sociology*, 63 (1957), 290–96; and Delbert C. Miller, "Industry and Community Power Structure," *American Sociological Review*, 23 (1958), 9–15.

7. See Robert A. Dahl, *Who Governs?* (New Haven: Yale University Press, 1961); Edward C. Banfield, *Political Influence* (New York: The Free Press, 1961); and Nelson W. Polsby, *Community Power and Political Theory* (New Haven: Yale University Press, 1963). Extensive current bibliographies of community power studies can be found in Roland Pellegrin,

"Selected Bibliography on Community Power Structure," *Southwestern Social Science Quarterly*, 48 (1967), 451–65, and Edward Keynes and David M. Ricci, *Political Power, Community, and Democracy* (Chicago: Rand McNally, 1970), pp. 255–77.

8. Heinz Eulau and Robert Eyestone, "Policy Maps of City Councils and Policy Outcomes: A Developmental Analysis," *American Political Science Review*, 62 (1968), 124–44.

9. Donald B. Rosenthal and Robert L. Crain, "Structure and Values in Local Political Systems: The Case of Fluoridation Decisions," *Journal of Politics*, 28 (1966), 169–96; and Amos H. Hawley, "Community Power and Urban Renewal Success," *American Journal of Sociology*, 68 (1963), 422–31.

10. Oliver P. Williams and Charles R. Adrian, *Four Cities* (Philadelphia: University of Pennsylvania Press, 1963), p. 295.

11. For a distinction between "weak mayor" and "strong mayor" city governments see William O. Winter, *The Urban Polity* (New York: Dodd, Mead, 1969), chap. 10.

12. Charles R. Adrian, "Leadership and Decision-Making in Manager Cities: A Study of Three Communities," *Public Administration Review*, 18 (1958), 208–13.

13. Kenneth Prewitt, "Political Ambitions, Volunteerism, and Electoral Accountability," *American Political Science Review*, 64 (1970), 5–17.

14. Kenneth Prewitt and Heinz Eulau, "Political Matrix and Political Representation: Prolegomenon to a New Departure from an Old Problem," *American Political Science Review*, 63 (1969), 427–41.

15. See also David R. Morgan and Samuel

A. Kirkpatrick, "Policy Variations, Political Recruitment, and Suburban Social Rank," *Sociological Quarterly*, 11 (1970), 452–62.

16. Dahl, *Who Governs?*, especially pp. 200–14.

17. Adrian, "Leadership and Decision-Making."

18. Gladys Kammerer, "Role Diversity of City Managers," *Administrative Science Quarterly*, 8 (1964), 421–42.

19. David A. Booth, "Are Elected Mayors a Threat to the Manager?", *Administrative Science Quarterly*, 12 (1968), 572–89.

20. Bruce Kovner, "The Resignation of Elgin Crull," in Edward C. Banfield (ed.), *Urban Government: A Reader in Administration and Politics*, rev. ed. (New York: The Free Press, 1969), pp. 316–21.

21. See Edward C. Banfield and James Q. Wilson, *City Politics* (Cambridge: Harvard University Press, 1963), chap. 2, for a discussion of the political function of city government.

22. See Leonard D. White, *The City Manager* (Chicago: University of Chicago Press, 1927).

23. John C. Bollens and John C. Ries, *The City Manager Profession: Myths and Realities* (Chicago: Public Administration Service, 1969), p. 2.

24. David A. Booth, *Council-Manager Government in Small Cities* (Chicago: International City Managers' Association, 1968), pp. 101–102.

25. Deil Wright, "The City Manager as a Development Administrator," in Robert Daland (ed.), *Comparative Urban Research* (Beverly Hills, Calif.: Sage, 1969), pp. 203–48.

26. John A. Gardiner, "Police Enforcement of Traffic Laws: A Comparative Analysis," in James Q. Wilson (ed.), *City Politics and Public Policy* (New York: John Wiley, 1968), pp. 151–72.

27. James Q. Wilson, "The Police and the Delinquent in Two Cities," in Stanton Wheeler (ed.), *Controlling Delinquency* (New York: John Wiley, 1967), pp. 9–30; and also James Q. Wilson, *Varieties of Police Behavior* (Cambridge: Harvard University Press, 1968).

28. Robert R. Alford, *Bureaucracy and Participation: Political Cultures in Four Wisconsin Cities* (Chicago: Rand McNally, 1969), chap. 8.

29. Martha Derthick, "Intercity Differences in Administration of the Public Assistance Program: The Case of Massachusetts," in Wilson (ed.), *City Politics and Public Policy*, pp. 243–66.

30. Wallace S. Sayre and Herbert Kaufman, *Governing New York City* (New York: Russell Sage, 1960), pp. 406–407.

31. John C. Bollens and Henry J. Schmandt, *The Metropolis: Its People, Politics and Economic Life*, 2nd ed. (New York: Harper & Row, 1970), p. 135.

32. Robert W. Winslow, *Crime in a Free Society: Selections from the President's Commission on Law Enforcement and Administration of Justice* (Belmont, Calif.: Dickenson, 1968), p. 313.

33. Glendon Schubert, *Judicial Policy-Making* (Glenview, Ill.: Scott, Foresman, 1965), p. 29. See also President's Commission on Law Enforcement and Administration of Justice, *The Challenge of Crime in a Free Society* (Washington, D.C.: Government Printing Office, 1967).

34. Stuart S. Nagel, "The Tipped Scales of American Justice," *Trans-action* (May/June 1966), pp. 4–9.

35. *Report of the National Advisory Commission on Civil Disorders* (New York: Bantam, 1968), pp. 338–43.

36. Kenneth M. Dolbeare, *Trial Courts in Urban Politics: State Court Policy Impact and Functions in a Local Political System* (New York: John Wiley, 1967).

1. City Councils

The Problem

IN SPITE OF common challenges stemming from the common environment shared by all cities in a metropolitan region, continued and even increasing social and economic differentiation among and within cities rather than homogenization and integration are the most significant features of the contemporary metropolitan scene.[1] Cities within the same metropolitan region are not only maintaining but also developing distinct and unique "public life styles."[2] Urban sociology and urban geography have raised a multitude of questions and given a multitude of answers in seeking to account for the fact that cities facing basically similar challenges from the environment react so differently to these challenges. Most relevant research deals with the problem of differentiation and its effect on the development of cities in terms of historical settlement patterns, economic location and growth, or geographical space distribution.[3]

But differences in municipal life styles may also be the result of differences in public policies deliberately pursued by local governments in the metropolitan area. If this is so, the common pressures from the environment are evidently interpreted differently in the process of public decision making that seeks to cope with them. It would seem, then, that metropolitan cities are in different stages of policy development. Leaving aside momentarily the meaning of "stages of policy development," we can ask a number of questions that may shed light on the relationship between environmental pressures and public policies designed to meet these pressures. If cities are in different stages of policy development, how can the stages be identified? Is policy development linear and "progressive," or is it reversible? Do the stages of policy development in fact correspond to relevant conditions of the environment? But if there are no differences in environmental challenges, what makes for arrested development in one city, while a similarly challenged city takes off or another is highly developed? On the other hand, if cities are in different stages of development, is it due to their possessing

Policy Maps of City Councils and Policy Outcomes: A Developmental Analysis*

Heinz Eulau
and Robert Eyestone

uneven resource capabilities by which environmental problems can be solved? But how can one explain why cities with equal resources adopt quite different public policies? What is the character of the policies designed to meet environmental challenges? Are they attempts to adjust the city to the changing environment, or are they attempts to control the environment, or both?

Questions like these in turn direct our attention to the need for exploring the policy perspectives of urban decision makers. How do municipal policy makers perceive their community's environment and problems stemming from environmental conditions? What are their short-term policy positions, and what are their long-range policy images of the future? Are their perceptions of problems, policy orientations, and expectations related to the city's stage of policy development? And if this is the case, what are we to make of the relationship from a theoretical point of view? Although we do not propose to deal with all of these questions, it seems to us that they provide the cutting edge of an empirical theory of urban public policy.

Reprinted with permission from The American Political Science Review, *62 (March 1968), 124–44.*

*The larger project of which this analysis is a part, the City Council Research Project, is sponsored by the Institute of Political Studies, Stanford University, and is supported by the National Science Foundation under contract GS 496.

The Project

This study of the policy maps of city councils in relationship to city policy development is part of a much larger project on municipal legislative bodies conducted in the ninety-odd cities of the San Francisco Bay metropolitan region since 1964.

The data used in this report come from the following sources: (1) city size, density, and growth data from the 1960 and 1965 Censuses of Population; (2) city per capita assessed valuation data and expenditure data for planning and amenties from the *Annual Report of Financial Transactions concerning Cities of California*, for the fiscal years 1958–59 to 1965–66, published by the State Controller; and (3) data concerning council policy maps from interviews with city councilmen conducted in 1966 and 1967.

The interviews, using both open-ended and closed questions, averaged about three hours in length. In addition, councilmen were asked, at the end of each interview, to fill out a written questionnaire. Interviews were held, as the tabulation shows, in eighty-nine cities located in eight counties around the San Francisco Bay. Two councils refused to cooperate altogether, and in four others not enough councilmen were interviewed to permit analysis at the council level. Inadequate budget data in the case of six cities incorporated after 1959 further reduced the number of councils available for this analysis to seventy-seven. One city, incorporated after interviewing had begun, has been excluded from the study as has been the city-county of San Francisco because its Board of Supervisors is a much more professionalized legislative body than the other councils of the region.

The Model

The model guiding the analysis is a partial one, and we shall not be dealing in the analysis with all of its relevant empirical components.[4] The model predicts city policy development as a response to external and internal features of the urban environment.

	Number of Councils	Number of Councilmen
Interview targets	89	488
Access refused	− 2	− 10
	87	478
Deficient council data	− 4	− 12
	83 (93%)	466
Interview refusals		− 31
		435 (89%)
No budget data available for analysis	− 6	
	77 (87%)	

The external features include, but are not exhausted by, city size, density, and growth as the most immediate symptoms of common challenges from the environment, as well as city resources as environmental constraints on policy outcomes. The internal features include, but are not exhausted by, the demands for certain policies made by individuals and groups as well as the policy orientations which local decision makers themselves bring to or formulate in the course of the policy-making process. The model seeks to order these component variables and relate them to each other in a theoretically meaningful manner.

The model assumes that city size, density, and growth as well as resources are antecedent variables; that individual or group demand and decision makers' policy orientations are intervening variables; and that policy outcomes and resultant stages of policy development are consequent variables. Of course, in empirical reality neither city size, density, or growth nor city resources are truly independent precisely because policies may be designed to control the city's environment or increase its resources. But for the purpose of short-term analysis we can assume these variables to be independent.

Although we shall not deal with individual or group demands in this paper, they are likely to be related to the city's demographic features. For instance, the larger a city's population, the more and more diverse demands are likely to be made on policy makers (and, moreover, the more and more diverse demands for policies coping with problems stemming from environmental challenges are likely to be made). On the other hand, decision makers' policy orientations should be independent of environmental variables, though they are likely to be related to the policy preferences of individuals or groups that are not independent of pressures from the environment.

Policy outcomes are assumed to follow each other in a characteristic sequence that constitutes the city's policy development. These outcomes are responses to environmental challenges, such as those occasioned by high population density or a high growth rate. Moreover, they are indicative of policy makers' willingness to utilize city resources. Changes in city size or density due to growth as well as in resource capability bring about changes in policy outcomes that move the city along from one stage to another in the development process. The process of policy development need not be unidirectional; at least temporary reversals are possible.

Environmental challenges may or may not be perceived by policy makers as "problems" requiring action. Even if problems are not perceived and no action is taken, there is a policy that is reflected in policy outcomes. Policy makers' sensitivity to environmental challenges is influenced by the demands that are made on them as well as by their own policy preferences and policy images. Therefore, city policy development is not only due to changes in the environment but is mediated by policy makers' orientations to action. For instance, whether or not resources are mobilized for development depends to a large extent on demands made on government as well as on the policy preferences of policy makers.

However, policy makers' perceptions of problems, policy positions, and policy images —their "policy maps," so to speak—are themselves not independent of policy development. Because policy development is cumulative in that past policy outcomes constrain current policy proposals—what is feasible and what is not—policy maps are likely to be formulated, consciously or unconsciously, within the restrictive context of

the stage of development in which a city is momentarily located. In other words, policy makers cannot do as they please. The model assumes, therefore, that decision makers' policy maps reflect as well as shape policy development.

Not all the propositions that can be derived from the model will be tested in this study. We present the model to give direction to the analysis. Particular hypotheses derived from the model will be introduced as we proceed. Our major objective is to demonstrate the utility of the typology of policy development that we construct from city budget data as indicators of policy outcomes and, indirectly, of public policy.

The Concepts and Measures

1. *Policy and policy outcomes. Policy* is defined as the relationship of a governmental unit to its environment. It finds expression in general programs and specific decisions, or in policy declarations of decision makers. But because a policy need not be declared to be a policy, analysis cannot rely on manifest statements or overt decisions alone but must concern itself with policy outcomes. By policy outcomes we mean the concrete manifestations of policy—revenues, expenditures, regulations, court decisions, the exertion of police power, and so on. Policy outcomes, then reflect the orientations of a policy makers, regardless of whether or not a conscious decision has been made. On the other hand, because policy outcomes may at times represent unanticipated results not intended by policy makers, policy analysis cannot altogether ignore policy declarations. In fact, the relationship between policy intentions and policy outcomes challenges the analyst of public policy.

To develop our concept of policy further, we conceive of public policy as a response of government to challenges or pressures from the physical and social environment. Changes in public policy either adjust or adapt the political system to environmental changes, or they bring about changes in the environment. Which course of action is chosen depends on a multitude of factors—the structure of the political system, its human and physical capabilities, the degree of mass or elite involvement in the political process, the vitality of private associations making public demands; and, last but not least, the perceptions, preferences, and orientations of policy makers.

The problematics of policy making arise out of the relationship between changes in the environment that require some response, the ways in which these changes are experienced as challenges by decision makers, and the values that decision makers may seek in formulating policy. Policy, then, is a response to environmental pressures, both physical and social, as well as anticipation of a future state of affairs. If this is the case, a change in policy is both causal and purposive: it is "caused" by environmental challenges, but it is also directed toward a goal and shaped by a purpose. The tension arising out of the simultaneous impact of causal and purposive "forcings" is a basic dilemma in the scientific study of politics.

Analysis of policy outcomes through time requires a classification of policies.[5] We distinguish between "adaptive" and "control" policies. The measure used as an indicator of an adaptive policy is the percentage of *total* government expenses spent for health, libraries, parks and recreation.[6] These major accounting categories used to report expenditures presumably include the major amenities offered by cities. A "high amenities" city differs from a city with a traditional services orientation in that it spends less of city income for fire and police services or public works.[7]

The measure used to indicate a city's control policy is the percentage of all *general* government expenses spent by the planning commission. *General* government expenses include essentially all administrative expenses and salaries *not* included under fire, police, or recreation categories, and so on.[8]

2. *Policy development and its measurement.* Policy outcomes are responses to changes and challenges in the environment. Policy development refers to a set of policy outcomes that follow each other sequentially

through time. If the annual outcomes are similar, we speak of the resulting profile as a *stage* of policy development. Three stages will be identified: *retarded, transitional,* and *advanced.*[9] The median of medians for all cities with respect to planning and amenities expenditures over a period of eight years serves as the criterion of similar or dissimilar outcomes.

The definition of a set of sequential and similar outcomes as a stage presupposes continuity and stability. But the conception of development implies that one stage may, sooner or later, be followed by a new stage. It is unlikely that one stage will suddenly yield to another. Not only may development revert; even if development is "progressive," the transformation from one stage to the next may involve a series of dissimilar outcomes—some outcomes characteristic of an earlier stage, others characteristic of a later stage. If this occurs, an eight-year profile cannot easily be assigned to one stage or another. Put differently, we cannot easily predict whether the system will remain in the earlier stage or move into a later stage.

To cope with this possibility, we define a set of sequential but dissimilar policy outcomes as a *phase* of development. The notion of phase suggests that the sequence is less clearly bounded and, perhaps, of shorter duration than a stage. As we are constructing three stages of development, we must provide for two phases—an *emergent* phase that indicates movement from the retarded to the transitional stage, and a *maturing* phase that is located between the transitional and advanced stages.

Figure 1 illustrates how annual policy outcomes are assigned to a stage or phase of policy development. If planning and amenities expenditures fall below the grand medians in every year of the eight-year sequence, the profile is classified as *retarded* (cell I); if one or the other type of expenditures falls above the grand medians, the profile is designated as transitional (cells II and III); and if both planning and amenities expenditures are above the medians in all eight years, the profile is being assigned to the *advanced* stage of development (cell IV).

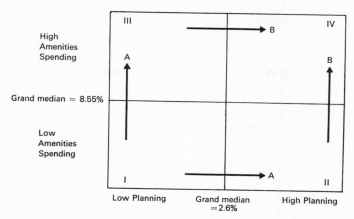

Figure 1. Categories of Policy Outcomes over Eight-year Period

If during the eight-year sequence expenditures move across the median lines, the profiles represent phases of development: outcomes moving from cell I to cells II or III (arrows A) are classified as *emergent*; those moving from cells I, II, or III into cell IV (arrows B) are designated as *maturing*.

Cases of "reversals" for which the model does not provide are being assigned to stages or phases of development in such a way that "reversal errors" are reduced as much as possible. This involves informed but hopefully not arbitrary assignment decisions.[10] We are satisfied that the reversals are not sufficient to invalidate the typology of policy development. As Table 1 shows, for the 82 cities whose policy profiles can be identified over an eight-year period, there were 572 opportunities for change in annual outcomes.[11] Of these opportunities eighty, or

14 percent, represented reversals from one year to the next. In the other 86 percent of opportunities, there either was no change, that is, all outcomes remained in the same stage over all eight years; or change occurred in the hypothesized ("progressive") direction. Reversals in stable stage cities are due, of course, to the assignment of some "impure" cases where reversals seem to be only temporary deviations from the regular pattern.

A validity test. In order to test the validity of the typological contructs and the underlying assumptions, we can divide the eight-year period into two four-year periods and assign each period's profile to either a stage or phase of policy development. Crosstabulation permits us to inspect the internal movement of the policy profiles from one period to the next. If our assumptions and

TABLE 1. Developmental Typology of City Policy Profiles with Opportunities for Change and Reversals

DEVELOPMENT TYPE	CITIES N =	OPPORTUNITIES N =	NUMBER OF REVERSALS				REVERSALS	
			(1)	(2)	(3)	(4)	N =	% =
Retarded	11	76	7	2			11	14
Emergent	14	98	5	5	1		18	18
Transitional	26	182	9	6		1	25	14
Maturing	15	104	5	6	1		20	19
Advanced	16	112	4	1			6	5
	82	572	30	20	2	1	80	14

TABLE 2. Policy Development of Cities in Developmental Sequence from 1958–61 to 1962–65

STATE OF DEVELOPMENT IN 1958–61	STATE OF DEVELOPMENT IN 1962–65				
	Retarded N = 11	Emergent N = 14	Transitional N = 26	Maturing N = 15	Advanced N = 16
Retarded N = 16	6	9			1
Emergent N = 16	4	2	7	3	
Transitional N = 24	1	3	14	5	1
Maturing N = 16			5	7	4
Advanced N = 10					10

assignments are reasonably valid, we should be able to predict, from knowledge of a profile's location on the development scale in the first four-year period, where it will be located in the second four-year period. We predict that cities in a stage of development are less likely to move than cities in a phase of development. We also predict that when there is movement, it is more likely to be in the hypothesized "progressive" direction than in a reversed direction. Table 2 presents the results.

It is readily evident that, with some exceptions, both predictions are supported by the data. Of the fifty cities in stages of development during the 1958–67 period, thirty or 60 percent remained in the same stage during the following 1962–65 period; but of the thirty-two cities in a phase of development during the earlier period, only nine or 28 percent remained there in the later period. If we consider the direction of movements, it appears that of the twenty cities in stages during the earlier period that did move, sixteen or 80 percent advanced in the expected direction. But this result is, of course, largely a function of the boundaries set to the typology: retarded cities can only move forward and advanced cities can only move backward. More significant, therefore, is the fact that none of the advanced cities reverted, suggesting that once this plateau is reached, institutionalization of policies makes reversal unlikely; and the further fact that of the ten transitional cities that did move, six moved forward and four backward. Similarly, of the fourteen emergent cities that moved, ten or 71 percent moved forward as

expected and only four returned to the retarded stage in the later period; but of the nine moving maturing cities, a bare majority of five reverted to the transitional stage. Of course, these results, whether "favorable" or not from the developmental standpoint, may be influenced by the original data. Some policy outcomes as measured are in some cases very close to the median of medians cutting point that serves as the criterion for assignment, so that we may be dealing here with errors over which we have no control. Nevertheless, we believe that the weight of the evidence is sufficient to warrant our interpretation of Table 2. It is also noteworthy that few of the movements, either forward or backward, exceed one step at a time. Of the twenty-six cities moving forward and having an opportunity to do so by *more* than one step (i.e., those retarded, emergent and transitional in the first period), twenty-one or 81 percent moved one step only; and of the nine cities moving backward and having an opportunity for more moves (i.e., those transitional and maturing in the first period), all but one reverted only one step.

Reversed development is an empirical fact of life. While stages of development as conceived by historians are inevitably consecutive and irreversible, policy development, is in fact, reversible. Although we assume that in general stages and phases follow each other in "progressive" order, an assumption that the results of Table 2 certainly do not falsify, no rigid assumptions need or should be made about the direction of change. Policy is the creation of men and can be changed by men, within certain constraints imposed by environmental necessities, in whatever direction they prefer. Otherwise the concept of policy would make little sense.

3. *Resource capability.* A city's resource capabilities can be measured in a variety of ways. Ideally, we would like to think of resource capability as the maximum amount of income a city can expect annually when serious efforts are made to tap all possible income sources, including current revenues from taxes, borrowed funds, grants in aid, or income from utilities, and so on. However, we have no way to determine whether such efforts have been made. Moreover, were we to use the readily available city income figures as a measure of resource capability, the measure would contravene our assumption that some cities are more pressed for revenue than others. Nor can we use a measure equivalent to per capita gross national product that is used in the comparative study of nations.[12] For a high proportion of the production of any city crosses city boundaries and is not available to support local government expenditures. Needed is a measure of the wealth remaining wholly within city limits and available to local taxation or such state taxation as is refundable to the city.

The measure we are using is, therefore, total assessed valuation per capita subject to local taxation for fiscal 1965–66, as determined by the California State Board of Equalization. In using this measure, we assume that wealth in the form of private, commercial, and industrial property will be a potential source of revenue, and that per capita assessed valuation is a rough indicator of a city's resource capability.[13] A city will hesitate to institute new programs or expand old ones if it has a low level of assessed valuation per capita, but may be more inclined to do so if it has a high level of valuation.

4. *Policy maps.* Policy, we must remember, is a theoretical concept imposed on observed reality. Regardless of whether specific decisions have been deliberately made or not, what we observe are policy outcomes from which city policy is inferred. If, as we shall suggest, policy outcomes as summarized in the typology of policy development are posi-

tively related to indicators of what we may consider environmental challenges, the presumption that the policy was intended to meet the pressures of the environment is strong, but it is only a presumption. And because it is only a presumption, the investigation of policy makers' "policy maps" becomes an important component of policy analysis.

What do we mean by *policy map?* In the first place, we assume that if policy is a response to environmental challenges, these challenges will have been perceived by policy makers. They may choose, consciously or unconsciously, not to act, but such nonaction is also a response that will be reflected in policy outcomes. By being perceived the environmental challenges become "problems" or "policy issues." In order to tap this facet of the policy map, we asked this question:

Mr. Councilman, before talking about your work as a councilman and the work of the council itself, we would like to ask you about some of the problems facing this community. In your opinion, what are the two most pressing problems here in (city)?

The policy map consists, secondly, of the policy maker's recommendations for action or "policy positions"—those preferences that he either brings into the policy-making situation or evolves in the course of decision making. Again, his not consciously entertaining a policy position on an issue is yet to be considered a policy orientation and a component of his policy map. We therefore asked this question:[14]

Now, looking toward the future, what one community-wide improvement, in your opinion, does this city "need most" to be attractive to its citizens?

Finally, we assume that the policy map includes the policy maker's "ends-in-view" or values—those hopes and expectations concerning the future which policy decisions are to bring about. The following question was designed to yield what one may think of as the "policy image":

Now, taking the broadest view possible, how do you see (city) in the future? I mean, what kind of a city would you personally like (city) to be in the next twenty-five years?

Whether these three components of the policy map constitute a consistent whole, a "perspective" as Harold Lasswell would call it,[15] is an empirical question not central to the present study, but one we shall speculate about in the conclusion. Needless to say, perhaps, knowledge of the policy map does not permit prediction about the outcome of decision making on any particular policy issue. But we proceed on the assumption that policy maps represent important linkages between environmental challenges and public policies.

5. *Units of analysis and interpretation.* Although the data on policy maps come from interviews with individuals, our analysis uses councils as the units of analysis. Decision making by legislative bodies is a collective act. Not the individual councilman but the council, as a whole or under the majority rule, is the effective policy maker. Past research on legislatures, following in the wake of voting studies, has analyzed the behavior of individuals *in* the legislature in order to make statements about the behavior *of* legislatures. This procedure presents serious outcomes as measured by budget data are due to collective decisions (or nondecisions), the legislative group rather than the individual legislator is the more viable unit of analysis. Council perceptions, positions, or images are therefore constructed or reconstructed from data about individuals or provided by individuals, permitting us to make statements about city councils and not about city councilmen. We shall report the rules followed in this procedure in the text or footnotes.[16] This type of analysis is of course made possible by the relatively large (though for satisfactory statistical purposes still all too small) number of legislative groups being investigated. As far as we know, no similar type of analysis using as many as eighty or so units has ever been undertaken in the comparative study of legislative bodies.

In reading and interpreting the tables, a number of methodological considerations must be kept in mind. In the first place, we are dealing with data that come from truly independent sources—the federal census reporting population characteristics, city budgets reporting financial allocations, and interviews with city councilmen. These different kinds of data are used to construct quite different properties of the units—city councils —that we are observing. The census yields data that are best interpreted as representing the council's "contextual" properties; the budget data are representative, in a very direct sense, of the council's "emergent" properties; and the interview data provide the basis for "aggregate" properties.[17] To relate properties as diverse as these is extraordinarily difficult. But for this reason one cannot simply write off even modest relationships between variables as not significant.

Second, the typology of policy development that serves as our major device for ordering the data is not a simple continuum. While the five types constitute an ordinal ranking on a scale from "more developed" to "less developed," they also represent qualitative differences associated with different levels of development. In other words, a city's movement from one stage into another may be due to structural changes in causal factors rather than simple gradual increases. This means that variables related to city policy development may well exhibit sharp changes at certain points in the developmental sequence rather than incremental changes from one stage to another. For instance, a council's orientation to action may change radically after it has left the retarded stage and entered the emergent phase and then not change at all. Also, variables need not change monotonically across the five developmental types. Development may be related, for instance, to city growth in the early stages or phases but may decline in the advanced cities. Or cities at the three intermediate levels of policy development may show characteristics not shared by the least and most developed cities. Or cities in the two phases of development may be more similar to each other than to cities in the immediate neighboring stages.

Finally, we are less impressed by "significant differences" in a statistical sense that we might find than by patterns in the distribution of the data that make theoretical sense. The small number of cases also makes difficult the controlling of one variable by another that is so necessary if spurious relationships and false interpretations are to be avoided. We have used the control technique in relating resource capability to policy development, but we have not done so with the interview data, largely because the frequencies of cases in particular cells of the tables would be greatly strained by the procedure. This makes it all the more necessary to view each table not as an isolated entity unrelated to any other table. Rather, it is the weight of all the tables inspected simultaneously that must be considered in making inferences or drawing conclusions.

The Analysis

1. *Environmental challenges and policy development.* City size, density, and growth rate are direct indicators of challenges from the environment that every city faces. They bring in their wake problems that the city council may seek to solve through policies that adapt the city to the environment or that control environmental pressures. As the typology of city policy development is built on outcomes that reflect such policies, it follows:

Hypothesis 1a: The larger a city's size, the more developed is city policy likely to be.
Hypothesis 1b: The greater a city's density, the more developed is city policy likely to be.
Hypothesis 1c: The greater a city's growth, the more developed is city policy likely to be.

Table 3 shows that the three hypotheses are not falsified by the data. Moreover, the data show a pattern of policy development that, with two exceptions, is highly linear. We have no explanation for the deviation from the pattern of the transitional cities in the low density category. With regard to growth we note, as we perhaps might have expected, a levelling-off of the effect of growth in the advanced stage, the terminus of development. Apparently, once policy

TABLE 3. Relationships between City Size, Density, and Growth and Policy Development*

			POLICY DEVELOPMENT		
	Retarded N = 11	Emergent N = 14	Transitional N = 26	Maturing N = 15	Advanced N = 16
Population Size	(%)	(%)	(%)	(%)	(%)
<10,000	82	79	35	13	0
10–50,000	18	21	46	67	44
>50,000	0	0	19	20	56
	100	100	100	100	100
Density					
<2,000	73	58	19	41	0
2–4,000	18	28	50	26	44
>4,000	9	14	31	33	56
	100	100	100	100	100
Growth Rate					
<10%	54	36	43	13	19
10–50%	46	49	39	47	62
>50%	0	14	19	40	19
	100	100	100	100	100

*Size and density data for 1965; growth rate for 1960–65.

development has reached the advanced stage, growth is likely to be marginal in its effect on city policy.

The data suggest that city councils adopt policies which are congruent with needs rooted in pressures from the environment. Whatever the declared policy objectives of city fathers, they tend to follow policies that either adapt the city to or seek to control the environment.

2. *Resource capability and policy development.* The resources available to a city government are an important constraint on the expenditures it can make and the policies it can follow. Resource capability is largely an objectively limiting factor, but it is also subjective in that its limiting effect is interpreted by the city council before it becomes a factor in the policy-making process. For instance, the council estimates how high a tax rate city residents are willing to approve. High resource capability is necessary for policy development, but it is not sufficient. Nevertheless, we hypothesize:

Hypothesis 2: The higher a city's resource capability, the more developed is city policy likely to be.

Table 4, Part A, shows that there is no support for the hypothesis. In fact, more of the retarded cities seem to have high resource capability than any of the other cities in various stages or phases of development. However, the distributions may be misleading. As we suggested, policy development is dependent on policy makers' willingness to mobilize resources, and their willingness to do so may depend on the intensity of pressures from the environment *regardless* of available resources. Therefore, one must control the relationship between resource capability and policy development by such indicators of environmental challenges as size, density, or growth rate. Table 4, B, reports the findings.

In the smaller cities, presumably less subject to environmental challenges, fewer of the more developed than of the less developed cities are low in resource capability, just as hypothesized; but development also declines in cities of the same size with high capability,

counter to the hypothesis. In the larger cities, on the other hand, resource capability is highly related to policy development in the advanced stage.

Controls for density reveal the same pattern even more distinctly. In the low-density, high capability cities policy development declines, counter to the hypothesis; but in the densely populated cities high resource capability is related to policy development across the continuum in linear order.

Finally, if resource capability is controlled by growth rate, the developmental process clearly follows the hypothesized pattern only in the high-growth cities with high assessed valuation (and again in linear fashion except for leveling off in the advanced stage). The data do not permit us to say anything about the slow-growing, low-capability cities; but in the slow-growth, high-capability and the high-growth, low-capability cities hypothesis 4 is clearly falsified.

Policy makers evidently respond to environmental pressures less in terms of the resources that are available than in terms of their willingness to mobilize these resources. It is for this reason that inquiry into policy makers' perceptions of city problems, policy positions, and policy images becomes an important part of policy analysis.

3. *Problem perceptions and policy development.* Environmental challenges are not self-evident. They become evident only if and when they give rise to "problems" that come to the attention of policy makers. The perception of a problem means that traditional ways of doing things—policies—are inadequate or at the very least that their adequacy is in question. It is through the perception of problems, then, that the policy process is set in motion. But, if policy makers do not respond to problems generated by environmental challenges, either by not perceiving them or not acting upon them, this does not mean that there is no policy. It simply means that prevailing policy continues.

In collegial bodies like legislatures or councils a problem is a problem if the members *between them* are aware of the problem, but it is not necessary for all or even most of

TABLE 4. Relationship between City Resource Capability and Policy Development

ASSESSED VALUATION PER CAPITA	POLICY DEVELOPMENT				
	Retarded N = 11	Emergent N = 14	Transitional N = 26	Maturing N = 15	Advanced N = 16
Part A	(%)	(%)	(%)	(%)	(%)
> $2,600	54	28	38	33	44
$1,700–2,600	18	44	24	47	25
< 1,700	27	28	38	20	31
	100	100	100	100	100
Part B					
Size < 25,000	(%)	(%)	(%)	(%)	(%)
< $1,700	27	28	24	13	6
> $1,700	73	72	39	54	6
Size > 25,000					
< $1,700	—	—	15	7	25
> $1,700	—	—	23	27	62
	100	100	100	100	100
Density					
< 2,000					
< $1,700	9	14	0	7	0
> $1,700	63	44	19	33	0
> 2,000					
< $1,700	19	14	38	13	32
> $1,700	9	28	43	47	68
	100	100	100	100	100
Growth					
< 10%					
< $1,700	9	0	19	0	6
> $1,700	46	36	23	13	13
> 10%					
< $1,700	18	28	19	20	25
> $1,700	27	36	39	67	56
	100	1000	100	100	100

the members to perceive it. Different members have access to different aspects of the environment. Because of varied membership elected collegial bodies can be more sensitive to the environment than administrative hierarchical organizations. "Problem diversity," therefore, refers to the absolute number of different problems articulated by a council, adjusted for comparison across councils by the total number of mentions in each council.[18] Because, as we have seen, the more developed cities face more severe environmental challenges, we formulate:

Hypothesis 3: The more diverse the prob-

lems perceived by a council, the more developed is city policy likely to be.

Table 5 shows that this hypothesis is falsified by the data. In fact, problem diversity is greater among the councils of the retarded cities where one might least expect it and declines almost linearly in the following stages and phases, though there is some leveling off at the more developed end of the development continuum.

How can one interpret this finding? One plausible answer is that policy develops in response to few but intensively felt problems, while a multitude of minor problems that are

TABLE 5. Relationship between Problem Diversity and Policy Development

DIVERSITY SCORE QUARTILE	POLICY DEVELOPMENT				
	Retarded N = 9	Emergent N = 12	Transitional N = 25	Maturing N = 15	Advanced N = 16
	(%)	(%)	(%)	(%)	(%)
I. (Most)	45	33	20	27	6
II.	22	17	28	20	44
III.	22	33	28	13	31
IV. (Least)	11	17	24	40	19
	100	100	100	100	100
Index	+34	+16	−4	−13	−13

not critical do not stimulate the policy process. If this is so, we should expect that problems are more "visible" to the council as a whole in the more developed than in the less developed cities. A measure of "problem visibility" must take account not only of the absolute number of problems that are articulated, but also of the number of councilmen who articulate any one problem.[19] We postulate:

Hypothesis 4: The more visible problems are to the council, the more developed is city policy likely to be.

Table 6 tends to support the hypothesis, although there is some dropping off at the advanced stage. One might expect this because, as the very concept "advanced" suggests, a council in this stage of policy development is likely to have the challenges stemming from the environment well in hand. As a result, not only are fewer problems perceived in this stage, but the few problems are so self-evident that, though of great urgency, they fail to stand out as particularly visible.

Problem visibility may be thought of as setting the council's legislative agenda. The more visible a problem, the more likely it is to be considered by the council. But the visibility is at most a necessary and not a sufficient condition for legislative action. In order to act, the council must, in fact, be agreed that the problem is a problem. We therefore measure the degree of council agreement on the single most visible problem as well as council agreement on the general policy area that seems most problematic.[20] We propose:

Hypothesis 5: The more agreement on the single most visible problem, the more developed is city policy likely to be.

Hypothesis 6: The more agreement on the

TABLE 6. Relationship between Problem Visibility and Policy Development

VISIBILITY SCORE QUARTILE	POLICY DEVELOPMENT				
	Retarded N = 9	Emergent N = 12	Transitional N = 25	Maturing N = 15	Advanced N = 16
	(%)	(%)	(%)	(%)	(%)
I. (High)	22	17	28	40	12
II.	11	33	24	13	45
III.	0	25	36	20	31
IV. (Low)	67	25	12	27	12
	100	100	100	100	100
Index	−45	−8	+16	+13	0

most visible problem area, the more developed is city policy likely to be.

Table 7 tends to support these hypotheses, but we note an interesting deviation from the expected patterns in the cities of the emergent phase. While on the single problem measure more councils in the emergent phase reveal high agreement, these councils are least agreed on the general area of problems facing their cities. We can only speculate on these results. It may be that being in the emergent phase is, on the one hand, a disorienting condition that makes it difficult to achieve agreement on the general area of problems that require action; but that, precisely because of this condition, high agreement can be reached on the single most urgent problem. However, we also note that all councils, regardless of level of policy development, can evidently reach agreement more readily on a specific problem than on a general area of related problems.

What kinds of problems or problem areas are most salient to city councils? And is such salience related to policy development? Although we do not propose to introduce a formal hypothesis, we are altogether unprepared for the results obtained. Taking all those councils where at least three councilmen had named the same problem, we obtain the findings reported in Table 8.

As Table 8 shows, no three councilmen in any council, whatever the city's stage or phase of development, articulated problems relating to amenities; and only a few councils on various levels of development mustered enough members who considered planning or zoning as especially pressing problems. We shall leave it to another occasion to interpret the full implications of the results reported in Table 8. Suffice it to say here that problems involving provisions for amenities clearly do not rank high on the agenda of problems considered pressing. Put differently, amenities appear to be luxuries that councils are willing to indulge in only after other urban problems, notably sewerage and drainage, financing of services and transportation, have been solved. But planning and zoning also do not stand out as pressing problems. Either these matters are being satisfactorily handled already, so that they are perceived as problems by only a few councils, or they are not

TABLE 7. *Relationship between Agreement on Specific Problem and General Problem Area and Policy Development*

SINGLE PROBLEM AGREEMENT	POLICY DEVELOPMENT				
	Retarded $N = 9$	Emergent $N = 12$	Transitional $N = 25$	Maturing $N = 15$	Advanced $N = 16$
	(%)	(%)	(%)	(%)	(%)
67–100%	22	50	36	47	46
51–66%	45	25	32	20	43
0–50%	33	25	32	33	13
	100	100	100	100	100
Index	−11	+25	+4	+14	+33
PROBLEM AREA AGREEMENT					
	(%)	(%)	(%)	(%)	(%)
67–100%	33	17	32	13	37
51–66%	0	8	16	54	13
0–50%	67	75	52	33	50
	100	100	100	100	100
Index	−34	−58	−20	−20	−13

TABLE 8.   Problems and Problem Areas Perceived as Pressing by City Councils

TYPES OF PROBLEMS PERCEIVED	POLICY DEVELOPMENT					
	Retarded N = 9	Emergent N = 12	Transitional N = 25	Maturing N = 15	Advanced N = 16	Total N = 77
Services & Utilities						
Sewerage & drainage	1	1	5	2	—	9
Sanitation & disposal	—	1	—	—	—	1
Water sources	1	—	1	—	1	3
Financing services	—	1	2	4	3	10
Total in area	2	3	8	6	4	23
Percent in area	22%	25%	32%	40%	25%	30%
Amenities						
Total in area	—	—	—	—	—	—
Promotion & Development						
Planning, master plan	—	1	—	—	3	4
Zoning & maintenance	2	1	4	—	—	7
Transportation & traffic	—	1	5	2	3	11
Attract business & industry	—	1	2	—	—	3
Urban renewal & development	—	1	—	—	3	4
Assessment and taxes	—	—	—	2	—	2
Total in area	2	5	11	4	9	31
Percent in area	22%	42%	44%	27%	57%	40%
Social & Remedial						
Water pollution	—	—	—	—	1	1
Race & ethnic problems	—	—	—	—	1	1
Educational problems	—	—	—	1	—	1
Housing	1	—	—	—	—	1
Total in area	1	—	—	1	2	4
Percent in area	11%	0%	0%	7%	12%	5%
Governmental & Intergovernmental						
Annexation	1	—	—	—	—	1
Local government personnel	—	1	—	—	—	1
Citizen participation	—	—	—	—	1	1
Total in area	1	1	—	—	1	3
Percent in area	11%	8%	0%	0%	6%	4%
Not classifiable	3	3	6	4	0	16
	34%	25%	24%	26%	0%	21%
Grand total	100%	100%	100%	100%	100%	100%

recognized as viable means for coping with environmental challenges.[21]

When asked why they considered a problem to be a problem, a variety of reasons were given by councilmen that could be coded into three categories—operational and financial, political, and inevitable or uncontrollable. Councils were characterized in terms of the dominant set of reasons that were given.[22] We do not entertain any particular hypothesis about how councils on various levels of development are likely to rationalize their city's problems. But we note two results in Table 9. First, great majorities of councils in all cities, regardless of level of policy development, attribute community problems to circumstances beyond their control. This is to say that a substantial number of problems, as we have speculated all along, have their roots in environmental conditions. But we also note that "political" reasons are given by more councils as we move from the retarded to the advanced stage of development. The linearity of the data suggests that

TABLE 9.   Reasons Given for Problems and Policy Development

TYPE OF REASONS	POLICY DEVELOPMENT*				
	Retarded $N = 9$	Emergent $N = 12$	Transitional $N = 25$	Maturing $N = 15$	Advanced $N = 16$
Operational- financial	(%) 22	(%) 8	(%) 36	(%) 20	(%) 25
Inevitable- uncontrollable	78	92	84	73	62
Political	11	17	12	27	38

*Percentages total more than 100 since any one council could give sets of reasons that are numerically tied.

politicization of the decision-making milieu in these cities may well be related to policy development. The more politicized the social environment, the more likely it seems to be that policy development takes place.

4. *Policy positions and policy development.* Once problems have been identified and agreed upon as agenda items, the legislature or council will seek to evolve a policy position. A policy position by the council, whether held by all members or only a majority, is of course an emergent property of the council following upon interaction, deliberation, and possibly compromise, and it is not simply the addition of individual members' policy preferences. What we are tapping, then, when we ask individual councilmen to suggest the "most needed" communitywide improvement and then aggregate these recommendations, is not the council's policy as it emerges in the voting situation, but rather the initial state of a council position before the legislative process has had an opportunity to affect the deci-

sional outcome.[23] But as actual council policy is reflected in the policy outcomes out of which the typology of policy development is constructed, inquiry into the hypothetical initial state of the policy process can shed light on the dynamics of policy making. We shall first explore the diversity and visibility of improvement recommendations made by councils in varying stages and phases of policy development. Again we stipulate:

Hypothesis 7: The more diverse improvements recommended in a council, the more developed is city policy likely to be.

And again, as with problem perceptions, we find the diversity hypothesis falsified by the data.[24] As Table 10 shows, highly diverse improvement proposals are just as likely to be made in the less developed as in the most developed councils. However, though problem and improvement proposal diversity is low in the more developed cities, and perhaps because of it, we expect that the improvement

TABLE 10.   Relationship between Improvement Diversity and Policy Development

IMPROVEMENT SCORE QUARTILE	POLICY DEVELOPMENT				
	Retarded $N = 9$	Emergent $N = 12$	Transitional $N = 25$	Maturing $N = 15$	Advanced $N=16$
I. (Most)	(%) 33	(%) 50	(%) 20	(%) 13	(%) 31
II.	33	17	36	33	0
III.	11	8	16	27	57
IV. (Least)	22	25	28	27	12
	100	100	100	100	100
Index	+11	+25	− 8	−14	+19

TABLE 11.   *Relationship between Improvement Visibility and Policy Development*

IMPROVEMENT SCORE QUARTILE	POLICY DEVELOPMENT				
	Retarded N = 9	Emergent N = 12	Transitional N = 25	Maturing N = 15	Advanced N = 16
	(%)	(%)	(%)	(%)	(%)
I. (High)	11	25	28	7	31
II.	22	17	16	46	31
III.	33	25	24	40	13
IV. (Low)	33	33	32	7	25
	100	100	100	100	100
Index	− 22	− 8	− 4	0	+ 6

recommendations that are made are highly visible in these cities. Hence:

Hypothesis 8: The more visible the improvements recommended in a council, the more developed is city policy likely to be.

Table 11 supports the hypothesis.[25] Recommendations for improvements are more visible in the developed than the less developed cities, and only in maturing and advanced cities do a majority of councils fall into the two upper visibility quartiles.

We expect on the basis of this finding that councils in the more developed cities are more agreed on what specific improvements or what general improvement areas are needed than councils in the less developed cities:

Hypothesis 9: The more agreement there is in a council on the single most needed improvement, the more developed is city policy likely to be.

Hypothesis 10: The more agreement there is in a council on a general improvement area, the more developed is city policy likely to be.

Table 12 presents the data.[26] They represent some interesting findings. In the first place, with respect to agreement on the single most visible improvement proposal made, there is a very low level of agreement regardless of a city's location on the policy development continuum. Only a few councils are highly agreed, and only a few more manage

to achieve better than simple majority agreement. In all types of city policy development, majorities of the councils fall below the majority criterion needed for agreement. Interestingly, and though the percentage differences are small, fewer councils in both types of "phase" cities are in the nonagreement category than councils in the "stage" cities. But, in general, we must consider Hypothesis 9 as being falsified by the data.

If we turn to the less demanding Hypothesis 10—less demanding because agreement is needed only on a general area rather than on a specific case of improvement—the data give only weak support to the hypothesis. Although few of the retarded councils are high on improvement area agreement and the more developed councils tend in the expected direction, the significant aspect of the table is that only one council in each of the two types of "phase" cities is unable to achieve a minimal level of agreement. The tendency already noted in connection with single improvement agreement is exaggerated under the less demanding condition of general improvement area agreement.

What are we to make of these unexpected findings? Are they merely due to random fluctuations in the data, or are they of theoretical significance? We must seek an explanation in the nature of the emergent and maturing phases of policy development as these were defined. Cities in these phases undergo sudden bursts of activity, reflected in policy outcomes, that move them from one stage into another. It would seem that this unfolding of policy-making "energy" is

TABLE 12. Relationship between Agreement on Specific Improvement and General Improvement Area and Policy Development

SINGLE IMPROVEMENT AGREEMENT	POLICY DEVELOPMENT				
	Retarded N = 9	Emergent N = 11*	Transitional N = 25	Maturing N = 15	Advanced N = 16
	(%)	(%)	(%)	(%)	(%)
67–100%	11	0	12	7	6
51–66%	0	36	20	33	19
0–50%	89	64	68	60	75
	100	100	100	100	100
Index	−78	−64	−56	−53	−69
IMPROVEMENT AREA AGREEMENT					
	(%)	(%)	(%)	(%)	(%)
67–100%	22	45	40	60	37
51–66%	45	45	28	33	44
0–50%	33	10	32	7	19
	100	100	100	100	100
Index	−11	+35	+ 8	+53	+18

*One council in this type could not be properly measured and had to be dropped from the tabulation.

greatly aided by *pre-decisional* agreement or at least by relatively little disagreement in councils as to what improvements or areas of improvement are most needed. This finding and out interpretation suggest that we are tapping a very real component of the policy process by aggregating individual responses.[27]

What types of improvement were recommended by the councils that are agreed? Because of the dispersion of single improvement recommendations, we shall present only the data on improvement areas.[28] What is of interest in the data presented in Table 13 is, first of all, that the improvement areas are quite different from the comparable problem areas of Table 8. Only one council in a maturing city suggested services and utilities as an area needing improvements. But while no council had perceived amenities as a *problem*, a fourth of the councils in each of the developmental types, except the retarded, reported that amenities constitute an area where improvements are needed.

TABLE 13. Relationship between Improvement Areas and Policy Development

IMPROVEMENT AREA	POLICY DEVELOPMENT				
	Retarded N = 9	Emergent N = 11	Transitional N = 25	Maturing N = 15	Advanced N = 16
Services and utilities	(%) 0	(%) 0	(%) 0	(%) 7	(%) 0
Promotion and development	0	8	4	14	25
Amenities	11	25	28	26	25
Less than 3 informants	89	67	68	53	50
	100	100	100	100	100

This discontinuity in council policy maps from problem perceptions to policy positions requires explanation. Does it mean that councils do not behave rationally? One might be inclined to think so, but discontinuity is not necessarily the same thing as inconsistency. Because amenities are not recognized as "problems," it does not follow that councils may not wish to pursue policies to obtain amenities for their cities. For policies, we argued, are not simple conditioned responses to environmental challenges; they are also the products of those ends-in-view, values, or images of the future that policy makers carry with them into the policy-making situation. While the policy positions articulated in response to the question about needed improvements may not be relevant to the problems that councils perceived and articulated, they are certainly not inconsistent with them. The results suggest that policy images are important components of the council's policy map as a whole.

5. *Policy images and policy development.* What kind of future a legislative body envisages is likely to color its perceptions of environmental challenges and its current policy preferences. But images of the future are also likely to be projections of current trends in a city's policy development. They tend to orient the council toward the future and may influence future development, but they are not independent of present tendencies. Moreover, the more limited the legislature's jurisdiction, the better-defined its image is likely to be. In the case of municipal councils whose tasks are well set by statutory requirements and limitations we can expect that long-range goals are well defined.

Because we know that policy development varies with demographic indicators of environmental challenges such as size, density, and growth, and because we also can assume that these indicators are highly related to ecological factors such as residential patterns or level of industrialization, we hypothesize:

Hypothesis 11a: The more developed a city's policy, the more will councils tend to envisage the city's future as "balanced" or industrial.

Hypothesis 11b: The less developed a city's policy, the more will councils tend to envisage the city's future as residential and/or recreational.

The ease with which it was possible to classify responses into the categories of "residential" or "recreational," on the one hand, and of "balanced" or "industrial," on the other hand, supports our speculation that long-range images or goals are likely to be well defined in legislative bodies with limited scopes of action.[29] As Table 14 shows, the reciprocal Hypotheses 11a and 11b are well supported by the data.

Because policy images are well defined, we hypothesize that there is a great deal of agreement within the councils on policy goals. But as, by definition, the less developed cities are engaged in a more limited range of activities than the more developed ones, we can expect the difference to be reflected in the level of agreement:

TABLE 14. Relationship between Policy Image and Policy Development

CONTENT OF IMAGE	POLICY DEVELOPMENT				
	Retarded N = 9	Emergent N = 12	Transitional N = 25	Maturing N = 15	Advanced N = 16
Residential-recreational	(%) 56	(%) 50	(%) 52	(%) 27	(%) 13
Split or non-classifiable	22	8	12	7	19
Balanced and/or industrial	22	42	36	66	68
	100	100	100	100	100

TABLE 15. *Relationship between Agreement on Policy Image and Policy Development*

POLICY IMAGE AGREEMENT	POLICY DEVELOPMENT				
	Retarded *N = 9*	*Emergent* *N = 12*	*Transitional* *N = 25*	*Maturing* *N = 15*	*Advanced* *N = 16*
	(%)	(%)	(%)	(%)	(%)
100%	78	67	52	53	50
67–99%	0	25	32	27	31
51–66%	0	0	4	13	0
Split or non-classifiable	22	8	12	7	19
	100	100	100	100	100

Hypothesis 12: The less developed a city's policy, the greater the proportion of councils reaching high agreement on the image of city future.

Table 15 supports the hypothesis. It not only supports it but reveals an extraordinarily high level of agreement, especially in the retarded and emergent cities where two-thirds and more of the councils are unanimously agreed on the policy image. But in the transitional, maturing, and advanced cities, too, most councils agree on long-range goals by overwhelming majorities. We are dealing here, it seems, with that substantive consensus on values that facilitates the democratic process of bargaining, compromise, and adjustment. It is within this consensus that disagreements over particular policies can be resolved and lasting community conflicts be reduced to manageable format. However, the fact that agreement on future goals is inversely related to policy development represents a profound dilemma for democratic theory.

Conclusions

A metropolitan city's development toward distinct and differentiated styles of social life is powerfully shaped by policies that are responses to challenges from the metropolitan environment. Whether a city stands still, moves forward to reach a new level of development, or reverts to an earlier state depends on the strength of such challenges as can be measured by city size, density or growth rate. In general, development involves the adoption of policies that either adapt the city to the changing environment or control the environment. In this process of adjustment and control through appropriate policies, the city's resource capabilities seem to play only a limited part. It appears that policy makers' willingness to tap city resources in order to adopt appropriate policies is a critical component of the policy development process.

Policy makers' willingness to set their city on a course of development depends on the content of their policy maps—how they perceive the problems facing the city, what preferences they entertain with regard to policy alternatives, and how they envisage the city's future. In general, it seems that municipal decision makers' policy maps constitute a consistent whole, although there may be discontinuities and deviations. It also appears, in general, that the various components of the policy map are meaningfully related to the stage or phase of city policy development. There is in the councils of a metropolitan region such as that around the San Francisco Bay a satisfactory level of agreement on what the problems are that cities in different stages of development face, and there is very high agreement on what the city's future should be like. There is less agreement, as one might expect, on the specific policies that should be adopted to obtain the goals that are envisaged, but there is sufficient agreement on the general area of issues that needs attention.

It has been the burden of our argument that the systematic study of public policy cannot be content with correlating indicators of environmental challenges or indicators of resource capability to policy outcomes. Rather, it was our assumption that policy development is greatly influenced by the predilections, preferences, orientations, and expectations of policy makers—in short, by the political process itself. The data presented in the analysis, though limited, confirm the validity of this assumption. Yet, as we noted, the fact that level of agreement on policy goals seems to be inversely related to policy development raises many problems for the policy maker. Not the least important is the question of how a developed community can maintain a sufficient consensus on public goals. In the city councils of the San Francisco Bay metropolitan region a high level of agreement on policy goals still exists. Whether it will continue to exist in the face of increasing differentiation of areas within the city challenges the urban political process.

Notes

1. See, for instance, the recent work by Oliver P. Williams *et al.*, *Suburban Differences and Metropolitan Policies: A Philadelphia Story* (Philadelphia: University of Pennsylvania Press, 1965).
2. Oliver P. Williams is a recent paper has argued that metropolitan regions are collections of small groups of residents and the economic superstructures necessary to sustain them. Each group is characterized by the choice of a distinctive life style, and because members of the various groups wish to live in congenial environments they tend to be found in similar locations throughout the region. Precisely where they are located is a matter of economics and the remnants of past land uses in the region, but the fact of congeniality is a major cause of similarity in location choice. See "A Framework for Metropolitan Political Analysis," prepared for the Conference on Comparative Research in Community Politics, held at Athens, Georgia, November 16–19, 1966.
3. See, for instance, F. Stuart Chapin, Jr., and Shirley F. Weiss (eds.), *Urban Growth Dynamics* (New York: John Wiley, 1962); Wilbur R. Thompson, *A Preface to Urban Economics* (Baltimore: Johns Hopkins University Press, 1965); the relevant literature is legion.

4. More complete studies, using multiple correlation and regression analyses, will appear in forthcoming publications of the City Council Research Project. But see also our earlier report: Robert Eyestone and Heinz Eulau, "City Councils and Policy Outcomes: Development Profiles." in James Q. Wilson (ed.), *City Politics and Public Policy* (New York: John Wiley, 1968).
5. Much classificatory activity, in the field of public policy analysis as elsewhere, is a game. Either the inventors of classifications and typologies do not make it clear just what analytical purpose the classification is to serve, or they may even imply that by having a classification they have explained something. We make this point to have it understood that we are not interested in justifying or defending the particular typology of policy development that we have constructed, but in examining its utility in the analysis at hand.
6. Since education and public welfare policies are not made at the city level in California, we cannot use expenditures in these areas as measures of policy outcomes.
7. The amenities measure is an attempt to tap Williams' and Adrian's concept of amenities. See Oliver P. Williams and Charles R. Adrian, *Four Cities: A Study in Comparative Policy Making* (Philadelphia: University of Pennsylvania Press, 1963), pp. 198–225.
8. Expenses by the planning commission include both expenses and outlays, therefore encompassing the range of items from paper supplies to salaries of full-time city planners to special outside studies commissioned by the city planning commission. California State law requires every city to have a planning commission, but this body may be, and frequently is, a standing committee of citizens appointed by the city council and incurring no expenses charged against the city. Therefore, the actual dollar amount spent by the planning commission would seem to be a good indicator of the extent of a city's commitment to the idea of planning as a way to control the environment. General government expenses are used as the percentage base rather than total government expenses in order to make planning definitionally independent of amenity expenditures.
9. It is important to keep in mind that while we are using categories reminiscent of such concepts as "traditional," "transitional," and "modern" used in the literature of comparative politics, our observations cover only a small segment of that part of the historical developmental process usually called "modern." It is all the more significant that, even within this small part, we can locate cities in clearly different stages of policy development. The suggests that a concept like "modern" disguises a great deal of the variance that more microscopic analysis can reveal. The point is that our stages "correspond" only analytically to similarly conceived stages used

in the long-term analysis of national development.

10. For a more detailed discussion of how the development typology was constructed and cities assigned to a stage or phase of policy development, see Eyestone and Eulau in Wilson, *op. cit.*

11. This calculation is made as follows: over eight years, each city's annual outcomes could change seven times. This would make for 82 × 7, or 547 opportunities for all cities. However, as we missed data for the first fiscal year in two cities, we must deduct two opportinities, giving us the 572 figure.

12. For a discussion of system capabilities, see Gabriel A. Almond, "A Developmental Approach to Political Systems," *World Politics*, 17 (January 1965), 195–203.

13. Assessed valuation includes private houses and property, commercial property and industrial property. From private property a city derives personal property revenues and a portion of state income tax revenues; from commercial property it receives property and sales tax revenues; and from industrial property it gets property tax revenues.

14. This is not the only question we asked in this connection. For instance, we also asked a great many closed "agree-disagree" questions, some of which we used in the earlier analysis, in Wilson, *op. cit.*

15. See Harold D. Lasswell and Abraham Kaplan, *Power and Society: A Framework for Political Inquiry* (New Haven: Yale University Press, 1950), p. 25.

16. This is not the place to discuss the methodological problems and procedures involved in "stepping up" the data from the level of the individual (microanalysis) to the level of the group (macroanalysis). Suffice it to say that our empirical results justify the viability of the procedures, although we would be the first to admit that many technical problems remain to be solved.

17. Paul F. Lazarsfeld has written in many places about the variety of "group properties" that need to be distinguished in analysis lest errors of inference be made. See, for instance, Paul F. Lazarsfeld, "Evidence and Inference in Social Research," in Daniel Lerner (ed.), *Evidence and Inference* (New York: The Free Press, 1959), pp. 117–25; or Paul F. Lazarsfeld and Herbert Menzel, "On the Relation between Individual and Collective Properties," in Amitai Etzioni, *Complex Organizations* (New York: Holt, Rinehart, and Winston, 1961), pp. 422–40. We are not dealing with the global, structural, or relational properties of councils in this analysis.

18. That is, the absolute number of individual problems named was divided by all problem responses made in a council. The resulting scores that could range from zero to one, were rank-ordered and divided into the quartile ranges used in the analysis.

19. That is, the number of problems named was multiplied by the number of respondents and divided by all responses squared. The resulting score was subtracted from one to rank-order the councils from high to low. The formula then is: $1 - NP \times NR/r^2$, where NP = number of problems, NR = number of respondents, and r = number of total responses.

20. The measure of agreement on a single problem is simply the proportion of councilmen among all respondents who mentioned the most frequent problem. For the measure of problem area agreement, the number of responses in the area receiving the most responses was divided by the number of responses in all areas. Five "problem areas" were provided for classification of individual problems: Services and Utilities, Amenities, Promotion and Development, Social and Remedial Problems, and Governmental and Intergovernmental Problems.

21. Our measure of salience, as mentioned in the text, was whether a problem or problem area was mentioned by at least three respondents. We shall not try to interpret the proportions obtained for the services and utilities as well as promotion and development areas across the developmental continuum because the results may be an artifact of council size. As five councils in the transitional stage, three in the maturing phase and seven in the advanced stage had more than five members (usually seven), and as no retarded or emergent council had more than five members, clearly any one problem had more of a chance to be named by at least three respondents in the more developed cities. But as, for instance, nine of the advanced councils had only five members, yet all advanced councils are accounted for in naming at least one problem, the council size factor does not seem to have too much of a distorting effect. But we note it as interesting that the more developed a city's policy, the more councils tend to mention problems related to utilities and services and to promotion and development.

22. The dominant set of reasons was simply defined as that set which included the most responses among all sets, regardless of absolute number.

23. We could argue our case more liberally on statistical grounds and possibly test it if we had more and numerically more diverse legislative bodies available for analysis: the larger a legislative body, the more likely it is that averaged individual preferences will approximate, if not correspond to, the preference of the collectivity.

24. The improvement diversity measure was constructed in the same way as the problem diversity measure. See footnote 18, above.

25. The improvement visibility measure was constructed in the same manner as the problem visibility measure. See footnote 19, above.

26. The improvement agreement measures are

the same as those used in connection with problem agreement. See footnote 20, above.

27. We would like to point out here that we had very similar results in the earlier study in which we used a *closed* agree-disagree scale measuring attitudes concerning the scope of government activity and in which we used *individual* councilmen as our units of analysis: see Eyestone and Eulau, in Wilson (ed.), *City Politics.*

28. An improvement area was assumed to be salient in council preferences if at least three respondents articulated problems in the area.

29. Because an "industrial" future was envisaged in only a handful of councils, we combined this category with the "balanced" category which implies that the council envisages a balance in residential, commercial, and industrial development.

2. Municipal Executives and Administrators

The City Manager in Legislative Politics: A Collision of Role Conceptions

Ronald O. Loveridge

Introduction*

THE "LOST WORLD of Municipal Government" has been rediscovered. Nothing less than an expansive assertion of research has rescued urban politics from the backwater of political science. Instead of a preoccupation with formal and prescriptive statements about "good government," urban politics has witnessed important developments in theory, method, and empirical studies.

The first discovery of municipal government dates to the Progressive Era when the politics of the city, under indictment by journalists and reformers, became the object of concerted popular reform. The political ideology of the reform movement was the ethos of "good government"—efficiency, honesty, impartiality. Many political scientists participated in the hue and cry for political change; scholars like Goodnow, Merriam, White, among others, both studied city politics and promoted its reform.

From the ferment of change, perhaps the outstanding structural legacy is the council-manager plan.[1] (First adopted by Dayton,

Reprinted with permission from Polity, *1 (Winter 1968), 213–36.*

Most of the data examined in this paper have been drawn, either directly or indirectly, from research of the City Council Research Project, Institute of Political Studies, at Stanford University. I am especially indebted to two colleagues, Charles Adrian and Francis Carney, for useful criticisms and suggestions on an earlier draft of this paper, which was delivered at the 1967 annual meeting of the Western Political Science Association in Tucson, Arizona.

Ohio, in 1914, the plan is now in effect in over 1,750 cities with a total population of approximately 45 million.) The plan became the immediate focus of scholarly attention. Early evaluations were almost uniformly favorable; these sentiments were well expressed by Harold Alderfer: "No system is perfect, but the council-manager form allows the best possible combination of democracy and efficiency in local government."[2] In much of the early writing and research, the major concern was to discuss, even "prove," why manager government is the best form of local government.

But after World War II, the city manager lost his preeminent status. The council-manager plan was initially conceived, justified, and popularly accepted on the premise of separation of politics and administration. The city manager was to be the administrator, the city council, the policy maker—so the advocates proposed.[3] When the dichotomy between politics and administration was debunked, the policy role of the city manager was open to close evaluation. While commending his administrative performance, political scientists frequently criticized the policy values of the city manager. Edward Banfield and James Q. Wilson in *City Politics*, for example, note that "managers ... tend to be conservative, unenterprising, and devoted to routine [and] ... the typical manager's mentality is probably still a good deal closer to that of the engineer than to that of the politician."[4] The recurring theme in most of the critiques is that the city manager exerts little or no policy leadership on non-routine decisions, is unresponsive to the needs and demands of the people, and in general acts to depoliticize the allocation of city values.

The "behavioral persuasion" further relegated the city manager to the sidelines of community research. Questions about the community political system, decision-making process, and leadership structure took priority over questions of "efficiency and economy" or of what is the preferred structure of local government. At best, the city manager was seen as one of many forces which act to mold public policy. The city manager was, in short, a favorite of traditional political science. To those of a different generation, the city manager is viewed more as another parameter in the urban political environment.

Why, then, should we as students of urban politics be interested in the policy role of the city manager? In council-manager cities, the city manager appears often in study after study as the most influential public official, elected or otherwise.[5] More than a popular administrator or a hired hand for the "power structure," a city manager emerges as a full-time professional committed to direct intervention in community affairs:

> To begin with, a major source of innovations are those professional occupational roles centrally concerned with community institutions. Part of the job of certain occupations is to constantly propose changes in community institutions. Such professionalized roles as city manager . . . carry within themselves the notion of constant improvement in the services involved.[6]

The prominent place of the manager in community decisions can be attributed to reasons beyond career obligations to report city problems and propose policy solutions. The manager's recognized expertise, position at the apex of city administration, and virtual monopoly of technical and other detailed information propel him, willingly or unwillingly, into a pivotal policy position. And, as suggested by a colleague, the city manager is probably the one local actor able to take a comprehensive view of the public interest *and* to exercise an important influence on other policy participants.

Because he provides executive leadership for the city's policy process, the analysis of the city manager's policy role is important for the study and practice of urban politics. If we assume that the behavior of political actors is conditioned by the conception of appropriate roles for themselves, how a city manager participates in the policy process should depend, in some measure, on values and expectations held for the manager's policy role. And as observed by Karl Bosworth: "Not only is he [city manager] inevitably in public view, but the range of his operations is broad, and the fate of his community may be determined in part by the public goals his thoughts lead him to set for his government."[7]

Problems and Procedures

Two definitions of the manager's policy role are especially crucial to its normative content and its influence on behavior—those of city managers *and* of city councilmen. First, city managers are the occupants of the focal position. How they interpret the policy role obviously conditions their policymaking activities; but more important to this paper, their conceptions of what a city manager should or should not do provide the central direction to the role's normative content. *The first objective is to examine the normative character of the policy role as defined by city managers.*

The city manager, unlike most political executives, is appointed and thus serves at the pleasure of the council. As expressed by one writer, "The manager is one of the most dispensable men in any political community."[8] Moreover, the content of a manager's policy activities has to be at least generally endorsed by the city councilmen. The dependence of the city manager on their approval guarantees councilmen a prominent place in defining what a city manager can do. *The second objective is to explore the expectations of councilmen for the city manager's policy role.*

The third and final objective is to analyze the role conflict between city managers and city councilmen. Is there disagreement? If so, what is the extent and kind of the disagreement? And what is the significance of such a disagreement for the city manager's involvement in the policy process?

To investigate the above objectives, the policy role conceptions of city managers and city councilmen will be examined. Such data are available for city managers and city councilmen in the San Francisco Bay region.[9] Of some 72 "centralized managed" cities, role data have been collected on 59 managers (82% of those possible) and 338 city councilmen (84% of those possible). An interest in policy conceptions is particularly suited to survey research, for role conceptions can be tapped by asking rather than observing—to this end, structured interviews and written questionnaires were both used.[10]

Intraposition Consensus and the Policy Role: The City Manager

In contrast to most American political executives, city managers should have relatively well-defined and agreed-upon conceptions of their policy role.[11] There are several reasons for clarity of role definition. First, the city charter or enabling ordinances provide a formal and often detailed specification of the duties of the city manager. Second, every city manager makes decisions on problems which directly commit the city government and which affect the community in important ways. The proper policy role is thus a normative question a city manager cannot really avoid. And, third, because of the long-standing controversy over the proper policy activities of the manager, the content of the policy role is frequently discussed at graduate school, at conferences, in the municipal literature, or at council sessions. For example, in commenting on an annual conference of the International City Managers' Association, two city managers observed: "The familiar, never answered questions concerning the philosophy of professional city management, the proper role of the council and manager, and the dearth of political leadership were discussed time and again."[12]

Agreement on the central values of the policy role result from three conditions peculiar to the city manager as a political executive. To begin, city managers view themselves and participate as members of a profession. The implications of being a professional are suggested by Banfield and Wilson:

> Whether or not he regards managing cities as his life's work, he knows that it is a profession and that what is "right" or "wrong"

both for him and the council is to be found in the professional Code of Ethics and in the "common law" that has grown up around it.[13]

A member of the city manager profession is exposed to new ideas, programs, and techniques. Such exposure occurs through print and through face-to-face contact at meetings, conferences, or conventions. The International City Managers' Association, for instance, holds national conferences, publishes a monthly journal as well as a variety of handbooks, offers training courses, supplies technical advice or materials, and reports on new municipal developments. And, in California, the League of California Cities acts as a clearinghouse for city managers. The league, among other things, sponsors an annual statewide convention, hosts semiannual conferences in northern and southern California, and encourages frequent county meetings. The effect of these activities is to lessen the parochialism of the city managers and to provide them with a set of general norms to guide public policy making.

The second reason for policy role agreement lies in the sequence of career choices and experiences common to many managers. Though not prescribed by a legally sanctioned professional education or apprenticeship, a set of common recruitment and socialization patterns now characterize the city manager. Furthermore, all evidence indicates that these patterns are becoming increasingly important criteria in city manager appointments.[14]

City managers tend to be college educated, usually with an undergraduate major in the social sciences—the most popular being political science. Especially, the younger managers have begun or completed M.A. work in public administration. For example, a manager in his early thirties gave this response: "While I was at University of California, I had intended to go to law school. For my undergraduate major in political science, I picked public administration as an option. During my senior year, I became acquainted with Howard Gardner of the League of California Cities. I took a seminar from him and decided that this was the field for me. Upon graduation, I did a year of graduate work at U.C. in public administration." And it is at graduate school where the prospective city manager is exposed to professional concepts, emphases, and values (see Table 1).

Table 1. Key Career Choices and Experiences of San Francisco Bay Area City Managers

Career Patterns	Percentage of City Managers (N=59)
College education (B.A. completed)	78 (46)
Social science major	58 (34)
M.A. work (or law school)	44 (26)
Appointment outside of city staff	76 (45)
Prior city management experience when appointed	68 (40)

Two other patterns reinforce a comparable policy ideology. One is that most city managers are appointed from outside the city staff. And, when appointed, they usually have had previous city management experience. Because most city councils review many applicants before hiring a manager, these professional credentials of mobility and experience loom as important. It should also be added that the high turnover rate—average tenure in a city is less than five years—further encourages a cosmopolitan rather than a local policy perspective. These career choices and experiences should fashion a set of general norms to guide participation in the public policy process.

The third and final reason—the city manager as a policy actor—has been the subject of continuous exhortation. The two most important sources are the International City Managers' Association and the municipal journals. The ICMA, parent body of the city manager profession, circulates good government memoranda and pamphlets. Probably, though, the most conspicuous and influential exhorters are the municipal magazines: *American City, Mayor and Manager, National Civic Review, Public Management, Western City.* These magazines repeatedly tell the city manager how he can or should be a more active and effective policy maker.

Any content analysis of commonplace themes would reveal almost unanimous agreement that the city manager should be a policy innovator and leader. As an innovator, the expectation emphasis is on new programs, policies, or problems. And as a leader, the focus is on the manager as a change agent, a professional activisit responsible for making what Selznick calls critical decisions.

To examine the policy role expectations held by the city managers, we used nine closed questions. These items were designed to discover the direction and content of city manager defined policy role conceptions.[15] We asked: "Now, ever since the council-manager plan was first adopted, there has been much disagreement over what a city manager should or should not do. Here are nine questions on the job of being a city manager. Read each question and then decide which one of the four answers most closely describes how you feel—do you strongly agree, tend to agree, tend to disagree, or strongly disagree?" (See Table 2 for a recapitulation of results.)

The level of consensus among city managers on many policy expectations is striking. While some disagreement exists, most city managers see themselves as active participants in the public policy process.[16] To be specific, on items 1–5 there is overwhelming agreement that the city manager should exercise executive leadership. And policy leadership is viewed as more than the staff role of advice giving. As expressed by one manager:

A city manager is obligated to bring his expertise, experience, and ability to the council. He should actively take part in policy recommendations. Common sense would seem to indicate that a full-time manager trained and experienced in municipal affairs should make recommendations to what is essentially an amateur, part-time council.

The managers believe they should be policy innovators and policy advocates. The municipal budget is regarded as an executive budget—and, as is often the case, many of the more important community decisions are embodied in that executive budget. Three out

TABLE 2. City Manager Expectations for the Policy Role

1. CITY MANAGER AS POLICY INNOVATOR
(A city manager should assume leadership in shaping municipal policies.)

	Agree			*Disagree*	
SA	TA	%	%	TD	SD
22	28	88	12	4	3

2. CITY MANAGER AS POLICY ADVOCATE
(A city manager should advocate major changes in city policies.)

	Agree			*Disagree*	
SA	TA	%	%	TD	SD
22	25	81	19	8	3

3. CITY MANAGER AS BUDGET CONSULTANT
(A city manager should consult with the council before drafting his own budget.)

	Agree			*Disagree*	
SA	TA	%	%	TD	SD
4	14	31	69	17	23

4. CITY MANAGER AS POLICY ADMINISTRATOR
(A city manager should act as an administrator and leave policy matters to the council.)

	Agree			*Disagree*	
SA	TA	%	%	TD	SD
4	9	22	78	33	12

5. CITY MANAGER AS POLICY NEUTRAL
(A city manager should maintain a neutral stand on any issues on which the community is divided.)

	Agree			*Disagree*	
SA	TA	%	%	TD	SD
4	10	24	76	33	11

6. CITY MANAGER AS POLITICAL ADVOCATE
(A city manager should advocate policies to which important parts of the community may be hostile.)

	Agree			*Disagree*	
SA	TA	%	%	TD	SD
6	26	55	45	21	5

7. CITY MANAGER AS POLITICAL LEADER
(A city manager should work through the most powerful members of the community to achieve policy goals.)

	Agree			*Disagree*	
SA	TA	%	%	TD	SD
8	23	53	47	18	9

8. CITY MANAGER AS POLITICAL RECRUITER
(A city manager should encourage people whom he respects to run for city council.)

	Agree			*Disagree*	
SA	TA	%	%	TD	SD
4	21	44	56	20	12

9. CITY MANAGER AS POLITICAL CAMPAIGNER
(A city manager should give a helping hand to good councilmen who are coming up for reelection.)

	Agree			*Disagree*	
SA	TA	%	%	TD	SD
1	14	25	75	33	11

of four managers reject the classic administration-politics dichotomy which assigns the manager only administrative responsibilities. And managers feel they should be involved in the resolution of controversial issues, which means taking a position rather than retiring behind the cloak of professional neutrality.

Somewhat less agreement is evinced on more politicized and community-related activities (items 6–9). On matters of community controversy, especially when there is powerful opposition, city managers are more reluctant to act as policy advocates. Nevertheless, over one half of the managers believed they should take policy positions even in the face of important opposition. As to possible tactics of manager involvement in controversial questions, one manager responded as follows:

> The real distinction is what you should do publicly in contrast to what you must do privately. A city manager should be more than a council adviser. He should urge and recommend policy. He should write policies for others to present. A city manager should definitely lead behind the scenes. But he should not lead publicly. . . . I think a city manager should be a faceless man in the community.

As to political leadership vis-a-vis the community power structure, a comparable distribution resulted. A slight majority of managers felt that the city manager should be a community leader and not simply a municipal executive, that he should work directly with the influential people of the community to facilitate the achievement of policy goals. Perhaps a more significant indicator of the strong policy role adopted by many managers is the normative expectation among 40 percent of the managers that they should "encourage people . . . to run for city council." In other words, 25 out of 58 respondents believe a proper function of the city manager is to influence the cast of legislators. But, finally, there is overall agreement on one prohibition: A city manager should not get involved in the political campaigns of city councilmen—though some city managers privately said they have written speeches and planned strategies for incum-

bent councilmen. Yet, in general, the one political activity most managers believe they should avoid is electioneering. Beyond this, the city manager has apparently few normative restrictions on the breadth or style of his involvement in the public policy process. The expectation portrait of the city manager's policy role that emerges, therefore, from the distributions of the nine questions is that of a strong political executive, expected to exert policy leadership on most demands or issues before the civic agenda.[17]

Intraposition Consensus and the Policy Role: City Councilmen

If a city manager also shapes his policy activities by taking into account the expectations of others with whom he interacts, no "other" is likely to be more concerned with or important to the city manager's policy role than the city council.[18] The policy-making style and discretion of the manager are, for one thing, largely contingent upon the council. And because the manager is dependent on council acceptance of his innovative and leadership activities, the city council should be able to exert strong demands on him for conformity to its goals, interests, and norms.

But why should the council be so crucial for the policy role of city managers? For most policies are, by and large, initiated from sources outside the council, and councils themselves tend to demonstrate little political leadership. As observed by one writer: "The evidence now available does not show the council to be a very strong agency and its major power does appear to reside in the fact that its acquiescence is needed."[19] Nevertheless, the council is still the critical group with whom the city manager must interact. Perhaps of most importance, the city manager's career depends on the desires and satisfactions of the legislative body—namely, the city council. At any time, the city manager can be dismissed by the council. The success of the manager depends on his rapport with the council, itself a product of highly personalized relations. In council meetings, informal working sessions, private meetings, or personal communications, the manager is subject to the continuous face-to-face influence of the council. On top of that, managers spend an estimated 30 to 40 percent of their time in meetings with the council, carrying out instructions of the council, and preparing reports for the council.

To examine city councilmen's expectations, we used both interview and questionnaire data. Before proceeding to analysis, we must comment on a problem of inference. First, it is unlikely that the expectation demands of the council are the sum of the expectations of city councilmen; certain councilmen, for instance, are more important than others. And, second, the expectations of councils vary from city to city; that is, in one city the council may expect the city manager to act as public leader and chief executive, while in another he may be expected to act as the chief administrator and council errand boy. Nevertheless, for lack of an alternative measure and because of the emphasis on general expectations, we will use the combined responses of city councilmen to measure the direction and content of their expectations for the city manager's policy role.

The focus first is on the general functional expectations expressed by city councilmen to one open-ended question: "Now, what about the city manager? What should he do, or not do, to be most effective in his relations with the Council? How about on policy matters?" Responses were coded into sanc-

tioned policy activities for the city manager, with up to five major functional expectations counted per councilman (see Table 3).

The policy image held by councilmen for the city manager seems much closer to a staff administrator than a political executive. The four most frequently mentioned expectations clearly support this interpretation. The city manager is, first, to be a good administrator; that is, he should maintain a smooth-running city administration and effectively carry out council policy. Second, in one way or another, many councilmen said a city manager should avoid direct involvement in the policy or political process of the city. Sometimes a councilman would curtly reply, "Carry out policies as determined by the council majority. Period." More commonly, however, councilmen would find cause to point out the subordinate or adviser role of the manager. The priority given to the third and fourth expectations again tends to stress the adviser role of the manager. He should be prepared to answer all questions and be able to give first-rate policy advice and to keep the council informed on all problems facing the city. The most accepted policy role as generalized by city councilmen for the city manager is that of the staff officer hired to give advice and information on city affairs as well as to implement council-passed policy.

Perhaps a better measure of the expectation map of city councilmen would be closed items, comparable to those asked of city managers. To this end, we will examine the results to nine general expectation questions.

TABLE 3. *Councilmen Expectations for Policy Role of City Manager*

Expectations for Manager	Percentage of Councilmen who Mention each Expectation (N=248)	
Be a good administrator	45	(156)
Leave policy (and politics) to council	43	(148)
Give good advice	41	(142)
Keep council informed	34	(119)
Work with council as a policy team	26	(091)
Identify policy problems	24	(085)
Be a good diplomat for city	22	(078)
Be a good public relations man for council	19	(066)
Be a professional	19	(065)
Avoid intracouncil politics	13	(044)

We asked: "Here are some statements which reflect different viewpoints about the job of city manager or top administrator. We would like to know how you feel about these viewpoints. Would you please read each one and then check just how much you generally agree or disagree with it?" (See Table 4 for a recapitulation of results.)

Again, most councilmen seem agreed upon the policy image of the city manager as a staff administrator as opposed to a political executive. Particularly noteworthy is that councilmen reveal greatest consensus on the classic dichotomy between politics and administration. To most councilmen, the city manager is viewed as the administrator, the council, the policy maker. Overall, the councilmen delimit the proper policy activities of the manager to those of council adviser. They object to claims of community or political leadership. A majority of councilmen even oppose any involvement which is represented as policy innovation or policy leadership. And, finally, one of the most vigorously pressed prerogatives of the city managers is that of the executive budget—which in fact is —written into the statutes or charters of many of the cities. However, even on this activity, only a hairline majority favored such arrangement. City councilmen, then, tend to define the policy role in a "narrow context" with the primary emphasis on the city manager as a source of information, not as a policy—much less political—leader.

Expectations for the Policy Role: An Interposition Comparison and Interpretation

City managers and city councilmen hold pointedly different conceptions for the policy role of the city manager. In itself, the lack of interposition consensus should not be unexpected. For role consensus between most focal and counter positions is far from unanimous. What is important is the kind and extent of disagreement. City managers largely share the policy values of the political executive—they are interested in formulating and defining the purposes of city government.

City councilmen, for the most part, regard the city manager as their man in city hall who administers the city and who is on tap for advice, information, and recommendations. We thus have two quite dissimilar sets of expectations of how the city manager should function as policy maker.[20]

For two sets of political actors who interact continuously on a face-to-face basis the general lack of consensus is surprising. To highlight this conflict in policy role ideologies, let us look at Table 5 and examine the differences in responses to six comparable items answered by both managers and city councilmen.

The disagreement percentages illustrate clearly the conflicting role definitions for the manager's policy activities. These disagreements center on the fundamental character of the city manager's participation in the policy process and, as such, cannot be dismissed as unimportant role conflicts. Rather, it would appear that managers and councilmen subscribe to two contrasting views of the city manager's policy role.

Whether attributing the policy role conflicts between managers and councilmen to differences in socialization and recruitment, development of language, standards of evaluation, or reference groups, the tendency of most writers is to dismiss such role disagreements as "image versus reality" conflicts. That is, while councilmen justify and explain the council-manager prerogatives in terms of the image of the manager as dealing primarily with administrative matters and leaving policy matters to the council, city managers, in practice, participate in most stages of the community policy process.[21] Furthermore, most political scientists see the city manager as acquiring actual leadership and dominance in the determination of public policy. From this conclusion, the city manager is continuously exhorted to "assume new responsibilities for leadership." An example—John Pfiffner writes: "From now on the city manager will have to become more of a human or social engineer and less of an efficiency engineer in the traditional sense."[22] Almost all of these evaluations or recommendations ignore or discount the policy

TABLE 4. *City Councilmen Expectations for the City Manager Policy Role*

1. CITY MANAGER AS POLICY ADMINISTRATOR
   (The city manager should act as an administrator and leave policy matters to the council.)

	Agree			*Disagree*	
A	TA	%	%	TD	D
205	54	87	13	32	7

2. CITY MANAGER AS POLITICAL LEADER
   (The city manager should work through the most powerful members of the community to achieve his policy goals.)

	Agree			*Disagree*	
A	TA	%	%	TD	D
9	26	12	88	85	176

3. CITY MANAGER AS POLITICAL CAMPAIGNER
   (The city manager should give a helping hand to good councilmen who are coming up for reelection.)

	Agree			*Disagree*	
A	TA	%	%	TD	D
21	33	18	82	48	195

4. CITY MANAGER AS POLICY ADVISER
   (The city manager should work informally with councilmen to prepare important policy proposals.)

	Agree			*Disagree*	
A	TA	%	%	TD	D
141	95	80	20	27	33

5. CITY MANAGER AS POLITICAL RECRUITER
   (The city manager should encourage people whom he respects to run for the council.)

	Agree			*Disagree*	
A	TA	%	%	TD	D
31	36	23	77	63	165

6. CITY MANAGER AS POLITICAL NEUTRAL
   (The city manager should maintain a neutral stand on any issues which may divide the community.)

	Agree			*Disagree*	
A	TA	%	%	TD	D
121	68	64	36	45	61

7. CITY MANAGER AS POLICY INNOVATOR
   (The city manager should assume leadership in shaping municipal policies.)

	Agree			*Disagree*	
A	TA	%	%	TD	D
48	77	42	58	59	122

8. CITY MANAGER AS POLITICAL ADVOCATE
   (The city manager should advocate policies even if important parts of the community seem hostile to them.)

	Agree			*Disagree*	
A	TA	%	%	TD	D
80	57	46	54	72	68

9. CITY MANAGER AS BUDGET CONSULTANT
   (The city manager should consult with the council before drafting his own budget proposal.)

	Agree			*Disagree*	
A	TA	%	%	TD	D
91	53	49	51	60	92

TABLE 5. Policy Expectation Disagreements between Managers and Council

1. CITY MANAGER AS POLICY ADMINISTRATOR

City Managers (%)		Percent Disagreement	City Councilmen (%)	
Agree	Disagree	%	Agree	Disagree
22	78	66	88	12

2. CITY MANAGER AS POLICY INNOVATOR

City Managers (%)		Percent Disagreement	City Councilmen (%)	
Agree	Disagree	%	Agree	Disagree
88	12	46	42	58

3. CITY MANAGER AS POLITICAL LEADER

City Managers (%)		Percent Disagreement	City Councilmen (%)	
Agree	Disagree	%	Agree	Disagree
53	47	41	12	88

4. CITY MANAGER AS POLICY NEUTRAL

City Managers (%)		Percent Disagreement	City Councilmen (%)	
Agree	Disagree	%	Agree	Disagree
24	76	40	64	36

5. CITY MANAGER AS POLITICAL RECRUITER

City Managers (%)		Percent Disagreement	City Councilmen (%)	
Agree	Disagree	%	Agree	Disagree
44	56	21	23	77

6. CITY MANAGER AS BUDGET CONSULTANT

City Managers (%)		Percent Disagreement	City Councilmen (%)	
Agree	Disagree	%	Agree	Disagree
31	69	18	49	51

expectations of the council for the city manager. This writer, on the other hand, contends that the policy role conflict between the manager and council is central to any explanation of the city manager's behavior as a policy maker.

To judge the importance of the policy role conflict, let us look at two kinds of responses made by city managers. First, the council is the city manager's most important reference group. One prominent manager has explained the relationship in these words: "I regard myself as the hired hand of the city council. In the last analysis I don't work for the public; I don't work for the individual citizens of the city; I work for the council." To identify the audience before whom a city manager tries to maintain or enhance his standing, the question was asked:

A city manager's reputation is said to be dependent on the approval of a number of different publics. Some publics, however, are probably more important than others. How would you rank the following on the importance to your reputation as a city manager:

administrative staff—
fellow city managers—
public-at-large—

council—
community groups—
professional management groups—

Of the 58 managers who responded, 42 managers (73%) ranked the council first and an additional 13 (23%) ranked it second. The data suggest that city managers are very sensitive to and dependent upon favorable council appraisal and that no other reference group is a serious rival to the council.[23]

Second, perhaps the most direct measure of the frequency and intensity of the policy role conflict can be found in the expressed frustrations of city managers. In field interviews with a sample of forty Bay Area managers, the question was asked: "What would you say are the two most pressing problems or frustrations you face as city manager?" Although responses could run the gamut from community problems to policy matters to personnel questions or to more personal feelings, over 60 percent (25) of the managers identified conflict with the city council as one of their two most important problems or frustrations. Conflict between managers and councils can result from sources other than policy role conflict; however, upon a rereading of the interview protocols, the main frustration of the managers appears to center on various aspects of the policy process.[24] For example, here are several illustrative responses:

I find it frustating that you have a highly trained professional, proficient in efficient and economic operations of city government, subject to the approval of a lay council. A group of men who typically have less education, who are affected by political pressures, who are relatively uninformed, and who invoke personalities will often reject almost out of hand ideas carefully developed and presented by the city manager.

The council is my number one gripe. When anything goes wrong, I am to blame—it is my judgment, my policies. I am the scapegoat when something goes wrong. . . . The council, too, often feels it is the expert on everything. Yet, they spend little time in studying problems.

The first problem would be the city council. Councilmen are not on the council long enough to become oriented into the job, to become aware of the need for open-minded evaluation of problems. . . . Councilmen often demonstrate the inability to recognize the long-range implications of some of their actions.

Effects of the differences in policy conceptions between managers and councilmen take myriad forms.[25] Tentative analysis of available data suggests the direction and character of certain general consequences. The city manager in confronting the gap between personal and council-sanctioned policy activities cannot react as an elected chief executive. Rather, publicly and to the council, he presents himself as a professional administrator. Policy activities of any legislative significance have to be camouflaged accordingly or carried out in an informal and indirect manner. Thus it is behind the scenes that the city manager strives to build, utilize, and husband his political resources to influence public policy decisions.

More important, evidence indicates that the normative expectations of city councilmen influence *how* the city manager expends his political resources on *what* policy questions. A pronounced impact on the direction and foci of policy innovation and leadership activities by city managers is the result. The overall effect was well explained in one city manager study as follows:

Managers were in substantial agreement on the areas where they should push hard for managerial policies and the areas where they should remain neutral or stay out altogether. They agreed that managers should assert themselves strongly on technical questions where the best policy is strongly or entirely dependent on factual data. They also strongly defended the responsibility of managers in fields of internal management.

The areas where the managers play a more limited role or stay out altogether include: partisan political issues; moral and regulatory issues; public versus private ownership; the internal operations of the city council; relations with independent boards and commissions and other governments, except as guided by council instructions; and issues where the city council is divided within itself.[26]

The city manager, in brief, is most likely to act as a political executive primarily in "safe" areas. But on policy problems of a controversial variety, he is expected by the council to act as staff adviser. In many ways, therefore, the city manager is a consensus politician par excellence; high priority is given to avoiding friction, criticisms, or opposition. Bounded by council sanctions and alert to their anticipated reactions, the city manager cannot initiate, fix priorities, or bargain for acceptance of policies as he believes he should. The city manager cannot introduce major policy decisions onto the civic agenda which do not have the implicit approval of the city council. Moreover, besides a real antagonism to the city manager as a community change agent, the city council expects the city manager to participate in a policy decision in accordance with the wishes and prejudices of the council—and not the abstract values of the public interest or of the city manager profession. One councilman put the expectations of many into these words:

The job of the city manager is carrying out the administration of city affairs within the policies laid down by the council. He shouldn't become involved in the political atmosphere of the community. For his job is carrying out council policies regardless of his personal feelings. . . . The council is an elected group supposedly reflecting the desires of the electorate. The manager is appointed by the council—it's a paid position; he is an employee of the city council!

Conclusion

City managers reveal a near consensus on the appropriate policy role orientation. Almost all managers believe they should participate in the initiation, formulation, and presentation of policy proposals. The textbook stereotype of the city manager as viewing himself as an "efficiency and economy" administrator is no longer accurate. Various changes ranging from differences in socialization and recruitment patterns to the complex needs and requirements of city governments have worked together to fashion a new set of general norms to guide the policy behavior of the city manager—namely, those of the political executive.

In contrast, city councilmen cleave to the image of the city manager as a staff administrator. The city manager's participation in the policy process tends to be delimited to those activities of adviser and political agent for the council. For city councilmen do not see the city manager as an independent policy participant; quite the contrary, he is more likely to be conceived as the "servant" of the council, acting at their pleasure and for their interests.

Probably the most important finding of this paper is the unusually dissimilar conceptions of the policy role held by city managers and city councilmen. Anyone who occupies a particular position has role partners who are differently located in the social structure and who, as a result, have differing values and expectations. But the kind and extent of disagreement between managers and councilmen—given the power of councilmen, their close and continuous interaction with the city manager, and the relative visability of the city manager's policy activities—

make this incidence of role conflict especially crucial. How the city manager resolves his conception of the political executive with the council's conception of the staff administrator probably takes a number of forms. We have developed two. One is the camouflaging of policy activity or confining all such activity to behind-the-scenes politicking. The other is ready involvement in "safe" policy areas and cautious retreat or withdrawal from more controversial questions. This question of role resolution deserves more extensive and systematic analysis because it explains much of the dynamics of the policy exchange between managers and councilmen.[27]

"If responsible management of economic development and the finding of the resources necessary to conduct desired programs for economic and social improvements are to be successfully achieved, we shall need," writes Duane Lockard, "great political ingenuity, courage, and leadership. . . . In short, the courage to plan ahead, the wit and leadership required to make enough people see the need of facing the realities of mass society may turn out to be the crucial challenge facing state and local government."[28] The city manager met the demand for improved administration of city goods and services—and still does. However, the data we have examined raise doubts as to the probable success of the manager in the areas of social conflict and economic progress and more generally the quality of city life. Though the city manager shares the values of the political executive tempered often with the best training that academics can provide, the role collision between manager and council severely handicaps his exercise of innovative public leadership of nonroutine decisions.[29]

Notes

1. "The origin of the council-manager plan," wrote Leonard White, "is imbedded in the revolution of the civic and business interests of the American city, aided and abetted by various forward-looking groups, against the waste, extravagance, and sometimes corruption which

characterized 'politician' government of the last century." Leonard White, *City Manager* (Chicago, 1927), p. ix.

2. Harold Alderfer, *American Local Government and Administration* (New York, 1956), p. 308. And even the pre-1945 great men of political science were enthusiastic about the successes of the council-manager plan; for example, Charles Merriam commented: "Permit me to say in language as plain as I can make it that city managers have made the outstanding contribution to public administration in the United States in the twentieth century." See Charles Merriam, "The City Manager of Today," *Public Management* (February 1950), p. 28.

3. The administration-politics dichotomy has had a strange yet important life history. Embraced by early writers as sound causal and normative theory, the dichotomy is now wholly rejected in academic circles. For a succinct perspective on the administration-politics dichotomy, see Wallace Sayre, "Premises of Public Administration: Past and Emerging," *Public Administration Review* (Spring 1958), pp. 102–105.

4. Edward Banfield and James Q. Wilson, *City Politics* (Cambridge, Mass. 1963), pp. 173, 174.

5. "Rule by amateurs," write Williams and Adrian, "is likely to mean that under most conditions, persons outside the legislative body must be depended upon to make the essential policy decisions in all but the formal sense." Oliver Williams and Charles Adrian, *Four Cities* (Philadelphia, 1963), p. 292; see pp. 305–308 for an excellent discussion of the manager as an influential outsider. See also Aaron Wildavsky, *Leadership in a Small Town* (Totawa, N.J., 1964); he concludes, "As a matter of course, therefore, we would expect a city manager who takes a broad view of his responsibilities, in a town without full-time elected officials, to be the most general activist and to appear in more decision areas than anyone else."

6. Peter Rossi, "Theory, Research, and Practice in Community Organization," in *Democracy in Urban America*, Oliver Williams and Charles Press (eds.), (Chicago, 1961), p. 388.

7. Karl Bosworth, "The Manager is a Politician," *Public Administration Review* (Summer 1958), p. 216. For a further discussion of the importance and implications of the city manager as a political executive, see the symposium in *Public Administration Review* (Summer 1958): Charles Adrian, "A Study of Three Communities," pp. 208–13; Dorothea Strauss Pealy, "Need for Elected Leadership," pp. 214–16; and Karl Bosworth, "Manager is a Politician." pp. 216–22.

8. Gladys Kammerer, Charles Farris, John DeGrove, and Alfred Clubok, *City Managers in Politics* (Gainesville, Fla., 1962), p. 81.

9. This paper is based on data to be used in a monograph—tentatively titled "City Managers in Legislative Politics"—on which I am currently working. The monograph is one in a series to be published by members of the City Council Research Project, Institute of Political Studies, at Stanford University, Heinz Eulau, director. The project, financed by a grant from the National Science Foundation, is investigating decision making in small legislative groups. Focusing primarily on city councils, we have been collecting interview data from over four hundred councilmen in the San Francisco Bay region (that is, the counties of Alameda, Contra Costa, Marin, Napa, San Francisco, San Mateo, Santa Clara, Solano, and Sonoma). However, my monograph is based not only on data from interviews with city councilmen but also on a questionnaire sent to all Bay Area city managers in December 1965, and to a lesser extent on forty field interviews conducted with Bay Area managers in the summer of 1964.

10. See the rationale of *The Legislative System* for relying on interview data in studying role conceptions: John Wahlke, Heinz Eulau, William Buchanan, and LeRoy Ferguson, *The Legislative System* (New York, 1962), particularly pp. 31–33. (The concept of role is especially prominent in American sociology, social psychology, and cultural anthropology.) Important summaries of the concept of role can be found in Neal Gross, Ward Mason, and Alexander McEachern, *Explorations in Role Analysis* (New York, 1958), pp. 11–69; and Theodore Sarbin, "Role Theory," in Gardner Lindzey (ed.), *Handbook of Social Psychology I*. (Reading, Mass., 1954), pp. 223–58. Two useful introductions to the relationship of expectations and behavior can be found in Robert Bierstedt, *Social Order* (New York, 1957); and Arnold Rose (ed.), *Human Behavior and Social Process* (Boston, 1962). More seminal works on the implications of the concept of role include George Mead, *Mind, Self, and Society* (Chicago, 1934); Ralph Linton, *Study of Man* (New York, 1936); and Talcott Parsons, *Social System* (Glencoe, Ill., 1951).

11. Where a study taps central, clearly defined expectation sets, role analysis becomes an especially valuable explanatory tool. See, for example, Alvin Gouldner, "Cosmopolitans and Locals," *Administrative Science Quarterly* (December 1957; March 1958), pp. 281–306, 444–80.

12. C. A. Harrell and D. G. Weiford, "City Manager and the Policy Process," *Public Administration Review* (Spring 1959), p. 102.

13. Banfield and Wilson, *City Politics*, p. 174.

14. See, for example, *Directory of City Managers 1964*, published by International City Managers' Association (1964), pp. 6–19.

15. The policy expectation items were devised and selected from an evaluation of the study's objectives and after a review of the city manager

literature—in particular, some questions were drawn from Jeptha Carrell, *Role of the City Manager* (Kansas City, 1962).

16. See Ronald O. Loveridge, "Role Orientations of an Urban Policy Maker" (Dittoed Paper, University of California, Riverside, 1956).

17. For a general description of the "most essential and characteristic functions" of a chief executive, see Edward Banfield, "The Training of the Executive," in Carl Friedrich and Seymour Harris (eds.), *Public Policy* (Cambridge, Mass., 1960), pp. 27–28.

18. For further and more detailed explanation, see Ronald O. Loveridge, "City Manager and Role Analysis" (unpublished doctoral dissertation, Stanford University, 1965), pp. 123–27.

19. Duane Lockard, *The Politics of State and Local Government* (New York, 1963), p. 325.

20. Between managers and councilmen, the clash in role conceptions appears consistent regardless of the structural or cultural characteristics of cities. Such variables as, for example, city size, socioeconomic status, or even political values do not generally change the conflicting interpretations of the policy role of the city manager.

21. For example, B. James Kweder, in a study of 21 North Carolina cities, states: "The perceptions of managers, mayors, and councilmen of the policy-making process in their cities clearly refutes the idea that policy making is something performed exclusively by the council. Not only do the managers participate actively in the process, they participate actively in every one of the six phases into which the policy-making process has been divided for this study. Moreover, in many cities the manager clearly emerges as the person who has the greatest influence over what is happening at every stage of the policy-making process." James Kweder, *The Roles of the Manager, Mayor, and Councilmen in Policy Making* (Chapel Hill, N.C., 1965), p. 31.

22. John Pfiffner, "The Job of the City Manager," *Public Management* (June 1961), p. 123.

23. Gladys Kammerer suggests that elected mayors or political bosses would also be important interpreters of the manager's policy role. See Gladys Kammerer, "Role Diversity of City Managers," *Administrative Science Quarterly* (March 1964), pp. 421–42.

24. For example, Jeptha Carrell distinguishes between six major sources of conflict between managers and councilmen: power prerogatives, personality clashes, political setting, policy-expediency differences, manager's inflexibility and rectitude, and communication and cognition difficulties. See Jeptha Carrell, "The City Manager and His Council: Sources of Conflict," *Public Administration Review* (December 1962), pp. 203–208.

25. Obviously, the policy environment of city politics is inordinately more complex than the interactions between manager and councilmen. The city is not a blank check on which the manager and his council can together or separately write their policy preferences. For an excellent essay on why cities adopt varied decisions and policies, see Robert Alford, "The Comparative Study of Urban Politics," in Leo Schnore and Henry Fagin (eds.), *Urban Research and Policy Planning*, (Beverly Hills, Calif., 1967), pp. 263–304. See also, James Q. Wilson, *City Politics and Public Policy* (New York, 1968); and a recent evaluative venture in the community power literature, Richard Merelman, "On the Neo-elitist Critique of Community Power," *American Political Science Review* (June 1968), pp. 451–60.

26. Clarence Ridley, *The Role of the City Manager in Policy Formulation* (Chicago, 1958).

27. For two excellent statements on the importance and mechanisms of the resolution of role conflict, see Robert Goods, "A Theory of Role Strain," *American Sociological Review* (August 1960), pp. 483–95; and Robert Merton, *Social Theory and Social Structure* (New York, 1957), pp. 225–386.

28. Lockard, *State and Local Government*, pp. 20, 22.

29. To foster community leadership, California managers now frequently propose an elected mayor or at least a mayor with greater responsibility and authority. This change violates a basic tenet of the Model City Charter of the National Municipal League but is seen as necessary to meet emerging community conflicts. A strong mayor—the managers hope—can speak out on political issues, build support for new policy directions, and focus attention on social questions. (To a 1968 ICMA Goals Questionnaire administered by the California League of Cities, almost 70 percent of the managers who responded said they favored a strong mayor who can exercise political leadership.)

Executive Leadership and Community Innovation: The Fluoridation Experience*

Donald B. Rosenthal and Robert L. Crain

THE CURRENT INTEREST in comparative urban politics owes much to the debate between Floyd Hunter and Robert Dahl over the locus of decision-making power in American cities.[1] One problem of these studies and others like them was that they focused on one city at a time. It was difficult to determine, therefore, how much of the argument flowed either from the peculiar features of the city selected or from the methodology employed. In an attempt to overcome this problem, recent studies have generated comparative schemes for interpreting differences among cities. Rather than pursuing the possibility that formal structures and types of governmental decision makers might constitute a significant dimension for differentiating community decisions, however, such comparisons have tended to emphasize sociological factors and community values.[2] The present study relies upon

"*Executive Leadership and Community Innova-tion*," by Donald B. Rosenthal and Robert L. Crain, is reprinted from Urban Affairs Quarterly, 1 (March 1966), 39–57, by permission of the publisher, Sage Publications, Inc.

*Research was made possible by a grant from the United States Public Health Service to National Analysis, Inc., of Philadelphia. The authors wish to thank Aaron J. Spector of National Analysis for his cooperation through the many phases of the study. They are grateful to Elihu Katz, who played a major part in the larger project.

a different approach. Given the *same issue* in every case, we report the relationship between the public position taken by the mayor and the outcome of the decision in 362 cities. We argue that the position taken by the mayor is crucial in understanding the decision a community makes with respect to fluoridation. In turn, the mayor is influenced by certain pressures operating in the community, but he is more than a mere pawn in the decision-making process.

The Problem

Over the past fifteen years, many cities have gotten into fierce controversies on the question of adding minute quantities of fluoride ion to the public water supply in order to reduce tooth decay in children. This process—fluoridation—has had the overwhelming support of medical and dental professionals and rarely has it been opposed by established interest groups. Nevertheless, fluoridation has not fared well in many cities. Often, the proposal was raised for consideration before the city council, a routine public hearing was scheduled and then an *ad hoc* committee of antifluoridationists would spring into action. They appeared before the councils of this country to warn against the evils of socialized medicine and to blame fluorides for every human ill from nymphomania to the destruction of car batteries. If the council then decided to put the issue to public referendum, a lengthy and often corrosive fight would break out and fluoridation was generally defeated.

Some of the social scientists who studied fluoridation controversies were attracted by this opportunity to look at mass behavior. The emphasis in many of these studies was upon the seemingly irrational behavior of the voter.[3] Yet there was something disquieting about such an approach. Should we accept without question the idea that fluoridation decisions are direct expressions of the psychological aberrations of a community over which political traditions and public leadership can have no control? We preferred, instead, to treat the fluoridation decision as one made in a political setting under the influence of *political leadership.*

This approach influenced our research in several ways: First, it suggested that the differences between decision-making patterns might be traced to differences in the concrete governmental systems. This encouraged us to undertake a large-scale comparative study. Second, it forced our attention away from the referendum campaign toward the process by which the government decided to put the issue up to public vote. Most of the research which had been done followed the course of steamy referendum campaigns.[4] But the referendum, though common, is still not the *typical* decision-making route for fluoridation. Therefore, we wanted to find out what the people inside City Hall were doing while the screaming was going on outside. There is no need to deny that referenda campaigns on fluoridation were marked by hysterical outbursts on occasion, but few studies have looked at the process by which that hysteria may have been "managed." In addition to holding a referendum, of course, a local political system might have adopted by governmental authority, a vote could have been taken within the city government setting aside the proposal, or some action could have been taken to bury the matter without bringing it to a vote.

Given these possible alternatives, it is clear that the *political setting* might make some difference. Findings on this point are reported elsewhere;[5] in general, fluoridation has a better chance of consideration and possible adoption where certain governmental conditions prevail; where the political structure centralizes decision-making authority; where mechanisms are available (political parties) for insulating decision makers from "irregular" pressures; and where there is a low level of *direct* citizen participation both as a general rule and specifically on the fluoridation decision.

Within different political structures, however, the position taken by *formal policy leaders*—the mayor or city manager—may vary. The ability of these leaders to influence community decisions is the subject of the present paper.

The Method

We attempted to make a comparative study of community decisions on fluoridation by using mailed questionnaires sent to local informants, who became "volunteer" members of our research team. Questionnaires were sent to the publisher of the largest local paper, the local health officer, and the city clerk in each of 1,186 cities. This number includes all cities from 10,000 to 500,000 in size which own their own water supplies or exercise ultimate control over its treatment. It excludes those cities which have naturally fluoridated water.

Each "informant" was asked for different information. The health officer described some of the details of the campaign; the publisher informed us about the local political system and provided judgments about such things as the level of controversy associated with the fluoridation decision;[6] if a referendum was held, the city clerk supplied us with the results of the vote, as well as with results from other recent referenda and elections.

Response rates varied from 35 percent to 58 percent but, by cross-checking the responses on the three questionnaires, we were able to estimate the kinds of biases that the variations in responses introduced.[7] Responses, on the whole, came more heavily from cities which had experienced considerable controversy. It is noteworthy that probably no more than 20 percent of cities in this survey population have not faced the fluoridation issue.

In the research, we focused upon differences among communities, both in population composition and in political structure. We also collected data on the conduct of the campaign: the characteristics of the leaders of the pro- and antifluoridation factions, the kinds of campaign literature, the support that each of the opposing groups had, and so on. Fluoridation is a highly public issue. Campaigns involve a great deal of voter "education," and referenda draw very heavy turnouts, often with more people voting on the question than voted for any of the offices at the same election.

The Major Findings

In terms of the magnitude of the correlation, the central finding of the study is that the position taken on fluoridation by the formal executive leadership (the mayor or city manager) virtually determines the decisions made by the government: if the mayor does not publicly support fluoridation, there is very little chance for its adoption. The basic relationship is demonstrated in Table 1 where "first decision," "second decision," and "third decision" refers to each time that the fluoridation issue came up. Since the process of decision making took place over a number of years, it was possible for different mayors to assume different positions. The results given here are for governmental action only. (We shall consider referenda results subsequently.)

It is clear that when the mayor favors fluoridation, adoption occurs in a majority of cases at the time of a first decision: 61 percent; when he is neutral there are almost no adoptions: 6 percent. When he openly opposes fluoridation, which occurs in the fewest instances, the result is much like that for taking no position. Only *positive* support seems to be correlated with favorable action. The same sort of difference exists between the governmental decision and the position taken by the city manager in council-manager systems.

That the position of the mayor and city manager is closely correlated with action taken by the political system may seem to be belaboring the obvious. After all, they are the most prominent figures in the local government, or at least an important part of it. Aside from all of the "community power structure" studies which indicate that the mayor is marginal to decision making, the finding is important because the mayor is *by no means* the only decision maker on the issue—in fact, it is usually the city council that has the formal responsibility in fluoridation actions. In many cities, furthermore, the mayor is not in a structurally powerful position: his post may be largely honorific; he may be a formally "weak" mayor with very few powers; he may be subordinate in prestige to the city manager.

Even if the executive is willing to take a position which influences governmental

TABLE 1. Mayor's Position and Government Decision for Each Time Fluoridation Came Up

Question: At the time (that fluoridation was considered) what position did the mayor and city manager take? (Favored fluoridation; opposed fluoridation; took no stand; don't know.)

MAYOR'S DECISION	PERCENTAGE OF CITIES				
	Administrative Adoption	Held Referenda	No Action	Total	N
First Decision					
Mayor opposed	10	17	73	100	30
Mayor neutral	6	16	78	100	141
Mayor favored	61	10	29	100	191
Second Decision					
Mayor opposed	(0) *	(50)	(50)	100	12
Mayor neutral	5	34	61	100	38
Mayor favored	33	28	39	100	46
Third Decision					
Mayor opposed	(0)	(43)	(57)	100	7
Mayor neutral	(0)	(30)	(70)	100	10
Mayor favored	38	10	52	100	21

*Where cases have a base of less than twenty we have placed them in parentheses.

TABLE 2. Mayor's Stand and Referendum Outcome (All "Rounds" of Consideration Combined) *

MAYOR'S STAND	REFERENDA CITIES ADOPTING	
	Percent	N
Opposed	7	14
Neutral	11	37
Favored	46	34

*As we saw in Table 1, early "rounds" of consideration had much the same effect as later rounds. The notion of rounds is admittedly, arbitrary but was necessary because fluoridation had peaks and troughs of public attention. In fact, some conflict arose between the reports of the health officers and those of the publishers because of differing conceptions of the time of these "rounds."

action, we might expect him to remain neutral when it came to a referendum. The political rewards for going out on a limb for fluoridation appear limited.[8] Still, in cities which held a referendum, slightly more than half the mayors took a stand. Table 2 gives the mayor's stand and the referenda results for all referenda, combining the three decisional "rounds" distinguished in the previous table. When the mayor favored fluoridation, it had an almost even chance of passing; when he opposed it or remained neutral, fluoridation won in only about 10 percent of the cases.

Thus, not only at the governmental level, but also where the public is brought into the decisional process, there is a strong correlation between the mayor's stand and the final community action. This finding is especially interesting since it runs contrary to the thesis advanced by James Coleman that negative votes on fluoridation are the product of citizen alienation from the local political system. Coleman argues that many people vote against fluoridation *just because* it is perceived as an opportunity to revolt against a government which doesn't care what "ordinary people" think. We maintain, on the other hand, that support for the measure from the political leadership of the community provides an important positive cue for voters.[9] Although the mayor's favorability does not result in a *majority* of referenda being passed, the difference between the mayor being favorable or neutral, or opposed, is striking. Thus these data point out the importance of the mayor as a symbolic leader of the community.

The Problem of Error and the Problem of Causality

We cannot automatically assume that the high correlations in these two tables demonstrate the power of the mayor. The correlation may simply be in error, or the correlation might be a spurious one. We see no reason to believe that the data are in serious error. It could be that the respondent (in this case the public health officer) simply remembers that the city passed fluoridation and the mayor signed the bill, and therefore assumes that the mayor must have supported it. However, we find that the vast majority of public health officers were strongly committed to fluoridation; it seems unlikely they would be willing to give credit for passage to a mayor who stayed out of the line of fire while they themselves were in the trenches.

The more serious problem is that of spurious correlation. It is possible that the agreement between the mayor's stand and the final outcome simply means that the mayor shrewdly guesses the way the wind is blowing and gets on the winning side. Methodologically, the problem is similar to the bandwagon problem in the analysis of roll-call votes to measure the power of a legislator.

It is possible to suggest a test for this question. Let us suppose that the mayor does not influence the decision and see whether the implications of this assumption contradict our data. Specifically, let us assume that the mayor adopts a cautious stance toward fluoridation and only after carefully determining the eventual outcome of the debate

TABLE 3. Mayor's Stand and Outcome

| MAYOR'S STAND | NUMBER OF DECISIONS | | | |
	Adopting Administratively	Adopting by Referendum	Rejecting by Referendum	Rejecting Administratively
Favor	139	16	18*	85*
Neutral or oppose†	14*	5*	47	172
Total	153	21	65	257

*The mayor's stand is on the losing side.
†We have combined "neutral" and "oppose" because their effects are approximately the same.

announces his own position on the winning side.

Table 3 reports on all 499 decisions in the 362 cities. Obviously, the mayor does not always guess the outcome correctly. In fourteen cases, he remains neutral when the city is "planning" to adopt administratively, and in 85 cases he favors fluoridation when it will not be adopted. In fact, in 103 of 122 "errors," the mayor tends to favor when fluoridation is going to be rejected. Given our Machiavellian assumption, this is the worst type of mistake to make; it would be more sensible to play it safe and remain neutral when the situation is not clearly predictable. Either these mayors are very optimistic about fluoridation, and err on the positive side in their predictions (an unlikely assumption) or else we have contradicted ourselves, and they are not "weathervanes" (simply responding to the way the public winds are blowing) but believe in taking the position which is recommended by the local health organizations.

This point is given a further test in a different way. As fluoridation's reputation for controversy spread, the rate of administrative adoptions dropped in the latter half of the 1950s.[10] This falling rate of administrative adoptions, however, did not affect the favorability of local mayors. What happened was that mayors remained nearly as favorable, on the whole, at the beginning of the decade as they were at the end, but they became less *effective*. This means that in the late campaigns the mayor was more likely to be caught supporting fluoridation when it was about to be rejected. But our "weathervane" assumption is now contradicted again, since we have no reason to assume that the

later mayors would be less sophisticated about fluoridation.

Clearly, then, the mayor plays an important role in the fluoridation decision. Why does he have so much influence, particularly in cities where he is not a political party leader or does not have much authority invested in his office? One possibility is that he is (in the eyes of both the city council and the voters) a symbol of the "public interest" and as such legitimizes the claim of the health specialists. In a situation like this the voter (and the city councilman) is faced with a difficult decision in which he may not have a very heavy investment. The mayor's stand thus serves as a welcome cue for making one's own decision.

If, on the other hand, the mayor refuses to take a position, he only heightens the ambiguity present in the issue. His neutrality nourishes the seeds of doubt planted by the antifluoridationists. Given the fact that "elites" remain largely passive on this issue and that most civic groups are neutral (with the exception of the Lions' Club or Jaycees who occasionally endorse the measure), opponents are able to create high visibility for themselves by their extremism; governmental neutrality, in effect, makes it easier for their claims to be regarded as respectable. Only the presence of recognized leadership on the side of the proponents can counteract this.[11]

Situational Factors

Now that we have located an actor who influences the decisional process, what are the factors which influence *him* and what are the conditions for maximizing his influence?

Obviously, the controversy which surrounds fluoridation is both a cause of mayoral caution and an impediment to his effectiveness. Controversy does not begin when fluoridation is turned over to the public for decision, but is promoted by opposition from the start of the decision process. Hesitancy by governmental leaders encourages the opponents to ask for a referendum and, in turn, increases the level of community conflict.

In practice, there is no easy empirical method for separating the extent to which controversy effects the mayors stand from the amount of controversy which is *caused* by the mayor taking a neutral or negative position. If we examine the relationship between the stand taken by the mayor and what we call the "heat of controversy,"[12] percentaging across the bottom in Table 4, we find that increased controversy reduces the proportion of mayors who take a favorable stand on fluoridation. When fluoridation is "hotly debated" mayors favor it only in 50 percent of the cases—thirty out of sixty instances. Their favorability increases to 63 percent (seventeen of twenty-seven cases) when fluoridation is "warmly discussed" and to 77 percent when controversy is low. Certainly the relationship is interesting, but it is somewhat less impressive than that between mayor's stand and outcome. Assuming that controversy effects the mayor's stand, which it surely does, holding controversy constant in Table 4 indicates that the mayor's stand is still strongly correlated with the community decision. As the table indicates, even when controversy is low, adoption is difficult

without the mayor's stand in favor of fluoridation. Controversy is itself a reflection of referenda campaigns, since no referenda are held where the mayor is neutral or opposed and the local "climate of opinion" is described as "calm." Under such conditions, fluoridation may be adopted administratively in 23 percent of the cases without mayoral support. This contrasts with conditions of high controversy where fluoridation decisions are made largely through referenda when the mayor is not favorable.

The small number of cases in so many of the cells must make us cautious about the specific findings, but what is important is that at each level of controversy, the mayor's stand appears to have consequences for the ultimate decision. The situation may be perceived as one of "expanding interferences" in which the mayor's influence has more "static" to overcome as controversy increases.

Aside from the mayor, the chief groups working for fluoridation in any community were the local health organizations. The kind of activity exhibited by such organizations has to be taken into account in understanding the attitude expressed by the mayor. These are the organizations which constitute the "interests" in the area of fluoridation.[13]

Our information on the positions taken by the local medical society, the local dental association, and the local health office was supplied by the health officer. There was uniform support for fluoridation from these sources but the medical society tended to be less militant than the others. Because of the

TABLE 4. Mayor's Stand, Heat of Controversy, and Outcome

OUTCOME	HOTLY DEBATED		WARMLY DISCUSSED		CALMLY OR VERY CALMLY DISCUSSED	
	Mayor Favors	Mayor Neutral or Opposed	Mayor Favors	Mayor Neutral or Opposed	Mayor Favors	Mayor Neutral or Opposed
	(%)	(%)	(%)	(%)	(%)	(%)
Administrative adoption	30	7	47	0	65	23
Held referendum	43	57	41	40	14	0
No action	27	37	12	60	21	77
Total (*N*)	100 (30)	101 (30)	100 (17)	100 (10)	100 (43)	100 (13)

*TABLE 5. Activity of Health Organizations and Mayor's Stand
Organizational Activity Index**

Mayor's Stand	Low (0–3)	High (4–6)
	(%)	(%)
Favor	46	61
Neutral or opposed	54	39
Total (N)	100 (100)	100 (271)

*The health officer was asked to describe the activity of the organization in terms of "very active; moderately active; inactive." For the index we assigned "2" points where the organization was active; "1" point if moderately active; "0" if not active. We then added all organizational scores together. The maximum for any city would then be a "6."

high degree of active support given fluoridation by these organizations, we attempted to measure their impact by developing an organizational index for each community which we compared to the mayor's stand. Table 5 indicates that where these organizations are more active in support of fluoridation, the mayor is also more likely to be favorable.

The Position of the Manager

Up to this point, we have been calling the executive in the local political system the "mayor." Much of what we have said applies equally to the city manager. In cities where the council-manager plan is in effect, it is impossible to say whether the manager influences the mayor or vice versa. It is likely that the manager is a leader in his own right on an issue like fluoridation. Table 6 compares the positions taken by mayors and managers in the same cities. Out of the 140 cases reported in the table, in only nine instances did one of the two men favor fluoridation while the other remained silent. From a handful of

cases, of course, it is difficult to place much reliance on a "finding" that the mayor seems the more powerful figure because cities are more likely to adopt if he stands alone than if the manager favors while the mayor is neutral.

There is little evidence here that managers were more reluctant to assume a policy position on fluoridation than were mayors. This, of course, runs counter to the classical notion, which has been under heavy attack in recent years, that the manager was to be a journeyman expert who would bring his expertise to bear in the making of community decisions, but would largely subordinate himself to the will of the political arm of the local government. As Eugene C. Lee has pointed out, in many manager cities "the administrative head of the city has assumed responsibility for what might be designated 'professional civic leadership.'" [14] The manager has become the person to see in many communities when a problem arises because he is formal head of the local administrative bureaucracy and technical *apparat*. This is especially true where an issue can be defined as a "nonpolitical"

TABLE 6. Percentage of Cities Adopting Administratively by Stands of the Mayor and Manager

POSITIONS TAKEN		PERCENTAGE OF CITIES ADOPTING ADMINISTRATIVELY	
Mayor	Manager	Percentage	N
Favor	Favor	63	73
Favor	Neutral	60	5
Neutral	Favor	0	4
Neutral	Neutral	10	50
One oppose, other neutral; or both oppose		0	8

matter, which is often the case. On a "technical" decision like fluoridation, therefore, the manager is particularly well placed to assume policy leadership.

While some critics of the manager plan, like Duane Lockard, argue that "an appointive executive who is not evidently subordinate may be less acceptable" as a policy leader for the community than an elected official charged with administration, there is little empirical evidence to support this view. Indeed, Lockard recognizes that the manager system has certain things working in its favor including: (1) a favorable reputation for efficient and honest administration; (2) the growing place of expertise and the expert in business and government; (3) the trend toward emphasizing executive leadership over legislative power.[15]

Fluoridation is just the kind of issue which allows the manager to take a public stand.[16] However, not all managers are publicly active on the issue. It is important to isolate some of the elements which may influence the kind of action which the manager chooses to take.

A Personal Factor: Professionalism

One of the factors which seems to play a major part in the manager's stand is the extent of his professionalization. While it is difficult to gather information on this aspect of the mayor's career, the manager's educational and employment history are available in the membership files of the International City Managers' Association. They were kind enough to permit us to make use of their data.

Professionalization may create attitudes more favorable toward innovation. Kammerer and her associates found in a study of council-manager cities in Florida that local political systems could be differentiated in terms of the professionalization of the manager (as well as the "climate of opinion" in the community).[17] Those managers who were "locals" (appointed from within the community to advance the interests of a particular political organization) were found to act in a "nonprofessional" manner. On the other hand, the professional manager was likely to use other city managers as a reference group, in addition to being concerned with how he was viewed by his own council. To be recommended for another position in a larger city, he must show his ability to "get things done." Or, as Williams and Adrian put it, referring to urban renewal programs, "the projects are the fulfillment of the administrator's dreams. To the city-manager and the planning director, they offer an opportunity to become identified with a major city project in which administrative magic may be performed."[18]

Because of the professionalized attitudes which some managers have, we might expect that managers would be even less likely to oppose fluoridation than mayors are. On the other hand, some managers may feel that they should maintain neutrality on a "question of policy." This may be one explanation of the finding in Table 7 that a mayor is more likely to favor fluoridation if the city

TABLE 7. *Form of Government and Mayor's Stand by Region (Percent of Mayors Favoring)* *

Region	Manager Cities	All Mayor Council Cities
Northeast	55 (18)	32 (59)
South	69 (52)	70 (27)
Midwest	77 (34)	61 (72)
West	46 (41)	36 (14)
Total	63 (145)	51 (172)

*Breakdowns by region are important because of the concentration of forms of government in particular regions. The commission form of government, for example, is concentrated in the East; the city-manager form predominates in the West. For further discussion of this point, see Crain, Katz, and Rosenthal, *op. cit.*, pp. 217–18.

has a manager than if it does not. While some managers may not have taken *public* stands, they may have exerted informal influence on the council or mayor.

To demonstrate that it is the professionalization of the managerial role and not simply the different structure of government in manager cities which accounts for fluoridation outcomes, we looked at the careers of 145 city managers and developed a scale of professionalism. The least professionalized managers are assumed to be those who went to college in the same state they are presently employed in, have never held a managerial post in another city, and have had adminstrative experience below the rank of manager in their present city. Some of these men will, no doubt, go on to other cities but these will be a minority. A middle group of men either have some graduate training or have worked in other cities. Finally, a small group are geographically mobile and have graduate degrees. In Table 8 the date of decision was used in the analysis as an index of the level of controversy. As we indicated earlier, the controversialness of fluoridation increased over time. We would not expect the "professional" manager to be moved much by controversy on the issue. This is exactly what we find.

The top line of Table 8 indicates a slight positive correlation between professionalization and favorability. When we look at the second and third lines, however, we find that it was the *nonprofessional* who was slightly more likely to take a public stand favorable to fluoridation *before* 1955. After

1955 this tiny difference is strongly reversed. In other words, the nonprofessional managers are equally (if not more) willing to support fluoridation when it is not controversial. The professional manager, however, is the main support of the "cause" when it is controversial. It is noteworthy that the nonprofessionalized managers seem to run for cover under conditions of controversy while a considerable number of the professionals hold their ground.

The willingness of the professionally oriented manager to continue to involve the city in late fluoridation efforts obscures the fact that as a political structure manager cities tend to "pioneer" in consideration of fluoridation. This proposition flows from the finding that the manager system is more likely to act early on fluoridation. Taken together, the three nonmanager systems (partisan mayor-council; nonpartisan mayor-council; commission) have a median consideration date of late 1953; the median for *all* manager systems is half a year earlier. This is consonant with the image of the manager as a man in touch with new developments effecting municipal government, and one more likely to have continuing contact with and respect for technical experts.

Conclusions

In the present paper, we have been pointing to only one aspect of community decision making on fluoridation which we

TABLE 8. *Professionalization of the Manager and His Position for Early and Late Decisions*

Early and Late Decisions	Local with No Graduate Schooling	Mobile or with Graduate Schooling	Professional Education
Percentage of managers favoring fluoridation, all cases	51 (53)	57 (79)	64 (11)
Percentage of managers favoring before 1955	69 (33)	65 (43)	— (1)
Percentage of managers favoring 1955 or later	20 (20)	47 (36)	70 (10)
Difference: early-late	49	18	—
Percentage of managers involved in late decisions	38 (53)	46 (79)	91 (11)

feel has been given inadequate consideration: the leadership function performed by the mayor and/or manager. Instead of fleeing the issue or suppressing it, American mayors and managers have frequently supported fluoridation even when to do so may have seemed politically unwise.[19]

Furthermore, we have found that the policy positions taken by these local political "stars" is crucial for the decision made by the local community. In some cases, mayors may be local "bosses," but such cities can only be a small proportion of all those which have passed on fluoridation. Instead, it would appear that these leaders provide important "cues" for both members of their own councils and for the public.

We do not contend, however, that the mayor is a completely free agent in this matter. For one thing, he is a man operating in a particular kind of political system. Second, his choices in politics are influenced by situational factors like level of controversy in the community. Unfortunately, because the literature had not prepared us for the importance of the local political system, we did not include any questions in the questionnaires on the social backgrounds of the mayors and managers, as we would do if the study were undertaken again.[20] We have been able to describe part of the social setting for the manager, particularly as he is embedded in a professionalized career commitment, but similar data is not available for American mayors. If these data were available, we would be interested in whether social differences among mayors create conditions for the expression of different attitudes on fluoridation. It remains to be seen whether systematic generalizations about institutionalized political actors can be developed for fluoridation and other issues. Studies along similar lines would have to establish the general utility of such an effort.

In any event, it is significant how little importance can be attributed to the presence of legitimacy-bestowing "influentials" in the fluoridation decision-making process. Many simply withdraw from the issue. This leaves the mayor in a position where he is more publicly visible and consequently more of a "leader" than he may appear to be when surrounded by these same persons on consensual "community projects" like new hospitals and the acquisition of new industry, where political leadership may be mainly a matter of acquiescence.[21]

Notes

1. Floyd Hunter, *Community Power Structure* (Chapel Hill: University of North Carolina Press, 1953); Robert Dahl, *Who Governs?* (New Haven: Yale University Press, 1961). For a review of much of this literature, see Robert Presthus, *Men at the Top* (New York: Oxford University Press, 1964), especially chap. 2.

2. Robert E. Agger, Daniel Goldrich, and Bert E. Swanson, *The Rulers and the Ruled* (New York: John Wiley, 1961); Oliver Williams and Charles Adrian, *Four Cities* (Philadelphia: University of Pennsylvania Press, 1963). Both the Agger volume and the study by Williams and Adrian discuss local politics but they make little use of formal structures and there is a tendency to treat mayors and managers as individuals rather than as actors within political roles.

3. Benjamin D. Paul, William A. Gamson, and S. Stephen Kegeles (eds.), "Trigger for Community Conflict: The Case of Fluoridation." *Journal of Social Issues*, 17, No. 4 (1961). In this special issue devoted to fluoridation there were few references to the political process. The contributors were either sociologists, psychologists, or specialists in public health. For a review and critique of the literature on fluoridation, particularly as it makes use of the concept of alienation, see Donald B. Rosenthal. "The Politics of Community Conflict" (unpublished Ph.D. dissertation. University of Chicago, 1964, especially chap. 2).

4. Particularly relevant to our work is Maurice Pinard. "Structural Attachments and Political Support in Urban Politics: The Case of Fluoridation Referendums," *American Journal of Sociology*. 68 (March 1963), 513–26.

5. Donald B. Rosenthal and Robert L. Crain, "Structure and Values in Local Political Systems," *Journal of Politics*, 28 (February 1966).

6. We asked the publisher: "Compared to other issues with which you are familiar, would you say that fluoridation was: 1) very calmly discussed; 2) calmly discussed; 3) warmly discussed; 4) hotly debated." We received 328 responses: 133 (41 percent) identified fluoridation as falling into the two calmer categories. Thus 59 percent of our respondents saw the fluoridation proposal as raising more than average

controversy. In fact, 113 (34 percent) indicated that the issue was "hotly debated."

7. Because we used three questionnaires and drew upon additional data, there is no standard case base. This, along with varying response rates, accounts for the variation in the number of cases in the tables.

8. We found few instances in which a connection could be traced between a position taken on fluoridation and political benefits to the actor. Indeed, one of the few cases in which fluoridation was brought into partisan politics boomeranged on the proposer. The health officer of a large city in northern New Jersey reported the following history of mayor activity: "The incumbent proposed fluoridation in order to get the support of labor. However, labor supported his opponent who was the City Commissioner in charge of the Health Bureau and who also supported fluoridation. The incumbent then campaigned against fluoridation and was defeated along with the referendum."

9. James S. Coleman, *Community Conflict* (New York: The Free Press, 1957). This view has been so widely accepted among writers on the subject that a further refinement went to the matter of whether administrative endorsements had to be actual or merely perceived before voters would vote against fluoridation. For this point, see Arnold Simmel, "A Signpost for Research on Fluoridation Conflicts: The Concept of Relative Deprivation," in Paul, Gamson, and Kegeles (eds.), "Trigger for Community Conflict," pp. 33–34.

10. The data is not presented here. A history of the declining popularity of fluoridation over the last fifteen years is provided in Robert L. Crain, "Fluoridation: The Diffusion of an Innovation among Cities," *Social Forces*, 44 (June 1966), 467–76.

11. For a consideration of the kinds of leadership available in most communities for the promotion of fluoridation, see Robert L. Crain, Elihu Katz, and Donald B. Rosenthal, *The*

Fluoridation Decision: Community Structure and Innovation (unpublished manuscript).

12. See footnote 6 for the wording of this item.

13. Fluoridation falls within the sphere of interest of these groups, but the generation of issues and their promotion by bureaucrats and associational complexes does not make them decisive decision makers. For a discussion of how issues are generated by local associations. See Edward C. Banfield, *Political Influence* (New York: The Free Press, 1960).

14. Eugene C. Lee, *The Politics of Non-Partisanship* (Berkeley: University of California Press, 1960), p. 152.

15. Duane Lockard, "The City Manager, Administrative Theory, and Political Power," *Political Science Quarterly*, 77 (March 1962), 236.

16. We do not mean that defining fluoridation as a technical issue is a wise move. This practice has backfired. Opponents of fluoridation have frequently accused the local health people of being part of a bureaucratic conspiracy directed from Washington.

17. Gladys M. Kammerer, Charles D. Farris, John M. DeGrove, and Alfred B. Clubock, *City Managers in Politics* (University of Florida Monographs: Social Sciences, No. 13; Gainesville, University of Florida Press, 1962).

18. Williams and Adrian, *Four Cities*, p. 160.

19. Whether supporting fluoridation is politically unwise is a difficult problem for future research. It may be that it is "wiser" to endure a brief flurry of protest rather than try to ride the fence through an extended period of acrimonious debate.

20. Governmental sponsorship of this project made an inquiry into politics at the local level difficult.

21. Losing efforts by "good government" groups to introduce metropolitan government despite opposition by the mayors of these large cities (St. Louis, Cleveland) emphasize the point made in the present article. Scott Greer, *Metropolitics* (New York: John Wiley, 1964).

A NEGLECTED but nevertheless highly crucial aspect of the role of the governmental administrator has been his involvement in the generating and guidance of legislative decisions. Although several accounts have been published over recent years about the relative importance of the executive and legislative branches of government in determining the final content of statutes, practically nothing has been put into print concerning the specific engendering or catalytic roles of administrators in the process of lawmaking.[1] . . . This essay seeks to examine the degree and character of administrative involvement in statute lawmaking with special reference to Los Angeles. The nature of the involvement of both the political and career sectors of the municipal administrative system in selected topical aspects of that jurisdiction's legislative process constitutes the core of the study. Prefatory analysis of the factors governing the context of this particular inquiry serves to provide a meaningful backdrop for relating its subsequent findings and implications.

The Rationale of Neglect

Writing nearly two decades ago, Professor Edwin E. Witte expressed the lament that relationships between administrative agencies and the legislative departments of our federal, state, and local governments were only imperfectly understood, particularly in matters of lawmaking. These relationships, he contended, were perceived by political scientists in terms of the order-making powers vested in administrative departments, and of the periodic associations arising pursuant to the structuring, financing, empowering, and surveillance of administrative activities by legislatures. The basic dimensions of this administrative-legislative relationship, according to traditional interpretation, assigned to the legislature "the working out of an acceptable compromise between conflicting positions taken by different groups in our society on proposals for legislation originating [in and] outside the legislature, most commonly with private organizations." The

The Career Public Service and Statute Lawmaking in Los Angeles

Harry W. Reynolds, Jr.

function of administrative departments, on the other hand, was "chiefly to supply the legislature and the executive on their request with information they need for the efficient discharge of their duties in relation to legislation, and to initiate minor bills designed to correct defects which have shown up in the laws that these departments administer."[2] Such an image of interaction reflected a disjunctive, largely segmental understanding of the phenomena of lawmaking; the administrative apparatus was felt to be subordinate to and only intermittently—perhaps even perfunctorily—associated with the legislative department and its decision-rendering processes.[3] . . .

The interest in separating politics from administration had as its object the elimination of values and normative judgments from the administrative act. With respect to the association of administrators with legislators in statute lawmaking, the identification through this dichotomy of policy formation with politics removed the policy process from consideration as a proper element impinging upon administration.[4] It also denoted the career civil servant as a value-neutral functionary largely unassociated with policymaking.

Notwithstanding the qualifications which

This is an edited version of an article which first appeared in Western Political Quarterly, *18 (September 1965), 621–39. Reprinted by permission of the University of Utah, copyright owners, and the author.*

were advanced against the forecited postulates by a growing number of researchers[5]— qualifications arising from empirical inquiries at many places in the political process— the verities of administrative-legislative relationships in statute lawmaking remained largely unexplored and imperfectly understood. A review of pertinent research in this area points up the gaps in our knowledge.

The Dimensions of Administrative Involvement: The Traditional Landscape

Approximately five decades of scholarship, measured from the turn of the twentieth century, have demonstrated the increasing importance of the American executive apparatus in determing the course and content of legislative enactments. Three echelons within this apparatus have been identified as distinct participants shaping and maneuvering the substantive decisions of legislative bodies—chief executives, department heads, or their facsimile, and the career civil service of the various levels of government. The nature of the participation of these particular executive categories in lawmaking, moreover, divides into three reasonably definable roles —as originators of legislation; as advisers or catalysts in the shaping of legislative proposals which were multifariously sired; and as calculated manipulators of the instruments and processes bringing about the enactment, modification, or rejection of pending legislation. . . .

The Career Administrator as Initiator of Legislation

The present study focuses upon the role of the career governmental administrator in the initiatory and enactment phases of 206 pieces of proposed legislation which have dealt with numerous substantive topics of concern to the city of Los Angeles. Introduced formally over a period of one month (March) in 1959 in the city council, these pieces of proposed legislation have been before the executive

and legislative organs of that city for much of the succeeding time, in the course of their enactment or rejection.

As Table 1 seeks to make clear, the variety which characterized the proposed legislation —that is, the difference in subject matter— has been considerable; their source or authorship is individually assignable to one of several distinct categories. Of central significance at this point is the strategic nature of the career governmental administrator's involvement in determining much of that proposed legislation's content and fate at the time of its drafting and introduction. The criteria for determining authorship, it should be stated, turn upon the ascertainment of the particular forces most controlling the substantive provisions of initial drafts of legislation.

In the case of the 50 bills attributed to departmental authorship, 38 are substantively the handiwork of career civil servants, 12 are the product of political-level leadership within the departments. The former category included proposed legislation in every subject-matter field identified in Table 1; the latter category embraced only three such fields.

The mechanics of bill drafting, where the career civil servant has been involved as initiator, followed a fairly standard course. This involvement has been characterized both by career-level initiative in framing particular policy proposals and in the vigorous advocacy of them, as embodied in drafts of legislation, before various echelons within the respective departments. The overwhelming majority of the bills drafted by career civil servants would appear from available evidence in this study to have been prompted by operational or administrative situations experienced by the careerists in the performances of their duties, and deemed to require some rectification through statutory means.

The prompting of situation and the administrators' response thereto in the form of drafted bills is illustrated in the following examples. With respect to one measure promoting safety in public recreation: "Some of the recreation supervisors got together and on the basis of their common experiences

TABLE 1. Legislative Proposals Introduced in Los Angeles City Council by Subject Matter and Source of Authorship*

(February 27–March 30, 1959)

Subject Matter Breakdown of Legislative Proposals†	Total No. of Bills by Topic	AUTHORSHIP OF PROPOSED LEGISLATION BY SOURCE						
		Private Citizen	Private Group	Mayor	Council	CAO‡	Dept. of City	Committee of City
Public Safety	16	3		1	1	8	8	3
Police	14	2		1			8	3
Fire							8	3
Traffic	2	1			1			
Public Works	89	19	8	5	6	15	19	17
Streets	67	16	7	3	6	8	13	14
Sidewalks	1						1	
Water power	3	1						2
Sewers	12	1		2		6	2	1
Rubbish	1		1					
Right of way	4	1				1	2	
Public buildings	1						1	
Building and Safety	9	2	2	1			2	2
Health and Welfare	14	3	1			3	5	2
Health	10	2				3	3	2
Recreation	4	1	1				2	
Planning	23	2	1			1	5	14
Personnel	10		4		1	4	1	
County, State, and Federal Affairs	20	1	2		1	5	9	2
Industry and Transportation	11		1					10
Finance (Authorization)	14	1	1	4	1	2	1	4
Totals	206	31	20	11	10	30	50	54
Percentages of Total		15.1	9.2	5.3	4.8	14.5	24.7	26.4

*The Los Angeles City Council is comprised of 15 members chosen for four-year terms in nonpartisan elections. Half the members are elected every two years. The council's business is transacted through 15 standing committees. The mayor is elected for four years, appoints 5-man boards to administer the city's 19 departments. With few exceptions all departmental personnel beneath the commissions is under the merit system.

†The legislation under consideration here relates substantively to questions of enlarging or modifying municipal services, and to matters of administrative authority, organization, and procedure. Revenue, appropriation, and private bills are omitted. In preparing this study, the writer has had access both to the complete legislative histories filed with the city clerk and to the impressions and memorabilia of legislators and interest groups participating in the lawmaking process of the city.

‡The CAO, or chief administrative officer, handles budgetary and organization and management matters. He is appointed by the mayor, confirmed by the council, answerable to both.

drafted a memorandum detailing their ideas on what this particular change should be. This is the substance of this bill which the department supports."[6] And concerning a street widening with mandatory off-street parking in a residential apartment neighborhood: "Our engineers in that district have pointed out for years that such a change would speed traffic flow. This bill embodies the recommendations they submitted to us, and from a technical point of view is workable."[7] . . .

The preceding groupings comprise probably three-fourths—or, as nearly as can be determined, thirty-eight—of the bills attributed to the initiation of the career administrative system. A second category includes twelve bills whose origin lay with the political level of administrative leadership within the municipal departments. In these circumstances, the contribution of the career system was primarily that of extractor of background information designed to support the need and feasibility of the desired legislative actions. In the case of five of these bills the recommendations of the career sector, primarily in matters surrounding the technical justification of proposed undertakings, were adverse, and duly overridden by the departmental leadership (i.e., the commissions in charge of the departments). . . .

What the foregoing analysis particularly suggests, of course, is the predominant importance of the career levels of administration within departments of the Los Angeles city government in the initiation of legislative proposals offered in the name of the city government. That the thirty-eight bills brought forth by career levels of administration were accepted in their principal substantive and procedural terms by higher departmental levels with no snags or changes to speak of is significant testimony to the pivotal and conclusive role of that career system in the formulation of legislative proposals within the executive apparatus of the city.[8]

The involvement of the career level of administration in the formulation of statutes by the other sources identified in Table 1 is also worthy of interpretation. Private citizens initiated thirty-one bills in every field but two listed in Table 1. In the case of twenty-seven of these pieces of proposed legislation, the great majority of them pertaining to public works projects,[9] a considerable amount of prior consultation between sponsors and the respective departments which would effectuate anticipated statutes was evident. Such consultation allowed the affected departments (through their career administrative echelons) to review in every instance the technical feasibility or justification of the desired statutory objectives, and in the case of fourteen projects actually to put the functional details into workable drafts of legislation. In the remaining thirteen instances it made possible a thoroughgoing review by these departmental technicians of the legislative drafts to insure like workability of ends and means.

Within both categories of consultation the available evidence suggests a great deal of qualifying of both the citizens' statutory drafts and the composition of the various

functional objectives which were hopefully to be achieved through statute, all as a consequence of the scrutiny of them by career-level administrators. Four bills initiated by private citizens were not subjected to any administrative clearance.

In referring to career administrative review and modification of bills, two questions suggest themselves—how and by whom? The evidence afforded by the present study indicates clearly that, in answer to the first query posed, administrative assistance was sought after and exploited in the case of private citizens on the basis of direct and continuing access to the points of effectual assistance in departmental hierarchies, and not through a downward traversing of the formal chains of command. Such direct subagency-clientele associations have been based on long-standing relationships which have flourished in an atmosphere of reciprocal good will and customer dependency. . . .

Much the same story arises from the review of the twenty bills spawned by the interest groups that were active within the time span of this study. Every subject-matter field but one listed in Table 1 was covered in these drafts of legislation. Departmental clearance was effected in every instance, including eleven bills drafted by the respective sponsoring groups and nine drawn up by the departments concerned to accommodate particular pressure groups requests and objectives. In these instances, departmental clearance again was effected primarily at the level of the technician. The eleven bills drawn up by the interest groups were reviewed at this level. The nine bills accommodating pressure group proposals were likewise authored at this source in the departments discharging the brunt of this service. . .

Eleven bills pertaining to four fields emerged from the mayor's office in the period covered by the study; ten bills in five fields emanated from the membership of the city council. The departments concerned assisted in the drafting of every bill embodying the substantive objectives sought by the mayor. Eight of the ten bills espoused by the municipal councilmen were similarly scrutinized as to their statutory language, and significant portions thereof written, by the pertinent departments at the legislators' request. Two bills within this category were drafted by individual councilmen and not cleared with the departmental staffs concerned substantively with their provisions. The case histories of mayoralty and councilmanic bills again leave no room for questioning the preeminent role of technicians in the departments in either the critical examination or the actual drafting of these proposals. Decisions made at this level were characteristically subjected to review according to the procedure and results noted previously in connection with most private submissions.

The thirty bills emanating from the chief administrator's office, and pertaining to six subject-matter fields listed in Table 1, were in each instance the product of administrative staff studies undertaken by appropriate municipal line departments in conjunction with the chief administrative officer. Accordingly, each draft of legislation accorded in some measure with the particular predilections of the career administrators knowledgeable in the substantive requirements pertaining thereto. The manner of appropriate departmental clearance was very much like that already noted, where comparable types of substantive legislation involving the same departments were extant. Administrative technicians entered reservations about the contents of three of the pieces of proposed legislation in this category at the time of drafting.

The final class of legislation, that initiated by committees of the city, included fifty-four bills pertaining to every subject category but one listed in Table 1. Over three-fourths of these bills dealt with public works, planning, and transportation items. The initiating groups were, in fact, advisory committees appointed by the mayor or the city council at different times to make recommendations concerning various topics of current governmental concern—for example, revising the building code, improving transportation facilities. Many of their proposals, when put in draft legislation form, were endorsed or cosponsored by one or more departmental commissioners. Within the period covered by

the study, there were seven committees which submitted their recommendations in the form of the numerous pieces of proposed legislation mentioned previously. These committees made little use of career-level personnel in the framing of tentative statutory drafts. Actual drafting in the above instances was undertaken by committee staffs composed of assorted persons among whom were a number of career administrators serving in interim, quasi-official capacities.

Clearly the position of the career administrators has been seen as a pivotal factor in convincing the political levels of departmental leadership and the city council of the worth of pressure group and individual citizen objectives desired by statute. Statements such as "If the administrators oppose us, we're sunk"; "We find the Council checks with the departments on our requests and lets itself be governed by what they say"; and "They (career administrators) do us many favors before the Council" are common, running through the case histories of bills espoused by these sources. . . .

The Career Administrator as Catalyst and Synthesizer

The foregoing data suggest a catalytic and synthesizing role for the career governmental administrator in statute lawmaking as well. This involvement took place according to various levels of intricacy, and pertained to occasional as well as multitudinous and repetitive items. The first and most elemental level concerned career administrators' assistance to sponsors of legislation—specifically, in rendering feasible from a technical point of view the language of legislative drafts which emanated from nondepartmental sources. Features of this career administrative role were reviewed previously. A corollary of this explicative involvement by administrators was the attempt to embody statutory objectives (written as well as unwritten) in practicable, achievable terms.

Of the 156 bills which emerged from six nondepartmental sources within the period of this study, 100 were reviewed and adapted in the manner referred to above. This includes sixty-four proposed statutes actually drafted *in toto* or almost *in toto* by administrative units to actualize the desired goals of outsiders. The drafting and review of these pieces of proposed legislation by the career levels of administration served inescapably to effect substantive or procedural modifications—albeit of an imperceptible nature in some instances—in the interest of enhancing the workability of the ensuing statutes.

The legislative histories of all of the 100 bills which were initiated by nondepartmental sources (and cleared administratively) indicate overwhelming finality for career-level decisions in regard to substantive and procedural syntheses.[10]

An analysis of twenty-six bills arising from nondepartmental sources revealed 138 substantive issues of varying intricacy which were referred to career-level administrators in four departments. Career administrative judgments were accepted conclusively in forty-six instances (e.g., the most feasible of several routes for a road, the content of updated safety criteria to be included in the building and safety code), due largely to the initiative of the careerists themselves. In the case of fifty-seven issues referred to career administrative units at the instigation of contending forces (pressure groups, departmental commissioners, private citizens, and the like) for resolution, career level judgments were similarly decisive, and accepted as final. Only with the remaining items in dispute did career administrators limitedly participate in their adjustment in accordance with strict guidelines laid down by political-level superiors....

The Career Administrator as Legislative Manipulator

The disposition of the 206 pieces of proposed legislation comprising this study at the hands of the Los Angeles City Council reinforces the central image of the career administrative system in the municipality's lawmaking process.

One broad measure of the importance of the career administrative system in the city council's acceptance or rejection of proposed legislation is the fate attending bills of whatever origin in accordance with their prior clearance, or substantive criticism, by the staffs of the municipal departments. Of 50 pieces of suggested legislation emanating from the municipal departments, 39 were approved by the city council. Twelve bills emanated from the political leadership of the departments, it will be recalled, and 38 from the career administrative system. Of these respective numbers, 9 and 30 were enacted into law. Twenty of 31 bills arising from private citizens passed the council, as did 14 of 20 pieces of proposed legislation brought up by pressure groups. Eight of the mayor's 11 bills, 9 of the city council's 10, and 22 of the chief administrative officer's 30 also were enacted. Six of the 54 proposed statutes brought forth by committees of the city received the approval of the council....

In all, fifty-eight bills supported by career administrative units within municipal departments did not pass. Only two of nineteen bills specifically opposed by some portion of the administrative system did pass. The position of the career administrative system vis-à-vis pending legislation was thus a paramount factor influencing city council decisions in a great many instances....

The greatest amount of effort by the administrative departments of Los Angeles in regard to legislation pending in the city council was exerted on behalf of those bills comprising the first four categories in Table 1. Thirty bills out of seventy-three in this group were singled out for special, sustained advocacy in which career administrative personnel played a part. Various techniques and approaches which embodied this advocacy may be identified:

1. *The personal cultivation of councilmen by the political and career levels of management in a number of city departments.* This was most commonly done by (1) personal visits from administrators to individual councilmen, openly to enlist their support for or sound out their sentiments concerning particular bills; (2) issuing a string of written messages (memoranda, position papers, and

routine commentaries) from departmental sources for the edification of councilmen, wherein departmental preferences were laid out and pertinent questions dealt with; and (3) utilization of outside mediaries—namely, the municipal newspapers, the mayor's office, influential and respected citizens, lobbyists—to communicate circumspectly to councilmen the particular feelings of the departments and to receive back in turn legislative reactions. . . .

2. *The exploitation of formal hearings by departmental administrators.* This tactic was employed rather exclusively in those situations where committees of the city council regularly held formal hearings to which administrators were given access. Only three committees have made such regularity a practice—those dealing with public works, planning, and health and welfare legislation. Within this limited setting, nevertheless, two municipal departments were successful in a number of instances in influencing councilmaniac thinking by means of well-planned and well-presented testimony from select witnesses, carefully supplemented with suitably arranged publicity. This committee cultivation saw the constant use of career-level personnel from the departments concerned as witnesses. With fairly elaborate precision, the presentations of general managers and bureau chiefs were buttressed numerically and in depth by statements from technicians, program specialists, and the like.

3. *The exploitation of particular events and circumstances by certain municipal administrators.* Application of this tactic was confined to a few instances where, in the judgment of certain departmental careerists and commissioners, the prospects for passage of select legislation would be augmented. Only three pending bills were spotlighted in this manner during the period covered by the study. Each piece of legislation pertained to some aspect of public safety, the cause of which was deemed to be better served if efforts were put forth to heighten public support for the bills in question. Evocation of this support took the form of administrative dramatizing of important, and in some cases crucial, circumstances whose recent occur-

rence suggested the need for remedial legislation. Presentations and exhortations were made in a carefully planned manner to civic clubs, parent-teacher meetings, and like associations in the city over a period of several weeks; career-level administrators sustained the brunt of the burden of justification and enlightenment. . . .

4. *The husbanding by career administrators of nongovernmental sources of community influence.* Besides having recourse to power centers in the community which might aid the passage of bills urgently needed because of pressing circumstances, career administrative echelons in four Los Angeles departments also have cultivated these kinds of instruments as a matter of general utility. Thus, within the period covered by the study, there was evidence of sustained contact by career and political levels of management with the press and civic clubs and organizations in the interest of relating their influence to the furtherance of departmental business of various kinds before the city. . . .

Interviews with councilmen suggest clearly that some administrative departments have established close and continuing contacts with them over a period of many years, wherein the individual and collective attitudes of legislators with regard to particular bills can be determined as a matter of course. Administrative support or opposition to pending legislation can be transmitted on a similar basis to the city council. Two councilmen pointed out that in the case of several departments the closeness and continuity of their contacts with the city council were such that relevant councilmanic attitudes regarding departmentally proposed legislation were ascertainable before the legislation was formally introduced. To other councilmen, similarly, the involvement of career administrators in these departments in rendering assistance to nongovernmental sponsors of draft legislation served as the best way of acquainting these sponsors authoritatively with known legislative feelings about particular proposals, thus heightening somewhat prospects for enactment. . . .

This conception of the dominance of the administrative system in selectively influencing the city council as to pending legislation, with a largely passive role for other contributing sources of bills, affords a meaningful insight into decision making in the municipal legislature. The reasons for this passivity, particularly on the part of political interest groups, are rooted in some measure in the political history of Los Angeles, where they have become traditional. In a narrow sense, they constitute a reaction to a blatant aggressiveness by some interest groups in earlier days which has become suspect in the public's mind. But in a more fundamental sense, the limited influence enjoyed by these groups and other contributors of legislation derives from the established practice of the city council to treat principally with the administrative departments in resolving questions about legislation that is before it for passage or rejection. . . .

The Mayor Decides

Of the 118 bills in this study which passed the city council, 109 were signed into law by the mayor. Among this number were all 39 which had originated with the departmental administrative systems, as well as 18 (of 20) begot by private citizens and twelve (of fourteen) engendered by political interest groups. Also approved were the eight bills emanating from the mayor's office which passed the council, as well as the seven (of nine) initiated by the council and the twenty (of twenty-one) stemming from the chief administrative officer. Only five of the six council-approved bills originating from other nongovernmental sources received executive sanction. The considerable success achieved by the administrative system in the matter of mayoralty approvals is attributable both to the long-standing influence exercised by various departments with skill and informality upon the mayor's office, and to a kindred sentiment between these two sources on behalf of the bulk of this legislation. From various interviews and legislative histories, there is considerable evidence of the dependence of the mayor's office upon departmental (i.e., career-level administrative) guidance in

the disposition of much of this pending legislation, and the uninterrupted (and usually unchallenged) counsel from this source which accordingly was proffered, often at the department's own initiative. Practically every bill signed, from whatever source, was one enjoying an earlier imprimatur of the career administrative system.

Conclusions

Clearly, the career level of administration in Los Angeles is active in all phases of statute lawmaking. It dominates the initiating, synthesizing, and legislative manipulation phases of bill enactment. This is accomplishes by controlling the substance of virtually all initial and amended drafts from all sources, giving embodiment to its own versions or proposals of legislation. Developing over a long period, this career administrative hegemony has derived from both a vigorous initiative by the bureaucracy on its own behalf and an indigenous monopoly of technical competence by administrators not readily imitated by other participants in the city's lawmaking process. Such preeminence on the part of the career administrative system has been largely self-directing. It focuses upon the council or the other parties interacting in the lawmaking process at various stages, undergoing no effective challenge from the political level of executive leadership or any other force capable of significantly upsetting established rules which have minimized the direct influence of citizens, interest groups, and even legislators and the collegial department headships, upon the final legislative products.

The present evidence suggests rather complete acceptance by the city council of the career administrative system's recommendations, substantive and procedural, in regard to legislation. Exceptions involve bills with intricate financial or touchy political concomitants, by and large. Substance *per se* affords no basis of significant correlation in the matter of passage or rejection, nor does corroborating or dissuasive staff (i.e., the chief administrator's) analyses, save as they sometime heighten councilmanic sensitivities on factors of cost. The analysis here presented casts a fuller quantitative and qualitative light on the variously perceived hypothesis of career administrative involvement in statute lawmaking. It poses, too, additional sub-hypotheses requiring further investigation in other settings to assure conclusive insights into the origin, scope, and impact of unneutrality.

Notes

1. The preparation of this study was facilitated by a research grant from the Research Council of the University of Southern California. Special acknowledgment must be accorded the office of the City Clerk of Los Angeles, without whose assistance pertinent materials would have been unavailable. On the paucity of prior studies dealing with the extent of administrative involvement in statute lawmaking, see especially O. Douglas Weeks, "Initiation of Legislation by Administrative Agencies," 9 *Brooklyn L. Rev.* (1940), 117–31; and Edwin E. Witte, "Administrative Agencies and Statute Lawmaking," *Public Administration Review*, 2 (Spring 1942), 116–17.

2. Witte, "Administrative Agencies and Statute Lawmaking," p. 116.

3. The literature of political science was slow to perceive the changing nature of the image. W. F. Willoughby could write in 1934: "A few years ago Congress would have resented the attempt on the part of the President to embody his proposals in the form of definite drafts of bills as an infringement on its function. Now the President boldly puts his proposals in this form, declares them to be administrative measures and takes the position that support of them is a test of party fealty." *Principles of Legislative Organization and Administration* (Washington, D.C.: Brookings, 1934), p. 68.

4. George A. Shipman, "The Policy Process:

An Emerging Perspective," *Western Political Quarterly*, 12 (June 1959), 538.

5. The main assaults by the empiricists upon the prevailing didacticism of political science in the decades just prior to and following the turn of the century are well depicted in such works as David Easton, *The Political System* (New York: Alfred A. Knopf, 1953), chaps. 1 and 2; Henry Commager, *The American Mind* (New Haven: Yale University Press, 1950), chap. 15. Pragmatism and a social adaptation of Darwinism constituted the new methodology of investigation; James Bryce, Woodrow Wilson, Charles Beard, Arthur Bentley, Charles Merriam, W. F. Willoughby, and Frank Goodnow were the principal fashioners of the revised perspective regarding politics. Yet while Bryce's *American Commonwealth*, rev. ed., (New York: The Macmillan Company, 1910) and Wilson's *Congressional Government* (New York: Meridian Books, 1956) sought to lay bare the realities of the process of lawmaking, they did so largely in descriptive and general terms.

6. Statement of senior recreation inspector, Los Angeles Recreation and Parks Department, before the City Council Committee on Health and Welfare, as reported in dossier No. 89316, Los Angeles City Clerk's Office, and recorded by the writer, March 30, 1959.

7. Statement of senior traffic engineer, Los Angeles Traffic Department, before the City Council Committee on Planning, as reported in dossier No. 89424, and recorded by the writer, December 29, 1959.

8. In the nineteen departments of the Los Angeles city government only two have officially constituted legislative liaison units which review legislative proposals from those departments and otherwise look after legislative business in the city council.

9. Sidewalk and sewer installations, alley and street pavings, and street lighting equipment, for the most part.

10. Procedural items were more common, running to several hundred. One bill alone had sixty-seven requiring administrative judgments; six bills had at least fifty such items each, and probably more.

3. Urban Courts

THE PURPOSE of this paper is to compare the behavior of, and especially the sentences imposed by, criminal court judges selected by radically different political processes.[1] It attempts to discover what happens when the selection of judges is taken "out of politics," as reformers have advocated. It also analyzes the relationship between a city's political system and a particular public policy—criminal court decisions. Thus it attempts to contribute to an understanding of the question, "What difference does it make who governs?" The cities studied are Minneapolis and Pittsburgh.

In the past, the study of urban government and urban politics focused on the administration of government services in cities. This focus was very apolitical both in fact and value. It stated that politics was, in fact, absent from the administration of urban government (unless nefariously brought in) and, more important, it ought to be absent. In recent years students of urban government have indicated, quite accurately, that the governments of our cities, particularly our larger cities, serve another function in addition to the administration of public goods and services; namely, a political function—the management of conflict in matters of public importance.[2] Their studies have shown the various ways in which conflict is managed in various cities. Some large cities (over 300,000 in population) have a "traditional" political system with (typically) a formally partisan city government, strong parties which rely on material rewards rather than issues to attract members and which have a generally working-class orientation toward politics (an emphasis on conferring material benefits upon individuals and an identification with local areas of the city, rather than the city "as a whole"), and a centralization of influence. Other large cities have a "good government" or reform political system with (typically) a formally non-partisan city government, weak parties which rely on nonmaterial rewards (primarily issues or personalities) and which have a generally middle-class orientation toward politics (an emphasis on government maximizing such values as efficiency, honesty, impartiality,

An Empirical Evaluation of Urban Political Systems: The Criminal Courts*

Martin A. Levin

professionalism, and an identification with the city "as a whole"), and a decentralization of influence.[3]

In short, these studies answered the question "Who governs?" However, even more recently, students of urban government have attempted to raise and answer a second and probably more important question: "What difference does it make who governs?"[4] In other words, what difference does it make to the average citizen whether he lives in a city with a "traditional" political system or a "good government" political system?[5]

It is very likely, as James Q. Wilson has argued, that the struggle for power in a city has little direct effect on the life of the average citizen, but that the services provides by the government once in power (such as the administration of criminal justice, education, and welfare) are very likely to directly and significantly affect him.[6] Moreover, it is possible that the policies followed in providing these services are closely related to—and, indeed, perhaps the product of—the city's political system. These policies can be viewed as the outputs of the city's political system, and the political processes of the city can be viewed as the inputs.[7]

This study attempts to ascertain what

*This paper is a revised and condensed version of an essay by the same title delivered at the Sixty-Fifth Annual Meeting of the American Political Science Association, New York City, September 1969, reprinted by permission of the author and the American Political Science Association. All of the footnotes containing the interview quotations have been deleted.

261

consequences differing political systems have on the decisions of the criminal court judges in Minneapolis and Pittsburgh and thus for the individuals that come into the courts. It also attempts to discover what happens when the selection of judges is taken "out of politics."

Judicial Selection Reform

For many years attorneys, their professional associations, many (but by no means all) judges, and reform-minded laymen have advocated taking the selection of judges out of politics. The proposals for doing this vary, but the model "merit selection plan" usually includes gubernatorial appointment of judges from a list of nominees selected by a nonpartisan nominating commission composed of lawyers and laymen (and, in some instances, judges). These appointees go before the voters at the next election without opposition and solely on the question of their retention. Another selection method designed to remove judges from politics, but which the reformers feel is less ideal, is the selection of judges in truly nonpartisan elections. This selection method, or some variation of it, is followed for trial court judges in fourteen states.

The advocates of reform selection base their argument on both procedural grounds (that judges are experts and should be selected by fellow experts in a nonpolitical manner)[8] and substantive grounds (that these expert, nonpolitical selection procedures will produce higher quality, more efficient, more independent, and therefore more impartial and just judges).[9] The criteria on which these reform advocates base their judgments of "more efficient," "more just," or of a "higher quality" are not always clear. Moreover, none of the reform advocates support their assertions with systematic evidence indicating that taking the selection of judges "out of politics" does, in fact, produce such judges, nor do they present evidence indicating that reform judicial selection has any consequences regarding what judges in fact do.[10]

The opponents of taking the selection of judges "out of politics" premise their argument on democratic values (e.g., popular participation and legitimizing judges' decisions), but they also fail to support their assertions with evidence that a political selection procedure would help attain such values. However, recently Edward Costikyan offered an empirical defense of political selection procedures and an empirical critique of reform selection procedures based on his experience as the Reform Democratic leader of Tammany Hall.[11] They are persuasive but inadequate because they focus primarily on selection procedures. His effort to present systematic evidence on the consequences of these procedures actually presents only his evaluation of the qualifications of a small number of judges selected by each method. It does not examine the nature of their judicial decisions and behavior.

The Evaluation of Selection Procedures and Political Systems on the Basis of Judicial Decisions

The arguments over judicial selection procedures do not systematically answer or even raise the crucial questions which the average urban resident might ask before approving one plan or another: What are the consequences of these different methods of judicial selection procedures? What effects, if any, do these different selection procedures have on the decisions of the criminal court judges? More specifically, what are their effects, if any, on the quality of justice in the criminal courts? In short, what difference does reform selection make to the individuals who come into the courts? These are the questions which this paper examines. To answer them, comparative research was undertaken on the criminal courts and political systems of Pittsburgh and Minneapolis. These cities represent two more or less opposed types of political systems (the "traditional" and the "good government," respectively) and both types of judicial selection systems (the political and the reform, respectively).[12]

Pittsburgh has a formally partisan and highly centralized city government. The Democratic party organization is strong, hierarchical, disciplined, highly cohesive, and attracts workers with material incentives.[13] It dominates city politics and is influential in state and national politics. Public and party offices are filled by party professionals whose career patterns are hierarchical and regularized. There is a high degree of centralization of influence, and the citizens tend to accept pro-union and liberal social welfare policies. There is wide acceptance of partisanship and party activity in almost every sphere of Pittsburgh local government. Indeed, there has been little public enthusiasm for efforts to take the selection of judges out of politics, and the parties view positions on the courts and their related agencies as primary sources of rewards for their workers.

There are nineteen judges on the Pittsburgh (Allegheny County) common pleas court (the trial court for both criminal and civil jurisdictions), and they are elected on a partisan basis for ten-year terms. Party designation appears on the ballot. In practice, the political parties, especially the Democratic party, dominate the selection of judges in Pittsburgh, and the local bar association usually plays a very limited role. The primaries and the general elections for judicial positions are dominated by the parties. When a court vacancy occurs, the governor appoints a successor who must stand for reelection at the next general election, and 52.6 percent of the nineteen incumbent judges in 1965 initially reached the bench in this manner. These interim appointments have also been controlled by the local parties. The Pittsburgh judges' career patterns also reflect the dominance of the parties and the limited role of the bar association in judicial selection. Almost all of the judges held a government position such as city solicitor, assistant prosecutor, city councilman, state legislator, or even congressman, prior to coming to the bench (all partisan offices are controlled by the parties). They were also active members of the party organization.

Minneapolis has a formally nonpartisan and structurally fragmented city government. The Democratic-Farmer-Labor (DFL) party and the Republican party play a significant but limited role in city politics. They are both formally (because of nonpartisan elections) and informally (because of the wide acceptance of nonpartisanship) limited. The parties are moderately weak, loosely organized, highly democratic and undisciplined. They attract workers through nonmaterial incentives. Thus the parties do not overcome the formal decentralization of authority in the city. Individuals (including "amateur" politicians) with the ability and willingness to work, but with little seniority in the party, can and do rise rapidly in the party and in city government. The citizens tend to be disposed toward conservative policies. Nonpartisanship in city politics is widely and strongly accepted by the people (and even by many party workers and some party leaders). Indeed, the electorate has had a strong negative response to candidates or incumbents who violate, or seem to violate, this ideal. This is especially true of the courts and their related agencies, and thus party leaders and workers tend not to regard them as a source of party rewards.

There are sixteen judges on the Minneapolis (Hennepin County) district court (the trial court for both criminal and civil jurisdictions), and they are formally elected for six-year terms on a nonpartisan basis. In practice, the political parties have almost no role in the selection of judges in Minneapolis, while the local bar association generally plays a major role. Prior to a judicial election the Minneapolis bar association polls its members and publicizes the results. The "winner" of the poll (or the second or third highest candidate) almost always wins the election. The governor makes appointments to interim vacancies, and 87.5 percent of the incumbent judges in 1965 initially reached the bench in this manner. When vacancies occur the Minneapolis bar association conducts a poll, and the Minnesota governors have closely adhered to the bar's preferences. The two DFL governors who have served in the last ten years have been significant exceptions to this pattern, but they were strongly criticized for this (even by some of their own party members) and had to carefully work around the bar association. Moreover, even during the administrations of these DFL governors, the party played almost no role in judicial selections because the governor's decisions were at the most influenced by "political" rather than "party" considerations (e.g., the appointees' relationship to these governors was personal rather than organizational). The Minneapolis judges' career patterns also reflect the minor role of the parties and the major role of the bar association in judicial selection. Prior to coming to the bench, 77.7 percent (14) of the incumbent Minneapolis judges in 1965 had been exclusively or predominantly in private legal practice (usually business-oriented, and often corporate, practices). Those who had held public positions before coming to the bench did not hold elective positions (with one exception) and were generally not active in either party. Thus the judicial selection system in each city seems to be a reflection of the political systems. Therefore, the political systems seem to indirectly determine the type of judicial personnel in each city.

The Criminal Courts

This study centers on the criminal court because its judges tend to be the focal point of the criminal justice system. Their decisions significantly affect the lives and often the freedom of the individuals that come into the court, the behavior of other justice officials, and they involve fundamental questions of social order. These decisions define—at least in part—society's response to deviance. . .

Furthermore, judges have a very high degree of discretion in criminal court sentencing decisions. Criminal statutes in Pennsylvania and Minnesota (as in most states) allow the judge the choice of incarcerating a convicted defendant or of granting probation in common felonies. If the judge decides to imprison him, the statutes also allow him freedom to set the term in prison within certain prescribed limits. This high degree of discretion presents an opportunity to study

the behavior of the judges affected by the fewest external variables, such as the actual degree of the defendant's guilt and the quality of police investigation and prosecution. (By contrast, conviction rates are not simply the products of the judges' discretion and are greatly affected by these three factors.)

To understand general and typical judicial behavior patterns in each city, the sentencing decisions in routine cases are compared statistically for the nine most common felony offenses[14] rather than for the highly publicized (and often unique) offenses of murder or white-collar crime such as embezzlement. To understand the judges' decision-making processes and courtroom behavior, open-ended interviews were conducted with all but one of the judges in both cities, and trials and courtroom proceedings were observed over several months in 1966. The judges' interview statements were cross-validated on the basis of their actual sentencing decisions, observation of their courtroom behavior, and interviews with over twenty criminal court participants in each city.

The Judges' Sentencing Decisions and Behavior Prior to Sentencing

There are significant differences in the sentencing decisions of the judges in each city. The decisions are more lenient in Pittsburgh than in Minneapolis.[15] White and Negro defendants receive both a greater percentage of probation and a shorter length of incarceration in Pittsburgh. This pattern persists when the defendants' previous record, plea, and age are also controlled, and it is rather consistent among all nine of the offenses compared. Table 1 indicates this pattern in general terms. For probation, when the sentencing decisions are controlled for type of prior record and race, there is a sufficient number of cases to compare the nine offenses in each city for twenty-six categories.[16] In twenty-two categories there is a greater percentage of probation in Pittsburgh, in two categories there is a greater percentage of probation in Minneapolis, and

TABLE 1. Summary of Comparison of Sentencing Decisions in Pittsburgh and Minneapolis

	Percentage of Probation: Comparison Between Cities for Offenses with Sufficient Cases		
	Number of offenses in which there is a greater percentage of probation in Pittsburgh	Number of offenses in which there is a greater percentage of probation in Minneapolis	Number of offenses in which there is no significant difference between cities
No prior record, whites	3	2	1
No prior record, Negroes	5	0	0
Prior record, whites	9	0	0
Prior record, Negroes	5	0	0
Total	22	2	1

	Length of Incarceration: Comparison Between Cities for Offenses with Sufficient Cases		
	Number of offenses in which there is a shorter length of incarceration in Pittsburgh	Number of offenses in which there is a shorter length of incarceration in Minneapolis	Number of offenses in which there is no significant difference between cities
No prior record, whites	1	1	0
No prior record, Negroes	2	0	1
Prior record, whites	6	1	0
Prior record, Negroes	4	0	0
Total	13	2	1

Note: Tables 1–4 are summaries of the data which appeared in the original version of this paper.

in one there is no significant difference between the cities. For incarceration, when type of prior record and race are controlled, there is a sufficient number of cases to compare the nine offenses for sixteen categories. In thirteen categories there is a shorter length of incarceration in Pittsburgh, in two there is a shorter length of incarceration in Minneapolis, and in one there is no significant difference between the cities. Throughout every aspect of the data the pattern runs almost entirely in one direction—greater leniency in Pittsburgh—and there are only some marginal variations in the degree of this greater leniency.

Although both white and Negro defendants receive more lenient sentences in Pittsburgh, in both cities whites receive a greater percentage of probation than Negroes in most categories and in Minneapolis whites receive a shorter length of incarceration than Negroes in most categories. In Pittsburgh Negroes receive a shorter length of incarceration than whites in almost all offenses.

On the whole, sentencing decisions for Negroes are more favorable in Pittsburgh than in Minneapolis, both in absolute terms and relative to whites. First, as Table 2 indicates in general terms, whites receive more lenient sentences than Negroes in more

TABLE 2. Summary of Comparison of Sentencing Decisions for Whites and Negroes in Pittsburgh and Minneapolis

	Percentage of Probation: Comparison Between Whites and Negroes for Offenses with Sufficient Cases					
	NUMBER OF OFFENSES IN WHICH WHITES RECEIVE A GREATER PERCENTAGE OF PROBATION THAN NEGROES		NUMBER OF OFFENSES IN WHICH NEGROES RECEIVE A GREATER PERCENTAGE OF PROBATION THAN WHITES		NUMBER OF OFFENSES IN WHICH THERE IS NO SIGNIFICANT DIFFERENCE BETWEEN THE RACES	
	Pitts.	Minn.	Pitts.	Minn.	Pitts.	Minn.
No prior record	4	5	1	1	1	1
Prior record	7	2	1	2	2	1
Total	11	7	2	3	3	2

	Length of Incarceration: Comparison Between Whites and Negroes for Offenses with Sufficient Cases					
	NUMBER OF OFFENSES IN WHICH WHITES RECEIVE A SHORTER LENGTH OF INCARCERATION THAN NEGROES		NUMBER OF OFFENSES IN WHICH NEGROES RECEIVE A SHORTER LENGTH OF INCARCERATION THAN WHITES		NUMBER OF OFFENSES IN WHICH THERE IS NO SIGNIFICANT DIFFERENCE BETWEEN THE RACES	
	Pitts.	Minn.	Pitts.	Minn.	Pitts.	Minn.
No prior record	0	0	2	1	0	3
Prior record	1	1	6	0	0	2
Total	1	1	8	1	0	5

categories in Minneapolis than in Pittsburgh. Second, in the instances of greater probation for whites, the differential between the races is larger in Minneapolis than in Pittsburgh. Third, Negroes receive more favorable sentences in absolute terms in Pittsburgh. As Table 3 indicates, Negroes in Pittsburgh receive a "high" percentage of probation and a "short" length of incarceration in more categories than Negroes in Minneapolis.[17] Indeed, as Table 4 indicates, Pittsburgh Negroes generally receive even more lenient sentences than whites in Minneapolis.

There are also significant differences in the judges' courtroom behavior prior to sentencing. Most nonjury trials in Pittsburgh are informal (e.g., witnesses stand at the front bar) and abbreviated, and most of the judges prefer this arrangement. Most of the Pittsburgh judges also prefer informal procedures for obtaining information concerning defendants (the defense attorney's trial presentation, individuals intervening with the judge outside of court, the court staff's knowledge about the defendant) rather than the presentence investigations of the probation department. Trials in Minneapolis are formal, deliberate, and unabbreviated, and all of the judges prefer this arrangement. They also use presentence investigations in almost every case, and most of them dislike utilizing any informal sources of information concerning the defendant.

The Judges' Decision-Making Processes

The behavior of the Pittsburgh and Minneapolis judges seems to be the indirect product of the cities' political systems. As noted, these systems seem to influence judicial selection. In each city the judges' socialization and recruitment patterns reflect the pattern of the cities' judicial selection system. These socialization and recruitment patterns,

TABLE 3. Summary of Comparison of Probation and Incarceration Patterns for Whites and Negroes in Pittsburgh and Minneapolis

	Proportion of Cases in which Whites and Negroes receive a "High" * Percentage of Probation in Pittsburgh and Minneapolis							
	Whites				Negroes			
	NUMBER OF OFFENSES IN WHICH WHITES RECEIVE A "HIGH" PERCENTAGE OF PROBATION		TOTAL NUMBER OF OFFENSES IN WHICH THERE IS A SUFFICIENT NUMBER OF CASES FOR ANALYSIS		NUMBER OF OFFENSES IN WHICH NEGROES RECEIVE A "HIGH" PERCENTAGE OF PROBATION		TOTAL NUMBER OF OFFENSES IN WHICH THERE IS A SUFFICIENT NUMBER OF CASES FOR ANALYSIS	
	Pitts.	Minn.	Pitts.	Minn.	Pitts.	Minn.	Pitts.	Minn.
No prior record	7	6	8	9	5	1	7	7
Prior record	7	1	10	8	3	0	10	5
Total	14	6	18	17	8	1	17	12

	Proportion of Cases in which Whites and Negroes receive a "Short" * Length of Incarceration in Pittsburgh and Minneapolis							
	Whites				Negroes			
	NUMBER OF OFFENSES IN WHICH WHITES RECEIVE A "SHORT" LENGTH OF INCAR- CERATION		TOTAL NUMBER OF OFFENSES IN WHICH THERE IS A SUFFICIENT NUMBER OF CASES FOR ANALYSIS		NUMBER OF OFFENSES IN WHICH NEGROES RECEIVE A "SHORT" LENGTH OF INCAR- CERATION		TOTAL NUMBER OF OFFENSES IN WHICH THERE IS A SUFFICIENT NUMBER OF CASES FOR ANALYSIS	
	Pitts.	Minn.	Pitts.	Minn.	Pitts.	Minn.	Pitts.	Minn.
No prior record	0	1	2	8	2	0	4	5
Prior record	3	1	8	8	6	0	8	4
Total	3	2	10	16	8	0	12	9

*See footnote 17 for the operational definition of these absolute terms.

TABLE 4. Comparison of Sentences for Pittsburgh Negroes and Minneapolis Whites

	Number of offenses in which Pittsburgh Negroes receive a greater percentage of probation than Minneapolis whites	Number of offenses in which Minneapolis whites receive a greater percentage of probation than Pittsburgh Negroes	Number of offenses in which there is no significant difference between the two groups
No prior record	2	2	2
Prior record	6	2	1
Total	8	4	3

	Number of offenses in which Pittsburgh Negroes receive a shorter length of incarceration than Minneapolis whites	Number of offenses in which Minneapolis whites receive a shorter length of incarceration than Pittsburgh Negroes	Number of offenses in which there is no significant difference between the two groups
No prior record	1	0	2
Prior record	7	0	0
Total	8	0	2

in turn, seem to influence the judges' decision-making processes in both cities and thus help determine judicial decisions. The Pittsburgh judges' decision making is typically characterized by an orientation toward the defendant, and it lacks an orientation toward punishment or deterrence. It is nonlegalistic in that it tends to be particularistic, pragmatic, and based on policy considerations. The Minneapolis judges typically tend to be more oriented toward "society" and its needs than toward the defendant. They are also more oriented towards the goals of their professional peers. Their decision making is legalistic and universalistic. Many of the Minneapolis judges seem aware of nonlegalistic factors that they might consider, but they do not seem to feel they are proper or relevant.

The Pittsburgh judges' decision-making processes seem to cumulatively contribute to lenient sentencing decisions, and the Minneapolis judges' seem to cumulatively contribute to severe decisions. The covariation of these decision-making processes and the ultimate substance of these decisions suggests this linkage, but it does not conclusively demonstrate it. Nevertheless, there seems to be enough evidence to suggest this linkage as the most reasonable and probably the best explanation.

These decision-making processes and the judges' courtroom behavior prior to sentencing very closely approximate two general models of decision making. The Minneapolis judges' behavior approximates a judicial decision-making model, and the Pittsburgh judges' approximates an administrative decision-making model.[18]

The judicial model of decision making has the following characteristics: (1) Decisions are made on the basis of the "best" evidence as defined under the laws of evidence. (2) Decisions are made on the basis of complete evidence as developed by the adversary system. (3) A judge feels that he must maintain physical distance from the parties to judge effectively and must maintain an image of detached objectivity because it is as important to appear just as to be just. (4) His decisions have a dichotomous specificity (yes-

no), and they must assign legal wrong to one of the two parties. (5) A judge deduces his decision by a formal line of reasoning from legal principles that exist, independent of policy considerations. (6) He evaluates his success by the degree to which his decisions have followed these procedures and by their satisfaction of abstract notions of justice and the law. He generally has a greater concern for procedure than for substantive issues, and thus is more concerned with satisfying "the law" as an abstract doctrine than arriving at "just" settlements of individual cases.

The administrative model of decision making has the following characteristics: (1) Decisions are made on the basis of the kind of evidence on which reasonable men customarily make day-to-day decisions. (2) Decisions are made on the basis of sufficient evidence gathered by the administrator's own investigation, and the length and depth of the investigation is determined by the resources available to him. (3) An administrator feels that he must seek intimate contact with the real world to be able to administer effectively. He feels that this is more important than maintaining an image of detached objectivity (i.e., "appearing just"). (4) He may adopt dichotomous (yes-no) or intermediate decisions. (5) He deduces his decision by pragmatic methods from the policy goals incorporated in the program he administers. He has greater concern for arriving at "just" settlements based on the particular merits of individual cases than for adherence to abstract notions of justice and the law. (6) He has a greater concern for substantive issues than for procedure, and thus he evaluates his success by the way the program he administers "fits" real world demands and supports.[19]

More specifically, sixteen of the eighteen Pittsburgh judges seem to be oriented toward the defendant. Their view of most defendants is benevolent, and they describe their decision making as usually "giving the benefit of the doubt" to the defendant. They feel that these "chances" are worth taking despite getting "taken in sometimes" because "some are rehabilitated." They explicitly seek to "help" them by emphasizing probation and parole. Moreover, they tend to feel that they have a "closeness" and "kinship with the people that come into criminal court," that they are "more human" than the judges of the past and that they have a "greater empathy and awareness of the [defendant's] problems" and "more insight into the different types of people" that come before them. Several of these judges express this empathy as part of their general attachment to the "underdog." Many explain this "closeness" as a product of their experiences in their previous careers in political parties and government.

The judges' image of their clients seems to have a crucial effect on their treatment of them. Their "closeness" and "empathy" with the defendant causes the Pittsburgh judges to stand apart from the law and to act as a buffer between it and the people upon whom it is enforced. Most of them act as if they view the law primarily as a constraint within which they have to operate to achieve substantive justice for the defendant.

Fourteen of the eighteen Pittsburgh judges do not seem to be oriented toward institutional rehabilitation, punishment, or deterrence. They act as if their decisions are, in part, based on the pragmatic standards of "Is the punishment effective?" and "Is it necessary?" These judges feel that prisons today are ineffective in achieving rehabilitation or even deterrence because of their low quality, and they feel that this policy consideration is relevant to their decision making. Thus they tend to be "reluctant" or "ashamed" of incarcerating defendants and "try to keep it to a minimum." They feel that rehabilitation is most likely to occur, if at all, within the family.

Their views on the gravity of several offenses—regardless of the standards of gravity of the law—also seem to contribute to their feeling that punishment may not be necessary in some instances. These views seem to be based on pragmatic and "realistic" criteria such as the actual background of the defendants and the actual effect of their acts. Thirteen of the eighteen Pittsburgh judges consider the defendant's background ("how he lives" and the heterogeneity and

"mill town" character of the population) in ascertaining the standards of proper conduct. Thus they often tend to base their sentencing decisions on the extralegal standards of the group in which the offense occurred (e.g., youths, Negroes, lower-income persons, homosexuals, or sex offenders). This tends to reduce the gravity of many acts in the judges' minds (e.g., certain types of violence, sex offenses such as sodomy, gambling cases), because they often are not repugnant to the standards of the group in which they usually occur.

The judges' focus on the actual effect of the defendants' acts often seems to cause them to act as if they view much of the defendants' behavior less as a criminal act than as a civil act or a tort.[20] Twelve of the eighteen Pittsburgh judges tend to view many acts as part of a dispute between two private parties rather than as a conflict between an individual and society as represented by the state. This perspective seems to be developed by the frequent "special" relationships between the defendant and the "victim": prior acquaintance and sometimes strong ties (e.g., as a relative, friend, or lover), the victim's physical or sexual provocation (e.g., in assault or rape cases), monetary provocation (e.g., in forged check or theft cases), or the "victim's" desire for revenge. This perspective also tends to reduce the gravity of many acts in the judges' minds, especially since it seems to contribute to the feeling that many of the defendants' acts are not threats to society.

Thirteen of the eighteen Pittsburgh judges feel that many crimes against property which do not involve violence are "minor," involve "only money," and are "less serious than [harm to] a human being." Some seem to feel that many crimes against property are in themselves not serious, even beyond the absence of physical harm, because the victims of these offenses sometimes have themselves to blame for their loss and because insurance coverage often mitigates the victims' loss.

The Pittsburgh judges' decision making is also nonlegalistic in that it tends to be particularistic.[21] Sixteen of the eighteen

Pittsburgh judges consider the individual defendant more than the offense, and they tend to focus on his personal characteristics (e.g., the "type of person" he is and his relationship with his family). They seem to base their sentencing decisions, in part, on the general criteria of the defendant's prior record, his offense, and the "type of person" he is, but they tend to act as if no general norm covers all individuals that fit one of these criteria. Within these general criteria they make numerous fine distinctions based on very diffuse and particularistic considerations (e.g., "how the defendant conducted himself" during the commission of the offense, how "cooperative" he was when arrested, or the culpability and background of the victim, such as the degree of actual consent or female provocation and the past "purity" of a victim in a rape case).22 They describe their decision making as "intuitive," "impressionistic," "unscientific," and "without rules of thumb," and they feel that "everything [about the defendant] counts."23

A final characteristic of their nonlegalistic decision making is the tendency of sixteen of the eighteen Pittsburgh judges to eschew a literal application of the law and prefer to exercise their discretion. They are critical of the law's inflexibilities and impracticalities, and they resist standardization of any of their sentencing decisions (even in offenses such as drunken driving and gambling).

Thirteen of the seventeen Minneapolis judges tend to be more oriented toward "society" and its needs and protection than toward the defendant. They tend to be critical of most defendants and often are resigned to their "criminality." For example, one judge explained his severe sentences for aggravated forgery: "I feel that once a fellow is a 'paper hanger' [i.e., a check forger], he'll always be one. So the best thing is to get him off the street." Thus they often seem inclined to "give up" on a defendant.

The Minneapolis judges' tendency to penalize defendants who plead not guilty with more severe sentences seems to be an indication of their greater concern for the needs of society than for the defendants'. Twelve of

the seventeen judges feel that trials should not be used by the "guilty" to escape a conviction. Thus if a defendant pleads not guilty and is then convicted, they feel that his plea indicated "the wrong attitude" or that he "wasn't repentant," and therefore they feel that he usually "deserves less consideration" in sentencing. They also feel this way because the defendant "has put the state through the expense of a trial."

Similarly, these thirteen judges also feel that, almost without exception, crimes against person are extremely grave. Indeed, sentences in all offenses are more severe in Minneapolis than in Pittsburgh, but this difference is much greater for armed robbery than for crimes against property. This seems to be a function of the Minneapolis judges' view of the extreme gravity of armed robbery and their tendency to base their decisions for this offense on an unqualified general standard. They also feel that most crimes against property are serious and represent threats to society and particularly to business.

Thirteen of the seventeen judges are also oriented toward their professional peers (e.g., correction authorities and law enforcement officials) and their goals. Although they want to exercise discretion, they are willing to sacrifice some of it to achieve both greater consistency in their sentences and the goals of some of these peers. In almost all instances in recent years, the effect of pursuing these goals has been more severe sentences. They explained that the city's police department felt that this uniform and rather severe policy was necessary to curb prostitution, which they felt was giving parts of the downtown section a "bad image." Most of the judges agreed to follow this pattern. Later, the mayor and the council made similar (though less concrete) suggestions to the judges concerning the necessity of curbing homosexual bars in the downtown area and again received a favorable response from the judges. In short, these judges tend to be more "enlightened" in terms of professional doctrine than benevolent toward the defendant. Indeed, many Minneapolis judges explained that the reason they rejected informal sources of information about the defendant (which tend to convey personal and mitigating information) and prefer the probation department's presentence investigations was that they "didn't want to become emotionally involved in individual cases." Thus the judges' orientation toward their professional peers and their lack of an orientation toward the defendant seem to be interrelated and mutually reinforcing, and they seem to cumulatively contribute to severe sentencing decisions.

Twelve of the seventeen Minneapolis judges believe in the effectiveness of institutional rehabilitation and penal deterrence, and thus are not reluctant to incarcerate defendants. Few of these judges are critical of the quality of prisons, but several complain about "the failure rate of the people we put on probation." Many of the judges spoke of the therapeutic effect of the "shock" of incarceration. To most of the judges a defendant's bad environment is a reason to have him undergo institutional rehabilitation rather than a factor that will mitigate their sentencing decision.

The decision making of thirteen of the seventeen Minneapolis judges is legalistic and universalistic, and this seems to reinforce the effect of their greater orientation toward society. They feel little "closeness" to the defendants and thus, instead of acting as a buffer between them and the law, they tend to act as if they are the law. The nature of the offense dominates their considerations. Some individual characteristics, such as the defendant's prior record, are considered, but only as a general standard, and they make few qualifications in their general standards. Thus, since they feel that defendants with a prior record deserve more severe treatment, their sentences for these defendants are much more severe than those for defendants with no prior record. Whether the offense is against person is another general standard that is followed with few qualifications and thus, as noted, sentences for offenses such as armed robbery are very severe. Personal characteristics tend to be considered only in unusual situations, and thus allowances or exceptions are infrequent. These judges also base their decisions on the standards of conduct prescribed by the law and tend to be highly critical of the standards of conduct of many defendants.[24]

The Judges' Socialization and Recruitment Patterns

The Pittsburgh judges' socialization and recruitment patterns seem to influence their decision-making processes. The pre-judicial careers of most of the Pittsburgh judges in political parties and government and their minority ethnic[25] and lower-income backgrounds seem to have contributed to the development of the characteristic which many successful, local professional politicians possess—the ability to empathize and to grasp the motives of others by entering imaginatively into their feelings.

This pre-judicial experience (reinforced by the lack of highly legalistic experiences) seems to have contributed to the nonlegalistic, particularistic character of their decision making, their focus on policy considerations, and their use of pragmatic criteria. In this experience in party- and policy-oriented government positions, general rules were usually subordinated to achieve more immediate ends (e.g., those of a constituent). In the milieu of the party organization, personal relationships were emphasized (especially with their constituents), and they seem to have focused on particular and tangible entities. Their successes in this milieu depended largely on their ability to operate within personal relationships. It depended on whom they knew rather than what they knew. Abstractions such as "the good of society as a whole" seem to have been of little concern to them.

Thus their client relationships were usually characterized by expedient, exceptional, benevolent, and affirmative decisions which were the antithesis of legalistic behavior. Their decisions focused on interpersonal relationships and involved a great deal of discretion with little attention given to general rules. Indeed, a primary task of a local party worker is to view a situation in personal terms, to dispense favors, and to make exceptions rather than apply legal rules. In short, it is usually his job to say "yes," particularly to an individual who has a problem or who is in trouble.[26] The Pittsburgh judges seem to have brought many of these patterns to the bench with them.

The legalistic pre-judicial careers of most of the Minneapolis judges and their middle-class Northern-European-Protestant backgrounds[27] seem to have contributed to the development of their greater orientation toward "society" than toward the defendant. In their careers few had contact with individuals from lower-income backgrounds. Their experience in private practice (usually business-oriented and often corporate practices) typically involved major societal institutions such as the law, corporations, and commercial transactions. Several of the judges, for example, mention their pre-judicial experiences as a source of their feeling that forgery of checks can disrupt the heart of business operations. As private attorneys they largely based their standards on those of the profession, and on the bench they often turn to "enlightened" professional doctrine as a source of their norms.

This pre-judicial experience (reinforced by their lack of party and policy experiences) seems to have contributed to the legalistic and universalistic character of their decision making and their eschewal of policy considerations. Rules were generally emphasized, especially legalistic ones. Learning to "get around" in these organizations involved skill in operating in a context of rules. Their success depended more on their objective achievements and skills than on personal relationships. Also, rules were used to maintain and protect these organizations. The Minneapolis judges seem to have brought many of these patterns to the bench with them.

Both the judges' social backgrounds and their pre-judicial career experiences seem to have influenced their decision making, but in both Minneapolis and Pittsburgh the latter seems to have been the more important influence. In both cities, when the judges' pre-judicial career experiences and their social backgrounds influence their decision making

in similar ways, they tend to reinforce each other. However, when they tend to influence their decision making in opposite ways, the impact of their career experiences seem to be predominant. The decision making of the few Pittsburgh judges with middle-class Protestant backgrounds who also had careers in party and government positions tends to be oriented toward the defendant—particularistic, pragmatic, and based on policy considerations. Unfortunately, all of the Pittsburgh judges with minority ethnic and lower-income backgrounds also had party and government careers, and thus this conclusion cannot be tested with both variables independently controlled, but it can be in Minneapolis. The decision making of the few Minneapolis judges with minority ethnic or lower-income backgrounds who also had predominantly legalistic careers tends to be oriented toward society, legalistic and universalistic. The decision making of the few Minneapolis judges with middle-class Northern-European-Protestant backgrounds who also had less legalistic careers tends to be less oriented toward society and less legalistic and universalistic than that of most of the other Minneapolis judges.

The covariation of the dominant socialization and recruitment patterns of the judges in each city and their decision-making processes suggests a causal linkage, but it does not demonstrate it. Nevertheless, there seems to be sufficient evidence to suggest this linkage as the best available explanation. Specifically, in each city the judges with socialization and recruitment patterns which differ from the dominant pattern tend to follow decision-making processes which significantly differ from those of most of the city's judges. In Pittsburgh the few judges with little party or policy experience tend to be less oriented toward the defendant, less particularistic, less pragmatic, and less policy-oriented than most of the other Pittsburgh judges. In Minneapolis the few judges with less legal experience and more political experience than most of their colleagues tend to be less oriented toward society and their professional peers, less legalistic, and less universalistic than most of the other Minneapolis judges.

The Explanatory Framework and Some Alternatives

Through their effect on judicial selection, the political systems of these cities seem to indirectly determine judicial behavior. This relationship is similar to the way a city's political system effects such services as police, education, welfare, and urban renewal. There usually is little day-to-day political direction of these services. However, many of the policies of those administering these services sometimes reflect the values of the political system. Often this seems to be a result of the selection by the political system of the top administrator of these services. For example, the mayor or city council's criteria and goals in selecting a police chief (e.g., the "most professional" man, an "outsider," an "insider" who gets along with the men in the department, or a man "close to the party") are likely to affect the subsequent policies that the chief pursues.[28] This also seems to be true of the school board or the mayor's choice of a school superintendent.

Recently, scholars have given a good deal of attention to the role of political factors in judicial decision making. However, political influence does not seem to shape the behavior of the Pittsburgh and Minneapolis judges in criminal court. Almost all common felony defendants have no influence because they are literally on the bottom rung of society: typically, they are young lower-income males, often from a minority group. In other cases in which defendants do have political influence these judges' decisions may be shaped by it (though it seems less likely to occur in Minneapolis). For example, organized labor is quite influential in Pittsburgh, and almost all of the Pittsburgh judges are wary of taking the "wrong" position in a case involving a union. This is indicated by their reluctance to preside over these cases (especially strike injunction requests). Usually, a judge who has several years before reelection will finally accept the case.

The Pittsburgh judges, in part, may be lenient because of their predominant minority ethnic backgrounds and the Minneapolis judges, in part, may be severe because of their Northern-European-Protestant backgrounds, but the relationship does not seem to be so direct. As noted, the judges' prejudicial career experiences seem to be a more dominant factor. Moreover, the crucial intervening variable seems to be the city's political system and its influence on judicial selection, recruitment, and socialization. Judges with these social and career backgrounds are recruited by the city's political and judicial selection systems.

Evaluation and Some Policy Implications

This analysis of the Pittsburgh and Minneapolis judges' decision making in criminal court indicates some of the consequences of these cities' political systems and methods of judicial selection. However, to more fully understand these consequences, some evaluation of these judges' decisions in themselves is necessary. Logically, such evaluation ought to be reduced to an analysis of the empirical effects of each court system: to what degree and in what manner does each pattern of decisions (more lenient in Pittsburgh and more severe in Minneapolis) affect the defendants and crime in the community, all other factor's being equal? Which type of sentencing has the greatest tendency to rehabilitate the defendant? Which further exacerbates his sense of injustice? Which further weakens the moral bind of the law on the defendant? Which type of sentencing and court procedures are most likely to deter future crime and future criminals?

Answers to these questions would greatly aid in evaluating these decisions. In fact, however, this type of analysis is presently not possible, and the reasons indicate some general problems in policy analysis. We have some knowledge about rates of crime, rehabilitation, and recidivism, and attitudes of defendants; and we have some fragmentary knowledge about their general causes. Nevertheless, it does not seem likely that we will be able to ascertain the precise effect of these court decisions on defendants and on crime in the community in general. First, these court decisions are at most only one of many causal factors of crime rates and of defendants' attitudes.[29] Second, we have almost no idea of the precise degree that each of these causal factors affects these rates and these attitudes. We are particularly weak in our knowledge of the precise degree to which criminal court decisions affect them.

More important, in the nature of the situation we are not likely to gain this knowledge in the near future. The range of causal factors is so broad and so complex. Many of them are so interrelated that it would be difficult to measure the precise contribution of each of these causal factors. Advances in methodology, such as regression analysis, are not likely to change this.[30]

It appears that we must be content with evaluating the Pittsburgh and Minneapolis criminal court judges directly in terms of their behavior—lenient decisions and informal procedures in Pittsburgh and more severe decisions and formal procedures in Minneapolis. It is possible to make a persuasive case for the Minneapolis criminal court in terms of the goals of equality and the "rule of law," all other things being equal. In actual policy situations, however, "all other things" are rarely equal. Realistic policy choices are never made in an ideal context, but in a real, and therefore imperfect, context. Most big-city criminal courts, including those in this study, operate in a context of a heterogeneous population, including a large proportion of lower-class and minority-group individuals. In this context, it is possible to make a persuasive case for the Pittsburgh criminal court whose judges often tend to base their decisions on the standards of conduct of the group in which the offense occurred. Indeed, the assumptions of the rule of law (that all men are equal or similar) seldom square with the realities of our urban context. Nevertheless, despite the benevolence of intention, criminal court decisions based on these extralegal standards may tend to have serious unintended consequences. This has been suggested by John Dollard with respect to criminal justice in the South. In explaining the high level of aggression

among poor Negroes in a small southern town in the 1930s, Dollard concludes that among the institutional features of southern life that sustain this aggression is the double standard of justice—viewing "Negro crime" as less serious than "white crime."[31]

This tension between the style of criminal court which may be preferable in an ideal context (relatively homogeneous cities) and the style which may be necessary because of the actual context (heterogeneous cities with large lower-class populations) and the difficulties inherent in the latter style seem to be the product of a more general tension in the larger cities of our society and in our theory of democracy. According to the rule of law and democratic theory, we ought to ignore class differences, but urban realities are such that it is difficult. For example, in their discussion of social class and mental illness, Hollingshead and Redlich state that if an upper-class husband beats his wife "this needs to be evaluated quite differently from similar occurrences in class V (the lower class)."[32] Since physical violence is a part of the lower-class culture, they feel there is no presumption that the lower-class wife-beater is mentally ill. The implication of this view is that public decision makers ought to recognize that acts which are behaviorally "the same" may be very different because they stem from different standards or cultures, and thus they may require different official responses to them.[33] However, this seems offensive to our theory of democracy, which assumes that we will be a society with one culture, not two. It assumes that we will be able and willing to live together under a single set of rules or standards. The idea that two sets of rules may be necessary—one for the middle class and the other for the lower class—cannot be reconciled to our theory.

This tension points to the central factor to be considered in any evaluation or policy prescription concerning the criminal courts in our large cities: the existence of "two cultures" in these cities—a large lower-class as well as the dominant middle-class culture. Although the Pittsburgh judges often tend to base their decisions, in part, on the existence of these two cultures, they usually fail to adhere to the "rule of law." On the other hand, the Minneapolis judges tend to adhere to the rule of law, but they fail to consider these two cultures. If these are shortcomings in both courts, it is important to recognize that they are largely a function of these two cultures—a factor external to these court systems. Thus any prescription for remedying these inadequacies should be directed primarily at this external factor and more basic cause. As long as these two cultures exist, there will be a tension in our theory of democracy, and the criminal courts will have to either ignore the rule of law or the realities of urban life.

Notes

1. The research on which this paper is based was conducted while the author was a V. O. Key, Jr. Fellow at the Joint Center for Urban Studies of M.I.T. and Harvard and was also supported by a Research Training Fellowship of the Social Science Research Council. I am indebted to James Q. Wilson, Martin Shapiro, and Frank Levy for their contributions to an earlier version of this paper.

2. The leading works which focus on the political function of city government are R. Dahl, *Who Governs?* (New Haven: Yale University Press, 1961); E. Banfield and J. Wilson, *City Politics* (Cambridge: Harvard University Press, 1963); and W. Sayre and H. Kaufman, *Governing New York City* (New York: Russell Sage Foundation, 1960).

3. These two descriptions are intended to indicate two "models" of urban political systems. For a discussion of these two models and other urban political systems see Banfield and Wilson, *City Politics*, especially chaps. 3, 8, 9, 11–13.

4. James Q. Wilson, "Problems in the Study of Urban Politics," in E. H. Buehrig (ed.), *Essays in Political Science* (Bloomington: Indiana University Press, 1964), p. 133.

5. Of course, the initial argument for the utility of an input-output model of politics was made by David Easton, "An Approach to the Analysis of Political Systems," *World Politics*, 9, (April 1957), 491–509; and *The Political System* (New York: Alfred A. Knopf, 1953).

6. Wilson, "Problems in the Study of Urban Politics," pp. 144–45.

7. Recently, there have been several significant empirical studies based on this mode of analysis. Most of these studies are included (or referred to) in J. Wilson (ed.), *City Politics and Public Policy* (New York: John Wiley, 1968).

8. For example, see A. Vanderbilt, *The Challenge of Law Reform* (Princeton, N.J.: Princeton University Press, 1955), p. 29.

9. For a typical statement of this view, see *Society and the Law* by F. James Davis, Henry Foster, C. Ray Jeffery, and E. Eugene Davis (New York: The Free Press, 1962), p. 205.

10. This is even true of the President's Commission on Law Enforcement and the Administration of Justice, which is empirically oriented in most of its reports. As if Holmes had never argued that "the life of law is not logic but experience," the commission report on courts merely asserts without supporting evidence that "merit selection plans provide a *more rational procedure* for selecting judges than popular election alone." President's Commission on Law Enforcement and the Administration of Justice, *The Challenge of Crime in a Free Society* (Washington, D.C.: Government Printing Office, 1967), chap. 5 (emphasis added).

11. Evidence supporting Costikyan's conclusions comes from a recent systematic survey of the attitudes of Missouri lawyers concerning the plan. (R. Watson, "Missouri Lawyers Evaluate the Merit Plan for Selection and Tenure of Judges," *American Bar Association Journal* [June 1966], p. 55.) See also Joel Grossman's findings on the political and conservative nature of the ABA's influence on the selection of federal judges. J. B. Grossman, *Lawyers and Judges* (New York: John Wiley, 1965), especially pp. 88–92, 196–98, and 208–15.

12. A second set of cities—one city with a "traditional" political system and reform judicial selection and another with a "good government" political system and a political judicial selection —would be required to more fully test the relationship between political systems and judicial decisions. This was beyond the limits of the resources of this study. Moreover, there seem to be few, if any, such cities. As this study indicates, a city's judicial selection system usually tends to reflect its political system.

13. For a detailed discussion of the political and judicial selection systems of both cities and of several other aspects of this paper, see Martin A. Levin, "Urban Political Systems and Judicial Behavior: The Criminal Courts of Pittsburgh and Minneapolis" (unpublished Ph.D. dissertation, Department of Government, Harvard University, 1969).

14. The nine offenses are burglary, grand larceny, aggravated robbery, simple robbery, aggravated assault, indecent assault, aggravated forgery, nonsufficient funds, and possession of narcotics. A random sample of all cases of these offenses for a particular set of years is compared (1958 to 1965 for Minneapolis and 1960 to 1965 for Pittsburgh).

15. This analysis is based on a comparison for both the frequency with which probation is

granted for an offense and the length of the term of incarceration (if the defendant does not receive probation) in the sentencing decisions of the Pittsburgh and Minneapolis judges.

16. A category is a subset of all the defendants for a particular offense. The subset is comprised of those defendants with a particular characteristic for which controls are introduced—race, prior record, type of plea, and age. Thus typical categories for a particular offense are "white, no prior record"; "Negro, no prior record, plea of not guilty"; "Negro, prior record, plea of not guilty, 17 to 21 years old." Of course, for most offenses there is not a sufficient number of cases in every category to make comparisons between cities or races.

17. For probation a "high percentage" is operationally defined as a frequency of 50.0 percent or greater. For incarceration a "short length" is operationally defined as a term of incarceration of 11.0 months or less.

18. These models are "ideal types" designed to abstract from reality the essence of a pattern of behavior. They are derived from many sources, especially C. G. Haines' discussion of "the mechanical theory" of judicial decision making and the "free legal decision," in "General Observations on the Effects of Judges," in G. Schubert (ed.), *Judicial Behavior* (Chicago: Rand McNally, 1964), pp. 40–49; Carl A. Auerbach et al., *The Legal Process* (San Francisco: Chandler, 1961), pp. 374, 591, 729–30, 734, 737, 749; K. C. Davis, *Administrative Law Treatise* (St. Paul: West, 1958), Vol. I: pp. 1, 7–8, 38–39, 40–42, 57, 94–99, Vol. II: pp. 173–74; Benjamin Cardoza, *The Nature of the Judicial Process* (New Haven: Yale University Press, 1921); Max Rheinstein's introduction to *Max Weber on Law in Economy and Society* (Cambridge: Harvard University Press, 1954); and Joel Grossman, *Lawyers and Judges* (New York: John Wiley, 1964), p. 19. I am indebted to Martin Shapiro for initially suggesting this comparison and for aid in its substantive development.

19. The administrative model of decision making fails to fully capture one major element of the Pittsburgh judges' behavior—their special emphasis on informalism and on personal and individualistic considerations. The model of Khadi justice described by Max Weber seems to capture this and other elements of their behavior: Weber describes Khadi justice as "popular justice" based on "free discretion" and appealing to "the sentiments of laymen" (especially the "underprivileged classes") because of its focus on the "concrete, ethical, or political considerations of substantial justice [rather than] formalism." Khadi justice involved eschewing written law and deciding on the basis of "practical value judgments." The source of modern Khadi justice is "the democratic ethos" and it springs from "irrational 'feelings' . . . normally insti-

gated or guided by party leaders or the press." (In Rheinstein, *Max Weber*, pp. 228–29, 318, 351–52, 354–56.)

20. According to legal doctrine, both criminal and tort law are directed to providing remedies for wrongs committed, but criminal law is directed to remedying wrongs committed against the public at large. Tort law is directed to remedying wrongs committed against an individual. For a discussion of this distinction, see David Matza, *Delinquency and Drift* (New York: John Wiley, 1963), pp. 169–72.

21. In sociological theory, an individual whose decision making is particularistic is oriented toward objects in light of their particular relationships—their relationship to him, his collectivity, or to other particular objects rather than their relationship to general standards. He does not act in conformity with general standards concerning differential treatment. His behavior is premised on considerations of person. T. Parsons and E. A. Shils, *Toward a General Theory of Action* (New York: Harper & Row, 1951), pp. 81–82.

22. An indication of how frequently the Pittsburgh judges fail to base their decisions on these general criteria is that their sentencing decisions for defendants with a prior record are only slightly less lenient than those for defendants without a prior record. By contrast, the Minneapolis judges usually base their decisions on these general criteria, and thus defendants with a prior record receive much more severe sentences than those without one.

23. In crimes against person, the nature of the offense tends to become the dominant criterion for the decisions of fourteen of the eighteen judges and thus tends to operate as a general standard. However, these judges significantly qualify the generality of this standard by making several distinctions—most of which are diffuse—among various types of crimes against person (e.g., the degree of viciousness involved in the violence, the degree of aggressiveness, the degree of passion, whether a weapon was involved, the degree of provocation involved, or whether the act caused an injury). A comparison of the Pittsburgh and Minneapolis judges' sentencing decisions for armed robbery indicates that the Pittsburgh judges frequently qualify this general standard and the Minneapolis judges almost always adhere to it.

24. Many of the Minneapolis judges seem to be aware of nonlegalistic factors that they might consider, but they do not seem to feel that they are proper or relevant. For example, they feel that the stability of lower-income families is the proper concern of public agencies other than the criminal court.

25. Four of the Pittsburgh judges are Jewish (two of whom were foreign born), seven are Catholic (one of whom is foreign born, three

have Irish backgrounds, two Italian, one Polish, one Hungarian), one is Negro, and six are white Protestants.

26. As Robert Merton has pointed out, "The political machine is a much more human system of partisan government, whose chief object soon became the circumvention of government by law. . . . The Machine, through its local agents, fulfills the important social function of humanizing and personalizing all manner of assistance." "The Latent Functions of the Machine," in *Social Theory and Social Structure*, rev. ed. (New York: The Free Press, 1957), pp. 73–75.

27. Fourteen of the Minneapolis judges are Protestants (several Lutherans and also Congregationalists, Episcopalians, Methodists, and Christian Scientists) and eight of them have Scandinavian backgrounds; two of the judges are Catholic and one is Jewish.

28. See James Q. Wilson's discussion of the relationship between a city's political system and police behavior, *Varieties of Police Behavior* (Cambridge: Harvard University Press, 1969), chap. 8, especially pp. 232–36.

29. Among the more salient of these many factors seem to be (1) the age distribution of the population (e.g., 72 percent of all those arrested for Part 1 crimes in the United States in 1965 were between the ages of 13 and 29); (2) the ease with which goods can be stolen (their easy availability as in self-service stores, and the degree of preventive measures such as the frequency of locking cars); (3) the degree of insurance coverage and the company's willingness to pay theft claims; (4) the degree of public support (to the extent of approving public expenditures) for government programs to curb crime; (5) the style, behavior, and level of effort of law enforcement agencies (police and prosecutors) and the courts; and (6) the social (the degree of education, family stability, class culture) and economic (the degree of unemployment, the general level of prosperity, the distribution of wealth) environment of the community. (For a thorough discussion of these factors and their relationships, see J. Q. Wilson, "Crime in the Streets." *The Public Interest* (Fall 1966), 26–35. Moreover, there may be several other major causal factors of which we presently have only limited awareness.

30. Regression analysis is designed to predict effects in a multivariate situation, but it is only effective in assessing the precise contribution of several variables if the data are "internally controlled" (i.e., if there is a good deal of independent variation among the explanatory variables). It is much less effective in doing this when the explanatory variables are highly correlated—i.e., multicollinearity. (For a technical discussion of multicollinearity, see J. Johnston, *Econometric Methods* [New York: McGraw-Hill, 1963], pp. 201–207.) However, this is precisely the nature of the data involved in recidivism rates and defendants' attitudes. For example, a city might have a large Negro population, a stagnant economy with few opportunities for unskilled labor, lenient judges, and a poor job counseling program in its probation department. All of these factors may effect the city's rate of recidivism, but all of them also seem to be highly interrelated. Moreover, this is frequently the nature of the data of real world policy analysis—especially in the evaluation of policy programs, which are often only one of the several factors affecting some output and often these factors are highly correlated.

31. "The formal machinery of the law takes care of the Negroes' grievances much less adequately than that of the whites, and to a much higher degree the Negro is compelled to make and enforce his own law, with other Negroes. . . . The result is that the individual Negro is, to a considerable degree, outside the protection of the white law, and must shift for himself. This leads to the frontier psychology. . . . [This] condoning of Negro violence . . . may be indulgent in the case of any given Negro, but its effect on the Negro group as a whole is dangerous and destructive. . . . So long as the law does not take over the protection of the Negro person he will have to do it himself by violent means." John Dollard, *Caste and Class in a Southern Town* (Garden City, N.Y.: Doubleday Anchor Books, 1957), pp. 274–79, 280, 281, as quoted in J. Q. Wilson, *Varieties of Police Behavior*, pp. 297–98.

32. A. B. Hollingshead and F. Redlich, *Social Class and Mental Illness* (New York: John Wiley, 1956), p. 127.

33. W. F. Whyte noted this problem in relation to the police. "There are prevalent in society two general conceptions of the duties of a police officer. Middle-class people feel that he should enforce the law without fear or favor. . . . On the other side are the people of Cornerville, who have different standards and have built up an organization whose perpetuation depends on the freedom to violate the law." *Street Corner Society*, 2nd ed. (Chicago: University of Chicago Press, 1955), pp. 136, 138.

V

Urban Policy Outputs

OUTPUTS ARE those binding decisions and policies made by the political authorities in response to various demands, supports, and apathy generated within the political system. They may take the form of broad policy directives, specific legislative acts, court decisions, or administrative rules or decisions made by bureaucrats. Urban policies provide a host of basic public services (e.g., education, welfare, public safety); regulate personal and group behavior (e.g., policing and inspection activities); and control the actions of public officials (e.g., regulating elections, barring discrimination). At a more abstract level of analysis, policy outputs, in the form of rewards and deprivations, provide basic incentives for members to support the political system. They provide the system with its primary means for responding to change by regulating and transforming its behavior. Outputs may also have consequences beyond the political system. In this sense they serve as transactions between the political system and its environment, as when political decisions affect the operation of the economy or regulate social behavior. In other instances, however, the impact of outputs may be felt only within the political system itself, an example of which would be a local ordinance establishing a personnel classification and pay plan for city employees.

Traditional Urban Policy Approaches

An interest in public policy is nothing new in political science. In the field of local government, traditional textbooks invariably devoted considerable attention to the various public services and activities of the municipality since, above all, the city was seen as a service-rendering agency. Therefore, a natural concern was shown for what benefits the municipal government confers and how it goes about administering them.

The examination of local services from this perspective was largely a descriptive undertaking, beginning perhaps with a history of the service area, the administrative activities surrounding it, the problems encountered in providing the service (usually lack of money or lack of jurisdiction), and frequently concluding with recommendations designed to improve the activity. Such areas as public works, public utilities, health, welfare, police, fire protection, and more recently housing, planning, and urban development are often treated in this fashion. In addition to these textbook discussions of urban services, a large body of case study literature has developed over the years. Although it has been concerned principally with decision-making processes, it has frequently explored various dimensions of specific policy areas. The focus in these studies is normally upon the process which affects a policy decision, such as what groups get involved, how they make their wishes known, the coalitions which form, the relationships among various political actors, the timing of decisions, and the formality of the decision process. Despite certain limitations, a number of important contributions to the understanding of the urban political process have come from case studies such as those of Detroit by Mowitz and Wright, of New York by Sayre and Kaufman, plus Banfield's several studies of Chicago, and Martin and others' study of Syracuse.[1] Although interesting and rich with detail, the in-depth study of a particular city along with entirely descriptive accounts of urban services administration are seriously deficient as a way of analyzing public policies. Ordinarily, for instance, case studies are theoretically barren, do not lend themselves to easy comparison, provide few broad generalizations, and are difficult, if not impossible, to replicate.[2] Strictly descriptive accounts suffer these same shortcomings and contribute almost nothing to the systematic accumulation of information so essential for the building of a scientific discipline.

Empirical Studies of Public Policy

Recent years have brought a renewed interest in public policy analysis on the part of empirically oriented political scientists. Influenced by the theoretical framework of systems analysis and using sophisticated statistical tools and a comparative approach, these scholars have been concerned principally with explaining the various influences on public policy at both the state and local level. As indicated in the introductory essay to this volume, a small group of scholars[3] have been responsible for leading the way in the investigation of the relationship between public policies and a variety of social, economic, and political factors. The model used in research of this type considers public policy as the dependent variable influenced by environmental forces. Or, in the words of Dye, policy outputs are the "result of *forces* brought to bear upon a *system* and causing it to make particular *responses*."[4] The approach ordinarily involves a multiple variable (multivariate) analysis where policies (often measured by expenditure data) are the dependent variables, socioeconomic characteristics are independent influences, and political structures and processes are intervening variables. The dependence of this kind of model for the analysis of public policy on a systems framework can be readily seen in Figure 1.

(Independent variables)　　　(Intervening variables)　　　(Dependent variable)

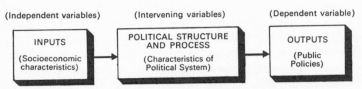

Figure 1.　A Partial Model for Policy Analysis

OPERATIONALIZING THE INPUT-OUTPUT MODEL

The model is operationalized by the use of selected variables (often from the census and other readily available sources) which are subjected to correlation-regression analysis producing simple, partial, and multiple correlation coefficients. A simple coefficient (r) reveals only the extent of correlation between two variables without taking into account possible outside influences. For example, in their pioneering study of the factors affecting welfare policies among the American states, Dawson and Robinson found that economic variables (especially the wealth of the state) and political variables (party competition) were both positively related to higher welfare benefits. Thus it was necessary to determine whether both relationships were valid or whether one variable might be "causing" the differences in the other two—to separate the real from the spurious relationship. In fact, the association between party competition and welfare policies turned out to be largely the product of the state's wealth. In other words, there was no real causal relationship between increased welfare benefits and greater party competion; they appeared related only because *both* were the result of wealth. In this case, then, party competition was not truly an intervening variable; the only valid relationship was between economic resources (i.e., wealth) and welfare policies.

The statistical technique employed to help discriminate between real and spurious associations is the *partial correlation coefficient*. These are interpreted in the same way as simple coefficients so that coefficients near zero indicate no independent relationship when the effects of other independent (or intervening) variables are "held out" or held constant. Thus when the contribution of other variables is controlled, the remaining partial coefficient indicates the unique relationship between that particular independent variable and the dependent variable. As an example, a simple coefficient of .60 between two variables (e.g., race and poverty) might drop to a partial coefficient of .08 when the effect of income on poverty is controlled.

Finally, the *multiple correlation coefficient* (R) expresses the extent to which *all* independent variables are associated with the dependent variable (policy outputs in these examples). The strength of the multiple coefficient (again, interpreted as the other coefficients) provides an indication of how good the model (at least, the variables being used in the model) is in explaining differences among governmental units with respect to various policy outputs. Frequently, the coefficient of determination, which is the multiple coefficient squared (R^2), is used to show what percentage of the variation in the dependent variable is explained by the operation of all the independent variables. For example, a multiple correlation coefficient of .50 means that only 25 percent of the variance in a particular dependent variable is attributable to fluctuations in the independent variables.

Following the lead of Dawson and Robinson, other scholars in the field of state politics began to employ the policy analysis model described above. Dye's research on the effects of a state's economic development and its political system on a series of policy areas marked a significant step forward in the application of an input-output policy analysis model. To represent the impact of a state's economic development, Dye chose four basic variables—urbanization, industrialization, wealth, and education. The influence of the state's political system was measured by level of interparty competition, division of two-party control (extent to which Democrats or Republicans control state government), level of voter participation, and degree of legislative malapportionment. The policy areas examined included the combined state and local spending for education, welfare and highways, tax and revenue policy, and public regulation policy. His book-length findings, presented in 1966, substantially confirmed the earlier, more limited analysis of welfare benefits by Dawson and Robinson. Dye concluded that not only was his model a very powerful tool for policy analysis, but that state political system characteristics "have relatively little independent effect on policy outcomes in the states." Levels of economic development were revealed to be considerably more influential in shaping public policy than political system characteristics.[5] A recent study of urban policy outputs using this basic approach reached the same conclusion—that political structure variables (form of government, type of ballot, council election, and administrative centralization) had "no impact" on urban policy as manifested primarily by various per capita city expenditure levels.[6] Conclusions such as these which have far-reaching consequences for political science have not gone unchallenged, as seen in the article by Lineberry and Fowler contained in this section. Recent research in state politics also suggests that while system resources may largely account for the amount of money spent, the "black box" or political structure may affect the *kinds* of policies adopted and, indeed, the level of expenditures for some.[7] Sharkansky has also discovered that local government spending is highly dependent on the level of economic resources, while spending by state governments is relatively independent of economic constraints.[8] Thus he has argued that state and local expenditures should be separated for purposes of analysis and not lumped together, as was done in Dye's 1966 work.

The discussion above rather clearly reveals that most policy research employing an input-output model has relied almost exclusively on expenditure variables as indicators of policy outputs. They are relatively easy to obtain, especially for the fifty states, and the argument has been advanced that levels of spending and their distribution among alternative functions of government reflect major commitments to specific goals and objectives —in short, basic policy choices.[9] Although there is increasing awareness that greater efforts must be made to analyze policy areas which are not best represented by governmental expenditures (e.g., law enforcement effectiveness, civil rights), a number of important findings have resulted from a focus on local fiscal behavior. The following is a listing of some of the more important propositions affecting urban politics which have come from this kind of research.[10] Note that some of the studies have incorporated a large number (N) of cities while others have a more limited comparative base.

1. Variations in local fiscal behavior (taxes and expenditures) for central cities ($N = 36$ metropolitan areas) can largely be accounted for by a limited number of socioeconomic and political system variables (Campbell and Sacks).

2. Central city per capita expenditures ($N = 198$) become higher as population size increases (Bahl).

3. Per capita taxes are greater in central cities ($N = 36$) than in suburbs (Campbell and Sacks).

4. Central cities ($N = 36$) spend relatively more than do suburban governments on noneducation public functions, whereas the latter spend a proportionately greater amount for education (Campbell and Sacks).

5. Findings on effects of population density on total per capita municipal expenditures have been mixed; however, density appears to be positively related to per capita police ($N = 670$) and fire expenditures ($N = 662$) (Rogers).

6. The more urban a community (less oriented toward family life style), the greater its per capita expenditures ($N = 670$) (Rogers).

7. Percent Catholic is positively related to total per capita municipal expenditures ($N = 51$) (Clark).

8. Decentralized decision making is positively associated with both total per capita spending and urban renewal expenditures ($N = 51$) (Clark).

9. Planning expenditures ($N = 190$) are largely unrelated to community socioeconomic variables (Lineberry), although greater expenditures ($N = 473$) appear positively correlated with population mobility and the presence of nonpartisan elections (Rogers).

10. Municipal expenditures in a group of suburbs ($N = 90$) are more closely related to community needs (reflected by percent of property in industrial and commercial use—requiring more services) than to community wealth (Williams et al.).

The above research largely reflects the influence of community social and economic forces on outputs, although occasionally the effects of certain political characteristics are noted. Expenditure studies of this type have at least two major limitations: (1) the lack of any measure of program or service quality; and (2) the lack of information concerning the effect or impact of spending on citizens of the community. The evaluation of public policy has become an almost separate part of the discipline of political science (usually found in the area of public administration) and only recently has serious attention been turned toward devices which might aid in judging the effectiveness of the policy process. One of the principal tools for this purpose is planning-programming-budgeting (PPB) about which there is a growing body of literature.[11] PPB has been most widely applied at the federal government level, especially in the area of national defense, although it is rapidly winning adherents at lower levels of government. PPB is basically a system of analysis designed to help management make better choices in allocating resources among alternative courses of action in attaining policy goals. It requires objectives to be specified, the measurement of a program output, and determination of program costs. PPB proceeds on assumptions ordinarily accepted by economists: that resources are scarce hence choices and cost are everywhere involved, that input-output and cost-benefit calculations can be determined for public activities; and that if alternative choices are carefully costed, one may show a relative advantage over others.[12] This new budgetary approach with its emphasis on program policy decisions is closely related to an earlier process for analyzing public policy outputs called *cost-benefit analysis*. In essence, the cost-benefit approach involves comparing the total annual cost of a particular government project to the gross annual benefits (ordinarily expressed in some quantifiable form, i.e., number of persons assisted, number of moving vehicle violations, etc.) which can then be expressed as a cost-benefit ratio. Probably the best results from cost-benefit analysis as applied to an area of government have come in the field of water resource development,[13] although applications have been proposed for such diverse areas as urban renewal and urban refuse collection.[14] Although the debate continues over the effectiveness of these techniques for evaluating policy outputs, their increased use at higher levels of government will virtually assure greater applications at the urban level as well.

Only a limited number of studies have attempted to assess the impact of social, economic, and governmental influences on more substantive (nonexpenditure) urban policy areas. A few generalizations have been forthcoming, however, as indicated by the following representative propositions derived from empirical research on certain substantive policy outputs.[15]

1. Fluoridation of water is more likely to be adopted ($N = 189$) when the local decision-making authority is centralized in a relatively strong executive such as a city manager or partisan mayor (Rosenthal and Crain).

2. Cities with a high proportion of managers, proprietors, and officials

in their labor force will have greater difficulties in instituting urban renewal ($N = 194$) because of the presumably more decentralized decision-
making processes (Hawley).

3. The level of commitment to local public health (measured by number
of local employees; $N = 331$ counties) can largely be explained by a
limited number of demographic variables which can be considered as
measures of urbanism (Palumbo and Williams).

4. The higher the social status of a particular group of suburbs ($N = 81$),
the greater the proportion of land zoned residential, and conversely the
lower the percentage of land zoned for industrial and commercial use
(Williams *et al.*).

Distinctions among Terms

The increased emphasis on the study of public policy has also resulted in
efforts to achieve certain conceptual distinctions among the terms used in
policy analysis. We mentioned previously Easton's basic distinction between policy outputs and outcomes, the former referring primarily to the
actions and decisions of political authorities and the latter referring to the
longer range, secondary consequences of those acts. In the policy analysis
literature, there is a tendency to use the terms policy output and outcome
almost interchangeably, although Sharkansky has differentiated between
public policy, policy outputs, and *policy impacts*.[16] The first (policy) refers
to actions taken by government while the second term (outputs) represents
service levels affected by those actions and policy impacts refers to the
effect the service has on a population. Sharkansky has operationalized
these terms by using government expenditures, size and nature of government staff, and physical facilities provided the staff as principal manifestations of public policy. Outputs are measured by the amount of benefits and
services provided per capita or per client; the units of service in relation to
size of population; the incidence of beneficiaries among political clients;
the rate at which a service is performed; or the frequency with which
people choose to use benefits or services. Policy impact shows the effects
of a government service and might be measured in the field of public
safety by state residents per motor vehicle death (road safety) or in
education by dropout rates or percentage of selective service registrants
passing the mental examination (exam success). One of Sharkansky's more
provocative findings has been that government spending levels (outputs)
do not necessarily determine the nature or quality of services provided
(impact).[17]

Developing Policy Typologies

Other research in the area of public policy has been concerned with
developing various policy typologies as a way of moving toward higher
levels of generality. Previous reference was made to policy typologies

which offered essentially nominal categories such as those of Lowi (distributive, redistributive, and regulatory) or those categories for urban policy
suggested by Froman (segmental and areal). Certain limitations seem to
inhere in such efforts as these—in part, because of difficulties in operationalizing the concepts to permit systematic comparison. As a way out of
this dilemma, a few efforts have been made to employ techniques such as
factor analysis in order to achieve broad policy categories which share
common underlying traits or "factors." The most promising research
using factor analysis to develop underlying policy areas or categories has
occurred in the field of state politics. Sharkansky and Hofferbert used a
twenty-six-variable factor analytic scheme as a way of generating two
basic state policy dimensions—welfare/education and highways/natural
resources. The authors reported that one principal socioeconomic factor
(affluence of the state) and one political factor (party competition/turnout)
had strong positive relationships to the welfare/education policy factor
while the second principal policy factor (highways/natural resources) was
negatively associated with a state's level of industrialization. The study
concluded that there is no single answer to the question, "Is it politics or
economics that has the greatest impact on public policy?"[18] Another
effort to use factor analysis to discover the basic components of public
policy among states has been by Robert Crew. Three factors were derived
which explained 60 percent of the total variance among expenditures for
eleven areas of activity. Crew labeled the factor which accounted for the
most variance "rurality," since it encompassed several policy areas (e.g.,
highways and natural resources) associated with a rural environment. The
broad policy area underlying the second principal factor seemed to be a
collective-individual dimension (e.g., high positive loadings on health and
libraries, negative relationship with expenditures for welfare). The third
factor was made up of those variables which related to maintenance of
public order or control (police protection, education, and libraries).[19]

More has been done with factor analysis in state than in urban politics.
Yet an early study limited to one region was done by Robert Wood using
this technique in which he reduced twenty community characteristic
variables to seven factors in order to explain variations in local governmental expenditures for sixty-four municipalities in five New Jersey
counties.[20] Palumbo and Williams used factor analysis to explore the
correlates of commitment to local public health,[21] and Masotti and Bowen
also used this device to identify the community social characteristics
associated with certain local public policies.[22]

Even the use of the most advanced research techniques does not solve
all the problems associated with public policy analysis. What does one do,
for example, with policy areas which do not easily lend themselves to
quantification? The surface has barely been scratched on this question and
considerable research remains to be done on those aspects of policy
making which have not yet been treated with quantitative tools.[23] Another
point has been raised in regard to the prevailing model of policy analysis,
which calls into question the exclusive use of policy as a dependent

variable. Froman has argued that we might significantly enrich the understanding of policy processes by reversing the orthodox explanatory relationships and consider policy to be an *in*dependent variable which might help to explain something else.[24] This idea comes close to the concept of "feedback" or the problem of reciprocal causation which political scientists have thus far largely ignored, at least insofar as systematic research is concerned. Undoubtedly, there will be further new developments and directions in policy analysis as this area continues to be one of the most promising and fruitful for political research.

The Articles

The articles in this section are representative of the best recent research focusing on urban policy outputs. Certain aspects of public policy at the local level are not covered, partly because so much policy research has relied heavily on output dimensions measured in terms of dollars and cents. Those policies which do not easily lend themselves to quantification —such as urban renewal, public housing, antipoverty, planning, zoning, or even law enforcement—have been slighted. Thus these selections must be regarded primarily as illustrative rather than as a comprehensive treatment of the whole panorama of urban policy outputs.

Lineberry and Fowler in the first selection offer a sophisticated analysis of a proposition which has aroused considerable controversy among specialists in urban politics—whether reform municipalities (e.g., nonpartisan, council-manager, at-large elections) exhibit different public policies than unreformed cities (e.g., partisan, mayor-council, ward elections). Their approach is to determine the impact of both socioeconomic variables and political institutions (structural variables) on outputs of city government. The authors' hypothesis that political structure will exert an independent influence on policy is tested for 200 cities using two measures of policy outputs—municipal revenues and expenditures. The data indicate that reformed cities generally spend and tax less than unreformed cities even though cities in these categories are not markedly different in terms of demographic variables. The authors also report that they are able to predict municipal outputs more exactly in unreformed than in reformed cities, suggesting that, as hypothesized, local political institutions do seem to play an important role in the political process—a role substantially independent of a city's demography.

The study by Crain and Rosenthal is concerned with the effects of community socioeconomic status on the level of citizen participation and, subsequently, the impact of citizen involvement on the adoption of certain community public policies. They find that communities with high status tend to have higher levels of citizen participation; in turn, this leads to increased controversy, decentralized decision making, and a tendency toward immobility on the part of local government. Using data from national surveys on a variety of policy areas—such as urban renewal, school desegregation, fluoridation of water, and so on—the authors conclude that when people get highly involved, which is most likely to happen in higher status cities, the adoption of controversial community policies may be delayed or avoided completely.

This study employs the gamma coefficient (γ) to describe the relationship among certain variables. Gamma is a measure of the direction and degree of association (correlation) between variables measured on an ordinal scale—that is, ranked data. With values ranging from -1 to $+1$, it indicates whether the variables relate positively (as one increases, the other increases) or negatively (as one variable increases, the other decreases), plus the strength of that relationship. For example, a perfect 1.0 value would represent a positive one-to-one correspondence between the two variables being compared.

Dye's article on education outputs stands as an almost classic example of recent systematic comparative research on public policy using an input-output model. Using sixty-seven large cities, he assesses the impact of school system structure (e.g., method of selecting school board members, city government control over school budgets) and urban environmental variables (wealth, white-collar employment, etc.) on educational outcomes (e.g., school expenditures, teachers' salaries, teacher-pupil ratios). A multivariate analysis reveals that, in general, community socioeconomic characteristics are more closely associated with educational policies than are political structure variables. The author does acknowledge that neither environmental nor structural variables are able to explain all the policy differences among the cities studied. In fact, only half the variation in as few as two policies (per pupil expenditure and private school enrollment) can be explained by the operation of all the variables combined.

Clarke's study is also concerned with only one basic policy—municipal reform. He sets out to examine the community characteristics related to the consideration of and adoption of new forms of local government for forty-three third-class cities in Pennsylvania which became possible under a change in state law. The setting for this study approaches a quasi-experimental situation since each city was provided the option of changing its form of government at the same time. The author's findings are similar to those of Lineberry and Fowler—that community policy decisions are associated with both socioeconomic variables and political process variables. In this instance, the local political variables (e.g., party competition, interest group strength, voter turnout) were even more important to the ultimate policy outcome (adoption or nonadoption of reform charters) than were the usual community social indicators. Clarke suggests that socioeconomic and political process variables may vary in their comparative explanatory value with the type of policy being considered. In this case, a policy concerned with governmental form was more influenced by political variables; in Dye's study of educational policies, the level of economic support for the local schools was more closely associated with community resource variables.

Notes

1. Robert J. Mowitz and Deil S. Wright, *Profile of a Metropolis* (Detroit: Wayne State University Press, 1962); Wallace S. Sayre and Herbert Kaufman, *Governing New York City* (New York: Russell Sage, 1960); Edward C. Banfield, *Political Influence* (New York: The Free Press, 1961); and Roscoe C. Martin *et al.*, *Decisions in Syracuse* (Bloomington: Indiana University Press, 1961).

2. See Morris Davis and Marvin G. Weinbaum, *Metropolitan Decision Processes: An Analysis of Case Studies* (Chicago: Rand McNally, 1969), chap. 1, for a discussion of the advantages and limitations of the case method.

3. See Richard E. Dawson and James A. Robinson, "Inter-Party Competition, Economic Variables, and Welfare Policies in the American States," *Journal of Politics*, 25 (1963), 265–89; Thomas R. Dye, *Politics, Economics and the Public: Policy Outcomes in the American States* (Chicago: Rand McNally, 1966); Richard I. Hofferbert, "The Relation between Public Policy and Some Structural and Environmental Variables in the American States," *American Political Science Review*, 60 (1966), 73–82; and Ira Sharkansky, *Spending in the American States* (Chicago: Rand McNally, 1968).

4. Dye, *Politics, Economics and the Public*, p. 3. Chapters 1 and 2 contain the clearest available explanation of this particular policy model along with an excellent description of the required statistical techniques. Our discussion of these concepts closely follows his analysis.

5. *Ibid.*, chap. 11, quotation from p. 293.

6. Chester B. Rogers, "Environment, System and Output: The Consideration of a Model," *Social Forces*, 48 (1969), 72–87.

7. Allan G. Pulsipher and James L. Weatherby, Jr., "Malapportionment, Party Competition and the Functional Distribution of Governmental Expenditures," *American Political Science Review*, 62 (1968), 1207–19; Charles F. Cnudde and Donald J. McCrone, "Party Competition and Welfare Policies in the American States," *American Political Science Review*, 63 (1969), 858–66; and Ira Sharkansky and Richard I. Hofferbert, "Dimensions of State Politics, Economics, and Public Policy," *ibid.*, pp. 867–79.

8. Ira Sharkansky, *The Politics of Taxing and Spending* (Indianapolis: Bobbs-Merrill, 1969), chap. 4.

9. Oliver P. Williams *et al.*, *Suburban Differences and Metropolitan Policies* (Philadelphia: University of Pennsylvania Press, 1965), p. 75.

10. These studies are: Alan K. Campbell and Seymour Sacks, *Metropolitan America* (New York: The Free Press, 1967); Roy W. Bahl, *Metropolitan City Expenditures* (Lexington: University of Kentucky, 1969); Rodgers, "En-

vironment, System and Output"; Terry N. Clark, "Community Structure, Decision Making, Budget Expenditures, and Urban Renewal in fifty-one American Communities," *American Sociological Review*, 33 (1968), 576–93; Robert Lineberry, "Community Structure and Planning Commitment: A Note on the Correlates of Agency Expenditures," *Social Science Quarterly*, 50 (1969), 723–30; and Williams *et al.*, *Suburban Differences and Metropolitan Policies*. Studies analyzing fiscal behavior for local educational systems have not been included.

11. A still useful introduction to PPB is David Novick (ed.), *Program Budgeting: Program Analysis and the Federal Budget* (Washington, D.C.: Government Printing Office, 1964; Cambridge: Harvard University Press, 1965). See also "Planning-Programming-Budgeting Symposium," *Public Administration Review*, 26 (1966), 243–319; and "Planning-Programming-Budgeting System Re-examined" (symposium), *ibid.*, 29 (1969).

12. Marshal Dimock and Gladys Dimlock, *Public Administration*, 4th ed. (New York: Holt, Rinehart, & Winston, 1969), p. 493.

13. See Robert Dorfman (ed.), *Measuring Benefits of Government Investments* (Washington, D.C.: Brookings Institution, 1965).

14. Resource Management Corporation, *Benefit-Cost Applications in Urban Renewal: Summary of the Feasibility Study* (Washington, D.C.: Government Printing Office, 1968); and Werner Z. Hirsch, "Cost Functions of an Urban Government Service: Refuse Collection," *Review of Economics and Statistics*, 47 (1965), 87–92.

15. These studies are Donald B. Rosenthal and Robert L. Crain, "Structure and Values in Local Political Systems: The Case of Fluoridation Decisions," *Journal of Politics*, 28 (1966), 169–96; Amos H. Hawley, "Community Power and Urban Renewal Success," *American Journal of Sociology*, 68 (1963), 42–31; Dennis J. Palumbo and Oliver P. Williams, "Predictors of Public Policy: The Case of Local Public Health," *Urban Affairs Quarterly*, 2 (1967), 75–92; and Williams *et al.*, *Suburban Differences and Metropolitan Policies*.

16. Ira Sharkansky, "Environment, Policy, Output and Impact: Problems of Theory and Method in the Analysis of Public Policy," in Sharkansky (ed.), *Policy Analysis in Political Science* (Chicago: Markham, 1970), pp. 61–79. Similar distinctions (between policy content, process, and outcome) appear in Austin Ranney, "The Study of Policy Content: A Framework for Choice," in Ranney (ed.), *Political Science and Public Policy* (Chicago: Markham, 1969), pp. 6–9.

17. Ira Sharkansky, "Government Expenditures and Public Services in the American States," *American Political Science Review*, 61 (1967), 1066–77.

18. Sharkansky and Hofferbert, "Dimensions of State Politics."

19. Robert E. Crew, Jr., "Dimensions of Public Policy: A Factor Analysis of State Expenditures," *Social Science Quarterly*, 50 (1969), 381–88.

20. Robert C. Wood, *1400 Governments* (Cambridge: Harvard University Press, 1961).

21. Palumbo and Williams, "Predictors of Public Policy."

22. Louis H. Masotti and Don R. Bowen, "Communities and Budgets: The Sociology of Municipal Expenditures," *Urban Affairs Quarterly*, 1 (1965), 39–58.

23. An early nonexpenditure urban policy output study is Joel Smith, *Some Social Aspects of Mass Transit in Selected American Cities* (East Lansing: Institute for Community Development and Services, Michigan State University, 1959). See also Donald J. McCrone and Charles F. Cnudde, "On Measuring Public Policy," in Robert Crew (ed.), *State Politics* (Belmont, Calif.: Wadsworth, 1968), pp. 523–30; and Thomas R. Dye, "Inequality and Civil-Rights Policy in the States," *Journal of Politics*, 31 (1969), 1080–97.

24. Lewis A. Froman, Jr., "The Categorization of Policy Contents," in Ranney (ed.), *Political Science and Public Policy*, pp. 43–44.

Reformism and Public Policies in American Cities*

Robert L. Lineberry and Edmund P. Fowler

A DECADE AGO, political scientists were deploring the "lost world of municipal government" and calling for systematic studies of municipal life which emphasized the political, rather than the administrative, side of urban political life.[1] In recent years, this demand has been generously answered and urban politics is becoming one of the most richly plowed fields of political research. In terms originally introduced by David Easton,[2] political scientists have long been concerned with inputs, but more recently they have focused their attention on other system variables, particularly the political culture[3] and policy outputs of municipal governments.[4]

The present paper will treat two policy outputs, taxation and expenditure levels of cities, as dependent variables. We will relate these policy choices to socioeconomic characteristics of cities and to structural characteristics of their governments. Our central research concern is to examine the impact of political structures, reformed and unreformed, on policy making in American cities.

Reprinted with permission from The American Political Science Review, 61 (September 1967), 701–17.
*The authors are indebted to Professors Robert T. Daland, James W. Prothro, William R. Keech, and James Q. Wilson for comments on an earlier draft of this paper. For assistance in statistical and methodological questions, the advice of Professor Hubert Blalock and Mr. Peter B. Harkins has been invaluable. The authors, of course, assume responsibility for all interpretation and misinterpretation.

Political Culture, Reformism, and Political Institutions

The leaders of the Progressive movement in the United States left an enduring mark on the American political system, particularly at the state and municipal level. In the states, the primary election, the referendum, initiative and recall survive today. The residues of this *Age of Reform*,[5] as Richard Hofstadter called it, persist in municipal politics principally in the form of manager government and at-large and nonpartisan elections. The reformers were, to borrow Banfield and Wilson's phrase, the original embodiment of the "middle class ethos" in American politics. They were, by and large, white Anglo-Saxon Protestants reacting to the politics of the party machine, which operated by exchanging favors for votes.[6]

It is important that we understand the ideology of these reformers if we hope to be able to analyze the institutions which they created and their impact on political decisions. The reformers' goal was to "rationalize" and "democratize" city government by the substitution of "community oriented" leadership. To the reformers, the most pernicious characteristic of the machine was that it capitalized on socioeconomic cleavages in the population, playing on class antagonisms and on racial and religious differences. Ernest S. Bradford, an early advocate of commission government with at-large elections, defended his plans for at-large representation on grounds that

> under the ward system of governmental representation, the ward receives the attention, not in proportion to its needs but to the ability of its representatives to "trade" and arrange "deals" with fellow members. ... Nearly every city under the aldermanic system offers flagrant examples of this vicious method of "part representation." The commission form changes this to representation of the city as a whole.[7]

The principal tools which the reformers picked to maximize this "representation of the city as a whole" were the commission, and later the manager, form of government, the nonpartisan election, and the election at-large. City manager government, it was argued, produced a no-nonsense, efficient, and business-like regime, where decisions could be implemented by professional administrators rather than by victors in the battle over spoils. Nonpartisan elections meant to the reformer that state and national parties, whose issues were irrelevant to local politics anyway, would keep their divisive influences out of municipal decision making. Nonpartisan elections, especially when combined with elections at large, would also serve to reduce the impact of socioeconomic cleavages and minority voting blocs in local politics. Once established, these institutions would serve as bastions against particularistic interests.

Banfield and Wilson have argued that the "middle class ethos" of the reformers has become a prevalent attitude in much of political life. The middle class stands for "public-regarding" virtues rather than for "private-regarding" values of the ethnic politics of machines and bosses. The middle class searches for the good of the "community as a whole" rather than for the benefit of particularistic interests.[8] Agger, Goldrich, and Swanson, in their study of two western and two southern communities, have documented the rise of a group they call the "community conservationists," who "see the values of community life maximized when political leadership is exercised by men representing the public at large, rather than 'special interests.' "[9] Robert Wood has taken up a similar theme in his penetrating analysis of American suburbia. The "no-party politics of suburbia" is characterized by "an outright reaction against partisan activity, a refusal to recognize that there may be persistent cleavages in the electorate and an ethical disapproval of permanent group collaboration as an appropriate means of settling disputes."[10] This ideological opposition to partisanship is a product of a tightly knit and homogeneous community, for "nonpartisanship reflects a highly integrated community life with a powerful capacity to induce conformity."[11]

Considerable debate has ensued over both the existence and the consequences of these two political ethics in urban communities. Some evidence has supported the view that reformed governments[12] are indeed found in cities with higher incomes, higher levels of education, greater proportions of Protestants, and more white-collar jobholders. Schnore and Alford, for example, found that "the popular image of the manager city was verified; it does tend to be the natural habitat of the upper middle class." In addition, manager cities were "inhabited by a younger, more mobile population that is growing rapidly."[13]

More recently, Wolfinger and Field correlated socioeconomic variables—particularly ethnicity and region—to political structures. They concluded that "the ethos theory is irrelevant to the South . . . inapplicable to the West . . . fares badly in the Northeast" and that support for the theory in the Midwest was "small and uneven."[14] Region proved to be a more important predictor of both government forms and of policy outputs like urban renewal expenditures than did the socioeconomic composition of the population.

In our view, it is premature to carve a headstone for the ethos theory. It is our thesis that governments which are products of the reform movement behave differently from those which have unreformed institutions, even if the socioeconomic composition of their population may be similar. Our central purpose is to determine the impact of both socioeconomic variables and political institutions (structural variables) on outputs of city governments. By doing this, we hope to shed some additional illumination on the ethos theory.

Research Design

Variables. The independent variables used in this analysis, listed in Table 1, consist of relatively "hard" data, mostly drawn from the U.S. census.[15] These variables were selected because they represent a variety of possible social cleavages which divide urban populations—rich vs. poor, Negro vs. white, ethnic vs. native, newcomers vs. old-timers.

We assume that such social and economic characteristics are important determinants of individual and group variations in political preferences. Data on each of these independent variables were gathered for each of the 200 cities in the sample.[16]

TABLE 1. Independent Variables

---

1. Population, 1960
2. Percent population increase or decrease, 1950–60
3. Percent nonwhite
4. Percent of native population with foreign-born or mixed parentage
5. Median income
6. Percent of population with incomes below $3,000
7. Percent of population with incomes above $10,000
8. Median school years completed by adult population
9. Percent high school graduates among adult population
10. Percent of population in white collar occupations
11. Percent of elementary school children in private schools
12. Percent of population in owner-occupied dwelling units

Our principal theoretical concern is with the consequences of variations in the structural characteristics of form of government, type of constituency, and partisanship of elections. The variable of government form is unambiguous. Except for a few small New England towns, all American cities have council-manager, mayor-council, or commission government. There is, however, somewhat more ambiguity in the classification of election type. By definition, a "nonpartisan election is one in which no candidate is identified on the ballot by party affiliation."[17] The legal definition of nonpartisanship conceals the wide variation between Chicago's and Boston's nominal nonpartisanship and the more genuine variety in Minneapolis, Winnetka, and Los Angeles.[18] We will quickly see, though, that formal nonpartisanship is not merely an empty legal nicety, but that there are very real differences

in the political behavior of partisan and nonpartisan cities, even though we are defining them in legal terms only.[19]

Our classification of constituency types into only two groups also conceals some variation in the general pattern. While most cities use either the at-large or the ward pattern of constituencies exclusively, a handful use a combination of the two electoral methods. For our purposes, we classified these with district cities.

The dependent variables in this study are two measures of public policy outputs. A growing body of research on local politics has utilized policy measures as dependent variables.[20] The present research is intended to further this study of political outputs by relating socioeconomic variables to expenditure and taxation patterns in cities with varying political structures.

The dependent variables are computed by a simple formula. The measure for taxation was computed by dividing the total personal income of the city into the total tax of the city, giving us a tax/income ratio. Similarly, dividing expenditures by the city's aggregate personal income gave us an expenditure/income ratio as the measure for our second dependent variable. These measures, while admittedly imperfect,[21] permit us to ask how much of a city's income it is willing to commit for public taxation and expenditures.

Hypothesis. Much of the research on city politics has treated reformed institutions as dependent variables. Although we shall briefly examine the social and economic differences between reformed and unreformed cities, our principal concern will be to explore the *consequences* for public policy of political institutions. From our earlier discussion of the political culture of cities we hypothesized that:

1. The relationship between socioeconomic cleavages and policy outputs is stronger in unreformed than in reformed cities.

This hypothesis focuses on the intention of the reformers to minimize the role of particularistic interests in policy making.

Reformed and Unreformed Cities: A Comparison

The economic and social contrasts between reformed and unreformed cities have been the subject of much research,[22] and for our purposes we may be brief in our treatment. We divided the independent variables into three groups, one measuring population size and growth, a second containing social class indicators and a third including three measures of social homogeneity. The means and standard deviations for each variable by institutional category are found in Table 2.

It should initially be noted that population size and growth rate fairly clearly separate the reformed from the unreformed cities. As Alford and Scoble have amply documented,[23] the larger the city, the greater the likelihood of its being unreformed; the faster its growth rate, the more likely a city is to possess manager government, nonpartisan and at-large elections. These differences are largely accounted for by the fact that very large cities are most likely to (1) have unreformed institutions and (2) be stable or declining in population. Since neither of these variables emerged as particularly important predictors of our output variables, we relegated them to secondary importance in the rest of the analysis.

The data in Table 2 indicate that reformed cities (at least those over 50,000) do not appear to be "the natural habitat of the upper middle class." While reformed cities have slightly more educated populations and slightly high proportions of white-collar workers and home ownership, unreformed cities have generally high incomes. In any case, whatever their direction, the differences are not large. What is striking is not the differences between the cities but the similarities of their class composition.

Homogeneity is easily one of the most ambiguous terms in the ambiguous language of the social sciences. We have followed Alford and Scoble who used three measures of homogeneity: for ethnicity, the percent of population native-born of foreign-born or mixed parentage; for race, the percent non-

white; and for religious homogeneity, the percent of elementary school children in private schools. The last measure, while indirect, was the only one available, since data on religious affiliation are not collected by the Census Bureau.

With the exception of race, reformed cities appear somewhat more homogeneous than unreformed cities. While the differences in homogeneity are more clear-cut than class differences, this hardly indicates that reformed cities are the havens of a socially homogeneous population. Although the average nonpartisan city has 16.9 percent of its children in private schools, this mean conceals a wide range—from 2 to 47 percent.

Our findings about the insignificance of class differences between reformed and unreformed cities are at some variance with Alford and Scoble's conclusions. There is, however, some support for the argument that reformed cities are more homogeneous. While we used cities with populations of over 50,000, their sample included all cities over 25,000; and varying samples may produce varying conclusions. The only other study to analyze cities over 50,000 was Wolfinger and Field's and our conclusions are generally consistent with theirs. We differ with them, however, on two important questions.

First, Wolfinger and Field argued that what differences there are between unreformed and reformed cities disappear when controls for region are introduced: "The salient conclusion to be drawn from these data is that one can do a much better job of predicting a city's political form by knowing what part of the country it is in than by knowing anything about the composition of its population."[24] Since regions have had different historical experiences, controls for region are essentially controls for history, and, more specifically, historical variation in settlement patterns. The problem with this reasoning, however, is that to "control" for "region" is to control not only for history, but for demography as well: to know what region a city is in *is* to know something about the composition of its population. Geographical subdivisions are relevant subjects

TABLE 2. *Comparison of the Means (and Standard Deviations) of Socioeconomic Characteristics of Reformed and Unreformed Cities*

INDEPENDENT VARIABLES	GOVERNMENT TYPE					
	Mayor-Council		Manager		Commission	
Population (10³)	282.5	(858.6)	115.7	(108.0)	128.6	(115.2)
% change, 1950–60	36.4%	(118.8)	64.1%	(130.4)	18.5%	(36.7)
Class:						
Median income	$6,199.	(1,005.0)	$6,131.	(999.6)	$5,425.	(804.4)
% under $3,000	15.3%	(7.0)	17.3%	(6.9)	21.5%	(7.9)
% over $10,000	16.9%	(7.2)	17.5%	(6.7)	12.5%	(3.7)
% high school graduates	40.7%	(10.8)	48.1%	(8.9)	41.6%	(10.4)
Median education (yrs.)	10.7	(1.1)	11.4	(.89)	11.0	(2.1)
% owner-occupied dwelling units	54.9%	(15.1)	57.3%	(13.6)	54.6%	(13.7)
% white collar	44.1%	(9.0)	48.1%	(7.1)	44.2%	(7.6)
Homogeneity:						
% nonwhite	10.6%	(11.5)	11.6%	(10.8)	16.5%	(14.9)
% native with foreign-born or mixed parentage	19.7%	(9.9)	12.4%	(8.3)	11.7%	(10.7)
% private school attendance	23.5%	(11.9)	15.3%	(11.8)	16.6%	(11.8)
	N = 85		N = 90		N = 25	

INDEPENDENT VARIABLES	ELECTION TYPE			
	Partisan		Nonpartisan	
Population:				
Population (10³)	270.8	(1,022.1)	155.8	(198.7)
% population increase 1950–60	17.1	(40.1)	58.3%	(136.1)
Class:				
Median income	$5,996	(904.5)	$6,074	(1,045.5)
% under $3,000	16.8%	(7.1)	17.2%	(7.2)
% over $10,000	16.1%	(6.1)	16.7%	(7.0)
% high school graduates	40.5%	(9.2)	45.3%	(10.6)
Median education (yrs.)	10.6	(1.1)	11.2	(1.2)
% owner-occupied dwelling units	51.5%	(14.4)	57.7%	(13.8)
% white collar	43.5%	(7.5)	46.7%	(8.2)
Homogeneity:				
% nonwhite	13.0%	(11.9)	11.5%	(11.8)
% native with foreign-born or mixed parentage	17.5%	(10.7)	14.7%	(9.6)
% private school attendance	24.1%	(13.6)	16.9%	(11.3)
	N = 57		N = 143	

INDEPENDENT VARIABLES	CONSTITUENCY TYPE			
	District		At-Large	
Population:				
Population (10³)	246.9	(909.8)	153.6	(191.2)
% population increase 1950–60	23.1%	(36.4)	59.1%	(143.7)
Class:				
Median income	$6,297	(965.2)	$5,942	(1,031.9)
% under $3,000	14.7%	(6.5)	18.2%	(7.6)
% over $10,000	17.7%	(7.1)	16.0%	(6.6)
% high school graduates	43.6%	(10.9)	44.4%	(10.4)
Median education (yrs.)	10.9	(1.1)	11.2	(1.2)
% owner-occupied dwelling units	55.1%	(14.4)	56.9%	(14.5)
% white collar	45.2%	(9.4)	46.3%	(7.5)
Homogeneity:				
% nonwhite	9.8%	(10.6)	13.0%	(12.3)
% native with foreign born or mixed parentage	18.9%	(9.4)	13.4%	(9.7)
% private school attendance	23.2%	(12.5)	16.6%	(11.7)
	N = 73		N = 127	

of political inquiry only because they are differentiated on the basis of attitudinal or socioeconomic variables. The South is not a distinctive political region because two surveyors named Mason and Dixon drew a famous line, but because the "composition of its population" differs from the rest of the country.

It is, therefore, difficult to unravel the meaning of "controlling" for "region" since regions are differentiated on precisely the kinds of demographic variables which we (and Wolfinger and Field) related to reformism. Cities in the Midwest, for example, have a much higher proportion of home ownership (64%) than cities in the Northeast (44%), while north-eastern cities have more foreign stock in their population (27%) than the Midwest (16%). Hence, to relate ethnicity to political reformism and then to "control" for "region" is in part to relate ethnicity to reformism and then to control for ethnicity. Consequently, we have grave reservations that the substitution of the gross and unrefined variable of "region" for more refined demographic data adds much to our knowledge of American cities. "Controlling" for "region" is much more than controlling for historical experiences, because region as a variable is an undifferentiated *potpourri* of socioeconomic, attitudinal, historical, and cultural variations.[25]

We also differ with Wolfinger and Field in their assertion that their analysis constitutes a test of the ethos theory. As we understand it, Banfield and Wilson's theory posits that particular attitudes are held by persons with varying sociological characteristics (ethnic groups and middle class persons, in particular) and that these attitudes include preferences for one or another kind of political institution. But relating the proportion of middle-class persons in a city's population to its form of government says nothing one way or another about middle class preferences. An important part of understanding, of course, is describing and it is certainly useful to know how reformed cities differ from unreformed cities.

In our view, however, such tests as Wolfinger and Field used cannot logically be called explanations, in any causal sense. The most obvious reason is that they violate some important assumptions about time order: independent variables are measured with contemporary census data, while the dependent variables are results of decisions made ten to fifty years ago. Moreover, this problem is multiplied by the difficulty of inferring configurations of political power from demographic data. Presumably, their assumption is that there is a simple linear relationship between sheer numbers (or proportions) of, say, middle-class persons and their political power: the larger the size of a group in the city's population, the easier it can enforce its choice of political forms. At least one prominent urban sociologist, however, has found empirical support for precisely the opposite proposition. Hawley concluded that the smaller the proportion of middle-class persons in a city, the greater their power over urban renewal policies.[26] Similarly, it may also be dubious to assume that the size of an ethnic population is an accurate indicator of influence of ethnic groups. Although we recognize the importance of describing the socioeconomic correlates of political forms, the logical problems involved suggest the need for a good deal of caution in interpreting these differences as explanations.[27]

In any case, the question of why the city adopts particular structures is of less interest to us than their consequences for public policy. It is to this analysis that we now turn.

Policy Outputs and the Responsiveness of Cities

We are now in a position to take three additional steps. First, we can compare the differences in policy outputs between reformed and unreformed cities. Second, we can assess the cumulative impact of socioeconomic variables on these policy choices. Finally, we can specify what variables are related in what ways to these output variables. In essence, we can now treat political institutions, not as dependent variables, but as factors which influence the *level* of expenditures and taxation and the *relationship* between cleavage variables and these outputs.

Differences between reformed and unreformed cities' outputs. Contrary to Sherbenou's conclusions about Chicago suburbs,[28] our data indicate that reformed cities both spend and tax less than unreformed cities, with the exception of expenditures in partisan and non-partisan cities. It appears that partisan, mayor-council, and ward cities are less willing to commit their resources to public purposes than their reformed counterparts. What is of more importance than the difference in outputs, however, is the relative responsiveness of the two kinds of cities to social cleavages in their population.

TABLE 3. *Mean Values of Tax/Income and Expenditure/Income Ratios, by Structural Characteristics*

Structural Variables	Taxes /Income	Expenditures /Income
Election type:		
Partisan	0.032	0.050
Nonpartisan	0.030	0.053
Government type:		
Mayor-council	0.037	0.058
Manager	0.024	0.045
Commission	0.031	0.057
Constituency type		
Ward	0.036	0.057
At-large	0.027	0.049

The responsiveness of cities. We have argued that one principal goal of the reform movement was to reduce the impact of partisan, socioeconomic cleavages on governmental decision making, to immunize city governments from "artificial" social cleavages—race, religion, ethnicity, and so on. As Banfield and Wilson put their argument, the reformers "assumed that there existed an interest ('the public interest') that pertained to the city 'as a whole' and that should always prevail over competing, partial (and usually private' interests."[29] The structural reforms of manager government, at-large, and nonpartisan elections would so insulate the business of governing from social cleav-

ages that "private regarding" interests would count for little in making up the mind of the body politic. But, amid the calls of the reformers for structural reforms to muffle the impact of socioeconomic cleavages, a few hardy souls predicted precisely the opposite consequence of reform: instead of eliminating cleavages from political decision making, the reforms, particularly the elimination of parties, would enhance the conflict. Nathan Matthews, Jr., a turn-of-the-century mayor of Boston, issued just such a warning:

> As a city is a political institution, the people in the end will divide into parties, and it would seem extremely doubtful whether the present system, however illogical its foundation be, does not in fact produce better results, at least in large cities, than if the voters divided into groups, separated by property, social or religious grounds.[30]

Matthews recognized implicitly what political scientists would now call the "interest aggregation" function of political parties.[31] Parties in a democracy manage conflict, structure it, and encapsulate social cleavages under the rubric of two or more broad social cleavages, the parties themselves. "Parties tend to crystallize opinion, they give skeletal articulation to a shapeless and jelly-like mass . . . they cause similar opinions to coagulate."[32] The parties "reduce effectively the number of political opinions to manageable numbers, bring order and focus to the political struggle, simplify issues and frame alternatives, and compromise conflicting interests."[33] Since parties are the agencies of interest aggregation, so the argument goes, their elimination makes for greater, not lesser, impact of social cleavages on political decisions.

Political scientists have recently confirmed Matthews' fears, at least with regard to electoral behavior in partisan and nonpartisan elections. Evidence points to the increased impact of socioeconomic cleavages on voting when a nonpartisan ballot is used than when the election is formally partisan. Gerald Pomper studied nonpartisan municipal elections and compared them with partisan elections for the New Jersey State Assembly in Newark. He concluded that the "goal of nonpartisanship is fulfilled, as party identification does not determine the outcome. In place of party, ethnic affiliation is emphasized and the result is 'to enhance the effect of basic social cleavages.' "[34] If (1) this is typical of other American cities and if (2) electoral cleavages can be translated effectively into demands on the government in the absence of aggregative parties, then we might assume that the reformed institutions would reflect cleavages more, rather than less, closely than unreformed ones.

Essentially, then, there are two contrasting views about the consequences of municipal reform. One, the reformers' ideal, holds that institutional reforms will mitigate the impact of social cleavages on public policy. The other argues that the elimination of political parties and the introduction of other reforms will make social cleavages more, rather than less, important in political decision making.

The measurement of responsiveness. We have hypothesized that socioeconomic cleavages will have less impact on the policy choices of reformed than unreformed governments. Thus one could do a better job of predicting a city's taxation and expenditure policy using socioeconomic variables in partisan, mayor, and ward cities than in nonpartisan, manager, and at-large cities. Operationally, we will test this hypothesis by using multiple correlation coefficients. Squaring these coefficients, called "multiple Rs," will give us a summary measure of the total amount of variation in our dependent variables explained by our twelve independent variables.[35] The results of the correlation analysis are summarized in diagrams 1 and 2.

DIAGRAM 1. Proportion of Variation Explained (R^2) in Taxation Policy with Twelve Socioeconomic Variables, by Institutional Characteristics*

Independent Variables	Structural Variables		Dependent Variable
	Reformed Institution:		
	Government: commission	62%	
	Government: council-manager	42%	
	Election: nonpartisan	49%	
	Constituency: at-large	49%	
Twelve Socioeconomic Variables			Tax/Income Ratio
	Unreformed Institution:		
	Government: mayor-council	52%	
	Election: partisan	71%	
	Constituency: ward/mixed	59%	

*In the total sample, the twelve independent variables explained 52 percent of the variation in taxes.

DIAGRAM 2. Proportion of Variation Explained (R^2) in Expenditure Policy with Twelve Socioeconomic Variables, by Institutional Characteristics*

Independent Variables	Structural Variables		Dependent Variable
	Reformed Institution:		
	Government: commission	59%	
	Government: council-manager	30%	
	Constituency: at-large	36%	
	Elections: nonpartisan	41%	
Twelve Socioeconomic Variables			Expenditure/Income Ratio
	Unreformed Institution:		
	Government: mayor-council	42%	
	Constituency: ward/mixed	49%	
	Elections: partisan	59%	

*In the total sample, the twelve independent variables explained 36 percent of the variation in expenditures.

On the whole, the results of the correlation analysis strikingly support the hypothesis, with the exception of commission cities. Thus, we can say, for example, that our twelve socioeconomic variables explain 71 percent of the variations in taxation policy in partisan cities, and 49 percent of the variation in nonpartisan cities. In commission cities, however, socioeconomic variables predict substantially more variation in both taxes and expenditures than in the unreformed mayor-council cities.[36] The anomaly of commission governments is interesting, for they present, as we will see, marked exceptions to virtually every pattern of relationships we found. The substantial explanatory power of these socioeconomic variables is not altered, but confirmed, by examining the variables independently. The rest of the correlations show a consistent pattern: reformed cities are less responsive to cleavages in their population than unreformed cities.

If one of the premises of the "political ethos" argument is that reformed institutions give less weight to the "private-regarding" and "artificial" cleavages in the population, that premise receives striking support from our analysis. Our data suggest that when a city adopts reformed structures, it comes to be governed less on the basis of conflict and more on the basis of the rationalistic theory of administration. The making of public policy takes less count of the enduring differences between white and Negro, business and labor, Pole and WASP. The logic of the bureaucratic ethic demands an impersonal, apolitical settlement of issues, rather than the settlement of conflict in the arena of political battle.

To Spend or Not to Spend

If efforts to expand or contract the scope of government stand at the core of municipal political life,[37] they are nowhere better reflected than in the taxation and expenditure patterns of cities. A generation ago, Charles Beard wrote, "In the purposes for which appropriations are made the policies of the city government are given concrete form—the culture of the city is reflected. Indeed, the history of urban civilization could be written in terms of appropriations, for they show what the citizens think is worth doing and worth paying for."[38] Pressures to expand and contract government regulations and services are almost always reflected one way or another in the municipal budget. Labor, ethnic groups, the poor, and the liberal community may press for additional services and these must be paid for; the business community may demand municipal efforts to obtain new industry by paring city costs to create a "favorable business climate"; or businessmen may themselves demand municipal services for new or old business. In any case, few political conflicts arise which do not involve some conflict over the budget structure.

Class variables and public policies. Part of the political rhetoric associated with the demand for a decrease in the scope of the national government is the argument that the initiative for policy making should rest more with the state and local governments. Opposition to high federal spending levels, as V. O. Key has demonstrated, is found more often among persons with middle-class occupations than among blue-collar workers.[39] It is not inconceivable that the middle-class argument about state and local responsibility might be more than political rhetoric, and that at the local level, middle-class voters are willing to undertake major programs of municipal services, requiring large outlays of public capital. Wilson and Banfield have argued that the "public regarding" upper-middle class voters in metropolitan areas are often found voting for public policies at variance with their "self-interest narrowly conceived," and that "the higher the income of a ward or town, the more taste it has for public expenditures of various kinds."[40] Similarly, a longitudinal study of voting patterns in metropolititan Cleveland found that an index of social rank was positively correlated with favorable votes on welfare referenda.[41] If these data reflect middle-class willingness to spend on a local level, they might indicate that the "states' rights" argument was more than ideological camouflage:

middle-class voters stand foursquare behind public expenditures at the local level even when they oppose those expenditures from the national government. Therefore, we hypothesized that:

2a. The more middle-class the city, measured by income, education and occupation, the higher the municipal taxes and expenditures.

In line with our general concern of testing the impact of political structures on municipal policies, we also hypothesized that:

2b. Unreformed cities reflect this relationship more strongly than reformed cities.

With respect to hypothesis 2a, the data in Table 4 on three middle-class indicators are unambiguous and indicate a strong rejection of the hypothesis. However we measure social class, whether by income, education, or occupation, class measures are negatively related to public taxes and expenditures.

It is possible, however, that income does not have a linear, but rather a curvilinear, relationship with municipal outputs. Banfield and Wilson argue that "In the city, it is useful to think in terms of three income groups— low, middle, and high. Surprising as it may seem to Marxists, the conflict is generally between an alliance of low-income and high-income groups on one side and the middle-income groups on the other."[42] If the relationships between income and expenditure

is curvilinear, then we should expect to find that proportions of both low- and high-income groups were positively correlated with outputs. Our data, however, lend no support to this notion of a "pro-expenditure" alliance. Rather, the proportion of the population with incomes below $3,000 is positively correlated with expenditures in all city types (although the relationships are small) and the proportion of the population in the above $10,000 bracket is negatively correlated with expenditures. Summing the two measures and correlating the combined measure with outputs produced no correlation greater than .15 and the relationships were as likely to be negative as positive. Tests for non-linearity also suggested that no such coalition exists in the cities in our analysis.

To be sure, aggregate data analysis using whole cities as units of analysis is no substitute for systematic survey data on middle-class attitudes, but it is apparent that cities with larger middle-class population have higher expenditures. As we emphasized earlier, the "ethos theory" deals with attitudes and the behavior of individuals, while our data deal with cities and their behavior. The coalition suggested by Banfield and Wilson, however, is not discernible at this level of aggregation in these cities.

Hypothesis 2b is not consistently borne out by the data. In fact, the relationships between middle-class variables and ouputs are, if anything, stronger in the reformed cities than in their unreformed counterparts. One would not want to make too much of the

TABLE 4. Correlations between Middle Class Characteristics and Outputs in Reformed and Unreformed Cities

CORRELATIONS OF	GOVERNMENT TYPE			ELECTION TYPE		CONSTITUENCY TYPE	
	Mayor-Council	Manager	Com-mission	Partisan	Non-partisan	Ward	At-large
Taxes with:							
Median income	−0.13	−0.24	−0.19	0.03	−0.19	−0.17	−0.22
White collar	−0.23	−0.12	−0.62	−0.21	−0.33	−0.30	−0.32
Median education	−0.36	−0.22	−0.08	−0.45	−0.24	−0.48	−0.18
Expenditures with:							
Median income	−0.19	−0.32	−0.43	−0.04	−0.32	−0.23	−0.34
White collar	−0.24	−0.23	−0.58	−0.18	−0.39	−0.32	−0.35
Median education	−0.32	−0.36	−0.26	−0.36	−0.38	−0.44	−0.32

data, but a large body of literature on city politics, which we discuss below, suggests that reformed institutions maximize the power of the middle class.

We originally assumed that the proportion of owner-occupied dwelling units constituted another measure of middle-class composition, but it soon became apparent that it was only weakly related to income, occupation, and education measures. Nevertheless, it emerged as the strongest single predictor of both expenditure and taxation policy in our cities. We hypothesized that:

3a. Owner-occupancy and outputs are negatively correlated, and

3b. Unreformed cities reflect this relationship more strongly than reformed cities.

Hypothesis 3a is consistently borne out in the data presented in Table 5. These relationships were only slightly attenuated when we controlled for income, education, and occupation. No doubt self-interest (perhaps "private-regardingness") on the part of the home owner, whose property is intimately related to the tax structure of most local governments, may account for part of this relationship. Moreover, home ownership is correlated (almost by definition) with lower urban population density. High density, bringing together all manner of men into the classic urban mosaic, may be itself correlated with factors which produce demands for higher expenditures—slums, increased needs for fire and police protection, and so on.

In confirmation of hypothesis 3a, the unmistakable pattern is for unreformed cities to reflect these negative relationships more strongly than the manager, nonpartisan, and at-large cities, although commission cities show their usual remarkably high correlations.

Homogeneity variables and public policies. Dawson and Robinson, in their analysis of state welfare expenditures, found strong positive relationships between the ethnicity of a state's population and the level of its welfare expenditures.[43] If this is symptomatic of a generalized association of ethnic and religious minorities with higher expenditures, we might find support for the hypothesis that:

4a. The larger the proportion of religious and ethnic minorities in the population, the higher the city's taxes and expenditures.

And, if our general hypothesis about the impact of political institutions is correct, then:

4b. Unreformed cities reflect this relationship more strongly than reformed cities.

The correlations between ethnicity, religious heterogeneity and outputs (see Table 6) are, with one exception, positive, as predicted by hypothesis 4a. These associations may reflect the substantial participation by ethnic groups in municipal politics long after the tide of immigration has been reduced to a trickle.[44] The relatively intense politicization of ethnic groups at the local level,[45] the appeals to nationality groups through "ticket balancing" and other means, and the resultant higher turnout of ethnic groups than other lower status groups,[46] may produce an influence on city government far out of proportion to their number.

We found when we related all twelve of our independent variables to outputs in

TABLE 5. *Correlations between Owner Occupancy and Government Outputs in Reformed and Unreformed Cities*

CORRELATIONS OF OWNER OCCUPANCY WITH:	GOVERNMENT TYPE			ELECTION TYPE		CONSTITUENCY TYPE	
	Mayor-Council	Manager	Commission	Partisan	Non-partisan	Ward	At-large
Taxes	−0.57	−0.31	−0.73	−0.64	−0.45	−0.56	−0.48
Expenditures	−0.51	−0.23	−0.62	−0.62	−0.40	−0.50	−0.40

TABLE 6.   Correlations between Ethnicity and Religious Heterogeneity and Outputs in Reformed and Unreformed Cities

CORRELATIONS OF	GOVERNMENT TYPE			ELECTION TYPE		CONSTITUENCY TYPE	
	Mayor-Council	Manager	Com-mission	Partisan	Non-partisan	Ward	At-large
Taxes with:							
Ethnicity	0.49	0.26	0.57	0.61	0.43	0.56	0.40
Private school							
attendance	0.38	0.15	0.37	0.33	0.37	0.41	0.25
Expenditures with:							
Ethnicity	0.36	0.02	0.21	0.48	0.21	0.44	0.13
Private school							
attendance	0.34	−0.01	0.07	0.25	0.24	0.40	0.05

various city types that the associations were much weaker in cities we have labeled reformed. The correlations for ethnicity and religious homogeneity show a generally similar pattern, with commission cities exhibiting their usual erratic behavior. The data, then, show fairly clear support for hypothesis 4b.

The third variable of our homogeneity indicators—percent of population nonwhite—had almost no relationship to variation in outputs, regardless of city type. We found the same weak correlations for the poverty income variable, which was, of course, strongly related to the racial variable. An easy explanation suggests that this is a consequence of the political impotence of Negroes and the poor, but one should be cautious in inferring a lack of power from the lack of a statistical association.

We have dealt in this section with factors which are positively and negatively related to spending patterns in American cities. While social class variables are associated negatively with outputs, two measures of homogeneity, private school attendance and ethnicity are related to higher taxes and spending. Examining the strengths of these correlations in cities with differing forms, we found some support for our general hypothesis about the political consequences of institutions, especially for the homogeneity variables and the home ownership variable. Interestingly, however, this was not the case with class variables.

Reformism as a Continuous Variable

The central thrust of our argument has been that reformed governments differ from their unreformed counterparts in their responsiveness to socioeconomic cleavages in the population. Logically, if the presence of one feature of the "good government" syndrome had the impact of reducing responsiveness, the introduction of additional reformed institutions should have an additive effect and further reduce the impact of cleavages on decision making. We therefore decided to treat "reformism" as a continuous variable for analytic purposes and hypothesized that:

5. The higher the level of reformism in a city, the lower its responsiveness to socioeconomic cleavages in the population.

We utilized a simple four-point index to test this hypothesis, ranging from the "least reformed" to the "most reformed." The sample cities were categorized as follows:

1. Cities with none of the reformed institutions (i.e., the government is mayor-council, elections are partisan, and constituencies are wards).
2. Cities with any one of the reformed institutions.
3. Cities with two of the reformed institutions.

4. Cities with three reformed institutions (i.e., the government is either manager or commission, elections are nonpartisan, and constituencies are at-large).

We can not overemphasize the crudity of this index as an operationalization of the complex and abstract concept of reformism. Nonetheless, we think some of the relationships we found are strongly suggestive that reformism may in reality be a continuous variable.

To test this hypothesis, we took four variables which had moderate-to-strong correlations with our dependent variables and computed simple correlations in each reform category. If our hypothesis is correct, the strength of the correlations in Table 7 should decrease regularly with an increase in reform scores. While there are some clear exception, to the predicted pattern of relationships, there is some fairly consistent support for the hypothesis. Even when the decreases in the strengths of the correlations is irregular, there is a clear difference between cities which we have labeled "most reformed" and "least reformed."

Again, we would not want to attach too much importance to the results of this rough-and-ready index. But, the patterns support our previous argument about the impact of reformism: the more reformed the city, the less responsive it is to socioeconomic cleavages in its political decision making.

A Causal Model and an Interpretation

A causal model. The implicit, or at times explicit, causal model in much of the research on municipal reformism has been a simple one: socioeconomic cleavages cause the adoption of particular political forms. A more sophisticated model would include political institutions as one of the factors which produce a given output structure in city politics. We hypothesize that a causal model would include four classes of variables: socioeconomic cleavages, political variables (including party registration, structure of party systems, patterns of aggregation, strength of interest groups, voter turnout, etc.), political institutions (form of government, type of elections, and types of constituencies), and political outputs. Diagram 3 depicts one possible causal model.

This study has of necessity been limited to

DIAGRAM 3. A Hypothesized Causal Model

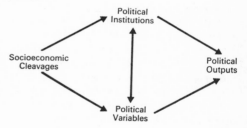

TABLE 7. Correlations between Selected Independent Variables and Output Variables by Four Categories of Reformism

CORRELATIONS OF	REFORM SCORES			
	1 (least reformed)	2	3	4 (most reformed)
Taxes with:				
Ethnicity	0.62	0.41	0.50	0.34
Private school attendance	0.40	0.32	0.28	0.25
Owner-occupancy	−0.70	−0.39	−0.54	−0.44
Median education	−0.55	−0.27	−0.32	−0.13
Expenditures with:				
Ethnicity	0.51	0.27	0.41	0.05
Private school attendance	0.46	0.23	0.16	0.08
Owner-occupancy	−0.67	−0.30	−0.54	−0.38
Median education	−0.49	−0.19	−0.38	−0.37

exploring the linkages between socioeconomic cleavages, political institutions, and political outputs. We found that political institutions "filter" the process of converting inputs into outputs. Some structures, particularly partisan elections, ward constituencies, mayor-council governments, and commission governments, operate to maximize the impact of cleavage indicators on public policies. We conclude by discussing some of the reasons why different structures have varying impacts on the conversion process.

An interpretation. Three principal conclusions may be derived from this analysis.

1. Cities with reformed and unreformed institutions are not markedly different in terms of demographic variables. Indeed, some variables, like income, ran counter to the popular hypothesis that reformed cities are havens of the middle class. Our data lent some support to the notion that reformed cities are more homogenous in their ethnic and religious populations. Still, it is apparent that reformed cities are by no means free from the impact of these cleavages.

2. The more important difference between the two kinds of cities is in their behavior, rather than their demography. Using multiple correlation coefficients, we were able to predict municipal outputs more exactly in unreformed than in reformed cities. The translation of social conflicts into public policy and the responsiveness of political systems to class, racial, and religious cleavages differs markedly with the kind of political structure. Thus political institutions seem to play an important role in the political process—a role substantially independent of a city's demography.

3. Our analysis has also demonstrated that reformism may be viewed as a continuous variable and that the political structures of the reform syndrome have an additive effect: the greater the reformism, the lower the responsiveness.

Through these political institutions, the goal of the reformers has been substantially fulfilled, for nonpartisan elections, at-large constituencies, and manager governments are associated with a lessened responsiveness of cities to the enduring conflicts of political life. Or, as Stone, Price, and Stone argued in their study of changes produced by the adoption of manager governments, the council after the reform "tended to think more of the community as a whole and less of factional interests in making their decisions."[47]

The responsiveness of a political institution to political conflicts should not be confused with the "responsibility" of a political system as the latter term is used in the great debate over the relative "responsibility" of party systems.[48] In fact, the responsiveness of political forms to social cleavages may stand in sharp contrast to "responsible government" on the British model. Presumably, in American cities, partisan elections, ward constituencies, and mayor-council governments maximize minority rather than majority representation, assuring greater access to decision makers than the reformed, bureaucratized, and "depoliticized" administrations.

Partisan electoral systems, when combined with ward representation, increase the access of two kinds of minority groups: those which are residentially segregated, and which may as a consequence of the electoral system demand and obtain preferential consideration from the councilmen; and groups which constitute identifiable voting blocs to which parties and politicians may be beholden in the next election. The introduction of at-large, nonpartisan elections has at least five consequences for these groups. First, they remove an important cue-giving agency—the party—from the electoral scene, leaving the voter to make decisions less on the policy commitments (however vague) of the party and more on irrelevancies such as ethnic identification and name familiarity.[49] Second, by removing the party from the ballot, the reforms eliminate the principal agency of interest aggregation from the political system. Hence, interests are articulated less clearly and are aggregated either by some other agency or not at all. Moreover, nonpartisanship has the effect of reducing the turnout in local elections by working class groups,[50] leaving officeholders freer from retaliation by these groups at the polls. Fourth, nonpartisanship may also serve to decrease the salience of "private-regarding" demands by increasing the relative political power of "public-regarding" agencies like the local press.[51] And when nonpartisanship is combined with election at-large, the impact of residentially segregated groups or groups which obtain their strength from voting as blocs in municipal elections is further reduced.[52] For these reasons, it is clear that political reforms may have a significant impact in minimizing the role which social conflicts play in decision making. By muting the demands of private-regarding groups, the electoral institutions of reformed governments make public policy less responsive to the demands arising out of social conflicts in the population.

The structure of the government may serve further to modify the strength of minority groups over public policy. It is significant in this respect to note that commission governments, where social cleavages have the greatest impact on policy choices, are the most decentralized of the three governmental types and that manager governments are relatively the most centralized.[53] From the point of view of the reformer, commission government is a failure and their number has declined markedly in recent years.[54] This greater decentralization of commission and of mayor-council governments permits a multiplicity of access points for groups wishing to influence decision makers.[55] It may also increase the possibilities for collaboration between groups and a bureaucratic agency, a relationship which has characterized administrative patterns in the federal government. As a result of this decentralization, group strength in local governments may be maximized.

It is important in any analysis of reformism to distinguish between the factors which produce the *adoption* of reformed institutions and the *impact* of the new political forms once they have been established. We can offer from our data no conclusions about the origins of reformed structures, for it is obviously impossible to impute causation, using contemporary census data, to events which occurred decades ago. Once a

city has institutionalized the reformers' ideals, however, a diffused attitude structure may be less helpful in explaining the city's public policy than the characteristics of the institutions themselves. With the introduction of these reforms, a new political pattern may emerge in which disputes are settled outside the political system, or in which they may be settled by the crowd at the civic club at the periphery of the system.[56] If they do enter the political process, an impersonal, "nonpolitical" bureaucracy may take less account of the conflicting interests and pay more attention to the "correct" decision from the point of view of the municipal planner.

These conclusions are generally consistent with the ethos theory developed by Banfield and Wilson. If one of the components of the middle-class reformer's ideal was "to seek the good of the community as a whole" and to minimize the impact of social cleavages on political decision making, then their institutional reforms have served, by and large, to advance that goal.

Notes

1. Lawrence J. R. Herson, "The Lost World of Municipal Government," *American Political Science Review*, 51 (June 1957), 330–45; Robert T. Daland, "Political Science and the Study of Urbanism," *ibid.*, 491–509.
2. David Easton, "An Approach to the Analysis of Political Systems," *World Politics*, 9 (April 1957), 383–400.
3. Edward C. Banfield and James Q. Wilson, *City Politics* (Cambridge: Harvard University Press and M.I.T. Press, 1963); see also James Q. Wilson and Edward C. Banfield, "Public-Regardingness as a Value Premise in Voting Behavior," *American Political Science Review*, 58 (December 1964), 876–87.
4. See, for example, Thomas R. Dye, "City-Suburban Social Distance and Public Policy," *Social Forces*, 4 (1965), 100–106; Raymond Wolfinger and John Osgood Field, "Political Ethos and the Structure of City Government," *American Political Science Review*, 60 (June 1966), 306–26; Edgar L. Sherbenou, "Class, Participation, and the Council-Manager Plan," *Public Administration Review*, 21 (Summer 1961), 131–35; Lewis A. Froman, Jr., "An Analysis of Public Policies in Cities," *Journal of Politics*, 29 (February 1967), 94–108.
5. New York: Alfred A. Knopf, 1955.

6. John Porter East. *Council Manager Government: The Political Thought of Its Founder, Richard S. Childs* (Chapel Hill: University of North Carolina Press, 1965). p. 18.

7. Ernest S. Bradford, *Commission Government in American Cities* (New York: The Macmillan Company, 1911), p. 165.

8. Banfield and Wilson, *City Politics*, p. 41.

9. Robert Agger, Daniel Goldrich, and Bert E. Swanson, *The Rulers and the Ruled* (New York: John Wiley, 1964), p. 21.

10. Robert C. Wood, *Suburbia: Its People and Their Politics* (Boston: Houghton Mifflin, 1959), p. 155.

11. *Ibid..* p. 154.

12. We refer to cities characterized by commission or manager government, nonpartisan elections, and at-large constituencies as "reformed." Our use of the term is historical and no value position on reformism's merits is intended. To refer to reformed cities as "public regarding" or "middle class" is, it seems, to assume what needs to be proved.

13. Leo Schnore and Robert Alford, "Forms of Government and Socio-Economic Characteristics of Suburbs," *Administrative Science Quarterly*, 8 (June 1963), 1–17. See also the literature cited in Froman, "Analysis of Public Policies in Cities."

14. Wolfinger and Field, "Political Ethos," pp. 325–26.

15. The source for the first nine variables is *The County and City Data Book* (Washington, D.C.: United States Bureau of the Census, 1962). For the last three variables, the source is Orin F. Nolting and David S. Arnold (eds.), *The Municipal Yearbook 1965* (Chicago: International City Managers' Association, 1965), pp. 98 ff.

16. We used a random sample of 200 of the 309 American cities with populations of 50,000 or more in 1960. All information on the forms of government and forms of election are drawn from *The Municipal Yearbook 1965*.

17. Banfield and Wilson, *City Politics*, p. 151.

18. For Minneapolis, see Robert Morlan, "City Politics: Free Style," *National Municipal Review*, 48 (November 1949), 485–90; Winnetka, Banfield and Wilson, *City Politics*, p. 140; Los Angeles, Charles G. Mayo, "The 1961 Mayoralty Election in Los Angeles: The Political Party in a Nonpartisan Election," *Western Political Quarterly*, 17 (1964), 325–39.

19. At least one other variable may produce a given institutional form in a city—the legal requirements of a state government, which vary from state to state and may even vary for different kinds of cities within the same state. We have not taken account of this variable because systematic information on comparative state requirements in this area was unavailable to us. However, Wolfinger and Field consulted several experts and eliminated cities which are not given free choice over their institutions. Nevertheless, a comparison of our figures with theirs revealed no important differences.

20. See footnote 4, *supra*.

21. We recognize that these are only rough indicators of city finance policies. Definitions of taxation vary from city to city and what may be financed from taxes in one city may be financed from fees in another. Expenditures present a more complex problem because the types and amounts of state transfer payments vary from state to state according to state laws, the division of governmental labor in a state, the incomes and sizes of cities, not to mention political factors at the state level. We think it important, however, that our independent variables explain a large proportion of the variation in municipal outputs as we measured them. No doubt one could explain an even larger proportion of the variation in measures which specify different functional responsibilities of cities. At least these measures constitute a starting point, and we hope others will improve on them.

The source of our output measures was the *County and City Data Book*.

22. See, for example, Robert Alford and Harry Scoble, "Political and Socio-Economic Characteristics of American Cities," *The Municipal Yearbook 1965*, pp. 82–97; Sherbenou, *Class, Participation;* John H. Kessel, "Governmental Structure and Political Environment," *American Political Science Review*, 56 (September 1962), 615–20.

23. Alford and Scoble, "American Cities." The particularly large differences found between the populations of reform and unreformed cities reflect the fact that New York City and several other urban giants are included in the sample.

24. Wolfinger and Field, "Political Ethos," p. 320.

25. In statistical parlance, the problem with "region" as an independent variable might be described as treating a complicated background variable as the first variable in a specific developmental sequence. But, as Blalock argues, *"one should avoid complex indicators that are related in unknown ways to a given underlying variable.* Geographical region and certain background variables appear to have such undesirable properties": Hubert M. Blalock, *Causal Inferences in Nonexperimental Research* (Chapel Hill: University of North Carolina Press, 1964), p. 164 (italics in original).

26. Amos Hawley, "Community Power and Urban Renewal Success," *American Journal of Sociology*, 68 (January 1963), 422–31.

27. See also the exchange between Banfield and Wilson and Wolfinger and Field in "Communications," *American Political Science Review*, 60 (December 1966), 998–1000.

28. Sherbenou, *Class, Participation*, pp. 133–34.

29. *Ibid.*, p. 139.

30. Quoted in Banfield and Wilson, *City Politics*, p. 154.

31. For a discussion of the concept of interest aggregation, see Gabriel Almond, "Introduction: A Functional Approach to Comparative Politics," in Gabriel Almond and James S. Coleman (eds.), *The Politics of Developing Areas* (Princeton, N.J.: Princeton University Press, 1960), pp. 38–45.

32. Maurice Duverger, *Political Parties* (New York: Science Editions, 1963), p. 378.

33. Frank J. Sorauf, *Political Parties in the American System* (Boston: Little, Brown, 1964), pp. 165–66.

34. Gerald Pomper, "Ethnic and Group Voting in Nonpartisan Municipal Elections," *Public Opinion Quarterly*, 30 (Spring 1966), p. 90; see also J. Leiper Freeman, "Local Party Systems: Theoretical Considerations and a Case Analysis," *American Journal of Sociology*, 64 (1958), 282–89.

35. It is possible that the difference between any two correlations may be a function of very different standard deviations of the independent variables. A quick look at Table 2, however, suggests that this is not likely to affect the relationships we find.

36. Wolfinger and Field, "Political Ethos," p. 312. "Omit the commission cities from consideration since this form does not figure in the ethos theory." Historically, however, commission government was the earliest of the structures advocated by the Progressives and is quite clearly a product of the reform era. While history tells us that commission cities can not legitimately be excluded from the fold of reformism, they appear to be its black sheep, characterized by low incomes, low population growth, and large proportions of nonwhites. In fact, they present a marked contrast to both mayor-council and manager cities.

37. Agger *et al.*, *Rulers and the Ruled*, pp. 4–14.

38. Charles A. Beard, *American Government and Politics*, 4th ed. (New York: The Macmillan Company, 1924), p. 727.

39. V. O. Key, *Public Opinion and American Democracy* (New York: Alfred A. Knopf, 1961), p. 124.

40. Wilson and Banfield, *City Politics*, p. 876. Footnote 5 in the same article conveniently summarized research supporting this proposition.

41. Eugene S. Uyeki, "Patterns of Voting in a Metropolitan Area: 1938–1962," *Urban Affairs Quarterly*, 1 (June 1966), 65–77.

42. Banfield and Wilson, *City Politics*, p. 35.

43. Richard E. Dawson and James A. Robinson, "The Politics of Welfare," in Herbert Jacob and Kenneth Vines (eds.), *Politics in the American States* (Boston: Little, Brown, 1965), pp. 398–401.

44. Raymond Wolfinger, "The Development and Persistance of Ethnic Voting," *American Political Science Review*, 59 (December 1965), 896–908.

45. Robert E. Lane, *Political Life* (New York: The Free Press, 1959), pp. 236–43.

46. *Ibid.*

47. Harold Stone, Don K. Price, and Kathryn Stone, *City Manager Government in the United States* (Chicago: Public Administration Service, 1940), p. 238.

48. The standard argument for party responsibility is found in the works of E. E. Schattschneider, especially, *Party Government* (New York: Farrar Rinehart, 1942), and in the report of the Committee on Political Parties of the American Political Science Association, *Toward a More Responsible Two-Party System* (New York: Rinehart, 1950).

49. See Pomper, "Ethnic and Group Voting"; and Freeman, "Local Party Systems."

50. Robert Salisbury and Gordon Black, "Class and Party in Partisan and Nonpartisan Elections: The Case of Des Moines," *American Political Science Review*, 57 (September 1963), 584–92.

51. One newspaperman said of nonpartisan politics that "you can't tell the players without a scorecard, and we sell the scorecards": Banfield and Wilson, *City Politics*, p. 157.

52. Oliver P. Williams and Charles Adrian, *Four Cities* (Philadelphia: University of Pennsylvania Press, 1963), pp. 56–57.

53. Alford and Scoble, "American Cities," p. 84.

54. In our view, the failure of the commission government to achieve the intended reforms is more plausible as an explanation of its demise than its administrative unwieldiness—the conventional explanation.

55. Williams and Adrian, *Four Cities*, pp. 30–31.

56. Carol E. Thometz discusses the role of the "Civic Committee" in decision making in Dallas: see *The Decision-Makers* (Dallas: Southern Methodist University Press, 1963).

THE STUDY OF community decision making and city politics is at the present time a search for the basic relationships—the small number of correlations which are so large and so consistent as to be of prime consideration in any analysis. Thus studies to date have concentrated on isolating the effects of such major factors as the impact of active and inactive civic elites,[1] of weak and strong party structures,[2] and of basic characteristics of the population.[3] In this paper, we advance one basic hypothesis dealing with the effect of the socioeconomic status of the population of the community upon the decision-making process.

Community Status as a Dimension of Local Decision Making*

Robert L. Crain
and Donald B. Rosenthal

Community Socioeconomic Status

In the analysis of the political behavior of individuals, socioeconomic status is an important variable, and it is hardly surprising that the average socioeconomic status of a community should be one of its most important characteristics. Given the differences in political values between higher- and lower-status persons, we might expect the distinguishing values held by local electorates to be the most important difference between high- and low-status communities. In contrast to low-status persons, we expect better educated and wealthier persons to endorse innovation and "progress"; to be more liberal on civil rights and civil liberties issues, to be more "public-regarding" in their attitudes toward government, to support the development of "amenities" such as recreational or cultural facilities, and to favor "reform" in government.[4] These are important differences, but the evidence indicates that there is something more important about the high-status community which often produces a completely unexpected set of outcomes. Highly educated and higher-status citizens are more active in political roles and in their participation in politics[5] and this has important consequences, regardless of what it is they want the government to do.

It seems to us that the "citizens"—persons who have no "special" political resources—influence government almost entirely through collective action. Thus, when we speak of citizen influence on government, we are thinking primarily of the action of organizations such as the PTA, the American Legion, neighborhood associations, fraternal societies, church groups, ethnic organizations, trade unions, amateur political clubs, and occupational associations, where the general membership does not have specialized political resources although individual members may. Among citizen-related groups, we are also including those *ad hoc* and informal groups organized to agitate concerning a particular decision. Thus the county medical society is better thought of as an elite group, rather than a citizens' group, because of the special status which flows to the organization as a result of the expertise of those involved in it.

Well-educated persons, and high-status persons in general, are more interested in politics and better informed; they are more likely to hear about a new issue in local politics. They are also more likely to feel efficacious about their ability to influence decisions, and have the time, money, and skills to participate in an effort to influence those decisions.[6] Finally, they are more likely to be

Reprinted with permission from American Sociological Review, *32 (December 1967), 970–85.*

We wish to thank Amos Hawley and Donald Matthews for permitting secondary analysis of their data, and Bruce C. Straits and David H. Klassen for their able assistance.

members of voluntary organizations which can play political roles. Furthermore, there is a multiplier effect; each person who becomes active in a voluntary organization is a resource who can be used to recruit others.

It follows that one major difference between high-status and low-status communities is the number of voluntary organizations, their size, and the number of people who can be mobilized in a campaign. We have only indirect evidence to support this proposition, but the point is nearly an obvious one. We suggest that this higher level of citizen participation in political activities, and in organizations which can become involved in local decision making, has the following effects:

1. Opposition to the existing government and its policies is easier to mobilize. Granted, the middle-class electorate may have, on the whole, less to gripe about, but they can organize more effectively even around minor grievances.

2. Political campaigns will be more issue-oriented, since the organizations of the middle-class community will often have special interests in particular issues, rather than reflecting generalized dissatisfactions; the groups will call attention to the issues, and also publicize the stands taken by the elected officials. If issues become more important, political leaders will be less able to depend on party or personal loyalty.

3. In all cities it seems likely that citizens' groups react to issues created by others, rather than introduce new issues of their own.[7] It is also easier to organize in opposition to a proposal than to organize in order to support it. The effect of these propositions is to create more opposition in middle-class cities to proposals advanced by the government (or by business or other groups) than in working-class communities.

4. Citizens who are interested and skilled in influencing government will apply pressures to break down the barriers which insulate the government from them; thus we would expect them to favor nonpartisanship, the referendum, and other "reform" measures.[8]

What are likely to be the effects of these

processes upon the men in decision-making positions?

1. One main effect should be to make government officials more cautious, since they will be unable to predict how citizens will respond to anything that they do. They may often perceive the citizenry as more opposed to a particular program than it is in fact, since the opposition will be more easily organized.

2. It is likely that many politicians subscribe to the "what have you done for us lately?" theory; that issue-oriented voters are quicker to punish than to reward; if the public is more or less evenly divided on an issue, the politician will lose votes no matter which side he takes. This leads to additional pressures to remain neutral or to prevent issues from arising.

3. Elected officials will wish to conform to the values of citizen participation by holding public meetings, listening attentively to petitioners, and permitting decisions to be made by referenda.

4. Since party loyalty is weaker, elected officials will themselves be less concerned with party loyalty; they are more likely to go to the mass media, or to publicize their position when it wins them votes, thereby increasing public discussion and controversy.

5. If an issue does arise and become controversial, the pressures on elected officials to remain neutral will increase; hence a controversial issue is more likely to result in nothing being done.

Taken together, this adds up to the following statement of relationships: Middle-class cities will have a less stable government, will be less willing to embark on controversial programs, and, when they do attempt to innovate, there will be higher levels of community debate and hence higher levels of controversy and a greater possibility of stalemate. In contrast, in low-status cities, citizens are less readily able to mobilize to influence the decision-making process; this may result in either government by a traditional political machine, or in a government heavily influenced by the local economic elite; but in any case there should be less controversy, and few programs, once begun, will be sidetracked. The data to be presented below support this interpretation, but with one important deviation: the argument does not apply to the cities with the very highest level of education. We shall consider that problem after we have examined the data.

There is some support in the literature for the present viewpoint.[9] Amos Hawley advances essentially the same argument when he says that high-status cities have more difficulty implementing urban renewal plans because power is more decentralized.[10] Many of these points are related to those advanced by Berelson, when he argues that apathy and seemingly blind party loyalty are functional for political stability.[11] Gusfield, in his critique of pluralist theories of democracy, points out the ways in which citizens' associations may serve to increase conflict and political extremism.[12] This does not mean that the mass society theory, as advanced by Kornhauser,[13] is directly in disagreement with our position: there is no disagreement with the proposition that unorganized mass participation can lend itself to extremism, but only concerning whether a large number of strong voluntary citizens' groups actually insulate the government and the voters from each other, as Kornhauser's pluralistic society model proposes.

In addition, David Greenstone and Paul Peterson find, in their current study of the poverty program in the four largest cities of the United States, that the weaker the political party organization, the slower the city is in obtaining federal funds; this supports our idea that such cities are likely to be "inefficient" in their decision-making processes.[14]

Urban Renewal

It seems clear that the "establishment" benefits from urban renewal. Businessmen concerned with saving the central business district, city fathers trying to keep the property tax base up, and developers looking for sites, all profit in obvious ways; both the elected public official and the government administrator are provided with a chance to demonstrate their ability in a highly visible

way. Given the possible ways that a city can provide matching funds, it also seems clear that, for many cities, the costs of an urban renewal project can be nearly zero. It is harder to say who pays for all the benefits, other than the person who pays federal income tax; but certainly the slum dweller and the owner of a home in a conservation area may think he is coming out on the short end. In the low-status city, the government and various elites will be able to arrive at an acceptable program and push it through; but in the high-status city, we argue that citizens' groups will be organized—some to protest the dangers of integration, others to complain about the failure to allow for Negro relocation, still others to prevent demolition of their own neighborhood, and others to complain about creeping socialism. The government program will be in danger of sinking under the weight of controversy.

Amos Hawley has already made this argument, saying that high socioeconomic status implies a decentralization of power. Since his presentation of data has been criticized, it is worthwhile presenting his data in a slightly different way.[15] The problem raised involves the possibility of a spurious correlation; high-status cities probably have less need for urban renewal, since a high-status population is probably living in better housing. Since the Census of Housing does not provide a perfect indicator of need for urban renewal, it is difficult to decide whether the association between community status and urban renewal "success" is causal or spurious.

The data are based upon 763 cities, all over 15,000 in population, and all in states which had enabling legislature for urban renewal during the period of study. Educational attainment is measured by the percentage of the population with four years of college, grouped into five categories. Of the 763 cities, 308 officially entered the urban renewal program. However, by 1962 (when these data were gathered), only 62 percent of the 308 had completed their first urban renewal project; and 42 cities (14 percent) had withdrawn from the program. In terms of our argument (and Hawley's), these "dropout" cities are important, since it is here that the impact of community opposition was apparently most successful. However, it is also true that the inability of a city to complete its first urban renewal project by 1962 suggests some impediment in the decision-making process, and, finally, some cities faced with citizen opposition may have chosen not to enter the program at all. Thus, all three indicators—entry, completion, and dropout—can be used as tests of our hypothesis.

As expected, well-educated cities are less likely to become involved in urban renewal: γ (entry, education) $= -.16$. Obviously, this could be because cities with well-educated populations simply have fewer slums or decaying business areas requiring renewal. Therefore, in order to test this alternative hypothesis, the size of the city and the age of its housing are introduced as "control" variables. Size of city reflects not only the opportunity to have slums, since there is more space, but also the presence of a city administration large enough to handle the task of submitting a proposal. Older and larger cities are more likely to have entered the program: γ (entry, housing age) $= +0.32$; γ (entry, size) $= +0.58$. Thus "educational attainment" might simply be a reflection of a factor like age of housing. However, when size and age of housing are used as controls,[16] the association between educational attainment and the probability of entering the urban renewal program decreases only very slightly: γ (entry, education; size, housing age) $= -.15$. Thus we argue that if education were merely a measure of *need* for urban renewal, the partial association, when we control for another measure of need such as age of housing, would necessarily decrease more than it has in this case. We conclude that education measures not need, but ability to act.

There are two other even more convincing approaches. First, if education is only a measure of need, it will have its most decisive impact on whether the city enters the program or not, not on what happens after that. To have entered the program at all asserts a need. But the data disagree; high education

is more strongly associated with dropping out of the program, or with failing to complete the first project by 1962 than it is with entrance. The simple gammas are only γ (dropout, education) $= +0.07$ and γ (completion, education) $= -0.16$, but when we again enter size and age of housing as controls, the partial associations increase and are higher than the association with entrance to the program: γ (dropout, education; size, housing age) $= +0.21$, and γ (completion, education; size, housing age) $= -0.24$, both higher than γ (entry, education; size, housing age).

If, on the other hand, we read education as a measure of the degree of decision-making inefficiency and uncertainty introduced by citizen participation, then the associations behave approximately as expected, at least when size and age are controlled; the well-educated city shows some hesitancy in entering the program, but it is most different from other cities when the time comes to work out the details of a concrete proposal. Citizen participation in the planning process means more opposition, more issues to be negotiated with more people, more chance of failure.

School Boards and School Desegregation in the North

In 1964 and 1965, graduate students were assigned the task of interviewing elites in eight northern cities and preparing case studies of the school desegregation issue.[17] With only eight case studies, and with only a limited amount of "hard" data, the material must be considered impressionistic at best. However, it seems to lend support to our argument, and, more important, it gives us some indication of the nature of the mechanism which links socioeconomic status to styles of decision making. After a series of staff discussions, agreement was reached on a ranking of the eight cities in terms of three variables:

Acquiescence is the extent to which the school system met the demands of the civil rights movement, both symbolic and "real";

the acquiescent school board was one which committed itself verbally to integration, treated the civil rights leaders with relatively little antagonism, and also adopted an integration program which numerically increased the number of students in integrated schools.

School Board Cohesiveness is the extent of agreement and cooperation among board members; it is based upon our knowledge of the public controversies, and upon the individual board member's response to sociometric questions, and his rating of how much agreement there is among the board members.

Strength of Political Parties is a measure of the ability of the parties' leadership to control party nominations for office; again it is measured impressionistically.

The socioeconomic status of the population (measured by the percent of the population who are high school graduates) is negatively associated with acquiescence; the Spearman rank-order correlation coefficient was − 0.46.

Why should cities with high-status populations be less likely to have school boards which acquiesce to the civil rights movement? Figure 1 presents the argument schematically. First, high-status cities tend to have weak political parties. (This rank correlation is − 0.77; although it may be exaggerated because of the poor quality of our measure of party strength, the association is strong.) The city with weak political parties has a school board which is generally more heterogeneous in social background than

that in a low-status city. The argument is simply that a weak political party deprives the government of freedom from public opinion—which may take the form of demanding ethnic representation, or anti-integration appointments, and which may change from one year to the next. Granted, a government which is insulated from the voters may use its freedom to appoint party hacks, but it may also appoint civic leaders; whichever it does, it will at least appoint a homogeneous board whose members can work together. Thus the presence of weak political parties is associated with low levels of school board cohesion, although, again, the rank-order correlation, − 0.90, is likely to be exaggerated. In addition, a high-status and participative public encourages intraboard conflict, since there is a ready audience for the ambitious board member and a following available for any member who wishes to rebel. The correlation between socioeconomic status of the city and board cohesion is − 0.74, but there is no association between the socioeconomic status of the city and the status of the school board.

To make the final link in the chain of causation, cohesive boards are much more acquiescent than boards with internal dissension. The main reason for this seems to be that the cohesive board can thrash out disagreement in the backroom rather than in public, and thus can avoid mobilizing the anti-integrationists. The cohesive board can ignore the wishes of the public. Granted it is possible for an extremely conservative but

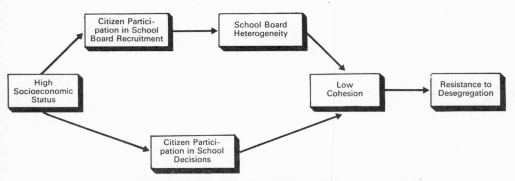

Figure 1. Schematic Presentation of Relation of Community Socioeconomic Status to Outcome of School Desegregation Issues in Northern Cities

cohesive board to refuse to acquiesce, but it would be rare indeed for a school board to be more conservative than the average white citizen; all of the school boards studied were more liberal than whites in general, on comparable questionnaire items.[18] Although school board members' attitudes are more important than board cohesion in determining acquiescence, cohesion is strongly correlated with acquiescence: $r = +.71$. The least acquiescent boards have had histories of severe conflict on other issues and close votes on the appointment of superintendents.

The Civil Rights Movement

The school desegregation study also collected information on the civil rights movement in each city. The civil rights movement is a special case of the mobilization of citizens to influence government. Our principal hypothesis is that the higher the status of the population, the more easily mobilized it is. This should result in a larger number of civil rights organizations, and more civil rights activity.

In general, the greater the competition between groups and individuals in the movement, the more militant the leadership—a completely unsurprising finding. The greatest competition seems to be in the two cities which have traditional political machines; the conflict is of course between the "establishment" and the direct action groups. If these two cities are excluded, a correlation ($r = 0.61$) appears between the socioeconomic status of the Negro population and militancy, in the remaining six cities, apparently because of the higher level of competition between civil rights groups and leaders in the high-status cities. The high-status cities also have civil rights movements which are more symbol-oriented, and more concerned with citywide issues; this is consistent with our image of the high-status community as one which is more responsive to ideological appeals, and which is more easily mobilized in support of vague or abstract "public-regarding" goals. In the South, data were gathered on only six cities, and

the differences between such cities as Montgomery, Alabama, and Miami, Florida, are so extreme as to make comparison difficult. However, it is true that high-status southern Negro communities tend to have more highly organized civil rights movements, more competition, a higher level of civil rights activity, and more ambitious goals—a pattern which is consistent with the northern data.

Falling Between Two Stools

Whether a compromise is a happy medium or whether it falls between two stools, folk wisdom warns us that many relationships are curvilinear. The data to be presented in the remainder of this paper are consistent with those presented earlier, except that in almost every case there is a reversal at the extreme upper tail of the distribution. Can we argue that if we only increase the educational level and the level of citizen participation enough, it will at some point begin to strengthen the structure of government, rather than continue to make it more unstable and susceptible to public opinion? We think so, although the argument is not an obvious one.

Both William Kornhauser and James S. Coleman have argued that citizen participation in voluntary associations brings stability to government, and prevents rancorous conflict.[19] We would modify that proposition to read that citizen participation *at a high and stable level* in formal associations has this effect, while moderate and irregular participation has the unstabilizing consequence described in the earlier section of this paper. We further argue that a high and stable level of participation occurs in only very highly educated communities.

Consider, for example, Rossi and Dentler's description of Hyde Park in Chicago, or William Whyte's description of Park Forest as examples of extremely high levels of education.[20] Citizen participation in these communities is very high—so high, in fact, that organizations which in other communities might have highly fluctuating memberships and a doubtful future at any time will be able to operate in a more permanent fashion. In addition, the number of organizations in the community should be greater. We think this has two important implications.

1. Channels of contact between the citizens and the government are regularized. Continued contact over a period of time between stable groups and the government tends to produce an accommodation between them: political leaders find it easy to check political actions out in advance with representatives of these groups, and the opportunity for negotiation and compromise is greater. Over a period of time, the general point of view, or values, of government officials will be closer to that of the population as a result of this contact.[21]

2. The response of the public will be predictable. The main reason for this is that, when a problem comes up, particular organizations already exist to take positions (few issues will require new organizations, although they may encourage the formation of groups representing coalitions between pre-existing groups); since groups are reasonably permanent, they have an established and relatively stable leadership and a partially articulated ideology which will determine their response. There are other reasons, as follows: (1) Since much of the population is already participating in local political organizations, there is less possibility of a revolt led by people who are relatively inactive in the community. Borrowing Kornhauser's and Coleman's words, the ratio of unattached but "available" people to those already attached is probably lower in very high-status cities. It is more difficult to subvert existing organizations, and also harder to form new ones, since there are fewer organizational vacuums to fill. (2) The leadership is more stable, since it is more highly developed, has more permanent bases of support, and is generally better known in the community. (3) The existing organizations can be used to exert influence, and even discipline, on their own members and on the rest of the community; its leadership will have more political experience, and more skills in developing support for their position. (4) It is assumed in these communities that

the poitison of the citizenry is known. People take it for granted that their city is liberal, pro-education, and anti–urban renewal. In fact a random sample of the population may not find much support for this conventional wisdom, but, if the participation level of the community has been high for a long period of time, it is likely that battles between opposing groups have been fought "to a finish" already, and the issue assumed settled.[22] (5) Existing organizations can be used by the government to communicate and exert influence on the citizens.

Neither of these points is very original; several have been stated in different form by either Coleman or Kornhauser. Our point of departure from their argument is that these conditions hold only when the population is *highly mobilized*. If many people in the community are willing to participate, but there are not enough to maintain a rather complete set of permanent and stable organizations, then not all these conditions will hold. Instead, when a new issue comes up, an existing organization may find its membership suddenly becoming more active and new leaders coming forth; the ideological position of the group may be subject to change. Or a new group may be organized, making its claim to be the group to specialize in a particular area, and previously unknown persons may become important leaders. Furthermore, it is more likely in these cities that the government will be out of touch with the population to a greater extent, and less able to use the structure of voluntary associations to develop support for its proposals. Of course, at the other extreme, the government of a very low-status community may take positions which are at variance with the population values but, if the community lacks the resources to organize in opposition, the government need not pay much attention.[23]

Fluoridation Controversies

Fluoridation — the addition of small amounts of fluoride to the public drinking water to reduce tooth decay among children

TABLE 1. *Decisions on Fluoridation by Community Educational Level**

DECISIONS	MEDIAN EDUCATIONAL LEVEL				
	8 years or less	9 years	10 years	11 years	12 years or more
Percent of cities adopting fluoridation without referenda	41	39	37	22	39
(N)	(63)	(99)	(100)	(66)	(66)
Of all other cities, percent holding referenda	29	26	38	46	32
(N)	(37)	(60)	(73)	(51)	(47)
Percent of cities with mayors publicly supporting fluoridation	61	64	57	45	57
(N)	(63)	(88)	(95)	(61)	(52)

*All data indirectly standardized (Stouffer's method)[25] by region.

—is a good test of our thesis.[24] Almost universally endorsed by the medical profession with the strong support of the federal government, and with few local government officials actually opposed to it, fluoridation has still had an unfortunate history of controversy and defeat. Apparently, it is the sort of program which is expendable if there is public opposition.

The data were gathered by a mail survey of public health officers, city clerks, and newspaper publishers in 1,086 American cities of over 10,000 population. The health officers, when asked, almost never said that public officials declined to support fluoridation because of their uncertainty about its medical effects; they did claim that unfavorable officials were concerned about public opposition. This, then, is a good test of the influence of public opinion on the government. National surveys have shown that well-educated persons are considerably more favorable to fluoridation than persons with low levels of education; our theory was developed because we found that the correlation for communities runs exactly counter to this, as shown in Table 1. In general, high-status cities are less likely to adopt fluoridation, and more likely to hold a referendum on the issue—except for the extreme upper group, which is more likely to adopt and less likely to hold a referendum. The data are standardized indirectly, to remove the differences between the four regions of the

TABLE 2. *Community Educational Level and Opposition Activity in Fluoridation Decisions*

OPPOSITION ACTIVITY	Educational Level					
	REFERENDA CAMPAIGNS			GOVERNMENTAL DECISIONS		
	9 years or less	10 years	11 years or more	9 years or less	10 years	11 years or more
Percent of cities with opposition literature	68	86	92	39	47	54
(N)	(40)	(36)	(52)	(179)	(111)	(124)
Percent of cities with opposition speakers (of all cities with meetings)	77	87	94	67	68	77
(N)	(35)	(31)	(47)	(109)	(69)	(90)
Percent of cities with imported opposition speakers (of all cities with opposition speakers)	56	56	71	55	62	64
(N)	(27)	(27)	(44)	(73)	(47)	(69)

country—the South, East, Midwest, and West. Observe that, since the percentage of cities holding referenda is based only upon nonadopting cities, it is statistically independent of the adoption rate; thus the data represent two independent findings. The last line of the table indicates that the proportion of mayors favoring fluoridation follows the same curve, mayors becoming less favorable as education increases until we reach the top group. This should not be read as independent evidence, however, since the mayor's position is very strongly associated with the outcome.

We have some data to clarify the mechanism which translates high educational attainment into defeats for fluoridation. In Table 2, we see one reason why well-educated cities have more difficulty with fluoridation; they simply have more opposition. The data are based upon the reports of the health officer; the limited number of cases means that we cannot separate out the extreme upper tail in this table or the next one. Since the antifluoridation movement uses a national (indeed, international) network of spokesmen, the use of imported talent is a measure of the sophistication of the opposition, just as is the use of printed literature and of public speakers.

Not only are well-educated cities more likely to have opposition, the government is more responsive to the opposition. The three indicators of level of opposition in Table 2 are combined in Table 3 into a single dichotomy, and the effect of opposition in cities of varying levels of education is examined. Whether one considers the prevention of administrative adoption, or the precipitation of a referendum, opposition has its greatest impact in high-status cities, as reflected in the percentage differences in the last line of each half of the table. Thus the data indicate that high-status cities have more citizen influence, are more responsive to that influence, and, in the case of fluoridation, the effect is strong enough to overcome the fact that high-status cities have populations which were initially more favorable to adoption.

Referenda Outcomes. The theory of the impact of level of education can be extended

to include referenda outcome as well. First, if fluoridation referenda are typical of all referenda, a referendum held after a political campaign is not simply a public opinion poll; the positions taken by government officials and by various organizations are important to the outcome. In addition, we would argue that the typical voter responds to high levels of noise from his fellow citizens in much the

TABLE 3. Community Educational Level, Opposition Activity, and Fluoridation Outcome*

Opposition Activity	Percent of Cities Adopting Administratively		
	EDUCATIONAL LEVEL		
	9 years or less	10–11 years	12 years or more
High	23	19	17
(N)	(70)	(109)	(44)
Low	37	36	38
(N)	(110)	(100)	(22)
Difference	−14	−17	−21
Opposition Activity	Percent of Cities Holding Referenda		
	EDUCATIONAL LEVEL		
	9 years or less	10–11 years	12 years or more
High	17	23	24
(N)	(70)	(109)	(44)
Low	11	10	6
(N)	(110)	(100)	(22)
Difference	+8	+13	+18

*Data standardized by region.

same way that the government official does— namely, by becoming confused and hesitant to support something "controversial." The hypothesis was tested on three types of referenda, as reported by city clerks in the fluoridation study; fluoridation votes, votes on school bonds or taxes, and votes on the last other referendum for public improvements. As Table 4 indicates, the school bond results do not fit the theory; they simply show that well-educated cities are slightly more likely to support the schools. The other

TABLE 4.   Community Educational Level and Referenda Results *

REFERENDA RESULTS	MEDIAN EDUCATION				
	8 years or less	9 years	10 years	11 years	12 years or more
Percent of school board referenda receiving less than 60% "yes" vote	62	44	54	50	45
(N)	(32)	(26)	(45)	(29)	(30)
Percent of other bond referenda receiving less than 60% "yes" vote	48	53	57	56	46
(N)	(47)	(46)	(65)	(58)	(64)
Percent of fluoridation referenda resulting in defeat	71	78	76	83	56
(N)	(34)	(53)	(67)	(52)	(53)

*Data standardized by region.

two types of referenda do conform, with the very low- and very high-status cities most likely to vote "yes."

The Structure of Local Politics

Generally speaking, the high-status city is more likely to have a "reformed" government with a city manager and with greater use of referenda, as shown in Table 5.[26] High-status cities are also less likely to use the now unfashionable commission form of government. However, if the high-status city has retained the mayor-council form, it is not more likely to have nonpartisan council elections. High-status cities also hold more referenda. Again, the data have been standardized to remove the effect of region. We are more interested, however, in the informal structure of government; here the curvilinear relation reappears. In the fluoridation survey, the local newspaper publisher was asked, "How influential are political parties in the elections for city council and mayor?" Looking first at partisan mayor-council cities we see that the publisher is more likely to rate the parties as "not too influential" or "not influential at all" in well-educated cities, again with a reversal when we move past a median of eleven years of schooling. When we look at manager and nonpartisan mayor-council cities as a second test, we see exactly the same pattern. In the next two rows we see that, as education increases, the number

of uncontested mayoralty elections declines, again with a reversal at the end, and the number of elections with three or more candidates for mayor increases, again reversing at the end. Thus we have at least four bits of evidence that cities with moderately high levels of education are the ones with the weakest and most open and fluid political structures. Why? We think it is another corollary of the general theory.

We noted at the beginning of the paper that the well-educated population should show more attention to issues, less party loyalty, more support for reform and for direct democracy. So far, so good. But why should very high-status cities have strong parties, uncontested elections, and the absence of third-party candidates? Looking again at our earlier discussion of the effect of very high levels of education and citizen participation, we see that several of the points made there would lead us to predict a greater structuring of politics in these cities. Political parties can be stronger because they have greater volunteer resources, because the leadership is better known, and because the leadership has a denser network of organizational affiliations to work through. There is also less danger of the party producing the sort of completely unacceptable candidate whose presence weakens party loyalty. And opposition may be suppressed because an organizational monolith has captured the available contributors and volunteer workers, or has permitted the incumbent to build

TABLE 5. *Community Educational Level and Political Structure*

POLITICAL STRUCTURE	EDUCATION LEVEL				
	8 years or less	9 years	10 years	11 years	12 years or more
Percent of cities with city manager government*	30	43	46	59	55
(N)	(229)	(259)	(259)	(166)	(174)
Percent of cities using commission governments*	20	14	14	13	12
(N)	(229)	(259)	(259)	(166)	(174)
Percentage of mayor-council cities with nonpartisan elections*	41	44	25	49	36
(N)	(113)	(120)	(110)	(58)	(50)
Percent of cities holding a referendum in past 12 years*	44	49	47	54	54
(N)	(129)	(136)	(159)	(104)	(112)
Of cities holding referenda, percent who held 6 or more in 12 years*	37	33	47	55	57
(N)	(53)	(64)	(74)	(58)	(62)
Percent of partisan mayor-council cities with "weak" parties	14	32	58	67	50
(N)	(22)	(22)	(31)	(9)	(8)
Percent of manager and nonpartisan mayor-council cities with "weak" parties	53	44	67	67	60
(N)	(36)	(43)	(60)	(48)	(60)
Percent of cities with uncontested mayoralty elections*	19	16	13	16	29
(N)	(72)	(71)	(76)	(45)	(49)
Percent of cities with 3 or more candidates in last mayoralty elections*	12	15	27	29	19
(N)	(72)	(71)	(76)	(45)	(49)

*Data standardized by region.

a strong following. One case comes immediately to mind: the ward surrounding the University of Chicago was the only one of fifty in Chicago where the incumbent alderman was unopposed in 1967—despite the considerable heterogeneity of the area, which includes low-income Negroes and wealthy whites as well as University faculty and students. The incumbent alderman, whose base has been the local precinct organization affiliated with Americans for Democratic Action, was formally endorsed by both the Republican and Democratic parties, despite the fact that the incumbent is highly controversial, and is the white alderman of a ward which has a very large Negro population. In this case, it seems reasonable that the willingness of the middle-class residents to partici-

pate at a very high level in amateur politics—and their loyalty to the independent party—has resulted in the growth of the functional equivalent of a political machine, has made it possible for the incumbent to be very well known in his ward, and has created a political climate which in another time or place might be called oppressively conformist.

Negro Registration in Southern Counties

The next case is possibly the most difficult one to argue. One assumes that the governments of southern counties are strongly opposed to the registration of Negroes. But if this is so, one must inquire why there are

Negroes registered in the South at all? If some counties have been quite successful in disenfranchising the Negro despite the federal government, why have others not been as fortunate? When we consider the problem, it becomes clear that there are reasons why a local government might not resist a Negro registration drive: it may need Democratic votes; it may need to gain the support of Negro elites; it may believe the Negro vote to be deliverable in local elections; it may find resistance simply more trouble than it is worth. Whatever the case in any particular county, it does seem clear that if a prospective Negro registrant were given his choice of submitting his application to the local registrar of voters, or to a referendum vote by his already enfranchised fellow citizens, he would surely choose to take his chances with the former. If, then, the citizens are more strongly opposed than the government to Negro registration, we predict, consistently with the other material presented, that the higher the educational level of the whites in the county, the more reluctant the government will be to permit Negro registration. This curious generalization is precisely the finding of Matthews and Prothro. We cannot improve very much on their explanation of the finding: "The higher the average education of the whites in a county, the more actively and effectively they seem to enforce the traditional mores of the region against Negro participation in elections. An increase in average schooling for whites in the South

seems to give them more of the skills they need to effectively express their anti-Negro sentiment."[27] They go on to note that white citizens' councils are more common in counties with higher levels of education, as an example of this. We had reexamined their data, and have standardized them to remove the interstate variation in Negro registration rates; this does not affect the pattern (see Table 6). Note that one half of the cases fall in the lowest-education group, which has the highest registration rate; above this point the curve is flat at the lower level. The data presented by Matthews and Prothro show that the counties with highest education have a slightly higher registration rate, but this finding disappears when state differences are removed by standardization.

Matthews and Prothro noted that segregationist organizations are more common in high-status counties; even when the data are standardized, this effect remains quite pronounced. This is as predicted by our argument, of course. More surprising, however, is the fact that incidents of racial violence are reported much more frequently from highly educated cities. The sources for these data are the *New York Times*, the *Southern Educational Reporting Service*, and the Southern Regional Council. It is possible that there is considerable over-reporting of incidents in high-status communities, but the relationship is so strong that we have included it despite our qualms about journalistic sources. Again, we argue that high levels

*TABLE 6. Educational Attainment of White Population and Political Characteristics of Southern Counties**

POLITICAL CHARACTERISTICS	MEDIAN YEARS OF SCHOOLING OF WHITES				
	8 years or less	9 years	10 years	11 years	12 years or more
Percent of Negroes registered to vote	34	27	28	28	28
Percent of counties with segregationist organization	15	27	30	34	38
Percent of counties with racial violence reported	6	8	18	23	40
Mean percent of votes for Strom Thurmond for President, 1948	23	27	28	29	23
(*N*)	(520)	(275)	(123)	(57)	(23)

*Data standardized by region.

of literacy, willingness to participate in community affairs, and organizational skill make it easier to mobilize the human resources necessary to throw rocks at schoolchildren, or burn a cross. At a minimum, a sufficiently dense network of association to permit likeminded persons to organize informally for social support would seem to be a necessity.

In the last row of this table we see another curvilinear relationship, although not a very strong one: the lowest and highest educated counties gave the fewest votes to Strom Thurmond's States' Rights candidacy. Our argument is simply that in these counties social control mechanisms to maintain loyalty to the national parties were most successful. It is in the moderately well-educated counties that the candidate who best represented the values of the citizenry was most successful.

Two Alternative Explanations

These data seem to lend little support to the most obvious alternative explanation—that the differences in the behavior of communities of differing status levels lie in the differences in the values of the residents, with the governments of middle-class cities doing "middle-class" things, while working-class cities produce working-class governmental outcomes. In the case of fluoridation, Negro voter registration, school desegregation, and probably urban renewal and bonds for municipal improvements, the correlation at the community level is the opposite of that at the individual level. The data strongly suggest that the community is a good deal more than the sum of its parts.

What about the reversal which sometimes occurs at the high end of the educational scale? It could be argued that, in the case of fluoridation, for example, the greater support for fluoridation among especially well-educated persons is sufficient to overcome the debilitating effects of high levels of citizen participation. But, in the case of party structure, we see no way in which the reversal at the high end of the scale could be attributed to the values of well-educated people: cer-

tainly, we see no reason why well-educated people should disapprove of three-way mayoralty races, or approve of uncontested elections and strong political parties.

A more difficult objection to deal with is the point that the cities at both extremes are more homogeneous and, accordingly, similar to each other and different from cities in the middle. The argument might go as follows: heterogeneity causes dissension and conflict, and conflict tends to make it difficult for the government to act. The hypothesis seems quite reasonable on its face—although no more so than the one we have advanced—but there are two problems. First, how do we explain the ability of city governments to act contrary to the wishes of a homogeneous public—for example, in registering voters in the poorest counties of the South? Second, we could determine at what median educational level the population is most heterogeneous in education only if we assume that education is a metric scale measuring social status—that the difference between 5 and 6 years of schooling is as important as the difference between 12 and 13 years. Without this assumption, there is no obvious argument which would establish that cities with a median educational level of 8 years are in fact more homogeneous in social status than a city with a median of 11 years.

The one important exception to our argument is Minar's[28] findings, and our own, regarding conflict over schools. Recall that we found that well-educated communities are more likely to approve school bonds. David Minar studied a group of Chicago suburbs, and found not only more favorable votes on school bond and tax referenda, but less competition in school board elections in the higher status suburbs. No doubt there are issues which are exceptions to our hypothesis, although we are disappointed that school board selection should be one of them. However, Minar's data are limited to a group of suburban school systems near Chicago; it may be that many of them are in the upper end of the educational distribution where the "reversal" might be in effect. At this time, we can only report that there is at least one apparent exception to our hypothesis.

Conclusions

If examples of the ecological fallacy (the inability to generalize from group data to individuals) are difficult to find, examples of what we might call the contextual fallacy (the inability to predict group action from the characteristics of individuals) are apparently common.

We have examined eight different community issues and found twenty-two cases which support our hypothesis that a city with a well-educated population is partly immobilized by high levels of citizen participation which prevent the government from exercising the authority to make decisions. In addition, we have found in ten of these cases a reversal at the high end of the educational distribution, where, we argue, the educational level is high enough to permit a decision-making process in which citizens play structured, consistent, and predictable roles.

No doubt there are certain issues in which the effect is different from the one shown here. We do not make any prediction, for example, about noncontroversial decisions, and some educational decisions may not follow the pattern of the issues presented here.

It should be observed that this paper only seems to give support to the idea that citizen participation is "bad." Granted the "intelligentsia" would conclude, on many of the issues described here that citizen participation has had unfortunate results—damaging children's teeth and preventing racial equality, for example. But there are no doubt other issues in which widespread citizen participation leads to "good" results. The only value-oriented conclusion one can legitimately draw from these data is a mere tautology: If public officials are going to do the right thing, the people should leave them alone while they do it.

Notes

1. The "power structure" literature is, of course, extensive. For a recent consideration of the polarization in American politics between the civic elite and the working-class (frequently ethnic) politicians, see David L. Westby, "The Civic Sphere in the American City," *Social Forces*, 45 (December 1966), 161–69.

2. Edward C. Banfield, *Political Influence* (New York: The Free Press, 1961); Edward C. Banfield and James Q. Wilson, *City Politics* (Cambridge: Harvard University Press and the M.I.T. Press, 1963); Charles R. Adrian, "Some General Characteristics of Nonpartisan Elections," *American Political Science Review*, 46 (September 1952), 766–76. For our own consideration of this problem in the context of fluoridation outcomes, see Donald B. Rosenthal and Robert L. Crain, "Structure and Values in Local Political Systems," in James Q. Wilson (ed.), *City Politics and Public Policy* (New York: John Wiley, 1968).

3. A summary of this literature and the development of a basis for distinguishing among local issues is available in Lewis A. Froman, "An Analysis of Public Policies in Cities," *Journal of Politics*, 29 (February 1967), 94–108. The present analysis, however, runs somewhat contrary to the argument advanced by Froman.

4. Samuel A. Stouffer, *Communism, Conformity and Civil Liberties* (Garden City, N.Y.: Doubleday, 1955); S. M. Lipset, *Political Man* (Garden City, N.Y.: Doubleday, 1960); Banfield and Wilson, *City Politics*.

5. Robert E. Lane, *Political Life* (New York: The Free Press, 1959), especially pp. 220–34; Lester Milbrath, *Political Participation* (Chicago: Rand McNally, 1965), pp. 114–28.

6. Most measures of alienation find that working-class persons score more highly. This may be due to a variety of factors, but the relationship with feelings of inefficacy and estrangement are clear.

7. We would hypothesize that middle-class communities are more readily structured to encourage bureaucratic professionals to initiate policy than are working-class communities. The result would be the kind of policy initiation base discussed by Banfield, in his *Political Influence*.

8. Froman, "Analysis of Public Policies in Cities."

9. Banfield and Wilson touch on this theme repeatedly in their works. In addition to *Political Influence* and *City Politics*, see James Q. Wilson, *The Amateur Democrat* (Chicago: University of Chicago Press, 1962).

10. Amos H. Hawley, "Community Power and Urban Renewal Success," *American Journal of Sociology*, 68 (January 1963), 422–31.

11. Bernard R. Berelson, Paul F. Lazarsfeld, and William N. McPhee, *Voting* (Chicago: University of Chicago Press, 1954).

12. Joseph R. Gusfield, "Mass Society and Extremist Politics," *American Sociological Review*, 27 (February 1962), 19–30.

13. William Kornhauser, *The Politics of Mass Society* (New York: The Free Press, 1957).

14. J. David Greenstone and Paul Peterson, "Reformers, Machines and the War on Poverty," in Wilson (ed.), *City Politics and Public Policy*.

15. Hawley, "Community Power"; Bruce C. Straits, "Community Adoption and Implementation of Urban Renewal," *American Journal of Sociology*, 71 (July 1965), 77–82.

16. The partial gamma is computed by taking the weighted average of the γ's in the subtables, using the total number of cases as the weight in each case.

17. The present section is based on a study reported in Robert L. Crain, *The Politics of School Desegregation* (Chicago: Aldine, 1968).

18. For example, 91 percent of the school board members disagreed with the statement, "White people have the right to keep Negroes out of their neighborhood if they want to, and Negroes should respect that right," compared to only 43 percent of the national population. The last figure is from Donald J. Treiman, "Status Discrepancy and Prejudice," *American Journal of Sociology*, 69 (May 1966), 651–64.

19. James S. Coleman, *Community Conflict* (New York: The Free Press, 1957).

20. Peter H. Rossi and Robert A. Dentler, *The Politics of Urban Renewal* (New York: The Free Press, 1962); William S. Whyte, *The Organization Man* (New York: Simon & Schuster, 1956).

21. To some extent, this argument may appear to run counter to the view of those who suggest that issues each have their individual spheres of action and individual actors. However, we are merely indicating that, while arenas may or may not differ, participation across-the-board by the public is more important in high-status communities.

22. At least in the few really high-status "participative" communities of the kind we are discussing here, it is likely that issues have not so much been suppressed as that the important parameters of the system have been regularly tested and that no elements capable of changing it have entered that system to cause its general reorientation. At lower levels of organization and education, problems of issue suppression described by Bachrach and Baratz, or Agger, Goldrich, and Swanson, might arise. Peter Bachrach and Morton S. Baratz, "Two Faces of Power," *American Political Science Review*, 56 (December 1962), 947–52; Robert E. Agger, Daniel Goldrich, and Bert E. Swanson, *The Rulers and the Ruled* (New York: John Wiley, 1964).

23. This argument has ramifications for other levels of political systems as well, if we accept the general proposition that greater citizen participation and political differentiation results in unstable or conflict-prone political life.

24. For a full report of that study see Robert L. Crain, Elihu Katz, and Donald B. Rosenthal, *The Politics of Community Conflict* (Indianapolis: Bobbs-Merrill, 1967).

25. Samuel A. Stouffer, "Standardization of Rates when Specific Rates are Unknown," in A. J. Jaffe (ed.), *Handbook of Statistical Methods for Demographers*, pp. 65–70.

26. These data are from the *Municipal Year Book* (Chicago: International City Managers' Association) (annual), for the cities in the fluoridation study.

27. Donald R. Matthews and James W. Prothro, *Negroes and the New Southern Politics* (New York: Harcourt, Brace & World, 1966), p. 128.

28. David W. Minar, "The Community Basis of Conflict in School System Politics," *American Sociological Review*, 31 (December 1966), 822–34.

Governmental Structure, Urban Environment, and Educational Policy*

Thomas R. Dye

ONE OF THE CENTRAL CONCERNS of political science is the identification of the forces shaping public policy, and this includes educational policy. Policy outcomes in education express important value commitments of a political system and these commitments are dependent variables which political science must endeavor to explain. Mounting concern over the achievements of public education, particularly the outputs of big-city school systems, accentuate the need for examining policy outcomes in public education. Fortunately, the mutual isolation of education and political science is rapidly breaking down, and it is possible to bring some of the conceptual tools of political science to a study of the forces shaping educational policy outcomes in the nation's major school systems.

The purpose of the research reported below was to explore some of the determinants of educational outcomes in sixty-seven of the nation's large cities. Specifically, we wished to assess the impact of the structure of city government and the structure of city school systems on education outcomes, and to compare the effect of these structural variables on educational outcomes with the effect of urban environmental variables. For example, does it make any significant

Thomas R. Dye, "Governmental Structure, Urban Environment, and Educational Policy." Reprinted from Midwest Journal of Political Science, 11 (1967), 353–80, by permission of the Wayne State University Press.

*This research was supported in part by a grant from the U.S. Office of Education and in part by the Office of General Research at the University of Georgia. I am grateful for the assistance given by Mr. Alfred K. Barr in preparing statistical materials for this research.

difference in educational outcomes whether the school board is elected or appointed, or whether school board members are selected by ward or at-large? Are school taxes or expenditures significantly affected by whether or not tax assessors are elected or appointed, or whether or not the city government exercises budgetary control over the school board? Does it make any difference in educational policy whether city elections are partisan or nonpartisan in character, or whether the city is under a mayor, manager, or commission form of government? Or are educational outcomes primarily a function of the economic character of a city—its size; and wealth; its income, education, and occupational level; and its racial composition?

A Model for the Analysis of Education Policy

Let us construct a variation of the Easton model to conceptualize the determinants of educational outcomes in the nation's cities.[1] We shall conceive of educational outcomes as the product of "inputs" brought to bear upon a "system" causing it to produce particular "outputs."

The value of Easton's model lies in the questions that it poses:

1. What are the significant dimensions of educational inputs, school systems, and educational outputs?
2. How do environmental inputs affect educational system structures? (Linkage A)
3. How do environmental inputs affect educational policy outcomes? (Linkage C)
4. How do structural variables affect educational policy outcomes? (Linkage B)
5. How do educational outputs affect, through feedback, system characteristics and inputs? (Linkage D)

This conceptual framework spotlights a central question of this study: Do structural variables in school politics independently influence educational outcomes? Or are educational outcomes determined by environmental variables without regard to structural variables? To state the question in another fashion: Assuming that environmental variables influence both the structure of city politics and educational outcomes, can structural variables be shown to influence educational outcomes once the effects of environmental variables are controlled?[2]

What factors in the urban environment are likely to generate policy demands upon city school systems? There is a great deal of social science literature which views size of a city as a crucial variable in urban affairs. Scott Greer argues effectively that increases in the scale of society bring about profound changes in culture and life style, changes which we should expect to be reflected in educational policy.[3] Even among central cities of metropolitan areas there are vast differences, both qualitative and quantitative, between New York with its eight million inhabitants, and Greenville, South Carolina, with 66,000 inhabitants—differences which result from size alone.

The kinds of demands made upon a school system should also vary according to the felt educational needs of the community and its aspirations for its children. Public opinion about what should go on in public schools should be an important input variable. Yet there is little reliable information about public opinion on school issues, and none which has been collected on a comparative basis for the 67 cities in our sample. Public demands, as specific opinions or attitudes toward the schools, are not easily studied.

In lieu of survey information on public opinion on school issues in all our cities, it was decided to use socioeconomic characteristics which could logically be related to expectations for educational services. For example, adult populations which themselves have attained a high level of education might be expected to seek a high level of educational services for their children. White-collar occupational groups might be expected to demand a kind of education which will enable their offspring to follow them into the middle class, while blue-collar occupation groups may be somewhat less sympathetic toward middle-class educational values. Median family income is obviously a measure of the ability to support education. But since people with higher incomes usually want more and better schooling for their children it can also be treated as a demand variable. Finally, it was also decided to treat the racial character of a city as an input variable for school systems. Even when socioeconomic status is controlled, it is not difficult to postulate a difference in attitude toward schools associated with skin color alone. Large Negro populations suggest the likelihood of segregated schools and a particular stance toward the school system growing out of that segregation. A large Negro population suggests that whites living in the city will hold particular views of the school system based upon the large Negro clientele.

In short, our approach is to use socio-

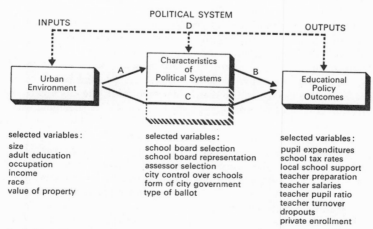

INPUTS	POLITICAL SYSTEM D	OUTPUTS

selected variables:
size
adult education
occupation
income
race
value of property

selected variables:
school board selection
school board representation
assessor selection
city control over schools
form of city government
type of ballot

selected variables:
pupil expenditures
school tax rates
local school support
teacher preparation
teacher salaries
teacher pupil ratio
teacher turnover
dropouts
private enrollment

Figure 1. A Model for the Analysis of Educational Policy Outcomes in American Cities

economic characteristics which on *a priori* grounds appear to be related to demands for educational services. We shall hypothesize that communities of higher socioeconomic status know the value of education, are more sophisticated in judging the quality of educational services, and know how to make their demands felt in the political system. In contrast, communities with people lower on the socioeconomic scale frequently place less value on education, are less able to judge educational services, and are less able to organize themselves to press their demands on the political system.

Associated with demand variables are those factors reflecting ability to finance public education. Inputs must be conceived to include measures of ability, as well as willingness, to support education. Median family income is one measure of ability. Property value plays an even more important role in city school finance. Most school districts in the United States use property taxes as their principal source of local school revenue. The base of these taxes is "assessed value," but the ration between "assessed value" and the true or "full value" of property is a policy outcome of the political system rather than a real limitation on resources. Hence "*full* value of property per pupil" is employed as an index of ability to finance education.

What political system variables should be incorporated into our analysis of educational outcomes? The problem is to guess what governmental arrangements will have an independent effect on educational policy if any. Certainly, the manner of selecting the school board, whether it is elected or appointed, would seem to be an important structural variable. Most city school boards in the United States are elected rather than appointed. In our sample of 67 school systems 54 were elected and only 13 were appointed; this finding parallels the results of more comprehensive surveys of city school districts which show that less than a quarter of the nation's city school boards are appointed.

It is important to note that there is a very significant difference in the social character of cities with appointed and elected school boards. Appointed school boards tend to be found in larger cities with lower socioeconomic populations, large Negro concentrations, and heavy property investment. Appointed school boards are found in New York, Chicago, Philadelphia, Baltimore, Pittsburgh, Birmingham, Jackson, Richmond, Norfolk, Buffalo, San Francisco, Seattle, and Fort Wayne. The populations of these thirteen cities, on the whole, have lower adult education levels, lower family incomes, and lower proportions of white-collar residents than cities with elected school boards. Moreover, these cities, on the whole, have significantly larger nonwhite populations than cities with elected school boards. On a per pupil basis there is also a greater investment in property in these thirteen cities than in cities with elected school boards. Could it be that appointed school boards are found in these cities because appointed boards can better protect heavy property investment from lower socioeconomic groups than elected boards?

The association between these environmental variables and the structure of school boards means that we must control for environmental variables in order to assess the *independent* effect of school board structure on educational policy. Another difficulty in assessing the effect of school board selection is formulating a directional hypothesis regarding the impact of this variable on educational policy. Let us assume that an elected board facilitates the expression of public demands in school policy, while an appointed board hinders public demands in favor of the policies of dominant interests in the city. In other words, let us assume that an elected board better represents voter opinion while an appointed board better represents the opinion of the city's elite. The problem still remains of determining what this means "policywise." If the city's voters are predominantly from low occupational, educational and income groups which lack great interest in education, an appointed board may result in greater educational expenditures and more quality education than one would ordinarily get from an elected board in such a city. On the other hand, if the city's voters are predominantly from middle occupational, educational, and income groups with high educational aspirations for their children, an appointed board may represent large city taxpayers who would keep educational expenditures lower than would be the case if the public had more access to the board.

Similar problems arise in estimating the effect of selecting school boards by wards or at large. Presumably, ward representation, whether elected or appointed, ties the school board member closer to a specific electorate than at-large representation. But the policy effects of this structural arrangement would depend upon the attitude of the electorate toward the public schools.

Since local finance depends heavily upon property assessments, it would seem appropriate to inquire whether an elected or appointed assessor has any impact on school finance. If any directional hypothesis is to be made about this variable, it would be that the effect of electing the assessor would be to keep down school revenue and expenditures. Presumably, an appointed assessor is freer to support schools with higher assessments.

In contrast to school board selection, the structure of school board representation (whether board members are selected by ward or at-large) and the method of selecting the school tax assessor (whether he is appointed or elected) appear unrelated to any of the environmental variables in our model. Only eight of our sixty-seven cities selected school board members by ward—Greenville, Salt Lake City, Dallas, Los Angeles, Springfield, Mass., Minneapolis, Providence, and Atlanta. The ratio in our sample of ward versus at-large representation corresponds to the nationwide ratio.

Whether or not the school board is financially independent of the city would seem to be an important structural variable in school politics, and which would have significant effect upon educational outcomes. The specific variable selected was whether or not a city government agency had the power to alter the school budget after its approval by the school board. Since it is unlikely that the city government would *increase* the school budget over the recommendations of the school board, it can be expected that city oversight of school budgets would have, if anything, a depressing effect on school revenue and expenditures. In contrast, financial independence would be expected to have a positive effect on school revenue and expenditures.

There is a slight tendency for cities with independent school budgets to have populations with higher education, occupation, and income than cities with municipal control over school budgets. There were fifteen cities in our sample in which the city government had review authority over the school board's budget. About a quarter of the nation's city school districts operate under such a structure. Analysis revealed that cities with municipal control, over school budgets tend to be larger cities with lower education, occupation, and income levels. There is no significant difference in racial composition or property value.

Our findings regarding urban environment and the structure of city government parallel those of John H. Kessel.[4] The mayor-council form of government is more frequently encountered in large cities with lower education and occupation characteristics. Manager government is found more frequently in middle-size cities with higher education and occupation characteristics. Cities with large Negro populations are more likely to have a mayor-council form of government than a manager form of government. Property investment—that is, the full value of property per pupil—is much higher in mayor-council cities than in manager cities.

There is not a great deal of social difference between partisan and nonpartisan cities. Even though there is considerable evidence to support the view than nonpartisanship is the structural preference of middle-class groups, and partisanship the preference of working-class, ethnic, and racial groups,[5] there appears to be little relationship between the social character of cities and partisan and nonpartisan elections. Over two-thirds of American cities operate nonpartisan elections for local offices, including school boards. There is only a slight tendency for the larger cities with lower socioeconomic populations to operate partisan elections.

These relationships between environmental variables and structural characteristics are important to keep in mind when exploring the effect of these different sets of variables or policy outcomes. The problem will be to sort out the effects of environmental variables on policy outcomes from the effects of structural variables. For example, it may turn out that appointed school boards spend more per pupil than elected school boards; but since we know that cities with appointed school boards have more property wealth at their disposal than cities with elected school boards, it may be that wealth rather than school board selection is the real determinant of educational expenditures. Policy differences between elected and appointed school boards may really be a product of their differing urban environments rather than different methods of selecting school board members. To identify the independent effect of structural variables, it will be necessary to control for the effect of environmental variables.

The Urban Environment and Educational Outcomes

THE COST OF TEACHING JOHNNY TO READ

Any analysis of educational outcomes must begin by explaining educational expenditures. No doubt the most important element explaining total dollar expenditures for school in each city is the number of children attending school. But this type of correlation belabors the obvious: the more children to be taught, the more money is needed for schools. By using *per pupil* expenditures rather than total or per capita expenditures, explanation can center on those factors which influence expenditures per unit of "need." Per pupil expenditures in effect hold constant for "need," and provide a measure of the city's willingness and ability to spend money for education. It may also be considered a rough measure of the quality of educational services provided.

In the 1963–64 school year, city school expenditures averaged $395 per pupil in the 67 school systems studied; this compares with $349 per pupil reported in James' study of American cities, and $369 for the national average.[6] This figure ranged from a low of

$213 in Greenville, South Carolina, to a high of $639 in Rochester, New York. Why is it that some cities spend three times as much on the education of each child as other cities?

Table 1 suggests that wealth is a principal determinant of educational expenditures in American cities. Both median family income and property value per pupil were significantly related to per pupil expenditures. Nonwhite populations were inversely related to expenditures: the larger the nonwhite proportion of the population, the lower the per pupil expenditures. Interestingly, per pupil expenditures were *not* related to the educational or occupational level of city populations.

However, larger cities spend significantly more for the education of each child than smaller cities.

How do these findings compare with previous studies? Prior to 1963, there was only one published study of local school expenditures which included cities from different states. This was Harvey Brazer's analysis of educational spending in the forty largest cities in the United States.[7] He, too, found that median family income was the most important factor in explaining differences in educational spending among cities, although he used per capita rather than per pupil figures. Earlier Werner Z. Hirsch had studied 26 school districts in St. Louis County and Sacks and Hellmuth had studied 32 school districts in metropolitan Cleveland.[8] Both reported income and property value as among their most influential variables in determining pupil expenditures.

In 1963, Jerry Miner examined the correlates of per pupil educational expenditures in 1,100 school districts responding to a mailed questionnaire.[9] His simple coefficient for median family income was .25, for property value .25, for adult education .17, and for nonwhite population − .27. All of these coefficients were significant in Miner's study; they tend to substantiate our own findings although they are somewhat lower in magnitude. In addition to these environmental variables, Miner also reported positive coefficients with cost elements, such as teachers' salaries and auxiliary services.

H. Thomas James' study in 1965 of 107

TABLE 1. The Social Character of Cities and Educational Policy Outcomes

Educational Policy Outcomes	Urban Environmental Variables											
	SIZE		EDUCATION		OCCUPATION		INCOME		NONWHITE		PROPERTY	
	Sim.	Par.	Sim.	Par.	Sim.	Par.	Sim.	Par.	Sim.	Par.	Sim.	Par.
Per pupil expenditures	0.40*	0.41*	−0.04	−0.13	−0.01	−0.02	0.47*	0.30*	−0.39*	−0.41*	0.32*	0.34*
Expenditures relative to income	−0.14	0.07	0.15	0.07	0.14	−0.02	−0.11	−0.06	−0.09	−0.02	−0.39*	−0.30*
School tax rate	0.03	0.04	0.22	−0.05	0.25	0.09	0.29*	0.25*	−0.31*	−0.16	−0.10	−0.16
Local school support	0.11	0.03	0.02	0.11	−0.08	−0.17	0.34*	0.25*	−0.17	−0.08	0.23	0.06
Teachers' salaries	0.31*	0.28*	−0.05	−0.17	−0.02	0.00	0.42*	0.29*	−0.30*	−0.26*	0.19	0.11
Teacher turnover	0.28*	0.17	0.15	−0.01	0.11	0.04	0.11	0.08	−0.08	0.02	−0.05	0.14
Teacher-pupil ratio	−0.03	−0.02	−0.07	0.02	−0.13	−0.15	−0.01	0.11	0.24*	0.25*	−0.02	−0.17
Teachers without degrees	0.05	−0.18	−0.45*	−0.31*	−0.36*	0.07	0.02	0.30*	0.05	−0.27*	0.07	−0.06
Teachers with master's	−0.01	0.02	0.23	0.17	0.15	−0.06	0.18	−0.02	−0.14	−0.05	0.21	0.20
Dropout rate	−0.12	−0.05	0.35*	0.26*	0.24*	−0.06	0.20	0.10	−0.04	0.10	0.07	0.01
Private school enrollment	0.25*	−0.04	−0.45*	−0.40*	−0.36*	0.07	0.23	0.38*	0.07	−0.01	0.45*	0.29*

Note: Figures are simple and partial correlation coefficients for 67 cities; partial coefficients show the correlations between policy variables and each environmental variable while controlling for all other environmental and structural variables; an asterisk indicates a significant relationship at the 0.05 level.

large school districts in the nation produced findings remarkably similar to our own regarding the determinants of per pupil expenditures.[10] His simple coefficients were as follows: median family income .55; property value .43; adult education .17; and nonwhite population − .41.

In short, scholars appear to agree that school expenditures are closely related to ability to finance public education. Wealth, as measured by income, property value, and size of city, is the principal determinant of how much is spent on the education of each child.

EDUCATIONAL "EFFORT"

Per pupil expenditures measure both the willingness and ability of a city to spend money for education. The next problem is to separate "willingness to spend" from "ability to spend" in order to roughly determine the sacrifice a city is making for education. School expenditures can be expressed relative to a city's ability to spend money. The most appropriate measure of ability to pay for education is probably the aggregate income of the city. Therefore, the measure "total public school expenditures as a per cent of aggregate income of the population" really holds constant for ability to spend and more directly measures the city's willingness to sacrifice personal income for public education. This is the city's educational "effort." The cities in our sample devoted an average of 4 percent of their aggregate personal income to public school expenditures; this approximates the national income share devoted to public schools.

It was expected that cities with higher socioeconomic status populations would sacrifice a greater share of their personal income for education. However, we were unable to produce any evidence to support this hypothesis. There was no relationship between population characteristics and educational effort. However, property investment was inversely associated with educational effort—the greater the property resources of a city, the smaller the proportion of personal income devoted to education. Or, in other

words, the fewer the property resources of a city, the larger the proportion of personal income devoted to education.

While per pupil expenditures increase with increases in property value, school expenditures as a percent of income declines. This means that cities with less taxable resources are required to put forth a greater effort in education than cities with greater resources. However, despite their greater effort, cities with less resources still end up spending less per pupil on education. In short, "richer" cities can provide better educations for their children with less of an economic sacrifice than that required of "poorer" cities to provide an inferior education for their children.

LOCAL SCHOOL SUPPORT

Per pupil expenditures for cities reflects the expenditure of money received from the state and federal government as well as money raised locally. In 1963–64 about 40 percent of all school funds came from state and federal sources, while 60 percent were raised at the local level from local sources. Prior to 1965 the federal government's contribution to public education was quite small: less than 4 percent of total public school expenditures. This meant that most nonlocal school revenue came from state governments.

The mean local share of school revenue for our 67 cities was 64.8 percent, slightly higher than the mean for all United States cities. Local school support ranged from a low 35 percent in Greenville to a high of 90 percent in Des Moines.

Income was the most important determinant of local school support followed by property value. The higher the median family income, the greater the local share of public school expenditures.

EFFECTIVE TAX RATES

To the taxpayer, perhaps the most important policy outcome in education is the school tax he must pay. Yet to date no published study in education or political science has examined the determinants of school tax rates. The National Educational Association reports that the mean school tax rate per

$1,000 of *assessed* value for 128 school systems with enrollments of $25,000 or more was $27.49.[11] Tax rate on assessed value varied from $11 per $1,000 to $184. The problem of course, is that ratios of assessed value to market value vary enormously in American cities, in our study from 8 percent to 100 percent. To determine effective tax rate, the outcome of greatest interest to the taxpayer, it is necessary to multiply the tax rate by the ratio of assessed value to market value. The resulting effective tax rate represents actual tax paid on market value. Of course, one must rely on local reporting of the ratio of assessed value to market value, and to the extent that cities misrepresent this ratio our figures are still subject to error.

The mean effective school tax rate for our 67 cities was $10.30; this compares with a mean of $10.00 for 128 large school systems reported by the NEA. Yet cities ranged from a low of $2.00 in Memphis and Montgomery to a high of $67.00 in Des Moines.

The effective school tax rate was, of course, closely related to the proportion of school revenue coming from local sources. The greater the local support for schools, the higher the tax rate. But what is the linkage between environmental circumstances and school taxes?

Income appears to be the most influential environmental variable affecting school tax rates. The higher the income level, the higher the school tax rate people seem to be willing to impose upon themselves. Educational level and white-collar employment are also related to school tax rates but only through their relationship to income. When other variables are controlled in partial coefficients, income remains associated with tax rates while the education and occupation relationships disappear. There is also some relationship between nonwhite population and school tax rates; large nonwhite populations are associated with lower school tax rates.

TEACHING IN CITY SCHOOLS

Nearly everyone can claim to have known at least one remarkable teacher. But it is difficult indeed to say precisely what it is that made that teacher remarkable. The assumption in this section is that teachers salaries, teacher turnover, teacher-pupil ratios, and teacher preparation levels are rough indices of this critical educational outcome—quality teaching.

The academic preparation of classroom teachers in large cities is substantially better than the preparation of all teachers in the United States. For example, teachers without a bachelors degree comprised nearly 10 percent of all teachers in the nation, but in our sample only 4.9 percent of classroom teachers had no bachelors degree. (This compares with 4 percent of all classroom teachers in a NEA survey of 140 large school systems.)[12] Four cities reported that less than one-fourth of 1 percent of their teachers had no bachelors degree—Columbus, Ohio; Dallas; Denver; and Forth Worth. Syracuse reported that over a quarter of their teachers had no degree; several New York and New Jersey cities reported large proportions of noncollege degree teachers.

It is very interesting to observe that it is *not* the resources of a city—income, property, and size—which influence teacher preparation levels. It is the education and occupation levels of the city's population which were more closely associated with the proportion of teachers with bachelor's degrees. Increases in education and income levels are associated with declines in the proportion of teachers without degrees. We might speculate that higher socioeconomic status populations demand teachers with better academic training than lower socioeconomic status populations which are less sophisticated in judging teacher preparation.

In obtaining teachers with advanced degrees, that is, master's or doctor's degrees, it again appeared that cities with better educated populations were more successful than cities with less educated populations. However, this relationship was not as pronounced as the relationship between adult education and teachers with bachelor's degrees. And no other environmental variable was significantly related to advanced teacher education.

Teachers' salaries in large city school districts are substantially above the national average in teachers' salaries. In 1964 the national average for classroom teachers salaries was $5,963, while the average for school districts with 25,000 or more pupils was $6,572. The average for our own sample was $6,613; salaries ranged from a low at $4,607 in Jackson, Mississippi, to a high of $9,054 in San Francisco.

This great variation in salaries paid city teachers was closely related to income levels in the cities. The higher the median family income, the higher the average classroom teacher salary. Salaries were also independently related to size of city with larger cities paying higher salaries. However, cities with large nonwhite populations tended to pay somewhat lower salaries; doubtlessly this represented the influence of southern cities with large nonwhite populations and low teachers' salaries.

The fact that teachers' salaries were more closely related to income levels than to property values suggests that it is not really the availability of taxable property which determines salary levels so much as the demand generated by high incomes in a city. School districts must pay salaries commensurate with general income levels in a city regardless of their taxable resources.

The teacher turnover rate—which includes retirement, resignation, dismissal, or promotion to a nonteaching position—was 11.4 percent for 140 large school systems in 1963–64; the comparable figure for our sample was 12.0. Turnover was as high as 18 percent in Syracuse and as low as 6 percent in Chicago. The only environmental variable to correlate significantly with teacher turnover was size. Larger cities tended to have less turnover than smaller cities.

One final measure of instructional quality is the teacher-pupil ratio, or the number of pupils enrolled per classroom teacher. The assumption underlying the use of this variable is that close and personal attention of a teacher at the elementary and secondary school level is a positive factor in a pupil's educational experience. A further assumption is that professional attention to individual needs cannot be given effectively by

teachers who face large classes. Hence, the greater the teacher-pupil ratio, the less desirable the classroom situation from an educational point of view.

Classrooms in large cities appear much more crowded than classrooms throughout the nation. In 1964–65 the teacher-pupil ratio for the nation's public schools was 25.1; but in our sample of city schools the average teacher-pupil ratio was 27.4. This ratio varied from a high of 31 in Detroit and Oklahoma City to a low of 22 in Rochester.

Interestingly, teacher-pupil ratios were unrelated to any environmental condition except the city's racial composition. Classrooms were more crowded in cities with larger nonwhite populations.

DROPOUTS

Evaluating the overall output of an educational system is made very difficult by the fact that there is little agreement on the objectives of public education. Is the goal of public education college preparation, vocational skill, emotional happiness, psychological adjustment, good automobile driving, the inculcation of spiritual values, the production of engineers and scientists, the cultivation of patriotism, the training of competent homemakers, or winning the Olympics? And even if we could measure any or all of these outputs, how could we tell whether the failure to achieve them was a product of educational policies or an outgrowth of other national problems?

One increasingly popular measure of educational output is the dropout rate. In this study it is expressed as the number of pupils who graduated in 1963 per 10th grades in 1960. Certainly, it can be argued that the child who does not complete at least 12 years of education in a highly technical society represents a national liability. At the very least, we should be able to obtain agreement that reducing dropouts is a valid educational objective.

A special study of the dropout problem in 128 large cities by the National Education Association reported that 708 out of every 1,000 10th graders in 1960 graduated in 1963;

the dropout rate for this time span was 29.2 percent.[13] In our own sample the retention rate was 711; the dropout rate was 28.9 percent. Apparently, big-city school systems suffer substantially higher dropout rates than the rest of the nation: the national average for the same time span was 76.0, a dropout rate of only 24.0 percent. Philadelphia had the highest dropout rate in our sample: only 53.4 percent of 10th graders stayed to graduate; 46.6 percent dropped out. Sacramento kept 94.0 percent of their 10th graders in school; only 6.0 percent dropped out.

It is interesting that the most important variable influencing dropouts is the education level of the adult population. It is not the resources of a city—income, property, or size—which affect dropouts; it seems to be the educational level of the parents. The higher the education level of the adult population, the more likely children are to stay in school until graduation. Wealth is not an important factor. In the next section, we shall try to see whether or not school policies affect dropout rates.

PRIVATE SCHOOL ENROLLMENT

Private school enrollment could be conceptualized as either an input variable in public school systems or as an educational outcome. Certainly, it would be plausible to conceive of the level of private school enrollment as influencing public attitudes, demands, and supports relative to public schools. On the other hand, one could just as easily conceive of the level of private school enrollment as a reaction to the quality of public school education and serve an educational outcome. As we explained earlier, a correlation coefficient cannot tell us in which direction the causal arrows point.

James' study of 107 city school systems reported a mean private school enrollment of 16.5 percent of all elementary students; in our sample the mean private school enrollment was 19.6 percent of all elementary students.[14] Pittsburgh appears to have the highest private enrollment of any city in the nation—46 percent; Chattanooga was lowest with 4 percent.

Private school enrollment is significantly related to several environmental variables. The pattern of these relationships is quite surprising. First of all, private enrollment is positively associated with wealth; increases in both income and property value are accompanied by increases in private enrollment. This indicates that private enrollment is partly a product of the resources available to parents; only cities which can afford the luxury of large private school enrollments do so. But private school enrollment is negatively associated with adult education level. (It is also negatively associated with white-collar employment, but since this association disappears in partial coefficients we may assume that it is a spurious relationship.) This is true even though income and education are positively correlated among our cities ($r = .40$). This suggests that if income is held constant, cities with well-educated adult populations will rely more upon public schools, while cities with less-educated adult populations will rely more upon private schools.

Relationships Among Educational Outcomes

Up to now we have been concerned with the effect of urban environmental variables on educational outcomes. We now turn to an examination of some of the more interesting relationships *among* educational outcomes in large cities.

First of all, let us observe the relationship between spending for public education and our other educational outcomes. Among large cities per pupil expenditures are positively associated with local school support, although the association is not particularly strong. Cities which rely more on local revenue spend more money per pupil. This means that per pupil expenditures are negatively associated with state (and federal) aid, since our local support measure is simply the inverse of the proportion of school funds coming from the state and federal government. Of course, federal and state aid does not "cause" lower per pupil expenditures. Many federal and state aid programs provide larger shares of intergovernmental revenue to poorer communities which spend less on their schools. The result of these compensatory programs of federal and state agencies is an inverse relationship between federal and state aid and per pupil expenditures.

Analysis does *not* permit us to say whether state aid leads to increases in per pupil expenditures or whether it is merely a substitute for local support. The consensus of scholars seems to be that there is *some* additive effect in state and federal aid but also *some* reduction in local effort.[15] The absence of positive correlation between state-federal aid and per pupil expenditures is not in itself evidence that such aid fails to generate increases in per pupil expenditures. Too many intervening variables—the compensatory nature of aid formulae, for example—obscure the effect of intergovernmental revenue on per pupil expenditures in a fifty-state analysis. Studies over time in particular school districts are probably the best way to ascertain the effect of state and federal aid on pupil expenditures and local school support.

As one might expect, educational spending is closely related to several cost factors in public schools. Per pupil expenditures increase with increases in teacher salaries, decreases in teacher-pupil ratios, and increases in the proportion of teachers with advanced degrees. Earlier, Jerry Miner reported that cost factors are "the most important determinant of both total and local per pupil expenditures."[16] However, this sort of statement really begs the question. All that this says is that higher cost factors result in higher per pupil expenditures. It would be quite startling if it were otherwise. And, of course, school tax rates are most closely related to local school support.

Teachers' salaries are related to proportion of teachers with advanced degrees. However, interestingly, neither teachers' salaries nor any other outcome measure is significantly related to teacher turnover. Apparently, turnover is strictly a function of the size of city (see Table 1) and the resulting occupational mobility that a large city provides.

It is interesting that the dropout rate, the only educational outcome we have which is derived directly from the students themselves, is *not* associated with any of the educational policies considered. Differences in dropout rates were not related to school expenditures, teacher salaries, teacher-pupil ratios, or other measures of educational quality. Yet earlier we observed that adult education levels had a profound impact on dropout rates. Apparently, it is the educational level of the parents rather than any policies of the schools which is the most important influence on the child.

Private school enrollment is positively correlated with pupil expenditures and teachers' salaries. This association is a product of the intervening effect of wealth. Wealthy populations can afford more for public education while at the same time sending larger proportion of their children to private schools. There is no evidence that private school enrollment reduces public school expenditures. Rather, private school enrollment is a product of resource levels, the same environmental factor which positively influences support for public schools. Moreover, the withdrawal of children from public schools in wealthy cities leaves more money available per pupil in public schools. However, it is interesting to note that a large private school enrollment is associated with decreases in educational "effort"—that is, in the proportion of personal income devoted to education.

System Variables and Educational Outcomes

Thus far, attention has been focused upon the relationships between environmental variables and educational outcomes. Now we turn to the problem of assessing the effect of system characteristics on educational outcomes. Of course, in assessing the effect of system characteristics, it is necessary to take into account the effect of environmental inputs, since these inputs have already been shown to influence both system characteristics and educational outcomes.

TABLE 2. Relationships among Educational Policy Outcomes

	Pupil Exp.	Exp. Income	School Taxes	Local Support	Teacher Salaries	Teacher Turnover	Pupil Ratio	No Degrees	Master's Degree	Dropouts
Per pupil expenditures	1.00									
Expenditures relative to income	0.00	1.00								
School tax rate	0.12	0.00	1.00							
Local school support	0.21	−0.23	0.43*	1.00						
Teachers' salaries	0.63*	0.06	0.26*	0.39*	1.00					
Teacher turnover	0.02	0.15	0.02	0.06	−0.08	1.00				
Teacher-pupil ratio	−0.40*	0.00	−0.10	0.07	0.05	−0.23	1.00			
Teachers without degrees	0.19	−0.15	−0.06	0.08	−0.02	−0.02	−0.08	1.00		
Teachers with master's	0.26*	−0.15	0.06	0.24	0.33*	0.05	−0.18	−0.19	1.00	
Dropout rate	0.02	−0.17	0.14	0.10	0.04	0.00	−0.04	−0.11	0.13	1.00
Private school enrollment	0.30*	−0.40*	0.06	0.39*	0.30*	0.09	−0.04	−0.38*	0.12	−0.06

Note: Figures are simple coefficients for 67 cities; an asterisk indicates a significant relationship at the 0.05 level.

Table 3 shows the relationships between structural characteristics of school systems and educational policy outcomes.[17] Perhaps the most striking feature of the table is absence of significant relationships, particularly in comparison with Table 1 where environmental variables were shown to be related to most of these same outcomes. On the whole, there seems to be little relationship between the structure of school systems and the policy outcomes we have selected. Certainly, we can say that structural characteristics seem to be less influential than environmental variables in determining policy outcomes.

Let us examine, first of all, what difference it makes whether school boards are elected or appointed. There were no significant differences in educational outcomes between school systems with elected and appointed boards. For example, the average per pupil expenditure for fifty-four elected school boards was $385 while the average for thirteen appointed boards was $408; statistically, this is not a significant difference. The same lack of differentiation between elected and appointed systems holds true for other policy variables. This means that the method of selecting school boards has no consistent directional impact on educational policy.

However, earlier we speculated that the effect of appointed versus elected school boards might vary depending upon the nature of the constituency. An appointed board in a low-status population city might result in higher educational expenditures than an elected board in such a city; whereas an appointed board in a high-status population city might result in lower expenditures than an elected board in such a city. Such an effect would be obscured in averages and in linear correlation analysis.

Unfortunately, we do not have enough cities with appointed boards (13) to state with great confidence whether this curvilinear hypothesis is true or not. However, available evidence fails to support our speculations on this point. There were no significant differences in educational expenditures of elected and appointed boards when high-status and low-status cities were considered separately.

For example, elected boards in cities with low adult education levels spent $420 per pupil while appointed boards in such cities spent $421 per pupil; elected board in cities with high adult education levels spent $421 per pupil while appointed boards in such cities spent $414 per pupil. These differences, although they run in the predicted directions, are not large enough to be significant.

It was not possible to ascertain any significant relationships between educational outcomes and the method of selecting school board members—whether they are selected by ward or at-large. Neither correlation analysis nor investigation of curvilinear relationships produced any evidence that this particular structural variable measurably influences educational policy.

There was a very slight relationship between school tax rates and the method of choosing the tax assessor. Electing the tax assessor tended to result in lower tax rates on the full market value of property. The average effective tax rate in the twenty-nine cities with appointed assessors was $11.90 per $1,000 of market value compared to only $9.40 in cities with elected assessors. The partial coefficient suggested that this relationship was an independent one, although the small size of the coefficient suggested that the relationship was subject to many exceptions. Tax rates were the only outcome noticeably affected by this structural variable.

Surprisingly, the independence of the school board from city budgetary control had no visible impact on school expenditures or school taxes or local school support. Contrary to our original hypothesis, school boards which were dependent upon city approval of their budgets do not necessarily spend less than independent boards. However, there was a significant relationship between the fiscal independence of school boards and the proportion of teachers without degrees. The fifteen dependent school boards had an average of 9.8 percent of their teachers without a college degree compared to 3.7 percent for the fifty-two independent school boards. Are we to conclude from this finding that fiscally independent school boards insist upon minimum professional

TABLE 3. *Structural Characteristics of School Systems and Educational Policy Outcomes*

	Structural Variables											
Educational Policy Outcomes	SCHOOL BOARD SELECTION		SCHOOL BOARD REPRESENTATION		ASSESSOR SELECTION		CITY CONTROL OF BUDGET		FORM OF GOVERNMENT		TYPE OF BALLOT	
	Sim.	Par.	Sim.	Par.	Sim.	Par.	Sim.	Par.	Sim.	Par.	Sim.	Par.
Per pupil expenditures	0.07	−0.15	0.05	0.01	0.02	0.01	0.19	0.23	−0.07	0.28*	0.08	0.12
Expenditures relative to income	−0.27	−0.11	−0.05	−0.11	0.04	0.09	−0.02	0.06	0.35*	0.25*	0.02	0.14
School tax rate	−0.07	0.10	0.05	−0.10	−0.14	−0.24	−0.07	−0.05	0.11	0.03	0.07	0.00
Local school support	−0.01	−0.08	0.05	−0.03	−0.06	0.10	0.10	0.09	−0.26	−0.20	−0.01	−0.01
Teachers' salaries	−0.02	−0.08	−0.05	−0.09	0.04	0.00	0.03	0.03	−0.01	−0.15	−0.10	−0.07
Teacher turnover	−0.28	−0.23	0.00	0.10	0.01	0.00	0.00	0.11	0.28*	0.25*	0.00	0.15
Teacher-pupil ratio	−0.02	0.08	−0.05	0.07	0.24	0.27	−0.33*	−0.36*	−0.04	−0.15	−0.23	−0.16
Teachers without degrees	0.23	0.09	0.00	0.06	−0.22	−0.23	0.45*	0.27*	−0.32*	−0.18	0.41*	0.23
Teachers with master's	−0.04	−0.07	0.11	0.05	0.09	0.05	−0.08	0.00	−0.06	−0.02	−0.02	0.08
Dropout rate	−0.09	−0.03	−0.03	−0.01	0.13	0.09	−0.09	0.02	0.02	−0.06	−0.08	0.07
Private school enrollment	0.18	−0.12	−0.04	−0.09	−0.16	−0.21	0.11	−0.08	−0.48*	−0.30*	0.20	0.12

Note: Figures are simple and partial correlation coefficients for 67 cities; partial coefficients show the correlations between policy variables and each structural variable while controlling for all other structural and environmental variables; an asterisk indicates a significant relationship at the 0.05 level.

qualifications while fiscally dependent school boards are more lax about such matters?

It seems to make little difference educationally whether a city operates under a partisan or nonpartisan style of politics. Correlation analysis failed to reveal any independent relationships between partisanship and educational policy outcomes. (The relationship between partisanship and teacher qualifications shown in the simple correlation disappeared when environmental factors were controlled.)

Interestingly, the structure of city government itself seemed to be more closely related to certain educational outcomes than structural variables relating directly to school boards. Controlling for environmental variables, including size and wealth, manager cities tend to spend more per pupil than nonmanager cities. (This relationship is obscured in simple coefficients because manager cities tend to be smaller cities and smaller cities tend to spend less per pupil than larger cities.) Of course, environmental factors still have a greater impact on school expenditures than form of government, but form of government also has some independent effect on expenditures. Moreover, form of government is also independently related to educational effort: manager cities spend a larger share of their personal income for education than nonmanager cities. Form of government also has some independent effect on private school enrollment: cities with mayors have higher private enrollments than cities with managers, even after controlling for the influence of environmental forces.

Of course, we do not mean to say that manager government "causes" higher pupil expenditures, greater educational effort, or lower private enrollments. But there is the association between this structural characteristic and these educational outcomes which exists independently of the environmental conditions incorporated in our model—size, wealth, income, occupation, adult education, and race. Even after discounting the influences of these environmental variables, we can say that manager government is associated with these policy outcomes. Probably, the same sociopolitical values which support

manager government also support higher school expenditures and commitments to public education.

In general, then, structural variables had relatively little impact upon educational outcomes. How does this finding compare with studies of other scholars in education and political science? The only studies to deal with structural variables were concerned with their impact on spending. H. Thomas James concluded that "governmental variables are unimportant as correlates of educational expenditures."[18] His analysis included the method of selecting school boards and their fiscal independence from the city. Preliminary findings from the Syracuse studies reported by Alan K. Campbell tend to confirm our belief that structural variables are relatively unimportant in educational policy: "Another general finding of particular importance for central cities is the lack of fiscal significance for city schools of the independence or dependence of their governmental systems. The finding is reported despite its negative character because of the tendency, in much popular literature about education, to attach great importance to governmental independence."[19]

Evaluating A Model: Multivariate Analysis

Now let us try to summarize the explanatory powers of our model. To what extent can educational outcomes in large cities be explained by reference to our model? How much of the total variation in educational outcomes can be attributed to all of the urban environmental variables and political system characteristics considered together?

Multiple correlation coefficients summarizing the effect of six environmental variables are shown in left-hand column of Table 4. These coefficients summarize the total effect on each outcome of size, wealth, education, occupation, race, income, board selection, board representation, assessor selection, board independence, type of ballot, and form of government.

The question of what is or is not a satis-

TABLE 4. *Urban Environment, Structural Variables, and Educational Policy Outcomes*

	Total Effect Environmental Variables and Structural Variables	Total Effect of Environmental Variables	Total Effect of Structural Variables	Effect of Environment Controlling for Structure	Effect of Structure Controlling for Environment
Per pupil expenditures	0.74	0.69	0.20	0.68	0.16
Expenditures relative to income	0.54	0.46	0.29	0.35	0.15
School tax rate	0.46	0.40	0.19	0.33	0.10
Local school support	0.49	0.43	0.31	0.26	0.11
Teachers' salaries	0.60	0.60	0.13	0.54	0.00
Teacher turnover	0.46	0.32	0.38	0.13	0.21
Teacher-pupil ratio	0.56	0.28	0.43	0.23	0.39
Teachers without degrees	0.69	0.52	0.58	0.26	0.35
Teachers with master's	0.35	0.33	0.14	0.24	0.03
Dropout rate	0.42	0.40	0.17	0.30	0.03
Private school enrollment	0.75	0.69	0.51	0.49	0.19

Note: Figures in the first column are multiple correlation coefficients based on all twelve independent variables; figures in the second column are multiple correlation coefficients based on six environmental variables only; figures in the third column are multiple correlation coefficients based on six structural variables only; figures in the fourth column are multiple-partial coefficients showing effect of six environmental variables while controlling for six structural variables; and figures in the last column are multiple-partial coefficients showing the effect of six structural variables while controlling for six environmental variables.

factory level of explanation is always very subjective. A multiple coefficient of .50 indicates that only 25 percent of the variation among cities has been explained by our model. Most of our policy outcomes are near or above that level of explanation. Since the systematic explanation of policy is a relatively recent endeavor of political scientists, perhaps we should be encouraged by this beginning effort. On the other hand, our coefficients indicate that neither environmental nor structural variables are able to explain all of the policy differences among cities. A multiple coefficient of .71 is required to explain half of the total variation in a policy measure. Only per pupil expenditures and private school enrollment can be explained at that level by the variables in our model.

This means we must examine educational decision making much more closely in order to understand the full range of forces influencing educational policy.

Returning to a central question posed at the beginning of our study, what are the linkages between urban environment, political system characteristics, and educational outcomes? We were unable to produce much evidence of a strong explanatory linkage between political system characteristics and educational outcomes. Urban environmental forces—size, wealth, and socioeconomic attributes of populations appeared to directly influence educational outcomes without being mediated by structural variables.

However, one further set of operations seems appropriate in order to confirm our belief that the character of political systems is less important than environmental forces in shaping education policy. Thus far, we have considered the policy impact of each independent variable separately. Now we want to compare the policy impact of all of our environmental variables considered together with the policy impact of all of our structural variables considered together.

The coefficients in the second and third columns in Table 4 show the total impact of six environmental variables and the total impact of six structural variables respectively. The coefficients in the last two columns in Table 4 are multiple-partial coefficients. They

show the policy impact of six environmental variables while controlling for six structural variables and of six structural variables while controlling for six environmental variables.

Again, the evidence seems conclusive: on the whole, urban environmental variables were more influential in determining educational policy outcomes than structural characteristics of political systems. There are only two policy outcomes for which structural variables appear more influential than environmental variables—teacher-pupil ratios and teachers without degrees. In addition, structural variables had some independent relationship with private school enrollment, but this relationship was not as close as the relationship between environmental variables and private school enrollment.

Of course, we are not justified in concluding from these operations that the structure of school systems never has any impact on educational policies. We can only say that the particular structural variables that we have studied do not appear to be as influential in determining a city's educational policy as its size, its wealth, and resources, and its educational and racial composition.

It may be that the policy outcomes we have considered are too crudely measured in aggregate data to reveal the subtle impact of political system variables. (However, it should be noted that the effect of environmental variables could be clearly observed in this crudely measured aggregate data.) Or it may be that some other politicial system variables not included in our study might someday be shown to have important independent effect on educational policy. For example, if comparable survey data on public attitudes toward education could be obtained for a number of cities, it might turn out that public attitudes independently influence policy choices even after controlling for the effect of a city's size and resources.

However, since a great deal of literature suggests that structural variables in the school system are influential in determining policy, these findings at least warn educators and political scientists against making simple assumptions about the policy consequences of political system characteristics. Hopefully, these findings will challenge educators and political scientists to continue research into the linkages between environmental variables, school systems, and educational policy.

Notes

1. David Easton, *A Systems Analysis of Political Life* (New York: John Wiley, 1965); *A Framework for Political Analysis* (Englewood Cliffs, N.J.: Prentice-Hall, 1965), pp. 23–76; and "An Approach to the Analysis of Political Systems," *World Politics*, 9 (April 1957), 383–400.

2. The selection of the sixty-seven cities was accomplished by what might be euphamistically called nonprobability sampling. The universe consisted of all cities which were the central cities of the nation's 212 standard metropolitan statistical areas (SMSAs). Since some SMSAs have more than one central city, the number of cities in the universe was really 242. The sixty-seven cities in this study were selected solely on the basis of availability of data on all of the environmental, structural, and policy variables. In other words, out of the 242 cities in the universe, complete sets of data were available for only sixty-seven cities.

This came about largely because the principle sources of data on educational outcomes, reports of the National Education Association, and U.S. Office of Education, are available only for "Selected" school districts. The basis for selection in this case appears to be the faithfulness of school administrators in returning forms and questionnaires. Data collected by the National Municipal League is also very spotty. Another problem is coterminality of school districts with census data. School districts frequently have boundaries which are not coterminous with the boundaries of any other political subdivision. Our sample included only those cities which were reasonably coterminous with a school district. Thus the problems of data sources restricted analysis to sixty-seven cities.

The only way to ascertain the extent of bias in

such a nonrandom sample is to compare characteristics of the sample with known characteristics of the universe. The following table indicates that our sample overrepresents larger cities with higher white-collar and income levels and larger nonwhite concentrations. This is not a particularly serious problem so long as we confine our generalizations to large cities.

Additional checks upon representativeness are found in the text where policy measures for the sample are compared with the same measures in larger samples from previous studies, or with reported national averages.

The principal sources of data were: U.S. Bureau of the Census, *County and City Data Book, 1962* (Washington, D.C.: Government Printing Office, 1962); Research Divisions—National Education Association, *Selected Statistics on Local School Systems 1963–64* (Washington, D.C.: NEA, 1966); Research Division—National Education Association, *Twenty-second Biennial Salary Survey of Public School Employees 1964–65* (Washington, D.C.: NEA, 1965); H. Thomas James, *Determinants of Educational Expenditures in Large Cities of the United States* (Palo Alto, Calif.: School of Education, Stanford University, 1966); International City Managers' Association, *Municipal Yearbook 1965* (Chicago: ICMA, 1965).

3. Scott Greer, *Governing the Metropolis* (New York: John Wiley, 1962), pp. 1–42.

4. John H. Kessel, "Governmental Structure and Political Environment," *American Political Science Review*, 56 (September 1962), 615–20.

5. Charles R. Adrian, "Some General Characteristics of Non-partisan Elections," *American Political Science Review*, 46 (September 1952), 766–76; Charles E. Gilbert, "Some Aspects of Non-partisan Elections in Large Cities," *Midwest Journal of Political Science*, 6 (November 1962), 345–63.

6. James, *Determinants of Educational Expenditures*, Appendix.

7. Harvey Brazer, *City Expenditures in the United States* (New York: National Bureau of Economic Research, 1959).

8. Werner Z. Hirsch, "Determinants of Public Education Expenditures," *National Tax Journal*, 13 (March 1960), 24–40; Seymour Sacks and

A COMPARISON OF CHARACTERISTICS OF SAMPLE OF 67 CITIES WITH KNOWN CHARACTERISTICS OF ALL CENTRAL CITIES OF METROPOLITAN AREAS

Characteristic	Means for 67 Sample Cities	Means for 242 Central Cities
Size: 1960 population	588,000	237,000
Median school completed by population over 25 in 1960	11.0 yrs.	11.0 yrs.
Occupation: percent in white-collar employment in 1960	46.4%	44.7%
Income: median family income, 1959	$5,979	$5,743
Nonwhite: percent nonwhite population in 1960	17.1%	14.0%

William F. Hellmuth, *Financing Government in a Metropolitan Area* (New York: The Free Press, 1960).

9. Jerry Miner, *Social and Economic Factors in Spending for Public Education* (Syracuse: Syracuse University Press, 1963).

10. James, *Determinants of Educational Expenditures.*

11. Research Division—National Education Association, *Selected Statistics of Local School Systems 1963–64* (Washington, D.C.: NEA, 1966).

12. *Ibid.*

13. Project School Drop-Out, National Education Association, *Holding Power of Large City School Systems* (Washington: NEA, 1964).

14. James, *Determinants of Educational Expenditures,* Appendix.

15. Edward F. Renshaw, "A Note on the Expenditure Effect of Aid to Education," *Journal of Political Economy,* 67 (April 1960), 170–74.

16. Miner, *Social and Economic Factors.*

17. The direction of the relationships can be understood by noting the values assigned structural variables: School board selection: 0 = elected, 1 = appointed; school board representation: 0 = by ward, 1 = at-large; assessor selection: 0 = appointed, 1 = elected; city control of budget: 0 = no city review, 1 = city review; form of government: 1 = mayor, 2 = commission, 3 = manager; type of ballot: 1 = nonpartisan, 2 = partisan.

18. James, *Determinants of Educational Expenditures.*

19. Alan K. Campbell, "The Socio-Economic, Political, and Fiscal Environment of Educational Policy-making in Large Cities" (Paper delivered at the 1966 annual meeting of the American Political Science Association, New York City, September 1966, p. 10).

IN RECENT YEARS, a growing body of research has used multivariate statistical techniques to examine the relationship between aggregate environmental characteristics and the public policies of state and local governments. This research has been concerned primarily with isolating or demonstrating the social, economic, and political correlates of either public policies (e.g., expenditures, revenues, and referenda issues) or governmental structures (viz., form of government, size of election districts, and type of ballot).[1]

One advantage of the aggregate approach, beyond the relative accessibility of data, is that it permits a systematic, comparative study of states or cities. On the local level, this comparative approach provides a convenient supplement to the earlier case study approach which was concerned with the political processes and issues of particular cities.

A number of hypotheses have been suggested by studies employing either the case study or aggregate approaches. In those observations dealing with government structure, attention is usually directed to the council-manager plan as an example of progressive government. That is, city governments which are reform-oriented are likely to be found in more affluent, better educated, homogeneous, middle-class cities. The notion is that the middle class prefers a more efficient, professional city administration. Conversely, the mayor-council plan is usually associated with older, machine-type politics which allegedly reflects the preferences of the less affluent, less-educated, working-class and ethnic minorities who are most concerned about political representation.[2]

The question of how to categorize commission government has presented a problem. Despite the fact that it was one of the earliest manifestations of the reform movement, its popularity has declined steadily, and it is rapidly fading into obscurity throughout most of the country.[3] Curiously enough, in spite of its decline in the last four decades and its rather marked politicization in those cities in which it does remain, scholars continue to consider both commission and council-manager governments ana-

Environment, Process, and Policy: A Reconsideration*

James W. Clarke

lytically as reform governments. Indications of the weaknesses in such a combination are apparent in some of the anomalous relationships revealed and recognized in a recent study by Lineberry and Fowler.[4]

General Statement of Problem

Two ideas emerge from the case and aggregate studies of public policies in cities. The results of the case studies suggest that political variables are important determinants of public policy. More specifically, political decision making and interaction processes appear to be the key variables which must be studied in order to understand policy outcomes.[5] Conversely, the results of aggregate comparative studies on the state and local levels indicate that policy outcomes are more closely associated with the social and economic characteristics of the units of analysis. These studies suggest that environmental rather than political variables appear to be much more important as policy determinants.[6]

There are several possible explanations for these somewhat contradictory conclusions. First, it may be that some variables are

Reprinted with permission from The American Political Science Review, 63 (December 1969), 1172–82.
*This research is a byproduct of a larger study supported by a U.S. Public Health Service Research Grant (IFS AP33, 924–01). Special thanks are due my graduate assistant, David H. Vomacka, for his help in processing these data.

ignored in either approach, thus exaggerating the importance of those variables which are considered. For example, most case studies ignore or at least do not treat systematically the social and economic variables employed in the aggregate approach. The opposite emphasis is present in the aggregate studies— that is, decision-making or process variables tend to be ignored. Second, and this applies mainly to the aggregate studies, it may be that the indicators which are used to measure process variables are simply too crude or insensitive to reflect the dimensions being considered. Attempts to quantify what are essentially behavioral variables frequently encounter this problem. Third, comparative studies of cities have been unable to control adequately for differences in local policies which may reflect state and federal restrictions rather than local prerogatives. Thus state laws limiting the discretion of city governments can only confound attempts to explain the policies of these governments if this factor is not considered. Closely related to this problem is the fact that controls for time are rarely employed. Particularly in studies of reformism, cities are often classified as reformist or not regardless of when or how the particular charter was adopted. It is unlikely that events such as these, many of which occurred around the turn of the century, can be considered the same as events occurring at mid-century.[7] Finally, it may be that environmental factors are important determinants of policies, such as revenue and expenditure policies, which are substantially dependent on the economic potential of communities. But are these same environmental variables equally important in influencing policies which reflect more closely the manifest political values of a community (e.g., elections for public office and certain referenda decisions)?

Lineberry and Fowler, in their study of reformism in American cities, suggest that

> the implicit, or at times explicit, causal model in much of the research on municipal reformism has been a simple one: socio-economic cleavages cause the adoption of particular political forms. A more sophisticated model would include political institutions as one of

the factors which produce a given output structure in city politics. We hypothesize that a causal model would include four classes of variables: socio-economic cleavages, political variables (including party registration, structure of party systems, patterns of aggregation, strength of interest groups, voter turnout, etc.), political institutions (form of government, type of elections and types of constituencies), and political output.[8]

This study represents an effort to examine, with one modification, such a model of reformism. That modification is that the single policy output, or dependent variable, in this study involves change or innovation in a political institution form of government.

Setting

Forty-three third-class cities in Pennsylvania have been selected for study. In 1957, the Optional Third-Class City Charter Law was signed providing all third-class cities with the option to adopt new municipal charters—either a mayor-council or council-manager plan.[9] If the local electorate chose to keep its existing commission form of government, which until 1957 had been required by state law, it could do so.[10] Under these conditions, the state laws of Pennsylvania provide a common legal framework for these cities. That is, in 1957, all forty-three cities were governed by commission governments, and all were provided with the same opportunity to adopt new charters under the law. This, perhaps more than anything else, directs attention to the characteristics of individual communities in seeking some explanation for their action or inaction on the charter question.[11]

The time period considered is the years from 1957, when the Optional Charter Law was adopted, through 1966. During this period, nine cities voted to adopt new charters. Six cities adopted the mayor-council plan. Three adopted the council-manager plan. Twelve other cities attempted unsuccessfully to adopt new charters.[12] There was no new charter activity in the remaining twenty-two cities.

Broadly defined, the dependent variable to

be examined is municipal reform or change. As indicated earlier, the usual and inappropriate distinction between reform and non-reform government is not used. Thus, both the new options, council-manager or mayor-council, are considered innovative or representative of political change, while the commission plan only represents the status quo.

The setting of this study approaches a quasi-experimental situation. All forty-three cities function within the constraints imposed by Pennsylvania law. Each city was provided with the same option, at the same time, to consider new charters. Furthermore, the controlled time period during which the cities were examined minimizes the effects of demographic or other environmental fluctuations. Control of these factors permits a more accurate assessment of the environmental and political influences on local public policy.

Research Design

The purpose of this study is to examine those variables which are related to the consideration and adoption of new political forms. In a broader perspective, the analysis deals with the correlates of political change on the local level. The general hypothesis is that variations in the social, economic, and political characteristics of communities are associated with the decision to alter or retain existing forms of government. The forty-three cities selected for the study are treated as a statistical population of third-class cities in Pennsylvania.[13]

The study attempts to answer two questions: (1) What are the correlates of charter-reform activity in the forty-three cities? (2) Among those cities which were active, what variables are associated with the outcomes of this activity? Twelve independent variables were selected for analysis because of their prominence in the local and state policy literature (see Table 1).[14] Aside from the familiar variables (1–8), variables 9–11 require some further clarification below:

Metropolitan classification. The cities are classified as central, independent, or suburban cities. A central city is the largest city

TABLE 1. *Independent Variables*

1. Population, 1960 (10^3)
2. Median gross rentals, 1960
3. Real estate values, 1960 (per capita)
4. Median income, 1960 (10^2)
5. Median school years completed by the adult population, 1960
6. Percentage white collar, 1960
7. Percentage nonwhite, 1960
8. Percentage of the native population of foreign or mixed parentage, 1960
9. Metropolitan classification, 1960
10. Employment-residence ratios, 1960
11. Percentage absentee-owned industry, 1965
12. Local interparty competition, 1955–66

of 50,000 or more, located within a Standard Metropolitan Statistical Area (SMSA). Suburbs are cities above 10,000 located within SMSA,s. Independent cities are cities above 10,000 located outside SMSA,s.[15] This classification is treated as a dichotomous variable comparing central and independent cities to suburbs.

Employment-residence ratios. This is the ratio of total employment to resident employment. It measures the extent to which a city is dependent upon a nonresident labor force.[16]

Percentage absentee-owned industry. The degree of absentee-owned industry is measured by the percentage of the total local work force employed by absentee-owned firms. The location of the firm's home office was used to determine whether the firm is absentee or locally owned—that is, if the home office is located outside the city, it is considered to be an absentee-owned firm.[17]

Local interparty competition. This variable is defined as the relative percentage of city elective offices held over the twelve-year time period by the minority party. This was determined by consulting the *Pennsylvania Manual* for the years included in the study and recording for each two-year period the number of offices held by both parties.[18] These numbers were then totaled for the twelve-year period and the percentage of local offices held by the minority party was calculated for each city. The index ranges from 0 (least competitive) to 50 percent (most competitive) where control was equally divided between the parties.

The dependent variable—charter reform activity—is treated as a dichotomous variable—that is, reform activity is dichotomized on the basis of its presence or absence in each city. The minimal condition required for a city to be classified as "active" was that it had, either by petition or ordinance, placed the question of whether or not to elect a charter study commission before the local electorate.[19]

Two methods were used to explore the second question. First, results were classified in terms of success—that is, either adoption or rejection of the charter proposals—and operationalized as a dichotomous variable.[20] Second, the percentage of the popular vote approving the proposal was used as the dependent variable in the twenty-two cases where the public did have an opportunity to vote on the issue.[21]

Four political process variables—type of proposal, city hall response, fear of the higher costs of reform government, and voter turnout—were included in the analysis. These variables are commonly considered in the case study literature on municipal reform and metropolitan reorganization,[22] but they are not often included systematically in comparative studies. They are treated in this analysis as dichotomous variables.[23]

As stated above, the twenty-two charter referenda occurred over the years from 1957 to 1966. Because of this extended time period, newspaper accounts seemed to offer the most reliable and comprehensive information concerning the campaigns. Local newspapers, in each of the cities in which the referenda occurred, were examined for the time period beginning with the ordinance or petition leading to the election of a charter study commission through to the date the referendum was held.[24]

The four process variables were defined as follows:

1. *Type of proposal.* This was defined and coded simply as either a mayor-council (1) or council-manager (0) plan.

2. *City hall response.* This variable was dichotomized as opposition (0) or lack of opposition (1) to the proposal. Opposition was defined subjectively as any number of councilmen or city employees who, actively and overtly, opposed the charter reform proposal to a degree, sufficient in itself, to keep the issue consistently before the public. In those cities where city hall was divided on the issue, the dominant response, in terms of publicity, was coded.

3. *Cost issue.* This variable was defined as either the presence (0) or absence (1) of a fear of higher costs under a reform government, as reflected in newspaper accounts and political advertisements.

4. *Voter turnout.* This variable was included in the analysis in a more conventional manner.[25] Voter turnout was defined as the percentage of the total registered voters in each community who voted on the local charter referendum.

Simple, partial, and multiple correlations are used to describe the relationships. In addition, cumulative coefficients of determination are reported to indicate the relative variation explained by each independent variable.

Reform and Socioeconomic Indicators: Some Propositions

There is a substantial body of literature which discusses the environmental correlates of municipal reform.[26] No attempt will be made here to discuss that literature. Rather, only the major conclusions will be summarized in the form of propositions.[27]

1. *Population size.* Larger cities are more likely to consider and adopt new charters than smaller cities (Alford and Scoble; Kessel).

2. *Social class.* Cities with larger middle-class populations—as measured by occupation, education, and income—are more likely to consider and adopt new charters (Banfield and Wilson; Schnore; Alford and Scoble; Kessel).

3. *Social heterogeneity*. Cities with larger non-white and ethnic populations are less likely to consider and adopt new charters (Banfield and Wilson; Kessel; Schnore and Alford; and Alford and Scoble).

4. *Economic potential*. Cities with greater economic potential—as measured by per capita market value of real estate, median gross rentals, and larger employment-residence ratios—are more likely to consider and adopt new charters (Williams and Adrian; Sherbenou).

5. *Absentee-owned industries*. Cities with greater proportions of the work force employed in absentee-owned firms are less likely to consider and adopt new charters.[28] (Williams and Adrian; Kessel).

6. *Metropolitan classification*. Central and independent cities are more likely to consider and adopt new charters than suburban cities. This proposition is drawn from Schnore's finding that the commission plan is more common in "older, less modernized" suburbs where many problems are not recognized or acknowledged.[29] Third-class suburban cities in Pennsylvania tend to fit this description. It may be also that the status quo or "care-

taker" orientation of some suburbs is a result of the suburban dependence on central city resources and services.[30]

7. *Interparty competition*. Cities with more competitive party structures are more likely to engage in reform activity but less likely to adopt new charters. There is a scarcity of research on local party competition from which to draw hypotheses. Proposition 7 is based on the suspicion that challenges to the controlling party, such as structural changes, are more likely in competitive cities because of the minority party's efforts to exploit any opportunity to weaken the control of the majority party. At the same time, it is doubtful that a weak minority party could mobilize sufficient support to carry a proposal which was opposed by the majority.

Reform Activity and Environmental Indicators: Some Findings

A step-wise correlation program was used to analyze these data.[31] In Table 2, the independent variables are ranked in terms of the relative variance produced in the dependent variable—reform *activity*. It is clear that metropolitan class and population size are the most important environmental correlates of reform activity. The remaining ten variables, in combination, contribute only an additional 22 percent to the explained variance in the dependent variable. It appears that the effects of social class and heterogeneity, economic potential, and absentee ownership are marginal in determining the presence or absence of charter reform activity.

Although the total variation explained by the environment is not high (55 percent), metropolitan classification and population size together account for 33 percent of the total variation. This finding provides some support for propositions 1 and 6, which, when combined, might be termed a stress-dependence hypothesis. That is, larger cities may generate greater demands for services which are not easily handled in the rather decentralized administrative structure inherent in commission governments. The resulting

TABLE 2. Cumulative Multiple Correlations between Selected Environmental Variables and Reform Activity in Forty-three Pennsylvania Cities

ENVIRONMENTAL VARIABLES	ACTIVITY INDEX		
	Multiple R	Multiple R^2	Increase in R^2
Metropolitan class	0.48	0.23	0.23
Population size	0.58	0.33	0.10
All variables *	0.74	0.55	0.22

Note : In this program, variables are ranked in terms of their overall explanatory power (i.e., the variance produced in the dependent variable). If a variable is unrelated to the dependent variable, it is excluded from the equation. When a number of independent variables are not truly independent—i.e., when they are highly intercorrelated—the importance of one or more of these variables may be minimized. For example, if variables A, B, and C are highly intercorrelated and their effects on variable D are being analyzed, the computer may rank variable A highly and, as a result, deemphasize the importance of variables B and C. This would result because B and C did not contribute a sufficient additional increment to the variance explained by A. For a more detailed explanation, see Hubert M. Blalock, *Social Statistics* (New York: McGraw-Hill, 1960), pp. 346–51.

* Variables which independently account for less than a 7 percent increase in R^2.

TABLE 3. Cumulative Multiple Correlations between Selected Environmental Variables and Reform Outcomes in Twenty-Five Attempts*

ENVIRONMENTAL VARIABLES	OUTCOMES (PASSAGE-DEFEAT)		
	Multiple R	Multiple R²	Increase in R²
Rentals	0.47	0.22	0.22
Metropolitan class	0.63	0.40	0.18
Absentee-ownership	0.73	0.53	0.13
Real estate values	0.78	0.60	0.07
All variables†	0.86	0.74	0.14

*See footnote 20.
†Variables which independently account for less than a 7 percent increase in R^2.

stress may provide at least the inclination to consider structural changes. Further, as indicated above, the dependence of suburban cities on central city resources may result in a reduction in demands placed on suburban governments and a corresponding status quo orientation.[32]

Environment Indicators and Reform Outcomes: Some Findings

Attention is now directed to this question: Once political change is formally considered, as reflected in the activity index, what are the environmental correlates of the results of this consideration (i.e., the variables associated with passage or defeat)? The results reported in Table 3 reveal that the relationship between outcomes and metropolitan class is consistent with the earlier findings, but the explanatory importance of population size has diminished. A possible explanation is that this is a consequence of the fact that larger cities tended to be active while smaller cities remained inactive (i.e., larger cities were more likely to attempt to exercise their new charter options than smaller cities). In this measure, where only active cities are considered, the variation in population size is not as great.

The effects of absentee ownership require some explanation. The relationship is negative.[33] It appears that there is a tendency to

reject new charter proposals in cities where a larger proportion of the local economy is controlled by absentee-owned firms.[34] This finding is consistent with proposition 5. Further, there is evidence of support for proposition 4. Economic potential, as reflected in rentals and real estate values, appears to be a factor of some importance. New charter proposals tend to have a higher probability of success in cities with greater economic potential.

The most important conclusion which can be drawn at this point is that central and independent cities with greater economic potential and lower levels of absentee ownership are more likely to adopt new charters. It is interesting to note that neither the social indicators nor interparty competition (propositions 2, 3 and 7) is associated with reformism as it is measured in two separate indices.

Environmental and Political Indicators and Referenda Outcomes: Some Propositions and Findings

Thus far, interparty competition was the only explicitly political variable included in the analysis.[35] Now the four additional political process variables are introduced in the analysis of twenty-two charter referenda: (1) type of proposal, (2) city hall response, (3) fear of excessive costs, and (4) voter turnout.[36] The dependent variable in this case is the percentage of the popular vote approving the new charter proposal.

The textbook literature on urban politics provides an abundant supply of insights into the politics of municipal reform.[37] In brief, it is suggested that council-manager proposals are usually opposed by incumbent city administrations and local politicians. This opposition often has its basis in the understandable reluctance to sacrifice or relinquish political influence (e.g., patronage) to a professional manager. Perhaps the most common criticism of the manager plan is that it costs too much. Opponents of manager proposals often exploit the public's fear of excessive costs during reform campaigns. If this

TABLE 4. Simple Correlations among Political Variables in Twenty-Two Campaigns

	City Hall Response	Type of Proposal	Cost Issue	Percent Voter Turnout
City Hall response (1 = support, 0 = opposition)	—	0.72	0.83	−0.53
Type of proposal (1 = mayor, 0 = manager)		—	0.76	−0.56
Cost issue (1 = no, 0 = yes)				−0.57

fear becomes a salient issue for the electorate, it is probable that it will be reflected in a higher voter turnout comprised of a disproportionately large number of negative voters.[38]

The following propositions are drawn from this literature:

8. City hall opposition is associated with council-manager proposals.

9. The fear of higher costs of reform government is associated with council-manager proposals and city hall opposition.

10. Higher voter turnouts are associated with council-manager proposals, city hall opposition, and the fear of higher costs.

11. Referendum defeat is associated with council-manager proposals, city hall opposition, fear of excessive costs, and larger voter turnouts.

Beyond examining these specific propositions, the overriding question raised here involves the relative importance of political process variables when they are evaluated simultaneously with the environmental set.

Propositions 8, 9, and 10 are examined in Table 4. The substantial association between these variables tends to confirm the hypothesized relationships, if one agrees with a logical sequence of events. That is, when council-manager proposals were offered, in most cases city hall responded negatively. Usually this opposition was mobilized in countercampaigns to dramatize the alleged excessive costs of council-manager government. Alerted to the alleged financial burden council-manager government would create, taxpayers expressed their fears by turning out

in larger numbers to vote against the proposal. It appears that if local public officials oppose a charter proposal and subsequently provide a nucleus for resistance, opposition in the community at large is more likely to develop.[39]

With reference to proposition 10, larger voter turnouts are clearly associated with council-manager proposals, city hall opposition, and the fear of excessive costs of reform government. Conversely, smaller voter turnouts are associated with mayor-council proposals, city hall support, or at least lack of opposition, and the absence of the cost issue.

Proposition 11 is considered in the final phase of the analysis, when both environmental and political variables are combined to assess their relative importance as correlates of referenda outcomes. The results reported in Table 5 provide evidence of the

TABLE 5. Cumulative Multiple Correlations between Selected Environmental and Political Variables and the Percentage Positive Vote in Twenty-two Referenda

ENVIRONMENTAL AND POLITICAL VARIABLES	PERCENTAGE POSITIVE VOTE		
	Multiple R	Multiple R²	Increase in R²
Cost issue	0.69	0.47	0.47
Population size	0.76	0.57	0.10
Type of proposal	0.82	0.68	0.11 *
Voter turnout	0.87	0.75	0.08
All variables†	0.98	0.96	0.21

*The apparent nonsequential ordering is due to rounding. The difference in R^2 between the second and third variables is 0.0033.

†Variables which independently account for less than a 7 percent increase in R^2.

rather striking relative importance of political process variables. Four of the sixteen variables included in the analysis, three political process variables, and population size account for 75 percent of the variation in the percentage positive vote—that is, the percentage of votes cast *for* the adoption of new charters.

Several conclusions can be drawn from these results. Of greatest significance is the relative strength of the political process variables. With the exception of population size (a positive relationship), the explanatory capacity of the environmental set of variables appears to be quite limited. Again, the weakness of association between the dependent variable and indicators of social class, social heterogeneity, and interparty competition is noteworthy in view of the importance accorded these variables in the literature. Beyond this, it appears safe to conclude that there is some empirical support for proposition 11.

With reference to proposition 11, perhaps some further clarification is due. A larger positive vote on the charter question is associated with mayor-council proposals, absence of the cost issue, and lower voter turnout.[40] The reduced importance of city hall response as an independent variable is a function of the statistical fact that this variable is highly correlated with two of the other process variables—namely, type of proposal and the cost issue (see Table 4). In the case of three such variables in a multiple correlation

equation, the explanatory overlap is considerable (see Note, Table 2).

Environmental and Political Variables: A Relative Assessment

Thus far, an attempt has been made to determine the correlates of variously defined dependent variables which measure different dimensions of structural change or reformism. The analysis has shown that, in general, the relative importance of environmental variables declined when political process variables were considered simultaneously in the analysis of referenda outcomes. Population size was the single exception.

At the conclusion of their study, Lineberry and Fowler suggest that "political institutions 'filter' the process of converting [socioeconomic] inputs into [political] outputs."[41] They hypothesize that political variables perform a similar "filter" or linkage function. If the Lineberry-Fowler model is valid, one would expect to find a convincing relationship between the environmental set and the political process variables. Table 6 shows that there is such a relationship between a sub-set of the environmental set and the political variables. More specifically, indicators of economic potential (rentals, income, real estate values, and employment-residence ratios) and race (percentage nonwhite) are most closely associated with the political

TABLE 6. Simple Correlations between Environmental and Political Variables in Twenty-two Referenda

Environment	Type of Proposal	City Hall Response	Cost Issue	Voter Turnout
Rentals	0.27	0.42	0.41	−0.53
Income	0.31	0.20	0.18	−0.52
Real estate values	0.35	0.14	0.33	−0.43
Employment-residence ratios	0.07	0 33	0.49	−0.39
Nonwhite	0.48	0.43	0.29	−0.32
Party competition	−0.03	−0.19	−0.20	0.20
Metro class	0.17	0.18	0.22	0.17
Absentee ownership	0.19	−0.11	−0.14	−0.16
Education	−0.13	0.06	0.11	−0.13
Ethnicity	−0.17	−0.25	−0.02	0.07
White collar	−0.28	0.00	−0.03	−0.07
Population	0.29	−0.01	0.11	−0.03

variables. Cities with greater economic potential and larger nonwhite populations are more likely to receive and vote on mayor-council proposals. Consequently, city officials are less likely to oppose these proposals and the cost issue remains dormant. This combination of events results in lower voter turnouts and greater acceptance potentials for reform proposals.

There is some evidence, reported earlier, that reform activity is less likely to occur in more racially diverse cities, namely, suburbs.[42] However, this evidence must now be qualified by adding that when reform activity does occur, the size of the nonwhite minority is positively associated with mayor-council proposals which have a greater probability of acceptance. It may be that economically viable and racially diverse cities find mayor-council government more compatible with a need to provide an arena for the arbitration of potentially conflicting interests.

Population size and metropolitan class, which were shown earlier to have some determinant effect on reform activity and outcomes (see Tables 2, 3 and 5), are not related in any meaningful way to the political variables. A plausible interpretation of this, noted earlier, is that population size and metropolitan class exert an independent influence on reformism.[43] Larger central and independent cities are more likely to consider and adopt reform policies simply as a result of a sheer physical need for administrative innovation. In short, their size, relative proximity to parasitic suburbs, or, as is the case with independent cities, their relative geographical isolation may provide sufficient pressures for structural change or administrative innovation regardless of other social, economic, and political variables. The remaining environmental indicators appear to be only tenuously related to the political variables.

Summary and Conclusions

An important feature of this study is its quasi-experimental design. Both the time sequence and legal constraints are uniform for each city included in the analysis. Thus any distortion, which is quite probable when these factors are not controlled, has been eliminated.

The findings reported are generally consistent with the linkage model hypothesized by Lineberry and Fowler.[44] The analysis has shown that some of the political variables recognized in the Lineberry and Fowler model—namely, structure of party systems (interparty competition), patterns of aggregation (type of proposal and cost issue), strength of interest groups (city hall response), and voter turnout—were, with the exception of interparty competition, important determinants of referenda outcomes. Beyond this, the relative importance of environmental variables declined when these political variables were considered simultaneously in the analysis. There is some evidence that these political variables function as intervening variables linking a subset of the environmental indicators to referenda outcomes. Finally, some standard social indicators—namely, education, ethnicity, and occupation—were shown to be conspicuously weak in their association with reformism throughout the analysis.

These findings suggest the importance of political process variables in comparative urban research. On the surface, it may seem that this finding is contrary to those of a number of studies which have indicated the limited influence of political variables on policy outputs at both the state and local levels.[45] A possible explanation for these somewhat divergent findings is that previous policy output research has been limited almost exclusively to analyses of revenue and expenditure policies which, quite plausibly, would be associated with variables reflecting the economic potential or the tax base of states and localities. However, the relationships which exist between these socioeconomic variables and policies which represent explicitly political values (e.g., candidate preferences or essentially noneconomic issues such as fluoridation and municipal reform) may not be as direct or important as they are in those policies which must be made within the parameters set by the economic potential of the state. It is probable, and certainly worthy of further research, that the explanatory importance of socioeconomic and political process variables will vary with the type of policy being considered. When noneconomic policies are considered, a stronger association is revealed between political process variables and, in this case, referenda outcomes. These process variables reflect the attitudinal and behavioral dimensions of city politics to a greater degree than the socioeconomic variables.

Another explanation for these differences is that perhaps too much consideration is being given to the relative availability of political data rather than the theoretical relevance of these data to the problem being examined. The result is that political variables are usually defined operationally in structural rather than behavioral or interactional terms. To this extent, the behavioral dimension of politics is being ignored, not assessed, in the policy output studies and the results may be simply a product of the methodology.

What this analysis has demonstrated is not that environmental variables are unimportant, but rather that their importance must be assessed in combination with relevant and meaningful political variables; that is, political process variables which are often recognized but rarely included in comparative urban research. Despite the reservations one may have about the validity of dichotomous variables in defining complex political phenomena, the costs of excluding such variables may far exceed the satisfaction which may be derived from more rigorously defined, more readily accessible, but inconsequential indicators. In short, an effort must be made to include those variables, which have been shown in the case study literature to have theoretical and political relevance, into aggregate comparative studies. The theoretical limitations of case study analysis are well known. More attention should now be directed to the explanatory limitations of simple input-output analysis in which no attempt is made to determine the independent and intervening effects of political process variables.

Notes

1. A good discussion of this literature can be found in Herbert Jacob and Michael Lipsky, "Outputs, Structure, and Power: An Assessment of Changes in the Study of State and Local Politics," *Journal of Politics*, 30 (May 1968), 510–38.

2. Perhaps the best known statement of this view is found in Edward C. Banfield and James Q. Wilson, *City Politics* (Cambridge: Harvard University Press and M.I.T. Press, 1963); and their article, "Public-Regardingness as a Value Premise in Voting Behavior," *American Political Science Review*, 58 (December 1964), 876–87.

3. Charles R. Adrian, *Governing Urban America*, 2nd ed., (New York: McGraw-Hill, 1961), pp. 214, 217–18.

4. For example, they found that commission governments did not fulfill the objectives of institutional reform—i.e., this form of government seems to reflect rather than reduce the impact of social cleavages. Robert L. Lineberry and Edmund P. Fowler, "Reformism and Public Policies in American Cities," *American Political Science Review*, 61 (September 1967), 701–16.

5. See, for example, Robert J. Mowitz and Deil S. Wright, *Profile of a Metropolis* (Detroit: Wayne State University Press, 1962); and Robert Dahl, *Who Governs? Democracy and Power in an American City* (New Haven: Yale University Press, 1961).

6. See, for example, Richard E. Dawson and James A. Robinson, "Interparty Competition, Economic Variables and Welfare Politics in the American States," *Journal of Politics*, 25 (May 1963), 265–98; Richard I. Hofferbert, "The Relation Between Public Policy and Some Structural and Environmental Variables in the American States," *American Political Science Review*, 60 (March 1966), 73–82; and Thomas R. Dye, "Governmental Structure, Urban Environment, and Educational Policy," *Midwest Journal of Political Science*, 11 (August 1967), 353–80. For an exception to this general finding, see Ira Sharkansky, "Economic and Political Correlates of State Government Expenditures: General Tendencies and Deviant Cases," *Midwest Journal of Political Science*, 11 (May 1967), 173–92. See also the discussion of this question in Jacob and Lipsky, "Outputs, Structure, and Power," pp. 511–17.

7. On this point, see Jacob and Lipsky, "Outputs, Structure, and Power," p. 518.

8. Lineberry and Fowler, "Reformism and Public Policies," p. 714.

9. Hereafter referred to as the Optional Charter Law.

10. Under the law, a city could place a proposal to elect a charter study commission before the voters either by ordinance or petition. If a commission were elected by popular vote, it

could, after a study period, recommend either a mayor-council or council-manager charter, or it could recommend retention of the existing commission plan. A recommendation for a new charter was then placed before the people in a referendum.

11. Other structural variables usually considered in studies such as this were not relevant. Pennsylvania law requires partisan, at-large elections in all third-class cities.

12. One of these cities, at the time of this writing, had not had the opportunity to vote. It was coded as an "active" rather than a new charter city.

13. The 1960 census populations of these cities range from 10,667 to 138,440. Five cities were excluded from the study because they have dropped below the legal population minimum of 10,000 required for third-class cities.

14. Variables 1 through 10 were taken from *The Municipal Yearbook 1963* (Chicago: International City Managers' Association, 1963); and *The County and City Data Book 1962* (Washington, D.C.: U.S. Department of Commerce, Bureau of Census, 1962). All data are taken from the 1960 census.

15. *The Municipal Yearbook 1963*, p. 97.

16. *Ibid.*, p. 92.

17. The employment information and home office location were taken from the *Pennsylvania Industrial Directory 1965* (Harrisburg, Pa.: Department of Internal Affairs, 1965).

18. "Lists of Public Officials" (Harrisburg, Pa.: Department of Property and Supplies), Vols. 92–97.

19. Twenty-one of the forty-three cities were defined as active.

20. Rejection was defined to include, in addition to electoral defeat, the failure of a charter study commission either to submit a recommendation or to recommend retention of the commission plan. One of these conditions was met in twenty-five cases involving twenty cities. Five cities experienced two campaigns. In the analysis, the second effort in these five cities was treated as a separate event.

21. The twenty-two referenda occurred in nineteen cities. Again, the second referendum in three of the cities was treated as a separate event with conditional changes treated as new information.

22. For example, see David A. Booth, *Metropolitics: The Nashville Consolidation* (East Lansing: Michigan State University, Institute for Community Development, 1963), pp. 37–56; and Brett Hawkins, "Public Opinion and Metropolitan Reorganization in Nashville," *Journal of Politics*, 28 (May 1966), 408–18.

23. The risks involved in dichotomizing such complex variables are recognized and accepted in view of the new information which may be revealed about the interrelationship of these variables and the standard environmental indicators in determining policy outcomes.

24. The duration of reform activity usually ranged from a year to eighteen months. Additional information on some campaigns was found in published and unpublished documents made available by the Bureau of Research and Information of the Pennsylvania Department of Community Affairs, Harrisburg, Pa.

25. For an analysis of the correlates of voter turnout, see Robert R. Alford and Eugene C. Lee, "Voting Turnout in American Cities," *American Political Science Review*, 62 (September 1968), 796–813.

26. Examples of such studies are: Edgar L. Sherbenou, "Class Participation, and the Council-Manager Plan," *Public Administration Review*, 21 (Summer 1961), 131–35; John H. Kessel, "Government Structure and Environment: A Statistical Note about American Cities," *American Political Science Review*, 56 (September 1962), 615–20; Oliver P. Williams and Charles R. Adrian, *Four Cities: A Study in Comparative Policy Making* (Philadelphia: University of Pennsylvania Press, 1963), pp. 287–88; Leo F. Schnore, *The Urban Scene: Human Ecology and Demography* (New York: The Free Press, 1965), pp. 184–99; Robert R. Alford and Harry M. Scoble, "Political and Socioeconomic Characteristics of American Cities," *The Municipal Yearbook 1965* (Chicago: International City Managers' Association), pp. 82–97; Charles S. Liebman, "Functional Differentiation and Political Characteristics of Suburbs," *American Journal of Sociology*, 66 (March 1961), 485–90; Raymond E. Wolfinger and John Osgood Field, "Political Ethos and the Structure of City Government," *American Political Science Review*, 60 (June 1966), 306–26; Thomas R. Dye, "Urban Political Integration: Conditions Associated with Annexation in American Cities," *Midwest Journal of Political Science*, 8 (November 1964), 430–46; Thomas R. Dye, Charles S. Liebman, Oliver P. Williams, and Harold Herman, "Differentiation and Cooperation in a Metropolitan Area," *Midwest Journal of Political Science*, 7 (May 1963), 145–55; and Amos H. Hawley, "Community Power and Urban Renewal Success," *American Journal of Sociology*, 68 (January, 1963) 422–31; and Leo F. Schnore and Robert R. Alford, "Forms of Government and Socio-Economic Characteristics of Suburbs," *Administrative Science Quarterly*, 8 (June 1963), 1–17.

27. The propositions listed are logically derived from the studies indicated in footnote 26, *supra*. These propositions are not empirically derived because most of this literature deals specifically with government structure rather than political change. Thus the results of the examination of these propositions do not bear directly on the findings from which they were derived.

28. See also Ernst A. Barth, "Community In-

fluence Systems: Structure and Change," *Social Forces*, 40 (October 1961); "Absentee-Owned Corporations and Community Power Structure," *American Journal of Sociology*, 61 (March 1956), 413–19; Robert O. Schulze, "The Role of Economic Dominants in Community Power Structure," *American Sociology Review*, 23 (February 1958), 3–9.

29. Schnore, *Urban Scene*, p. 190.

30. See, for example, Amos Hawley, "Metropolitan Populations and Municipal Expenditures in Central Cities," *Journal of Social Issues*, 7 (1951), 100–108. The reference to "caretaker" government is taken from the Williams and Adrian typology, *Four Cities*.

31. For a brief explanation, see Note, Table 2. A complete description of the program is available in W. J. Dixon (ed.), *Biomedical Computer Programs* (Los Angeles: Health Sciences Computing Facility, Department of Preventive Medicine and Public Health, School of Medicine, University of California, 1964), pp. 49–59.

32. A further justification for this explanation is that population size is not strongly associated with any other environmental variable, and is only marginally associated with metropolitan classification ($r = .33$). It is possible that ethnicity ($r = -.49$) and race (percentage nonwhite, $r = .33$) are exerting an indirect influence through metropolitan classification. These correlations indicate that there is a tendency for the suburban cities to have larger ethnic and nonwhite populations. But, the correlations between both these variables and the activity index are low, although directionally consistent ($r_e = .29$) ($r_{nw} = .25$), and they proved to be rather inconsequential in the step-wise analysis.

33. The partial correlation coefficient between absentee ownership and activity outcomes is $-.45$.

34. Recall that rejection here does not necessarily mean electoral defeat, but any of the means of rejection indicated earlier, *supra*, footnote 20.

35. Incomplete newspaper coverage is the reason other political variables were not included. Newspaper coverage improved greatly after it was established that a referendum would be held.

36. Recall again that "reform outcomes" (passage defeat) refer to the twenty-five cases in which decisions were made either by the charter commission (e.g., recommendation to retain the commission plan) or in a referendum. At this point, *only* referenda decisions (defined as the percentage of the vote for the proposal) are considered.

37. See, for example, Adrian, *Governing Urban America*, chap. 8; and Edward C. Banfield and James Q. Wilson, *City Politics*, chap. 13.

38. A study of fluoridation referenda indicates that higher voter turnout is associated with the defeat of these referenda. See Maurice Pinard, "Structural Attachments and Political Support in Urban Politics: The Case of Fluoridation Referendums," *American Journal of Sociology*, 68 (March 1963), 513–26.

39. This is consistent with the findings that the position of the mayor is closely associated with the outcomes of fluoridation referenda. See David B. Rosenthal and Robert L. Crain, "Executive Leadership and Community Innovation: The Fluoridation Experience," *Urban Affairs Quarterly*, 1 (March 1966), 39–57.

40. The simple correlation between voter turnout and the percentage positive vote is negative, $r = -.53$.

41. Lineberry and Fowler, "Reformism and Public Policies, p. 715.

42. See footnote 32, *supra*.

43. *Supra*, pp. 1177–78.

44. *Loc. cit.*

45. See, for example, Herbert Jacob, "The Consequence of Malapportionment: A Note of Caution," *Social Forces*, 43 (December 1964), 256–61; Thomas R. Dye, "Malapportionment and Public Policy in the States," *Journal of Politics*, 27 (August 1965), 586–601; and *Politics, Economics and the Public: Policy Outcomes in the American States* (Chicago: Rand McNally, 1966); Richard I. Hofferbert, "The Relation Between Public Policy and Some Structural and Environmental Variables in the American States," *American Political Science Review*, 60 (March 1966), 73–82; and Jacob and Lipsky, "Outputs, Structure, and Power," 511–17.

VI

Feedback

LAWS, REGULATIONS, and other forms of official political decisions (i.e., outputs) are not merely randomly determined. Political authorities—whether they be legislators contemplating a new law, administrators fashioning a new procedure, or judges arriving at a legal decision—are presumed to have some objective or goal in mind which they anticipate will result from their action. As outlined previously, urban policies are the outcome of a variety of demands and supporting situations which constantly feed into the decision centers. In a democratic society, at least, those in positions of local authority are expected to take these stimuli into account as they arrive at public policy decisions. The degree to which officials are responsive to various inputs may vary, yet it seems safe to assume that public leaders (even in a dictatorship) do engage in a continuous evaluation process by which they seek to determine whether their decisions and policies are accomplishing the desired objectives. Even in common parlance, the term *feedback* is applied to this process by which groups or individuals gather information about past, present, or projected behavior as a way of deciding whether to continue or change existing behavior to arrive at some predetermined goal.

The feedback concept as employed in social science research comes primarily from the field of *cybernetics*, or the science of control and communication. Karl Deutsch has defined the term as a "communications' network that produces action in response to an input of information, and *includes the results of its own action in the new information by which it modifies its subsequent behavior*."[1] Even more simply, Norbert Wiener, one of the pioneers in the field of cybernetics, describes feedback as "the property of being able to adjust future conduct by past performances."[2] Illustrations of the feedback principle have come primarily from the physical world. A favorite mechanical analogy of a controlled feedback system is the thermostat which regulates the temperature in a building.[3] Deutsch, however, uses the example of a modern antiaircraft system equipped with radar tracking and computing devices which "senses" an object in the air and, through continuous adjustment, shoots it down.[4] In his application of these concepts from the physical world to the political system, David Easton considers feedback as the basic property which gives the system its dynamic quality. Feedback not only permits the political system to survive by adjusting to its surroundings, but it enables the system to explore and discover new ways of dealing with its problems. On the basis of information about past and present behavior, the system may select, reject, or emphasize one pattern of behavior over another.[5] In this way, outputs may be generated to deal with current or projected levels of stress to guarantee system survival and perhaps even the necessary support for those individual decision makers who may wish to continue in public office. As Easton suggests, "Predictions about the effects of outputs on the membership of a political system are the stock in trade of the practicing politician as well as the scholar."[6]

Though systematic analyses of the feedback process in politics have been virtually nonexistent, political scientists have long been concerned with questions of how public opinion and public policy are related. Some of the general findings regarding this opinion-policy linkage, which would normally be discussed as part of the input process, may be useful in our understanding of feedback since this latter process may be considered as a special category of input. The late V. O. Key, Jr., an eminent political scientist with a long-time interest in public opinion, discussed a model of government involving a two-way interaction process between citizens and officials even though he was not explicitly using a systems framework.[7] A concern of this model was the identification of various factors which might influence this two-way interaction—in particular, those things which affect citizen participation or involvement. Key mentions, first, that the size of the "attentive public" may vary from issue to issue. Second, the government may frequently act so as to anticipate negative or resistive action. As Key indicates, "Many governmental actions generate not a ripple of reaction; to some degree that consequence occurs because decision-makers have correctly estimated the temper of those to be affected by action."[8] Thus where feedback does not develop, government may be most attuned to public sentiment. Third, the rapidity with which the public responds to government action may vary considerably. In some situations, reaction may be immediate and unambiguous; in other instances, public response may emerge slowly and without precise form. And, finally, linkages between government and citizen will always be affected by imperfections in the flow of information. Some of these may result from deliberate misrepresentation by public authorities while plain lack of attentiveness may lead to confusion in other instances. While Key does not present his model in hypothesis form, his general observations about the political linkage process should be useful guides in developing more precise conceptual models of the feedback process as used in systems analysis.

The actual operation of the feedback process as applied to the political system is circular and dynamic, as suggested in Figure 1.

The political system engages in exchanges with various other systems through the output linkage. These surrounding or adjacent systems respond in some manner to the stimuli emanating from the political authorities and, in turn, generate some form of reaction which may return to the political system as a new input. The concept of feedback implies that the political system has access to information indicating the effects its outputs may produce in other systems so that it may anticipate certain reactions and plan accordingly. If, somehow, the public policies did not have the

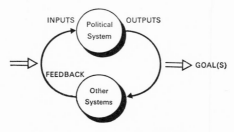

Figure 1. The Political Feedback Process

expected impact on other systems, the political system, through feedback, may modify its behavior through follow-up outputs which may move the political system closer to its desired goals. Thus the process is dynamic and continuous. Also, it should be noted that feedback does not always operate through the environment; in fact, it may return directly to the political system if the policy output has largely political consequences.

Analyzing the feedback process in greater detail, we find at least three basic requirements which appear to be essential parts of the operation— communication, goals, and the capacity to act. There can be no feedback without channels of communication to transmit information about events and situations to those in a position to officially act. Goals, in some form, must exist in light of which decisions can be made to modify or redirect the behavior of the system if necessary. And those in positions of authority must have both the capacity and the will to cause the system to move in the direction which the information indicates is necessary to achieve the goals. In other words, the system must be capable of responding to stress by changing its behavior if need be.

Message transmission is not only the first step in the feedback process but the *sine qua non* as well. No matter what happens in the environment as a result of political action, it cannot affect the decision makers in any purposeful way unless they have ways of learning about it. No information, no corrective action, or in Easton's words:

> Returning information about the state of the system, its distance from desired goals, and about past and continuing effects of action already taken, enables the decision centers of the system to engage in any corrective action perceived as feasible and necessary to achieve the goals.[9]

Although provision for an adequate information gathering process is essential, it is by no means easily done. On the urban scene, certain groups which have a sizable stake in the political process, such as the business community, may actually be sought out by public officials for their opinions on various policies and proposals. On the other hand, arousing other segments in order to get reaction on policy matters may be next to impossible. Certain issues, of course, stimulate more concern on the part of citizens than others. Open housing, for instance, has been one of the most controversial and emotionally charged domestic policies of recent years. Perhaps in areas such as this, decision makers can expect maximum feedback on current and proposed policy changes. Yet, in Toledo where an open housing referenda was held in 1967, a city primary turnout record was set, but 64 percent of the adult population did *not* vote. Moreover, only 40 percent of those questioned in that community felt that the election outcome would affect them personally, and only 16 percent felt a great personal stake in it.[10] The greatest problem in the functioning of the feedback process, however, is between ghetto residents and representatives of city government, including the police. Virtually every study of civil disturbance in one of the nation's cities touches upon this important problem. One of two things (or some of both) seems to be happening: either low-income residents generate little feedback for urban policy makers to respond to, or decision makers are not particularly motivated to pay much attention to "noise" from the ghetto. The President's Riot Commission concluded that the urban violence which erupted in a number of large cities during the summer of 1967 was foreshadowed by an accumulation of unresolved grievances by ghetto residents against local authorities—including, but not limited to, the police. The report quoted from a Senate Subcommittee on Employment, Manpower and Poverty presented just prior to the Detroit riot:

> Area residents . . . complain almost continually that their demands for program changes are not heeded, that they have little voice in what goes on.[11]

Partially in response to this acknowledged lack of communication between ghetto dweller and city hall, the Report of the Commission on the Causes and Prevention of Violence recommended that the federal government allocate seed money to certain states and localities for purposes of establishing citizens' grievance agencies.[12]

Two recent federally financed urban programs, Community Action Agencies and Model Cities, have explicitly recognized the importance of providing ways for the poor to make their views known concerning projects presumably designed for their benefit. Legislation establishing both programs contains provisions for widespread citizen participation from the "target" areas. A recent study of the model cities program in several locales noted that certain neighborhood participation groups organized because of model cities have even been successful in influencing various federally funded projects outside the scope of the model cities program. In one city, for example, the residents used model city machinery as the means of forcing the city to reconsider a rezoning action that would have concentrated high-rise apartments in one section of the model neighborhood. In another, urban renewal was for the first time brought under surveillance of affected local neighborhoods. All problems of communication between low-income groups and public officials have not been rectified, of course, but the conclusion Sundquist and Davis reached in their study of community decision making in model cities was that planning and program execution would henceforth be carried on *with* as well as *for* residents in poverty areas.[13]

No matter how good the communications channels, information by itself is valueless unless those in positions to act know what to do with it. This underlines the importance of goals and objectives. Easton sees feedback information as serving the broad purpose of permitting the authorities to act intelligently in meeting any possible loss of support.[14] Thus specific goal attainment is not emphasized in his work since his basic concern is with systemic survival. Yet in much of the cybernetic-oriented literature there is considerably more interest in the part which feedback plays in the system's goal attainment and goal direction. Deutsch, for example, stresses that any simple feedback mechanism implies a "purpose" or "goal" which may range from efforts to achieve some short-range temporary condition to the attainment of higher order, long-range purposes such as systems survival.[15]

In the area of urban politics, this goal-seeking process might embrace those immediate efforts to win passage of a forthcoming municipal bond issue or the long-range objective of creating the kind of community life in which amenities are bountiful. We noted previously that local elected officials frequently have "policy maps" or broad municipal objectives for their communities, such as maintenance of only traditional services or provision of urban amenities. Few cities, however, have gone as far as Dallas in setting forth a series of explicit short-range and longer-term goals for the community. Beginning in June 1966, a number of Dallas citizens met as a planning committee to draft a series of goals for Dallas which were published and served as the basis for a series of meetings, attended by 6,380 people, held late that year. Of the twelve basic areas of concern, at least nine in some way directly involved local governmental agencies (city government, design of the city, health, welfare, etc.).[16] Most cities and their municipal governments are far less self-conscious about goals. Nevertheless, some local polities appear to have both short-term and longer-range goals, even if only to preserve the status quo. Others, however, seem to be almost without concrete objectives, just drifting as it were from one problem or crisis to another without any real overriding goals. In those instances where goal-directed behavior is intermittent or almost nonexistent, the feedback process functions largely to insure system persistence rather than in pursuit of well-defined governmental purposes. Municipal political systems can not only change strategies or tactics necessary to achieve immediate objectives but also may consciously modify the goals both for the short run and over a longer time span.

Perhaps the fact that the urban system must have the capacity to redirect or modify its behavior for the feedback process to operate fully is too obvious for comment. Nevertheless, without this final step in the feedback cycle—the actual modification of behavior—the process is not complete. The degree to which a municipality may, in fact, change courses to meet perceived needs or new goals may vary not only between communities but in the same community through time. In some cities, the local board of education may have an almost perfect record in providing virtually every physical facility needed within the local school system. And yet that same group of decision makers may find it extremely difficult to move ahead with effective plans for ending racial segregation within that system. Or the local city council may recognize that unless immediate steps are taken to alleviate oppressive conditions in the ghetto areas civil disorder is virtually inevitable. Still, lack of funds or fear of white backlash may immobilize those who must act if change is to occur. Another example illustrating the difficulty in redirecting the urban system concerns the twin problems of "sunk costs" and bureaucratic inertia. Sunk costs may include previous large-scale commitments to physical development which, once completed, cannot be changed without enormous expense. Or a new set of political decision makers may take office pledged to redefine and redirect activities of municipal government only to find that the acts of previous administrations have irrevocably bound them to a course of action they would otherwise not have chosen. The commitment of large bureaucratic structures to existing patterns of behavior may have the same effect. More than one incoming "reform" administration has been stymied by the inability to overcome bureaucratic resistance. Thus certain impediments to goal attainment or system redirection are almost sure to be encountered in some form or another; some may yield fairly easily while other obstacles may block "progress" for decades.

Political science is notably devoid of efforts to systematically analyze the feedback process. Ira Sharkansky has given some attention to the concept of policy "impacts"—that is, the effects certain policy outcomes (namely, public services) have on various populations. In the field of education, for example, Sharkansky suggests that policy impact might be measured by the intellectual skills acquired by students or by the earning power of former students. He does not, in this particular study, seek to empirically analyze the policy impact concept nor to trace the further reaction that changes in educational policies might have on the political system.[17] Robert Salisbury, in his analysis of educational policies among the states, observed a phenomenon which might suggest the operation of feedback although he does not discuss his findings in that context. Salisbury noted that, once a state had achieved a certain level of economic development, further expenditures for education seemed to be dependent primarily upon the educational leadership and group activity within that state. In other words, his analysis suggested that, given a certain economic level, a previous willingness to spend for education (a policy output) may tend to produce an active educational leadership (a policy impact) which, in turn, seems committed to spending even more for educational purposes (feedback effect).[18]

A particularly noteworthy exception to the lack of attention to the feedback process by empirical social scientists is the recent paper presented to the 1969 American Political Science Association by Fowler and Lineberry.[19] Their stated purpose was to explain output-environment linkages, using Canadian cities as the units of analysis together with comparative data from U.S. cities. The authors recognized that almost all previous urban research using a systems model has assumed one-way causality (with public policy as the dependent variable) partly because of the methodological difficulties which arise in statistical efforts to unravel reciprocal causation. Using tax and expenditure data from all Canadian cities of over 50,000 and eight community characteristic variables (primarily socioeconomic), they sought to test not only the strength of certain relationships (using multivariate analysis) but also the *direction* of influence. Since it was not statistically possible to directly measure causation, the technique employed to determine two-way or reciprocal relationships (two-stage least-squares estimation of regression coefficients) permitted only statistical inferences regarding the direction of causality. In particular, Fowler and Lineberry dealt with the potential reciprocal effects of voting turnout and tax and spending levels, and the reciprocal relationship between home-owner occupancy and municipal spending and taxation. In the first instance, the nature of the two-way relationship between voter turnout and revenue and expenditure policies led the authors to conclude that political participation may have a more complex relationship to public policy than previous theory had recognized. Rather than finding a one-way "causal arrow" flowing from turnout to policy, they suggested that political participation may be both a protest against more taxation and higher spending as well as a positive response stemming from the desired results (public improvements) of greater spending. The following diagram might help explain the relationship. In this situation, there is both a positive and negative relationship between turnout and spending operating simultaneously. That is, increased turnout may be drawing voters into the system who are opposed to greater spending, while at the same time a group of voters may be attracted who wish to continue or improve public services by increasing levels of spending. Obviously, this is a complex situation, but one which may more realistically describe the relation-

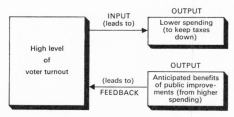

Figure 2. Reciprocity between Turnout and Spending

ship between these two variables than the ordinary assumption that the causal direction is strictly one way.

With respect to the relationship between expenditure and tax policies and owner occupancy, the findings supported previous research indicating that higher levels of home ownership in a city are associated with lower taxes and spending. Which causes which? The usual assumption is that home ownership leads to demands for lower taxes and spending. Fowler and Lineberry suggested, however, that it is just as plausible to hypothesize that high taxes may discourage home ownership. The hypothesized reciprocal relationship between owner occupancy and municipal spending and taxation was supported by the Canadian city data but not by the U.S. data. Although this study was intended to be exploratory and the authors urge caution in interpreting their inferences, it nevertheless stands as an important and provocative effort to systematically operationalize the feedback concept derived from systems analysis.

The original essay by Fowler and Lineberry found in this section attempts to fit the concept of feedback into the broader context of urban politics. The authors emphasize some of the complexities in the analysis of feedback and discuss its operation in light of three theories of urban politics. They also consider how urban policy makers seek to cope with the feedback process as a way of insuring the survival of the local political system.

Notes

1. Karl Deutsch, *The Nerves of Government: Models of Political Communication and Control* (New York: The Free Press, 1963), p. 88.

2. Norbert Wiener, *The Human Uses of Human Beings*, rev. ed. (New York: Doubleday Anchor, 1954), p. 33.

3. Alfred Kuhn, *The Study of Society: A Unified Approach* (Homewood, Ill.: Richard D. Irwin and Dorsey Press, 1963), p. 46.

4. Deutsch, *Nerves of Government*, p. 81.

5. David Easton, *A Systems Analysis of Political Life* (New York: John Wiley, 1965), p. 370.

6. *Ibid.*, p. 409.

7. V. O. Key, Jr., *Public Opinion and American Democracy* (New York: Alfred A. Knopf, 1961), pp. 411–14. An extended treatment of linkage models is found throughout Norman R. Luttbeg (ed.), *Public Opinion and Public Policy: Models of Political Linkage* (Homewood, Ill.: Dorsey Press, 1968).

8. Key, *Public Opinion and American Democracy*, p. 413.

9. Easton, *Systems Analysis of Political Life*, p. 370.

10. Howard D. Hamilton, "Direct Legislation: Some Implications of Open Housing Referenda," *American Political Science Review*, 64 (1970), 124–37.

11. *Report of the National Advisory Commission on Civil Disorders* (New York: Bantam edition, 1968), p. 286.

12. *To Establish Justice, To Insure Domestic Tranquility: Final Report of the National Commission on the Causes and Prevention of Violence* (Washington, D.C.: Government Printing Office, 1969), pp. 107–17.

13. James L. Sundquist with David W. Davis, *Making Federalism Work: A Study of Program Coordination at the Community Level* (Washington, D.C.: Brookings Institution, 1969), pp. 107–17.

14. Easton, *Systems Analysis of Political Life*, p. 364.

15. Deutsch, *Nerves of Government*, p. 93.

16. *Goals for Dallas*, rev. 2nd ed. (Dallas: Southwest Center for Advanced Studies, 1967).

17. Ira Sharkansky, "Environment, Policy, Output and Impact: Problems of Theory and Method in the Analysis of Public Policy," in Sharkansky (ed.), *Policy Analysis in Political Science* (Chicago: Markham, 1970), pp. 61–79.

18. Robert Salisbury, "State Politics and Education," in Herbert Jacob and Kenneth N. Vines (ed.), *Politics in the American States* (Boston: Little, Brown, 1965), p. 353.

19. Edmund P. Fowler and Robert L. Lineberry, "Canadian City Politics: Public Policy Analysis and the Problem of Reciprocal Causation" (Paper delivered at the annual meeting of the American Political Science Association, New York, 1969).

POLITICAL SCIENTISTS typically concern themselves with demands on the political system, with the conversion of those demands into public policy, and with the actual implementation of those policies. To use David Easton's language, *inputs, conversion mechanisms,* and *outputs* have been the major focus of political scientists. But to speak of the political system as consisting solely of these elements implies that it is merely a conveyer belt, rather than a system of interrelated parts. A conveyer belt is a closed system, mechanically processing items and making no change in its own operations. But a system with *feedback* from its outputs to its inputs is an open system, which enables a system to adapt its behavior to its environment.[1] Through feedback, a political system can generate the resources to make its policies self-corrective; or, if the feedback process is unsuccessful, policies can contribute to the self-destruction of the system. Feedback is not necessarily "democratic." We cannot say that the more feedback there is, the more decision makers take the needs of the common man into account. Indeed, an excess of feedback may produce an overload on the system, making it impossible for any demands to be heeded.

For feedback to occur, several conditions have to be met:

1. A public policy is enunciated or implemented.
2. The policy must have some impact on the environment of the political system.
3. The environment, or some elements within it, must respond to the policy impact with enthusiasm, opposition, or indifference.
4. The environmental response must be directed toward the political system in the form of new demands or supports.

These conditions are cumulative in that each of them depends upon the existence of the previous condition(s). The first critical distinction is that between *policy* and *impact*. A policy without an impact is, in effect, no policy at all. By impact we mean the changes in the environment actually produced by the policy.[2] An urban renewal project, for ex-

Patterns of Feedback in City Politics*

Edmund P. Fowler and Robert L. Lineberry

ample, may have several impacts: raising land values and tax values in the renewal area; slowing the tide of middle-class migration to suburbia; and displacement and relocations of low-income citizens living on renewal sites. The kinds of impacts a policy has produce *responses* of individuals or groups within the environment. A group of citizens perceiving favorable impacts may "feed back" their support to the political decision makers; a group disadvantaged by a policy may respond with nonsupport and demands for policy reversal. Urban renewal may generate favorable responses from real estate and construction interests, but negative responses from relocated individuals who are "given a few dollars and told to get lost"[3] by renewal agencies. But a response triggered by a policy impact does not guarantee eventual feedback to policy makers. A response to policy impacts may be nothing more than a psychological reaction. Persons displaced by a new superhighway or an urban renewal project may experience grief, dissatisfaction, or general malaise[4] without doing anything about their response. Or neighborhood groups may be formed specifically to challenge and reverse the renewal or highway project.[5] Only when there is some behavioral manifestation of a response to a policy's impact do we say that feedback has occurred.

Our conception of the feedback process can be visually depicted—albeit in very

*An original essay, written especially for this volume.

stylized form—in Figure 1. The model contained there indicates the four components of the feedback process: public policies, policy impacts, responses, and the feedbacks themselves. We reiterate that this process is cumulative. If a policy produces little impact, if an impact produces little or no response, if the response is not translated into political action, then the feedback process is attenuated.

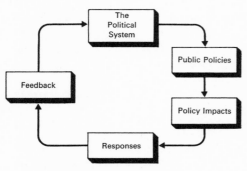

Figure 1. The Feedback Process

The Study of Feedback

There is very little about feedback in the literature of urban politics. Indeed, there is a tendency on the part of both scholars and practitioners to assume that the enunciation of policy itself is the alpha and omega of the political system. Even more commonly, political scientists and political decision makers focus almost exclusively on the level of expenditures as public policy. We can hardly blame political scientists for stopping at the water's edge by investigating mainly financial decisions of local governments. After all, political decision makers usually behave as if the size of the public budget is the central policy issue. Ralph Huitt has observed that the "American way with an issue is to debate it fiercely for years on an abstract level, then plump billions of dollars into it the day after it is enacted."[6] This suggests that the American concern for monetary standards applies no less to the public than the private sector.

More recently, however, there has been a significant concern with the impact of public policies. David Easton, in his seminal formulation of systems analysis in political science, distinguished between the "outputs" and "outcomes" of a policy.[7] Ranney, Sharkansky, and others have further refined the distinction between the policy *per se* and the *impact* of the policy.[8] What is now known about policy impact is sobering. It is clear, for example, that the amount of money spent on a policy is only distantly related to the level of services provided to the public.[9] Several studies on traffic enforcement cast doubt upon the proposition that vigorous law enforcement reduces accident rates.[10] Unquestionably, the most impressive study of policy impact is James S. Coleman's *Equality of Educational Opportunity.*[11] Studying the effects of various factors on pupil achievement and motivation, Coleman concluded that many of the most important determinants of educational impact were unrelated to public policy. This is no place to explore his careful and elaborate conclusions, but it is sobering indeed to learn that "the educational resources provided by a child's fellow students are more important for his achievement than the resources provided by the school board."[12] Although the study of policy impact is still in its infancy, enough evidence has accumulated to suggest that there is no one-to-one relationship between public policies and the actual reduction in the incidence of the problems which policy is supposed to affect.

But if there is little systematic attention being given to policy impact, there is even less devoted to public responses to policy and to feedback itself. One is tempted to attribute the relative absence of research on feedback to the relative absence of feedback among the urban citizenry. There is ample evidence that the typical American voter is apathetic about politics and possesses little information about what government is doing. The man on the street cares little about urban public policy because (1) it does not affect him, or (2) he fails to see how it affects him, or (3) his general interest in politics is so low that he does not activate himself, even if he perceives the effect of a policy. The low turnouts in municipal elections provide further evidence of the skimpy attentiveness of the urban citizenry.[13] Even in the hotly contested race between white Hugh Addonizio and black Kenneth Gibson for the 1970 mayoral election, only about 40 percent of the city's adult population appeared at the polls. If the drama and publicity associated with election campaigns does not stimulate intense interest in local politics, then day-to-day policy making presumably stimulates even less attention to urban affairs.

But to say that citizen awareness and activities in local politics is low is not to argue that feedback does not appear and at times assume a critical importance. To say that political scientists have written little explicitly about feedback does not mean that there has been nothing to write, or that they have not—like M. Jourdain and prose—been describing feedback in other terms. To be sure, it is difficult to examine the feedback process empirically. Explaining why one among dozens or hundreds of policy decisions prompts sustained feedback is almost like explaining the behavior of a computer spitting out random numbers. The myriad ways in which policy responses can sometimes become energized as feedback is not, even to careful students of local politics, readily comprehensible. But it is sometimes easy to see feedback in operation. The powerful effect of a single incident of public policy— the use of police to quell racial disturbances at Texas Southern University in Houston— on black attitudes is illustrated by Table 1. Surveys made in the black community before and after the violent black-police confrontation indicates clearly the effect of policy on individual and group attitudes. Attitudes supportive of the police declined significantly and critical attitudes increased. The effects of the police actions on black community sentiment appear to be immediate and plainly perceptible.

But this simple instance of response to policy activity may be deceptive. More typically, responses to policies are remote rather than immediate, indirect rather than direct, and mixed rather than decisive. Public policies may be delayed in their effects, "just as nuclear radiation from a surface H-bomb

TABLE 1. Responses of Black Community Samples to Questions Regarding Police, Before and After Police Actions at Texas Southern University, Houston, Texas*

QUESTION	RESPONSES Before TSU Violence	After TSU Violence
	%	%
1. In Houston, how would you say that the police treat Negroes—very well, fairly well, fairly badly, or very badly?		
Very well/fairly well	52	24
Fairly badly/very badly	37	67
Don't know	11	9
2. What kind of job do you think the police chief is doing?		
Excellent/good	30	8
Not so good/poor	44	73
Not sure	26	19

*Source: Blair Justice, *Detection of Potential Community Violence*, U.S. Department of Justice, Law Enforcement Assistance Administration, June 1968, p. 38.

blast can cause radioactive particles to 'float' to distant sites and 'settle' on them months later."[14] As the radiation analogy suggests, the effects of a policy may not be immediately apparent to an observer. Rather, reactions to one policy may "spill over" into other policy domains. The cumulative satisfactions or dissatisfactions with policies may give sustenance to, or prompt revolt against, the political system as a whole.

We have tried to emphasize some of the complexities in the analysis of feedback. In the next section, we use three theories of urban politics to emphasize different aspects of the feedback process. After that, we suggest some means of coping with feedback.

Three Theories and Feedback

There are many theories of urban government, almost as many as there are writers on the subject. But three of these theories—the theory of reform, the group theory of politics, and structural-functional theory—can be combined to illustrate the operation of the feedback process. The theory of reform directs our attention to the institutional mechanisms for processing feedback. Institutions are not neutral in their implications for the transmission of feedback. Rather, all feedback is distorted as it reenters the system. The nature of this distortion is a function of urban political institutions. The reform movement in urban politics was particularly concerned with the structure of institutions. Reformers reacted against machine politics and against the widespread corruption associated with the machine. Businessmen, Yankee old-stock groups, and intellectuals led the "good government" crusade. Intellectually, the reformers represented the first fruits of an era new in American political thought, when the dominant political metaphor was changing from a mechanistic, Newtonian model of thought to an evolutionary mode based upon Evolutionary Darwinism.[15] Woodrow Wilson, himself a leading political scientist and reformer, put the new metaphor in these terms:[16]

> The government of the United States was constructed upon the Whig theory of political dynamics, which was a sort of unconscious copy of the Newtonian theory of the universe. . . . The trouble with the theory is that government is not a machine, but a living thing. It falls, not under the theory of the universe, but under the theory of organic life. It is accountable to Darwin, not to Newton. It is modified by its environment, necessitated by its task, shaped to its functions by the sheer pressures of life.

With such an evolutionary metaphor, it was not difficult to think of men as malleable by institutional reform. To the Conservative Darwinist, the intellectual progeny of Herbert Spencer, man was subject to immutable laws of history and his behavior was reformable only marginally. To the Reform Darwinist, however, human behavior could be changed by modifying human institutions.[17] Thus reformers in city politics had a baker's dozen of institutional changes—at-large elections, nonpartisan politics, city manager government, civil service coverage, and other alterations—to promote their brand of democracy and accountability.

Today cities may be classified according to the degree to which their institutional arrangements reflect the reformers' preferences for "businesslike" and "apolitical" government.[18] But, intentionally or unintentionally, reformed governments differ from unreformed governments in the kinds of feedback they process. Several characteristics of reformed and unreformed institutions bear upon the feedback process:

1. Electoral participation is lower in reformed than unreformed cities.
2. Nonpartisan elections weaken party organizations and make the formulation and identification of issues by voters more difficult.
3. Bureaucratization and the city manager system remove policy determination from the hands of elected office holders, who are more accountable to feedback from electorates.
4. At-large elections make it more difficult for representatives of minority groups to win elections.

Thus reformed institutions appear to reduce at least certain kinds of feedback processing. In particular, it may be more difficult for groups with lower-than-average access to decision makers to articulate feedback through the regular input mechanisms. One student of the politics of reform in Toledo observes that

> in an urban society it is important that cities have political systems which are responsive to the diverse groups within them, yet capable of decisive action. This study suggests that reform institutions, when used in a large city, facilitate neither of these conditions. The lower-income and minority groups whose fate is crucial to the future of American cities are likely to find political access difficult under reform institutions. Nor are the skills of business and administrative officials readily available for the service of the community.[19]

A second general theory of government, the structural-functional theory, has been applied to local politics by Harold Kaplan in his study of metropolitan Toronto.[20] This theory directs our attention to the functions performed by governments and their impact on feedback. Kaplan emphasizes the tensions between two functions, integration and adaptation. While both elements are present to some degree in every system, any particular urban system will emphasize one over the other. The integrative role is played by those most interested in the survival of the system, while the adaptive role is shouldered by those who see the system as an instrument of change, regardless of internal conflict within it.[21] Emphasis on one or the other function will, we hypothesize, produce different kinds, and perhaps even different amounts, of feedback. A system primarily concerned with integration designs its policies explicitly to encourage positive feedback. Adaptive systems, on the other hand, are willing to pay the price of negative feedback in order to secure other goals. The leaders of Toronto Metro, for example, engaged in a "bricks and mortar" policy designed in part to win support for the Metro system. This integrative policy can be contrasted with the adaptive policy of fluoridation of municipal water supplies. Fluoridation is intended to deal with the distinctly "environmental" and "nonpolitical" problem of tooth decay, particularly among children. Few public policies can match fluoridation in the intensity and polarization of the feedback it generates. Crain and his associates estimate that "fluoridation was a public issue—often a stormy one—in over 3,000 cities in the United States and that fluoridation was rejected by more than half of them. By the end of 1960, the issue had been submitted to public referendum some 600 times, and the voters had rejected it over 60 percent of the time."[22] The examples of intense and polarized feedback arising from adaptive policies—such as urban renewal, public housing, civil rights policies, and zoning—could be easily multiplied. We hypothesize that adaptive policies generate more intense and polarized feedback than integrative policies.

The group theory of politics emphasizes the variable impact of policies on different groups and the consequent variations in feedback to the system. Kornhauser's group theory attempts to explain democratic systems and their stability through the interaction of three elements: masses, elites, and intermediary groups.[23] Stated simply, his theory defines two polar extremes of society. In the mass society, individuals are atomized and there is little development of secondary groups. In pluralist society, there are well-developed networks of secondary groups, which serve as buffers between masses and elites, as well as channels for processing demands on the system. Typically, in the urban political system, there is little regularized feedback from the masses *per se*. Yet the masses are not always quiescent or passive. V. O. Key, Jr., has tried to put mass behavior in some perspective by arguing that masses ordinarily permit a broad range of discretion on alternative policies formulated by the elities. Within this range, the decision makers are free to hammer out policies. However, there are "opinion dikes" beyond which elites cannot go without incurring sanctions from the masses.[24] The difficulty, of course, is the determination of the exact boundaries of permissibility. While citizens accept most policy without a murmer, some elite decisions—for example, fluoridation and open housing ordinances[25] —are met by antagonism at the mass level, often expressed through the referendum. At other times, mass reaction may be characterized by protests, anomic outbursts of street violence, or the "nay-saying" of alienated voters in a referendum. In analyzing mass feedback, it is important to remember that the resources for influencing decision makers are very crude (e.g., the election) or underdeveloped (e.g., because of low rates of participation). Moreover, as the reform theory suggests, the particular institutional channels of input may blur rather than sharpen the representation of mass opinion.

More important for the ongoing operation of the urban political system is the feedback from secondary groups and from the elites. Indeed, some writers argue that a political system with direct linkages between elites and masses is unstable and thus undesirable.[26] James S. Coleman notes that cities where citizens' needs are not aggregated by organized groups will have more rancorous conflict and even violence.[27] Thus secondary groups play a vital role in the transmission of feedback to decision makers. The rub is, however, that certain classes of citizens—particularly well-educated and well-to-do ones—are more likely than others to be organized into groups which have access to decision makers. "The business or upperclass bias of the pressure system shows up everywhere,"[28] particularly in urban government.

These three theories of urban government —the reform theory, the group theory of politics, and the structural-functional theory —each suggests elements which can be pieced together to form a rudimentary outline of the feedback process. Structural-functional theory identifies the importance of variation in policies in producing feedback; group theory suggests the impact of policies on, and the subsequent responses of, masses, secondary groups, and elites; and the theory of reform demonstrates the role of institutional mechanisms in facilitating or muting the expression of feedback.

Coping with Feedback

Political systems must cope with feedback in order to survive. Yet even the identification of feedback is no simple matter. Like fallout, responses to one policy can affect distant political phenomena. Easton describes some policy responses as being "stored and released" at a later time.[29] Reactions to a chain of government actions may spill over to become an emotionally laden evaluation of the system as a whole. Conversely, evaluation of the system may be so colored, either positively or negatively, as to virtually guarantee a favorable or unfavorable response to any given policy. Relations between city officials and ghetto dwellers (or between college administrators and students) are sometimes so strained that any action of one side seems merely to confirm the others' perception of "intransigence," "bad faith," or "duplicity." In the final analysis, the feedback from a single policy may be less important than the long-run responses to the cumulative policy process.

To cope effectively with feedback, decision makers would need enormous informational resources. They would want to identify at least four dimensions of feedback: amount, direction, intensity, and polarity. Both too much and too little feedback can be seriously dysfunctional. Too little feedback implies a system which is isolated from its environment; yet too much might immobilize the system by the press of conflicting demands. When New York City is described as "ungovernable," it is implied that there are more demands, and more feedback from policies, than can be processed through the system. But the amount of feedback may be less important than the other dimensions. The system can absorb much more positive than negative feedback. While any particular policy will generate both positive and negative responses, the degree to which one or the other side activates its attitudes is variable. Typically, a positive response to policy produces little feedback, for people get more exercised by negative actions of government. (Sometimes indifference or silence is interpreted as positive feedback—witness the Nixon administration's invocation of the "silent majority.") Reporting positive feedback may be a little like reporting "nonevents" in the news. Much conventional wisdom—supported by some research on fluoridation and open housing referenda[30]— holds that "antis" and "nay sayers" are more likely to be activated than supporters. Often, differential activation is a function of *intensity*. Two sides intensely committed to their positions may produce a *polarization* of feedback. Polarized opinions, whether blacks versus whites in the city or radicals versus conservatives on the campus, are difficult for decision makers to handle. High-intensity, extremely polarized conflicts are doubly likely to escalate.

One might think that urban decision makers were constantly searching out new techniques of identifying responses to policy impacts in order to anticipate feedback. One could imagine the utilization of careful economic and sociological studies of the impact of policies, together with extensive employment of public opinion sampling to gauge public reactions. Instead, urban officials typically respond to feedback only when it confronts them directly. Once policy is made, decision makers adopt a *laissez faire* attitude about it: unless seriously disruptive, feedback can be directly attributed to the policy, retain it, and add to it incrementally. Even the urban riots of the 1960s—surely the most forceful expressions of feedback in a generation—produced few significant changes in the policy choices of urban governments.[31]

Notes

1. Ludwig van Bertalanffy, *General System Theory* (New York: George Braziller, 1968), pp. 42–44.
2. See the discussion of policy impact in Robert L. Lineberry and Ira Sharkansky, *Politics and Urban Public Policy* (New York: Harper & Row, 1971), chap. 6, 7–10, *passim*.
3. Jeanne Lowe, *Cities in a Race with Time* (New York: Random House, 1967), p. 207.
4. Marc Fried, "Grieving for a Lost Home," in Leonard J. Duhl (ed.), *The Urban Condition* (New York: Basic Books, 1963), pp. 151–71.
5. Alan Lupo and Edmund P. Fowler, "The Highway and the People," *Boston Globe Sunday Magazine*, March 8, 1970, pp. 8–17.
6. "Rationalizing the Policy Process," *Social Science Quarterly*, 50 (December 1969), 485.
7. David Easton, *A System Analysis of Political Life* (New York: John Wiley, 1965), pp. 348–52.
8. Austin Ranney, "The Study of Policy Content," in Ranney (ed.), *Political Science and Public Policy* (Chicago: Markham, 1968), chap. 1; Ira Sharkansky, "Environment, Policy, Output, and Impact," in Sharkansky (ed.), *Policy Analysis in Political Science* (Chicago: Markham, 1970), chap. 4.
9. Ira Sharkansky, "Government Expenditures and Public Services in the American States," *American Political Science Review*, 61 (December 1967), 1066–77.
10. See, e.g., Robert P. Shumate, *The Long-Range Effect of Enforcement on Driving Speeds* (Washington, D.C.: International Association of Chiefs of Police, 1960).
11. Washington, D.C.: Government Printing Office, 1966.
12. James S. Coleman, "Toward Open Schools," *Public Interest*, No. 9 (Fall 1967), p. 21.
13. Robert R. Alford and Eugene C. Lee, "Voting Turnout in American Cities," *American Political Science Review*, 62 (September 1968), 796–813.
14. Blair Justice, *Detection of Potential Community Violence*, U.S. Department of Justice, Law Enforcement Assistance Administration, June 1968, p. 53.

15. On the shifting metaphors, see the imaginative treatment in Martin Landau, "On the Use of Metaphor in Political Science," *Social Research*, 28 (Fall 1961), 331–53; and Henry S. Commager, *The American Mind* (New Haven: Yale University Press, 1950), pp. 320–25.
16. Quoted in *ibid.*, p. 323.
17. The distinction between Conservative Darwinists, whose hearts were with Herbert Spencer, and the Evolutionary Darwinists like Lester Ward and Woodrow Wilson is pointed out in Eric Goldman, *Rendezvous with Destiny* (New York: Vintage Books, 1952), pp. 71–76.
18. See Robert L. Lineberry and Edmund P. Fowler, "Reformism and Public Policies in American Cities," *American Political Science Review*, 61 (September 1967), 701–16.
19. Jean L. Stinchcombe, *Reform and Reaction: City Politics in Toledo* (Belmont, Calif.: Wadsworth, 1968), p. 232.
20. Harold Kaplan, *Urban Political Systems* (New York: Columbia University Press, 1967), chap. 1.
21. Robert Agger and his associates, however, identify a major political grouping in local politics which they call "community conservationists." Their principal ideological preferences appear to strike a balance between integrative, low-tension decision making and adaptive policies. See *The Rulers and the Ruled* (New York: John Wiley, 1964), pp. 21–32.
22. Robert L. Crain et al., *The Politics of Community Conflict* (Indianapolis: Bobbs-Merrill, 1969), p. 4.
23. William Kornhauser, *The Politics of Mass Society* (New York: The Free Press, 1959); Joseph Gusfield, "Mass Society and Extremist Politics," *American Sociological Review*, 27 (February 1962), 19–30.
24. V. O. Key, Jr., *Public Opinion and American Democracy* (New York: Alfred A. Knopf, 1961), pp. 552–53.
25. Crain *et al.*, *Politics of Community Conflict*; Howard D. Hamilton, "Direct Legislation: Some Implications of Open Housing Referenda," *American Political Science Review*, 64 (March 1970), 124–37.
26. Kornhauser, *Politics of Mass Society*.
27. James S. Coleman, *Community Conflict* (New York: The Free Press, 1957), pp. 19–21.
28. E. E. Schattschneider, *The Semi-Sovereign People* (New York: Holt, Rinehart & Winston, 1960), p. 31.
29. Easton, *System Analysis of Political Life*, pp. 421–28.
30. Hamilton, "Direct Legislation," and the literature cited in his footnote 5.
31. Urban America and the Urban Coalition, *One Year Later: An Assessment of the Nation's Response to the Crisis Described by the National Advisory Commission on Civil Disorders* (New York: Praeger, 1969).

VII

Postscript

AS THE PERCEPTIVE STUDENT has undoubtedly noted by this point, we have not yet reached the millennium in the application of a systems approach to urban politics. We hope the strengths of this particular framework for political analysis have become evident from reading the articles and the accompanying commentary. Perhaps the major strength of a systems orientation lies in its comprehensive nature and its flexible structure which permit the development of a variety of specific paradigms for analysis— such as the popular input-output model. In its general outline, the systems approach is highly abstract, allowing its conceptual elements to be arranged in many ways to fit the contours of the particular subject area to which it is being applied. Yet we must also recognize the various shortcomings and inadequacies which have plagued those who have attempted to operationalize and use this model in actual analysis. Several of the articles contained in this volume illustrate different approaches to operationalizing a systems model. Some have been more successful than others; none represent the ultimate in devising imaginative indicators for the various political concepts represented in the model being used. In fact, there are those who would argue that in many respects, no matter how well done, certain basic deficiencies emerge in the way researchers have applied the systems model to state and local politics.

The concluding article in this volume by Philip Coulter raises some important questions concerning the adequacy of previous systems-based research of this type. Coulter acknowledges that the shift from a descriptive, case study literature in urban politics to a more comparative, behavioral orientation has been, by and large, a healthy change. His principal concern seems to be with some of the conceptual and methodological shortcomings which characterize the newer research, partially resulting from the very rapid transition from the older approach to the newer. He specifically identifies seven weaknesses in community policy studies (based on a systems approach) and suggests various ways to deal with them, including "a circumspect return to the use of case studies." Coulter's essay performs the valuable service of reminding us that we still have a long way to go in developing truly effective approaches and models to assist in understanding the complex political arrangements and behavior found in modern urban America.

Comparative Community Politics and Public Policy: Problems in Theory and Research*

Philip B. Coulter

THE STUDY OF public policy outcomes in American community political systems has, in the last decade, progressed very quickly from case studies to comparative systems analyses. The earlier intensive case studies, which examined one policy decision or several often idiosyncratic decisions usually in one community, tended to assume that each community is *sui generis*. Rather suddenly, the more "behaviorally" oriented students of local government policy adopted, at least implicitly, a general systems analysis of framework and began to compare policy outcomes of literally hundreds of communities. Although the change in direction is in general a healthy one,[1] the transition period was probably too brief, and the brevity has apparently inhibited the thoughtful reflection on questions of concepts, classification, measurement, theory, and causation that is essential to productive research.

Despite the fact that the more recent studies have begun to illuminate more precisely the comparative dimensions of community public policy outcomes, they are, by and large, characterized by a number of serious

Reprinted with permission from Polity, 3 (Fall 1970), 22–43.
*The author wishes to express his gratitude to Professors Irving Howards and David Booth, both of the University of Massachusetts, for their helpful comments and suggestions on an earlier draft of this paper.

inadequacies which will, if perpetuated, misdirect subsequent research in this area. The purpose of this essay is to identify and discuss some of these inadequacies and to suggest what may be more sensible avenues of future inquiry.[2] None of the criticisms offered here is revolutionary. Quite to the contrary, most involve conventional questions of theory and methodology that are well understood by social scientists. Yet their neglect in policy studies is apparent. It is hoped that these criticisms and suggestions will provide insights that are all too frequently absent in this area of political science. Before detailing seven weaknesses in community policy studies, it is useful to review briefly the theoretical scheme usually employed in ordering and analyzing the data.

Public policy is considered to be the "dependent" variable, variations in which are to be accounted for by a set of "independent" environmental or social structural variables that are presumed to cause or correlate with patterns of policy outcomes. Many of the more recent studies have sought to account for an additional proportion of the variation in the dependent policy variable by including consideration of some set of "intervening" variables which come between environmental inputs and policy outputs. Environmental variables usually consist of population characteristics from census materials: percent homeowners, "ethnics," low-income earners, various education levels, and others. Most of the policy outcomes examined are per capita expenditure levels extracted from municipal budgets—such as total expenditures and expenditures on specific policy areas such as public health, education, urban renewal, and welfare. The set of intervening variables is usually either a nominal scale which divides local governments into executive types (mayor-council, manager-council, or commission form), or an ordinal scale which categorizes governments on a continuum from "unreformed" to "reformed."[3]

The basic assumption is that patterns of government policy outputs are a reflection of environmental properties of the community.

The extent to which the community's environment tends to be homogeneous or heterogeneous (in terms of the various population characteristics) is taken to be an indicator of the extent to which there are social cleavages in the community from which emerge demands or pressures on government for policy decisions. In addition, the same kinds of environmental variables are employed to account for variations in the incidence of types of executive arrangements and degrees of governmental reform. Thus the theoretical schema of community policy studies resembles that of Easton's political system paradigm.[4] Environmental variables which presumably measure cleavages comprise "inputs" (demands and support) which are "processed" by the political system (that is, formal governmental institutions), which produce "outputs" in the form of policies and decisions. By constructing measures of input, system, and output variables, and subjecting these measures to quantitative analysis, much of the variation in the incidence of governmental forms and policy outcomes is presumably accounted for. Figure 1 below graphically presents the

the findings of this body of research are often contradictory and ambiguous, mainly because of certain methodological, conceptual, and technological shortcomings.[6] These interrelated problems are now dealt with in detail.

Inference of Linkages and Inattention to Process Variables

Among the problems prevalent in community policy studies, the way in which substantive connections among the variables are established is perhaps the most serious. The approach taken by most authors has been to construct numerous quantitative measures of community population characteristics, form of government, and policy outputs and to perform correlation analyses on these data to determine the extent to which there is covariance among different levels of the phenomena being measured. The results usually indicate that the incidence of forms of government or degrees of reform does tend to vary systematically with certain measures of environmental homogeneity and heterogeneity.[7]

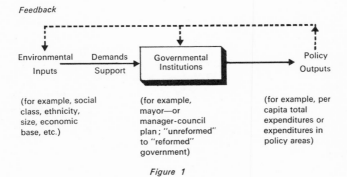

Feedback

Environmental Inputs — Demands Support → Governmental Institutions → Policy Outputs

(for example, social class, ethnicity, size, economic base, etc.)

(for example, mayor—or manager-council plan; "unreformed" to "reformed" government)

(for example, per capita total expenditures or expenditures in policy areas)

Figure 1

variables and their hypothesized interrelationships.

Although this description of the mode of analysis most often used is slightly oversimplified, it does express in general terms the kinds of assumptions which underlie much of community policy research and the hypothesis that are tested.[5] Unfortunately,

Further, levels of policy outputs are found to vary concomitantly with the indicators of environmental properties and to some lesser extent with governmental characteristics.[8] The relationships identified are described in linear terms, and the correlation coefficients are occasionally impressively high.[9] Thus a certain proportion of the total variation in the dependent variable (governmental forms and/or policy outcomes) is said to be "explained" by the independent variables. Of course, the "residual" (that is, the variation in the dependent variable unaccounted for by the independent variables) is usually attributed to the influence of variables not included in the regression equation, chance, idiosyncratic "situational" variables,[10] or otherwise "explained away." But the real problem is that the identification and measurement of a close statistical relationship between sets of variables is not explanation. Rather, it is the high level of correlation itself that is to be explained through the identification and explication of the substantive political linkages between two or more related phenomena.

With regard to correlations between environmental and policy variables, for example, the explanation usually offered is that heterogeneous environments are more conducive to the formation of social cleavages in the population (based on class, status, race, occupational structure, etc.), and that the size of the resultant differential social groupings, and the needs which each presumably has, produce demands on government for certain decisions and policy outputs.[11] That is, social differentiation produces social cleavages, which in turn produce demands on government, which in turn produce varying levels of policy outputs. Herein lies an inferential leap. How does a "cleavage" make a demand? How does government respond to a cleavage?[12] *Cleavage* is an artificial, theoretical construct which the researcher imposes on the data for the sake of order. How are community environmental and governmental characteristics transformed into patterns of policy performance? The bulk of the policy literature gives little or no attention to an empirical explanation of how this conversion occurs. The inferential leap from a few demographic characteristics to levels of expenditure in various policy areas occasions at least two difficulties. How are environmental characteristics converted into demands, and how are demands converted into forms of government and/or policies? The usual way of handling these problems

has been to impute certain governmental and policy preferences to various groups on the basis of their social and economic characteristics, and to assume that these preferences are by and large reliably and accurately reflected in governmental form and performance. Thus it is assumed that aggregate socioeconomic characteristics produce and give shape to political attitudes, and that these attitudes are faithfully focused on government in the form of political "pressure." In turn, such pressures determine in large part the organizational framework of government and constitute stimuli to which government responds with policies. Although this set of assumptions may make sense, the empirical nature of the political linkages among variables is largely unexplored, and the *ersatz* explanations offered are *ex posto facto* and *ad hoc.*[13]

Thus there is precious little attention given to the character of the political process(es) involved in the formation of public policy. Although many studies, both theoretical and empirical, have illuminated a wide variety of process variables,[14] their finding have been virtually ignored in community policy research. Apparently, either political process variables are considered unimportant or measures of process variables are unavailable in community data compendia (more likely the latter). The relationship between political decision processes and structures has been well documented. It simply cannot be assumed that these are unrelated to the conversion of environmental variables into policies. In fact, it seems highly likely that local governmental institutions and policies are, to a great extent, influenced independently by process variables. If this is true, it is certainly useful to know whether a community's pattern of political processes constitutes a polyarchy, a bargaining arrangement, a hierarchy, a price system, an anonymous or kaleidoscopic arrangement, a combination of these, or what. Further, it cannot be assumed that each input is managed by the same set of processes or that outputs are the products of the same set of processes. Yet it is apparently assumed that the political processes operative in communities are either unimportant or practically identical (since no empirical description is undertaken), and both inputs and outputs are assumed to be related to process in the same way.

Public Expenditures as Policy Outputs

Most studies have conceived of policy outputs in terms of the level of governmental expenditures—either total expenditures per capita or per capita total expenditures for some particular function or service, such as health, welfare, urban renewal, and education.[15] To be sure, these constitute important measures of the way in which local governments allocate scarce resources in their efforts to control and adapt to their environments. Yet there are at least two serious drawbacks involved in this regard. First, attempting to account for variations in the levels of total municipal expenditures (adjusted for population size) seems patently erroneous because total budget figures conceal so much more than they reveal. A community's total annual budget comprises the aggregate of its individual, disaggregated policy expenditures, and as such it covers up significant priorities given to various governmental activities. To construct a measure of the total amount of erotic affection manifested by a random sample of French lovers is not very enlightening, unless it can also be known how much of it is devoted to wives and how much to mistresses! Measures of gross expenditures summarize a wide variety of fiscal inconsistencies and conflicts. Although total per capita spending is a precise, quantitative, easily accessible datum, and although it appears to be linearly related to environmental or other kind of variables, it is not really very informative if the substance of policy is the object of explanation.

Second, the use of per capita expenditures even for individual policies is questionable. Although it is indicative of the relative levels of dollars-and-cents commitment of communities to solve perceived problems, it falls short of measuring the qualitative aspects of public policies. If policy is to be conceived as the total set of government actions vis-à-vis its environment, it is essential to explore not only government behavior (as measured by policy spending) but the impact of government programs on the citizenry—clients and recipients.[16] Does per capita spending on education deflate the high school "dropout" figure or increase proportions of high school graduates who attend college? Does welfare spending increase the mean or per capita income? Does a public health appropriation decrease the incidence of communicable diseases? In short, does spending in any of the policy areas have an impact on levels of input (demand and support) into the system?[17] If policy means efforts directed toward environmental control, more must be known about the quality of that control. Although the answers to these kinds of questions would seem (hopefully) to be affirmative, the comparative literature has not sought to demonstrate policy's qualitative impact. This leads to consideration of the conventionally used concept *feedback*. Although it is at least implicitly acknowledged in much of the literature that policy outputs can and do have substantial (and presumably measurable) impact on environment and government itself, the nature of that impact has been largely unexplored. One implication, among others, of the notion of feedback is that the substance of policy, by directly or indirectly controlling environment or adapting government, has a cumulative impact on subsequent policy outcomes. The extent to which this "force-of-custom" effect promotes continuity (or inhibits discontinuity) of policy patterns, and under what kinds of circumstances, has not been expounded at the level of comparative analysis. In short, although many studies have claimed to examine policy "outcomes," none has really done so on a comparative basis. A policy outcome should be kept distinct from a policy "output." An *outcome* refers to the consequences, intended or unintended, of an output, and it includes the way in which environment is controlled or the political system is adapted through the authoritative actions of government. Use of the term policy outcome implies (as it should) a conception of policy as an independent variable whose impact on the environment and political system is to be identified and measured. The comparative study of policy *outcomes* (as defined here) demands close attention.

In terms of the *level* and even the *direction* of policy expenditures, however, budget figures do represent interesting outputs of community political systems. But what of policy outcomes which allocate "values" rather than material resources and hence do not appear in budgets? This sort of policy has received some explicit comparative attention, but only recently.[18] Policies directed toward fluoridation of municipal water supplies or toward desegregation of public school systems are prime examples of local government actions which involve no substantial allocation of funds, but which are extremely important policy outcomes. It cannot automatically be assumed that input and process (or system) variables are identically related to policies which allocate values and those which allocate material resources.

*Failure to Differentiate
Policy Types*

Closely related to the previous point about the allegedly misplaced reliance on total and individual policy-area expenditures per capita, is a virtual absence of the use of policy typologies. Most studies make no attempt to categorize policies on the basis of criteria of similarities and dissimilarities. Two research efforts which do try to employ a taxonomic scheme empirically are provocative. Froman[19] distinguished between "areal" policies (that is, single actions which affect the entire community simultaneously) and "segmental" policies (that is, continuing programs which affect different, smaller segments of the community at different times). He classified adoption of council-manager plan and non-partisan elections, annexation, intermunicipal cooperation, educational services, and fluoridation as *areal*. The three *segmental* policies were urban renewal, total per capita expenditures, and welfare. Areal policies

were found to be associated with greater environmental homogeneity, and segmental policies with greater heterogeneity. Clark[20] has suggested that policies can be typed in terms of the extent to which they are "fragile" (that is, newer and more susceptible to opposition strategies) and "less fragile" (that is, older, more familiar, and more customary).

The point is, as Froman and Clark suggest, that inputs (and, by implication, processes) are not necessarily associated with individual policy outputs, and certainly not with categories of outputs, in the same fashion. The literature of political science provides numerous policy typologies which might well be usefully employed in comparative community studies. Lowi[21] has developed an interesting typology of public policies as "distributive," "regulatory," or "redistributive." A *distributive* policy is the aggregate result of many disaggregated, individualized (pork barrel) decisions, no one of which comprises a general form of consistent government action. *Regulatory* policies are similar in that they are applied to specific individuals and firms, yet all regulatory decisions must be made with reference to a broader, more general rule. Also, they are concerned with the specification and enforcement of proper behavior, rather than distributing material perquisites. Policies of *redistribution* involve broad categories of individuals, and these kinds of decisions tend to be closely interrelated. The impact of redistributive policies tends to fall on broad categories of people, such as "haves and have-nots," "bourgeoisie and proletariat," the well organized and the poorly organized. In the arena of redistributive policies, indulged and deprived come into direct confrontation.

Another policy typology potentially useful in comparative community studies is that of Almond and Powell who identify four kinds of policy.[22] *Regulative* policy "refers to the political system's exercise of control over behavior of individuals and groups . . . [and] the employment of legitimate coercion to control behavior." Including government expenditures, "the distributive [policy] . . . refers to the allocation of goods, services, honors, statutes, and opportunities of various kinds to individuals and groups in the society. It is the activity of the political system as a dispenser . . . of benefits among individuals and groups." *Extractive* policy "refers to the range of system performance in drawing material and human resources from the [environment]." Finally, there is *symbolic* policy which involves "the rate of *effective* flow from the political system into the society. . . . [including] affirmations of values by elites; displays of flags, troops, and military ceremony; visits by royalty or high officials; and statements of policy or intent by political leaders." Despite the apparent usefulness of these and other available policy typologies,[23] none has been employed in the comparative study of local public policies.

What is needed is the construction of policy taxonomies based on several important criteria or dimensions of policy. Most research in community (and especially state) policy outputs has been regrettably remiss in this task. Such studies have examined a rather narrow range of individual expenditure totals, and are, for this reason, strangely reminiscent of earlier case studies in some ways. As mentioned earlier, typologies of environment (homogeneous-heterogeneous) and governmental forms (unreformed-reformed) have been developed. However, as will be made evident below, further refinement in independent and intervening variables is also necessary.

Inadequate Quantitative Analysis

The array of quantitative techniques available to those who would use them is now vast. Yet in comparative policy studies, researchers have, with only a few exceptions, failed to use the statistical technology fully and comparatively. Three such techniques have been used: cross tabulation, factor analysis, and correlation analysis.[24] Since the purpose of all of these is to identify and measure relationships among variables, all are, of course, relevant to policy studies. Cross tabulation is no doubt the weakest of the three (for both aggregate and survey

data), since statistical measures of the strength of relationship between variables are less precise and informative.[25] Factor analysis "clusters" a set of variables on the basis of the strength of their interrelationships, and a given cluster is assumed to be "caused" by or to reflect the influence of an underlying factor or dimension of commonality. This technique is more precise, but results are more difficult to interpret.[26]

Most of the studies have relied on some sort of correlation analysis, usually simple and/or partial and multiple correlation coefficients, and in one case path coefficients.[27] Simple correlations measure the degree of covariance between two variables. Partial correlations do the same while holding the influence of one or more other independent variables "constant." Multiple correlations measure the relationships between one dependent and a set of independent variables and also demonstrate the extent to which each of the independent variables contributes to the "explanation" of the variation in the dependent variable. Path correlations presumably identify routes of causation of dependent variable variation through a chain of independent and intervening variables. If precision in the measurement of relationships among environmental, political system (or process), and policy variables is the intention, it makes sense to subject the data to the widest possible variety of analytical techniques. If this were done, it would be easier to separate the spurious from the real relationships; to determine what single variables and what interrelated combinations of variables are really statistically related to policy outputs, to what extent, and under what kinds of conditions.[28] In short, most data have been underanalyzed; comparative statistical treatment is needed.

Two other technical difficulties deserve mention. First, there is evident in almost every case the assumption of linearity in the statistical relationships. It is easy enough to perform nonlinearity tests on the data. Second, there is a tendency to confuse correlation with causation and/or explanation. Causes must be identified and explanations must be supplied by the researcher. No matter how vigorously the data are manipulated, the researcher must be aware of the caveats pertaining to the attribution of causation supplied by both statisticians and philosophers of social science.[29] Modesty and caution must prevail.

Political Ethos: Tempest in a Teapot

Perhaps the most controversial concept in community political studies at this time is "political ethos." There is considerable conflict among political scientists in regard to the extent to which ethos influences collective decisions about forms of government and public policy.[30] Since the various protagonists on this and related questions have recently exploited each other's alleged weaknesses publicly, their arguments will not be summarized here. However, certain assumptions held implicitly by all warring camps deserve brief comment.

It is regrettable that none of the research on community political ethos (or culture) has employed either the insights of anthropology and sociology or the more recent empirical and theoretical work of students of cross-national political cultures.[31] Because of this negligence, community political culture studies have, on the whole, lacked precision and credibility.[32] Questions about the relationship, if any, between political values and political behavior have been couched in terms which threaten to inhibit progress in the explanation of community government and policy. If one assumes that political culture is an abstraction of political values implicit in and manifested by patterns of political behavior, and infers the existence of certain underlying normative orientations from behavior, then it is one thing. This is what most political ethos studies have done. If, on the other hand, political beliefs and values which people hold are specifically sought out, measured, and related to patterns of political behavior, government, and policy outcomes, then whatever the results, at least less inference is involved. The former method tends to prove the importance of political ethos by inferentially assuming it

and subsuming it in a tautology. The latter approach, while not assuming the existence or importance of political culture, may find it—but may find that it has only limited expression in terms of shaping the contours of given political systems or types of policy outcomes. It is necessary to examine the extent to which political cultural values have an "independent" impact on behavior, institutions, and policies. This simply cannot be done by inferring values from configurations of political "interests" in the environment. That the two are related is probably true, but this offers no absolution for those who would measure one and attribute influence to the other.

Survey data have proved much more useful in cross-national studies, especially in attempting to link preferences with policies in contemporary national politics.[33] In American community studies, the use of current aggregate data (for example, on ethnicity and income) to try to explain the incidence of existing governmental forms which were adopted at various times in the last half century seems to make little sense.[34] Similarly, there is in almost all cases the assumption of linear relationships between configurations of demographic data and political power. It cannot be assumed that the size of various demographic groupings (to which are attributed political cultural values) is an accurate indicator of their political power in the community. Finally, in the ethos literature, it is increasingly easier to identify the "good guys" (public-regarding) and the "bad guys" (private-regarding). By borrowing so heavily from historian Richard Hofstadter,[35] advocates of the political ethos theory may have biased subsequent research.[36]

Regionalism: The Transcendental Potpourri

When all the available environmental and governmental data have been exhausted in attempting to account for policy variations, there has been a tendency to try to reduce the unexplained variation by introducing the concept of "regionalism." This is done ordinarily by performing the same statistical manipulations again while holding region constant—that is, by running correlations within regions.[37] That the meaning of regionalism can be known and measured in terms of boundary lines of groups of contiguous states seems to be an unwarranted assumption. What exactly is being held constant when statistical controls for regionalism are applied? Nobody seems to know for sure, but it is possible to speculate on this question. Controlling for the influence of region probably involves holding constant the impact of various (unknown) aspects of geography, demography, common historical experiences, economic development, culture, attitudes, and behavior. It is simply not known to what extent this is true. If it is true, what is the relative strength of the contribution of each dimension of regionalism to an explanation of the dependent variable? Until much more is known about the empirical nature of regionalism as (set of) variable(s), it seems risky to attribute to it much explanatory power. It is an ambiguous and elusive concept.

It should be added that regionalism has recently begun to receive closer empirical attention, mainly in connection with state policy outputs and mainly by Sharkansky.[38] He, in particular, has begun to explicate some of the components of regionalism (such as types and levels of economic activity) and to relate regionalism to policy outcomes with a clearer understanding of what is being done. However, even Sharkansky feels compelled to add a disclaimer.

> By itself, "regionalism" is not a satisfying explanation for public policy. . . . The saliency of the regional variables *seems* to reflect the importance of shared historical experiences and the regional orientations of state and local authorities. Insofar as public officials receive many of their policy cues from regional, rather than national reference groups, it is necessary to weigh heavily the *likelihood* that historical experiences shared by neighboring states have had a lasting impact on public policies.[39] (Italics added).

Sharkansky prudently exercises caution when he "makes no claim to identify the specific features associated with each region (independent of current economic levels) that provide the explanation of current policies."[40] Unfortunately, not all researchers in this field have demonstrated Sharkansky's understanding in the use of regionalism.

Governmental Institutions as Intervening Variables

Some of the community studies have considered the influence of a set of intervening variables which may reflect, suppress, or distort environmental pressures. Almost all of this research has posited various characteristics of formal governmental institutions as constituting the intervening variables. The quantitative measures of these governmental features are based on type of executive arrangement (mayor, manager, or commission), electoral system (partisan or nonpartisan), or degree of "reform."[41] In addition, there has been considerable effort devoted to the explanation of the incidence of these characteristics among communities as a function of community environmental properties.

The position argued here is that it seems impractical to employ governmental institutions as either dependent or intervening variables. Both the experience of the political practitioner and the research of the political scientist have repeatedly demonstrated that the nature of a community's formal governmental structure as set forth in the municipal charter of incorporation may bear little relation to the important patterns of community politics.[42] In terms of political orientations, participation, and power, calling Boston's electoral system nonpartisan has not made it so.[43] Those who expect Schenectady to behave as the International City Managers' Association says a manager-council city should behave are quickly and profoundly disappointed.[44] Similar examples are legion, and the evidence is compelling. That institutional arrangements are crucial must be proved, not assumed. However, this assumption underlies much of the community policy research. It may be valid, but it may also be invalid. Yet the question is rarely even raised.

A more productive and realistic, though probably more difficult, approach would be to postulate a set of "political regime" variables as a function of environmental pressures and as an intervening influence between environment and policy.[45] Political regime (that is, what is conventionally called structure of political power and elite) could, for example, be defined and empirically measured in terms of four criteria: size of the political elite; the extent to which its personnel are cohesive or divided on questions of values, strategies, goals, and policies; the nature of the relationship between elite and mass; and the relative scope of political elite influence over the range of policy areas. Defined in this way, regime seems much more likely than governmental institutions to be shaped by environmental demands. And the real intervening influence on policy outcomes is more likely to be political regime than formal institutions. It is, of course, possible that governmental institutions and officials are a more or less important part of political regime, but this must be empirically determined. Because of either convenience (institutional data are easily accessible, regime data are not) or misconception (formal institutions are uniformly important), only a handful of comparative studies has sought to conceptualize and measure the influence of regime variables, such as elite values.[46] Their efforts suggest some exciting and productive directions for future research.

The now vast body of community power structure literature indicates the kinds of political regimes that have actually been identified and those that are theoretically conceivable. An obviously useful example is found in Dahl's typology of regimes so familiar to students of urban politics: "covert integration by economic notables," "an executive-centered 'grand coalition of coalitions,' " the "coalition of chieftains," "independent sovereignties with spheres of influence," and "rival sovereignties fighting it out."[47] Similar examples from other studies include such types as monolithic or pyra-

midal, polylithic, countervailing, caucus rule, triarchy, and amorphous.[48] Common to all these conceptualizations of political regime is a commitment to the discovery of the configuration of the political elite and the determination of how policies are made, rather than an assumption that patterns of political influence and policy making are exactly congruent with the lines of formal authority. It is obviously important to explore the relationship between political regime structure variables and political process variables.

Although considerably less inclusive than the "regime" approach suggested here, the recent research of Eulau and Crain points in the right direction. Growing out of studies of the eighty-eight communities in the San Francisco Bay area, the conceptualizations and empirical findings of Eulau et al.,[49] are impressive. They consider the "vitality" and "diversity" of interest group life and the political orientations (or values) of city councilmen (as probable members of the political elite) as two intervening variables at least partially responsible for the translation of environmental pressures into policies. Second, they compare communities in terms of stages and phases of policy development ("retarded," "emergent," "transitional," "maturing," and "advanced"). Thus they employ a rather sophisticated developmental policy typology. Crain[50] has made use of quantitative and qualitative data on attitudes and characteristics of policy makers (for example, school board members and others) in the comparative study of patterns of community school desegregation. Crain, Katz, and Rosenthal[51] employ similar kinds of data in their comparative study of community decision making on fluoridation proposals. Future research ought to take into account not only the values and attitudes of policy makers, but the structure of the political regime and process of political elite (and perhaps electoral) decision making.

Summary and Conclusions

I have argued that the study of political public policy suffers from at least seven serious deficiencies. They are basically of three types: reliance on inference where descriptive and qualitative data are essential; failure to apply quantitative analysis thoroughly; and the postulation and measurement of interrelationships among improper and inadequate kinds of variables. Numerous suggestions which might profitably redirect policy studies have been offered, including increased attention to political linkages and political processes, examination of a greater variety of policies within taxonomic frameworks, more rigorous comparative measurement of the strength of variable associations, use of both aggregate and survey data which are more adequately descriptive of the variables and their relationships, and the substitution of political regime for governmental institutions as the set of intervening variables.

Further, at the risk of being ejected from the profession, I am prepared to argue the need for a circumspect return to the use of case studies. However, I would insist that community policy case studies fulfill at least three criteria. First, they should be explicitly comparative in design—they should ask the same kinds of questions and use the same kinds of data in studying policy. Second, they should be constructed so as to supply the missing quantitative and especially qualitative data which describe political linkages and emphasize transformation processes. Third, they should be devised in such a way that their results can be easily integrated with and will lend empirical, evidentiary support to the more abstract, quantitative, aggregate analysis of community political systems.

Future research which takes these criticisms and suggestions into account might yield clearer and more precise results and begin to resolve some of the disagreements and discrepancies in the policy literature. In addition to satisfying the natural curiosity of political scientists and achieving more "scientific rigor," the results might also prove more useful to policy makers, who are no doubt as confounded in the making of policy as we are in studying it.

Notes

1. Critical commentary on the development of the study of local government and politics can be found in Lawrence Herson, "The Lost World of Municipal Government," *American Political Science Review*, 51 (June 1957), 330–45; William Anderson, "Municipal Government: No Lost World," *American Political Science Review*, 51 (September 1957), 776–83; Robert T. Daland, "Political Science and the Study of Urbanization," *American Political Science Review*, 51 (June 1957), 491–509; Wallace S. Sayre and Nelson W. Polsby, "American Political Science and the Study of Urbanization," in Philip M. Hauser and Leo F. Schnore (eds.), *The Study of Urbanization* (New York: John Wiley, 1965), 115–57; and Norton E. Long, "Political Science and the City," in Leo F. Schnore and Henry Fagin (eds.), *Urban Research and Policy Planning* (Beverly Hills, Calif.: Sage Publications, 1967), 243–63.

2. Although this discussion centers only on the scholarly literature in the area of community politics and public policy, much of what is said applies with equal force to recent research in state politics and public policy.

3. An "unreformed" municipal government is usually defined as one which has retained a mayor-council plan, partisan elections, a larger city council, members of which are elected from wards, and has a patronage system for the recruitment of appointive officials. A "reformed" government is characterized by its manager-council form, nonpartisan elections, a smaller council, members of which are elected at-large, and a civil service bureaucracy.

4. Cf. David Easton's development of political systems theory in *The Political System* (New York: Alfred A. Knopf, 1953); *A Framework for Political Analysis* (Englewood Cliffs, N.J.: Prentice-Hall, 1965); and *A Systems Analysis of Political Life* (New York: John Wiley, 1965).

5. For a summary and synthesis of much of the literature in this area, see Philip Coulter, "Community Politics: The Policy Perspective," in James A. Riedel (ed.), *New Perspectives on State and Local Politics* (Waltham, Mass.: Blaisdell, 1971); Herbert Jacob and Michael Lipsky, "Outputs, Structure, and Power: An Assessment of Changes in the Study of State and Local Politics," *Journal of Politics*, 30 (May 1968), 510–39; and John H. Fenton and Donald W. Chamberlayne, "The Literature Dealing With Relationships Between Political Processes, Socioeconomic Conditions, and Public Policies in the American States: A Bibliographical Essay," *Polity*, 1 (Spring 1969), 388–405.

6. It should be noted that some differences in findings can be explained as a result of the use of different data—that is, different samples of communities of different sizes.

7. Research which has studied these various relationships includes the following: Lewis Froman, "An Analysis of Public Policies in Cities," *Journal of Politics*, 29 (February 1967), 94–109; John Kessel, "Governmental Structure and Political Environment; A Statistical Note About American Cities," *American Political Science Review* 56 (September, 1962) 615–20; Leo Schnore and Robert Alford, "Forms of Government and Socioeconomic Characteristics of Suburbs " *Administrative Science Quarterly* 8 (June 1963), 1–17; Edgar Sherbenou, "Class, Participation, and the Council-Manager Plan," *Public Administration Review*, 21 (Summer 1961), 131–35; Robert Alford and Harry Scoble, "Political and Socioeconomic Characteristics of Cities," in *The Municipal Yearbook, 1965* (Chicago: International City Managers' Association, 1965), 82–97; Raymond E. Wolfinger and John Osgood Field, "Political Ethos and the Structure of City Government," *American Political Science Review*, 60 (June 1966), 306–26; Robert L. Lineberry and Edmund P. Fowler, "Reformism and Public Policies in American Cities," *American Political Science Review*, 61 (September 1967), 701–17; Phillips Cutright, "Nonpartisan Electoral Systems in American Cities," *Comparative Studies in Society and History*, 5 (January 1963), 212–26.

8. Studies which attempt to account for policy variations with environmental and/or governmental variables include James Q. Wilson and Edward C. Banfield, "Public-Regardingness as a Value Premise in Voting Behavior," *American Political Science Review*, 58 (December 1964), 876–87; Wolfinger and Field, "Political Ethos"; Lineberry and Fowler, "Reformism and Public Policies"; Froman, "Analysis of Public Policies"; Thomas R. Dye, "Urban Political Integration: Conditions Associated with Annexation in American Cities," *Midwest Journal of Political Science*, 8 (November 1964), 430–46; Dye *et al.*, "Differentiation and Cooperation in a Metropolitan Area," *Midwest Journal of Political Science*, 7 (May 1963), 145–55; Robert C. Wood, *1400 Governments* (Garden City, N.Y.: Doubleday, 1964), chaps. 2–3; Lewis H. Masotti and Don R. Bowen, "Communities and Budgets: The Sociology of Municipal Expenditures," *Urban Affairs Quarterly*, (December 1965), 39–59; Thomas R. Dye, "Urban School Integration: A Comparative Analysis," *Urban Affairs Quarterly*, 4 (December 1968), 141–67; Otto A. Davis, "Empirical Evidence of Political Influence upon the Expenditure Policies of Public Schools," in Julius Margolis (ed.), *The Public Economy of Urban Communities* (Washington, D.C.: Resources of the Future, 1965), 92–112; Dennis J. Palumbo and Oliver P. Williams, "Predictors of Public Policy: The Case of Local Public Health," *Urban Affairs Quarterly*, 2 (June 1967), 75–93; Amos Hawley, "Community Power and Urban Renewal Success," *American Journal of Sociology*, 68 (January 1963), 422–31; and Maurice Pinard, "Structural Attachments and Political Support in Urban Politics: The Case of Fluoridation Referendums," *American Journal of Sociology*, 68 (March 1963), 513–26.

9. For example, Lineberry and Fowler, "Reformism and Public Policies," 709, statistically account for 52 percent of the variation in municipal taxation policy. Robert Wood, *1400 Governments*, p. 41, accounts for 96 percent of the variance in total operating expenditures.

10. Robert Alford suggests ways in which "situational" factors might be built into this type of research in "The Comparative Study of Urban Politics," in Schnore and Fagin (eds.), *Urban Research and Policy Planning*, 264–71.

11. The clearest and most elaborate argument relating environment to forms of government is in Kessel, "Governmental Structure," and Alford and Scoble, "Political and Socioeconomic Characteristics of Cities." There is a troublesome assumption implicit in all this literature that "homogeneous" environments cannot or do not make "demands." Similarly, the possibility that two communities could be homogeneous but quite different (for example, an upper-middle-class suburb and a working-class mill town) is never discussed. It should be noted that none of the policy studies acknowledges the possibility that its findings may be limited in validity to the post–New Deal period.

12. For additional discussion of this point, see the two "Communications" by Wolfinger and Field, and Lineberry and Fowler, *American Political Science Review*, 62 (March 1968), 227–31.

13. An awareness of the need to examine political "linkages" is shown by Martha Derthick, "Intercity Differences in Administration of the Public Assistance Program: The Case of Massachusetts," in James Q. Wilson (ed.), *City Politics and Public Policy* (New York: John Wiley, 1968), 243–67; and by J. David Greenstone and Paul E. Peterson, "Reformers, Machines, and the War on Poverty," in Wilson (ed.), *City Politics and Public Policy*, 267–93. Further discussion of the utility of case study data appears below.

14. Studies suggestive of the use of "process" variables include R. B. Wilson, "System and Process: Polar Concepts for Political Research," *Western Political Quarterly*, 14 (September 1961), 748–63; Robert A. Dahl and Charles E. Lindblom, *Politics, Economics, and Welfare* (New York: Harper & Brothers, 1953); Peter Rossi, "Power and Community Structure," *Midwest Journal of Political Science*, 4 (November 1960), 390–401; Harold Lasswell, "The Decision Process: Seven Categories of Functional Analysis," in Nelson W. Polsby *et al.*, *Politics and Social Life* (Boston: Houghton Mifflin, 1963),

93–105; and Robert E. Agger *et al.*, *The Rulers and the Ruled* (New York: John Wiley, 1964), chap. 2 and *passim*.

15. Examples of community studies which examine per capita total expenditures are cited in footnote 8. For comparison, see the state policy studies: Thomas R. Dye, *Politics, Economics, and the Public: Policy Outcomes in the American States* (Chicago: Rand McNally, 1966); Richard E. Dawson and James A. Robinson, "Inter-party Competition, Economic Variables, and Welfare Policies in the American States," *Journal of Politics*, 25 (May 1963), 265–89; Richard I. Hofferbert, "The Relation Between Public Policy and Some Structural and Environmental Variables in the American States," *American Political Science Review*, 60 (March 1966), 73–82; and John H. Fenton, *People and Parties in Politics* (Glenview, Ill.: Scott, Foresman, 1966), chap. 2.

16. For evidence on the impact of a federal, but locally administered, program on the recipients, see Daniel P. Moynihan, *Maximum Feasible Misunderstanding* (New York: The Free Press, 1969).

17. Greenstone and Peterson, "War on Poverty," demonstrate, for a public welfare program in four big cities, that different kinds of communities have different kinds of inputs, and that outputs can differ in degree and even in kind when inputs are similar.

18. Two recent major works examine "value" allocation policies: Robert L. Crain, *The Politics of School Desegregation* (Chicago: Aldine, 1968); and Robert L. Crain, Elihu Katz, and Donald B. Rosenthal, *The Politics of Community Conflict: The Fluoridation Decision* (Indianapolis: Bobbs-Merrill, 1969). See also the following essays in Wilson's *City Politics and Public Policy*: John A. Gardiner, "Police Enforcement of Traffic Laws," 151–73; and Herbert Jacob, "Wage Garnishment and Bankruptcy Proceedings in Four Wisconsin Cities," 197–215.

19. Froman, "Analysis of Public Policies," 101–109.

20. Terry N. Clark, "Community Structure, Decision Making, Budget Expenditures and Urban Renewal in 51 American Communities," *American Sociological Review*, 33 (August 1968), 576–94.

21. Theodore J. Lowi, "American Business, Public Policy, Case Studies, and Political Theory," *World Politics*, 16 (July 1964), 677–93.

22. Gabriel A. Almond and G. Bingham Powell, *Comparative Politics: A Developmental Approach* (Boston: Little, Brown, 1966), 190–212.

23. Cf. James S. Coleman, *Community Conflict* (Glencoe, Ill.: The Free Press, 1957); Murray Edleman, "Symbols and Political Quiescence," *American Political Science Review*, 54 (September 1960), 695–704; Ernest A. T. Barth and Baha Abu-Laban, "Community Power and a Typology of Social Issues," *Social Forces*, 24 (February 1959), 29–32: Lewis A. Froman, "The Categorization of Policy Contents," in Austin Ranney (ed.), *Political Science and Public Policy* (Chicago: Markham, 1968), 41–55; and Robert H. Salisbury, "The Analysis of Public Policy: A Search for Theories and Roles," in Ranney (ed.), *Political Science and Public Policy*, 151–79.

24. Examples of cross-tabulation studies include Kessel, "Governmental Structure," and Cutright, "Nonpartisan Electoral Systems." Among the factor analysis studies are Wood, *1400 Governments*, and Masotti and Bowen, "Communities and Budgets." Correlation analysis studies include Lineberry and Fowler "Reformism and Public Policies"; Froman, "Analysis of Public Policies; and Yong H. Cho, "The Effect of Local Governmental Systems on Local Policy Outcomes in the United States," *Public Administration Review*, 27 (March 1967), 31–39.

25. The cross-tabulation studies rarely employ the available approximate measures of variable interrelationship strength, such as the contingency and phi coefficients. See John E. Freund, *Modern Elementary Statistics* (Englewood Cliffs, N.J.: Prentice-Hall, 1962), 349–51; and George A. Ferguson, *Statistical Analysis in Psychology and Education* (New York: McGraw-Hill, 1959), 194–210.

26. This difficulty is discussed in Phillip M. Gregg and Arthur S. Banks, "Dimensions of Political Systems: Factor Analysis of 'A Cross-Polity Survey'," *American Political Science Review*, 59 (September 1965), 604–07.

27. Clark, "51 American Communities," alone has performed path coefficient analysis. It should be mentioned also that another sophisticated comparative statistical treatment is that of Palumbo and Williams, "Predictors of Public Policy."

28. Studies of state policy outcomes might also be improved and the disagreements resolved through comparative statistical analysis.

29. Cf. W. G. Runciman, *Social Science and Political Theory* (Cambridge, England: Cambridge University Press, 1963), 123–35.

30. See Edward C. Banfield and James Q. Wilson, *City Politics* (Cambridge: Harvard University Press and M.I.T. Press, 1963) chap. 3, and *passim;* Wolfinger and Field, "Political Ethos"; Lineberry and Fowler, "Reformism and Public Policies"; and Wilson and Banfield, "Public-Regardingness." See also, footnote 12. Additional research which investigates political culture and local politics includes: Samuel C. Patterson, "The Political Cultures of the American States," *Journal of Politics*, 30 (February 1968), 187–210; Oliver P. Williams and Charles R. Adrian, *Four Cities: A Study in Comparative Policy Making* (Philadelphia: University of Pennsylvania Press, 1963); and Edgar

Litt, *The Political Cultures of Massachusetts* (Cambridge: M.I.T. Press, 1965).

31. These include Gabriel A. Almond and Sidney Verba, *The Civic Culture* (Princeton, N.J.: Princeton University Press, 1963); Almond and Powell, *Comparative Politics*, 50–73; and Lucian W. Pye and Sidney Verba (eds.), *Political Culture and Political Development* (Princeton, N.J.: Princeton University Press, 1965). The more relevant anthropological-sociological literature includes Clyde Kluckhohn, "Culture and Behavior," in Gardner Lindzey (ed.), *Handbook of Social Psychology*, Vol. 2 (Reading, Mass.: Addison-Wesley, 1954); and Ralph Linton, *The Cultural Background of Personality* (New York: D. Appleton-Century, 1945), especially pp. 32–37.

32. Of course, even members of the discipline (anthropology) which claims the concept "culture" as their own experience considerable disagreement on its meaning. Cf. Alfred L. Kroeber and Clyde Kluckhohn, "Culture: A Critical Review of Concepts and Definitions," *Papers of the Peabody Museum*, 47 (1952), 24–270.

33. See especially Pye and Verba (eds.); *Political Culture.*

34. See Wilson and Banfield, "Public-Regardingness," Wolfinger and Field, "Political Ethos," and Lineberry and Fowler, "Reformism and Public Policies."

35. Richard Hofstadter, *The Age of Reform* (New York: Alfred A. Knopf, 1955), p.9.

36. Research which provides new and more empirically defensible insights into local political cultures is Robert R. Alford and Harry M. Scoble, *Bureaucracy and Participation: Political Cultures in Four Wisconsin Cities* (Chicago: Rand McNally, 1969).

37. Cf. Wolfinger and Field, "Political Ethos"; and Dye, "Urban School Integration."

38. Ira Sharkansky, "Regionalism, Economic Status and the Public Policies of American States," *Social Science Quarterly*, 49 (June 1968), 9–27. Also in the same volume are Charles R. Adrian, "Regional Analysis in Political Science," 27–39; and Clarence E. Ayres, "Some Reflections on Regionalism," 36–43. Sharkansky searches further for the meaning of regionalism in "The Utility of Elazar's Political Culture: A Research Note," *Polity*, 2 (Fall 1969), 66–83.

39. Sharkansky, "Regionalism," pp. 25–26.

40. *Ibid.*, p. 26.

41. Cf. Lineberry and Fowler, "Reformism and Public Policies"; Wolfinger and Field, "Political Ethos"; Vincent L. Marando, "Inter-Local Cooperation in a Metropolitan Area: Detroit," *Urban Affairs Quarterly*, 4 (December 1968), 185–201.

42. Cf. Oliver P. Williams and Charles R. Adrian, "The Insulation of Local Politics Under the Nonpartisan Ballot," *American Political Science Review*, 53 (December 1959), 1052–63; and Banfield and Wilson, *City Politics*, 148–50.

43. Cf. Edward C. Banfield, *Big City Politics* (New York: Random House, 1965), pp. 37–51.

44. Cf. Philip B. Coulter, "The Urban Political Elite: Power and Decision Making in Schenectady," unpublished doctoral dissertation, Department of Political Science, State University of New York at Albany, 1966.

45. Clark, "51 American Communities," is the only researcher to experiment with this notion on a comparative basis.

46. Cf. Agger *et al.*, *Rulers and the Ruled;* Robert Presthus, *Men at the Top* (New York: Oxford University Press, 1964); and William V. D'Antonio and William H. Form, *Influentials in Two Border Cities: A Study in Community Decision-Making* (South Bend, Ind.: University of Notre Dame Press, 1965).

47. Robert A. Dahl, *Who Governs? Democracy and Power in an American City* (New Haven: Yale University Press, 1961), pp. 169–223.

48. Cf. Rossi, "Power and Community Structure"; Roscoe C. Martin *et al.*, *Decisions in Syracuse* (Bloomington: Indiana University Press, 1961); and Coulter, "Urban Political Elite."

49. Robert Eyestone and Heinz Eulau, "City Councils and Policy Outcomes: Developmental Profiles," in Wilson (ed.), *City Politics and Public Policy*, pp. 37–67; and Heinz Eulau and Robert Eyestone, "Policy Maps of City Councils and Policy Outcomes: A Developmental Analysis," *American Political Science Review*, 62 (March 1968), 124–44.

50. Crain, *Politics of School Desegregation*, and Robert L. Crain and James J. Vaneko, "Elite Influence in School Desegregation," in Wilson (ed.), *City Politics and Public Policy*, pp. 127–49.

51. Crain, Katz, and Rosenthal, *Fluoridation Decision;* and Donald B. Rosenthal and Robert L. Crain, "Structure and Values in Local Political Systems: The Case of Fluoridation Decisions," *Journal of Politics*, 28 (February 1966), 169–96.

BOOKS

Abbott, David W., Louis H. Gold, and Edward T. Rogowsky. *Police, Politics, and Race: The New York City Referendum on Civilian Review.* Cambridge: Harvard University Press, 1969.

Adrian, Charles R., and Charles Press. *Governing Urban America,* 3rd ed. New York: McGraw-Hill, 1968.

———. *Public Attitudes and Metropolitan Decision Making.* Pittsburgh: Institute of Local Government, University of Pittsburgh, 1962.

Agger, Robert, Daniel Goldrich, and Bert Swanson. *The Rulers and the Ruled.* New York: John Wiley, 1964.

Alford, Robert R. *Bureaucracy and Participation: Political Culture in Four Wisconsin Cities.* Chicago: Rand McNally, 1969.

Altshuler, Alan A. *The City Planning Process: A Political Analysis.* Ithaca, N.Y.: Cornell University Press, 1966.

———. *Community Control: The Black Demand for Participation in Large American Cities.* New York: Pegasus, 1970.

Babcock, Richard F. *The Zoning Game: Municipal Practices and Policies.* Madison: University of Wisconsin, 1966.

Bachrach, Peter, and Morton S. Baratz. *Power and Poverty: Theory and Practice.* New York: Oxford University Press, 1970.

Bahl, Roy W. *Metropolitan City Expenditures: A Comparative Analysis.* Lexington: University of Kentucky Press, 1969.

Bailey, Harry A., Jr. (ed.). *Negro Politics in America.* Columbus, Ohio: Charles A. Merrill, 1967.

Bailey, Stephen K. *et al. Schoolmen and Politics.* Syracuse: Syracuse University Press, 1962.

Banfield, Edward C. *Big City Politics.* New York: Random House, 1965.

———. *Political Influence.* New York: The Free Press, 1961.

———. *The Unheavenly City: The Nature and the Future of Our Urban Crisis.* Boston: Little, Brown, 1970.

——— (ed.). *Urban Government,* rev. ed. New York: The Free Press, 1969.

———, and Morton Grodzins. *Government and Housing in Metropolitan Areas.* New York: McGraw-Hill, 1958.

———, and James Q. Wilson. *City Politics.* New York: Vintage Books, 1963.

Bayley, David H., and Harold Mendelsohn. *Minorities and the Police: Confrontation in America.* New York: The Free Press, 1969.

Bendiner, Robert. *The Politics of Schools: A Crisis in Self-Government.* New York: Harper & Row, 1969.

Bish, Robert L. *The Public Economy of Metropolitan Areas.* Chicago: Markham, 1971.

Bloomberg, Warner, Jr., and Henry J. Schmandt

Selected Bibliography

(ed.). *Power, Poverty and Urban Policy.* Beverly Hills, Calif.: Sage, 1968.

Bollens, John C. (ed.). *Exploring the Metropolitan Community.* Berkeley and Los Angeles: University of California Press, 1961.

———, and Henry J. Schmandt. *The Metropolis: Its People, Politics, and Economic Life,* 2nd ed. New York: Harper & Row, 1970.

Bonjean, Charles, Terry Clark, and Robert Lineberry (eds.). *Community Politics.* New York: The Free Press, 1971.

Booth, David A. *Metropolitics: The Nashville Consolidation.* East Lansing: Institute for Community Development, Michigan State University, 1963.

Boskoff, Alvin, and Harmon Zeigler. *Voting Patterns in a Local Election.* Philadelphia: J. B. Lippincott, 1964.

Brazer, Harvey E. *City Expenditures in the United States.* New York: National Bureau of Economic Research, 1959.

Campbell, Alan K. (ed.). *The States and the Urban Crisis.* Englewood Cliffs, N.J.: Prentice-Hall, 1970.

———, and Seymour Sacks. *Metropolitan America: Fiscal Patterns and Governmental Systems.* New York: The Free Press, 1967.

Chevigny, Paul. *Police Power: Police Abuses in New York City.* New York: Pantheon, 1969.

Clark, Terry N. (ed.). *Community Structure and Decision Making: Comparative Analysis.* San Francisco: Chandler, 1968.

Coleman, James S. *Community Conflict.* New York: The Free Press, 1957.

Conant, Ralph W. *The Politics of Community Health.* Washington, D.C.: Public Affairs Press, 1968.

Connery, Robert H. *et al. The Politics of Mental Health: Organizing Community Mental Health in Metropolitan Areas.* New York: Columbia University Press, 1968.

——— (ed.). *Urban Riots: Violence and Social Change.* New York: Academy of Political Science, Columbia University, 1968.

———, and Demetrios Caraley (eds.). *Governing the City: Challenges and Options for New York.* New York: Praeger, 1969.

———, and Richard H. Leach. *The Federal Government and Metropolitan Areas.* Cambridge: Harvard University Press, 1960.

Coulter, Philip B. (ed.). *Politics of Metropolitan Areas: Selected Readings.* New York: Thomas Y. Crowell, 1967.

Crain, Robert L. *The Politics of School Desegregation: Comparative Case Studies of Community Structure and Policy Making.* Chicago: Aldine, 1968.

———, Elihu Katz, and Donald B. Rosenthal. *The Politics of Community Conflict: The Fluoridation Decision.* Indianapolis: Bobbs-Merrill, 1969.

Crecine, John P. *Governmental Problem Solving: A Computer Simulation of Municipal Budgeting.* Chicago: Rand McNally, 1969.

Crouch, Winston W., and Beatrice Dinerman. *Southern California Metropolis: A Study in Development of Government for a Metropolitan Area.* Berkeley: University of California Press, 1963.

Dahl, Robert A. *Who Governs? Democracy and Power in an American City.* New Haven: Yale University Press, 1961.

Daland, Robert T. (ed.). *Comparative Urban Research: The Administration and Politics of Cities.* Beverly Hills, Calif.: Sage, 1969.

Danielson, Michael N. *Federal-Metropolitan Politics and the Commuter Crisis.* New York: Columbia University Press, 1965.

——— (ed.). *Metropolitan Politics.* Boston: Little, Brown, 1966.

Davis, Morris, and Marvin G. Weinbaum. *Metropolitan Decision Processes: An Analysis of Case Studies.* Chicago: Rand McNally, 1969.

Derthick, Martha. *The Influence of Federal Grants: Public Assistance in Massachusetts.* Cambridge: Harvard University Press, 1970.

Dobriner, William M. *Class in Suburbia.* Englewood Cliffs, N.J.: Prentice-Hall, 1963.

Doig, Jameson W. *Metropolitan Transportation Politics and the New York Region.* New York: Columbia University Press, 1966.

Dolbeare, Kenneth. *Trial Courts in Urban Politics.* New York: John Wiley, 1967.

Downes, Bryan T. (ed.). *Cities and Suburbs.* Belmont, Calif.: Wadsworth, 1971.

Downs, Anthony. *Urban Problems and Prospects.* Chicago: Markham, 1970.

Duncan, Otis Dudley *et al. Metropolis and Region.* Baltimore: Johns Hopkins Press, 1960.

Dye, Thomas R., and Brett W. Hawkins (eds.). *Politics in the Metropolis,* 2nd ed. Columbus, Ohio: Charles Merrill, 1971.

Easton, David. *A Framework for Political Analysis.* Englewood Cliffs, N.J.: Prentice-Hall, 1965.

———. *The Political System.* New York: Alfred A. Knopf, 1953.

———. *A Systems Analysis of Political Life.* New York: John Wiley, 1965.

Edwards, T. Bentley, and Frederick M. Wirt. *School Desegregation in the North.* San Francisco: Chandler, 1968.

Eldersveld, Samuel J. *Political Parties: A Behavioral Analysis.* Chicago: Rand McNally, 1964.

Eley, Lynn W., and Thomas W. Casstevens (eds.). *The Politics of Fair-Housing Legislation: State and Local Case Studies.* San Francisco: Chandler, 1968.

Eyestone, Robert. *The Threads of Public Policy: A Study in Policy Leadership.* Indianapolis: Bobbs-Merrill, 1971.

Fiser, Webb. *Mastery of the Metropolis,* Englewood Cliffs, N.J.: Prentice-Hall, 1962.

Fitch, Lyle C. *et al. Urban Transportation and Public Policy.* San Francisco: Chandler, 1964.

Flinn, Thomas A. *Local Government and Politics.* Glenview, Ill.: Scott, Foresman, 1969.

Freeman, Linton C. *Patterns of Local Community Leadership.* Indianapolis: Bobbs-Merrill, 1968.

——— *et al. Local Community Leadership.* Syracuse: University College of Syracuse, 1960.

——— *et al. Metropolitan Decision Making.* Syracuse: University College of Syracuse, 1962.

Friesema, H. Paul. *Communications, Coordination, and Control Among Local Governments in the Siouxland: A Study in Intergovernmental Relations.* Iowa City: Institute of Public Affairs, University of Iowa, 1965.

Gans, Herbert J. *The Levittowners: Ways of Life and Politics in a New Suburban Community.* New York: Pantheon Books, 1967.

Gardiner, John A. *Traffic and the Police: Variations in Law Enforcement Policy.* Cambridge: Harvard University Press, 1969.

Gilbert, Charles E. *Governing the Suburbs.* Bloomington: Indiana University Press, 1967.

Gittell, Marilyn. *Participants and Participation: A Study of School Policy in New York City.* New York: Praeger, 1968.

———, and Alan Hevesi (eds.). *The Politics of Urban Education.* New York: Praeger, 1969.

Goodall, Leonard E. *The American Metropolis.* Columbus, Ohio: Charles E. Merrill, 1968.

Goodman, Jay S. (ed.). *Perspectives on Urban Politics.* Boston: Allyn and Bacon, 1970.

Gottman, Jean. *Megalopolis.* New York: Twentieth Century Fund, 1961.

Greer, Scott. *The Emerging City: Myth and Reality.* New York: The Free Press, 1962.

———. *Governing the Metropolis.* New York: John Wiley, 1962.

———. *Metropolitics: A Study of Political Culture.* New York: John Wiley, 1963.

———. *Urban Renewal and American Cities: The Dilemma of Democratic Intervention.* Indianapolis: Bobbs-Merrill, 1965.

———, *et al.* (ed.). *The New Urbanization.* New York: St. Martin's, 1968.

Gulick, Luther H. *The Metropolitan Problem and American Ideals.* New York: Alfred A. Knopf, 1962.

Hadden, Jeffrey K., and Edgar F. Borgatta. *American Cities: Their Social Characteristics.* Chicago: Rand McNally, 1965.

Hauser, Phillip M., and Leo F. Schnore (eds.). *The Study of Urbanization.* New York: John Wiley, 1965.

Hawkins, Brett W. *Nashville Metro: The Politics of City-County Consolidation.* Nashville, Tenn.: Vanderbilt University Press, 1966.

———. *Politics and Urban Policies.* Indianapolis: Bobbs-Merrill, 1971.

Hawley, Amos H., and Basil G. Zimmer. *The Metropolitan Community: Its People and Government.* Beverly Hills, Calif.: Sage, 1970.

Herman, Harold. *New York State and the Metropolitan Problem.* Philadelphia: University of Pennsylvania Press, 1963.

Hirsch, Werner Z. (ed.). *Urban Life and Form.* New York: Holt, Rinehart, & Winston, 1963.

Hoover, Edgar M., and Raymond Vernon. *Anatomy of a Metropolis: The Changing Distribution of People and Jobs Within the New York Metropolitan Region.* Cambridge: Harvard University Press, 1959.

Hunter, Floyd. *Community Power Structure.* Chapel Hill: University of North Carolina Press, 1953.

Jacob, Philip E., and James V. Toscano (eds.). *The Integration of Political Communities.* Philadelphia: J. B. Lippincott, 1964.

Janowitz, Morris (ed.). *Community Political Systems.* New York: The Free Press, 1961.

———. *The Community Press in an Urban Setting,* 2nd ed. Chicago: University of Chicago Press, 1967.

Jennings, M. Kent. *Community Influentials: The Elites of Atlanta.* New York: The Free Press, 1964.

Joiner, Charles A. *Organizational Analysis: Political, Sociological, and Administrative Process of Local Government.* East Lansing: Institute for Community Development, Michigan State University, 1964.

Jonassen, Christen F., and Sherwood H. Peres. *Interrelationships Among Dimensions of Community Systems.* Columbus: Ohio State University Press, 1959.

Kammerer, Gladys. *The Urban Political Community.* Boston: Houghton Mifflin, 1963.

———, et al. *City Managers in Politics: An Analysis of Manager Tenure and Termination.* Gainesville: University of Florida, 1962.

Kaplan, Harold. *Urban Political Systems: A Functional Analysis of Metro Toronto.* New York: Columbia University Press, 1967.

Kimbrough, Ralph B. *Political Power and Educational Decision Making.* Chicago: Rand McNally, 1964.

Klonoski, James R., and Robert Mendelsohn (eds.). *The Politics of Local Justice.* Boston: Little, Brown, 1970.

Kornhauser, Arthur. *Detroit as the People See It.* Detroit: Wayne State University Press, 1962.

Kotler, Milton. *Neighborhood Government: The Local Foundations of Political Life.* Indianapolis: Bobbs-Merrill, 1969.

Kramer, Ralph M. *Participation of the Poor: Comparative Community Case Studies in the War on Poverty.* Englewood Cliffs, N.J.: Prentice-Hall, 1969.

Ladd, Everett C., Jr. *Ideology in America: Change and Response in a City, a Suburb, and a Small Town.* Ithaca, N.Y.: Cornell University Press, 1969.

———. *Negro Political Leadership in the South.* Ithaca, N.Y.: Cornell University Press, 1966.

Larsen, Christian, et al. *Growth and Government in Sacramento.* Bloomington: Indiana University Press, 1965.

Lee, Eugene C. *The Politics of Nonpartisanship: A Study of California City Elections.* Berkeley and Los Angeles: University of California Press, 1960.

Levin, Murray B. *The Alienated Voter: Politics in Boston.* New York: Holt, Rinehart, and Winston, 1960.

Lineberry, Robert L., and Ira Sharkansky. *Urban Politics and Public Policy.* New York: Harper and Row, 1971.

Long, Norton E. *The Polity.* Chicago: Rand McNally, 1962.

Loveridge, Ronald O. *City Managers in Legislative Politics.* Indianapolis: Bobbs-Merrill, 1971.

Lowe, Jeanne. *Cities in a Race with Time.* New York: Vintage, 1968.

Lowi, Theodore J. *At The Pleasure of the Mayor.* New York: The Free Press, 1964.

Lowry, Ritchie. *Who's Running this Town?* New York: Harper & Row, 1965.

Maass, Arthur (ed.). *Area and Power: A Theory of Local Government.* New York: The Free Press, 1959.

Makielski, Stanislaw J., Jr. *The Politics of Zoning: The New York Experience.* New York: Columbia University Press, 1966.

Margolis, Julius (ed.). *The Public Economy of Urban Communities.* Baltimore: Johns Hopkins Press, 1965.

Martin, Roscoe C. *Government and the Suburban School.* Syracuse: Syracuse University Press, 1962.

———. *Grass Roots,* 2nd ed. University: University of Alabama Press, 1964.

———. *Metropolis in Transition: Local Government Adaptation to Changing Urban Needs.* Washington, D.C.: Housing and Home Finance Agency, 1963.

———, et al. *Decisions in Syracuse.* Bloomington: Indiana University Press, 1961.

Marx, Gary T. *Protest and Prejudice: A Study of Belief in the Black Community.* New York: Harper & Row, 1967.

Masotti, Louis H. *Education and Politics in*

Suburbia. Glenview, Ill.: Scott Foresman, 1969.

————, and Don R. Bowen (eds.). *Riots and Rebellion: Civil Violence in the Urban Community.* Beverly Hills, Calif.: Sage, 1968.

May, Richard, Jr., *et al. Zoning Controversies in the Suburbs: Three Case Studies.* Washington, D.C.: Government Printing Office, 1968.

McCandless, Carl A. *Urban Government and Politics.* New York: McGraw-Hill, 1970.

Meyer, John F., John F. Kain, and M. Wohl. *The Urban Transportation Problem.* Cambridge: Harvard University Press, 1965.

Meyerson, Martin, and Edward C. Banfield. *Politics, Planning, and the Public Interest.* New York: The Free Press, 1955.

Mowitz, Robert J., and Deil S. Wright. *Profile of a Metropolis.* Detroit: Wayne State University Press, 1962.

Moynihan, Daniel P. *Maximum Feasible Misunderstanding: Community Action in the War on Poverty.* New York: The Free Press, 1969.

Murphy, Thomas P. *Metropolitics and the Urban County.* Washington, D.C.: Washington National Press, 1970.

Muth, Richard F. *Cities and Housing.* Chicago: University of Chicago Press, 1969.

Netzer, Dick. *Economics and Urban Problems.* New York: Basic Books, 1970.

————. *The Urban Fiscal Problem.* Pittsburgh: University of Pittsburgh Press, 1967.

Niederhoffer, Arthur. *Behind the Shield: The Police in Urban Society.* Garden City, N.Y.: Doubleday, 1967.

Owen, Wilfred. *The Metropolitan Transportation Problem.* Washington, D.C.: Brookings Institution, 1966.

Perloff, Harvey S., and Lowdon Wingo, Jr. (eds.). *Issues in Urban Economics.* Baltimore: Johns Hopkins Press, 1968.

Polsby, Nelson W. *Community Power and Political Theory.* New Haven: Yale University Press, 1963.

Press, Charles R. *Main Street Politics.* East Lansing: Institute for Community Development, Michigan State University, 1962.

Presthus, Robert V. *Men at the Top.* New York: Oxford University Press, 1964.

Prewitt, Kenneth. *The Recruitment of Political Leaders.* Indianapolis: Bobbs-Merrill, 1970.

Rabinovitz, Francine. *City Politics and Planning.* New York: Atherton, 1969.

Ranney, David C. *Planning and Politics in the Metropolis.* Columbus, Ohio: Charles E. Merrill, 1969.

Rogers, David. *The Management of Big Cities.* Beverly Hills, Calif.: Sage, 1971.

Rossi, Peter, and Robert A. Dentler. *The Politics of Urban Renewal.* New York: The Free Press, 1961.

Ruchelman, Leonard I. (ed.). *Big City Mayors:*

The Crisis in Urban Politics. Bloomington: Indiana University Press, 1969.

Sacks, Seymour, and William F. Hellmuth, Jr. *Financing Government in a Metropolitan Area.* New York: The Free Press, 1961.

Sayre, Wallace S., and Herbert Kaufman. *Governing New York City: Politics in the Metropolis,* New York: Russell Sage Foundation, 1960.

Schaller, Howard G. (ed.). *Public Expenditure Decisions in the Urban Community.* Baltimore: Johns Hopkins Press, 1963.

Schmandt, Henry J., Paul Steinbecker, and George D. Wendel. *Metropolitan Reform in St. Louis.* New York: Holt, Rinehart, and Winston, 1961.

Schnore, Leo F., and Henry Fagin (eds.). *Urban Research and Policy Planning,* Vol. 1. Beverly Hills, Calif.: Sage, 1967.

Seashore, Stanley, and Robert McNeill (eds.). *Management of the Urban Crisis: Government and the Behavioral Sciences.* New York: The Free Press, 1971.

Skolnick, Jerome H. *Justice Without Trial: Law Enforcement in Democratic Society.* New York: John Wiley, 1966.

————. *The Politics of Protest: Violent Aspects of Protest and Confrontation.* Washington, D.C.: Government Printing Office, 1969.

Sofen, Edward. *The Miami Metropolitan Experiment,* Bloomington: Indiana University Press, 1963.

Stinchcombe, Jean L. *Reform and Reaction: City Politics in Toledo.* Belmont, Calif.: Wadsworth, 1968.

Sundquist, James L. (ed.). *On Fighting Poverty: Perspectives from Experience.* New York: Basic Books, 1969.

————. *Making Federalism Work: A Study of Program Coordination at the Community Level.* Washington, D.C.: Brookings Institution, 1969.

Sussman, Marvin (ed.). *Community Structure and Analysis.* New York: Thomas Y. Crowell, 1959.

Sweeney, Stephen B. (ed.). *Metropolitan Analysis: Important Elements of Study and Action.* Philadelphia: University of Pennsylvania Press, 1958.

Syed, Anwar. *The Political Theory of American Local Government.* New York: Random House, 1966.

Talbot, Allan. *The Mayor's Game: Richard Lee of New Haven and the Politics of Change.* New York: Praeger, 1970.

Thompson, Wilbur R. *A Preface to Urban Economics.* Baltimore: Johns Hopkins Press, 1965.

Vernon, Raymond. *Metropolis 1985.* New York: Doubleday Anchor Books, 1963.

Vidich, Arthur J., and Joseph Bensman. *Small Town in Mass Society.* Princeton, N.J.: Princeton University Press, 1958.

Walsh, Annmarie H. *The Urban Challenge to Government*. New York: Praeger, 1969.

Warren, Robert O. *Government in Metropolitan Regions: A Reappraisal of Fractionated Political Organization*. Davis: Institute of Governmental Affairs, University of California, 1966.

Warren, Roland L. (ed.). *Politics and the Ghettos*. New York: Atherton, 1969.

Watson, Richard A. *The Politics of Urban Change*. Kansas City, Mo.: Community Studies, 1963.

Weaver, Robert C. *Dilemmas of Urban America*. Cambridge: Harvard University Press, 1965.

———. *The Urban Complex*. Garden City, N.Y.: Doubleday Anchor Books, 1966.

Wildavsky, Aaron. *Leadership in a Small Town*. Totowa, N.J.: Bedminster Press, 1965.

Willbern, York. *The Withering Away of the City*. University: University of Alabama Press, 1964.

Willhelm, Sidney M. *Urban Zoning and Land-Use Theory*. New York: The Free Press, 1962.

Williams, Oliver P. *Metropolitan Political Analysis: A Social Access Approach*. New York: The Free Press, 1971.

———, and Charles R. Adrian. *Four Cities: A Study in Comparative Policy Making*. Philadelphia: University of Pennsylvania Press, 1963.

———, et al. *Suburban Differences and Metropolitan Policies: A Philadelphia Story*. Philadelphia: University of Pennsylvania Press, 1965.

Wilson, James Q. *The Amateur Democrat*. Chicago: University of Chicago Press, 1962.

——— (ed.). *City Politics and Public Policy*. New York: John Wiley, 1968.

——— (ed.). *The Metropolitan Enigma*, rev. ed. Cambridge: Harvard University Press, 1968.

———. *Negro Politics*. New York: The Free Press, 1960.

——— (ed.). *Urban Renewal: The Record and the Controversy*. Cambridge: Harvard University Press, 1966.

———. *Varieties of Police Behavior*. Cambridge: Harvard University Press, 1968.

Wingo, Lowdon, Jr. (ed.). *Cities and Space*. Baltimore: Johns Hopkins Press, 1963.

Winter, William O. *The Urban Polity*. New York: Dodd, Mead, 1969.

Wolf, Eleanor P., and Charles N. Lebeaux. *Change and Renewal in an Urban Community*. New York: Praeger, 1969.

Wood, Robert C. *Suburbia: Its People and Their Politics*. Boston: Houghton-Mifflin, 1958.

Woodbury, Coleman (ed.). *The Future of Cities and Urban Redevelopment*. Chicago: University of Chicago Press, 1953.

Zimmer, Basil G., and Amos H. Hawley. *Metropolitan Area Schools: Resistance to District Reorganization*. Beverly Hills, Calif.: Sage, 1968.

ARTICLES

Abelson, Robert P., and Alex Bernstein. "A Computer Simulation Model of Community Referendum Controversies." *Public Opinion Quarterly*, 27 (1963), 93–122.

Abney, F. Glen, and Larry B. Hill. "Natural Disasters as a Political Variable: The Effect of a Hurricane on an Urban Election." *American Political Science Review*, 60 (1966), 974–81.

Adrian, Charles R. "Leadership and Decision Making in Manager Cities." *Public Administration Review*, 18 (1958), 208–13.

———. "Metropology: Folklore and Field Research." *Public Adminstration Review*, 21 (1961), 148–57.

———. "Some General Characteristics of Nonpartisan Elections." *American Political Science Review*, 46 (1952), 766–76.

———. "A Typology of Nonpartisan Elections." *Western Political Quarterly*, 12 (1959), 449–58.

Aiken, Michael, and Robert R. Alford. "Community Structure and Innovation: The Case of Public Housing." *American Political Science Review*, 64 (1970), 843–64.

———. "Community Structure and Innovation: The Case of Urban Renewal." *American Sociological Review*, 35 (1970), 650–65.

Alford, Robert R. "Bureaucracy and Participation in Four Wisconsin Cities." *Urban Affairs Quarterly*, 5 (1969), 5–30.

———, and Eugene C. Lee. "Voting Turnout in American Cities." *American Political Science Review*, 62 (1968), 796–613.

———, and Harry M. Scoble. "Community Leadership, Education and Political Behavior." *American Sociological Review*, 33 (1968), 259–72.

———, and Harry M. Scoble. "Sources of Local Political Involvement." *American Political Science Review*, 62 (1968), 1192–1206.

Bachrach, Peter. "A Power Analysis: The Shaping of Anti-Poverty Policy in Baltimore." *Public Policy*, 18 (1970), 155–86.

———, and Morton Baratz. "Decisions and Nondecisions: An Analytical Framework." *American Political Science Review*, 57 (1963), 632–42.

———, and Morton Baratz. "Two Faces of Power," *American Political Science Review*, 56 (1962), 947–52.

Banfield, Edward C. "The Politics of Metropolitan Area Organizations." *Midwest Journal of Political Science*, 1 (1957), 77–91.

Banovetz, James M. "Metropolitan Subsidies: An Appraisal. " *Public Administration Review*, 25 (1965), 297–301.

Bebout, John E., and Harry C. Bredemeier. "American Cities as Social Systems." *Journal of the American Institute of Planners*, 29 (1963), 64–76.

Beckman, Norman, and Page L. Ingraham. "The States and Urban Areas." *Law and Contemporary Problems*, 30 (1965), 76–102.

Beyle, Thad L. "Contested Elections and Voter Turnout in a Local Community: A Problem in Spurious Correlation." *American Political Science Review*, 59 (1965), 111–16.

Bittner, Egon. "The Police on Skid-row: A Study of Peace-keeping." *American Sociological Review*, 32 (1967), 699–715.

Black, Donald J., and Albert J. Reiss, Jr. "Police Control of Juveniles." *American Sociological Review*, 35 (1970), 63–77.

Black, Gordon S. "A Theory of Professionalization in Politics." *American Political Science Review*, 64 (1970), 865–78.

Blank, Blanche D., Rita J. Immerman, and C. Peter Rydell. "A Comparative Study of an Urban Bureaucracy." *Urban Affairs Quarterly*, 4 (1969), 343–54.

Bolan, Richard S. "Community Decision Behavior." *Journal of the American Institute of Planners*, 35 (1969), 301–10.

Booms, Bernard H. "City Governmental Form and Public Expenditure Levels." *National Tax Journal*, 19 (1966), 187–99.

Booth, David A. "Are Elected Mayors a Threat to Managers?" *Administrative Science Quarterly*, 12 (1968), 572–89.

———, and Charles R. Adrian. "Elections and Community Power." *Journal of Politics*, 25 (1963), 107–18.

Burke, Edmund M. "Citizen Participation Strategies." *Journal of the American Institute of Planners*, 34 (1968), 287–94.

Burkhead, Jesse. "Uniformity in Governmental Expenditures and Resources in a Metropolitan Area." *National Tax Journal*, 14 (1961), 337–48.

Campbell, Alan K., and Seymour Sacks. "Administering the Spread City." *Public Administration Review*, 24 (1964), 141–53.

Carrell, Jeptha J. "The City Manager and His Council: Sources of Conflict." *Public Administration Review*, 22 (1962), 203–08.

Cho, Yong H. "The Effect of Local Governmental Systems on Local Policy Outcomes in the United States." *Public Administration Review*, 27 (1967), 31–38.

———. "Fiscal Implications of Annexation: The Case of Metropolitan Central Cities in Texas." *Land Economics*, 45 (1969), 368–72.

Chute, Charlton F. "The Honolulu Metropolitan Area: A Challenge to Traditional Thinking." *Public Administration Review*, 18 (1958), 36–47.

Clark, Terry N. "Community Structure, Decision Making, Budget Expenditures, and Urban Renewal in 51 American Communities." *American Sociological Review*, 33 (1968), 576–93.

Cleveland, F. N. "Congress and Urban Problems." *Journal of Politics*, 28 (1966), 289–307.

Coke, James G., and Charles S. Liebman. "Political Values and Population Density Control." *Land Economics*, 37 (1961), 347–61.

Colcord, Frank C., Jr. "Decision Making and Transportation Policy: A Comparative Analysis." *Southwestern Social Science Quarterly*, 48 (1967), 373–97.

Conway, M. Margaret. "Political Participation in a Nonpartisan Local Election." *Public Opinion Quarterly*, 33 (1969), 425–30.

———. "Voter Information Sources in a Nonpartisan Local Election." *Western Political Quarterly*, 21 (1968), 69–77.

Crain, Robert L. "Fluoridation: The Diffusion of an Innovation Among Cities." *Social Forces*, 44 (1966), 467–76.

———, and Donald B. Rosenthal. "Structure and Values in Local Political Systems: The Case of Fluoridation Decisions." *Journal of Politics*, 28 (1966), 169–95.

———, and David Street. "School Desegregation and School Decision Making." *Urban Affairs Quarterly*, 2 (1966), 64–82.

Curran, S. J., and J. Donald. "The Metropolitan Problem: Solution from Within." *National Tax Journal*, 16 (1963), 216–21.

Cutright, Phillips. "Nonpartisan Electoral Systems in American Cities." *Comparative Studies in Society and History*, 5 (1963), 212–26.

Daland, Robert T. "Political Science and the Study of Urbanism." *American Political Science Review*, 51 (1957), 491–509.

Davies, David. "Financing Urban Functions and Services." *Law and Contemporary Problems*, 30 (1965), 127–61.

Davis, Otto A., and George Haines, Jr. "A Political Approach to a Theory of Public Expenditure: The Case of Municipalities." *National Tax Journal*, 19 (1966), 259–75.

———, and Andrew B. Whinston. "The Economics of Urban Renewal." *Law and Contemporary Problems*, 26 (1961), 78–92.

Derge, David R. "Metropolitan and Outside Alignments in Illinois and Missouri Delegations." *American Political Science Review*, 52 (1958), 1051–65.

Downes, Bryan T. "Issue Conflict, Factionalism, and Consensus in Suburban City Councils." *Urban Affairs Quarterly*, 4 (1969), 477–97.

———. "Municipal Social Rank and the Characteristics of Local Political Leaders." *Midwest Journal of Political Science*, 12 (1968), 514–38.

———. "The Social Characteristics of Riot Cities: A Comparative Study." *Social Science Quarterly*, 49 (1968), 504–20.

Downs, Anthony. "Metropolitan Growth and Future Political Problems." *Land Economics*, 37 (1961), 311–20.

Dugger, George S. "Relation of Local Government Structure to Urban Renewal." *Law and Contemporary Problems*, 26 (1961), 59–69.

Dye, Thomas R. "City-Suburban Social Distance and Public Policy." *Social Forces*, 44 (1965), 100–106.

———. "The Local-Cosmopolitan Dimension and the Study of Urban Politics." *Social Forces*, 41 (1963), 239–46.

———. "Metropolitan Integration by Bargaining Among Suburban Areas." *American Behavioral Scientist*, 5 (1962), 11–13.

———. "Urban Political Integration: Conditions Associated with Annexation in American Cities." *Midwest Journal of Political Science*, 8 (1964), 430–46.

———. "Urban School Segregation: A Comparative Analysis." *Urban Affairs Quarterly*, 4 (1968), 141–66.

Eliot, Thomas H. "Toward an Understanding of Public School Politics." *American Political Science Review*, 52 (1959), 1032–50.

Erbe, William. "Social Involvement and Political Activity: A Replication and Elaboration." *American Sociological Review*, 29 (1964), 198–215.

Eulau, Heinz. "The Informal Organization of Decisional Structures in Small Legislative Bodies." *Midwest Journal of Political Science*, 13 (1969), 341–66.

Feinberg, M. S. "The Implications of Core-City Decline for the Fiscal Structure of the Core-City." *National Tax Journal*, 17 (1964), 213–31.

Floro, George K. "Continuity in City-Manager Careers." *American Journal of Sociology*, 61 (1955), 240–46.

Fogelson, Robert M. "From Resentment to Confrontation: The Police, the Negroes, and the Outbreak of the Nineteen-Sixties Riots." *Political Science Quarterly*, 83 (1968), 217–47.

Form, William H. "Organized Labor's Place in the Community Power Structure." *Industrial Labor Relations Review*, 12 (1959), 526–39.

Freeman, J. Lieper. "Local Party Systems: Theoretical Considerations and a Case Analysis." *American Journal of Sociology*, 64 (1958), 282–89.

Friesema, H. Paul. "Interjurisdictional Agreement in Metropolitan Areas." *Administrative Science Quarterly*, 15 (1970), 242–50.

———. "The Metropolis and the Maze of Local Government." *Urban Affairs Quarterly*, 2 (1966), 68–90.

Froman, Lewis A., Jr. "An Analysis of Public Policies in Cities." *Journal of Politics*, 29 (1967), 94–108.

Frost, Richard T. "Stability and Change in Local Party Politics." *Public Opinion Quarterly*, 25 (1961), 221–35.

Gabis, Stanley. "Leadership in a Large Manager City: The Case of Kansas City." *Annals*, 353 (1964), 52–63.

Gamson, William. "The Fluoridation Dialogue:

Is it Ideological Politics." *Public Opinion Quarterly*, 26 (1962), 526–37.

———. "Rancorous Conflict in Community Politics." *American Sociological Review*, 31 (1966), 71–80.

Geschwender, James A. "Civil Rights Protest and Riots: A Disappearing Distinction." *Social Science Quarterly*, 49 (1968), 474–84.

Gittell, Marilyn. "Metropolitan Mayor: Dead End." *Public Administration Review*, 23 (1963), 20–24.

Gordon, Daniel N. "Immigrants and Municipal Voting Turnout: Implications for the Changing Ethnic Impact on Urban Politics." *American Sociological Review*, 35 (1970), 665–81.

———. "Immigrants and Urban Governmental Form in American Cities, 1933–1960." *American Journal of Sociology*, 74 (1969), 158–71.

"Governing Megacentropolis: A Symposium." *Public Administration Review*, 30 (1970), 473–520.

Grant, Daniel R. "Government of Interstate Metropolitan Areas." *Western Political Quarterly*, 8 (1955), 90–107.

———. "The Metropolitan Government Approach: Should, Can and Will It Prevail?" *Urban Affairs Quarterly*, 3 (1968), 103–10.

———. "Metropolitics and Professional Political Leadership: The Case of Nashville." *Annals* 353 (1964) 73–81.

———. "Urban and Suburban Nashville: A Case Study in Metropolitanism." *Journal of Politics* 17 (1955) 82–99.

Greene Lee S. "City Bosses and Political Machines." *Annals* 353 (1964) 115–30.

Greer Scott. "The Social Structure and Political Process of Suburbia." *American Sociological Review* 25 (1960) 514–26.

———. "The Social Structure and Political Process of Suburbia: An Empirical Test." *Rural Sociology* 27 (1962) 439–59.

———, and Peter Orleans. "The Mass Society and the Parapolitical Structure." *American Sociological Review*, 27 (1962), 634–46.

Gutman, Robert. "Urban Studies as a Field of Research." *American Behavioral Scientist*, 6 (1963), 9–14.

Hadden, Jeffry K., Louis H. Masotti, and Victor Thiessen. "The Making of the Negro Mayors 1967." *Trans-action* (January/February 1968) pp. 21–30.

Hagensick, A Clarke. "Influences of Partisanship and Incumbency on a Nonpartisan Elections System." *Western Political Quarterly*, 17 (1964), 117–24.

Hahn, Harlan. "Ethos and Social Class Referenda in Canadian Cities." *Polity*, 2 (1970), 295–315.

Hamilton, Howard D. "Direct Legislation: Some Implications of Open Housing Referenda." *American Political Science Review*, 64 (1970), 124–37.

Harrell, C. A., and D. G. Weiford. "The City Manager and the Policy Process." *Public Administration Review*, 19 (1959), 101–107.

Hawkins, Brett W. "Fringe-City Life-Style Distance and Fringe Support of Political Integration." *American Journal of Sociology*, 74 (1968), 248–55.

——. "Life Style, Demographic Distance and Voter Support of City-County Consolidation." *Southwestern Social Science Quarterly*, 48 (1967), 325–37.

Hawley, Amos H. "Community Power and Urban Renewal Success." *American Journal of Sociology*, 68 (1963), 422–31.

——. "Metropolitan Population and Municipal Government Expenditures in Central Cities." *Journal of Social Issues*, 7 (1951), 100–108.

Hirsch, Werner Z. "Determinants of Public Education Expenditures." *National Tax Journal*, 13 (1960), 29–40.

——. "Expenditure Implications of Metropolitan Growth and Consolidation." *Review of Economics and Statistics*, 41 (1959), 232–41.

——. "Local Versus Areawide Urban Government Services." *National Tax Journal*, 17 (1964), 331–39.

Holden, Matthew, Jr. "The Governance of the Metropolis as a Problem in Diplomacy." *Journal of Politics*, 26 (1964), 627–48.

Holloway, Harry. "Negro Political Strategy: Coalition or Independent Power Politics." *Social Science Quarterly*, 49 (1968), 534–48.

Horton, John E., and Wayne Thompson. "Powerlessness and Political Negativism: A Study of Defeated Referendums." *American Journal of Sociology*, 67 (1962), 485–93.

Huckshorn, Robert J., and Charles E. Young. "Study of Voting Splits on City Councils in Los Angeles County." *Western Political Quarterly*, 13 (1960), 479–97.

Jacob, Herbert. "Initial Recruitment of Elected Officials in the United States: A Model." *Journal of Politics*, 24 (1962), 703–16.

Jaros, Dean, and Robert I. Mendelsohn. "The Judicial Role and Sentencing Behavior." *Midwest Journal of Political Science*, 11 (1967), 471–88.

Jennings, M. Kent. "Public Administrators and Community Decision Making." *Administrative Science Quarterly*, 8 (1963), 18–43.

——, and Harmon Zeigler. "Class, Party, and Race in Four Types of Elections." *Journal of Politics*, 28 (1966), 391–407.

Jonassen, Christen. "Functional Unities in 88 Community Systems." *American Sociological Review*, 26 (1961), 399–407.

Jones, Garth N. "Integration of Political Ethos and Local Government Systems: The Utah Experience with Council-Manager Govern-

ment." *Human Organizations*, 23 (1964), 210–23.

Jones, Victor. "The Organization of a Metropolitan Region." *University of Pennsylvania Law Review*, 105 (1957), 538–52.

Kammerer, Gladys. "Role Diversity of City Managers." *Administrative Science Quarterly*, 8 (1964), 421–42.

——, and John De Grove. "Urban Leadership During Change." *Annals*, 353 (1964), 95–106.

Kaufman, Walter C., and Scott Greer. "Voting in a Metropolitan Community: An Application of Social Area Analysis." *Social Forces*, 38 (1960), 196–204.

Kee, Woo Sik. "Central City Expenditures and Metropolitan Areas." *National Tax Journal*, 18 (1965), 337–53.

——. "City-Suburban Differentials in Local Government Fiscal Effort." *National Tax Journal*, 21 (1968), 183–214.

——. "Suburban Population Growth and Its Implications for Core City Finance." *Land Economics*, 43 (1967), 202–11.

Kessel, John H. "Governmental Structure and Political Environment." *American Political Science Review*, 56 (1962), 615–20.

Kish, Leslie. "Differentiation in Metropolitan Areas." *American Sociological Review*, 19 (1954), 388–98.

Krueckberg, Donald A. "A Multivariate Analysis of Metropolitan Planning." *Journal of the American Institute of Planners*, 35 (1969), 319–25.

Lamanna, R. A. "Value Consensus Among Urban Residents." *Journal of the American Institute of Planners*, 31 (1964), 317–23.

Levin, Murray, and K. Eden. "Political Strategy for the Alienated Voter." *Public Opinion Quarterly*, 26 (1962), 47–63.

Levy, Burton. "Cops in the Ghetto: A Problem of the Police System." *American Behavioral Scientist*, 12 (1968), 31–34.

Liebman, Charles S. "Electorates, Interest Groups and Local Government Policy." *American Behavioral Scientist*, 5 (1961), 8–11.

——. "Functional Differentiation and Political Characterists of Suburbs." *American Journal of Sociology*, 66 (1961), 485–90.

——, et al. "Social Status, Tax Resources, and Metropolitan Cooperation." *National Tax Journal*, 16 (1963), 573–79.

Lindquist, Emory. "Socioeconomic Status and Political Participation." *Western Political Quarterly*, 17 (1964), 608–15.

Lineberry, Robert L. "Community Structure and Planning Commitment: A Note on the Correlates of Agency Expenditures." *Social Science Quarterly*, 50 (1969), 723–30.

Lockard, Duane. "The City Manager, Administrative Theory and Political Powers." *Political Science Quarterly*, 72 (1962), 224–36.

Long, Norton. "The Local Community as an Ecology of Games." *American Journal of Sociology*, 44 (1958), 251–61.

Lupsha, Peter A. "On Theories of Urban Violence." *Urban Affairs Quarterly*, 4 (1969), 273–96.

Luttbeg, Norman. "The Structure of Beliefs Among Leaders and the Public." *Public Opinion Quarterly*, 32 (1968), 398–410.

Lyden, Fremont James, and Jerry V. Thomas. "Citizen Participation in Policy Making: A Study of a Community Action Program." *Social Science Quarterly*, 50 (1969), 631–42.

Mann, Lawrence D. "Studies in Community Decision Making." *Journal of the American Institute of Planners*, 30 (1964), 58–65.

Marshall, Dale Rogers. "Who Participates in What? A Bibliographic Essay on Individual Participation in Urban Areas." *Urban Affairs Quarterly*, 4 (1968), 201–23.

Masotti, Louis H., and Don R. Bowen. "Communities and Budgets: The Sociology of Municipal Expenditures." *Urban Affairs Quarterly*, 1 (1965), 39–58.

Masters, Nicholas A. "The Politics of Union Endorsement of Candidates in the Detroit Area." *Midwest Journal of Political Science*, 1 (1957), 136–50.

Mayo, Charles G. "1961 Mayoralty Election in Los Angeles: The Political Party in a Nonpartisan Election." *Western Political Quarterly* 17 (1964), 325–37.

McDill, Edward L., and Jeanne Clare Ridley. "Status, Anomia, Political Alienation, and Political Participation." *American Journal of Sociology*, 58 (1962), 205–17.

Miller, S. M., and Martin Rein. "Participation, Poverty, and Administration." *Public Administration Review*, 29 (1969), 15–25.

Minar, David W. "The Community Basis of Conflict in School System Politics." *American Sociological Review*, 31 (1966), 822–34.

Morgan, David R. "Community Social Rank and Attitudes Toward Suburban Living." *Sociology and Social Research*, 55 (1971), 401–13.

Moynihan, Daniel P. "The Relation of Federal to Local Authorities." *Daedalus*, 96 (1967), 801–808.

Norton, James A. "Referenda Voting in a Metropolitan Area." *Western Political Quarterly*, 16 (1963), 195–212.

Nourse, Hugh O. "Economics of Urban Renewal." *Land Economics*, 42 (1966), 65–74.

Ostrom, Vincent, Charles M. Tiebout, and Robert O. Warren. "The Organization of Government in Metropolitan Areas: A Theoretical Inquiry." *American Political Science Review*, 55 (1961), 831–42.

Paletz, David L., and Robert Dunn. "Press Coverage of Civil Disorders: A Case Study of Winston-Salem, 1967." *Public Opinion Quarterly*, 33 (1969), 328–45.

Palumbo, Dennis J., and Oliver P. Williams. "Predictors of Public Policy: The Case of Local Public Health." *Urban Affairs Quarterly*, 2 (1967), 75–92.

Pellegrin, Roland. "Selected Bibliography on Community Power Structure." *Southwestern Social Science Quarterly*, 48 (1967), 451–65.

Peterson, Paul E. "Forms of Representation: Participation of the Poor in the Community Action Program." *American Political Science Review*, 64 (1970), 491–507.

Pidot, George B. "A Principal Components Analysis of the Determinants of Local Government Fiscal Patterns." *Review of Economics and Statistics*, 51 (1969), 176–88.

Piliavin, Irving, and Scott Briar. "Police Encounters with Juveniles." *American Journal of Socioligy*, 70 (1964), 206–14.

Pinard, Maurice. "Structural Attachments and Political Support in Urban Politics: The Case of Fluoridation Referendums." *American Journal of Sociology*, 68 (1963), 513–26.

Plaut, Thomas. "Analysis of Voting Behavior on a Fluoridation Referendum." *Public Opinion Quarterly*, 23 (1959–60), 213–22.

Pomper, Gerald. "Ethnic and Group Voting in Nonpartisan Municipal Elections." *Public Opinion Quarterly*, 30 (1966), 79–87.

Press, Charles. "Attitudes Toward Annexation in a Small City Area." *Western Political Quarterly*, 16 (1963), 271–78.

———. "Efficiency and Economy Arguments for Metropolitan Reorganization." *Public Opinion Quarterly*, 38 (1964), 584–94.

Prewitt, Kenneth. "Political Ambitions, Volunteerism, and Electoral Accountability." *American Political Science Review*, 64 (1970), 5–17.

———, and Heinz Eulau. "Political Matrix and Political Representation: Prolegomenon to a New Departure from an Old Problem." *American Political Science Review*, 63 (1969), 427–41.

Rosenthal, Donald B., and Robert L. Crain. "Structure and Value in Local Political Systems: The Case of Fluoridation Decisions." *Journal of Politics*, 28 (1966), 169–96.

Roth, Marian, and G. R. Boynton. "Communal Ideology and Political Support." *Journal of Politics*, 31 (1969), 167–85.

Sacks, Seymour, and David Ranney. "Suburban Education: A Fiscal Analysis." *Urban Affairs Quarterly*, 2 (1966), 103–19.

Salisbury, Robert H. "Schools and Politics in the Big City." *Harvard Educational Review*, 37 (1967), 408–24.

———. "St. Louis Politics: Relationships Among Interests, Parties, and Governmental Structure." *Western Political Quarterly*, 13 (1960), 498–506.

———. "Urban Politics: The New Convergence of Power." *Journal of Politics*, 26 (1964), 775–97.

Salisbury, Robert H., and Gordon Black. "Class and Party in Partisan and Non-Partisan Elections." *American Political Science Review*, 57 (1963), 584–92.

Sapolsky, Harvey M. "The Fluoridation Controversy," *Public Opinion Quarterly*, 33 (1969), 240–49.

Schmandt, Henry J. "The City and the Ring." *American Behavioral Scientist*, 4 (1960), 17–19.

———, and G. Ross Stephens. "Local Government Expenditure Patterns." *Land Economics*, 39 (1963), 397–406.

———, and G. Ross Stephens. "Measuring Municipal Output." *National Tax Journal*, 13 (1960), 369–75.

Schnore, Leo F. "The Functions of Metropolitan Suburbs." *American Journal of Sociology*, 61 (1956), 453–58.

———. "Measuring City-Suburban Status Differences." *Urban Affairs Quarterly*, 3 (1967), 95–108.

———. "Socio-Economic Status of Cities and Suburbs." *American Sociological Review*, 28 (1963), 76–85.

———, and Robert R. Alford. "Forms of Government and Socioeconomic Characteristics of Suburbs." *Administrative Science Quarterly*, 8 (1963), 1–17.

———, and Harry Sharp. "Racial Changes in Metropolitan Areas, 1950–1960." *Social Forces*, 41 (1963), 247–53.

Scott, Thomas M. "The Diffusion of Urban Governmental Forms as a Case of Social Learning." *Journal of Politics*, 30 (1968), 1091–1108.

———. "Metropolitan Governmental Reorganization Proposals." *Western Political Quarterly*, 21 (1968), 252–61.

Sears, David O., and T. M. Tomlinson. "Riot Ideology in Los Angeles: A Study of Negro Attitudes." *Social Science Quarterly*, 49 (1968), 485–503.

Seidler, Murray. "Some Participant Observer Reflections on Detroit's Community Action Program." *Urban Affairs Quarterly*, 5 (1970), 183–205.

Shapiro, Harvey. "Economics of Scale and Local Government Finance." *Land Economics*, 39 (1963), 175–86.

Sherbenou, Edgar L. "Class, Participation, and the Council-Manager Plan." *Public Administration Review*, 21 (1961), 131–35.

Sigel, Roberta S., and H. Paul Friesema. "Urban Community Leaders' Knowledge of Public Opinion." *Western Political Quarterly*, 18 (1965), 881–95.

Smith, Lincoln. "The Manager System and Collectivism." *American Journal of Economics and Sociology*, 24 (1965), 21–38.

Smith, Paul A. "The Games of Community Politics." *Midwest Journal of Political Science*, 9 (1965), 37–60.

Stephens, G. Ross. "The Suburban Impact of Earnings Tax Policies." *National Tax Journal*, 22 (1969), 313–33.

———, and Henry J. Schmandt. "Revenue Patterns of Local Government." *National Tax Journal*, 15 (1962), 432–36.

Stone, Clarence N. "Local Referendums: An Alternative to the Alienated-Voter Model." *Public Opinion Quarterly*, 29 (1965), 213–22.

Straits, Bruce C. "Community Adoption and Implementation of Urban Renewal." *American Journal of Sociology*, 71 (1965), 77–82.

Templeton, Frederic. "Alienation and Political Participation: Some Research Findings." *Public Opinion Quarterly*, 30 (1966), 249–61.

Thompson, Wayne E., and John E. Horton. "Political Alienation as a Force in Political Action." *Social Forces*, 38 (1960), 190–95.

Tiebout, Charles M. "A Pure Theory of Local Expenditures." *Journal of Political Economy*, 54 (1956), 416–24.

Tropman, John E. "Critical Dimensions of Community Structure." *Urban Affairs Quarterly*, 5 (1969), 215–32.

Uyeki, Eugene S. "Patterns of Voting in a Metropolitan Area, 1938–62," *Urban Affairs Quarterly*, 1 (1966), 65–77.

Vanecko, James J. "Community Mobilization and Institutional Change: The Influence of the Community Action Program in Large Cities." *Social Science Quarterly*, 50 (1969), 609–30.

Walker, Jack L. "Protest and Negotiation: A Case Study of Negro Leadership in Atlanta." *Midwest Journal of Political Science*, 7 (1963), 99–124.

Warren, Robert O. "A Municipal Services Market Model of Metropolitan Organization." *Journal of the American Institute of Planners*, 30 (1964), 193–204.

———. "Political Form and Metropolitan Reform." *Public Administration Review*, 24 (1964), 180–87.

Warren, Roland L. "Toward a Typology of Extra-Community Controls Limiting Local Community Autonomy." *Social Forces*, 34 (1956), 338–41.

Watson, Richard A., and John H. Romani. "Metropolitan Government for Metropolitan Cleveland: An Analysis of the Voting Record." *Midwest Journal of Political Science*, 5 (1961), 365–90.

Watson, Walter B. *et al.* "Metropolitan Decentralization Through Incorporation. *Western Political Quarterly*, 28 (1965), 198–207.

Wells, Lloyd M. "Social Values and the Political Orientations of City Managers." *Social Science Quarterly*, 48 (1967), 443–50.

Westby, David L. "The Civic Sphere in the American City." *Social Forces*, 45 (1966), 161–69.

Westley, William A. "Violence and the Police." *American Journal of Sociology*, 59 (1955), 34–41.

Willhelm, Sidney M., and Gideon Sjoberg.

"Economics vs. Protective Values in Urban Land Use Change." *American Journal of Economics and Sociology*, 19 (1960), 151–60.

Williams, J. Allen, Jr. "The Effects of Urban Renewal Upon a Black Community." *Social Science Quarterly*, 50 (1969), 703–12.

Williams, Oliver P. "Life Style Values and Political Decentralization in Metropolitan Areas." *Southwestern Social Science Quarterly*, 47 (1967), 299–310.

———. "A Typology for Comparative Local Government." *Midwest Journal of Political Science*, 5 (1961), 150–64.

Wilson, James Q. "The Strategy of Protest: Problems of Negro Civic Action." *Journal of Conflict Resolution*, 5 (1961), 291–303.

———. "Planning and Politics: Citizen Participation in Urban Renewal." *Journal of the, American Institute of Planners*, 29 (1963) 210–36.

———, and Edward C. Banfield. "Public-Regardingness as a Value Premise in Voting Behavior." *American Political Science Review*, 58 (1964), 876–87.

Wirt, Frederick M. "The Political Sociology of American Suburbia: A Reinterpretation." *Journal of Politics*, 27 (1965), 647–66.

Wolfinger, Raymond E. "The Development and Persistence of Ethnic Voting." *American Political Science Review*, 59 (1965), 896–909.

———. "Reputation and Reality in the Study of Community Power." *American Sociological Review*, 25 (1960), 636–44.

———, and John O. Field. "Political Ethos and the Structure of City Government." *American Political Science Review*, 60 (1966), 306–26.

Zald, Mayer N., and Thomas A. Anderson. "Secular Trends and Historical Contingencies in the Recruitment of Mayors: Nashville as Compared to New Haven and Chicago." *Urban Affairs Quarterly*, 3 (1968), 53–68.

Zikmund, Joseph, and Robert Smith. "Political Participation in an Upper-Middle Class Suburb." *Urban Affairs Quarterly*, 4 (1969), 443–58.

Zimmer, Basil G., and Amos H. Hawley. "Local Government as Viewed by Fringe Residents." *Rural Sociology*, 23 (1958), 363–70.

Zimmerman, Joseph F. "Metropolitan Reform in the U.S.: An Overview." *Public Administrative Review*, 30 (1970), 531–43.

Zisk, Betty, Heinz Eulau, and Kenneth Prewitt. "City Councilmen and the Group Struggle: A Typology of Role Orientation." *Journal of Politics*, 27 (1965), 618–46.

Index